FOUNDATIONS OF THE COPTIC LANGUAGE

VOLUME ONE

FR. ANDREAS ST. MACARIUS

A monk of the Monastery of St. Macarius the Great

Scetis, Egypt

Translation by

St. Mary and St. Moses Abbey

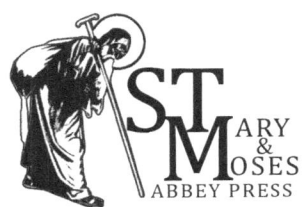

Foundations of the Coptic Language: Volume One

by Fr. Andreas St. Macarius
A monk of the Monastery of St. Macarius the Great - Scetis, Egypt

Translation by St. Mary and St. Moses Abbey

Copyright © 2025 Coptic Orthodox Diocese of the Southern United States.

All rights reserved.

Designed & Published by:
St. Mary & St. Moses Abbey Press
101 S Vista Dr., Sandia, TX 78383
stmabbeypress.com

Printed in the United States of America

Library of Congress Control Number: 2025934671

Cover design by St. Mary and St. Moses Abbey

Cover image: A scanned page from the Coptic Psalmody manuscript from the Monastery of Baramous.

Contents

Forward	vii
Introduction	ix
The Coptic Language	1
Lesson 1: Indefinite Articles	21
Lesson 2: Definite Articles	26
Lesson 3: The Plural Definite Article & Genitive Construction	30
Lesson 4: Near Demonstrative Adjectives and Pronouns	34
Lesson 5: Separate Personal Pronouns	37
Review Exercises 1	40
Exam 1	42
Lesson 6: Far Demonstrative Pronouns	44
Lesson 7: Possessive	48
Lesson 8: Possessive or Attributive Pronouns	52
Exercises and Applications	57
Lesson 9: Three Notes on the Possessive Adjectives and Pronouns	61
Lesson 10: The Definite Article as a Relative Pronoun, and Vice Versa	65
Review Exercises 2	69
Exam 2	71
General Exam on Lessons 1-10	73

Lesson 11:	Verbs	75
Lesson 12:	The Subject and Object Marks	80
Lesson 13:	The Future Tense	85
Lesson 14:	The Past Tense	90
Lesson 15:	Applications	95
Review Exercises 3		100
Exam 3		102
Lesson 16:	Classification of Verbs	104
Lesson 17:	Kinds of Verbs	110
Lesson 18:	Special Verbs	115
Lesson 19:	Agent Nouns	120
Lesson 20:	Verbal and Abstract Nouns	125
Review Exercises 4		130
Exam 4		132
Lesson 21:	The Morphological Forms of the Verb	134
Lesson 22:	The Forms (Tenses) of the Simple Verbs [Part 1]	139
Lesson 23:	The Forms (Tenses) of the Simple Verbs [Part 2]	144
Lesson 24:	The Forms (Tenses) of the Simple Verbs [Part 3]	149
Lesson 25:	The Forms (Tenses) of the Simple Verbs [Part 4]	155
Review Exercises 5		160
Exam 5		162
Lesson 26:	The Forms (Tenses) of the Derived Verbs	164
Lesson 27:	The Imperative Mood	169
Lesson 28:	Verb Tenses in the Indicative Mood	176

Lesson 29:	Verbs in the Past Tense	181
Lesson 30:	Verbs in the Future Tense	187
Review Exercises 6		192
Exam 6		194
Lesson 31:	Adjectives	196
Lesson 32:	Place of Adjectives with Respect to Described Nouns	203
Lesson 33:	Degrees of Description	208
Lesson 34:	Numbers [Part 1]	212
Lesson 35:	Numbers [Part 2]	218
Review Exercises 7		223
Exam 7		225
Appendix A:	Answers of the Lessons' Exercises	228
Appendix B:	Comprehensive Table of Frequently-Used Verb Forms	273
Appendix C:	Bibliography	287

Forward

The Coptic language is the language of our fathers and forefathers, since the time before the entrance of Christianity into Egypt. It is the language in which the fathers of most of the land of Egypt read the Holy Scriptures, both Old and New Testaments. It is the language in which the fathers of Coptic monasticism wrote their sayings and in which their biographies were written. It is also the language in which we enjoy the prayers of the Divine Liturgy and the daily Psalmody to the present day.

Learning the Coptic language is no longer a national duty, so that we may preserve the language of the forefathers, as much as it is a religious duty, so that we may understand our Coptic heritage which has reached us through the centuries, and so that we may practice our life in the Church with understanding and awareness, according to the commandment of St. Paul the Apostle: "I will pray with the spirit, and I will also pray with the understanding."[1]

We thank God that in the past [few] years there has been a breakthrough in learning the Coptic language, and there has been interest in our Coptic heritage, a general Egyptian interest, as a heritage of all Egyptians, to the extent that our national universities and institutions have organized symposiums and conferences to study and commemorate this heritage. Although we have great joy in this interest, greater is the responsibility which has been placed upon us to study our heritage and to give of our time and effort to study our language and delve deeper into it.

Since the time I began studying the Coptic language, I have read many books and booklets which explain the grammar of the language, and as I delved deeper into the study, I felt that most of the books that explain this grammar were just books for beginners. And very few of them explain the language for those who desire to dive into its depths, and sadly these few are not currently available in our libraries.

And the book *Foundations of the Coptic Language* by the reverend monk, Fr. Andreas of the Monastery of St. Macarius is one of those rare books, which delves into the depths of the language, and it explains all its grammar to you in a plain way, making its mysteries clear to you, even putting your hand on the keys of the language's literature and syntax.

I pray that this book be a good helper to you in progressing in studying the language, thanking the author who exerted a great effort, that the book may be released in this interesting and profitable form. Through the intercession of our Mother, the Virgin, St.

---

1 1 Corinthians 14:15.

Mary, and the great saint Abba Macarius, and through the prayers of His Holiness Pope Tawadrous II, and to our Lord be the glory always.

Abba Epiphanius
Bishop and Abbot of the Monastery of St. Macarius
The Glorious Feast of the Ascension
13th of Pashons, 1731 AM (21st of May, AD 2015)

Introduction

How deep are the prayers and praises of the Church in the Coptic language! For truly they have a special taste and powerful effect within the human soul. How joyful is the person who practices these prayers and praises, while they understand what they are saying in the Coptic language! For they soar on high on the spiritual and heavenly [things], and taste the sweetness of the eternal [things], while they are still in the body. They summon the future, to live it from now.

I must confess that when my spiritual father, the late Fr. Matthew the Poor, charged me with [the tast of] teaching the Coptic language for beginners, I began preparing lessons, lesson by lesson. And one of the elders of the monastery, who was adept at the Coptic language, advised me to prepare questions for every lesson, which may be answered and corrected, so that the benefit may be full. It never came to my mind that these lessons would go out of the monastery; but the Lord permitted that they be published, and so the first edition was released. The lovers of learning rushed at it, and the subsequent printings followed one after another, for the seekers multiplied.

In this revised edition, the following was done: 1. The first ten lessons were reworded; 2. Some minor changes were made in the remaining lessons; 3. Some grammar terms were introduced with their meaning in the Coptic language; 4. The answers for the questions of the exercises, reviews, and exams were added at the end of this book.

I would like to offer special thanks to our beloved bishop, H.G. Abba Epiphanius, for the effort and time which he gave to review this book, word for word, despite the lack of his time. May the holy Lord keep him for us, with His Holiness Pope Tawadros II, for many years and long, quiet times, that they may offer fiery prayers for the sake of all.

May the holy Lord bless this work and make it fruitful in the life of many, that all may enjoy the depth of the prayers and praises of the holy Church, and that many may be encouraged to read and translate our Coptic heritage, which was set in writing hundreds of years ago and is awaiting the children of the Church to bring it out to light. May the desired fruits be multiplied through the intercessions and prayers of our Mother St. Mary and the great saint Abba Macarius and all the saints of the Church, and to our holy Lord be all glory and honor and worship, from now and forever. Amen.

The monk Andreas of the monastery of St. Macarius
25th of May 2015

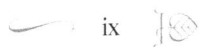

ϯⲛⲁⲧⲱⲃϩ ϧⲉⲛ ⲡⲓⲡⲛⲉⲩⲙⲁ,
ϯⲛⲁⲧⲱⲃϩ ⲇⲉ ⲟⲛ ϧⲉⲛ ⲡⲓⲕⲉϩⲏⲧ.
ϯⲛⲁⲉⲣⲯⲁⲗⲓⲛ ϧⲉⲛ ⲡⲓⲡⲛⲉⲩⲙⲁ,
ϯⲛⲁⲉⲣⲯⲁⲗⲓⲛ ⲇⲉ ⲟⲛ ϧⲉⲛ ⲡⲓⲕⲉϩⲏⲧ.

I will pray with the spirit,
and I will also pray with the understanding.
I will sing with the spirit,
and I will also sing with the understanding.
(1 Corinthians 14:15)

The Coptic Language

The Coptic language is the latest stage of the common dialect of the ancient Egyptian language.

At the entrance of the Christian religion into Egypt, the Coptic language continued to be used as a spoken language, [along] with the ancient Greek language, through which the Gospel was preached, until the eleventh century AD.

As the Arabic language spread increasingly after the entrance of Islam into the land of Egypt, the use of the Coptic language began to decline; nevertheless, the people of Upper Egypt continued speaking it, especially in some regions such as Niqada, Qos, Akhmim and its neighboring regions.

The use of this language among the commoners ended completely only around the beginning of the eighteenth century, but it is still in use until now in the Coptic churches, in their religious services.

Many and varied Coptic words and terms were introduced into the spoken Arabic language, and we currently use them in our daily life.

The Coptic language was written with Greek letters for a period of time before Christianity. And the Coptic language used all the letters of the Greek alphabet, with the pronunciation and characteristics it had at that time. To the Greek alphabet, seven other letters were added, taken from the Demotic writing, to express the pronunciation of seven sounds that do not exist in the Greek language.

When the Holy Scriptures were translated from the Greek language to the Coptic language, they saw that it was advisable to keep all the Greek words that had something to do with the new doctrine, or that expressed sheer Christian thoughts [or ideas]. This also took place when the Holy Scriptures were translated to the rest of the European languages. At the same time with these words, several other Greek words seeped into the Coptic language, for although there were words that had similar meaning in the [Coptic] language, their use was for the sake of appearing knowledgeable, and to give a special polish to an expression; for the custom was that everything, from which the fragrance of the Greek may be smelled, denoted progress and civilization, and what made this custom spread all the more is the aversion to everything related to the old, the pagan. And so these Greek words were introduced into the Coptic language, without being "Copticized" or becoming Coptic according to the grammar of the language, for the nouns remained in the subject form, and the verbs in the infinitive [form]; and so they are defective and cannot be conjugated.

And it happened just before the eleventh century, when the Copts perceived that the use of their language and its prevalence began to decline and that it was on the verge of vanishing, that they began to write and record it in volumes, and they wrote for it dictionaries and grammar guides. They called the first kind of publications the "Ladder," and the second kind the "Offering."

When the Copts began learning the Arabic language, they first wrote it with Coptic letters.

And about the eighteenth century when the knowledge of the Coptic language was close to vanishing, the Copts wrote their language with Arabic letters, and this was the final step in the life of the language.

In the second half of the twentieth century, a remarkable interest in the Coptic language began within the Coptic Church and in the homes of some families. May God make it fruitful, so that every Copt may understand the prayers and praises of the Church, thereby they become partners of the heavenly chorus.

The Coptic Language

The Coptic Alphabet

Upper case	Lower case	Name of letter		Pronunciation
(1) Letters taken from the Greek language: 25 in number				
Ⲁ	ⲁ	ⲁⲗⲫⲁ	Alpha	|a|
Ⲃ	ⲃ	ⲃⲏⲧⲁ	Beta, veta	|b|, |v|
Ⲅ	ⲅ	ⲅⲁⲙⲙⲁ	Jamma, gamma	|g|, |gh|, |n|
Ⲇ	ⲇ	ⲇⲉⲗⲧⲁ	Delta	|d|
Ⲉ	ⲉ	ⲉⲓ	Ei	|e|
Ⲋ	ⲋ	ⲥⲟⲩ	Sou	#6
Ⲍ	ⲍ	ⲍⲏⲧⲁ	Zeta	|z|
Ⲏ	ⲏ	ⲏⲧⲁ	Eta	|ee|
Ⲑ	ⲑ	ⲑⲏⲧⲁ	Theta	|th| as in "theology"
Ⲓ	ⲓ	ⲓⲱⲧⲁ	Iota	|i|
Ⲕ	ⲕ	ⲕⲁⲡⲡⲁ	Kappa	|k|
Ⲗ	ⲗ	ⲗⲟⲩⲗⲁ	Lola	|l|
Ⲙ	ⲙ	ⲙⲓ	Mi	|m|
Ⲛ	ⲛ	ⲛⲓ	Ni	|n|
Ⲝ	ⲝ	ⲝⲓ	Xi	|x|
Ⲟ	ⲟ	ⲟ	Short o	|o|
Ⲡ	ⲡ	ⲡⲓ	Pi	|p|
Ⲣ	ⲣ	ⲣⲟ	Ro	|r|
Ⲥ	ⲥ	ⲥⲓⲙⲁ	Cima	|s|
Ⲧ	ⲧ	ⲧⲁⲩ	Tav	|t|
Ⲩ	ⲩ	ⲩⲯⲓⲗⲟⲛ	Epsilon	|u|, |v|
Ⲫ	ⲫ	ⲫⲓ	Phi	|ph|
Ⲭ	ⲭ	ⲭⲓ	Ki, khi, shi	|k|, |kh|, |sh|
Ⲯ	ⲯ	ⲯⲓ	Psi	|ps|
Ⲱ	ⲱ	ⲱ	Aw	|au|

(2) Letters taken from the Demotic language (ancient Egyptian): 7 in number					
Ϣ	ϣ	ϣⲁⲓ	Shai	|sh|
Ϥ	ϥ	ϥⲁⲓ	Fai	|ph|
Ϧ	ϧ	ϧⲁⲓ	Khai	|kh|
Ϩ	ϩ	ϩⲱⲣⲓ	Hori	|h|
Ϫ	ϫ	ϫⲁⲛϫⲁ	Janja	|g|, |j|
Ϭ	ϭ	ϭⲓⲙⲁ	Chima	|ch|
Ϯ	ϯ	ϯ	Ti	|ti|

The vowels are seven in number: ⲁ, ⲉ, ⲏ, ⲓ, ⲟ, ⲩ, and ⲱ.

Pronunciation of the letters of the Coptic alphabet

The letters of the Coptic alphabet are divided into the following categories.

[1] Consonants (ϩⲁⲛϣⲱⲗϩ ⲉⲩϩⲟⲩⲣⲱⲟⲩ):

    1. Lips-articulated letters: ⲃ, ⲡ, ⲫ, ϥ

    2. Pharyngeal letters: ⳉ, ⲕ, ϫ, ϧ, ϩ

    3. Dental letters: ⲇ, ⲑ, ⲥ, ⲧ, ϯ

    4. Palatal letters: ϣ, ϫ, ϭ

    5. Lingual [i.e. of the tongue] letters: ⲗ, ⲣ

    6. Nasal letters: ⲙ, ⲛ

    7. Dual letters: ⲍ, ⳉ, ⲯ

[2] Vowels (ϩⲁⲛϣⲱⲗϩ ⲉⲩⲥⲙⲓⲕⲟⲛ):

    1. Letter sounding like |a|: ⲁ

    2. Letters sounding like |o|: ⲟ, ⲱ

    3. Letters sounding like |i|: ⲉ, ⲏ, ⲓ, ⲩ

✠ The Coptic Language ✠

Pronunciation of the consonant letters

1. Letters pronounced from the lips [i.e. the lips are the active site of articulation]: ⲃ, ⲡ, ⲫ, ϥ

The letter ⲃ has two sounds:

1. It is pronounced |v| if it is the first letter in a word or if it is followed by a vowel; for example:

ⲃⲁⲗ	eye	ⲃⲱⲕ	servant	ⲃⲁⲕⲓ	city	ⲃⲓⲣ	basket
ⲛⲓⲃⲉⲛ	every	ⲛⲟⲃⲓ	sin	ⲥⲁⲃⲉ	wise	ⲉ̀ⲃⲓⲁⲓⲕ	servants

2. It is pronounced |b| if it comes at the end of a word or if it is followed by a consonant; for example:

ϩⲱⲃ	work	ⲛⲏⲃ	master	ⲟⲩⲁⲃ	holy	ⲟⲩⲏⲃ	priest
ⲛⲟⲩⲃ	gold	ⲗⲱⲃϣ	interpretation	ϭⲏⲃⲥ	lamp	ⲧⲱⲃϩ	petition, prayer

As for proper nouns, it is pronounced |b|; for example:

ⲓⲁⲕⲱⲃ	Jacob	ⲓⲱⲃ	Job	Ⲁⲃⲣⲁⲁⲙ	Abraham	Ⲃⲁⲥⲓⲗⲓⲟⲥ	Basil

The letter ⲡ is pronounced |p|; for example:

ⲡⲓ	"the" definite article	ϣⲏⲡ	accepted	ϣⲱⲡⲓ	become	ⲡⲉ	to be

The letters ⲫ and ϥ: there is no difference between them, and they are pronounced the same way, that is |f| or |ph|; for example:

ⲫⲁⲓ	this (mas.)	ⲫⲉ	heaven	ⲫⲏ	that	Ⲫ̇ⲛⲟⲩϯ	God
ϥⲁⲓ	to lift up, to carry	ⲛⲓϥⲓ	breath	ⲥⲏϥⲓ	sword	ⲟⲩⲛⲟϥ	joy

2. Letters pronounced from the pharynx: ⲅ, ⲕ, ⲭ, ϭ, ϩ

The letter ⲅ has three sounds:

1. It is pronounced as |g| if it is followed by a vowel that sounds like |i| (ⲏ, ⲓ, ⲩ, ⲉ):

ⲁⲅⲓⲟⲥ	holy, saint	ⲅⲏ	earth	ⲅⲩⲙⲛⲁⲥⲓⲁ	sport (gymnastics)
ⲅⲉⲛⲟⲥ	race	ⲅⲉⲛⲉⲁ̀	generation	ⲙⲟⲛⲟⲅⲉⲛⲏⲥ	only-begotten

2. It is pronounced as |gh| if it is followed by a vowel that sounds like |o| and |a| (ⲱ, ⲟ, ⲁ):

ⲁⲅⲁⲡⲏ	love	ⲅⲁⲣ	because	ⲁⲅⲱⲛ	struggle, war

It is also pronounced |gh| if it is followed by consonants, for example:

ⲅ̀ⲣⲁⲫⲏ	writing	ⲅ̀ⲛⲟⲫⲟⲥ	fog, mist, or gloom	ⲁⲛⲁⲅⲛⲱⲥⲓⲥ	reading

3. It is pronounced |n| if it is followed by a pharyngeal letter (ⲅ, ⲕ, ⲭ, ⳍ):

ⲁⲅⲅⲉⲗⲟⲥ	angel	ⲁⲛⲁⲅⲕⲏ	necessity	ⲉⲅⲭⲟⲥ	spear
ⲥⲁⲗⲡⲓⲅⳍ	horn [trumpet]			ⲉⲩⲁⲅⲅⲉⲗⲓⲟⲛ	gospel

And there is a word that has all three sounds of the letter ⲅ: ⲅⲟⲅⲅⲩⲗⲏ (turnip). The words that contain the letter ⲅ are all Greek words in origin.

The letter ⲕ has one sound, that is ordinary |k|; for example:

ⲕⲁϣ	pen	ⲕⲁⲥ	bone	ⲕⲁϩⲓ	land
ⲕⲁⲡ	string	ⲕⲉⲙⲕⲉⲙ	timbrel	ⲕⲱϣ	to break
ⲛⲁⲕϩⲓ	pangs	ⲕⲱⲣϥ	to abolish	ⲛⲉⲕⲛⲁⲓ	your mercies

The letter ⲭ has three sounds:

1. It is pronounced as |k| in the Coptic words only, for example:

ⲭ̀ⲣⲱⲙ	fire	ⲭⲏⲙⲓ	Egypt	ⲭⲱⲡ	to hide, to conceal
ⲭⲁⲕⲓ	darkness	ⲭ̀ⲗⲟⲙ	crown	ⲭⲱ	to leave behind, to place

2. It is pronounced as |sh| if it is followed by the |i| sounding vowels (ⲏ, ⲓ, ⲩ, ⲉ), and also in the Greek words, like:

ⲯⲩⲭⲏ	soul	ⲭⲓⲱⲛ	snow	ⲭⲉⲣⲉ	hail
ⲓⲥⲭⲩⲣⲟⲥ	strong	ⲁⲣⲭⲏ	chief	ⲉⲩⲭⲏ	supplication, prayer

3. It is pronounced |kh| in the Greek words if it is followed by the |a| and |o| sounding vowels (ⲱ, ⲟ, ⲁ) or consonants:

ⲭⲁⲣⲓⲥ	grace	ⲭⲟⲣⲟⲥ	chorus	ⲭ̀ⲣⲓⲥⲧⲟⲥ	Christ, anointed
ⲭ̀ⲣⲟⲛⲟⲥ	time	ⲙⲟⲛⲁⲭⲟⲥ	monk	ⲗⲩⲭⲛⲓⲁ	lampstand, lighthouse

The letter ϧ is pronounced as |kh|:

ϧⲉⲛ	in, with	ⲥ̀ϧⲁⲓ	to write	ⲉ̀ϧⲟⲩⲛ	inward
ⲉⲃⲟⲗϧⲉⲛ	from	ϧⲟⲙϧⲉⲙ	to crush	ϧⲁⲧⲉⲛ	at, beside, in front of, near

The letter ϩ is pronounced as |h|:

ϩⲁ	to	ϩⲱⲛ	command	ϩⲟⲛϩⲉⲛ	to command
ϩⲱⲥ	to praise	ⲛⲟϩⲉⲙ	to rescue	ϩⲓⲟⲩ̀ⲓ	to throw, to cast

3. Letters pronounced between the teeth: ⲇ, ⲑ, ⲥ, ⲧ, ϯ

The letter ⲇ:

1. It is pronounced as |d| in the proper nouns that come from the Hebrew language:

ⲇⲁⲩⲓⲇ	David	ⲓⲟⲩⲇⲁⲥ	Judas	ⲇⲁⲛⲓⲏⲗ	Daniel

2. It is pronounced as |th| as in "the" in the Greek words and the Greek proper nouns:

ⲇⲱⲣⲟⲛ	offering	ⲇⲓⲁⲕⲟⲛ	servant	Ⲑⲉⲟⲇⲱⲣⲟⲥ	Theodore
ⲇⲓⲡⲛⲟⲛ	dinner	ⲇⲓⲁⲃⲟⲗⲟⲥ	devil	ⲇⲉ	but, while, whereas

There is not a single original word in the Bohairic dialect that includes this letter.

The letter ⲑ has two sounds:

1. It is pronounced as |th| as in "thanks":

ⲑⲁⲓ	this [fem.]	ⲡⲁⲑⲟⲥ	pain	ⲑⲉⲗ	hill, plateau
ⲑⲟⲙ	straw mat	ⲡⲁⲣⲑⲉⲛⲟⲥ	virgin	ⲑⲱⲕ	yours, belongs to you

2. It is pronounced as |t| if it is preceded by one of the following letters (ⲥ, ϣ, ⲧ, ⲙ); for example:

ⲥ̀ⲑⲟⲓ	smell	ⲧⲉⲙⲑⲁⲙ	mule	ⲥ̀ⲑⲉⲣⲧⲉⲣ	trembling

| ϣⲑⲏⲛ | shirt | ⲁⲥⲑⲉⲛⲏⲥ | weak | ⲥⲑⲟⲓⲛⲟⲩϥⲓ | incense |

It is to be noted in the pronunciation of ⲑ as |t| that it is pronounced as a soft |tah| as in "toy" if followed by the vowels ⲟ or ⲱ in the words ⲥⲑⲟⲓ and ϣⲑⲱⲣⲧⲉⲣ (turmoil, disturbance).

The letter ⲥ has three sounds:

1. It is pronounced as |s|:

| ⲥⲓⲙ | grass | ϧⲏⲃⲥ | lamp | ϫⲉⲃⲥ | ember [coal] | ⲥⲓ | satisfied [of food] |

2. It is pronounced as |sah| if it is followed by one of the letters (ⲱ, ⲟ, ⲁ), for example:

| ⲥⲟⲛⲓ | thief | ⲥⲱⲙⲁ | body | ⲥⲱ | to drink | ⲥⲁ | direction, side |
| ⲥⲟⲛ | brother | ⲥⲱⲛⲓ | sister | ⲥⲁⲃⲉ | wise | ⲥⲁϫⲓ | to speak |

3. It is pronounced as |z| if it is followed by the letter ⲙ in the Greek words only:

| ⲕⲟⲥⲙⲟⲥ | world | ⲡⲗⲁⲥⲙⲁ | creation | ⲡⲓⲣⲁⲥⲙⲟⲥ | trial, temptation |

As for the Coptic words, it is pronounced as |s|, and it is a common mistake that the two Coptic words ⲥⲙⲁⲣⲱⲟⲩⲧ and ⲥⲙⲟⲩ are pronounced with a |z|.

The letter ⲧ has four sounds:

1. It is usually pronounced |t|:

| ⲓⲱⲧ | father | ⲧⲏⲃ | finger | ⲧⲉⲛϩ | wing | ⲙⲱⲓⲧ | way, road |
| ⲥⲱⲧⲏⲣ | savior | ϩⲏⲧ | heart | ⲙⲉⲛⲣⲓⲧ | beloved | ⲥⲱⲧⲉⲙ | to hear |

2. It is pronounced as |tah| if it is followed by the letters (ⲱ, ⲟ, ⲁ), for example:

| ⲧⲁⲗϭⲟ | healed | ⲧⲁϫⲣⲟ | to confirm | ⲧⲱⲃϩ | request, supplication |
| ⲧⲁⲓⲟ | honor | ⲕⲁⲧⲁ | according | ⲧⲟⲩⲃⲟ | to purify, to cleanse |

3. It is pronounced as |d| in Greek words if it is preceded by the letter ⲛ, for example:

| ⲉⲛⲧⲟⲗⲏ | commandment | ⲗⲉⲛⲧⲓⲟⲛ | handkerchief | ⲟⲛⲧⲱⲥ | truly, indeed |

4. It is pronounced as |dh| if it is preceded by ⲛ and followed by one of the letters (ⲱ, ⲟ, ⲁ):

| ⲡⲁⲛⲧⲱⲛ | all | ⲡⲁⲛⲧⲁ | all | ⲡⲁⲛⲧⲟⲕⲣⲁⲧⲱⲣ | all-mighty |

The letter ϯ is a syllabic letter, consisting of two letters ϯı, and it is pronounced |ti|:

ⲛⲟⲩϯ	god	ϯ	to give	ϯ	"the" definite article
ⲛⲓϣϯ	great	ϯⲱⲟⲩ	to glorify	ϯ	I (pronoun)

4. Palatal letters: ϣ, ϫ, ϭ

The letter ϣ is pronounced |sh|, emphatic always:

ϣⲁ	to, until	ϣⲟⲙⲧ	three	ϣⲱⲗⲉⲙ	to smell	ϣⲉ	hundred, wood
ϣⲱ	sand	ϣⲁϣϥ	seven	ⲟⲩⲱϣⲧ	to worship	ϣⲁⲓ	feast, to rise
ⲱϣ	to read	ⲟⲩⲱϣ	to want	ϣⲉⲙϣⲓ	to serve	ϣⲟⲩ	abundant, a lot
ϣⲟ	thousand	ⲙⲏϣ	a lot	ϣⲱⲟⲩϣⲓ	sacrifice	ϣⲟⲩϣⲟⲩ	to boast, pride

The letter ϫ has two sounds:

1. It is pronounced as |g| if it is followed by the letters ⲱ, ⲟ, ⲁ or a consonant letter:

ϫⲱⲙ	book	ⲉ̀ϫⲱⲣϩ	eve	ϩⲟϫϩⲉϫ	to be annoyed
ϫⲟⲙ	power	ϩⲟⲗϫ	sweet	ⲟⲩϫⲁⲓ	salvation, health

2. It is pronounced as |j| if it is followed by the letters ⲏ, ⲓ, ⲩ, ⲉ:

ϫⲉ	because	ϫⲓϫ	hand	ϫⲁϫⲓ	enemy	ϫⲉⲙϯⲡⲓ	to taste
ϫⲏⲕ	perfect	ϫⲏⲣ	pillar	ϫⲓⲙⲓ	to find	ϫⲓⲛϫⲏ	free [of charge]

The letter ϭ has one sound, pronounced as |ch|:

ϭⲓ	to take	ϭⲣⲟ	victory	ⲧⲁⲗϭⲟ	to heal	ϭⲁⲗⲟϫ	foot
ϭⲱⲙ	garden	ϫⲁϭⲏ	left	ϭⲱⲣⲉⲙ	to indicate	ϭⲁⲗⲁⲩϫ	feet

5. Lingual Letters [i.e. articulated by the tongue]: ⲗ, ⲣ

The letter ⲗ has one sound |L|; for example:

ⲗⲁⲥ	tongue	ⲗⲁⲙⲡⲁⲥ	lamp	ⲑⲱⲗⲉⲃ	defilement, blemish
ⲗⲁⲟⲥ	people	ⲑⲉⲗⲏⲗ	to rejoice	ⲁⲧⲑⲱⲗⲉⲃ	without defilement

The letter ⲣ has one sound |r|; for example:

ⲣⲁⲛ	name	ⲣⲏ	sun	ⲣⲓ	room, cell	ⲓ̇ⲣⲓ	to make, to become
ⲣⲁ	deed	ⲣⲱ	mouth	ⲣⲁϣⲓ	to rejoice	ⲣⲱⲙⲓ	human [being]

6. Nasal letters: ⲛ, ⲙ

The letter ⲙ has one sound |m|; for example:

ⲙⲉⲓ	to love	ⲓⲟⲙ	sea	ⲙⲁ	place	ⲙⲏ	question article
ⲙⲏϣ	a lot	ⲙⲱⲟⲩ	water	ⲙⲉⲛⲣⲓⲧ	beloved	ⲥⲙⲏ̀	sound, voice

The letter ⲛ has one sound |n|; for example:

ⲛⲁⲓ	mercy	ⲛⲁⲛ	to us	ⲛⲟⲃⲓ	sin	ⲛⲟⲩⲃ	gold
ⲛⲟⲩϯ	god	ⲥⲓⲛⲓ	to cross, to pass	ϯⲛⲟⲩ = ⲛⲩⲛ			now

7. Dual letters: ⲍ, ⲝ, ⲯ

The letter ⲍ is pronounced as |z|:

ⲍⲱⲏ̀	life	ⲁⲛⲍⲏⲃ	school	ⲍⲱⲟⲛ	living creature
ⲍⲉⲛⲍⲉⲛ	lizard	Ⲍⲁⲭⲁⲣⲓⲁⲥ	Zacharias	ⲍⲱⲛⲏ	girdle, belt

The letter ⲝ is a compound letter, composed of ⲕⲥ together and is pronounced as |x|, for example:

ⲥⲁⲣⲝ	flesh	ⲁⲝⲓⲟⲥ	worthy	ⲗⲓⲝ	cover, veil	ⲑⲟⲩⲝ	pierce or stab

The letter ⲯ is a compound letter, composed of ⲡⲥ together and is pronounced as |ps|, and words containing it are few:

| ⲯⲩⲭⲏ | soul | ⲯⲁⲗⲙⲟⲥ | psalm | ⲯⲩⲭⲟⲥ | cold, frost |
| ⲯⲓⲧ | nine | ⲯⲁⲗⲧⲏⲥ | psalmist | ⲯⲁⲗⲓⲁ | psali (praise or spiritual song) |

Pronunciation of the vowel letters

The pronunciation of vowels is of paramount importance in the Coptic language, in clarifying similar words, to avoid confusion of their meaning; for it is noted that the difference in the lengthening [of the pronunciation] between ⲓ and ⲏ is double. Likewise, confusion between ⲟ and ⲱ has become widespread, even among those who have mastered the language, a matter that spoils the meaning of a word and the beauty of its pronunciation; therefore, perfecting the pronunciation of the vowels is necessary, and one should be accustomed to doing that from the beginning.

There are seven vowels in the Coptic language, which are divided into the following.

1. Letters that are short in length of pronunciation: ⲁ, ⲉ, ⲟ

The letter ⲁ:

1. It is pronounced as a prolonged |a| if the Jinkim mark is placed on it; for example:

| ⲁ̀ⲙⲟⲩ | to come | ⲁ̀ⲙⲏⲛ | truly | ⲁ̀ⲣⲉϩ | to keep, preserve | ⲁ̀ⲛⲟⲕ | I (pronoun) |
| ⲁ̀ⲙⲁϩⲓ | majesty | ⲁ̀ⲙⲉⲛϯ | hades | ⲁ̀ⲗⲟⲩ | boy, young man | ⲁ̀ⲛⲟⲛ | we (pronoun) |

It is also pronounced as a prolonged |a| if it comes at the beginning of two-letter words; for example:

| ⲁϣ | what | ⲁϥ | meat, fly | ⲁⲛ | no, not (negative particle) |

2. It is pronounced as a short |a| at the beginning of words consisting of three letters or more, and likewise at the beginning of three-letter syllables; for example:

| ⲁϫⲡ | hour | ⲁⲛⲁⲧⲟⲗⲏ | east | ⲁⲑⲙⲟⲩ | immortal |
| ⲁⲗⲗⲁ | but | ⲉ̀ⲃⲓⲁⲓⲕ | servants | ⲁⲛⲁⲥⲧⲁⲥⲓⲥ | resurrection |

3. It is pronounced as an emphasized short |a| when it comes in the middle of the word or its end, for example:

| ⲃⲁⲗ | eye | ⲫⲁⲓ | this | ⲥⲁ | direction, side | ⲕⲁⲧⲁ | according to |

The letter ⲉ:

1. It is pronounced |e| as in "essence" at the beginning of a word or syllable:

ⲉⲙⲓ	to know, to understand	ⲉⲃⲟⲗϧⲉⲛ	from	ⲫⲏⲧ	that who	ⲉⲛⲕⲟⲧ	to lie down, to sleep, to pass away

2. It is pronounced in the middle and end of a word as |ai| in the word "aim," for example:

| ⲡⲉ | to be | ⲃⲉⲣⲓ | new | ϧⲉⲛ | in, with | ⲃⲉⲛⲓ | palm tree |
| ⲙⲉⲓ | to love | ϩⲉⲙⲥⲓ | to sit | ⲛⲉⲙ | and, with | ⲛⲉϩⲥⲓ | to wake up |

The letter ⲟ: It is pronounced as a short, snatched |o| and has no lengthening.

1. At the beginning of a word it is pronounced as in "on," for example:

| ⲟⲥϧ | harvest | ⲟⲛ | also | ⲟϣϫ | painted |
| ⲟⲣⲫⲁⲛⲟⲥ | orphan | ⲟⲣⲑⲟⲇⲟⲍⲓⲁ | | upright opinion [orthodox] | |

If a Jinkim mark is placed on it at the beginning of a word or syllable, it gives it a slight lengthening:

| ⲟ̀ϩⲓ | to stand | ⲟ̀ⲛⲓ | to resemble | ⲟ̀ϫⲓ | to wrong, to deceive |

2. In the middle of the word, it is pronounced as "look, foot, cook," for example:

| ϫⲟⲙ | power | ⲑⲟⲙ | straw mat | ⲥⲟⲛ | brother | ⲉⲛⲕⲟⲧ | to lie down, to sleep |

3. At the end of a word or syllable, it is pronounced as "Rome":

| ⲣⲟ | door | ⲙⲟϣⲓ | to walk | ⲙ̀ⲑⲟ | in front of, before |

2. The vowels that are long in the length of their pronunciation: ⲏ, ⲱ

The letter ⲏ:

1. It is pronounced as a long |i| as in "feel" if it comes in the middle of a word or its end, for example:

| ϣⲏⲡ | acceptable | ϫⲏⲣ | pillar | ⲣⲏ | sun | ⲓⲏⲥ | fast, active |
| ϣⲏⲕ | deep | ϫⲏⲕ | perfect | ϫⲏ | placed | ⲙⲏ | question particle |

2. It is pronounced as a short |i| as in "Enoch," if it comes in the beginning of a word or syllable, for example:

| ⲏⲣⲡ | wine | Ⲏⲥⲁⲏⲁⲥ | Isaiah | Ⲏⲣⲱⲇⲏⲥ | Herod |

The letter ⲱ:

This letter is considered one of the most important letters that gives the Coptic language a special emphatic ring. It is different from the letter **ⲟ** that has a short lengthening, in that it is pronounced at the pharynx and is emphatic with a long lengthening.

1. At the beginning of the word, it is pronounced as in "song," for example:

| ⲱⲙⲥ | baptism | ⲱ̀ⲛⲓ | stone | ⲱⲥϧ | harvest | ⲱⲛϧ | life, to live |

2. In the middle of the word, it is pronounced as in "goal," for example:

| ϫⲱⲙ | book | ⲥⲱϯ | to save | ⲥⲱⲛⲓ | sister | ϣⲱⲡⲓ | to become |

3. At the end of the word, it is pronounced as in "go," for example:

| ⲃⲱ | tree | ⲥⲱ | to drink | ϣⲱ | sand | ⲭⲱ | to leave behind, to place |

3. The vowels ⲓ and ⲩ:

The letter ⲓ: This letter is used as a vowel and as a half consonant.

1. It has a short lengthening, meaning not elongated, if it comes at the end of the word; for example:

| ϣⲏⲣⲓ | son | ⲙⲁϩⲓ | arm | ⲣⲓ | room, cell | ⲡⲓ | "the" definite article |

2. It has a long lengthening, that is elongated, if it comes in the middle of the word; for example:

| ⲛⲓⲙ | who | ⲕⲓⲙ | to move | ⲙⲓⲥⲓ | to beget | ϫⲓⲙⲓ | to find |

It is noted that in the last two examples, that the middle iota is long while the one at the end is snatched, short.

3. It is pronounced as |ee| if it is preceded or followed by another vowel; for example:

ⲓⲱⲧ	father	ϫⲟⲓ	ship	ⲓⲟϩ	moon	ⲓⲱⲛⲁ	Jonah
ⲓⲱϯ	dew	ⲱⲓⲕ	bread	ⲓⲱⲃ	Job	ⲓⲟⲩⲇⲁⲥ	Judas
ⲓⲉⲍⲉⲕⲓⲏⲗ	Ezekiel	ⲓⲟⲣⲇⲁⲛⲏⲥ	Jordan	ⲓⲉⲣⲉⲙⲓⲁⲥ	Jeremiah

4. It is pronounced as short |i| if it comes at the beginning of the word and is followed by a consonant:

Ⲓⲥⲁⲁⲕ	Isaac	ⲓ̀ϥⲧ	nail	ⲓ̀ⲣⲓ	to make, to become
ⲓ̀ϣⲓ	to crucify	ⲓⲭⲑⲩⲥ	fish	ⲓ̀ⲛⲓ	to offer, to bring
Ⲓⲥⲣⲁⲏⲗ	Israel	ⲓⲥⲭⲩⲣⲟⲥ	strong	ⲓ̀ⲃ̄	devil, demon

And sometimes it is pronounced |ya| as in "yard," for example:

ⲓⲥϫⲉ	if	ⲓⲥ	O, behold	ⲓⲥϫⲉⲛ	from, since

The letter ⲩ: this letter has three sounds.

1. It is pronounced as |v| if it is preceded by one of the letters ⲁ or ⲉ:

ⲙⲁⲩ	mother	ⲉⲩⲭⲁⲣⲓⲥⲧⲓⲁ	thanksgiving	ⲛⲁⲩ	to see, to look
Ⲉⲩⲁ	Eve	ⲉⲩⲁⲅⲅⲉⲗⲓⲟⲛ	gospel	ⲙⲉⲩⲓ̀	thought, to think
ⲉⲩⲗⲟⲅⲓⲁ	blessing	ⲙ̀ⲕⲁⲩϩ	suffering	ϣⲁϥⲉⲣ	deserts

2. It is pronounced as |ee| as in "feel" if it is preceded by a consonant, for example:

ϩⲩⲙⲛⲟⲥ	praise	ⲑⲩⲥⲓⲁ	sacrifice	ⲕⲩⲣⲓⲟⲥ	master, lord

3. It is pronounced as |i| as in "if" if it comes at the beginning of the word; for example:

ⲩⲓⲟⲥ	son	ⲩⲡⲉ	behold	ⲩⲡⲟⲙⲟⲛⲏ	patience
ⲩⲯⲓⲥⲧⲟⲥ	height	ⲩⲙⲛⲟⲗⲟⲅⲓⲁ		praise, glorification

The sound ⲟⲩ:

It is a famous and important sound in Coptic words, and it is pronounced as follows.

1. At the beginning of the word or syllable, it is pronounced |oo| as in "boot," for example:

ⲟⲩⲣⲟ	king	ⲟⲩⲣⲱⲟⲩ	kings	ⲟⲩⲧⲁϩ	fruit
ⲟⲩⲛⲟϥ	joy	ⲟⲩϫⲁⲓ	salvation	ⲓⲁⲣⲱⲟⲩ	rivers
ⲉ̀ϩⲟⲟⲩ	day, daytime		ⲟⲩ	indefinite article for singular	

2. In the middle of the word, it is pronounced |oo| as in "food," for example:

| ϣⲟⲩⲣⲏ | censer | ⲛⲟⲩⲃ | gold | ⲧⲟⲩⲃⲟ | to purify |
| ⲣⲟⲩϩⲓ | evening | ⲉϧⲟⲩⲛ | inward | ⲛⲟⲩϥⲓ | beneficial, good |

3. At the end of the word, it is pronounced |oo| as in "taboo" with lengthening, for example:

| ϯⲛⲟⲩ | now | ⲥⲙⲟⲩ | to bless | ⲟⲩⲛⲟⲩ | hour, time |
| ⲥⲓⲟⲩ | star | ⲛ̀ϧⲏⲧⲟⲩ | in them | ⲥⲏⲟⲩ | time, era |

4. It is pronounced |ou| as in "Omega" if it is followed by a vowel, for example:

ⲟⲩⲏⲃ	priest	ⲟⲩⲁⲓ	one [mas.]	ⲟⲩⲁⲃ	pure, holy
ⲟⲩⲏⲛ	open	ⲟⲩⲓ	one [fem.]	ⲫⲏⲟⲩⲓ	heavens
ⲁⲗⲱⲟⲩⲓ	children	ⲟⲩⲉⲓ	to be far	ⲟⲩⲓⲛⲁⲙ	right [as in right hand]

But it is pronounced as an independent syllable if it is followed by the letter ⲱ; for example:

| ⲟⲩⲱⲓⲛⲓ | light | ⲟⲩⲱⲛϩ | to confess | ⲟⲩⲱϣⲧ | to worship |
| ⲟⲩⲱⲙ | to eat | ⲟⲩⲱⲛ | to open | ⲟⲩⲱϣ | to want, to desire |

The Dual Sounds:

Dual sounds consist of two vowels forming one syllable. In the Coptic language, there are the following dual sounds:

ⲁⲓ	ⲫⲁⲓ	this	ⲑⲁⲓ	this	ⲛⲁⲓ	mercy, those
ⲉⲓ	ⲙⲉⲓ	to love	ⲉⲣⲫⲉⲓ	temple	ⲟⲩⲉⲓ	to be far
ⲟⲓ	ⲕⲟⲓ	field	ⲥ̀ⲟⲟⲓ	smell	ϫⲟⲓ	boat, ship
ⲏⲓ	ⲙⲏⲓ	true	ⲙⲉⲑⲙⲏⲓ	truth	ⲏⲓ	home, house
ⲱⲓ	ⲓⲱⲓ	to wash	ϥⲱⲓ	hair	ⲡ̀ϣⲱⲓ	the height
ⲁⲩ	ⲙⲁⲩ	mother	ⲥ̀ⲛⲁⲩ	two	ⲛⲁⲩ	to see, to look
ⲉⲩ	ⲙⲉⲩⲓ	thought	ϣⲁϥⲉⲩ	deserts	ⲉⲩⲭⲏ	supplication, prayer

✠ Foundations of the Coptic Language ✠

The Pronunciation and Writing of the Greek Words Used in Coptic Texts

As for the Greek words that are introduced into the Coptic language, the Copts pronounce them according to the modern Greek way. And the effect of this pronunciation extended to the way they were spelled; for they wrote them according to the pronunciation. And most of the dual sounds vanished and were substituted with single vowels.

1. The dual sound ⲁⲓ is written and pronounced ⲉ, for example:

The word ⲕⲉ instead of ⲕⲁⲓ (the conjunction "and")

The word ⲇⲓⲕⲉⲟⲥ instead of ⲇⲓⲕⲁⲓⲟⲥ (righteous, just)

And so are all the verbs which come in the infinitive middle voice and passive voice in the Greek language like ⲭⲁⲣⲓⲍⲉⲥⲑⲉ instead of ⲭⲁⲣⲓⲍⲉⲥⲑⲁⲓ (to grant)

2. Likewise, the dual sound ⲉⲓ is written and pronounced ⲓ in the infinitive active voice, for example:

ⲁⲅⲓⲁⲍⲓⲛ instead of ⲁⲅⲓⲁⲍⲉⲓⲛ (to sanctify)

ⲛⲏⲥⲧⲉⲩⲓⲛ instead of ⲛⲏⲥⲧⲉⲩⲉⲓⲛ (to fast)

3. The letter ⲏ and the dual sound ⲟⲓ are also pronounced ⲓ, for example:

ⲉⲛ ⲧⲓⲥ ⲩⲯⲓⲥⲧⲓⲥ instead of ⲉⲛ ⲧⲟⲓⲥ ⲩⲯⲓⲥⲧⲟⲓⲥ (on high)

The result is that there are five different ways to express the |i| sound in the various Greek words, and they are: ⲩ, ⲓ, ⲏ, ⲉⲓ, ⲟⲓ. Because of this difficulty which has emerged, this led to exchanging one letter for another in these words when writing the Greek texts in Coptic letters.

When the Copts used the Greek words beginning with ⲁ vowel that had on it a soft breathing mark (an |h| breathing,), they placed the Coptic letter ϩ before it when they wrote it in Coptic, for example:

| ὅπως → ϩⲟⲡⲱⲥ (so that) | εἰρήνη → ϩⲓⲣⲏⲛⲏ (peace) |
| ἵνα → ϩⲓⲛⲁ (so that) | ἐλπίς → ϩⲉⲗⲡⲓⲥ (hope) |

It is to be noted that this rule applies to some Greek words but not all the Greek words beginning with a vowel with a soft breathing mark (an |h| breathing). For there are words, at the beginning of which the letter ϩ was not written, for example:

| ἅγιος → ⲁⲅⲓⲟⲥ (holy) | ἄξιος → ⲁⲍⲓⲟⲥ (worthy) |

The Jinkim Mark (ϪⲒⲚⲔⲒⲘ)

It is a dot or a small dash that is placed on a consonant to add a soft |e| sound before the letter and it is pronounced on its own, so that it may give its sound in the word. It is also placed on a vowel, to indicate that it is pronounced independently, and it gives it lengthening in pronunciation.

There are nine letters on which the Jinkim mark is not placed:

Ⲃ, Ⲇ, Ꙅ, Ⲍ, Ⲗ, Ⲝ, Ⲣ, Ⲯ, Ϯ.

As for the letters on which the Jinkim mark is placed, they are:

Ⲁ̇, Ⲅ̇, Ⲉ̇, Ⲏ̇, Ⲑ̇, Ⲓ̇, Ⲕ̇, Ⲙ̇, Ⲛ̇, Ⲟ̇, Ⲡ̇, Ⲥ̇, Ⲧ̇, Ⲩ̇, Ⲫ̇, Ⲭ̇, Ⲱ̇, Ϣ̇, Ϥ̇, Ϧ̇, Ϩ̇, Ϫ̇, Ϭ̇.

Each of these letters, when the Jinkim mark is placed on it, is pronounced as an independent syllable.

Syllables

A syllable is a part of a word that the tongue can utter all at once. It consists of a consonant letter or more, with a vowel or a dual sound. Also, the syllable may consist of a single vowel or dual sound. And in the Coptic language, there are two types of syllables:

1. The open syllable, which ends with a vowel; for example:

| ⲤⲰ | to drink | ⲤⲈ | yes | ⲤⲀ | direction, side | ⲤⲒ | to be satisfied |

2. The closed (locked) syllable, which ends with a consonant; for example:

| ⲤⲞⲚ | brother | ϦⲈⲚ | in, with | ⲢⲀⲚ | name | ⲒⲰⲦ | father |

Words may consist of one, two, or three syllables, and perhaps more, which are called multi-syllable words.

1. One-syllable words:

| ⲘⲀ | place | ϢⲀ | to | ⲖⲀⲤ | tongue | ⲤⲰⲚⲦ | to create |
| Ⳉⲱ | to place | ϨⲰⲂ | work | ⲂⲰⲔ | servant | ⲤⲰⲦⲠ | to choose |

2. Two-syllable words:

| ⲘⲒⲤⲒ | to beget | ⲤⲀϪⲒ | to speak | ⲢⲰⲘⲒ | human [being] | ϦⲞⲘϦⲈⲘ | to crush |
| ϪⲒⲘⲒ | to find | ⲀⲤⲠⲒ | language | ⲤⲞⲖⲤⲈⲖ | to adorn, to console |

3. Three-syllable words:

| ⲙⲉⲧⲟⲩⲣⲟ | kingdom | ϣⲉⲡϩ̀ⲙⲟⲧ | to thank | ⲁⲅⲅⲉⲗⲟⲥ | angel |
| ⲉⲣϩ̀ⲙⲟⲧ | to grant | ϯⲟⲩⲱϣⲧ | I worship | ⲡⲓⲧⲟⲩⲃⲟ | purity |

4. Multi-syllable words:

ⲧⲉⲕⲙⲉⲧⲟⲩⲣⲟ	your kingdom	ϯⲙⲉⲧⲙⲁⲓⲣⲱⲙⲓ	the love of mankind
ⲡⲓⲡⲣⲟⲫⲏⲧⲏⲥ	the prophet	ⲁⲣⲭⲏⲇⲓⲁⲕⲟⲛ	archdeacon
ⲡⲉⲕⲙⲁⲛ̀ϣⲱⲡⲓ	your dwelling	ⲉⲧⲥⲙⲁⲣⲱⲟⲩⲧ	the blessed

✠ The Coptic Language ✠

Ⲡⲓϣⲗⲏⲗ ⲛ̀ⲧⲉ Ⲡⲓϭⲟⲓⲥ	The Lord's Prayer
Ϧⲉⲛ ⲫ̀ⲣⲁⲛ ⲙ̀Ⲫⲓⲱⲧ ⲛⲉⲙ Ⲡ̀ϣⲏⲣⲓ ⲛⲉⲙ Ⲡⲓⲡ̀ⲛⲉⲩⲙⲁ ⲉⲑⲟⲩⲁⲃ ⲟⲩⲛⲟⲩϯ ⲛ̀ⲟⲩⲱⲧ. ⲁⲙⲏⲛ.	In the name of the Father and the Son and the Holy Spirit, one God. Amen.
ⲁⲣⲓⲧⲉⲛ ⲛ̀ⲉⲙⲡ̀ϣⲁ ⲉⲛⲭⲱ ⲙ̀ⲙⲟⲥ ϧⲉⲛ ⲟⲩϣⲉⲡ̀ϩⲙⲟⲧ ϫⲉ:	Make us worthy to pray thankfully:
ⲡⲉⲛⲓⲱⲧ ⲉⲧ ϧⲉⲛ ⲛⲓⲫⲏⲟⲩⲓ:	Our Father who art in heaven,
ⲙⲁⲣⲉϥⲧⲟⲩⲃⲟ ⲛ̀ϫⲉ ⲡⲉⲕⲣⲁⲛ:	hallowed be Thy name.
ⲙⲁⲣⲉⲥⲓ ⲛ̀ϫⲉ ⲧⲉⲕⲙⲉⲧⲟⲩⲣⲟ:	Thy kingdom come,
ⲡⲉⲧⲉϩⲛⲁⲕ ⲙⲁⲣⲉϥϣⲱⲡⲓ:	Thy will be done,
ⲙ̀ⲫ̀ⲣⲏϯ ϧⲉⲛ ⲧ̀ⲫⲉ ⲛⲉⲙ ϩⲓϫⲉⲛ ⲡⲓⲕⲁϩⲓ:	on earth as it is in heaven.
ⲡⲉⲛⲱⲓⲕ ⲛ̀ⲧⲉ ⲣⲁⲥϯ ⲙⲏⲓϥ ⲛⲁⲛ ⲙ̀ⲫⲟⲟⲩ:	Give us this day our daily bread
ⲟⲩⲟϩ ⲭⲁ ⲛⲏⲉⲧⲉⲣⲟⲛ ⲛⲁⲛ ⲉ̀ⲃⲟⲗ	and forgive us our trespasses,
ⲙ̀ⲫ̀ⲣⲏϯ ϩⲱⲛ ⲛ̀ⲧⲉⲛⲭⲱ ⲉ̀ⲃⲟⲗ ⲛ̀ⲛⲏⲉⲧⲉ ⲟⲩⲟⲛ ⲛ̀ⲧⲁⲛ ⲉ̀ⲣⲱⲟⲩ:	as we forgive those who trespass against us
ⲟⲩⲟϩ ⲙ̀ⲡⲉⲣⲉⲛⲧⲉⲛ ⲉ̀ϧⲟⲩⲛ ⲉ̀ⲡⲓⲣⲁⲥⲙⲟⲥ:	and lead us not into temptation,
ⲁⲗⲗⲁ ⲛⲁϩⲙⲉⲛ ⲉ̀ⲃⲟⲗϩⲁ ⲡⲓⲡⲉⲧϩⲱⲟⲩ:	but deliver us from the evil one.
ϧⲉⲛ Ⲡⲓⲭ̀ⲣⲓⲥⲧⲟⲥ Ⲓⲏⲥⲟⲩⲥ ⲡⲉⲛϭⲟⲓⲥ:	In Christ Jesus our Lord.
ϫⲉ ⲑⲱⲕ ⲧⲉ ϯⲙⲉⲧⲟⲩⲣⲟ ⲛⲉⲙ ϯϫⲟⲙ ⲛⲉⲙ ⲡⲓⲱⲟⲩ ϣⲁ ⲉ̀ⲛⲉϩ: ⲁⲙⲏⲛ.	For Thine is the kingdom, and the power, and the glory, forever. Amen.

✠ Foundations of the Coptic Language ✠

\multicolumn{6}{c}{**Abbreviated Words**}					
Word	Abbr.	Meaning	Word	Abbr.	Meaning
ⲁⲗⲗⲏⲗⲟⲩⲓⲁ	ⲁⲗ	Alleluia	Ⲙⲓⲭⲁⲏⲗ	Ⲙⲓⲭⲁ	Michael
ⲁⲙⲏⲛ	ⲁⲙ	Amen	Ⲡⲁⲩⲗⲟⲥ	Ⲡⲁⲩ	Paul
ⲁⲡⲟⲥⲧⲟⲗⲟⲥ	ⲁⲡⲟⲥ	Apostle	Ⲡⲉⲧⲣⲟⲥ	Ⲡⲉⲧ	Peter
ⲁⲣⲓⲡⲣⲉⲥⲃⲉⲩⲓⲛ	ⲁⲣⲓ	Intercede	Ⲡⲓϭⲟⲓⲥ	Ⲡⲟ̅ⲥ̅, Ⲡϭ̅ⲥ̅	The Lord
Ⲇⲁⲩⲓⲇ	ⲇⲁⲇ	David	Ⲡⲓ̅ⲭⲣⲓⲥⲧⲟⲥ	Ⲡ̅ⲭ̅ⲥ̅	The Christ
ⲇⲟⲝⲁⲥⲓ	ⲇⲟⲝ	Glory be to you	ⲡⲁⲣⲑⲉⲛⲟⲥ	ⲡⲁⲣⲑ	Virgin
ⲉⲑⲟⲩⲁⲃ	ⲉⲟⲩ	Holy	ⲡ̅ⲛⲉⲩⲙⲁ	ⲡⲛⲁ	Spirit
ⲉⲩⲁⲅⲅⲉⲗⲓⲟⲛ	ⲉⲩⲁⲅ	The Gospel	ⲡⲣⲁⲝⲓⲥ	ⲡⲣⲁ	Acts
Ⲑⲉⲟⲥ, Ⲑⲉⲟⲩ	ⲑⲥ, ⲑⲩ	God (Gr.)	ⲥⲧⲁⲩⲣⲟⲥ	⳨	Cross
Ⲓⲉⲣⲟⲩⲥⲁⲗⲏⲙ	Ⲓ̅ⲗⲏⲙ	Jerusalem	ⲥⲧⲁⲩⲣⲟⲥ	ⲥⲣⲥ	Cross
Ⲓⲏⲥⲟⲩⲥ	Ⲓ̅ⲏ̅ⲥ̅	Jesus	ⲥⲩⲛ ⲑⲉⲱ	ⲥⲩⲛ	In the name of God
Ⲓⲥⲣⲁⲏⲗ	Ⲓⲥⲗ	Israel	ⲥⲱⲧⲏⲣ	ⲥⲱⲣ	Savior
Ⲓⲱⲁⲛⲛⲏⲥ	Ⲓⲱⲁ	John	ⲧⲱⲃϩ	ⲧⲱⲃ	Pray
Ⲓⲱⲁⲛⲛⲏⲛ	Ⲓⲱⲛ	John	ⲩⲓⲟⲥ, ⲩⲓⲟⲩ	ⲩⲥ, ⲩⲩ	Son
ⲕⲉⲫⲁⲗⲉⲟⲛ	ⲕⲉⲫ	Chapter	Ⲫ̇ⲛⲟⲩϯ	Ⲫ̇ϯ	God (Cop.)
ⲕⲩⲣⲓⲉ ⲉ̇ⲗⲉⲏⲥⲟⲛ	ⲕⲉ, ⲕⲉⲛ	Lord have mercy	ⲭⲉⲣⲉ	ⲭⲉ	Hail
ⲕⲩⲣⲓⲟⲥ, ⲕⲩⲣⲓⲟⲩ	ⲕⲥ, ⲕⲩ	The Lord (Gr.)	ⲭⲉⲣⲟⲩⲃⲓⲙ	ⲭⲉⲣ	Cherubim
Ⲗⲟⲩⲕⲁⲥ	Ⲗⲟⲩⲕ	Luke	ⲭⲣⲟⲛⲟⲥ	ⲭⲣ	Time
Ⲙⲁⲣⲕⲟⲥ	Ⲙⲁⲣ	Mark	ⲯⲁⲗⲙⲟⲥ	ⲯⲁⲗ	Psalm
ⲙⲁⲣⲧⲩⲣⲟⲥ	ⲯⲉ	Martyr	ϣⲁ ⲉ̇ⲃⲟⲗ	ϣⲃⲗ	etc.
Ⲙⲁⲧⲑⲉⲟⲥ	Ⲙⲁⲧ	Matthew	ϣ̇ⲗⲏⲗ	ϣⲗ	Pray
ⲙⲉⲛⲉⲛⲥⲁ	ⲙⲉ	After	ϭⲟⲓⲥ	ϭⲥ, ⲟⲥ	Lord (Cop.)

The First Lesson
ⲡⲓϩⲟⲩⲓⲧ ⲛ̀ϣⲱ

✠

ⲛⲓⲛ̀ϫⲁⲓ ⲛ̀ⲁ̀ⲧⲥⲱⲟⲩⲛ

INDEFINITE ARTICLES

A noun, when it enters into a sentence, must be preceded by either an indefinite article or definite article. Indefinite articles are the following:

ⲟⲩ: It is placed before singular masculine and singular feminine nouns, and it is connected to the noun.

ϩⲁⲛ: It is placed before plural nouns of both genders, and it is connected to the noun.

1. Nouns that do not change in plural:

Masculine nouns (ϩⲱⲟⲩⲧ) that <u>do not change</u> in plural			
Singular ⲟⲩⲱⲧ		Plural ⲙⲏϣ	
ⲟⲩⲓⲟϩ	A moon	ϩⲁⲛⲓⲟϩ	Moons
ⲟⲩⲕⲁϣ	A pen	ϩⲁⲛⲕⲁϣ	Pens
ⲟⲩⲣⲁⲛ	A name	ϩⲁⲛⲣⲁⲛ	Names
ⲟⲩⲣⲏ	A sun	ϩⲁⲛⲣⲏ	Suns
ⲟⲩⲣⲱⲙⲓ	A man, human	ϩⲁⲛⲣⲱⲙⲓ	Men, humans
ⲟⲩⲥⲓⲟⲩ	A star	ϩⲁⲛⲥⲓⲟⲩ	Stars
ⲟⲩⲥⲙⲟⲩ	A blessing	ϩⲁⲛⲥⲙⲟⲩ	Blessings
ⲟⲩⲧⲁⲓⲟ	A honor	ϩⲁⲛⲧⲁⲓⲟ	Honors

Foundations of the Coptic Language

ⲟⲩⲧⲱⲟⲩ	A mountain	ϩⲁⲛⲧⲱⲟⲩ	Mountains
ⲟⲩⲱϣ	A lesson	ϩⲁⲛⲱϣ	Lessons
ⲟⲩϣⲏⲣⲓ	A son	ϩⲁⲛϣⲏⲣⲓ	Sons
ⲟⲩϣⲓⲛⲓ	A question	ϩⲁⲛϣⲓⲛⲓ	Questions
ⲟⲩ̀ϣⲗⲏⲗ	A prayer	ϩⲁⲛϣⲗⲏⲗ	Prayers
ⲟⲩ̀ϣϣⲏⲛ	A tree	ϩⲁⲛϣϣⲏⲛ	Trees
ⲟⲩϩⲱⲥ	A praise, hymn	ϩⲁⲛϩⲱⲥ	Praises
ⲟⲩϫⲱⲙ	A book	ϩⲁⲛϫⲱⲙ	Books

Feminine nouns (ⲥϩⲓⲙⲓ) that <u>do not change</u> in plural			
Singular ⲟⲩⲧ		Plural ⲛⲏϣ	
ⲟⲩⲃⲁⲕⲓ	A city	ϩⲁⲛⲃⲁⲕⲓ	Cities
ⲟⲩⲃⲱⲕⲓ	A maidservant	ϩⲁⲛⲃⲱⲕⲓ	Maidservants
ⲟⲩⲕⲩⲑⲁⲣⲁ	A harp	ϩⲁⲛⲕⲩⲑⲁⲣⲁ	Harps
ⲟⲩⲙⲁⲩ	A mother	ϩⲁⲛⲙⲁⲩ	Mothers
ⲟⲩⲛⲏⲥⲧⲓⲁ	A fast	ϩⲁⲛⲛⲏⲥⲧⲓⲁ	Fasts
ⲟⲩⲡⲁⲣⲑⲉⲛⲟⲥ	A virgin	ϩⲁⲛⲡⲁⲣⲑⲉⲛⲟⲥ	Virgins
ⲟⲩⲣⲓ	A room, cell	ϩⲁⲛⲣⲓ	Rooms, cells
ⲟⲩⲥⲱⲛⲓ	A sister	ϩⲁⲛⲥⲱⲛⲓ	Sisters
ⲟⲩϣⲉⲣⲓ	A daughter	ϩⲁⲛϣⲉⲣⲓ	Daughters
ⲟⲩϣⲟⲩⲣⲏ	A censer	ϩⲁⲛϣⲟⲩⲣⲏ	Censers
ⲟⲩϫⲓϫ	A hand	ϩⲁⲛϫⲓϫ	Hands
ⲟⲩ̀ϭⲣⲟⲙⲡⲓ	A dove	ϩⲁⲛϭⲣⲟⲙⲡⲓ	Doves

2. Nouns that change in plural:

Masculine nouns (ϥϩⲓⲙⲓ) that <u>change</u> in plural			
Singular ⲟⲩⲱⲧ		Plural ⲙⲏϣ	
ⲟⲩⲁⲗⲟⲩ	A child, youth	ϩⲁⲛⲁⲗⲱⲟⲩⲓ	Children, youths
ⲟⲩⲃⲱⲕ	A servant	ϩⲁⲛⲉ̀ⲃⲓⲁⲓⲕ	Servants
ⲟⲩⲓⲱⲧ	A father	ϩⲁⲛⲓⲟϯ	Fathers
ⲟⲩⲥⲟⲛ	A brother	ϩⲁⲛⲥⲛⲏⲟⲩ	Brothers
ⲟⲩⲓⲁⲣⲟ	A river	ϩⲁⲛⲓⲁⲣⲱⲟⲩ	Rivers
ⲟⲩⲓⲟⲙ	A sea	ϩⲁⲛⲁⲙⲁⲓⲟⲩ	Seas
ⲟⲩϣⲁϥⲉ	A desert	ϩⲁⲛϣⲁϥⲉⲣ	Deserts
ⲟⲩϧⲉⲗⲗⲟ	An elder, old [man]	ϩⲁⲛϧⲉⲗⲗⲟⲓ	Elders, old [men]

Feminine nouns (ⲥϩⲓⲙⲓ) that <u>change</u> in plural			
Singular ⲟⲩⲱⲧ		Plural ⲙⲏϣ	
ⲟⲩⲫⲉ	A heaven, sky	ϩⲁⲛⲫⲏⲟⲩⲓ	Heavens, skies
ⲟⲩⲁ̀ⲫⲉ	A head	ϩⲁⲛⲁ̀ⲫⲏⲟⲩⲓ	Heads
ⲟⲩⲥϩⲓⲙⲓ	A woman	ϩⲁⲛϩⲓⲟⲙⲓ	Women

Sample sentences:

ⲁ̄ ϩⲁⲛϣⲗⲏⲗ ⲛⲉⲙ ϩⲁⲛϩⲱⲥ ⲛⲉⲙ ϩⲁⲛⲛⲏⲥⲧⲓⲁ.
Prayers and praises and fasts.

ⲃ̄ ⲟⲩⲫⲉ ⲛⲉⲙ ⲟⲩⲣⲏ ⲛⲉⲙ ⲟⲩⲓⲟϩ ⲛⲉⲙ ϩⲁⲛⲥⲓⲟⲩ.
A sky and a sun and a moon and stars.

ⲅ̄ ⲟⲩⲕⲁϩⲓ ⲛⲉⲙ ϩⲁⲛⲧⲱⲟⲩ ⲛⲉⲙ ϩⲁⲛⲓⲁⲣⲱⲟⲩ ⲛⲉⲙ ϩⲁⲛⲁⲙⲁⲓⲟⲩ.
A land and mountains and rivers and seas.

ⲇ̄ ϩⲁⲛⲃⲁⲕⲓ ⲛⲉⲙ ϩⲁⲛϯⲙⲓ ⲛⲉⲙ ϩⲁⲛϣⲁϥⲉⲣ.
Cities and villages and deserts.

ⲉ̄ ⲟⲩⲓⲱⲧ ⲛⲉⲙ ⲟⲩⲙⲁⲩ ⲛⲉⲙ ϩⲁⲛϣⲏⲣⲓ ⲛⲉⲙ ϩⲁⲛϣⲉⲣⲓ.
A father and a mother and sons and daughters.

ⲉ̄ ⲟⲩⲣⲱⲙⲓ ⲛⲉⲙ ⲟⲩⲥ̀ϩⲓⲙⲓ ⲛⲉⲙ ϩⲁⲛⲁⲗⲱⲟⲩⲓ̀.
A man and a woman and children.

ⲍ̄ ϩⲁⲛⲥ̀ⲛⲏⲟⲩ ⲛⲉⲙ ϩⲁⲛⲥⲱⲛⲓ.
Brothers and sisters.

ⲏ̄ ϩⲁⲛⲙⲱⲓⲧ ⲛⲉⲙ ϩⲁⲛϣϣⲏⲛ ⲛⲉⲙ ϩⲁⲛⲏⲓ.
Roads and trees and houses.

ⲑ̄ ⲟⲩⲱϣ ⲛⲉⲙ ⲟⲩϫⲱⲙ ⲛⲉⲙ ⲟⲩⲕⲁϣ.
A lesson and a book and a pen.

ⲓ̄ ϩⲁⲛⲉ̀ⲃⲓⲁⲓⲕ ⲛⲉⲙ ϩⲁⲛⲃⲱⲕⲓ.
Menservants and maidservants.

ⲓ̄ⲁ̄ ϩⲁⲛⲓⲟϯ ⲛⲉⲙ ϩⲁⲛϧⲉⲗⲗⲟⲓ ⲛⲉⲙ ϩⲁⲛⲙⲟⲛⲁⲭⲟⲥ.
Fathers and elders and monks.

ⲓ̄ⲃ̄ ⲟⲩⲡⲁⲣⲑⲉⲛⲟⲥ ⲛⲉⲙ ⲟⲩϭ̀ⲣⲟⲙⲡⲓ ⲛⲉⲙ ⲟⲩϣⲟⲩⲣⲏ.
A virgin and a dove and a censer.

Exercises

1. Write the meaning of the following words:

1	ⲟⲩϣ̀ⲗⲏⲗ	2	ϩⲁⲛϫⲓϫ	3	ⲟⲩⲧⲁⲓⲟ
4	ϩⲁⲛⲫⲏⲟⲩⲓ̀	5	ⲟⲩⲃⲁⲕⲓ	6	ϩⲁⲛⲉ̀ⲃⲓⲁⲓⲕ
7	ⲟⲩⲃⲱⲕ	8	ϩⲁⲛⲣⲓ	9	ⲟⲩⲫⲉ
10	ϩⲁⲛϣⲏⲣⲓ	11	ⲟⲩϣⲟⲩⲣⲏ	12	ϩⲁⲛⲥⲱⲛⲓ
13	ⲟⲩⲛⲏⲥⲧⲓⲁ	14	ϩⲁⲛϩⲱⲥ	15	ⲟⲩⲥⲟⲛ
16	ϩⲁⲛϣⲉⲣⲓ	17	ⲟⲩⲁ̀ⲫⲉ	18	ϩⲁⲛⲣⲁⲛ
19	ⲟⲩⲕⲑⲁⲣⲁ	20	ϩⲁⲛⲣⲱⲙⲓ	21	ⲟⲩⲥ̀ϩⲓⲙⲓ
22	ϩⲁⲛϣϣⲏⲛ	23	ⲟⲩϣⲓⲛⲓ	24	ϩⲁⲛⲥ̀ⲛⲏⲟⲩ
25	ⲟⲩⲥⲓⲟⲩ	26	ϩⲁⲛⲓⲟϯ	27	ⲟⲩϫⲱⲙ
28	ϩⲁⲛⲕⲁϣ	29	ⲟⲩⲣⲏ	30	ϩⲁⲛⲡⲁⲣⲑⲉⲛⲟⲥ
31	ⲟⲩϭ̀ⲣⲟⲙⲡⲓ	32	ϩⲁⲛϩⲓⲟⲙⲓ	33	ⲟⲩϧⲉⲗⲗⲟ
34	ϩⲁⲛⲧⲱⲟⲩ	35	ⲟⲩⲣⲓ	36	ϩⲁⲛϣⲁϥⲉⲣ
37	ⲟⲩⲃⲱⲕⲓ	38	ϩⲁⲛⲙⲁⲩ	39	ⲟⲩⲥ̀ⲙⲟⲩ

2. Write the plural form of the following nouns:

	Singular	Plural		Singular	Plural
1.	ⲟⲩⲓⲱⲧ		2.	ⲟⲩⲓⲁⲣⲟ	
3.	ⲟⲩⲃⲱⲕ		4.	ⲟⲩⲁⲗⲟⲩ	
5.	ⲟⲩⲥⲟⲛ		6.	ⲟⲩⲓⲟⲙ	
7.	ⲟⲩϣⲁϥⲉ		8.	ⲟⲩⲥϩⲓⲙⲓ	
9.	ⲟⲩϥⲉ		10.	ⲟⲩⲁϥⲉ	
11.	ⲟⲩϧⲉⲗⲗⲟ		12.	ⲟⲩⲛⲏⲥⲧⲓⲁ	
13.	ⲟⲩⲓⲟϩ		14.	ⲟⲩⲥⲓⲟⲩ	

Lesson 2
ⲡⲓϣ ⲙ̄ⲙⲁϩ B̄
ⲛⲓⲛϫⲁⲓ ⲛ̀ⲥⲱⲟⲩⲛ
DEFINITE ARTICLES

1. The Masculine Singular Noun (ⲡⲓϩⲱⲟⲩⲧ ⲛ̀ⲟⲩⲱⲧ)

ⲡⲓ: a strong article, which is in general used before any masculine, singular noun.

ⲫ: a weak article, which is used before a masculine, singular noun that begins with one of the following letters: ⲃ, ⲓ, ⲗ, ⲙ, ⲛ, ⲟ, ⲣ.

ⲡ̀: a weak article, which is used before a masculine, singular noun that begins with letters other than the abovementioned.

ⲡⲓⲃⲱⲕ	= ⲫⲃⲱⲕ	The servant	ⲡⲓⲉⲛⲉϩ	= ⲡ̀ⲉⲛⲉϩ	The eternity, the age
ⲡⲓⲓⲟϩ	= ⲫⲓⲟϩ	The moon	ⲡⲓⲏⲓ	= ⲡ̀ⲏⲓ	The home, the house
ⲡⲓⲗⲁⲥ	= ⲫⲗⲁⲥ	The tongue	ⲡⲓⲕⲁϩⲓ	= ⲡ̀ⲕⲁϩⲓ	The earth
ⲡⲓⲙⲟⲩ	= ⲫⲙⲟⲩ	The death	ⲡⲓⲥⲟⲛ	= ⲡ̀ⲥⲟⲛ	The brother
ⲡⲓⲙⲱⲟⲩ	= ⲫⲙⲱⲟⲩ	The water	ⲡⲓⲱⲓⲕ	= ⲡ̀ⲱⲓⲕ	The bread
ⲡⲓⲛⲁϩϯ	= ⲫⲛⲁϩϯ	The faith	ⲡⲓⲱⲛϧ	= ⲡ̀ⲱⲛϧ	The life
ⲡⲓⲛⲟⲃⲓ	= ⲫⲛⲟⲃⲓ	The sin	ⲡⲓϣⲃⲱⲧ	= ⲡ̀ϣⲃⲱⲧ	The rod
ⲡⲓⲛⲟⲩϯ	= ⲫⲛⲟⲩϯ	The God	ⲡⲓϣⲏⲣⲓ	= ⲡ̀ϣⲏⲣⲓ	The son

Lesson 2 ✠ Definite Articles ✠

ⲡⲓⲣⲁⲛ = ⲫⲣⲁⲛ	The name	ⲡⲓϣϩⲏⲛ = ⲡⲓϣϩⲏⲛ	The tree
ⲡⲓⲣⲏ = ⲫⲣⲏ	The sun	ⲡⲓⲭⲱⲙ = ⲡⲭⲱⲙ	The book
ⲡⲓⲣⲱⲙⲓ = ⲫⲣⲱⲙⲓ	The man	ⲡⲓϭⲟⲓⲥ = ⲡϭⲟⲓⲥ	The master, the lord

Note 1:

The masculine, singular nouns, beginning with the syllable **ⲟⲩ** or the letter **ⲓ**, and are followed by a vowel, takes the definite article **ⲫ̀**; but if they are followed by a consonant, then they take the definite article **ⲡ̀**, for example:

ⲡⲓⲟⲩⲁⲓ = ⲫⲟⲩⲁⲓ	The one	ⲡⲓⲟⲩⲛⲟϥ = ⲡⲟⲩⲛⲟϥ	The joy
ⲡⲓⲟⲩⲱⲓⲛⲓ = ⲫⲟⲩⲱⲓⲛⲓ	The light	ⲡⲓⲟⲩⲣⲟ = ⲡⲟⲩⲣⲟ	The king
ⲡⲓⲟⲩⲏⲃ = ⲫⲟⲩⲏⲃ	The priest	ⲡⲓⲟⲩⲧⲁϩ = ⲡⲟⲩⲧⲁϩ	The fruit
ⲡⲓⲓⲁⲣⲟ = ⲫⲓⲁⲣⲟ	The river	ⲡⲓⲟⲩϫⲁⲓ = ⲡⲟⲩϫⲁⲓ	The salvation
ⲡⲓⲓⲟϩ = ⲫⲓⲟϩ	The moon	ⲡⲓⲓϥⲧ = ⲡⲓϥⲧ	The nail

2. The Feminine Singular Noun (ϯⲥϩⲓⲙⲓ ⲛ̀ⲟⲩⲱⲧ)

ϯ: a strong article, which is generally used before any feminine, singular nouns.

ⲑ̀: a weak article, which is used before a feminine, singular noun that begins with one of the following letters: ⲃ, ⲓ, ⲗ, ⲙ, ⲛ, ⲟ, ⲣ.

ⲧ̀: a weak article, which is used before a feminine, singular noun that begins with letters others than the abovementioned.

ϯⲃⲁⲕⲓ = ⲑ̀ⲃⲁⲕⲓ	The city	ϯⲁⲣⲭⲏ = ⲧ̀ⲁⲣⲭⲏ	The beginning
ϯⲃⲱⲕⲓ = ⲑ̀ⲃⲱⲕⲓ	The maidservant	ϯⲁⲫⲉ = ⲧ̀ⲁⲫⲉ	The head
ϯⲗⲱⲓϫⲓ = ⲑ̀ⲗⲱⲓϫⲓ	The reason	ϯⲡⲁⲣⲑⲉⲛⲟⲥ = ⲧ̀ⲡⲁⲣⲑⲉⲛⲟⲥ	The virgin
ϯⲙⲁⲩ = ⲑ̀ⲙⲁⲩ	The mother	ϯⲥⲱⲛⲓ = ⲧ̀ⲥⲱⲛⲓ	The sister
ϯⲛⲉϫⲓ = ⲑ̀ⲛⲉϫⲓ	The belly, the womb	ϯⲥϩⲓⲙⲓ = ⲧ̀ⲥϩⲓⲙⲓ	The woman
ϯⲛⲏⲃ = ⲑ̀ⲛⲏⲃ	The lady	ϯⲫⲉ = ⲧ̀ⲫⲉ	The heaven, the sky

ϯⲣⲓ = ⲉ̀ⲣⲓ		The room, the cell	ϯⲫⲟⲣϣⲓ = ⲧ̀ⲫⲟⲣϣⲓ		The table
ϯⲃⲓⲣ = ⲉ̀ⲃⲓⲣ		The palm-leaves basket	ϯⲯⲩⲭⲏ = ⲧ̀ⲯⲩⲭⲏ		The soul
ϯⲗⲩⲭⲛⲓⲁ = ⲉ̀ⲗⲩⲭⲛⲓⲁ		The lampstand	ϯϣⲉⲣⲓ = ⲧ̀ϣⲉⲣⲓ		The daughter
ϯⲙⲁϫⲧ = ⲉ̀ⲙⲁϫⲧ		The intestine, guts	ϯϣⲟⲩⲣⲏ = ⲧ̀ϣⲟⲩⲣⲏ		The censer
ϯⲛⲁϩⲃⲓ = ⲉ̀ⲛⲁϩⲃⲓ		The neck, the shoulder	ϯϫⲓϫ = ⲧ̀ϫⲓϫ		The hand
ϯⲣⲟⲙⲡⲓ = ⲉ̀ⲣⲟⲙⲡⲓ		The year	ϯϭⲁⲗⲟϫ = ⲧ̀ϭⲁⲗⲟϫ		The foot

Note 2:

The feminine, singular nouns beginning with the syllable ⲟⲩ or the letter ⲓ, and are followed by a vowel, take the definite article ⲉ̀; but if they are followed by a consonant, then they take the definite article ⲧ̀, for example:

ϯⲟⲩⲓ̀ = ⲉ̀ⲟⲩⲓ̀		The one	ϯⲟⲩⲣⲱ = ⲧ̀ⲟⲩⲣⲱ		The queen
ϯⲓⲁⲗ = ⲉ̀ⲓⲁⲗ		The mirror	ϯⲟⲩⲛⲟⲩ = ⲧ̀ⲟⲩⲛⲟⲩ		The hour
ϯⲓⲟⲡⲓ = ⲉ̀ⲓⲟⲡⲓ		The job	ϯⲟⲩⲃⲁϣ = ⲧ̀ⲟⲩⲃⲁϣ		The whiteness
ϯⲓⲱⲣⲉⲙ = ⲉ̀ⲓⲱⲣⲉⲙ		The sight	ϯⲓⲣⲓⲥ = ⲧ̀ⲓⲣⲓⲥ		The rainbow

Note 3:

The weak definite articles (ⲧ̀, ⲉ̀, ⲡ̀, ⲫ̀) define the word in a less specific way, while the strong definite articles (ϯ, ⲡⲓ) define the meaning of the word more precisely, for they point to the person or thing themselves.

Lesson 2 ✣ *Definite Articles* ✣

Exercises

1. Translate the following to the English language:

ā ⲫⲛⲟⲩϯ ⲛⲉⲙ ⲫⲣⲱⲙⲓ.
b̄ ⲫⲛⲟⲃⲓ ⲛⲉⲙ ⲫⲙⲟⲩ.
ḡ ⲫⲛⲁϩϯ ⲛⲉⲙ ⲡⲓⲟⲩⲱⲓⲛⲓ.
d̄ ⲡⲓⲣⲏ ⲛⲉⲙ ⲡⲓⲓⲟϩ.
ē ⲡⲓⲥⲟⲛ ⲛⲉⲙ ϯⲥⲱⲛⲓ.
s̄ ⲡϣⲏⲣⲓ ⲛⲉⲙ ϯϣⲉⲣⲓ.
z̄ ϯⲃⲱⲕⲓ ⲛⲉⲙ ϯⲙⲁⲩ.
h̄ ⲧⲫⲉ ⲛⲉⲙ ⲡⲕⲁϩⲓ.
ø̄ ⲫⲙⲟⲩ ⲛⲉⲙ ⲡⲱⲛϧ.
ī ⲟⲩⲣⲱⲙⲓ ⲛⲉⲙ ϩⲁⲛϣⲏⲣⲓ.
īā ⲟⲩⲟⲩⲣⲟ ⲛⲉⲙ ϩⲁⲛⲉ̀ⲃⲓⲁⲓⲕ.

2. Translate the following to the Coptic language:

1. The bread and the water.
2. Prayers and fasts.
3. The lord and the servant.
4. The fruit and the life.
5. The head and the foot.
6. Elders and virgins.
7. The censer and the table.
8. The salvation and the joy.
9. A brother and a sister.
10. The belly and the tongue.
11. The cell and the heaven.

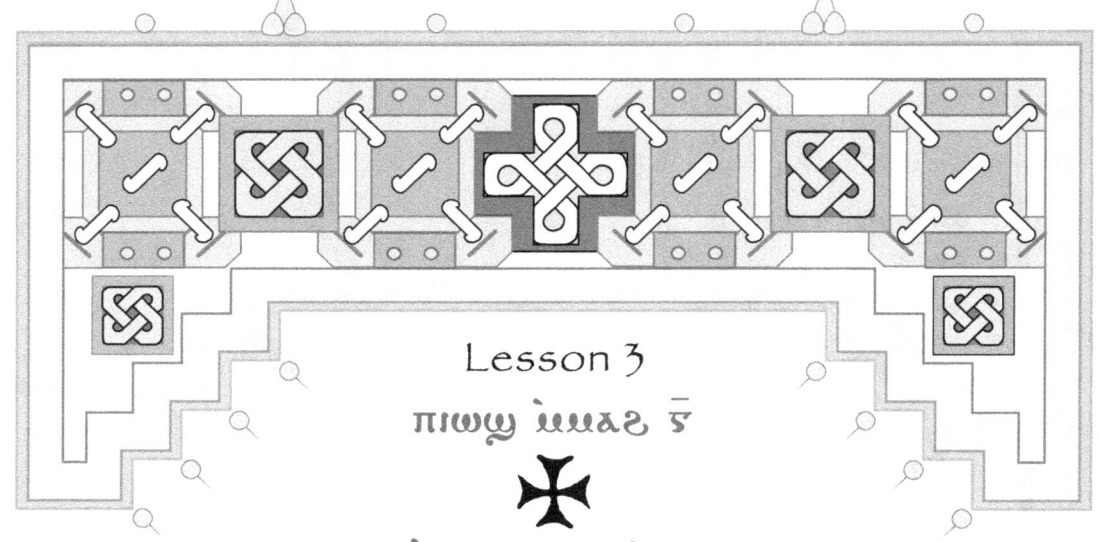

Lesson 3
ⲡⲓⲱϣ ⲙⲙⲁϩ $\bar{\text{ⲅ}}$

✠

ⲡⲓⲙⲏϣ ⲛ̀ⲣⲁⲛ ⲛⲉⲙ ϯⲙⲉⲧⲧⲟⲩϥ

THE PLURAL DEFINITE ARTICLE
AND THE GENITIVE CONSTRUCTION

1. The Plual Definite Article

ⲛⲓ is used in general to define plural nouns for both genders, for example:

ⲡⲓϣⲏⲣⲓ	The son	ⲛⲓϣⲏⲣⲓ	The sons
ⲡⲓϫⲱⲙ	The book	ⲛⲓϫⲱⲙ	The books
ϯⲥⲱⲛⲓ	The sister	ⲛⲓⲥⲱⲛⲓ	The sisters
ϯⲃⲁⲕⲓ	The city	ⲛⲓⲃⲁⲕⲓ	The cites

The form of most nouns does not change between the singular and plural forms, like the previous examples; however, there are nouns that have a different form in plural than that in singular, for example:

Singular ϩⲟⲩⲧ		Plural ⲙⲏϣ	
ⲡⲓⲁⲗⲟⲩ	The you, the child	ⲛⲓⲁⲗⲱⲟⲩⲓ̀	The children
ϯⲁ̀ⲫⲉ	The head	ⲛⲓⲁ̀ⲫⲏⲟⲩⲓ̀	The heads
ⲡⲓⲃⲱⲕ	The servant	ⲛⲓⲉ̀ⲃⲓⲁⲓⲕ	The servants
ⲫⲓⲁⲣⲟ	The river	ⲛⲓⲓⲁⲣⲱⲟⲩ	The rivers

Lesson 3 ✠ The Plural Definite Article and the Genitive Construction ✠

ⲫⲓⲟⲙ	The sea	ⲛⲓⲁⲙⲁⲓⲟⲩ	The seas
ⲫⲓⲱⲧ	The father	ⲛⲓⲓⲟϯ	The fathers
ⲡⲓⲙⲉⲛⲣⲓⲧ	The beloved	ⲛⲓⲙⲉⲛⲣⲁϯ	The beloved
ⲡⲓⲟⲩⲣⲟ	The king	ⲛⲓⲟⲩⲣⲱⲟⲩ	The kings
ⲡⲓⲥⲟⲛ	The brother	ⲛⲓⲥⲛⲏⲟⲩ	The brothers
ϯⲥϩⲓⲙⲓ	The woman	ⲛⲓϩⲓⲟⲙⲓ	The women
ϯⲫⲉ	The heaven	ⲛⲓⲫⲏⲟⲩⲓ	The heavens
ⲡϣⲁϥⲉ	The desert	ⲛⲓϣⲁϥⲉⲩ	The deserts
ⲡⲓϧⲉⲗⲗⲟ	The elder	ⲛⲓϧⲉⲗⲗⲟⲓ	The elders
ⲡⲓϩⲁⲗⲏⲧ	The bird	ⲛⲓϩⲁⲗⲁϯ	The birds
ⲡⲓϩⲱⲃ	The work	ⲛⲓϩⲃⲏⲟⲩⲓ	The works
ϯϭⲁⲗⲟϫ	The foot	ⲛⲓϭⲁⲗⲁⲩϫ	The feet

2. The Genitive or Possessive Construction

For possessive construction, there are articles that are used to add two nouns one to another.

ⲛ̀ⲧⲉ is the general article for the possessive construction, and it comes unconnected [i.e. separate] between the first noun (modified) and the second noun (modifier).

ⲡⲏⲓ ⲛ̀ⲧⲉ ⲛⲓⲁⲅⲅⲉⲗⲟⲥ	The house of the angels
ⲡϭⲟⲓⲥ ⲛ̀ⲧⲉ ⲛⲓϫⲟⲙ	The Lord of hosts
ⲡⲓϫⲱⲙ ⲛ̀ⲧⲉ Ⲙⲁⲣⲕⲟⲥ	The book of Mark

ⲛ̀ is an article for the possessive construction, and it comes connected to the beginning of the second noun (modifier).

ⲑⲙⲁⲩ ⲛ̀Ⲓⲏⲥⲟⲩⲥ	The mother of Jesus
ϯϣⲉⲣⲓ ⲛ̀Ⲥⲓⲱⲛ	The daughter of Zion
ϯⲁⲫⲉ ⲛ̀Ⲓⲱⲁⲛⲛⲏⲥ	The head of John

✠ Foundations of the Coptic Language ✠

Two important notes:

1. ⲛ̀ is changed to ⲙ̀ if the second noun begins with one of the following five letters: ⲯ, ⲃ, ⲫ, ⲙ, ⲡ.

ⲙ̀:

ⲡϣⲏⲣⲓ ⲙ̀ⲫⲣⲱⲙⲓ	The Son of Man
ⲫⲣⲁⲛ ⲙ̀Ⲫⲓⲱⲧ	The name of the Father
ⲡϫⲱⲙ ⲙ̀Ⲡⲉⲧⲣⲟⲥ	The book of Peter

2. ⲛⲓ is changed to ⲛⲉⲛ as a definite article for the plural first noun, in case of the presence of ⲛ̀ or ⲙ̀ as a possessive article connected to the second noun.

ⲛⲉⲛ:

ⲛⲉⲛϣⲏⲣⲓ ⲙ̀Ⲡⲓⲥⲣⲁⲏⲗ	The sons of Israel
ⲛⲉⲛⲣⲱⲙⲓ ⲙ̀Ⲫⲛⲟⲩϯ	The men of God
ⲛⲉⲛϫⲱⲙ ⲛ̀ϯⲉⲕⲕⲗⲏⲥⲓⲁ	The books of the Church

Exercises

1. Translate the following to the English language:

1. ⲛⲓⲓⲟϯ ⲛⲉⲙ ⲛⲓⲥⲛⲏⲟⲩ.
2. ⲛⲓⲟⲩⲣⲱⲟⲩ ⲛⲉⲙ ⲛⲓⲉ̀ⲃⲓⲁⲓⲕ.
3. ϩⲁⲛϩⲉⲗⲗⲟⲓ ⲛⲉⲙ ϩⲁⲛⲁⲗⲱⲟⲩⲓ.
4. ⲛⲓⲁⲙⲁⲓⲟⲩ ⲛⲉⲙ ⲛⲓⲁⲣⲱⲟⲩ.
5. ⲟⲩϩⲁⲗⲏⲧ ⲛⲉⲙ ϩⲁⲛϩⲁⲗⲁϯ.
6. ⲛⲓⲫⲏⲟⲩⲓ̀ ⲛⲉⲙ ⲛⲓϣⲁϥⲉⲩ.
7. ϩⲁⲛⲣⲱⲙⲓ ⲛⲉⲙ ϩⲁⲛϩⲓⲟⲙⲓ.
8. ϩⲁⲛϫⲓϫ ⲛⲉⲙ ϩⲁⲛⲃⲁⲗⲁⲩϫ.
9. ⲡⲕⲁϩⲓ ⲛⲉⲙ ⲛⲓⲉ̀ⲃⲛⲏⲟⲩⲓ̀.
10. ϯⲯⲩⲭⲏ ⲛⲉⲙ ⲫⲛⲁϩϯ.
11. ⲛⲓⲉ̀ⲃⲓⲁⲓⲕ ⲛ̀ⲧⲉ ⲡ̀ϭⲟⲓⲥ.
12. ϯⲃⲁⲕⲓ ⲛ̀ⲧⲉ Ⲫⲛⲟⲩϯ.
13. ⲛⲉⲛϣⲏⲣⲓ ⲛ̀Ⲥⲓⲱⲛ.
14. ⲛⲓⲟⲩⲣⲱⲟⲩ ⲛ̀ⲧⲉ ⲡ̀ⲕⲁϩⲓ.
15. ⲛⲓϣⲏⲗ ⲛ̀ⲧⲉ ⲛⲓⲓⲟϯ.
16. ⲛⲓϩⲁⲗⲁϯ ⲛ̀ⲧⲉ ⲧ̀ⲫⲉ.
17. ⲛⲉⲛϩ̀ⲃⲏⲟⲩⲓ̀ ⲙ̀ⲡⲓⲣⲱⲙⲓ.
18. ⲡ̀ⲱⲓⲕ ⲛ̀ⲧⲉ ⲡ̀ⲱⲛϧ.
19. ⲛⲓⲓⲟϯ ⲛ̀ⲧⲉ ⲛⲓϣⲁϥⲉⲩ.
20. ⲛⲓⲣⲟⲙⲡⲓ ⲛ̀ⲧⲉ ⲡ̀ⲱⲛϧ.

Lesson 3 ✠ The Plural Definite Article and the Genitive Construction ✠

2. Put the suitable definite article for the plural noun [ⲛⲓ or ⲛⲉⲛ]:

1. .... ϧⲉⲗⲗⲟⲓ ⲛ̀ⲧⲉ ϯⲃⲁⲕⲓ.
2. .... ⲉ̀ⲃⲓⲁⲓⲕ ⲙ̀ⲡⲟⲩⲣⲟ.
3. .... ϭⲁⲗⲁⲩϫ ⲛ̀ⲛⲓⲙⲁⲑⲏⲧⲏⲥ.
4. .... ⲥ̀ⲛⲏⲟⲩ ⲛ̀ⲧⲉ Ⲡϭⲟⲓⲥ.
5. .... ⲙⲉⲛⲣⲁϯ ⲛ̀Ⲓⲏⲥⲟⲩⲥ.
6. .... ⲁⲅⲅⲉⲗⲟⲥ ⲙ̀Ⲫϯ.

3. Translate the following to the Coptic language:

1. The birds and the heavens.
2. The brothers and the sisters.
3. Rivers and seas.
4. Fathers and mothers.
5. The head and the feet.
6. The books and the works.
7. Beloved (pl.) and brothers.
8. The sons of light.
9. The faith of men.
10. The monks of the desert.
11. The works of the Lord.
12. The fruit of life.
13. The hand of God.
14. The joy of the beloved (pl.).

Lesson 4
ⲡⲓⲱϣ ⲙ̀ⲙⲁϩ ⲇ̄

ⲡⲓϫⲓⲛϭⲱⲣⲉⲙ

NEAR DEMONSTRATIVE ADJECTIVES AND PRONOUNS

1. Near demonstrative adjectives (ⲛⲓ̀ⲥⲙⲟⲧ ⲛ̀ϭⲱⲣⲉⲙ ⲉⲧϩⲱⲛⲧ)

They come connected (ⲉⲩⲧⲟⲙϥ) to the indicated noun.

For the singular masculine (ⲛ̀ϩⲱⲟⲩⲧ ⲛ̀ⲟⲩⲱⲧ), ⲡⲁⲓ- (this):

ⲡⲁⲓⲉ̀ϩⲟⲟⲩ	This day	ⲡⲁⲓⲣⲱⲙⲓ	This man
ⲡⲁⲓϫⲱⲙ	This book	ⲡⲁⲓⲥⲟⲛ	This brother

For the singular feminine (ⲛ̀ⲥϩⲓⲙⲓ ⲛ̀ⲟⲩⲱⲧ), ⲧⲁⲓ- (this):

ⲧⲁⲓϣⲟⲩⲣⲏ	This censer	ⲧⲁⲓϣⲉⲣⲓ	This daughter
ⲧⲁⲓⲯⲩⲭⲏ	This soul	ⲧⲁⲓϣⲉⲗⲉⲧ	This bride

For the plural both genders (ⲛ̀ⲑⲟ ⲥ̀ⲛⲁⲩ ⲙ̀ⲙⲏϣ), ⲛⲁⲓ- (These):

ⲛⲁⲓϣⲏⲣⲓ	These sons	ⲛⲁⲓⲥⲱⲛⲓ	These sisters
ⲛⲁⲓⲥⲛⲏⲟⲩ	These brothers	ⲛⲁⲓⲣⲟⲙⲡⲓ	These years

Lesson 4 ✣ Near Demonstrative Adjectives and Pronouns ✣

Notes on demonstrative adjectives:

1. A demonstrative adjective is written with the indicated noun as one word.

2. ⲡⲁⲓ-, ⲧⲁⲓ-, ⲛⲁⲓ- take the place of the demonstrative adjective and the definite article together.

2. Near demonstrative pronouns (ⲛⲓⲙⲉⲩⲓ ⲛ̀ϭⲱⲣⲉⲙ ⲉⲧϩⲱⲛⲧ)

They come separate (ⲉⲩⲫⲟⲣϫ) from the indicated noun.

For the singular masculine, ⲫⲁⲓ (this):

ⲫⲁⲓ ⲟⲩⲁⲗⲟⲩ ⲡⲉ.	This is a boy.
ⲫⲁⲓ ⲟⲩϧⲉⲗⲗⲟ ⲡⲉ.	This is an elder.
ⲫⲁⲓ ⲟⲩⲕⲁϣ ⲡⲉ.	This is a pen.

For the singular feminine, ⲑⲁⲓ (this):

ⲑⲁⲓ ⲟⲩϣⲉⲣⲓ ⲧⲉ.	This is a daughter.
ⲑⲁⲓ ⲟⲩϣⲟⲩⲣⲏ ⲧⲉ.	This is a censer.
ⲑⲁⲓ ⲟⲩⲉⲕⲕⲗⲏⲥⲓⲁ ⲧⲉ.	This is a church.

For the plural both genders, ⲛⲁⲓ (these):

ⲛⲁⲓ ϩⲁⲛⲣⲱⲙⲓ ⲛⲉ.	These are men.
ⲛⲁⲓ ϩⲁⲛⲥⲱⲛⲓ ⲛⲉ.	These are sisters.
ⲛⲁⲓ ϩⲁⲛϩⲁⲗⲁϯ ⲛⲉ.	These are birds.
ⲛⲁⲓ ϩⲁⲛϣϣⲏⲛ ⲛⲉ.	These are trees.

A rule: the demonstrative pronoun is always used with the "to be" verbs [ⲡⲉ, ⲧⲉ, ⲛⲉ]. If the indicated noun is preceded by an indefinite article, the "to be" verb is placed after the noun, but if it is preceded by a definite article, then the "to be" verb comes before it, according to the following examples:

| ⲫⲁⲓ ⲟⲩⲭⲱⲙ ⲡⲉ. | This is a brother. | ⲫⲁⲓ ⲡⲉ ⲡⲓⲭⲱⲙ. | This is the book. |
| ⲑⲁⲓ ⲟⲩⲃⲁⲕⲓ ⲧⲉ. | This is a city. | ⲑⲁⲓ ⲧⲉ ϯⲃⲁⲕⲓ. | This is the city. |

ⲛⲁⲓ ϩⲁⲛϩⲉⲗⲗⲟⲓ ⲛⲉ. These are elders.	ⲛⲁⲓ ⲛⲉ ⲛⲓϩⲉⲗⲗⲟⲓ. These are the elders.

Exercises

1. Translate the following to the English language:

ⲁ̅ ⲫⲁⲓ ⲡⲉ ⲡϣⲏⲣⲓ ⲙ̀ⲫⲣⲱⲙⲓ.

ⲃ̅ ⲑⲁⲓ ⲧⲉ ⲑⲙⲁⲩ ⲛ̀ⲓⲏⲥⲟⲩⲥ.

ⲅ̅ ⲛⲁⲓ ⲛⲉ ⲛⲓⲟϯ ⲛ̀ⲧⲉ ϯⲉⲕⲕⲗⲏⲥⲓⲁ.

ⲇ̅ ⲡⲁⲓⲉϩⲟⲟⲩ ⲡⲉ ⲡϣⲁⲓ ⲛ̀ⲛⲓⲁⲡⲟⲥⲧⲟⲗⲟⲥ.

ⲉ̅ ⲧⲁⲓⲛⲏⲥⲧⲓⲁ ⲧⲉ ϯⲛⲏⲥⲧⲓⲁ ⲛ̀ⲧⲉ ϯⲡⲁⲣⲑⲉⲛⲟⲥ.

ⲋ̅ ⲛⲁⲓⲭⲱⲙ ⲛⲉ ⲛⲓⲭⲱⲙ ⲛ̀ⲧⲉ ⲡⲁⲓⲙⲟⲛⲁⲭⲟⲥ.

ⲍ̅ ⲫⲁⲓ ⲡⲉ ⲡⲓⲁⲅⲓⲟⲥ ⲙⲁⲣⲕⲟⲥ ⲡⲓⲁⲡⲟⲥⲧⲟⲗⲟⲥ.

ⲏ̅ ⲑⲁⲓ ⲧⲉ ϯϩⲓⲕⲱⲛ ⲛ̀ⲧⲉ ϯⲁⲅⲓⲁ ⲙⲁⲣⲓⲁ ϯⲡⲁⲣⲑⲉⲛⲟⲥ.

ⲑ̅ ⲛⲁⲓ ⲛⲉ ⲛⲓⲙⲟⲛⲁⲭⲟⲥ ⲙⲁⲝⲓⲙⲟⲥ ⲛⲉⲙ ⲇⲟⲙⲉⲇⲓⲟⲥ.

ⲓ̅ ⲡⲁⲓⲣⲱⲙⲓ ⲡⲉ ⲫⲓⲱⲧ ⲛ̀ⲧⲉ ⲡⲁⲓϣⲁϥⲉ.

ⲓ̅ⲁ̅ ⲫⲁⲓ ⲟⲩⲥⲟⲛ ⲡⲉ.

ⲓ̅ⲃ̅ ⲑⲁⲓ ⲟⲩⲣⲓ ⲧⲉ.

ⲓ̅ⲅ̅ ⲛⲁⲓ ϩⲁⲛϩⲁⲗⲁϯ ⲛⲉ.

ⲓ̅ⲇ̅ ⲛⲁⲓ ϩⲁⲛⲥⲛⲏⲟⲩ ⲛⲉ.

2. Translate the following to the Coptic language:

1. This is the Word of the Father.

2. This is the bride of Christ.

3. These are the elders of the desert.

4. This man is the father of the monks.

5. This church is the church of the angel.

6. These words are the words of life.

7. This is the pen of brother Lukas.

8. This is a home.

9. These are sons.

10. This is heaven.

11. These are trees.

Lesson 5
ⲡⲓⲱϣ ⲙ̀ⲙⲁϩ ⲉ̄

✠

ⲛⲓⲙⲉⲧⲓ̀ ⲛ̀ⲟⲩⲟⲛ ⲉⲧⲫⲟⲣϫ

Separate Personal Pronouns

ⲁⲛⲟⲕ	I	ⲛ̀ⲑⲟⲕ	You (mas.)	ⲛ̀ⲑⲟϥ	He
		ⲛ̀ⲑⲟ	You (fem.)	ⲛ̀ⲑⲟⲥ	She
ⲁⲛⲟⲛ	We	ⲛ̀ⲑⲱⲧⲉⲛ	You (pl.)	ⲛ̀ⲑⲱⲟⲩ	They

The separate personal pronouns are used to form noun sentences with the "to be" verb, for example:

ⲁⲛⲟⲕ ⲡⲉ ⲫ̀ⲟⲩⲱⲓⲛⲓ ⲙ̀ⲡⲓⲕⲟⲥⲙⲟⲥ.	I am the light of the world. (John 8:12)
ⲛ̀ⲑⲟⲕ ⲡⲉ Ⲡⲭ̅ⲥ̅ ⲡ̀ϣⲏⲣⲓ ⲙ̀Ⲫ̀ϯ.	You are the Christ the Son of God.
ⲛ̀ⲑⲟ ⲧⲉ ϯϣⲟⲩⲣⲏ ⲛ̀ⲛⲟⲩⲃ.	You are the censer of gold.
ⲛ̀ⲑⲟϥ ⲡⲉ ⲡⲓⲣⲏ ⲛ̀ⲧⲉ ϯⲇⲓⲕⲉⲟⲥⲩⲛⲏ.	He is the Sun of righteousness.
ⲛ̀ⲑⲟⲥ ⲧⲉ ⲑ̀ⲙⲁⲩ ⲛ̀Ⲓⲏⲥⲟⲩⲥ.	She is the mother of Jesus.
ⲁⲛⲟⲛ ϩⲁⲛⲥ̀ⲛⲏⲟⲩ ⲛⲉ.	We are brothers.
ⲛ̀ⲑⲱⲧⲉⲛ ϩⲁⲛⲓⲟϯ ⲛⲉ.	You are fathers.
ⲛ̀ⲑⲱⲟⲩ ⲛⲉ ⲛⲓϧⲉⲗⲗⲟⲓ ⲛ̀ⲧⲉ ⲡ̀ϣⲁϥⲉ.	They are the elders of the desert.
ⲁⲛⲟⲕ ⲡⲉ ϯⲁⲛⲁⲥⲧⲁⲥⲓⲥ ⲛⲉⲙ ⲡⲓⲱⲛϧ.	I am the resurrection and the life.
ⲛ̀ⲑⲟⲕ ⲡⲉ ⲡⲓⲟⲩⲏⲃ ⲛ̀ⲧⲉ ⲧⲁⲓⲉⲕⲕⲗⲏⲥⲓⲁ.	You are the priest of this church.

ⲛ̀ⲑⲟ ⲟⲩϣⲉⲣⲓ ⲛ̀ⲧⲉ ⲡⲓⲥⲟⲛ Ⲓⲁⲕⲱⲃ ⲧⲉ.	You are a daughter of the brother Jacob.
ⲛ̀ⲑⲟϥ ⲡⲉ ⲡⲓϧⲉⲗⲗⲟ ⲛ̀ⲧⲉ ⲡⲁⲓⲧⲱⲟⲩ.	He is the elder of this mountain.
ⲛ̀ⲑⲟⲥ ⲧⲉ ϯⲥⲱⲛⲓ ⲛ̀ⲧⲉ ⲛⲁⲓⲁ̀ⲗⲱⲟⲩ̀ⲓ.	She is the sister of these children.
ⲁⲛⲟⲛ ⲛⲉ ⲛⲓϣⲏⲣⲓ ⲛ̀ⲧⲉ ⲛⲓⲁ̀ⲅⲓⲟⲥ.	We are the sons of the saints.
ⲛ̀ⲑⲱⲧⲉⲛ ϩⲁⲛⲙⲉⲛⲣⲁϯ ⲛⲉ.	You are beloved.
ⲛ̀ⲑⲱⲟⲩ ⲛⲉ ⲛⲓⲥⲛⲏⲟⲩ ⲛ̀ⲧⲉ Ⲡϭⲟⲓⲥ.	They are the brothers of the Lord.

Asking About Animate and Inanimate [Objects]

1. ⲛⲓⲙ is used, meaning "who," to ask about an animate [object]:

ⲛⲓⲙ ⲡⲉ ⲫⲁⲓ?	Who is this?
ⲫⲁⲓ ⲡⲉ ⲡⲓⲟⲩⲏⲃ.	This is the priest.
ⲫⲁⲓ ⲟⲩⲟⲩⲏⲃ ⲡⲉ.	This is a priest.
ⲛⲓⲙ ⲧⲉ ⲑⲁⲓ?	Who is this?
ⲑⲁⲓ ⲧⲉ ϯⲥⲱⲛⲓ.	This is the sister.
ⲑⲁⲓ ⲟⲩⲥⲱⲛⲓ ⲧⲉ.	This is a sister.
ⲛⲓⲙ ⲛⲉ ⲛⲁⲓ?	Who are these?
ⲛⲁⲓ ⲛⲉ ⲛⲓⲙⲟⲛⲁⲭⲟⲥ.	These are the monks.
ⲛⲁⲓ ϩⲁⲛⲙⲟⲛⲁⲭⲟⲥ ⲛⲉ.	These are monks.

2. ⲁϣ is used, meaning "what," to ask about an inanimate [object]:

ⲁϣ ⲡⲉ ⲫⲁⲓ?	What is this?
ⲫⲁⲓ ⲡⲉ ⲡⲓⲕⲁϣ.	This is the pen.
ⲫⲁⲓ ⲟⲩⲕⲁϣ ⲡⲉ.	This is a pen.

Lesson 5 ✠ Separate Personal Pronouns ✠

ⲁϣ ⲧⲉ ⲑⲁⲓ?	What is this?
ⲑⲁⲓ ⲧⲉ ϯϣⲟⲩⲣⲏ.	This is the censer.
ⲑⲁⲓ ⲟⲩϣⲟⲩⲣⲏ ⲧⲉ.	This is a censer.

ⲁϣ ⲛⲉ ⲛⲁⲓ?	What are these?
ⲛⲁⲓ ⲛⲉ ⲛⲓϣϣⲏⲛ.	These are the trees.
ⲛⲁⲓ ϩⲁⲛϣϣⲏⲛ ⲛⲉ.	These are trees.

Exercises

1. Write the meaning of the following:

1. ⲡⲁⲓⲉϩⲟⲟⲩ	2. ⲧⲁⲓⲡⲁⲣⲑⲉⲛⲟⲥ	3. ⲛⲁⲓϩⲉⲗⲗⲟⲓ
4. ⲧⲁⲓⲛⲏⲥⲧⲓⲁ	5. ⲛⲁⲓϩⲁⲗⲁϯ	6. ⲡⲁⲓϫⲱⲙ
7. ⲛⲁⲓⲁⲗⲱⲟⲩⲓ̈	8. ⲡⲁⲓⲱⲛϧ	9. ⲧⲁⲓϫⲟⲙ

2. Translate the following to the English language:

ⲁ̅ ⲁⲛⲟⲕ ⲡⲉ ⲡⲓⲱⲓⲕ ⲛ̀ⲧⲉ ⲡⲱⲛϧ.
ⲃ̅ ⲛ̀ⲑⲟⲕ ⲡⲉ ⲡⲟⲩⲣⲟ ⲛ̀ⲧⲉ ⲛⲓⲟⲩⲣⲱⲟⲩ.
ⲅ̅ ⲛ̀ⲑⲟ ⲧⲉ ϯϣⲉⲣⲓ ⲛ̀Ⲥⲓⲱⲛ.
ⲇ̅ ⲛ̀ⲑⲟϥ ⲡⲉ ⲧⲁⲫⲉ ⲛ̀ϯⲉⲕⲕⲗⲏⲥⲓⲁ.
ⲉ̅ ⲛ̀ⲑⲟⲥ ⲧⲉ ϯϣⲉⲗⲉⲧ ⲙ̀Ⲡⲓⲭⲣⲓⲥⲧⲟⲥ.
ⲋ̅ ⲁⲛⲟⲛ ⲛⲉ ⲛⲓϣⲏⲣⲓ ⲛ̀ⲧⲉ ⲛⲓⲙⲁⲣⲧⲩⲣⲟⲥ.
ⲍ̅ ⲛ̀ⲑⲱⲧⲉⲛ ⲛⲉ ⲛⲉⲛⲉ̀ⲃⲓⲁⲓⲕ ⲙ̀Ⲡ̅ⲟ̅ⲥ̅.
ⲏ̅ ⲛ̀ⲑⲱⲟⲩ ⲛⲉ ⲛⲓⲙⲉⲛⲣⲁϯ ⲛ̀ⲧⲉ Ⲡ̅ⲭ̅ⲥ̅.

3. Translate the following to the Coptic language:

1. She is the mother of the light.	5. You are the brothers of the Lord.
2. You are the Savior of the world.	6. They are the birds of the sky.
3. He is the God of mankind.	7. I am a son.
4. You are the Virgin and the Mother.	8. We are brothers.

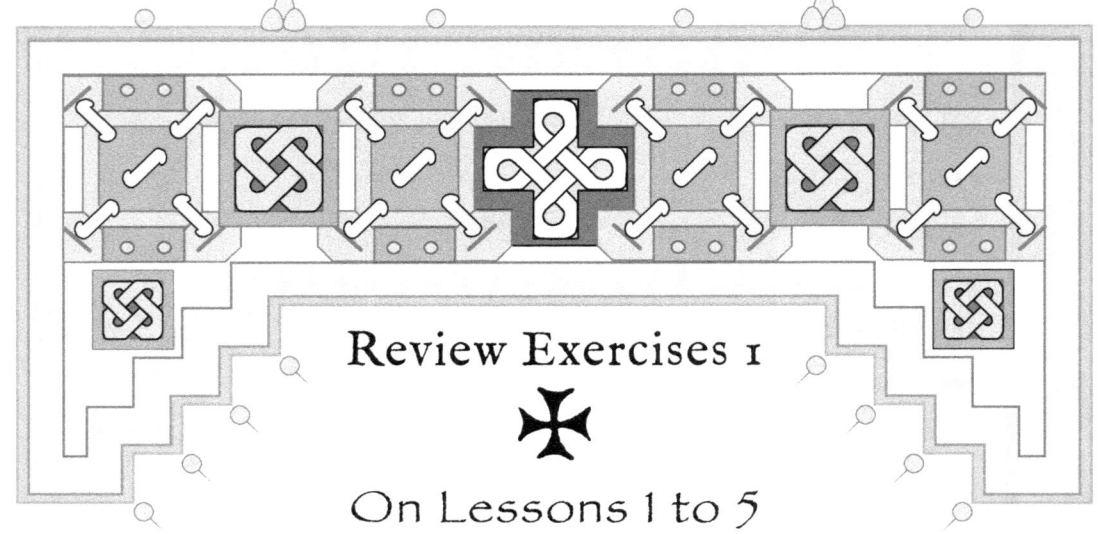

Review Exercises 1
On Lessons 1 to 5

1. Put the appropriate definite article for the following words:

ⲓⲟϯ	ϫⲓϫ	ⲥⲟⲛ	ⲥ̀ϩⲓⲙⲓ	ⲫⲛⲟⲩϯ
ϧⲁⲗⲟϫ	ⲃⲱⲕ	ⲫⲉ	ⲥ̀ⲛⲏⲟⲩ	ⲟⲩⲣⲟ
ⲉ̀ⲃⲓⲁⲓⲕ	ⲃⲁⲕⲓ	ⲉ̀ⲃⲛⲟⲩϯ	ϩⲉⲗⲗⲟⲓ	ϣⲁϥⲉ
ϩⲁⲗⲏⲧ	ⲙⲉⲛⲣⲁϯ	ⲓⲁⲣⲟ	ϩⲓⲟⲙⲓ	ⲟⲩⲣⲱⲟⲩ
ϩⲱⲃ	ⲟⲩⲣⲱ	ⲁⲙⲁⲓⲟⲩ	ⲃⲱⲕⲓ	ⲁⲗⲱⲟⲩⲓ

2. Write the meaning of the following words:

1. ⲡⲁⲓⲙⲟⲛⲁⲭⲟⲥ	2. ⲛⲁⲓϩⲁⲗⲁϯ	3. ⲡⲁⲓⲛⲁϩϯ
4. ⲧⲁⲓⲡⲁⲣⲑⲉⲛⲟⲥ	5. ⲡⲁⲓⲛⲁⲓ	6. ⲧⲁⲓⲣⲓ
7. ⲛⲁⲓⲛⲟⲃⲓ	8. ⲧⲁⲓⲯⲩⲭⲏ	9. ⲛⲁⲓⲣⲱⲙⲓ
10. ⲧⲁⲓϩⲓⲣⲏⲛⲏ	11. ⲡⲁⲓⲱⲓⲕ	12. ⲧⲁⲓϣⲉⲣⲓ

3. How do you ask about:

ⲟⲩϫⲱⲙ	ⲁϣ ⲡⲉ ⲫⲁⲓ?	ⲫⲁⲓ ⲟⲩϫⲱⲙ ⲡⲉ.
ϯⲙⲁⲩ	ⲛⲓⲙ ⲧⲉ ⲑⲁⲓ?	ⲑⲁⲓ ⲧⲉ ϯⲙⲁⲩ.
ⲡⲓϣⲏⲣⲓ		
ϩⲁⲛϣϣⲏⲛ		

Review Exercises 1 ✠ On Lessons 1 to 5 ✠

ⲧϣⲟⲩⲣⲏ		
ⲛⲓⲙⲟⲛⲁⲭⲟⲥ		
ⲟⲩⲥⲱⲛⲓ		
ⲡⲓⲣⲏ		
ϩⲁⲛⲓⲟϯ		

4. Translate the following to the English language:

1. ⲡⲓⲟⲩⲱⲓⲛⲓ ⲛⲉⲙ ⲡⲓⲭⲁⲕⲓ.
2. ⲫⲛⲟⲃⲓ ⲛⲉⲙ ⲡⲓⲟⲩϫⲁⲓ.
3. ϩⲁⲛϣⲗⲏⲗ ⲛⲉⲙ ϩⲁⲛⲛⲏⲥⲧⲓⲁ.
4. ⲛⲓⲫⲏⲟⲩⲓ ⲛⲉⲙ ⲡⲕⲁϩⲓ.
5. ϩⲁⲛⲁⲙⲁⲓⲟⲩ ⲛⲉⲙ ϩⲁⲛⲓⲁⲣⲱⲟⲩ.
6. ⲟⲩϣⲏⲣⲓ ⲛⲉⲙ ⲟⲩϣⲉⲣⲓ.
7. ⲛⲓϩⲱⲥ ⲛ̀ⲧⲉ ⲛⲓⲙⲟⲛⲁⲭⲟⲥ.
8. ⲡ̀ⲟⲩⲛⲟϥ ⲛ̀ⲛⲓⲥⲛⲏⲟⲩ.
9. ⲛⲉⲛⲉ̀ⲃⲓⲁⲓⲕ ⲙ̀Ⲡ̀ϭⲟⲓⲥ.
10. Ⲧ̀ϫⲓϫ ⲙ̀Ⲫϯ.
11. ⲡ̀ⲏⲓ ⲛ̀ⲧⲉ ⲛⲓⲁⲅⲅⲉⲗⲟⲥ.
12. ⲛⲓϩⲁⲗⲁϯ ⲛ̀ⲧⲉ ⲧ̀ⲫⲉ.
13. ⲫⲁⲓ ⲡⲉ ⲡⲓⲟⲩⲱⲓⲛⲓ.
14. ⲑⲁⲓ ⲧⲉ ϯϣⲟⲩⲣⲏ.
15. ⲛⲁⲓ ⲛⲉ ⲛⲓⲟⲩⲧⲁϩ.
16. ⲫⲁⲓ ⲟⲩⲓⲁⲣⲟ ⲡⲉ.
17. ⲑⲁⲓ ⲟⲩⲉⲕⲕ̀ⲗⲏⲥⲓⲁ ⲧⲉ.
18. ⲛⲁⲓ ϩⲁⲛϫⲱⲙ ⲛⲉ.
19. ⲁⲛⲟⲕ ⲟⲩϣⲏⲣⲓ ⲡⲉ.
20. ⲛ̀ⲑⲱⲧⲉⲛ ϩⲁⲛⲓⲟϯ ⲛⲉ.
21. ⲛ̀ⲑⲟⲥ ⲟⲩⲥⲱⲛⲓ ⲧⲉ.
22. ⲁⲛⲟⲛ ϩⲁⲛⲙⲉⲛⲣⲁϯ ⲛⲉ.
23. ⲛ̀ⲑⲟϥ ⲡⲉ ⲡⲓⲙⲉⲛⲣⲓⲧ.
24. ⲛ̀ⲑⲟ ⲧⲉ ϯⲡⲁⲣⲑⲉⲛⲟⲥ.

5. Translate the following to the Coptic language:

1. This is the priest of the desert.
2. These are fathers and brothers.
3. This is the mother of the light.
4. These are the angels of heaven.
5. We are the sons of the Church.
6. You are the Son of God.
7. He is the Savior of the world.
8. She is the city of God.
9. You are the daughter of Zion.
10. You are the brothers of the Lord.

Exam 1

On Lessons 1 to 5

1. Write the meaning of the following words:

1. ⲟⲩϫⲱⲙ	2. ϩⲁⲛⲣⲓ	3. ⲟⲩⲣⲱⲙⲓ
4. ϩⲁⲛⲣⲁⲛ	5. ⲟⲩⲃⲱⲕ	6. ϩⲁⲛⲣⲟⲙⲡⲓ
7. ⲟⲩϣⲏⲛ	8. ϩⲁⲛⲛⲏⲥⲧⲓⲁ	9. ⲟⲩⲃⲁⲕⲓ
10. ϩⲁⲛϣⲏⲣⲓ	11. ⲟⲩⲓⲟϩ	12. ϩⲁⲛⲛⲟⲃⲓ

2. For the following singular, masculine nouns, put the appropriate definite article, either ⲡ̀ or ⲫ̀:

ϭⲟⲓⲥ	ⲙⲟⲩ	ϣⲏⲣⲓ	ⲣⲁⲛ
ⲛⲁϩϯ	ⲗⲁⲥ	ⲱⲛϧ	ⲥⲟⲛ
ⲛⲟⲩϯ	ⲱⲓⲕ	ⲟⲩⲣⲟ	ⲟⲩϫⲁⲓ
ⲕⲁϩⲓ	ⲛⲟⲃⲓ	ⲃⲱⲕ	ⲏⲓ

3. For the following singular, feminine nouns, put the appropriate definite article, either ⲧ̀ or ⲑ̀:

ⲥⲱⲛⲓ	ⲫⲉ	ⲃⲁⲕⲓ	ⲁ̀ⲫⲉ
ⲛⲉϫⲓ	ⲙⲁⲩ	ϫⲓϫ	ⲃⲱⲕⲓ
ⲣⲓ	ϣⲉⲣⲓ	ϭⲁⲗⲟϫ	ϣⲟⲩⲣⲏ

Exam 1 ✣ On Lessons 1 to 5 ✣

4. Write the singular of the following plural nouns:

1. ιοϯ →	2. ⲫⲛⲟⲩⲓ →	3. ⲙⲉⲛⲣⲁϯ →
4. ⲟⲩⲣⲱⲟⲩ →	5. ϩⲁⲗⲁϯ →	6. ⲉ̀ⲃⲓⲁⲓⲕ →
7. ϧⲉⲗⲗⲟⲓ →	8. ϣⲁϥⲉⲣ →	9. ⲁⲗⲱⲟⲩⲓ →
10. ϩⲓⲟⲙⲓ →	11. ⲓⲁⲣⲱⲟⲩ →	12. ⲥ̀ⲛⲏⲟⲩ →

5. Put the appropriate demonstrative pronoun:

1. .... ⲟⲩⲓⲱⲧ ⲡⲉ.	2. .... ⲛⲉ ⲛⲓϧⲉⲗⲗⲟⲓ.
3. .... ⲟⲩϣⲟⲩⲣⲏ ⲧⲉ.	4. .... ⲡⲉ ⲡⲓⲟⲩⲏⲃ.
5. .... ϩⲁⲛⲥ̀ⲛⲏⲟⲩ ⲛⲉ.	6. .... ⲧⲉ ϯⲡⲁⲣⲑⲉⲛⲟⲥ.

6. Write the meaning of the following words:

ⲁ̄	ⲧⲁⲓⲫⲉ	ⲃ̄	ⲛⲁⲓϫⲱⲙ	ⲅ̄	ⲡⲁⲓϣⲏⲣⲓ
ⲇ̄	ⲛⲁⲓϫⲓϫ	ⲉ̄	ⲧⲁⲓⲥⲱⲛⲓ	ⲋ̄	ⲛⲁⲓⲛⲟⲃⲓ
ⲍ̄	ⲡⲁⲓⲣⲏ	ⲏ̄	ⲡⲁⲓⲱⲓⲕ	ⲑ̄	ⲧⲁⲓⲙⲁⲩ

7. Translate the following to the English language:

ⲁ̄ ⲛ̀ⲑⲱⲟⲩ ⲛⲉ ⲛⲉⲛⲓⲟϯ ⲛ̀ϯⲉⲕⲕⲗⲏⲥⲓⲁ.
ⲃ̄ ⲁⲛⲟⲛ ⲛⲉ ⲛⲉⲛϣⲏⲣⲓ ⲙ̀ⲡⲓⲟⲩⲱⲓⲛⲓ.
ⲅ̄ ⲛ̀ⲑⲟϥ ⲡⲉ ⲡⲓⲁⲅⲅⲉⲗⲟⲥ ⲛ̀ⲧⲉ Ⲡ̄ⲓ̄ϭ̄ⲟⲓⲥ.
ⲇ̄ ⲛ̀ⲑⲟ ⲧⲉ ⲑ̀ⲙⲁⲩ ⲛ̀Ⲓⲏⲥⲟⲩⲥ.
ⲉ̄ ⲛ̀ⲑⲟⲕ ⲡⲉ Ⲡ̄ⲓ̄ϭ̄ⲟⲓⲥ ⲛ̀ⲧⲉ ⲛⲓϫⲟⲙ.
ⲋ̄ ⲁⲛⲟⲕ ⲡⲉ ⲡⲓⲟⲩⲱⲓⲛⲓ ⲙ̀ⲡⲓⲕⲟⲥⲙⲟⲥ.
ⲍ̄ ⲛ̀ⲑⲟⲥ ⲧⲉ ϯϣⲉⲣⲓ ⲛ̀ⲧⲉ Ⲥⲓⲱⲛ.
ⲏ̄ ⲛ̀ⲑⲱⲧⲉⲛ ⲛⲉ ⲛⲓⲉ̀ⲃⲓⲁⲓⲕ ⲛ̀ⲧⲉ Ⲫⲛⲟⲩϯ.

8. Translate the following to the Coptic language:

1. The bread of life.
2. The light of the Lord.
3. The house of the angels.
4. The joy of the brothers.

Lesson 6
ⲡⲓⲱϣ ⲙ̀ⲙⲁϩ ⲋ̄

ⲚⲒⲘⲈⲨⲒ Ⲛ̀ϬⲰⲢⲈⲘ Ⲙ̀ⲠⲈⲐⲞⲨⲎⲞⲨ

Far Demonstrative Pronouns

For the masculine singular: **ⲪⲎ** (that).

For the feminine singular: **ⲐⲎ** (that).

For the plural both genders: **ⲚⲎ** (those).

Examples:

ⲁ̄	ⲪⲎ ⲞⲨⲆⲒⲀⲔⲞⲚ ⲠⲈ.	That is a deacon.
ⲃ̄	ⲐⲎ ⲞⲨⲠⲀⲢⲐⲈⲚⲞⲤ ⲦⲈ.	That is a virgin.
ⲅ̄	ⲚⲎ ϨⲀⲚⲘⲞⲚⲀⲬⲞⲤ ⲚⲈ.	Those are monks.
ⲇ̄	ⲪⲎ ⲠⲈ ⲠⲒⲞⲨⲎⲂ.	That is the priest.
ⲉ̄	ⲐⲎ ⲦⲈ ϮⲘⲀⲨ.	That is the mother.
ⲋ̄	ⲚⲎ ⲚⲈ ⲚⲒⲞϮ.	Those are the fathers.

The Relative Pronouns (ⲚⲒⲘⲈⲨⲒ ⲈⲦⲦⲞⲘϤ)

They are Ⲉ̀, ⲈⲦ, ⲈⲦⲈ. Each of them can be translated to "who," "which," or "that," for singular and plural, masculine and feminine.

Lesson 6 ✣ Far Demonstrative Pronouns ✣

The words ⲦⲎ and ⳘⲘⲀⲨ are adverbs of place, meaning "there."

"Who [is] there" or "who [are] there" = ⲈⲦⲦⲎ = ⲈⲦⲈ ⳘⲘⲀⲨ. There are no far demonstrative adjectives, and instead of them these two words are used: ⲈⲦⲦⲎ and ⲈⲦⲈ ⳘⲘⲀⲨ, and they cannot be conjugated.

The far demonstrative pronouns (ⲚⲎ, ⲐⲎ, ⲪⲎ) are added to the relative pronouns (Ⲉ̀, ⲈⲦ, ⲈⲦⲈ), to give them the character of specificity, and to form the following compound forms, which are called the demonstrative relative pronouns:

ⲪⲎⲈ̀	that who (mas.)	ⲐⲎⲈ̀	that who (fem.)	ⲚⲎⲈ̀	those who (pl.)
ⲪⲎⲈⲦ	that who (mas.)	ⲐⲎⲈⲦ	that who (fem.)	ⲚⲎⲈⲦ	those who (pl.)
ⲪⲎⲈ̀ⲦⲈ	that who (mas.)	ⲐⲎⲈ̀ⲦⲈ	that who (fem.)	ⲚⲎⲈ̀ⲦⲈ	those who (pl.)

In the examples above, for the masculine and feminine, the translation "who" is used for rational beings, and "which" for irrationals.

Sample Phrases:

ⲠⲒⲢⲰⳘⲒ ⲪⲎⲈ̀ⲦⲈ ⳘⲘⲀⲨ	"That man" or "The man who is there"
ⲠⲒⲢⲰⳘⲒ Ⲉ̀ⲦⲈ ⳘⲘⲀⲨ	"That man" or "The man who is there"
ⲠⲒⲢⲰⳘⲒ ⲈⲦⲦⲎ	"That man" or "The man who is there"

ϮⲤⲒⲔⲰⲚ ⲐⲎⲈ̀ⲦⲈ ⳘⲘⲀⲨ	"That icon" or "The icon which is there"
ϮⲤⲒⲔⲰⲚ Ⲉ̀ⲦⲈ ⳘⲘⲀⲨ	"That icon" or "The icon which is there"
ϮⲤⲒⲔⲰⲚ ⲈⲦⲦⲎ	"That icon" or "The icon which is there"

ⲚⲒⲤⲚⲎⲞⲨ ⲚⲎⲈ̀ⲦⲈ ⳘⲘⲀⲨ	"Those brothers" or "The brothers who are there"
ⲚⲒⲤⲚⲎⲞⲨ Ⲉ̀ⲦⲈ ⳘⲘⲀⲨ	"Those brothers" or "The brothers who are there"
ⲚⲒⲤⲚⲎⲞⲨ ⲈⲦⲦⲎ	"Those brothers" or "The brothers who are there"

ⲚⲒⲤⲰⲚⲒ ⲚⲎⲈ̀ⲦⲈ ⳘⲘⲀⲨ	"Those sisters" or "The sisters who are there"
ⲚⲒⲤⲰⲚⲒ Ⲉ̀ⲦⲈ ⳘⲘⲀⲨ	"Those sisters" or "The sisters who are there"
ⲚⲒⲤⲰⲚⲒ ⲈⲦⲦⲎ	"Those sisters" or "The sisters who are there"

For irrationals, they are translated as follows:

ⲛⲓϫⲱⲙ ⲛⲏⲉ̀ⲧⲉ ⲙ̀ⲙⲁⲩ	"Those books" or "The books which are there"
ⲛⲓϫⲱⲙ ⲉ̀ⲧⲉ ⲙ̀ⲙⲁⲩ	"Those books" or "The books which are there"
ⲛⲓϫⲱⲙ ⲉⲧⲧⲏ	"Those books" or "The books which are there"

Examples:

ⲁ̄ ⲡⲓϧⲉⲗⲗⲟ ⲫⲏⲉ̀ⲧⲉ ⲙ̀ⲙⲁⲩ ⲡⲉ ⲫⲓⲱⲧ ⲛ̀ⲧⲉ ⲛⲁⲓⲙⲟⲛⲁⲭⲟⲥ.
The elder who is there is the father of these monks.

ⲃ̄ ϯⲛⲏⲃ ⲑⲏⲉ̀ⲧⲉ ⲙ̀ⲙⲁⲩ ⲧⲉ ⲑⲙⲁⲩ ⲛ̀ⲧⲉ ⲛⲁⲓⲥⲱⲛⲓ.
The lady who is there is the mother of these sisters.

ⲅ̄ ⲛⲓⲟⲩⲏⲃ ⲛⲏⲉ̀ⲧⲉ ⲙ̀ⲙⲁⲩ ⲛⲉ ⲛⲓⲟϯ ⲛ̀ⲧⲉ ⲧⲁⲓⲉⲕⲕⲗⲏⲥⲓⲁ.
The priests who are there are the fathers of this church.

The definite article is added to the relative pronoun ⲉⲧ, to form:

ⲡⲉⲧ (ⲡⲉⲑ)	That who (mas.)	ⲑⲉⲧ	That who (fem.)	ⲛⲉⲧ	Those who (pl.)

Exercises

1. Write the meaning of the following:

ⲁ̄	ⲡⲁⲓϫⲱⲙ		ⲍ̄	ⲡⲓϫⲱⲙ ⲫⲏⲉ̀ⲧⲉ ⲙ̀ⲙⲁⲩ
ⲃ̄	ⲧⲁⲓϣⲟⲩⲣⲏ		ⲏ̄	ϯϣⲟⲩⲣⲏ ⲑⲏⲉ̀ⲧⲉ ⲙ̀ⲙⲁⲩ
ⲅ̄	ⲛⲁⲓⲙⲟⲛⲁⲭⲟⲥ		ⲑ̄	ⲛⲓⲙⲟⲛⲁⲭⲟⲥ ⲛⲏⲉ̀ⲧⲉ ⲙ̀ⲙⲁⲩ
ⲇ̄	ⲡⲓⲥⲟⲛ ⲉⲧⲧⲏ		ⲓ̄	ⲡⲓⲟϩ ⲉ̀ⲧⲉ ⲙ̀ⲙⲁⲩ
ⲉ̄	ϯⲥⲱⲛⲓ ⲉⲧⲧⲏ		ⲓⲁ̄	ϯϩⲓⲕⲱⲛ ⲉ̀ⲧⲉ ⲙ̀ⲙⲁⲩ
ⲋ̄	ⲛⲓⲟϯ ⲉⲧⲧⲏ		ⲓⲃ̄	ⲛⲓⲣⲓ ⲉ̀ⲧⲉ ⲙ̀ⲙⲁⲩ

2. Translate the following to the English language:

ⲁ̄ ⲫⲁⲓ ⲟⲩⲓⲱⲧ ⲡⲉ ⲟⲩⲟϩ ⲛⲏ ϩⲁⲛϣⲏⲣⲓ ⲛⲉ.
ⲃ̄ ⲑⲁⲓ ⲟⲩϩⲓⲕⲱⲛ ⲧⲉ ⲟⲩⲟϩ ⲫⲏ ⲟⲩϫⲱⲙ ⲡⲉ.
ⲅ̄ ⲛⲁⲓ ϩⲁⲛⲥⲛⲏⲟⲩ ⲛⲉ ⲟⲩⲟϩ ⲑⲏ ⲟⲩⲥⲱⲛⲓ ⲧⲉ.
ⲇ̄ ⲫⲏ ⲡⲉ ⲡⲓⲟⲩⲏⲃ ⲟⲩⲟϩ ⲛⲁⲓ ⲛⲉ ⲛⲓⲇⲓⲁⲕⲟⲛ.

Lesson 6 ✠ Far Demonstrative Pronouns ✠

ⲉ̄ ⲑⲏ ⲧⲉ ϯϣⲟⲩⲣⲏ ⲟⲩⲟϩ ⲫⲁⲓ ⲡⲉ ⲡⲓⲉⲣⲫⲉⲓ.

ⲋ̄ ⲛⲏ ⲛⲉ ⲛⲓⲓⲟϯ ⲟⲩⲟϩ ⲑⲁⲓ ⲧⲉ ϯⲙⲁⲩ.

ⲍ̄ ⲡⲓⲣⲱⲙⲓ ⲫⲏⲉ̀ⲧⲉ ⲙ̀ⲙⲁⲩ ⲡⲉ ⲡⲓⲟⲩⲣⲟ ⲛ̀ⲧⲉ ⲧⲁⲓⲃⲁⲕⲓ.

ⲏ̄ ϯⲥϩⲓⲙⲓ ⲑⲏⲉ̀ⲧⲉ ⲙ̀ⲙⲁⲩ ⲧⲉ ⲑⲙⲁⲩ ⲛ̀ⲛⲁⲓⲁ̀ⲗⲱⲟⲩⲓ̀.

ⲑ̄ ⲛⲓⲥⲛⲏⲟⲩ ⲛⲏⲉ̀ⲧⲉ ⲙ̀ⲙⲁⲩ ⲛⲉ ⲛⲓϣⲏⲣⲓ ⲛ̀ⲧⲉ ⲡⲁⲓⲟⲩⲏⲃ.

ⲓ̄ ⲛⲓⲙ ⲡⲉ ⲫⲏ? ⲛ̀ⲑⲟϥ ⲡⲉ ⲫⲓⲱⲧ ⲛ̀ⲛⲁⲓⲙⲟⲛⲁⲭⲟⲥ.

ⲓ̄ⲁ ⲛⲓⲙ ⲧⲉ ⲑⲏ? ⲛ̀ⲑⲟⲥ ⲧⲉ ϯϣⲉⲣⲓ ⲛ̀ⲧⲁⲓⲥⲱⲛⲓ.

ⲓ̄ⲃ ⲛⲓⲙ ⲛⲉ ⲛⲏ? ⲛ̀ⲑⲱⲟⲩ ⲛⲉ ⲛⲉⲛⲓⲟϯ ⲙ̀ⲡⲁⲓϣⲁϥⲉ.

Lesson 7

ⲡⲓⲱϣ ⲙ̇ⲙⲁϩ ⲍ̄

✠

ⲡⲓⲁⲙⲟⲛⲓ

POSSESSIVE

Possessive or Attributive Adjectives (ⲛⲓⲥ̇ⲙⲟⲧ ⲛ̇ⲁⲙⲟⲛⲓ)

So long as there is possession or attribution, then there is a "possessed" (attributed) and a "possessor" (attributed to). Therefore, the possessive or attributive pronoun includes what indicates the possessed and what indicates the possessor. And usually the possessive adjective begins with the letter that indicates the possessed.

1. The possessed:

Either it is singular masculine, and is expressed in the possessive adjective [form] by the letter ⲡ; or it is singular feminine, and is expressed in the possessive adjective [form] by the letter ⲧ; or it is plural, and is expressed in the possessive adjective [form] by the letter ⲛ.

2. The possessor:

Either the first person, whether singular (ⲁⲛⲟⲕ "I") or plural (ⲁⲛⲟⲛ "we"); or the second person, (ⲛ̇ⲑⲟⲕ "you" mas.), or (ⲛ̇ⲑⲟ "you" fem.), (ⲛ̇ⲑⲱⲧⲉⲛ "you" pl.); or the third person, (ⲛ̇ⲑⲟϥ "he"), or (ⲛ̇ⲑⲟⲥ "she"), (ⲛ̇ⲑⲱⲟⲩ "they").

The following table shows the possessive adjectives, without being connected to the possessed noun. As for the table after that, it shows the possessive adjectives connected to the possessed nouns.

Lesson 7 ✣ Possessive ✣

Possessor	Possessed		
	Singular masculine	Singular feminine	Plural
	ⲡ″	ⲧ″	ⲛ″
ⲁⲛⲟⲕ	ⲡⲁ- My	ⲧⲁ- My	ⲛⲁ- My
ⲛ̀ⲑⲟⲕ	ⲡⲉⲕ- Your (mas.)	ⲧⲉⲕ- Your (mas.)	ⲛⲉⲕ- Your (mas.)
ⲛ̀ⲑⲟ	ⲡⲉ- Your (fem.)	ⲧⲉ- Your (fem.)	ⲛⲉ- Your (fem.)
ⲛ̀ⲑⲟϥ	ⲡⲉϥ- His	ⲧⲉϥ- His	ⲛⲉϥ- His
ⲛ̀ⲑⲟⲥ	ⲡⲉⲥ- Her	ⲧⲉⲥ- Her	ⲛⲉⲥ- Her
ⲁⲛⲟⲛ	ⲡⲉⲛ- Our	ⲧⲉⲛ- Our	ⲛⲉⲛ- Our
ⲛ̀ⲑⲱⲧⲉⲛ	ⲡⲉⲧⲉⲛ- Your (pl.)	ⲧⲉⲧⲉⲛ- Your (pl.)	ⲛⲉⲧⲉⲛ- Your (pl.)
ⲛ̀ⲑⲱⲟⲩ	ⲡⲟⲩ- Their	ⲧⲟⲩ- Their	ⲛⲟⲩ- Their

Possessor	Possessed		
	Singular masculine	Singular feminine	Plural
	ⲡ″	ⲧ″	ⲛ″
ⲁⲛⲟⲕ	ⲡⲁⲓⲱⲧ My father	ⲧⲁⲥⲱⲛⲓ My sister	ⲛⲁϫⲱⲙ My books
ⲛ̀ⲑⲟⲕ	ⲡⲉⲕⲓⲱⲧ Your father	ⲧⲉⲕⲥⲱⲛⲓ Your sister	ⲛⲉⲕϫⲱⲙ Your books
ⲛ̀ⲑⲟ	ⲡⲉⲓⲱⲧ Your father	ⲧⲉⲥⲱⲛⲓ Your sister	ⲛⲉϫⲱⲙ Your books
ⲛ̀ⲑⲟϥ	ⲡⲉϥⲓⲱⲧ His father	ⲧⲉϥⲥⲱⲛⲓ His sister	ⲛⲉϥϫⲱⲙ His books
ⲛ̀ⲑⲟⲥ	ⲡⲉⲥⲓⲱⲧ Her father	ⲧⲉⲥⲥⲱⲛⲓ Her sister	ⲛⲉⲥϫⲱⲙ Her books
ⲁⲛⲟⲛ	ⲡⲉⲛⲓⲱⲧ Our father	ⲧⲉⲛⲥⲱⲛⲓ Our sister	ⲛⲉⲛϫⲱⲙ Our books
ⲛ̀ⲑⲱⲧⲉⲛ	ⲡⲉⲧⲉⲛⲓⲱⲧ Your father	ⲧⲉⲧⲉⲛⲥⲱⲛⲓ Your sister	ⲛⲉⲧⲉⲛϫⲱⲙ Your books
ⲛ̀ⲑⲱⲟⲩ	ⲡⲟⲩⲓⲱⲧ Their father	ⲧⲟⲩⲥⲱⲛⲓ Their sister	ⲛⲟⲩϫⲱⲙ Their books

✠ Foundations of the Coptic Language ✠

Notes:

1. The dash written after each possessive adjective in the first table indicates that the word that precedes the dash does not come separate, but rather it has an ending, to form a complete word with the possessed noun.

2. The two diagonal dashes after the first letter of the possessive adjective (ⲡ″, ⲧ″, ⲛ″) indicate that what expresses the possessor's pronoun should be put in their place.

Vocabulary (ⲥⲁⲛⲥⲁϧⲓ):

ⲧⲁⲫⲉ	The head	ⲡⲓϭⲗⲱⲧ	The kidney	ϯϣⲃⲱⲃⲓ	The throat
ⲡⲓϩⲟ, ⲡϩⲟ	The face	ⲡⲓϣⲱⲃϣ	The arm	ϯϭⲁⲗⲟϫ	The foot
ⲡⲓⲃⲁⲗ	The eye	ⲡⲓⲕⲱⲓ	The elbow	ϯⲕⲉⲗⲓ	The knee
ⲡⲓϣⲁⲓ	The nose	ⲡⲓⲥⲱⲙⲁ	The body	ϯⲯⲩⲭⲏ	The soul
ⲡⲓⲙⲁϣϫ	The ear	ϯⲥⲁⲣⲝ	The flesh	ⲡⲓⲛⲟⲩⲥ	The mind
ⲡⲓⲗⲁⲥ	The tongue	ϯⲛⲉϫⲓ	The womb, the belly	ⲡⲓⲙⲉⲩⲓ	The thought
ⲛⲓⲛⲁϫϩⲓ	The teeth	ϯⲛⲁϩⲃⲓ	The shoulder	ⲡⲓⲧⲏⲃ	The finger
ⲡⲓϩⲏⲧ	The heart	ϯϫⲓϫ	The hand	ϯⲃⲏⲧ	The rib
ϯⲙⲉⲥⲧⲉⲛϩⲏⲧ	The breast	ⲛⲓⲥⲫⲟⲧⲟⲩ	The lips	ⲡⲓⲗⲟⲅⲓⲥⲙⲟⲥ	The sense

Exercises

1. Write the meaning of the following:

1. ⲡⲁⲛⲟⲩϯ
2. ⲡⲉⲛϭⲟⲓⲥ
3. ⲧⲉⲕⲁⲫⲉ
4. ⲛⲉⲥϫⲓϫ
5. ⲛⲉϥⲃⲁⲗ
6. ⲡⲉⲕϩⲟ
7. ⲡⲉϥϣⲁⲓ
8. ⲡⲉⲙⲁϣϫ
9. ⲡⲉⲛⲗⲁⲥ
10. ⲡⲉϥⲛⲁⲓ
11. ⲧⲉⲕϩⲓⲣⲏⲛⲏ
12. ⲛⲉⲧⲉⲛⲛⲁϫϩⲓ
13. ⲧⲟⲩϣⲃⲱⲃⲓ
14. ⲡⲟⲩϩⲏⲧ
15. ⲛⲉⲛⲥⲁⲣⲝ
16. ⲧⲉⲛⲉϫⲓ
17. ⲛⲁϭⲗⲱⲧ
18. ⲡⲉⲕϣⲱⲃϣ
19. ⲡⲁⲕⲱⲓ
20. ⲡⲉϥⲧⲏⲃ
21. ⲛⲉⲥϭⲁⲗⲁⲩϫ
22. ⲧⲁⲕⲉⲗⲓ
23. ⲧⲉϥⲯⲩⲭⲏ
24. ⲡⲉⲛⲙⲉⲩⲓ
25. ⲡⲟⲩⲛⲟⲩⲥ
26. ⲛⲁⲗⲟⲅⲓⲥⲙⲟⲥ
27. ⲧⲉϥⲛⲁϩⲃⲓ
28. ⲧⲉⲕϣⲃⲱⲃⲓ
29. ⲛⲉϥϣⲏⲣⲓ
30. ⲡⲟⲩⲟⲩⲣⲟ
31. ⲧⲉⲥⲙⲁⲩ
32. ⲛⲁⲥⲫⲟⲧⲟⲩ
33. ⲡⲉⲕⲣⲁⲛ
34. ⲧⲉⲥⲱⲛⲓ
35. ⲧⲟⲩⲙⲁⲩ
36. ⲛⲉⲧⲉⲛⲣⲁⲛ

Lesson 7 ✠ Possessive ✠

2. Translate the following to the Coptic language:

1.	Their teeth	6.	Your (mas.) brother	11.	Our God	16.	Your (mas.) mercy
2.	Our mind	7.	Your (fem.) head	12.	Their life	17.	My Lord
3.	His name	8.	Her ears	13.	Your (fem.) soul	18.	Your (mas.) eyes
4.	Our feet	9.	My heart	14.	Our fingers	19.	His tongue
5.	Their sons	10.	His peace	15.	My fathers	20.	Your (pl.) sister

3. Translate the following to the English language:

ā ⲡⲥⲱϯ ⲛ̀ⲧⲉ ⲛⲉⲛⲯⲩⲭⲏ.

B̄ ⲡⲉⲕⲛⲁⲓ ⲛⲉⲙ ⲧⲉⲕϩⲓⲣⲏⲛⲏ.

ḡ ⲧⲁⲥⲱⲛⲓ ⲟⲩⲟϩ ⲧⲁϣⲫⲉⲣⲓ.

ⲇ̄ ⲛⲓϣⲏⲣⲓ ⲛ̀ⲧⲉ ⲛⲉⲕⲉⲩⲭⲏ.

ē ⲛⲁⲛⲟⲃⲓ ⲛⲉⲙ ⲛⲁⲁ̀ⲛⲟⲙⲓⲁ.

ⲋ̄ ⲡⲉⲛⲛⲟⲩϯ ⲛⲉⲙ ⲡⲉⲛⲟⲩⲣⲟ.

z̄ ⲡⲉⲕⲱⲟⲩ ⲛⲉⲙ ⲡⲉⲕⲧⲁⲓⲟ.

ⲏ̄ Ⲫⲁⲣⲁⲱ̀ ⲛⲉⲙ ⲛⲉϥϩⲁⲣⲙⲁ.

ⲑ̄ ⲡⲟⲩⲧⲁϩ ⲛ̀ⲧⲉ ⲧⲉⲛⲉⲭⲓ.

ī Ⲉ̀ⲗⲓⲥⲁⲃⲉⲧ ⲧⲉⲥⲥⲩⲅⲅⲉⲛⲏⲥ.

ⲓ̄ⲁ ⲛⲉⲕϫⲱⲙ ⲛⲉⲙ ⲛⲉⲕⲕⲁϣ.

ⲓ̄ⲃ ⲧⲉⲥⲱⲛⲓ ⲛⲉⲙ ⲛⲉⲥϣⲉⲣⲓ.

ⲓ̄ⲅ Ⲕⲟⲥⲙⲁ ⲛⲉⲙ ⲛⲉϥⲥⲛⲏⲟⲩ ⲛⲉⲙ ⲧⲟⲩⲙⲁⲩ.

Lesson 8

ⲡⲓⲱϣ ⲙⲙⲁϩ ⲏ̄

✠

ⲛⲓⲙⲉⲧⲓ ⲛ̀ⲁⲙⲟⲛⲓ

Possessive or Attributive Pronouns

Introduction

In the demonstrative adjectives we used: **ⲡⲁⲓ-** for singular masculine, and **ⲧⲁⲓ-** for singular feminine.

In the demonstrative pronouns we used: **ⲫⲁⲓ** for singular masculine, and **ⲑⲁⲓ** for singular feminine.

In the possessive adjectives we used: **ⲡ″** for singular masculine, and **ⲧ″** for singular feminine.

In the possessive pronouns we use: **ⲫ″** for singular masculine, and **ⲑ″** for singular feminine.

1. The full form of the possessive or attributive pronouns

Singular masculine		Singular feminine		Plural (both genders)	
ⲫⲱⲓ	belongs to me, mine	ⲑⲱⲓ	belongs to me	ⲛⲟⲩⲓ	belong to me
ⲫⲱⲕ	belongs to you (mas.), yours	ⲑⲱⲕ	belongs to you (mas.)	ⲛⲟⲩⲕ	belong to you (mas.)
ⲫⲱ	belongs to you (fem.), yours	ⲑⲱ	belongs to you (fem.)	ⲛⲟⲩ	belong to you (fem.)
ⲫⲱϥ	belongs to him, his	ⲑⲱϥ	belongs to him	ⲛⲟⲩϥ	belong to him

Lesson 8 ✣ Possessive or Attributive Pronouns ✣

ⲫⲱⲥ	belongs to her, hers	ⲑⲱⲥ	belongs to her	ⲛⲟⲩⲥ	belong to her
ⲫⲱⲛ	belongs to us, ours	ⲑⲱⲛ	belongs to us	ⲛⲟⲩⲛ	belong to us
ⲫⲱⲧⲉⲛ	belongs to you (pl.), yours	ⲑⲱⲧⲉⲛ	belongs to you (pl.)	ⲛⲟⲩⲧⲉⲛ	belong to you (pl.)
ⲫⲱⲟⲩ	belongs to them, theirs	ⲑⲱⲟⲩ	belongs to them	ⲛⲟⲩⲟⲩ	belong to them

Examples:

ⲫⲱⲕ ⲡⲉ ⲡⲓⲱⲟⲩ ⲛⲉⲙ ⲡⲓⲧⲁⲓⲟ.
Yours is the glory and the honor.

ⲛⲓⲫⲏⲟⲩⲓ ⲛⲉⲙ ⲡⲕⲁϩⲓ ⲛⲟⲩⲕ ⲛⲉ Ⲫϯ.
The heavens and the earth are Yours, O God.

The possessive pronouns often come after the demonstrative relative pronouns [ⲫⲏⲉⲧⲉ, ⲑⲏⲉⲧⲉ, ⲛⲏⲉⲧⲉ], and then the letter ⲛ̅ is introduced to the noun that follows. And this composition is unique to the Coptic language, and it signifies specificity; for example:

ⲫⲏⲉⲧⲉ ⲫⲱⲛ ⲛ̅ⲟⲩϫⲁⲓ.	That salvation which is ours.
ⲑⲏⲉⲧⲉ ⲑⲱⲕ ⲛ̅ⲉⲕⲕⲗⲏⲥⲓⲁ.	That church which is yours.
ⲛⲏⲉⲧⲉ ⲛⲟⲩϥ ⲙ̅ⲙⲁⲑⲏⲧⲏⲥ.	Those students who are his.

2. The imperfect form of the possessive pronouns

These do not have conjugation with the personal pronouns.

Singular masculine (ⲛϩⲱⲟⲩⲧ ⲛ̅ⲟⲩⲱⲧ):   ⲫⲁ

Singular feminine (ⲛ̅ⲥϩⲓⲙⲓ ⲛ̅ⲟⲩⲱⲧ):   ⲑⲁ

Plural both genders (ⲛⲑⲟ ⲥⲛⲁⲩ ⲙ̅ⲙⲏϣ):   ⲛⲁ

✣ It comes with the meaning of "of" or "owner of":

ⲛⲓⲥⲉⲣⲁⲫⲓⲙ ⲛⲁ ⲡⲓⲋ̅ ⲛ̅ⲧⲉⲛϩ.	The seraphim with (owner of) the six wings.
ⲫⲁ ⲡⲓⲁⲙⲁϩⲓ.	To whom the majesty belongs (owner of the majesty).

✛ It comes with the meaning of "possession of" or "belonging to":

ⲡⲓⲱⲟⲩ ⲫⲁ ⲡⲉⲛⲛⲟⲩϯ ⲡⲉ.	The glory belongs to our God. Or, The glory is our God's.
ⲡⲓⲕⲁϩⲓ ⲫⲁ Ⲡⳇϭⲟⲓⲥ ⲡⲉ.	The earth is possession of the Lord. Or, The earth is the Lord's.

✛ Attributive and possessive:

ⲛⲁ ⲧ̇ⲫⲉ ⲛⲉⲙ ⲛⲁ ⲡ̇ⲕⲁϩⲓ.	The heavenly and the earthly.
Ⲙⲓⲭⲁⲏⲗ ⲡⲁⲣⲭⲱⲛ ⲛ̇ⲛⲁ ⲛⲓⲫⲏⲟⲩⲓ̇.	Michael the head of the heavenly.
ⲛⲁ Ⲭⲏⲙⲓ.	The Egyptians.
ⲛⲁ Ⲫϯ.	The matters of God (what belongs to God).
ⲛⲁ ϯⲧⲁⲍⲓⲥ.	Ritualists.
ⲫⲁ ⲡⲓⲣⲟ.	The doorkeeper (the one associated with the door).

✛ Sometimes it comes with the meaning of "son":

ⲛⲁ ϯⲣⲉⲙϩⲉ.	Children of the free (Galatians 4:31).

Note: The possessive pronoun, whether in its full or imperfect form, is used to prevent repetition of the "possessed" noun, for example:

ⲡⲉϥⲱⲟⲩ ⲛⲉⲙ ⲫⲁ ⲡⲉϥⲓⲱⲧ.	His glory and of His Father's.
ⲧⲉⲕⲣⲓ ⲛⲉⲙ ⲑⲱⲓ ⲧⲉ.	Your cell and my own.
ϩⲁⲛⲧⲉⲛϩ ⲙ̇ⲫⲣⲏϯ ⲛ̇ⲛⲁ ⲟⲩϭⲣⲟⲙⲡⲓ.	Wings like a dove's.
ⲧⲉϥⲥⲙⲏ ⲙ̇ⲫⲣⲏϯ ⲛ̇ⲑⲁ ⲟⲩⲙⲟⲩⲓ̇ ⲧⲉ.	His voice is like a lion's.
ⲛⲉϥⲃⲁⲗ ⲙ̇ⲫⲣⲏϯ ⲛ̇ⲛⲁ ⲟⲩⲁϧⲱⲙ ⲛⲉ.	His eyes are like the eagle's.

Lesson 8 ✠ Possessive or Attributive Pronouns ✠

Exercises

1. Put the appropriate possessive adjective or pronoun in the blank:

e.g.	ⲫⲁⲓ ⲡⲉ ⲡⲁϣⲏⲣⲓ.	ⲡⲁϣⲏⲣⲓ ⲡⲉ ⲫⲱⲓ.
ⲁ̄	ⲑⲁⲓ ⲧⲉ ⲧⲉϥⲣⲓ.	ⲧⲁⲓⲣⲓ ⲧⲉ . . . . . .
ⲃ̄	ⲛⲁⲓ ⲛⲉ ⲛⲉⲥⲓⲟϯ.	ⲛⲁⲓⲟϯ ⲛⲉ . . . . . .
ⲅ̄	ⲫⲁⲓ ⲡⲉ ⲡⲉⲕⲣⲁⲛ.	ⲡⲁⲓⲣⲁⲛ ⲡⲉ . . . . . .
ⲇ̄	ⲑⲁⲓ ⲧⲉ ⲧⲉⲛⲥⲱⲛⲓ.	ⲧⲁⲓⲥⲱⲛⲓ ⲧⲉ . . . . . .
ⲉ̄	ⲛⲁⲓ ⲛⲉ ⲛⲟⲩⲓⲟϯ.	ⲛⲁⲓⲟϯ ⲛⲉ . . . . . .
e.g.	ⲫⲏⲉⲧⲉ ⲫⲱⲛ ⲛ̀ⲟⲩϫⲁⲓ	= ⲡⲉⲛⲟⲩϫⲁⲓ.
ⲋ̄	ⲛⲏⲉⲧⲉ ⲛⲟⲩⲧⲉⲛ ⲛ̀ⲓⲟϯ	= . . . . . . ⲓⲟϯ.
ⲍ̄	ⲑⲏⲉⲧⲉ ⲑⲱⲟⲩ ⲙ̀ⲙⲁⲩ	= . . . . . . ⲙⲁⲩ.
ⲏ̄	ⲫⲏⲉⲧⲉ ⲫⲱⲕ ⲛ̀ⲥⲟⲛ	= . . . . . . ⲥⲟⲛ.
ⲑ̄	ⲑⲏⲉⲧⲉ ⲑⲱⲥ ⲛ̀ϣⲉⲣⲓ	= . . . . . . ϣⲉⲣⲓ.
ⲓ̄	ⲛⲏⲉⲧⲉ ⲛⲟⲩⲛ ⲛ̀ⲥⲛⲏⲟⲩ	= . . . . . . ⲥⲛⲏⲟⲩ.

2. Translate the following to the English language:

ⲁ̄ ⲧⲁⲓⲛⲏⲥⲧⲓⲁ ⲧⲉ ⲑⲁ ϯⲡⲁⲣⲑⲉⲛⲟⲥ.
ⲃ̄ ⲡⲁⲓϣⲁⲓ ⲡⲉ ⲫⲁ ⲛⲓⲙⲁⲣⲧⲩⲣⲟⲥ.
ⲅ̄ ⲫⲁ ϯⲕⲩⲑⲁⲣⲁ ⲡⲉ Ⲇⲁⲩⲓⲇ.
ⲇ̄ ⲑⲱⲕ ⲧⲉ ϯϫⲟⲙ ⲛⲉⲙ ⲡⲓⲱⲟⲩ.
ⲉ̄ ⲛⲓⲫⲏⲟⲩⲓ̀ ⲛⲉⲙ ⲡ̀ⲕⲁϩⲓ ⲛⲉ ⲛⲟⲩⲕ, Ⲫϯ.
ⲋ̄ ⲛⲁⲓⲁⲗⲱⲟⲩⲓ̀ ⲛⲉ ⲛⲟⲩⲧⲉⲛ, ⲱ̀ ⲛⲁⲙⲉⲛⲣⲁϯ.
ⲍ̄ ⲡⲁⲓⲉϩⲟⲟⲩ ⲡⲉ ⲫⲁ ⲡⲓⲁⲅⲓⲟⲥ Ⲙⲁⲝⲓⲙⲟⲥ.
ⲏ̄ ⲧⲁⲓⲉⲕⲕⲗⲏⲥⲓⲁ ⲧⲉ ⲑⲁ ϯⲁⲅⲓⲁ Ⲙⲁⲣⲓⲁ ϯⲡⲁⲣⲑⲉⲛⲟⲥ.
ⲑ̄ ⲛⲓϫⲱⲙ ⲉ̀ⲧⲉ ⲙ̀ⲙⲁⲩ ⲛⲉ ⲛⲟⲩϥ.

✠ Foundations of the Coptic Language ✠

Simplified Summary

Singular masculine	Singular feminine	Plural (both genders)	
ⲟⲩ	ⲟⲩ	ϩⲁⲛ	Indefinite article
ⲡ, ⲫ	ⲧ, ⲑ	ⲛ	The distinguishing letters
ⲡⲓ- (the)	ϯ- (the)	ⲛⲓ- (the)	General definite articles (strong)
ⲡ̀-, ⲫ̀- (the)	ⲧ̀-, ⲑ̀- (the)	ⲛⲉⲛ- (the)	Specific definite articles
ⲡⲉ (is)	ⲧⲉ (is)	ⲛⲉ (are)	To be verbs
ⲡⲁⲓ- (this)	ⲧⲁⲓ- (this)	ⲛⲁⲓ- (these)	Near demonstrative adjectives
ⲫⲁⲓ (this)	ⲑⲁⲓ (this)	ⲛⲁⲓ (these)	Near demonstrative pronouns
ⲫⲏ (that)	ⲑⲏ (that)	ⲛⲏ (those)	Far demonstrative pronouns
ⲫⲁ	ⲑⲁ	ⲛⲁ	Possessive pronouns (imperfect form)
ⲡ"	ⲧ"	ⲛ"	Possessive adjectives
ⲫ"	ⲑ"	ⲛ"	Possessive pronouns (full form)

Personal pronoun (possessor)	Possessive adjectives			Possessive pronouns (full form)		
	Possessed			Possessed		
	Singular masculine	Singular feminine	Plural	Singular masculine	Singular feminine	Plural
ⲁⲛⲟⲕ	ⲡⲁ-	ⲧⲁ-	ⲛⲁ-	ⲫⲱⲓ	ⲑⲱⲓ	ⲛⲟⲩⲓ
ⲛ̀ⲑⲟⲕ	ⲡⲉⲕ-	ⲧⲉⲕ-	ⲛⲉⲕ-	ⲫⲱⲕ	ⲑⲱⲕ	ⲛⲟⲩⲕ
ⲛ̀ⲑⲟ	ⲡⲉ-	ⲧⲉ-	ⲛⲉ-	ⲫⲱ	ⲑⲱ	ⲛⲟⲩ
ⲛ̀ⲑⲟϥ	ⲡⲉϥ-	ⲧⲉϥ-	ⲛⲉϥ-	ⲫⲱϥ	ⲑⲱϥ	ⲛⲟⲩϥ
ⲛ̀ⲑⲟⲥ	ⲡⲉⲥ-	ⲧⲉⲥ-	ⲛⲉⲥ-	ⲫⲱⲥ	ⲑⲱⲥ	ⲛⲟⲩⲥ
ⲁⲛⲟⲛ	ⲡⲉⲛ-	ⲧⲉⲛ-	ⲛⲉⲛ-	ⲫⲱⲛ	ⲑⲱⲛ	ⲛⲟⲩⲛ
ⲛ̀ⲑⲱⲧⲉⲛ	ⲡⲉⲧⲉⲛ-	ⲧⲉⲧⲉⲛ-	ⲛⲉⲧⲉⲛ-	ⲫⲱⲧⲉⲛ	ⲑⲱⲧⲉⲛ	ⲛⲟⲩⲧⲉⲛ
ⲛ̀ⲑⲱⲟⲩ	ⲡⲟⲩ-	ⲧⲟⲩ-	ⲛⲟⲩ-	ⲫⲱⲟⲩ	ⲑⲱⲟⲩ	ⲛⲟⲩⲟⲩ

Exercises & Applications
On the Seventh & Eighth Lessons

1. Write the meaning of the following:

1. ⲡⲁⲣⲁⲛ	8. ⲡⲉⲥϣⲏⲣⲓ	15. ⲛⲉⲕⲉⲩⲭⲏ	22. ⲡⲉⲥⲛⲟⲩϯ
2. ⲡⲟⲩϩⲏⲧ	9. ⲧⲉⲥⲩⲅⲅⲉⲛⲏⲥ	16. ⲡⲁϭⲟⲓⲥ	23. ⲛⲉⲧⲉⲛⲣⲁⲛ
3. ⲧⲉϥϩⲓⲕⲱⲛ	10. ⲡⲉⲕⲟⲩϫⲁⲓ	17. ⲛⲁϭⲟⲓⲥ	24. ⲧⲟⲩϣⲃⲱⲃⲓ
4. ⲡⲉⲛⲛⲟⲩϯ	11. ⲡⲉⲧⲉⲛⲟⲩⲣⲟ	18. ⲡⲉⲕϩⲟ	25. ⲡⲉϣⲏⲣⲓ
5. ⲧⲁⲙⲉⲗⲉⲧⲏ	12. ⲧⲉϥⲙⲏϯ	19. ⲡⲉϥⲱⲟⲩ	26. ⲧⲉϥⲙⲁⲩ
6. ⲛⲉⲛⲛⲟⲃⲓ	13. ⲡⲟⲩⲕⲁϩⲓ	20. ⲡⲉⲧⲁⲓⲟ	27. ⲧⲉⲙⲏⲧⲣⲁ
7. ⲧⲁϩⲓⲣⲏⲛⲏ	14. ⲡⲉϥⲓⲱⲧ	21. ⲛⲟⲩϫⲁϫⲓ	28. ⲛⲉⲛⲯⲩⲭⲏ

2. Translate the following to the Coptic language:

1. My brother	6. Her father	11. My sins	16. Your (mas.) spirit
2. Your (mas.) mercy	7. Our mother	12. Your (mas.) glory	17. My fathers
3. Our king	8. His sister	13. His face	18. Her Lord
4. Your womb	9. My God	14. Your (pl.) sons	19. Their words
5. Her sisters	10. Your (pl.) queen	15. His books	20. Your (mas.) peace

3. Complete the missing parts in the following table, according to the given example in the first row:

ⲁⲛⲟⲕ	ⲡⲁϩⲏⲧ	ⲧⲁⲯⲩⲭⲏ	ⲛⲁϫⲓϫ	ⲫⲱⲓ	ⲛⲟⲩⲓ
………	ⲡⲉⲕϩⲏⲧ	……ⲯⲩⲭⲏ	……ϫⲓϫ	………	………
………	……ϩⲏⲧ	ⲧⲉⲯⲩⲭⲏ	……ϫⲓϫ	………	………
………	……ϩⲏⲧ	……ⲯⲩⲭⲏ	ⲛⲉϥϫⲓϫ	………	………
………	……ϩⲏⲧ	……ⲯⲩⲭⲏ	……ϫⲓϫ	ⲫⲱⲥ	………
………	……ⲥⲟⲛ	……ⲥⲱⲛⲓ	……ⲥⲛⲏⲟⲩ	………	ⲛⲟⲩⲛ
ⲛ̀ⲑⲱⲧⲉⲛ	……ⲥⲟⲛ	……ⲥⲱⲛⲓ	……ⲥⲛⲏⲟⲩ	ⲫⲱⲧⲉⲛ	………
………	……ⲥⲟⲛ	ⲧⲟⲩⲥⲱⲛⲓ	……ⲥⲛⲏⲟⲩ	………	ⲛⲟⲩⲟⲩ

4. Complete; put the suitable possessive pronoun or adjective in the blanks:

1.	ⲫⲁⲓ ⲡⲉ ⲡⲁϫⲱⲙ.	ⲡⲁⲓϫⲱⲙ ⲡⲉ ⲫⲱⲓ.
2.	ⲫⲁⲓ ⲡⲉ ⲡⲉⲕⲣⲁⲛ.	ⲡⲁⲓⲣⲁⲛ ⲡⲉ ⲫⲱⲕ.
3.	ⲫⲁⲓ ⲡⲉ ⲡⲉⲛⲓ̀.	ⲡⲁⲓⲛⲓ̀ ⲡⲉ ………… .
4.	ⲫⲁⲓ ⲡⲉ ……ϣⲏⲣⲓ.	ⲡⲁⲓϣⲏⲣⲓ ⲡⲉ ⲫⲱϥ.
5.	ⲫⲁⲓ ⲡⲉ ⲡⲉⲥⲥⲟⲛ.	ⲡⲁⲓⲥⲟⲛ ⲡⲉ ………… .
6.	ⲫⲁⲓ ⲡⲉ ……ϩⲱⲃ.	ⲡⲁⲓϩⲱⲃ ⲡⲉ ⲫⲱⲛ.
7.	ⲫⲁⲓ ⲡⲉ ⲡⲉⲧⲉⲛⲕⲁϩⲓ.	ⲡⲁⲓⲕⲁϩⲓ ⲡⲉ ………… .
8.	ⲫⲁⲓ ⲡⲉ ……ⲓⲱⲧ.	ⲡⲁⲓⲱⲧ ⲡⲉ ⲫⲱⲟⲩ.
9.	ⲑⲁⲓ ⲧⲉ ⲧⲁⲣⲓ.	ⲧⲁⲓⲣⲓ ⲧⲉ ⲑⲱⲓ.
10.	ⲑⲁⲓ ⲧⲉ ⲧⲉⲕϫⲓϫ.	ⲧⲁⲓϫⲓϫ ⲧⲉ ………… .
11.	ⲑⲁⲓ ⲧⲉ ……ϣⲉⲣⲓ.	ⲧⲁⲓϣⲉⲣⲓ ⲧⲉ ⲑⲱ.
12.	ⲑⲁⲓ ⲧⲉ ⲧⲉϥⲃⲁⲕⲓ.	ⲧⲁⲓⲃⲁⲕⲓ ⲧⲉ ………… .
13.	ⲑⲁⲓ ⲧⲉ ……ⲃⲱⲕⲓ.	ⲧⲁⲓⲃⲱⲕⲓ ⲧⲉ ⲑⲱⲥ.
14.	ⲑⲁⲓ ⲧⲉ ⲧⲉⲛⲥⲱⲛⲓ.	ⲧⲁⲓⲥⲱⲛⲓ ⲧⲉ ………… .
15.	ⲑⲁⲓ ⲧⲉ ……ⲫⲟⲣϣⲓ.	ⲧⲁⲓⲫⲟⲣϣⲓ ⲧⲉ ⲑⲱⲧⲉⲛ.
16.	ⲑⲁⲓ ⲧⲉ ⲧⲟⲩⲉⲕⲕⲗⲏⲥⲓⲁ.	ⲧⲁⲓⲉⲕⲕⲗⲏⲥⲓⲁ ⲧⲉ ………… .

Exercises & Applications ✠ On the Seventh & Eighth Lessons ✠

17.	ⲛⲁⲓ ⲛⲉ ⲛⲁⲃⲁⲗ.	ⲛⲁⲓⲃⲁⲗ ⲛⲉ............ .
18.	ⲛⲁⲓ ⲛⲉ........ⲙⲁϣϫ.	ⲛⲁⲓⲙⲁϣϫ ⲛⲉ ⲛⲟⲩⲕ.
19.	ⲛⲁⲓ ⲛⲉ ⲛⲉⲥⲛⲏⲟⲩ.	ⲛⲁⲓⲥⲛⲏⲟⲩ ⲛⲉ........... .
20.	ⲛⲁⲓ ⲛⲉ........ⲉ̀ⲃⲓⲁⲓⲕ.	ⲛⲁⲓⲉ̀ⲃⲓⲁⲓⲕ ⲛⲉ ⲛⲟⲩϥ.
21.	ⲛⲁⲓ ⲛⲉ ⲛⲉⲥⲓⲟϯ.	ⲛⲁⲓⲓⲟϯ ⲛⲉ........... .
22.	ⲛⲁⲓ ⲛⲉ........ϩ̀ⲃⲏⲟⲩⲓ̀.	ⲛⲁⲓϩ̀ⲃⲏⲟⲩⲓ̀ ⲛⲉ ⲛⲟⲩⲛ.
23.	ⲛⲁⲓ ⲛⲉ ⲛⲉⲧⲉⲛϧⲉⲗⲗⲟⲓ.	ⲛⲁⲓϧⲉⲗⲗⲟⲓ ⲛⲉ........... .
24.	ⲛⲁⲓ ⲛⲉ........ⲙⲉⲛⲣⲁϯ.	ⲛⲁⲓⲙⲉⲛⲣⲁϯ ⲛⲉ ⲛⲟⲩⲟⲩ.

5. Complete, putting the suitable possessive pronoun or adjective in the blanks:

1.	ⲫⲏⲉ̀ⲧⲉ ⲫⲱⲓ ⲛ̀ⲥⲟⲛ	=	ⲡⲁⲥⲟⲛ
2.	ⲫⲏⲉ̀ⲧⲉ........ⲛ̀ϣⲏⲣⲓ	=	ⲡⲉⲕϣⲏⲣⲓ
3.	ⲫⲏⲉ̀ⲧⲉ ⲫⲱ ⲛ̀ⲣⲱⲙⲓ	=	........ⲣⲱⲙⲓ
4.	ⲫⲏⲉ̀ⲧⲉ........ⲛ̀ⲓⲱⲧ	=	ⲡⲉϥⲓⲱⲧ
5.	ⲫⲏⲉ̀ⲧⲉ ⲫⲱⲥ ⲛ̀ϫⲱⲙ	=	........ϫⲱⲙ
6.	ⲫⲏⲉ̀ⲧⲉ........ⲛ̀ⲟⲩϫⲁⲓ	=	ⲡⲉⲛⲟⲩϫⲁⲓ
7.	ⲫⲏⲉ̀ⲧⲉ ⲫⲱⲧⲉⲛ ⲛ̀ⲟⲩⲏⲃ	=	........ⲟⲩⲏⲃ
8.	ⲫⲏⲉ̀ⲧⲉ........ⲛ̀ⲕⲁϩⲓ	=	ⲡⲟⲩⲕⲁϩⲓ
9.	ⲑⲏⲉ̀ⲧⲉ........ⲛ̀ⲥⲱⲛⲓ	=	ⲧⲁⲥⲱⲛⲓ
10	ⲑⲏⲉ̀ⲧⲉ ⲑⲱⲕ ⲛ̀ⲉⲕⲕⲗⲏⲥⲓⲁ	=	........ⲉⲕⲕⲗⲏⲥⲓⲁ
11.	ⲑⲏⲉ̀ⲧⲉ........ⲛ̀ϣⲉⲣⲓ	=	ⲧⲉϣⲉⲣⲓ
12.	ⲑⲏⲉ̀ⲧⲉ ⲑⲱϥ ⲙ̀ⲯⲩⲭⲏ	=	........ⲯⲩⲭⲏ
13.	ⲑⲏⲉ̀ⲧⲉ........ⲛ̀ⲣⲓ	=	ⲧⲉⲥⲣⲓ
14.	ⲑⲏⲉ̀ⲧⲉ ⲑⲱⲛ ⲙ̀ⲙⲁⲩ	=	........ⲙⲁⲩ
15.	ⲑⲏⲉ̀ⲧⲉ........ⲙ̀ⲃⲁⲕⲓ	=	ⲧⲉⲧⲉⲛⲃⲁⲕⲓ
16.	ⲑⲏⲉ̀ⲧⲉ ⲑⲱⲟⲩ ⲛ̀ⲁϫⲡ	=	........ⲁϫⲡ
17.	ⲛⲏⲉ̀ⲧⲉ ⲛⲟⲩⲓ ⲛ̀ϫⲱⲙ	=	........ϫⲱⲙ
18.	ⲛⲏⲉ̀ⲧⲉ........ⲛ̀ⲁⲡⲟⲥⲧⲟⲗⲟⲥ	=	ⲛⲉⲕⲁⲡⲟⲥⲧⲟⲗⲟⲥ

19.	ⲛⲏⲉⲧⲉ ⲛⲟⲩ ⲛⲁⲗⲱⲟⲩⲓ	=	.... ⲁⲗⲱⲟⲩⲓ
20.	ⲛⲏⲉⲧⲉ .... ⲙ̀ⲙⲁⲑⲏⲧⲏⲥ	=	ⲛⲉϥⲙⲁⲑⲏⲧⲏⲥ
21.	ⲛⲏⲉⲧⲉ ⲛⲟⲩⲥ ⲛ̀ⲕⲁϣ	=	.... ⲕⲁϣ
22.	ⲛⲏⲉⲧⲉ .... ⲛ̀ⲓⲟϯ	=	ⲛⲉⲛⲓⲟϯ
23.	ⲛⲏⲉⲧⲉ ⲛⲟⲩⲧⲉⲛ ⲙ̀ⲙⲉⲛⲣⲁϯ	=	.... ⲙⲉⲛⲣⲁϯ
24.	ⲛⲏⲉⲧⲉ ⲛⲟⲩⲟⲩ ⲛ̀ⲥⲛⲏⲟⲩ	=	.... ⲥⲛⲏⲟⲩ

6. Choose from the column on the right what suits every word in the column on the left:

ⲡⲉⲕⲣⲁⲛ	ⲑⲱ	ⲧⲟⲩⲃⲁⲕⲓ	ⲛⲟⲩ	ⲡⲁⲥⲙⲟⲩ	ⲛⲟⲩⲥ
ⲛⲟⲩⲥⲁϫⲓ	ⲛⲟⲩⲛ	ⲛⲉⲓⲟϯ	ⲫⲱϥ	ⲛⲉⲥϫⲱⲙ	ⲫⲱⲟⲩ
ⲧⲉⲙⲁⲩ	ⲫⲱⲧⲉⲛ	ⲡⲉϥϩⲏⲧ	ⲑⲱⲧⲉⲛ	ⲧⲉⲕϩⲓⲣⲏⲛⲏ	ⲑⲱⲛ
ⲡⲉⲧⲉⲛⲓⲱⲧ	ⲛⲟⲩⲓ	ⲛⲉⲕⲃⲁⲗ	ⲫⲱⲥ	ⲡⲟⲩⲛⲟⲩϯ	ⲫⲱ
ⲧⲉϥⲣⲓ	ⲑⲱⲥ	ⲧⲁⲛⲉϫⲓ	ⲑⲱⲟⲩ	ⲛⲉϥϣⲏⲣⲓ	ⲫⲱⲓ
ⲛⲉⲛϫⲁϫⲓ	ⲑⲱϥ	ⲡⲉⲥⲗⲁⲥ	ⲫⲱⲛ	ⲧⲉⲛⲥⲱⲛⲓ	ⲛⲟⲩⲧⲉⲛ
ⲧⲉⲥϣⲉⲣⲓ	ⲛⲟⲩⲟⲩ	ⲧⲉⲧⲉⲛⲁⲥⲡⲓ	ⲑⲱⲓ	ⲛⲉⲧⲉⲛϫⲓϫ	ⲑⲱⲕ
ⲛⲁⲥⲛⲏⲟⲩ	ⲫⲱⲕ	ⲡⲉⲛⲥⲱⲧⲏⲣ	ⲛⲟⲩⲕ	ⲡⲉⲣⲁⲛ	ⲛⲟⲩϥ

7. Translate the following passage to the English language:

Ⲱ Ⲓⲏⲥⲟⲩⲥ, ⲛ̀ⲑⲟⲕ ⲡⲉ ⲡⲉⲛⲛⲟⲩϯ ⲛⲉⲙ ⲡⲉⲛⲥⲱⲧⲏⲣ ⲛⲉⲙ ⲡⲉⲛⲟⲩⲣⲟ. ⲛ̀ⲑⲟⲕ ⲡⲉ ⲡⲓⲙⲱⲓⲧ ⲛⲉⲙ ϯⲙⲉⲑⲙⲏⲓ ⲛⲉⲙ ⲡⲓⲱⲛϧ. ⲛ̀ⲑⲟⲕ ⲡⲉ ⲡⲓⲱⲓⲕ ⲛ̀ⲧⲉ ⲡⲉⲛⲱⲛϧ ⲛⲉⲙ ⲡⲓⲟⲩⲱⲓⲛⲓ ⲛ̀ⲧⲉ ⲡⲉⲛⲕⲟⲥⲙⲟⲥ. ⲡⲉⲕⲓⲱⲧ ⲡⲉ ⲡⲉⲛⲓⲱⲧ. ⲡⲉϥⲑⲣⲟⲛⲟⲥ ⲡⲉ ϧⲉⲛ ⲧ̀ⲫⲉ. ⲡⲓⲕⲁϩⲓ ⲡⲉ ⲡⲓⲙⲁ ⲛ̀ⲧⲉ ⲛⲉϥϭⲁⲗⲁⲩϫ.

Ⲁⲛⲟⲛ ⲡⲉ ⲡⲉⲕⲗⲁⲟⲥ. ⲁⲛⲟⲛ ⲛⲉ ⲛⲉⲕϣⲏⲣⲓ ⲛⲉⲙ ⲛⲉⲕⲙⲉⲛⲣⲁϯ. ⲧⲉⲕⲙⲁⲩ ⲧⲉ ϯⲁⲅⲓⲁ Ⲙⲁⲣⲓⲁ ϯⲡⲁⲣⲑⲉⲛⲟⲥ. ⲛ̀ⲑⲟⲥ ⲧⲉ ⲧⲉⲛⲙⲁⲩ ⲛⲉⲙ ⲡ̀ϣⲟⲩϣⲟⲩ ⲙ̀ⲡⲉⲛⲅⲉⲛⲟⲥ.

Ⲱ Ⲙⲁⲣⲓⲁ, ⲛ̀ⲑⲟ ⲧⲉ ⲧⲉⲛⲟⲩⲣⲱ, ϯⲟⲩⲣⲱ ⲛ̀ⲧⲉ ⲛⲁ ⲛⲓⲫⲏⲟⲩⲓ ⲛⲉⲙ ⲛⲁ ⲡ̀ⲕⲁϩⲓ. ⲛ̀ⲑⲟ ⲧⲉ ϯϣⲟⲩⲣⲏ ⲛ̀ⲛⲟⲩⲃ. ⲡⲉϣⲏⲣⲓ ⲡⲉ ⲡⲉⲛϭⲟⲓⲥ. ⲁⲛⲟⲛ ⲛⲉ ⲛⲉϣⲏⲣⲓ.

Ⲁⲛⲟⲕ ⲡⲉ ⲡⲉⲕⲃⲱⲕ, ⲱ Ⲓⲏⲥⲟⲩⲥ. ⲛⲁⲥⲛⲏⲟⲩ ⲛⲉ ⲛⲉⲕⲉ̀ⲃⲓⲁⲓⲕ. ⲛⲓⲁ̀ⲅⲓⲟⲥ ⲛⲉ ⲛⲉⲛⲓⲟϯ. ⲁⲛⲟⲛ ⲛⲉ ⲛⲟⲩϣⲏⲣⲓ ⲛⲉⲙ ⲛⲟⲩⲙⲉⲛⲣⲁϯ. ⲡⲉⲛⲱⲛϧ ⲡⲉ ϧⲉⲛ ⲧⲉⲕϫⲓϫ, ⲱ ⲡⲉⲛϭⲟⲓⲥ.

Lesson 9

ⲡⲓⲱϣ ⲙⲙⲁϩ ⲑ̄

Three Notes on the Possessive Adjectives and Pronouns

The First Note

Some members of the human body and some nouns do not accept the definite articles; therefore, they consequently do not accept the previously-studied possessive adjectives. Rather, they accept the pronoun of the possessor at their end:

1. The nouns ending by a vowel: ⲭⲱ" (head), ⲣⲱ" (mouth), ϩⲑⲏ" (heart). See Column 1 in the table below for an example of joining the personal pronouns to them.

2. The nouns ending by a consonant:

   (a) Nouns ending by the letter ⲧ: ⲣⲁⲧ" (foot), ⲓⲁⲧ" (eye), ⲧⲟⲧ" (hand), ϣⲏⲧ" (belly, womb), ϩⲏⲧ" (beginning). See Column 2 below for an example of joining the personal pronouns to them.

   (b) Nouns ending by the letter ⲛ: ⲣⲉⲛ" (name), ⲕⲉⲛ" (bosom), ⲥⲟⲩⲉⲛ" (price). See Column 3 below for an example of joining the personal pronouns to them.

3. The word ϩⲣ" (face): See Column 4 below for an example of joining the personal pronouns to it.

Examples for joining personal nouns to the above-mentioned nouns:

Column 1		Column 2		Column 3		Column 4	
ⲭⲱⲓ	My head	ⲣⲁⲧ	My foot	ⲕⲉⲛⲧ	My bosom	ϩⲣⲏⲓ	My face
ⲭⲱⲕ	Your (m.) head	ⲣⲁⲧⲕ	Your (m.) foot	ⲕⲉⲛⲕ	Your (m.) bosom	ϩⲣⲁⲕ	Your (m.) face
ⲭⲱ	Your (f.) head	ⲣⲁϯ	Your (f.) foot	ⲕⲉⲛⲓ	Your (f.) bosom	ϩⲣⲉ	Your (f.) face
ⲭⲱϥ	His head	ⲣⲁⲧϥ	His foot	ⲕⲉⲛϥ	His bosom	ϩⲣⲁϥ	His face
ⲭⲱⲥ	Her head	ⲣⲁⲧⲥ	Her foot	ⲕⲉⲛⲥ	Her bosom	ϩⲣⲁⲥ	Her face
ⲭⲱⲛ	Our head	ⲣⲁⲧⲉⲛ	Our foot	ⲕⲉⲛⲧⲉⲛ	Our bosom	ϩⲣⲁⲛ	Our face
ⲭⲱⲧⲉⲛ	Your (pl.) head	ⲣⲁⲧⲉⲛ-ⲑⲏⲛⲟⲩ	Your (pl.) foot	ⲕⲉⲛ-ⲑⲏⲛⲟⲩ	Your (pl.) bosom	ϩⲣⲉⲛ-ⲑⲏⲛⲟⲩ	Your (pl.) face
ⲭⲱⲟⲩ	Their head	ⲣⲁⲧⲟⲩ	Their foot	ⲕⲉⲛⲟⲩ	Their bosom	ϩⲣⲁⲩ	Their face
m. = masculine; f. = feminine.							

The Second Note: When the possessed noun is indefinite

To attribute it to a possessor (an owner), we cannot in this case use the previous articles which indicate possession (ⲡ″, ⲧ″, ⲛ″, ⲫⲱ″, ⲑⲱ″, ⲛⲟⲩ″); rather, the genitive article ⲛ̀ⲧⲉ is used in the following way:

ⲟⲩϫⲱⲙ ⲛ̀ⲧⲉ Ⲡⲉⲧⲣⲟⲥ.	A book of Peter; one of Peter's books.

To attribute the indefinite possessed noun to the personal pronouns that indicate the first person, second person, and third person, singular and plural, we use the genitive article ⲛ̀ⲧⲉ while attaching it to the pronouns, in the following way:

ⲟⲩϣ̀ⲫⲏⲣ ⲛ̀ⲧⲏⲓ	One of my friends; a friend of mine.
ⲟⲩϫⲱⲙ ⲛ̀ⲧⲁⲕ	One of your (mas.) books; a book of yours.
ⲟⲩⲥⲟⲛ ⲛ̀ⲧⲉ	One of your (fem.) brothers; a brother of yours.
ϩⲁⲛⲓⲟϯ ⲛ̀ⲧⲁϥ	Fathers of his; some of his fathers.
ⲟⲩϣⲉⲣⲓ ⲛ̀ⲧⲁⲥ	One of her daughters; a daughter of hers.
ϩⲁⲛⲥⲛⲏⲟⲩ ⲛ̀ⲧⲁⲛ	Some of our brothers; brothers of ours.

Lesson 9 ✣ Three Notes on the Possessive Adjectives and Pronouns ✣

| ⲟⲩⲥⲱⲛⲓ ⲛ̀ⲧⲱⲧⲉⲛ | A sister of yours (pl.); one of her sisters. |
| ϩⲁⲛϩ̀ⲃⲏⲟⲩⲓ̀ ⲛ̀ⲧⲱⲟⲩ | Deeds of theirs; some of their deeds. |

The Third Note: When the possessed noun is defined by the relative noun ⲉⲧ (ⲉⲑ)

In this case also we use the genitive article ⲛ̀ⲧⲉ while attaching it to the personal pronouns, such as:

ⲫⲏⲉⲑⲟⲩⲁⲃ ⲛ̀ⲧⲁⲕ	Your saint; the saint who is yours.
ⲛⲏⲉⲑⲟⲩⲁⲃ ⲛ̀ⲧⲁϥ	His saints; the saints who are his.
ⲛⲏⲉⲧⲟⲛϧ̀ ⲛ̀ⲧⲱⲟⲩ	Their living (ones); the living (ones) who are theirs.
ⲑⲏⲉⲑⲙⲱⲟⲩⲧ ⲛ̀ⲧⲁⲥ	Her dead (fem.); the dead (fem.) who is hers.
ⲛⲏⲉⲑⲛⲁϩϯ ⲛ̀ⲧⲁⲛ	Our believers; the believers who are ours.

A sample phrase:

| ϧⲉⲛ ⲫ̀ⲟⲩⲱⲓⲛⲓ ⲛ̀ⲧⲉ ⲛⲏⲉⲑⲟⲩⲁⲃ ⲛ̀ⲧⲁϥ. | In the light of His saints. |

Exercises

1. Write the meaning of the following:

1. ⲛⲁ ⲛⲓⲫⲏⲟⲩⲓ̀	7. ⲡⲉⲕⲣⲁⲛ	13. ⲣⲁⲧⲕ
2. ⲫⲁ ⲡⲓⲣⲟ	8. ⲧⲉϥϩⲓⲣⲏⲛⲏ	14. ⲕⲉⲛϥ
3. ⲑⲁ ⲡⲁⲓⲏⲓ	9. ⲛⲉⲛⲓⲟϯ	15. ⲧⲟⲧ
4. ⲛⲁ ⲡ̀ⲕⲁϩⲓ	10. ⲛⲉⲧⲉⲛⲥⲛⲏⲟⲩ	16. ⲣⲱⲛ
5. ⲛⲁ ⲭⲏⲙⲓ	11. ⲡⲟⲩⲟⲩⲣⲟ	17. ⲁⲩⲣⲏϫⲥ
6. ⲑⲁ ⲧⲁⲓⲉⲕⲕⲗⲏⲥⲓⲁ	12. ⲧⲉⲛⲃⲁⲕⲓ	18. ϫⲱⲟⲩ

19. ϩⲁⲛϫⲱⲙ ⲛ̀ⲧⲏⲓ	25. ⲛⲏⲉⲧⲉ ⲛⲟⲩⲕ ⲙ̀ⲙⲁⲑⲏⲧⲏⲥ
20. ⲟⲩⲥⲟⲛ ⲛ̀ⲧⲁϥ	26. ⲑⲏⲉⲧⲉ ⲑⲱⲧⲉⲛ ⲛ̀ⲥⲱⲛⲓ
21. ϩⲁⲛϩ̀ⲃⲏⲟⲩⲓ̀ ⲛ̀ⲧⲁⲛ	27. ⲫⲏⲉⲧⲉ ⲫⲱϥ ⲛ̀ⲥⲱⲛⲧ
22. ⲟⲩϣⲉⲣⲓ ⲛ̀ⲧⲁⲥ	28. ⲛⲏⲉⲧⲉ ⲛⲟⲩⲥ ⲛ̀ϣⲏⲣⲓ

23. ϩⲁⲛⲓⲟϯ ⲛ̀ⲧⲱⲟⲩ	29. ⲑⲏⲉ̀ⲧⲉ ⲑⲱⲛ ⲙ̀ⲙⲁⲩ
24. ⲟⲩⲓⲱⲧ ⲛ̀ⲧⲱⲧⲉⲛ	30. ⲫⲏⲉ̀ⲧⲉ ⲫⲱⲓ ⲛ̀ⲥⲁϧ

2. Translate the following to the English language:

ⲁ̄ ⲡⲓⲥⲱⲙⲁ ⲛ̀ⲧⲉ Ⲡϭⲟⲓⲥ ⲛⲉⲙ ⲡⲉϥⲥⲛⲟϥ.

ⲃ̄ ⲛⲓϣⲗⲏⲗ ⲛ̀ⲧⲉ ⲛⲓⲙⲟⲛⲁⲭⲟⲥ ⲛⲉⲙ ⲛⲟⲩϩⲱⲥ.

ⲅ̄ ⲡⲉⲛϭⲟⲓⲥ ⲛⲉⲙ ⲡⲉⲛⲛⲟⲩϯ ⲛⲉⲙ ⲡⲉⲛⲟⲩⲣⲟ.

ⲇ̄ ⲡⲓⲣⲱⲙⲓ ⲫⲏⲉ̀ⲧⲉⲙ̀ⲙⲁⲩ ⲡⲉ ⲡⲉⲧⲉⲛⲟⲩⲏⲃ.

ⲉ̄ ⲛⲏ ⲛⲉ ⲛⲟⲩϣⲏⲣⲓ ⲛⲉⲙ ⲛⲟⲩϣⲉⲣⲓ.

ⲋ̄ ⲧⲁⲓϩⲓⲕⲱⲛ ⲧⲉ ⲑⲁ ϯⲡⲁⲣⲑⲉⲛⲟⲥ.

ⲍ̄ ⲫⲱⲓ ⲡⲉ ⲡⲓⲕⲁϩⲓ ⲧⲏⲣϥ.

ⲏ̄ ⲛⲁⲓ ⲛⲉ ⲛⲁ ϯⲧⲁⲝⲓⲥ ⲛ̀ⲧⲉ ϯⲉⲕⲕⲗⲏⲥⲓⲁ ⲉ̀ⲧⲉⲙ̀ⲙⲁⲩ.

ⲑ̄ ⲛⲉⲧⲉⲛϣⲏⲣⲓ ⲛⲉ ⲛⲁⲥ̀ⲛⲏⲟⲩ ⲛⲉⲙ ⲛⲁⲙⲉⲛⲣⲁϯ.

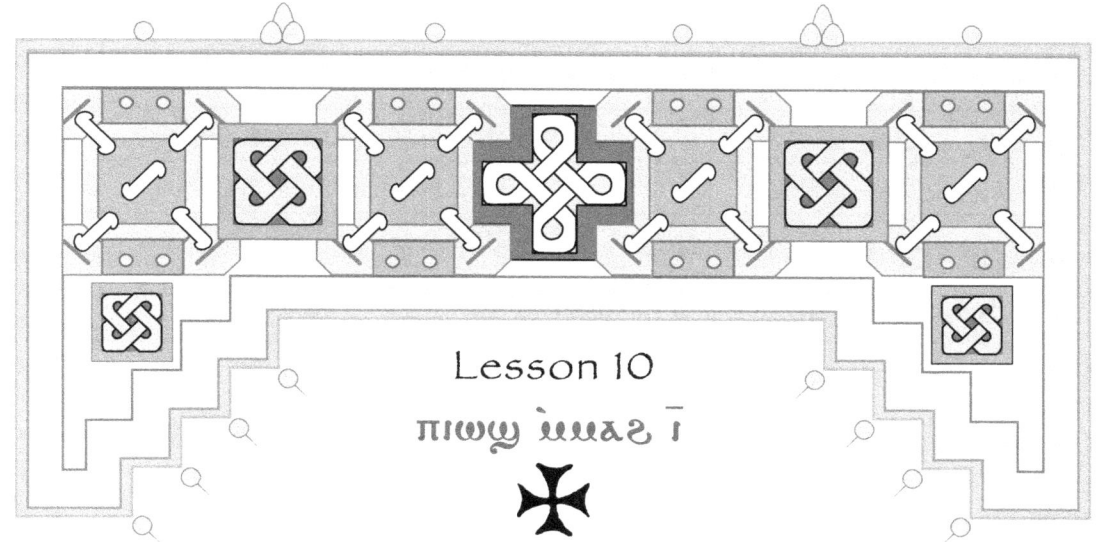

Lesson 10
ⲡⲓⲱϣ ⲙ̄ⲙⲁϩ ⲓ̄

USING THE DEFINITE ARTICLE AS A RELATIVE PRONOUN, AND VICE VERSA

1. Using the general definite article as a relative pronoun

The strong general definite articles (ⲡⲓ, ϯ, ⲛⲓ) come with the meaning of relative pronouns if they are directly followed by a preposition, so ⲡⲓ would mean "who/which" (mas.), ϯ "who/which" (fem.), and ⲛⲓ "who/which" (pl.).

Examples of prepositions:

ⲉⲑⲃⲉ	For the sake	ϧⲁ	under, about
ϣⲁ	to, until	ϧⲉⲛ	in, with
ϩⲓϫⲉⲛ	on, above	ⲉⲃⲟⲗϧⲉⲛ	from
ⲉⲃⲟⲗϩⲓⲧⲉⲛ	by, through	ϧⲁⲧⲉⲛ	at

Examples:

ⲡⲓⲗⲟⲅⲟⲥ ⲡⲓⲉⲃⲟⲗϧⲉⲛ Ⲫⲓⲱⲧ	The Word who is from the Father.
ϯϩⲓⲣⲏⲛⲏ ϯⲉⲃⲟⲗϧⲉⲛ ⲛⲓⲫⲏⲟⲩⲓ́	The peace which is from the heavens.
ⲛⲓⲉⲃⲟⲗϧⲉⲛ ⲡⲥⲉⲃⲓ	Who are from the circumcision.
ⲡⲓⲃⲉⲭⲉ ⲡⲓⲉⲃⲟⲗϧⲉⲛ ⲛⲓⲫⲏⲟⲩⲓ́	The reward that is from the heavens. (The heavenly reward).

ⲡⲓϣⲁ ⲉ̀ⲛⲉϩ	Who [which] is forever. (Eternal).
ⲛⲓⲉ̀ⲃⲟⲗϩⲓⲧⲉⲛ Ⲫϯ	Who [that] are through God.
ⲛⲓϫⲱⲙ ⲛⲓϩⲓϫⲉⲛ ϯⲧⲣⲁⲡⲉⲍⲁ	The books which are on the table.
ϯⲥⲱⲛⲓ ϯϧⲁⲧⲉⲛ ⲡⲓⲣⲟ ⲛ̀ⲧⲉ ⲡⲓⲉⲣⲫⲉⲓ	The sister who is at the door of the sanctuary.
ⲛⲓⲥⲛⲏⲟⲩ ⲛⲓⲃⲉⲛ ⲡⲓⲏⲓ ⲫⲏⲉⲧⲉⲙⲙⲁⲩ	The brothers who are in that house.

2. Using the relative pronoun as a definite article

The relative pronoun ⲉⲧ (ⲉⲑ) is translated as a definite article if the noun that is desired to be defined is an adjective derived from a verb, or what is called the qualitative form of the verb, for example:

ⲡⲓⲡ̀ⲛⲉⲩⲙⲁ ⲉⲑⲟⲩⲁⲃ   The Holy Spirit

Here the relative pronoun ⲉⲑ is translated as a definite article before the qualitative form ⲟⲩⲁⲃ.

Verb	Meaning	The derived adj.	Meaning	The adj. defined by ⲉⲧ	Combined meaning (sing., pl., mas., fem.)
ϫⲱⲕ	To perfect	ϫⲏⲕ	Perfect	ⲉⲧϫⲏⲕ	The perfect
ⲧⲁⲓⲟ	To honor	ⲧⲁⲓⲏⲟⲩⲧ	Honored	ⲉⲧⲧⲁⲓⲏⲟⲩⲧ	The honored
ⲥⲙⲟⲩ	To bless	ⲥⲙⲁⲣⲱⲟⲩⲧ	Blessed	ⲉⲧⲥⲙⲁⲣⲱⲟⲩⲧ	The blessed
ⲧⲟⲩⲃⲟ	To purify	ⲧⲟⲩⲃⲏⲟⲩⲧ	Pure	ⲉⲧⲧⲟⲩⲃⲏⲟⲩⲧ	The pure
ⲧⲟⲩⲃⲟ	To sanctify	ⲟⲩⲁⲃ	Holy	ⲉⲑⲟⲩⲁⲃ	The holy

ϯⲡⲁⲣⲑⲉⲛⲟⲥ ⲉⲧⲧⲁⲓⲏⲟⲩⲧ	The honored virgin.
ⲫⲏⲉⲧϣⲟⲡ ϧⲉⲛ ⲡⲓⲟⲩⲱⲓⲛⲓ	He who exists in the light.
ⲡⲓⲛⲁϩϯ ⲉⲧϫⲏⲕ ⲉ̀ⲃⲟⲗ	The perfect faith.

Lesson 10 ✣ Using the Definite Article as a Relative Pronoun, and Vice Versa ✣

The letter ⲧ is replaced with ⲑ before the nouns and derived adjectives beginning with the letters ⲙ, ⲛ, or ⲟ:

ⲉⲑⲟⲩⲁⲃ	The holy	ⲉⲑⲛⲏⲟⲩ	The coming	ⲉⲑⲙⲱⲟⲩⲧ	The dead (sing.)
ⲉⲑⲟⲩⲏⲛ	The open	ⲉⲑⲛⲁϩϯ	The believer	ⲉⲑⲙⲟϣⲓ	The (one) walking
ⲑⲏⲉⲑⲙⲉϩ ⲛ̀ϩⲙⲟⲧ	The full of grace	ⲛⲏⲉⲑⲙⲱⲟⲩⲧ	The dead (pl.)		

Important Note:

If the noun, which we want to describe using the relative pronoun, is an indefinite noun, then the adjective in this case accepts ⲉϥ (for singular masculine), ⲉⲥ (for singular feminine), ⲉⲩ (for plural).

Examples:

ⲟⲩϩⲏⲧ ⲉϥⲟⲩⲁⲃ A pure heart	ⲟⲩⲗⲁⲟⲥ ⲉϥⲟϣ Many people
ⲟⲩⲡⲁⲣⲑⲉⲛⲟⲥ ⲉⲥⲧⲁⲓⲏⲟⲩⲧ An honored virgin	ⲟⲩⲑⲩⲥⲓⲁ ⲉⲥϣⲏⲡ An acceptable sacrifice
ϩⲁⲛⲁⲅⲅⲉⲗⲟⲥ ⲉⲩⲟⲩⲁⲃ Pure angels	ϩⲁⲛϩⲏⲧ ⲉⲩⲥⲟⲩⲧⲱⲛ Upright hearts
ⲟⲩⲙⲱⲟⲩ ⲉϥⲃⲏⲗ ⲉ̀ⲃⲟⲗ A flowing water	ⲟⲩϩⲁⲡ ⲉϥⲥϧⲏⲟⲩⲧ A written judgment
ⲟⲩⲁⲓ ⲡⲉ ⲉ̀ⲃⲟⲗϧⲉⲛ ⲥ̀ⲛⲁⲩ: ⲟⲩⲙⲉⲑⲛⲟⲩϯ ⲉⲥⲧⲟⲩⲃⲏⲟⲩⲧ ⲛⲉⲙ ⲟⲩⲙⲉⲧⲣⲱⲙⲓ ⲉⲥⲟⲩⲁⲃ. One out of two: a holy divinity and a pure humanity.	

Exercises

1. Write the meaning of the following phrases:

ⲁ̄   ⲟⲩⲣⲱⲙⲓ ⲉϥⲧⲁⲓⲏⲟⲩⲧ.

ⲃ̄   ⲟⲩⲙⲱⲓⲧ ⲉϥⲥⲟⲩⲧⲱⲛ.

ⲅ̄   ⲟⲩⲥⲛⲟⲩ ⲉϥϣⲏⲡ.

ⲇ̄   ϩⲁⲛϫⲱⲙ ⲉⲩⲟϣ.

ⲉ̄   ϩⲁⲛⲣⲱⲟⲩ ⲉⲩⲟⲩⲏⲛ.

ⲋ̄   ⲟⲩϫⲓϫ ⲉⲥⲧⲟⲩⲃⲏⲟⲩⲧ.

ⲍ̄   ⲡⲉⲛϭⲟⲓⲥ ⲉⲑⲛⲏⲟⲩ.

✠ Foundations of the Coptic Language ✠

ⲏ̄ ⲡⲓⲣⲱⲙⲓ ⲉⲧϫⲏⲕ ⲉ̀ⲃⲟⲗ.
ⲑ̄ Ⲫϯ ⲫⲏⲉⲧϫⲟⲣ.
ⲓ̄ ϯⲡⲁⲣⲑⲉⲛⲟⲥ ⲉⲑⲙⲉϩ ⲛ̀ⲧⲁⲓⲟ.
ⲓ̄ⲁ̄ ⲛⲓⲥⲛⲏⲟⲩ ⲉⲧⲥⲙⲁⲣⲱⲟⲩⲧ.
ⲓ̄ⲃ̄ ⲡⲉⲕϩⲁⲧ ⲉⲑⲙⲉϩ ⲛ̀ⲭⲁⲣⲓⲥⲙⲁ.

2. Translate the following:

ⲁ̄ ⲡⲓⲣⲱⲙⲓ ⲡⲓⲉ̀ⲃⲟⲗϧⲉⲛ Ⲭⲏⲙⲓ.
ⲃ̄ ϯⲥⲱⲛⲓ ϯⲉ̀ⲃⲟⲗϧⲉⲛ ⲧⲁⲓⲃⲁⲕⲓ.
ⲅ̄ ⲛⲓⲙⲟϯ ⲛⲓⲉ̀ⲃⲟⲗϧⲉⲛ ⲡⲁⲓϣⲁϥⲉ.
ⲇ̄ ⲡⲓϫⲱⲙ ⲡⲓϩⲓϫⲉⲛ ⲧⲁⲓⲧⲣⲁⲡⲉⲍⲁ ⲡⲉ ⲫⲱⲕ.
ⲉ̄ ϯϩⲓⲕⲱⲛ ϯϩⲓϫⲉⲛ ⲧϫⲟⲓ ⲉ̀ⲧⲉⲙ̀ⲙⲁⲩ ⲧⲉ ⲑⲁ ϯⲡⲁⲣⲑⲉⲛⲟⲥ.
ⲋ̄ ⲛⲓⲁ̀ⲗⲱⲟⲩⲓ̀ ⲛⲓⲃⲉⲛ ⲡⲓⲏⲓ ⲉⲧⲧⲏ ⲛⲉ ⲛⲟⲩⲧⲉⲛ.
ⲍ̄ ⲫⲁⲓ ⲡⲉ ⲡⲓⲥⲟⲛ ⲉⲑⲛⲏⲟⲩ ⲡⲓⲉ̀ⲃⲟⲗϩⲓⲧⲉⲛ ⲡⲉⲛⲟⲩⲣⲟ.
ⲏ̄ ⲑⲁⲓ ⲧⲉ ϯϣⲉⲣⲓ ⲉⲧⲥⲙⲁⲣⲱⲟⲩⲧ ϯⲉ̀ⲃⲟⲗϧⲉⲛ ϯⲉⲕⲕⲗⲏⲥⲓⲁ ⲉⲧⲧⲏ.
ⲑ̄ ⲛⲁⲓ ⲛⲉ ⲛⲓϧⲉⲗⲗⲟⲓ ⲉⲧⲧⲁⲓⲏⲟⲩⲧ ⲛⲓⲉ̀ⲃⲟⲗϧⲉⲛ ⲛⲓⲧⲱⲟⲩ ⲉⲑⲟⲩⲁⲃ ⲛ̀ⲛⲏⲉ̀ⲧⲉⲙ̀ⲙⲁⲩ.

Review Exercises 2
On Lessons 6 to 10

1. Write the meaning of the following:

ā	ⲡⲓⲟⲩⲱⲓⲛⲓ ⲫⲏⲉⲧⲉⲙⲙⲁⲩ	ⲏ̄	ⲛⲁ ⲛⲓⲫⲏⲟⲩⲓ
ⲃ̄	ϯⲉⲕⲕⲗⲏⲥⲓⲁ ⲉⲧⲉⲙⲙⲁⲩ	ⲑ̄	ⲫⲁ ⲡⲓⲱⲟⲩ
ⲅ̄	ⲛⲓⲙⲟⲛⲁⲭⲟⲥ ⲉⲧⲧⲏ	ī	ⲑⲁ ⲡⲁⲓⲙⲁ
ⲇ̄	ⲡⲉϥⲛⲁⲓ ⲛⲉⲙ ⲧⲉϥϩⲓⲣⲏⲛⲏ	ⲓⲁ̄	ϩⲁⲛⲓⲟϯ ⲛ̀ⲧⲏⲓ
ⲉ̄	ⲛⲉⲕⲥⲁϫⲓ ⲛⲉⲙ ⲛⲉⲕϩⲃⲏⲟⲩⲓ	ⲓⲃ̄	ⲟⲩⲥⲟⲛ ⲛ̀ⲧⲁϥ
ⲋ̄	ⲡⲉⲛⲟⲩⲣⲟ ⲛⲉⲙ ⲧⲉⲛⲟⲩⲣⲱ	ⲓⲅ̄	ϩⲁⲛϫⲱⲙ ⲛ̀ⲧⲱⲟⲩ
ⲍ̄	ⲛⲟⲩⲛⲟⲃⲓ ⲛⲉⲙ ⲛⲟⲩⲁⲛⲟⲙⲓⲁ	ⲓⲇ̄	ⲟⲩⲃⲁⲕⲓ ⲛ̀ⲧⲱⲧⲉⲛ

2. Put the suitable possessive pronoun or adjective in the blank:

ⲫⲏⲉⲧⲉ ⲫⲱⲛ ⲛ̀ⲟⲩϫⲁⲓ	=	…..ⲟⲩϫⲁⲓ	ⲫⲏⲉⲧⲉ …..ⲛ̀ⲥⲟⲛ	=	ⲡⲉⲧⲉⲛⲥⲟⲛ
ⲛⲏⲉⲧⲉ ⲛⲟⲩϥ ⲛ̀ϣⲏⲣⲓ	=	……ϣⲏⲣⲓ	ⲛⲏⲉⲧⲉ …..ⲛ̀ⲥⲱⲛⲓ	=	ⲛⲉⲥⲥⲱⲛⲓ
ⲑⲏⲉⲧⲉ ⲑⲱⲟⲩ ⲙ̀ⲙⲁⲩ	=	……ⲙⲁⲩ	ⲑⲏⲉⲧⲉ …..ⲛ̀ϣⲉⲣⲓ	=	ⲧⲟⲩϣⲉⲣⲓ
ⲫⲏⲉⲧⲉ ⲫⲱⲓ ⲛ̀ⲓⲱⲧ	=	……ⲓⲱⲧ	ⲫⲏⲉⲧⲉ …..ⲛ̀ϫⲱⲙ	=	ⲡⲉⲕϫⲱⲙ
ⲛⲏⲉⲧⲉ ⲛⲟⲩⲧⲉⲛ ⲙ̀ⲃⲁⲗ	=	……ⲃⲁⲗ	ⲛⲏⲉⲧⲉ …..ⲛ̀ⲓⲟϯ	=	ⲛⲁⲓⲟϯ
ⲑⲏⲉⲧⲉ ⲑⲱⲕ ⲛ̀ϫⲓϫ	=	…..ϫⲓϫ	ⲑⲏⲉⲧⲉ …..ⲛ̀ⲣⲓ	=	ⲧⲉⲣⲓ

✠ Foundations of the Coptic Language ✠

3. Write the meaning of the following:

1. ⲣⲱⲛ	7. ϩⲑⲏⲕ	13. ⲁⲩⲣⲏϫϥ
2. ⲕⲉⲛⲧ	8. ϩⲣⲁϥ	14. ⲣⲁⲧⲉⲛ-ⲑⲏⲛⲟⲩ
3. ⲣⲁⲧⲕ	9. ϧⲏⲧⲥ	15. ϩⲣⲁⲛ
4. ϫⲱϥ	10. ⲧⲟϯ	16. ⲕⲉⲛϥ
5. ⲧⲟⲧⲟⲩ	11. ϫⲱⲧⲉⲛ	17. ⲧⲟⲧⲕ
6. ϧⲏⲧⲉⲛ	12. ⲥⲟⲩⲉⲛⲥ	18. ⲓⲁⲧϥ

4. Write the meaning of the following phrases:

1. ⲛⲓⲉⲃⲟⲗϧⲉⲛ ⲧⲫⲉ	7. ⲟⲩϩⲏⲧ ⲉϥⲥⲟⲩⲧⲱⲛ
2. ⲡⲓⲉⲃⲟⲗϩⲓⲧⲉⲛ Ⲫϯ	8. ⲡⲓⲣⲱⲙⲓ ⲉⲧⲧⲁⲓⲏⲟⲩⲧ
3. ϯⲉⲃⲟⲗϧⲉⲛ Ⲭⲏⲙⲓ	9. ϩⲁⲛⲁⲅⲅⲉⲗⲟⲥ ⲉⲩⲟⲩⲁⲃ
4. ⲡⲓϣⲁ ⲉⲛⲉϩ	10. ϯⲡⲁⲣⲑⲉⲛⲟⲥ ⲉⲑⲟⲩⲁⲃ
5. ⲛⲓϩⲓϫⲉⲛ ⲡⲓⲕⲁϩⲓ	11. ⲟⲩⲟⲩⲥⲓⲁ ⲉⲥϣⲏⲡ
6. ϯⲉⲃⲟⲗϧⲉⲛ ⲧⲁⲓⲃⲁⲕⲓ	12. ⲛⲓⲥⲛⲏⲟⲩ ⲉⲧⲥⲙⲁⲣⲱⲟⲩⲧ

5. Translate the following to the English language:

ⲁ̅ ⲡⲓⲣⲱⲙⲓ ⲫⲏⲉⲧⲉⲙⲙⲁⲩ ⲡⲉ ⲡⲟⲩⲓⲱⲧ.
ⲃ̅ ϯⲉⲕⲕⲗⲏⲥⲓⲁ ⲉⲧⲉⲙⲙⲁⲩ ⲧⲉ ⲑⲁ ϯⲡⲁⲣⲑⲉⲛⲟⲥ.
ⲅ̅ ⲛⲓⲥⲛⲏⲟⲩ ⲉⲧⲧⲏ ⲛⲉ ⲛⲉⲛⲥⲛⲏⲟⲩ.
ⲇ̅ ⲡⲉⲛϭⲟⲓⲥ ⲛⲉⲙ ⲡⲉⲛⲛⲟⲩϯ ⲛⲉⲙ ⲡⲉⲛⲥⲱⲧⲏⲣ ⲡⲉ Ⲓⲏⲥⲟⲩⲥ.
ⲉ̅ ⲛⲁϫⲱⲙ ⲛⲉⲙ ⲛⲉⲕϫⲱⲙ ⲛⲉ ϧⲉⲛ ⲧⲁⲓⲣⲓ.
ⲋ̅ ⲛ̅ⲑⲟϥ ⲛⲉⲙ ⲛⲉϥϣⲏⲣⲓ ⲛⲉ ⲙ̅ⲙⲁⲩ.
ⲍ̅ ⲡⲓϣⲁⲓ ⲉⲑⲛⲏⲟⲩ ⲡⲉ ⲫⲁ ⲛⲓⲙⲁⲣⲧⲩⲣⲟⲥ.
ⲏ̅ Ⲫⲱⲕ ⲡⲉ ⲡⲓⲱⲟⲩ ⲛⲉⲙ ⲡⲓⲧⲁⲓⲟ.
ⲑ̅ ⲛⲓϩⲓⲕⲱⲛ ⲛⲓϩⲓϫⲉⲛ ϯϫⲟⲓ ⲉⲧⲧⲏ ⲛⲉ ⲛⲁ ⲛⲓⲁⲅⲓⲟⲥ.
ⲓ̅ ⲛⲏ ⲛⲉ ⲛⲓϣⲏⲣⲓ ⲉⲧⲥⲙⲁⲣⲱⲟⲩⲧ ⲛⲓⲉⲃⲟⲗϩⲓⲧⲉⲛ ⲛⲓϧⲉⲗⲗⲟⲓ ⲉⲧⲧⲁⲓⲏⲟⲩⲧ.

6. Translate the following to the Coptic language:

1. This is a father and those are brothers.	3. These books are ours.
2. My spirit and my soul and my body.	4. The Virgin (the) full of glory.

Exam 2
On Lessons 6 to 10

1. Write the meaning of the following:

1. ⲡⲓϩⲁⲗⲏⲧ ⲫⲏⲉ̀ⲧⲉⲙⲙⲁⲩ	6. ⲛⲓϣⲏⲣⲓ ⲉⲧⲧⲏ	11. ⲡⲟⲩⲥⲙⲟⲩ
2. ϯϣⲟⲩⲣⲏ ⲑⲏⲉ̀ⲧⲉⲙⲙⲁⲩ	7. ⲡⲉϥⲛⲁⲓ	12. ⲡⲉⲛⲛⲟⲩϯ
3. ⲛⲓϣϣⲏⲛ ⲛⲏⲉ̀ⲧⲉⲙⲙⲁⲩ	8. ⲛⲁⲛⲟⲃⲓ	13. ⲛⲉⲥϣⲗⲏⲗ
4. ⲡⲓⲣⲱⲙⲓ ⲉⲧⲧⲏ	9. ⲛⲉⲧⲉⲛϩⲟ	14. ⲡⲉⲕⲧⲁⲓⲟ
5. ϯⲥⲱⲛⲓ ⲉⲧⲧⲏ	10. ⲧⲉϥⲯⲩⲭⲏ	15. ⲡⲁⲥⲱⲧⲏⲣ

2. Complete with the suitable possessive pronouns and adjectives:

1. ⲫⲁⲓ ⲡⲉ ⲡⲁϣⲏⲣⲓ.	ⲡⲁⲓϣⲏⲣⲓ ⲡⲉ …… .	
2. ⲑⲁⲓ ⲧⲉ …… ⲣⲓ.	ⲧⲁⲓⲣⲓ ⲧⲉ ⲑⲱϥ.	
3. ⲛⲁⲓ ⲛⲉ ⲛⲉⲥⲓⲟϯ.	ⲛⲁⲓⲓⲟϯ ⲛⲉ …… .	
4. ⲫⲁⲓ ⲡⲉ …… ⲥⲟⲛ.	ⲡⲁⲓⲥⲟⲛ ⲡⲉ ⲫⲱⲛ.	
5. ⲑⲁⲓ ⲧⲉ ⲧⲉⲧⲉⲛⲥⲱⲛⲓ.	ⲧⲁⲓⲥⲱⲛⲓ ⲧⲉ …… .	
6. ⲛⲁⲓ ⲛⲉ …… ϫⲱⲙ.	ⲛⲁⲓϫⲱⲙ ⲛⲉ ⲛⲟⲩⲕ.	
7. ⲫⲁⲓ ⲡⲉ ⲡⲟⲩⲟⲩⲣⲟ.	ⲡⲁⲓⲟⲩⲣⲟ ⲡⲉ …… .	
8. ⲑⲁⲓ ⲧⲉ …… ⲙⲁⲩ.	ⲧⲁⲓⲙⲁⲩ ⲧⲉ ⲑⲱ.	
9. ⲛⲁⲓ ⲛⲉ ⲛⲁⲥⲛⲏⲟⲩ.	ⲛⲁⲓⲥⲛⲏⲟⲩ ⲛⲉ …… .	

10. ϫⲱⲓ = ... ⲁ̀ⲫⲉ	14. ϧⲏⲧⲕ = ... ⲛⲉϫⲓ	18. ⲧⲟⲧ = ... ϫⲓϫ
11. ⲧⲟⲧⲕ = ... ϫⲓϫ	15. ϫⲱϥ = ... ⲁ̀ⲫⲉ	19. ϩ̀ⲣⲁϥ = ... ϩⲟ
12. ⲣⲁⲧϥ = ... ϭⲁⲗⲟϫ	16. ⲓⲁⲧⲥ = ... ⲃⲁⲗ	20. ϩⲑⲏⲛ = ... ϩⲏⲧ
13. ϩ̀ⲣⲁⲕ = ... ϩⲟ	17. ϧⲏⲧ = ... ⲛⲉϫⲓ	21. ⲣⲁⲧⲉⲛ = ... ϭⲁⲗⲁⲩϫ

3. Put the suitable definite article in the blank:

ⲫⲁ ⲧ̀ⲫⲉ	=	......ⲁⲅⲅⲉⲗⲟⲥ ...ⲉ̀ⲃⲟⲗϧⲉⲛ ⲧ̀ⲫⲉ.
ⲛⲁ Ⲭⲏⲙⲓ	=	......ⲣⲱⲙⲓ ...ⲉ̀ⲃⲟⲗϧⲉⲛ Ⲭⲏⲙⲓ.
ⲑⲁ Ⲫϯ	=	......ⲡⲁⲣⲑⲉⲛⲟⲥ ...ⲉ̀ⲃⲟⲗϩⲓⲧⲉⲛ Ⲫϯ.

4. Write the meaning of the following phrases:

1. ⲡⲉⲛⲛⲟⲩϯ ⲉⲑⲛⲏⲟⲩ.
2. ⲡⲓϧⲉⲗⲗⲟ ⲉⲧⲧⲁⲓⲏⲟⲩⲧ.
3. ⲛⲉⲛⲓⲟϯ ⲉⲧⲥ̀ⲙⲁⲣⲱⲟⲩⲧ.
4. ⲛⲓⲧⲱⲟⲩ ⲉⲑⲟⲩⲁⲃ.
5. ⲟⲩϫⲓϫ ⲉⲥⲧⲟⲩⲃⲏⲟⲩⲧ.
6. ϩⲁⲛⲁⲅⲅⲉⲗⲟⲥ ⲉⲩⲟⲩⲁⲃ.
7. ⲟⲩϫⲱⲙ ⲉϥⲟⲩⲏⲛ.
8. ϩⲁⲛϣⲏⲣⲓ ⲉⲩⲟϣ.

5. Translate the following to the English language:

ⲁ̄ ⲛ̀ⲑⲟϥ ⲡⲉ Ⲫⲛⲟⲩϯ ⲛ̀ⲧⲉ ⲛⲉⲛⲓⲟϯ.
ⲃ̄ ⲡⲉϥⲣⲁⲛ ⲡⲉ Ⲉⲙⲙⲁⲛⲟⲩⲏⲗ.
ⲅ̄ ⲧⲉϥⲙⲁⲩ ⲧⲉ ϯⲡⲁⲣⲑⲉⲛⲟⲥ ⲉⲑⲟⲩⲁⲃ.
ⲇ̄ ⲱ̀ Ⲙⲁⲣⲓⲁ ⲑ̀ⲙⲁⲩ ⲙ̀ⲡⲉⲛⲛⲟⲩϯ: ⲫⲱ ⲡⲉ ⲡⲓⲧⲁⲓⲟ. ⲑⲱ ⲧⲉ ϯⲇⲟⲝⲟⲗⲟⲅⲓⲁ.
ⲉ̄ ⲫⲏ ⲟⲩϫⲱⲙ ⲡⲉ ⲟⲩⲟϩ ⲑⲏ ⲟⲩϩⲓⲕⲱⲛ ⲧⲉ.
ⲋ̄ ⲛⲓϧⲉⲗⲗⲟⲓ ⲉⲧⲧⲏ ⲛⲉ ⲛⲉⲛⲓⲟϯ ⲛ̀ⲛⲁⲓϣⲁϥⲉⲣ.
ⲍ̄ ⲫⲁⲓ ⲡⲉ ⲡⲓⲥⲟⲛ ⲡⲓⲉ̀ⲃⲟⲗϧⲉⲛ ϯⲉⲕⲕⲗⲏⲥⲓⲁ ⲉ̀ⲧⲉⲙⲙⲁⲩ.

6. Translate the following to the Coptic language:

1. My heart and my tongue and my senses.
2. The heavenly and the earthly.
3. A blessed brother and a pure angel.

General Exam
On Lessons 1 to 10

1. Write the meaning of the following:

1.	ⲟⲩϫⲱⲙ	7.	ϩⲁⲛϫⲱⲙ
2.	ⲡⲓϫⲱⲙ	8.	ⲛⲓϫⲱⲙ
3.	ⲡⲁⲓϫⲱⲙ	9.	ⲛⲁⲓϫⲱⲙ
4.	ⲡⲓϫⲱⲙ ⲉ̀ⲧⲉⲙ̀ⲙⲁⲩ	10.	ⲛⲓϫⲱⲙ ⲉⲧⲧⲏ
5.	ⲡⲉϥϫⲱⲙ	11.	ⲛⲉⲧⲉⲛϫⲱⲙ
6.	ⲟⲩϫⲱⲙ ⲛ̀ⲧⲏⲓ	12.	ϩⲁⲛϫⲱⲙ ⲛ̀ⲧⲁⲥ

2. Choose from the left column the suitable number for each word on the opposite right column:

1.	ⲛⲁⲓⲟϯ	ⲫⲱⲥ	9.	ⲧⲁⲣⲓ	ⲛⲟⲩⲕ
2.	ⲧⲟⲩⲙⲁⲩ	ⲑⲱ	10.	ⲡⲉⲛⲗⲁⲥ	ⲫⲱⲟⲩ
3.	ⲡⲉⲥⲣⲁⲛ	ⲛⲟⲩⲛ	11.	ⲛⲉⲕⲁ̀ⲗⲱⲟⲩⲓ̀	ⲛⲟⲩ
4.	ⲧⲉⲥⲱⲛⲓ	ⲫⲱⲧⲉⲛ	12.	ⲧⲉϥϫⲟⲙ	ⲑⲱⲥ
5.	ⲛⲉϥϣⲏⲣⲓ	ⲛⲟⲩⲓ	13.	ⲡⲟⲩⲕⲁϩⲓ	ⲫⲱⲛ
6.	ⲡⲉⲧⲉⲛⲟⲩⲣⲟ	ⲑⲱⲕ	14.	ⲛⲉⲧⲉⲛϣⲗⲏⲗ	ⲑⲱϥ
7.	ⲧⲉⲕϩⲓⲣⲏⲛⲏ	ⲑⲱⲟⲩ	15.	ⲛⲉⲥⲁϫⲓ	ⲛⲟⲩⲧⲉⲛ
8.	ⲛⲉⲛϫⲓϫ	ⲛⲟⲩϥ	16.	ⲧⲉⲥϣⲉⲣⲓ	ⲑⲱⲓ

3. Put the suitable definite article in the blank:

ⲛⲁ ⲛⲓⲫⲏⲟⲩⲓ.	= ... ⲡⲛⲉⲩⲙⲁ ... ⲉ̀ⲃⲟⲗϧⲉⲛ ... ⲫⲏⲟⲩⲓ.
ⲫⲁ Ⲫ̇ⲓⲱⲧ.	= ... ⲗⲟⲅⲟⲥ ... ⲉ̀ⲃⲟⲗϧⲉⲛ Ⲫ̇ⲓⲱⲧ.
ⲑⲁ Ⲡ̇ϭⲟⲓⲥ.	= ... ⲥⲱⲛⲓ ... ⲉ̀ⲃⲟⲗϩⲓⲧⲉⲛ Ⲡ̇ϭⲟⲓⲥ.

4. Write the meaning of the following phrases:

1. ⲡⲓⲣⲱⲙⲓ ⲉⲑⲛⲁϩϯ	5. ⲛⲓⲣⲱⲟⲩ ⲉⲑⲟⲩⲏⲛ
2. ⲟⲩϩⲏⲧ ⲉϥⲟⲩⲁⲃ	6. ϩⲁⲛϣⲏⲣⲓ ⲉⲩⲟϣ
3. ⲧⲉⲕϩⲓⲣⲏⲛⲏ ⲉⲧϫⲏⲕ	7. ⲡⲉⲛϭⲟⲓⲥ ⲉⲧϫⲟⲣ
4. ⲟⲩⲡⲁⲣⲑⲉⲛⲟⲥ ⲉⲥⲧⲁⲓⲏⲟⲩⲧ	8. ⲛⲓⲥⲛⲏⲟⲩ ⲉⲧⲥⲙⲁⲣⲱⲟⲩⲧ

5. Complete with the suitable possessive adjectives:

1. ⲭⲱϥ = ... ⲁ̀ⲫⲉ	4. ϧⲏⲧⲥ = ... ⲛⲉϫⲓ	7. ⲓⲁϯ = ... ⲃⲁⲗ
2. ϩⲣⲁⲕ = ... ϩⲟ	5. ϧⲑⲏⲧⲉⲛ = ... ϩⲏⲧ	8. ⲣⲉⲛⲟⲩ = ... ⲣⲁⲛ
3. ⲣⲁⲧ = ... ϭⲁⲗⲟϫ	6. ⲧⲟⲧⲉⲛ = ... ϫⲓϫ	9. ϩⲣⲏⲓ = ... ϩⲟ

6. Translate the following to the English language:

ⲁ̄ ⲁⲛⲟⲛ ⲡⲉ ⲡⲉϥⲗⲁⲟⲥ ⲟⲩⲟϩ ⲛ̀ⲑⲱⲟⲩ ⲛⲉ ⲛⲉⲛⲓⲟϯ.
ⲃ̄ ⲫⲁⲓ ⲟⲩⲣⲱⲙⲓ ⲡⲉ ⲟⲩⲟϩ ⲛⲏ ϩⲁⲛϣⲏⲣⲓ ⲛ̀ⲧⲁϥ ⲛⲉ.
ⲅ̄ ⲛⲓⲙ ⲧⲉ ⲑⲁⲓ? ⲛ̀ⲑⲟⲥ ⲧⲉ ⲧⲉⲛⲙⲁⲩ ⲉⲑⲟⲩⲁⲃ.
ⲇ̄ ⲛⲓⲫⲏⲟⲩⲓ ⲛⲉⲙ ⲡ̀ⲕⲁϩⲓ ⲛⲉ ⲛⲟⲩⲕ, ⲱ̀ ⲡⲉⲛⲛⲟⲩϯ.
ⲉ̄ ⲫⲏ ⲟⲩⲁ̀ⲗⲟⲩ ⲡⲉ ⲟⲩⲟϩ ⲑⲏ ⲟⲩⲡⲁⲣⲑⲉⲛⲟⲥ ⲧⲉ.
ⲋ̄ ⲫⲱⲕ ⲡⲉ ⲡⲓⲱⲟⲩ ⲛⲉⲙ ⲡⲓⲧⲁⲓⲟ ⲛⲉⲙ ϯⲉⲩⲭⲁⲣⲓⲥⲧⲓⲁ.
ⲍ̄ ⲡⲓⲙⲟⲛⲁⲭⲟⲥ ⲉⲧⲧⲏ ⲡⲉ ⲡⲓϧⲉⲗⲗⲟ ⲛ̀ⲧⲉ ⲡⲁⲓϣⲁϥⲉ.
ⲏ̄ ⲛⲁⲓ ⲛⲉ ⲛⲓⲟⲩⲏⲃ ⲛⲓⲉ̀ⲃⲟⲗϩⲓⲧⲉⲛ ϯⲉⲕⲕⲗⲏⲥⲓⲁ ⲉ̀ⲧⲉⲙⲙⲁⲩ.

7. Translate the following to the Coptic language:

1. Your head and your eyes and your thought.

2. The Egyptians and their sons.

3. Pure angels and a blessed sister.

Lesson 11
ⲡⲓⲱϣ ⲙ̄ⲙⲁϩ ⲓⲁ
✠
ⲡⲓⲣⲁ

VERBS

The Declarative Form (ⲡⲓⲣⲏϯ ⲛ̄ⲧⲁⲙⲟ)

It is the form that informs about an event in the past, or is happening in the present, or will happen in the future in the affirmative case; or it did not happen in the past, is not happening in the present, or will not happen in the future in the negative case.

The tense of the verb (ⲡⲓⲥⲏⲟⲩ ⲛ̄ⲧⲉ ⲡⲓⲣⲁ)

The verb occupies part of the tense. The main tenses of the verb are present, past, and future. And for each tense of these three, there are several categories to determine the time wherein it happened with marks that specify the time of the action more precisely.

The conjugation of the verb in the first present tense or the existential state (ⲡⲓⲣⲓⲕⲓ ⲛ̄ⲧⲉ ⲡⲓⲣⲁ ϧⲉⲛ ⲡⲓⲥⲏⲟⲩ ⲉⲧϣⲟⲡ)

It indicates that the event is happening while it is talked about. Its mark is that the subject pronoun is placed directly before it. And the conjugation is as follows:

ϯϩⲱⲥ	I praise.	ⲕϩⲱⲥ	You (mas.) praise.	ϥϩⲱⲥ	He praises.
		ⲧⲉϩⲱⲥ	You (fem.) praise.	ⲥϩⲱⲥ	She praise.
ⲧⲉⲛϩⲱⲥ	We praise.	ⲧⲉⲧⲉⲛϩⲱⲥ	You (pl.) praise.	ⲥⲉϩⲱⲥ	They praise.

✠ Foundations of the Coptic Language ✠

Notes:

1. The plural form of the first, second, and third person in the Coptic language is used to indicate the dual and plural in both genders, as it is in the English language.

2. Sometimes the letter ϫ takes the place of the letter ⲕ with respect to the second person, singular masculine, if it begins with one of the letters ⲙ, ⲛ, or ⲟⲩ, for example:

ϫⲙⲉⲓ	You love	ϫⲛⲁⲩ	You look	ϫⲟⲩⲱϣ	You want
ϫⲙⲟⲥϯ	You hate	ϫⲛⲁϩϯ	You believe	ϫⲟⲩⲱⲙ	You eat

3. The negative form of this tense is formulated with the negative particle ⲁⲛ, and it is inserted after the verb, for example:

ϯⲥϧⲁⲓ ⲁⲛ.	I do not write.	ⲕⲥϧⲁⲓ ⲁⲛ.	You (mas.) do not write.

To emphasize the negative form, the letter ⲛ̀ is inserted before the subject pronoun, while ⲁⲛ comes after the verb, for example:

ⲛ̀ϯⲥϧⲁⲓ ⲁⲛ.	I never write.
ⲛ̀ϥ̀ⲥϧⲁⲓ ⲁⲛ.	He never writes.
ⲛ̀ⲑⲟϥ ⲛ̀ϥ̀ⲟⲩⲱⲙ ⲁⲛ ⲛⲉⲙ ⲡⲁⲓⲣⲱⲙⲓ.	He eats with this person.

Verbs (ϩⲁⲛⲣⲁ):

ϣⲗⲏⲗ	To pray	ϩⲱⲥ	To praise	ϯ	To give	ϩⲉⲙⲥⲓ	To sit
ⲥⲙⲟⲩ	To bless	ⲱϣ	To read	ϭⲓ	To take, to be granted	ⲛⲉϩⲥⲓ	To wake up
ⲁⲣⲉϩ	To keep	ⲥϧⲁⲓ	To write	ⲛⲁⲩ	To see	ⲥⲱⲧⲉⲙ	To hear
ϣⲉⲙϣⲓ	To serve	ⲕⲁϯ	To understand	ⲙⲟϣⲓ	To walk	ϣⲱⲗⲉⲙ	To smell
ⲟⲩⲱϣⲧ	To worship	ⲕⲱϯ	To seek	ⲥⲓⲛⲓ	To cross, To pass	ϭⲱⲣⲉⲙ	To point
ⲟⲩⲱϣ	To want; to wish	ⲟⲩⲱⲙ	To eat	ⲙⲓⲥⲓ	To beget	ⲭⲱⲗⲉⲙ	To hasten
ⲟⲩⲱⲣⲡ	To send	ⲥⲱ	To drink	ϣⲓⲛⲓ	To ask	ⲛⲟϩⲉⲙ	To rescue, to save
ⲓ̀	To come	ⲙⲉⲓ	To love	ⲕⲓⲙ	To move	ⲥⲱⲧⲡ	To choose
ⲛⲁϩϯ	To believe	ⲙⲟⲥϯ	To hate	ⲓ̀ⲣⲓ	To make, to do	ⲧⲁⲙⲟ	To inform; to tell

Lesson 11 ✠ Verbs ✠

Exercises

1. Write the meaning of the following verbs:

1. ⲧⲉⲛⲥϧⲁⲓ	10. ⲥⲉϩⲱⲥ	19. ⲧⲉⲧⲉⲛⲥⲱ
2. ϥⲕⲓⲙ	11. ϯϣⲓⲛⲓ	20. ⲥⲉⲃⲓ
3. ⲧⲉⲟⲩⲱϣⲧ	12. ϥⲛⲟⲃⲉⲙ	21. ⲧⲉⲛⲕⲁϯ
4. ϫⲛⲁⲩ	13. ⲧⲉⲙⲟϣⲓ	22. ϥϣⲉⲙϣⲓ
5. ⲧⲉⲧⲉⲛⲓ	14. ⲧⲉⲛⲥⲙⲟⲩ	23. ⲥⲙⲓⲥⲓ
6. ⲥⲙⲟⲥϯ	15. ϯⲛⲉϩⲥⲓ	24. ⲧⲉⲭⲱⲗⲉⲙ
7. ⲧⲉⲛⲕⲱϯ	16. ⲧⲉⲧⲉⲛϯ	25. ⲧⲉⲛⲥⲓⲛⲓ
8. ⲥⲉⲟⲩⲱⲙ	17. ϥϣⲗⲏⲗ	26. ⲕϩⲉⲙⲥⲓ
9. ⲧⲉⲱϣ	18. ⲕⲁⲣⲉϩ	27. ϯⲛⲁϩϯ

2. Translate (ⲃⲱⲗ ⲉⲃⲟⲗ):

ⲁ̄   ϯⲱϣ ⲁⲛ, ⲁⲗⲗⲁ ϯⲥϧⲁⲓ.
ⲃ̄   ϫⲟⲩⲱⲙ ⲁⲛ, ⲁⲗⲗⲁ ⲕⲥⲱ.
ⲅ̄   ⲧⲉⲥⲁϫⲓ ⲁⲛ, ⲁⲗⲗⲁ ⲧⲉⲥⲱⲧⲉⲙ.
ⲇ̄   ϥⲁⲣⲉϩ ⲁⲛ, ⲁⲗⲗⲁ ϥⲕⲁϯ.
ⲉ̄   ⲥⲛⲁⲩ ⲁⲛ, ⲁⲗⲗⲁ ⲥϣⲱⲗⲉⲙ.
ⲋ̄   ⲧⲉⲛⲟⲩⲱⲣⲡ ⲁⲛ, ⲁⲗⲗⲁ ⲧⲉⲛⲓ.
ⲍ̄   ⲧⲉⲧⲉⲛϭⲓ ⲁⲛ, ⲁⲗⲗⲁ ⲧⲉⲧⲉⲛϯ.
ⲏ̄   ⲥⲉϩⲉⲙⲥⲓ ⲁⲛ, ⲁⲗⲗⲁ ⲥⲉϣⲗⲏⲗ.
ⲑ̄   ⲛ̄ⲧⲉⲛⲙⲟⲥϯ ⲁⲛ, ⲁⲗⲗⲁ ⲧⲉⲛⲙⲉⲓ.

3. Sample sentences for translation and memorization:

ⲁⲛⲟⲕ ϯⲥⲁϫⲓ ϧⲉⲛ ⲡⲁⲗⲁⲥ,
   ϯⲥⲱⲧⲉⲙ ϧⲉⲛ ⲛⲁⲙⲁϣϫ,
   ϯⲛⲁⲩ ϧⲉⲛ ⲛⲁⲃⲁⲗ,
   ϯϣⲱⲗⲉⲙ ϧⲉⲛ ⲡⲁϣⲁⲓ,
   ϯⲟⲩⲱⲙ ϧⲉⲛ ⲛⲁⲛⲁϫϩⲓ,
   ϯⲥⲱ ϧⲉⲛ ⲣⲱⲓ,
   ϯϭⲱⲣⲉⲙ ϧⲉⲛ ⲡⲁⲧⲏⲃ,

ϯⲉⲣϩⲱⲃ ϧⲉⲛ ⲛⲁϫⲓϫ,
ϯⲙⲟϣⲓ ϧⲉⲛ ⲛⲁⲃⲁⲗⲁⲩϫ,
ϯⲥϧⲁⲓ ϧⲉⲛ ⲡⲁⲕⲁϣ,
ϯⲕⲁϯ ϧⲉⲛ ⲡⲁⲛⲟⲩⲥ,
ϯⲱϣ ϧⲉⲛ ⲡⲁϫⲱⲙ ⲉⲑⲟⲩⲁⲃ,
ϯϣⲗⲏⲗ ⲉⲃⲟⲗϧⲉⲛ ⲡⲁϩⲏⲧ,
ϯϩⲱⲥ ⲛⲉⲙ ⲛⲁⲓⲟϯ ⲛⲉⲙ ⲛⲁⲥⲛⲏⲟⲩ.

You may repeat these sentences by starting with other subject pronouns, instead of ⲁⲛⲟⲕ, while changing what is required to be changed, for example: ⲛ̀ⲑⲟⲕ, ⲛ̀ⲑⲟ, ⲛ̀ⲑⲟϥ, ⲛ̀ⲑⲟⲥ, ⲁⲛⲟⲛ, ⲛ̀ⲑⲱⲧⲉⲛ, ⲛ̀ⲑⲱⲟⲩ.

4. Answer, once in the affirmative form and then in the negative form, according to the given example:

ⲙⲏ ⲡⲁⲓϫⲱⲙ ⲡⲉ ⲡⲉⲕϫⲱⲙ?	ⲥⲉ, ⲡⲁⲓϫⲱⲙ ⲡⲉ ⲡⲁϫⲱⲙ.
	ⲙ̀ⲙⲟⲛ, ⲡⲁⲓϫⲱⲙ ⲡⲉ ⲁⲛ ⲡⲁϫⲱⲙ.
ⲙⲏ ⲧⲁⲓⲣⲓ ⲧⲉ ⲧⲉⲕⲣⲓ?	ⲥⲉ,
	ⲙ̀ⲙⲟⲛ,
ⲙⲏ ⲛⲁⲓⲥⲛⲏⲟⲩ ⲛⲉ ⲛⲉⲕⲥⲛⲏⲟⲩ?	ⲥⲉ,
	ⲙ̀ⲙⲟⲛ,
ⲙⲏ ⲕ̀ⲥϧⲁⲓ ϧⲉⲛ ⲡⲓⲉ̀ϫⲱⲣϩ?	ⲥⲉ,
	ⲙ̀ⲙⲟⲛ,
ⲙⲏ ⲕϩⲉⲙⲥⲓ ϯⲛⲟⲩ?	ⲥⲉ,
	ⲙ̀ⲙⲟⲛ,

5. Translate to the English language:

ā ⲟⲩⲓⲱⲧ ⲛⲉⲙ ϩⲁⲛϧⲉⲗⲗⲟⲓ ⲛⲉⲙ ϩⲁⲛⲥⲛⲏⲟⲩ.
ḇ ϯϣⲟⲩⲣⲏ ⲧⲉ ϧⲉⲛ ⲧ̀ϫⲓϫ ⲙ̀ⲡⲓⲟⲩⲏⲃ.
ḡ ⲛ̀ⲑⲱⲧⲉⲛ ⲛⲉ ⲡⲓⲟⲩⲱⲓⲛⲓ ⲛ̀ⲧⲉ ⲡⲓⲕⲟⲥⲙⲟⲥ.
ḏ ϯⲡⲁⲣⲑⲉⲛⲟⲥ Ⲙⲁⲣⲓⲁ ⲧⲉ ⲑ̀ⲙⲁⲩ ⲛ̀Ⲓⲏⲥⲟⲩⲥ.
ē ⲛ̀ⲑⲟⲥ ⲧⲉ ⲧ̀ϣⲉⲣⲓ ⲛ̀Ⲥⲓⲱⲛ.

Lesson 11 ✠ Verbs ✠

ⲋ̄ ⲁⲛⲟⲛ ⲛⲉ ⲛⲓⲉ̀ⲃⲓⲁⲓⲕ ⲛ̀ⲧⲉ Ⲡⲓⲭⲣⲓⲥⲧⲟⲥ.
ⲍ̄ ⲛ̀ⲑⲟϥ ⲡⲉ ⲡⲓϣ̇ⲱⲏⲛ ⲛ̀ⲧⲉ ⲡⲓⲱⲛϧ.
ⲏ̄ ⲫⲁⲓ ⲟⲩⲁ̀ⲗⲟⲩ ⲡⲉ, ⲁⲗⲗⲁ ⲑⲏ ⲟⲩⲡⲁⲣⲑⲉⲛⲟⲥ ⲧⲉ.
ⲑ̄ ⲑⲁⲓ ⲧⲉ ⲧⲉⲕⲁϫⲡ, ⲑⲏ ⲧⲉ ⲑⲏⲉ̀ⲧⲉ ⲑⲱⲓ.
ⲓ̄ ⲛⲁⲓ ϩⲁⲛϫⲱⲙ ⲛ̀ⲧⲁϥ ⲛⲉ, ⲁⲗⲗⲁ ⲛⲏ ⲛⲉ ⲛⲏⲉ̀ⲧⲉ ⲛⲟⲩⲥ.
ⲓⲁ̄ ⲡⲁⲓⲣⲱⲙⲓ ⲡⲓⲉ̀ⲃⲟⲗϧⲉⲛ ⲧⲁⲓⲃⲁⲕⲓ ⲡⲉ ⲡⲉⲧⲉⲛⲓⲱⲧ.
ⲓⲃ̄ ⲛⲁⲓϩⲓⲕⲱⲛ ⲛⲓϩⲓϫⲉⲛ ϯϫⲟⲓ ⲛⲉ ⲛⲁ ⲛⲉⲛⲓⲟϯ ⲉⲑⲟⲩⲁⲃ.

Lesson 12
ⲡⲓⲱϣ ⲙⲙⲁϩ ⲓⲃ

The Subject and Object Marks

1. The Subject Mark

If the subject comes after the verb, it is preceded by the particle ⲛ̀ϫⲉ, which means "I mean."

ⲡⲓⲙⲟⲛⲁⲭⲟⲥ ϥ̀ϣⲗⲏⲗ.	The monk prays.
ϥ̀ϣⲗⲏⲗ ⲛ̀ϫⲉ ⲡⲓⲙⲟⲛⲁⲭⲟⲥ.	He prays, I mean, the monk.
ⲛⲓⲥⲛⲏⲟⲩ ⲥⲉϩⲱⲥ.	The brothers praise.
ⲥⲉϩⲱⲥ ⲛ̀ϫⲉ ⲛⲓⲥⲛⲏⲟⲩ.	They praise, I mean, the brothers.

2. The Object Marks (ⲛⲓⲙⲏⲓⲛⲓ ⲙ̀ⲡⲉⲧⲟⲩⲁⲓϥ)

They are ⲛ̀, ⲙ̀, and ⲉ̀, and these come after the verb, attached to the beginning of the object, to point to it.

1. Objects are usually preceded by the letter ⲛ̀ as a mark for the object, for example:

ϥ̀ⲥⲟⲗⲥⲉⲗ ⲛ̀ⲛⲉⲛⲯⲩⲭⲏ.	He consoles our souls.
ϯⲙⲉⲓ ⲛ̀ⲛⲓⲥⲛⲏⲟⲩ.	I love the brothers.

2. If the object begins with the letters ⲯ, ⲃ, ⲫ, ⲙ, ⲡ, or the letter ⲛ̀ changes to ⲙ̀, for example:

Lesson 12 ✣ The Subject and Object Marks ✣

ⲥ̀ⲟⲩⲱⲙ ⲙ̀ⲡⲓⲱⲓⲕ.   She eats the bread.

ⲧⲉⲛⲟⲩⲱϣⲧ ⲙ̀ⲫ̀ⲓⲱⲧ.   We worship the Father.

ⲧⲉⲛⲟⲩⲱⲙ ⲙ̀ⲡⲓⲥⲱⲙⲁ ⲙ̀ⲡⲉⲛⲥⲱⲧⲏⲣ ⲟⲩⲟϩ ⲧⲉⲛⲥⲱ ⲙ̀ⲡⲉϥⲥⲛⲟϥ.
We eat the Body of our Savior and drink His Blood.

3. The letter ⲉ̀ is used as a mark for the object with some special verbs, for example:

ϩⲱⲥ ⲉ̀	To praise	ⲉ̀ⲙⲓ ⲉ̀	To know	ϣⲓⲛⲓ ⲉ̀	To asks about, to greet
ⲥ̀ⲙⲟⲩ ⲉ̀	To bless	ⲛⲁϩϯ ⲉ̀	To believe	ⲧⲁⲙⲟ ⲉ̀	To inform, to tell
ⲛⲁⲩ ⲉ̀	To see, to look	ⲙⲉⲩⲓ ⲉ̀	To think, to mention	ϯϩⲟ ⲉ̀	To ask, to beseech
ⲥⲱⲧⲉⲙ ⲉ̀	To hear	ⲁ̀ⲣⲉϩ ⲉ̀	To keep, to guard	ⲙⲟⲩϯ ⲉ̀	To call
ϣⲱⲗⲉⲙ ⲉ̀	To smell	ϣⲁⲣⲓ ⲉ̀	To hit	ⲉⲣϩⲉⲗⲡⲓⲥ ⲉ̀	To hope
ϫⲟⲙϫⲉⲙ ⲉ̀	To touch	ⲉⲣϩⲱⲃ ⲉ̀	To work	ⲉⲣⲃⲟⲏⲑⲓⲛ ⲉ̀	To help, to support

Examples

ⲁ̅	ϯϩⲱⲥ ⲉ̀Ⲡ̀ϭⲟⲓⲥ.	I praise the Lord.
ⲃ̅	ⲕ̀ⲥⲙⲟⲩ ⲉ̀ⲫ̀ⲣⲁⲛ ⲙ̀ⲡⲉⲛⲛⲟⲩϯ.	You (mas.) bless the name of our God.
ⲅ̅	ϥⲙⲟⲩϯ ⲉ̀Ⲡ̀ϭⲟⲓⲥ ⲛ̀ⲥⲏⲟⲩ ⲛⲓⲃⲉⲛ.	He calls the Lord always.
ⲇ̅	ⲧⲉⲁ̀ⲣⲉϩ ⲉ̀ⲛⲓⲉⲛⲧⲟⲗⲏ ⲛ̀Ⲓⲏⲥⲟⲩⲥ.	You (fem.) keep the commandments of Jesus.
ⲉ̅	ⲥ̀ⲉⲣϩⲉⲗⲡⲓⲥ ⲉ̀Ⲡ̀ϭⲟⲓⲥ.	She puts her hope [in] the Lord.
ⲋ̅	ⲧⲉⲛⲥⲱⲧⲉⲙ ⲉ̀ϯⲥⲙⲏ ⲙ̀ⲫ̀ⲛⲟⲩϯ.	We hear the voice of God.
ⲍ̅	ⲧⲉⲧⲉⲛϣⲁⲣⲓ ⲉ̀ϯϣⲁⲩ ⲁⲛ.	You (pl.) do not hit the cat.
ⲏ̅	ⲥⲉⲉⲣϩⲱⲃ ⲉ̀ⲡⲓϩⲱⲃ ⲙ̀Ⲡⲓϭⲟⲓⲥ.	They work the work of the Lord.
ⲑ̅	ϯϯϩⲟ ⲉ̀Ⲡ̀ϭⲟⲓⲥ ⲉ̀ⲃⲟⲗϧⲉⲛ ⲡⲁϩⲏⲧ ⲧⲏⲣϥ. I ask the Lord with all my heart.	
ⲓ̅	Ⲫϯ ϥ̀ⲉⲣⲃⲟⲏⲑⲓⲛ ⲉ̀ⲡⲉϥⲗⲁⲟⲥ ϧⲉⲛ ⲛⲟⲩϩⲟϫϩⲉϫ. God helps His people in their hardships.	

The object marks when they are joined to the personal pronouns (when the object is a pronoun)

The mark of the object can be conjugated to the pronouns that come as objects as follows:

✠ `ⲛ` and `ⲙ` change to `ⲙⲙⲟ`″ when they are connected to pronouns.

✠ `ⲉ` changes to `ⲉⲣⲟ`″ when it is connected to pronouns.

`ⲙⲙⲟⲓ`	`ⲉⲣⲟⲓ`	Me	`ⲙⲙⲟⲥ`	`ⲉⲣⲟⲥ`	Her
`ⲙⲙⲟⲕ`	`ⲉⲣⲟⲕ`	You (sing. mas.)	`ⲙⲙⲟⲛ`	`ⲉⲣⲟⲛ`	Us
`ⲙⲙⲟ`	`ⲉⲣⲟ`	You (sing. fem.)	`ⲙⲙⲱⲧⲉⲛ`	`ⲉⲣⲱⲧⲉⲛ`	You (pl.)
`ⲙⲙⲟϥ`	`ⲉⲣⲟϥ`	Him	`ⲙⲙⲱⲟⲩ`	`ⲉⲣⲱⲟⲩ`	Them

Examples:

ⲁ̄ `ϯⲙⲉⲓ ⲙ̀ⲡⲁⲛⲟⲩϯ ⲟⲩⲟϩ ϯϣⲉⲙϣⲓ ⲙ̀ⲙⲟϥ.`
I love my God and serve Him.

ⲃ̄ `ϥϩⲱⲥ ⲉ̀Ⲡⲓϭⲟⲓⲥ ⲟⲩⲟϩ ϥ̀ⲥⲙⲟⲩ ⲉ̀ⲣⲟϥ.`
He praises the Lord and blesses Him.

ⲅ̄ `ⲧⲉⲛϩⲱⲥ ⲉ̀ⲣⲟⲕ, ⲧⲉⲛⲥⲙⲟⲩ ⲉ̀ⲣⲟⲕ, ⲧⲉⲛϣⲉⲙϣⲓ ⲙ̀ⲙⲟⲕ, ⲧⲉⲛⲟⲩⲱϣⲧ ⲙ̀ⲙⲟⲕ.` We praise You, we bless You, we serve You, we worship You.

ⲇ̄ `ϥϣⲓⲛⲓ ⲉ̀ⲣⲟⲕ ⲛ̀ϫⲉ Ⲡⲉⲧⲣⲟⲥ.`
He greets (asks about) you, I mean, Peter.

ⲉ̄ `ϯⲛⲁⲩ ⲉ̀ⲣⲟϥ ⲁⲛ, ⲁⲗⲗⲁ ⲛ̀ⲑⲟϥ ϥ̀ⲛⲁⲩ ⲉ̀ⲣⲟⲓ.`
I do not see him, but he sees me.

Exercises

1. Begin the following sentences with the verb:

ⲁ̅ ⲡⲓⲁ̀ⲗⲟⲩ ϥⲱϣ.

ⲃ̅ ⲛⲓⲉ̀ⲃⲓⲁⲓⲕ ⲥⲉϣⲉⲙϣⲓ.

ⲅ̅ ϯⲥⲱⲛⲓ ⲥ̀ⲉⲙⲥⲓ.

2. Put the suitable object mark:

ⲁ̅ ⲕⲥⲱ .... ⲡⲓⲙⲱⲟⲩ.

ⲃ̅ ⲧⲉⲛⲥ̀ⲙⲟⲩ .... ⲫⲣⲁⲛ ⲙ̀ⲡⲉⲛⲛⲟⲩϯ.

ⲅ̅ ⲧⲉⲥϭⲁⲓ .... ⲡⲓⲱϣ.

ⲇ̅ ⲧⲉⲧⲉⲛⲁ̀ⲣⲉϩ .... ⲛⲓⲯⲁⲗⲙⲟⲥ.

ⲉ̅ ϯⲙⲉⲓ ...... ⲛⲓⲥ̀ⲛⲏⲟⲩ.

ⲋ̅ ⲥ̀ⲙⲓⲥⲓ .... ⲡⲉⲥϣⲏⲣⲓ.

ⲍ̅ ϥⲥⲟⲗⲥⲉⲗ .... ⲛⲉⲛⲯⲩⲭⲏ.

ⲏ̅ ⲥⲉϭⲓ .... ⲛⲟⲩⲭⲱⲙ.

3. Choose a verb from the right column that is suitable for the sentence in the left column:

ⲁ̅ ⲥ̀ ..... ⲁⲛ ⲉ̀ϯϣⲁⲩ.	ⲛⲁⲩ
ⲃ̅ ⲧⲉ ..... ⲙ̀ⲡⲓⲱⲓⲕ.	ϩⲱⲥ
ⲅ̅ ϥ ..... ⲙ̀ⲡⲉϥⲛⲟⲩϯ.	ⲟⲩⲱⲙ
ⲇ̅ ⲧⲉⲛ ..... ⲉ̀ⲡⲉⲛϭⲟⲓⲥ.	ϣⲓⲛⲓ
ⲉ̅ ⲧⲉⲧⲉⲛ ..... ⲛ̀ⲛⲉⲧⲉⲛϣ.	ⲥⲱⲧⲉⲙ
ⲋ̅ ϯ ..... ⲉ̀ϯⲥⲙⲏ ⲛ̀ⲧⲫⲉ.	ϣⲁⲣⲓ
ⲍ̅ ⲥⲉ ..... ⲉ̀ⲛⲟⲩϣⲏⲣⲓ.	ϣⲉⲙϣⲓ
ⲏ̅ ϫ ..... ⲉ̀ⲡⲉⲕⲥⲟⲛ.	ⲱϣ

4. Make the object a pronoun, and change what needs to be changed in the following sentences:

ⲁ̅ ϯϩⲱⲥ ⲉ̀ⲡⲁⲛⲟⲩϯ.

ⲃ̅ ϫⲛⲁⲩ ⲉ̀ⲛⲉⲕⲥ̀ⲛⲏⲟⲩ.

    ḡ   ⲧⲉⲥⲱⲧⲉⲙ ⲉ̀ⲧ̀ⲥⲙⲏ ⲙ̀Ⲫϯ.

    ⲇ̄   ϥ̀ⲥϧⲁⲓ ⲛ̀ⲛⲉϥϣ.

    ⲉ̄   ⲥ̀ⲱϣ ⲙ̀ⲡⲉⲥϫⲱⲙ.

    ⲋ̄   ⲧⲉⲛⲙⲉⲓ ⲙ̀ⲡⲉⲛⲓⲱⲧ.

    ⲍ̄   ⲥⲉⲭⲱ ⲛ̀ϯⲙⲉⲑⲙⲏⲓ.

    ⲏ̄   ⲧⲉⲧⲉⲛⲥⲙⲟⲩ ⲉ̀ⲫⲣⲁⲛ ⲙ̀Ⲡⲓϭⲟⲓⲥ.

5. Translate the following to the English language:

    ⲁ̄   ⲧⲉⲧⲉⲛⲁ̀ⲣⲉϩ ⲉ̀ⲛⲓⲉⲛⲧⲟⲗⲏ ⲙ̀Ⲡⲓϭⲟⲓⲥ.

    ⲃ̄   ⲛ̀ⲑⲱⲟⲩ (ⲛⲓⲉⲛⲧⲟⲗⲏ) ⲛⲉ ⲫⲙⲱⲓⲧ ⲛ̀ⲧⲉ ⲡⲱⲛϧ.

    ḡ   ⲧⲉⲛⲙⲉⲓ ⲙ̀ⲡⲓⲟⲩⲱⲓⲛⲓ ⲟⲩⲟϩ ⲧⲉⲛⲙⲟⲥϯ ⲛ̀ⲛⲉⲛϩⲃⲏⲟⲩⲓ̀ ⲙ̀ⲡⲓⲭⲁⲕⲓ.

    ⲇ̄   ϥϩⲱⲥ ⲉ̀ⲡⲉϥϭⲟⲓⲥ ⲛⲉⲙ ⲛⲉϥⲥⲛⲏⲟⲩ.

    ⲉ̄   ⲡⲓⲟⲩⲏⲃ ⲛⲉⲙ ⲛⲓⲇⲓⲁⲕⲟⲛ ⲥⲉϣⲗⲏⲗ ϧⲉⲛ ⲡⲓⲉⲣⲫⲉⲓ.

    ⲋ̄   ϯⲛⲁϩϯ ⲉ̀ⲣⲟⲕ, ⲱ̀ ⲡⲁⲛⲟⲩϯ, ϯⲉⲣϩⲉⲗⲡⲓⲥ ⲉ̀ⲣⲟⲕ ⲟⲩⲟϩ ϯϣⲉⲙϣⲓ ⲙ̀ⲙⲟⲕ.

    ⲍ̄   ⲕⲱϣ ϧⲉⲛ ⲡⲉⲕϫⲱⲙ ⲉⲑⲟⲩⲁⲃ ⲟⲩⲟϩ ⲕ̀ⲥϧⲁⲓ ⲛ̀ⲛⲓⲥⲁϫⲓ ⲛ̀ⲧⲉ Ⲡⲓϭⲟⲓⲥ.

    ⲏ̄   ⲥⲉⲧϩⲟ ⲉ̀ⲡⲟⲩⲛⲟⲩϯ ⲉ̀ⲃⲟⲗϧⲉⲛ ⲛⲟⲩϩⲏⲧ.

    ⲑ̄   ⲧⲉⲛϭⲓ ⲙ̀ⲡⲉϥⲥⲱⲙⲁ ⲛⲉⲙ ⲡⲉϥⲥⲛⲟϥ ⲉⲧⲧⲁⲓⲏⲟⲩⲧ.

    ⲓ̄   ⲧⲉⲛⲙⲟⲩϯ ⲉ̀ⲣⲟϥ ⲛ̀ⲥⲏⲟⲩ ⲛⲓⲃⲉⲛ.

    ⲓ̄ⲁ   Ⲫϯ ϥ̀ⲥⲱⲧⲉⲙ ⲉ̀ⲛⲉϥⲉ̀ⲃⲓⲁⲓⲕ ⲟⲩⲟϩ ϥ̀ⲛⲟϩⲉⲙ ⲙ̀ⲙⲱⲟⲩ ⲉ̀ⲃⲟⲗϧⲉⲛ ⲛⲟⲩϫⲁϫⲓ.

Lesson 13
ⲡⲓⲱϣ ⲙⲙⲁϩ ⲓⲅ

✠

ⲡⲓⲥⲏⲟⲩ ⲉⲑⲛⲏⲟⲩ

The Future Tense

The First Future Tense

The form of the first future [tense] consists of the same pronouns of the first present [tense], with the addition of the future mark **ⲛⲁ** to each of them, except in the singular feminine second person, **ⲣⲁ** is used instead of **ⲛⲁ**.

ϯⲛⲁⲓ	I will come.	ⲭⲛⲁⲓ	You (mas. sing.) will come.	ϥⲛⲁⲓ	He will come.
		ⲧⲉⲣⲁⲓ	You (fem. sing.) will come.	ⲥⲛⲁⲓ	She will come.
ⲧⲉⲛⲛⲁⲓ	We will come.	ⲧⲉⲧⲉⲛⲛⲁⲓ	You (pl.) will come.	ⲥⲉⲛⲁⲓ	They will come.

Examples:

ϥⲛⲁⲓ ⲛϫⲉ ⲡϣⲏⲣⲓ ⲙⲫϯ.   The Son of God will come.

ⲥⲉⲛⲁⲓ ⲛϫⲉ ⲛⲓⲙⲁⲣⲧⲩⲣⲟⲥ.   The martyrs will come.

ⲧⲉⲣⲁⲙⲓⲥⲓ ⲛⲈⲙⲙⲁⲛⲟⲩⲏⲗ.   You will give birth to Emmanuel.

The negative form of this future [tense] is formulated exactly as the first present tense, that is, by the particle **ⲁⲛ**, and to emphasize the negative form we use **ⲛ̀...ⲁⲛ**, for example:

ϥⲛⲁⲓ ⲛ̀ϫⲉ ⲡⲉⲑⲛⲏⲟⲩ ⲟⲩⲟϩ ϥⲛⲁⲱⲥⲕ ⲁⲛ.	"He who is coming will come and will not tarry" (Hebrews 10:37).
ⲧⲉⲛⲛⲁϭⲓⲥⲓ ⲁⲛ ⲉ̀ⲛⲉϩ.	We will never toil.
ⲛ̀ϯⲛⲁⲙⲟⲥϯ ⲁⲛ ⲛ̀ϩⲗⲓ.	I will never hate anyone.

It is noted that the future mark is derived from the verb **ⲛⲟⲩⲓ̀**, meaning "going to."

ⲉ̀ might come as a preposition, meaning "to," and it changes to **ⲉ̀ⲣⲟ"** to accept and be conjugated to the connected personal pronouns, for example:

ϥⲛⲁⲓ̀ ⲉ̀ⲣⲟⲓ.	He will come to me.	ⲧⲉⲛⲛⲁⲓ̀ ⲉ̀ⲣⲟⲕ.	We will come to you.

These three are similar in conjugation when connected to the personal pronouns:

ⲛ̀ (preposition meaning "to")		ⲛⲉⲙ (with)		ⲛ̀ⲧⲉ (genitive article)	
ⲛⲏⲓ	To me	ⲛⲉⲙⲏⲓ	With me	ⲛ̀ⲑⲏⲓ	Belongs to me, mine
ⲛⲁⲕ	To you (sing. mas.)	ⲛⲉⲙⲁⲕ	With you (sing. mas.)	ⲛ̀ⲧⲁⲕ	Belongs to you (sing. mas.), yours
ⲛⲉ	To you (sing. fem.)	ⲛⲉⲙⲉ	With you (sing. fem.)	ⲛ̀ⲧⲉ	Belongs to you (sing. fem.), yours
ⲛⲁϥ	To him	ⲛⲉⲙⲁϥ	With him	ⲛ̀ⲧⲁϥ	Belongs to him, his
ⲛⲁⲥ	To her	ⲛⲉⲙⲁⲥ	With her	ⲛ̀ⲧⲁⲥ	Belongs to her, hers
ⲛⲁⲛ	To us	ⲛⲉⲙⲁⲛ	With us	ⲛ̀ⲧⲁⲛ	Belongs to us, ours
ⲛⲱⲧⲉⲛ	To you (pl.)	ⲛⲉⲙⲱⲧⲉⲛ	With you (pl.)	ⲛ̀ⲧⲱⲧⲉⲛ	Belongs to you (pl.), yours
ⲛⲱⲟⲩ	To them	ⲛⲉⲙⲱⲟⲩ	With them	ⲛ̀ⲧⲱⲟⲩ	Belongs to them, theirs

Lesson 13 ✠ The Future Tense ✠

Examples:

ⲁ̄	`ⲕϯ ⲛⲁϥ ⲙ̀ⲡⲓϫⲱⲙ.`	You (sing. mas.) give to him the book.
ⲃ̄	`ϥϯ ⲛⲁⲛ ⲛ̀ⲧⲉϥϩⲓⲣⲏⲛⲏ.`	He gives to us His peace.
ⲅ̄	`Ⲡ̀ϭⲟⲓⲥ ⲛⲉⲙⲉ.`	The Lord [be] with you.
ⲇ̄	`ⲙⲏ ⲧⲉⲧⲉⲛⲛⲁϩⲱⲥ ⲉⲪϯ ⲛⲉⲙⲁⲛ?`	Will you (pl.) praise God with us?
ⲉ̄	`ⲧⲉⲣⲁϩⲉⲙⲥⲓ ⲛⲉⲙⲱⲟⲩ (ⲛⲉⲙ ⲛⲓⲁⲅⲓⲟⲥ).`	You (sing. fem.) will sit with them.
ⲋ̄	`ϯⲛⲁϣⲗⲏⲗ ϧⲉⲛ ϯⲉⲕⲕⲗⲏⲥⲓⲁ ⲛⲉⲙ ⲛⲁⲓⲟϯ ⲛⲉⲙ ⲛⲁⲥⲛⲏⲟⲩ.` I will pray in the church with my fathers and my brothers.	
ⲍ̄	`ⲧⲁϩⲓⲣⲏⲛⲏ ⲁⲛⲟⲕ: ϯϯ ⲙ̀ⲙⲟⲥ ⲛⲱⲧⲉⲛ: ϯϩⲓⲣⲏⲛⲏ ⲙ̀ⲡⲁⲓⲱⲧ: ϯⲭⲱ ⲙ̀ⲙⲟⲥ ⲛⲉⲙⲱⲧⲉⲛ.` My peace I give to you (pl.); the peace of My Father I leave with you (pl.).	
ⲏ̄	`ⲧⲉⲛϯ ⲛⲉ ⲙ̀ⲡⲓⲭⲉⲣⲉⲧⲓⲥⲙⲟⲥ ⲛⲉⲙ Ⲅⲁⲃⲣⲓⲏⲗ ⲡⲓⲁⲅⲅⲉⲗⲟⲥ.` We give you greeting with Gabriel the angel.	
ⲑ̄	`ϩⲁⲛϫⲱⲙ ⲛ̀ⲧⲱⲟⲩ` Books of yours	`ⲟⲩⲥⲟⲛ ⲛ̀ⲧⲱⲧⲉⲛ` A brother of yours (pl.)
	`ⲟⲩϣⲏⲣⲓ ⲛ̀ⲧⲁϥ` A son of his	`ⲛⲏⲉⲑⲟⲩⲁⲃ ⲛ̀ⲧⲁⲕ` Those saints of yours
	`ϩⲁⲛⲓⲟϯ ⲛ̀ⲧⲁⲛ` Fathers of ours	`ⲟⲩϣⲉⲣⲓ ⲛ̀ⲧⲁⲥ` A daughter of hers

Exercises

1. Put the following sentences in the future tense:

ⲁ̄ ⲕ̀ⲓ ⲉ̀ϯⲉⲕⲕⲗⲏⲥⲓⲁ.
ⲃ̄ ⲧⲉⲛϩⲱⲥ ⲛⲉⲙ ⲛⲉⲛⲥⲛⲏⲟⲩ.
ⲅ̄ ⲧⲉⲥϭⲁⲓ ⲙ̀ⲡⲉⲥϣ.
ⲇ̄ ⲕ̀ⲥⲁϫⲓ ⲛⲉⲙⲱⲟⲩ.
ⲉ̄ ⲧⲉⲁⲣⲉϩ ⲉ̀ⲛⲓⲉⲛⲧⲟⲗⲏ.
ⲋ̄ ⲧⲉⲧⲉⲛⲛⲁⲩ ⲉ̀ⲧⲫⲉ.

2. Answer once in the affirmative form and then in the negative form:

ⲁ̄	ⲙⲏ ϥⲛⲁⲓ̀ ⲛ̀ϫⲉ ⲡⲓⲟⲩⲏⲃ?	ⲥⲉ,
		ⲙ̀ⲙⲟⲛ,
ⲃ̄	ⲙⲏ ϫⲛⲁⲩ ⲉ̀ⲡⲓⲁⲅⲅⲉⲗⲟⲥ?	ⲥⲉ,
		ⲙ̀ⲙⲟⲛ,
ⲅ̄	ⲙⲏ ⲧⲉⲧⲉⲛⲥⲱ ⲙ̀ⲡⲓⲉ̀ⲣⲱϯ?	ⲥⲉ,
		ⲙ̀ⲙⲟⲛ,
ⲇ̄	ⲙⲏ ϯⲱϣ ⲙ̀ⲡⲁⲓϫⲱⲙ?	ⲥⲉ,
		ⲙ̀ⲙⲟⲛ,
ⲉ̄	ⲙⲏ ⲥⲉⲛⲁⲁ̀ⲣⲉϩ ⲉ̀ⲛⲟⲩⲱϣ?	ⲥⲉ,
		ⲙ̀ⲙⲟⲛ,

3. Write the meaning of the following words:

1. ⲫⲏⲉⲧⲓ̀ⲣⲓ
2. ⲑⲏⲉⲧⲥⲱⲧⲉⲙ
3. ⲛⲏⲉⲧϩⲱⲥ
4. ⲫⲏⲉⲧϣⲓⲛⲓ
5. ⲑⲏⲉⲧϯ
6. ⲛⲏⲉⲧⲙⲟϣⲓ

4. Write the meaning of the following phrases:

ⲁ̄ ϯϫⲱ ⲛⲱⲧⲉⲛ.
ⲃ̄ ⲕ̀ϣⲗⲏⲗ ⲉ̀ⲣⲟϥ.
ⲅ̄ ⲧⲉⲥⲱⲧⲉⲙ ⲛⲉⲙⲁⲥ ⲉ̀ⲡⲓⲥⲁϫⲓ ⲙ̀Ⲫⲛⲟⲩϯ.

Lesson 13 ✟ The Future Tense ✟

- ⲁ̄ ⲫϯ ⲛⲁⲛ ⲛⲉⲙⲱⲟⲩ.
- ⲉ̄ ϩⲁⲛϣⲏⲣⲓ ⲛ̀ⲧⲁⲥ.
- ⲋ̄ ⲧⲉⲛⲁⲣⲉϩ ⲉ̀ⲣⲱⲟⲩ.
- ⲍ̄ ⲧⲉⲧⲉⲛⲛⲁϣⲉⲙϣⲓ ⲙ̀ⲙⲟϥ.
- ⲏ̄ ⲥⲉϯ ⲛⲁⲕ ⲛⲉⲙⲁⲛ.
- ⲑ̄ ⲟⲩⲓⲱⲧ ⲛ̀ⲧⲱⲟⲩ.
- ī ⲛⲏⲉⲑⲟⲩⲁⲃ ⲛ̀ⲧⲁϥ.
- ⲓⲁ̄ ϩⲁⲛⲥⲱⲛⲓ ⲛ̀ⲧⲉ.

5. Translate the following to the English language:

- ⲁ̄ ϥⲛⲟϩⲉⲙ ⲛ̀ϫⲉ Ⲡϭⲟⲓⲥ ⲙ̀ⲡⲉϥⲗⲁⲟⲥ.
- ⲃ̄ ϯⲥⲱⲧⲡ ⲙ̀ⲙⲱⲧⲉⲛ, ⲱ̀ ⲛⲁⲙⲉⲛⲣⲁϯ.
- ⲅ̄ ⲧⲉⲛⲉⲣϩⲓⲁⲗⲡⲓⲥ ⲉ̀ⲣⲟⲕ, ⲱ̀ ⲡⲉⲛⲛⲟⲩϯ.
- ⲇ̄ ⲥⲛⲁⲙⲓⲥⲓ ⲛ̀ⲟⲩⲁⲗⲟⲩ.
- ⲉ̄ ⲧⲉⲣⲁϩⲉⲙⲥⲓ ⲛⲉⲙ ⲛⲓⲁⲡⲟⲥⲧⲟⲗⲟⲥ.
- ⲋ̄ ⲭ̀ⲛⲁϭⲓ ⲛ̀ⲟⲩϩⲙⲟⲧ ⲛⲉⲙ ⲛⲉⲕⲥ̀ⲛⲏⲟⲩ.
- ⲍ̄ ⲧⲉⲧⲉⲛⲥⲱⲧⲉⲙ ⲉ̀ⲧⲉϥⲥⲙⲏ ⲛ̀ϫⲱⲗⲉⲙ.
- ⲏ̄ ⲥⲉⲛⲁⲕⲱϯ ⲛ̀ⲥⲁ ⲡ̀ϩⲟ ⲛ̀ⲧⲉ Ⲡϭⲟⲓⲥ.
- ⲑ̄ Ⲫϯ ϥⲟⲩⲱⲣⲡ ⲛⲁⲛ ⲙ̀ⲡⲉϥϣⲏⲣⲓ.
- ī ⲧⲉⲛⲥⲱⲧⲡ ⲙ̀ⲡⲓⲙⲱⲓⲧ ⲛ̀ⲧⲉ ⲡ̀ⲱⲛϩ.
- ⲓⲁ̄ ⲥⲉⲙⲉⲓ ⲛ̀ⲛⲟⲩⲓⲟϯ ⲛⲉⲙ ⲛⲟⲩⲥ̀ⲛⲏⲟⲩ.
- ⲓⲃ̄ ⲱ̀ ⲡⲉⲛⲥⲱⲧⲏⲣ, ⲕ̀ⲓⲣⲓ ⲛⲉⲙⲁⲛ ⲕⲁⲧⲁ ⲡⲉⲕⲛⲁⲓ.

Lesson 14
ⲡⲓⲱϣ ⲙ̄ⲙⲁϩ ⲓ̄ⲇ̄

✠

ⲡⲓⲥⲏⲟⲩ ⲉⲧϭⲓⲛⲓ

The Past Tense

The Past Perfect Tense

The past perfect tense indicates that the event is past and completely done; therefore, it is used in narrating history, for it expresses the occurrence of the action once in the past. The mark of this tense is the letter **ⲁ**.

ⲁ Ⲫϯ ⲑⲁⲙⲓⲟ ⲙ̀ⲡⲓⲣⲱⲙⲓ.	God created the human [being].
ⲁ ϯⲡⲁⲣⲑⲉⲛⲟⲥ ⲙⲓⲥⲓ ⲙ̀Ⲡⲭ̄ⲥ̄.	The Virgin gave birth to Christ.
ⲁ ⲛⲓⲓⲟⲩⲇⲁⲓ ⲓϣⲓ ⲛ̀Ⲓⲏⲥⲟⲩⲥ.	The Jews crucified Jesus.

The connected personal pronouns are attached to the mark of the past perfect as follows:

ⲁⲓⲱϣ	I read	ⲁⲕⲱϣ	You (sing. mas.) read	ⲁϥⲱϣ	He read
		ⲁⲣⲉⲱϣ	You (sing. fem.) read	ⲁⲥⲱϣ	She read
ⲁⲛⲱϣ	We read	ⲁⲧⲉⲧⲉⲛⲱϣ	You (pl.) read	ⲁⲩⲱϣ	They read

Examples:

ⲁ̄	ⲁⲓⲛⲁⲩ ⲉ̀ⲡⲉⲕⲥⲟⲛ ⲛ̀ⲥⲁϥ ⲟⲩⲟϩ ⲁⲓⲥⲁϫⲓ ⲛⲉⲙⲁϥ.	I saw your brother yesterday and I spoke with him.

Lesson 14 ✣ The Past Tense ✣

ⲃ̄	ⲁⲕⲛⲟϩⲉⲙ ⲙ̀ⲡⲉⲕⲗⲁⲟⲥ ⲉ̀ⲃⲟⲗϧⲉⲛ ⲛⲟⲩⲛⲟⲃⲓ.	You saved Your people from their sins.
ⲅ̄	ⲁⲣⲉⲙⲓⲥⲓ ⲛⲁⲛ ⲛ̀ⲉⲙⲙⲁⲛⲟⲩⲏⲗ.	You bore to us Emmanuel.
ⲇ̄	Ⲫϯ ⲁϥⲑⲁⲙⲓⲟ ⲛ̀ⲧⲫⲉ ⲛⲉⲙ ⲡ̀ⲕⲁϩⲓ.	God created the heaven and the earth.
ⲉ̄	ⲁⲥⲙⲓⲥⲓ ⲙ̀ⲙⲟϥ, ⲁϥⲥⲱⲧ ⲙ̀ⲙⲟⲛ.	She gave birth to Him, [so] He saved us.
ⲋ̄	ⲁⲛⲛⲁϩϯ ⲉ̀ⲣⲟⲕ ⲟⲩⲟϩ ⲁⲛⲉⲣϩⲉⲗⲡⲓⲥ ⲉ̀ⲣⲟⲕ.	We believed in You and had hope in You.
ⲍ̄	ⲁⲧⲉⲧⲉⲛⲕⲁϯ ⲙ̀ⲡⲁⲓⲱϣ.	You (pl.) understood this lesson.
ⲏ̄	ⲛⲓⲓⲟⲩⲇⲁⲓ ⲁⲩⲓϣⲓ ⲙ̀ⲡⲉⲛⲥⲱⲧⲏⲣ.	The Jews crucified our Savior.

Note: We can write each sentence in five different ways without changing the meaning:

ⲁ̄	ⲁ Ⲫϯ ⲑⲁⲙⲓⲟ ⲙ̀ⲡⲓⲣⲱⲙⲓ.	God created the human [being].
ⲃ̄	Ⲫϯ ⲁϥⲑⲁⲙⲓⲟ ⲙ̀ⲡⲓⲣⲱⲙⲓ.	God created the human [being].
ⲅ̄	ⲁϥⲑⲁⲙⲓⲟ ⲛ̀ϫⲉ Ⲫϯ ⲙ̀ⲡⲓⲣⲱⲙⲓ.	God created the human [being].
ⲇ̄	ⲁϥⲑⲁⲙⲓⲟ ⲙ̀ⲡⲓⲣⲱⲙⲓ ⲛ̀ϫⲉ Ⲫϯ.	He created the human [being], I mean, God.
ⲉ̄	ⲁϥⲑⲁⲙⲓⲟ ⲙ̀ⲡⲓⲣⲱⲙⲓ.	He created the human [being].

The negative form of the past perfect tense:

The negative form is formulated with the mark ⲙ̀ⲡⲉ, as follows:

ⲙ̀ⲡⲉ ⲡⲓⲁ̀ⲗⲟⲩ ⲥⲱ ⲙ̀ⲡⲓⲉ̀ⲣⲱϯ.	The child did not drink the milk.
ⲙ̀ⲡⲉ ϩ̀ⲗⲓ ⲛⲁⲩ ⲉ̀ⲣⲟϥ ⲉ̀ⲛⲉϩ.	No one ever saw him.
ⲙ̀ⲡⲉ ⲛⲓⲥ̀ⲛⲏⲟⲩ ϭⲓ ⲛ̀ⲛⲟⲩϫⲱⲙ.	The brothers did not take their books.

The mark ⲙ̀ⲡⲉ is transformed to ⲙ̀ⲡ" to accept the connected personal pronouns, as follows:

ⲙ̀ⲡⲓⲥⲁϫⲓ	I did not speak.	ⲙ̀ⲡⲉⲕⲥⲁϫⲓ	You (sing. mas.) did not speak.	ⲙ̀ⲡⲉϥⲥⲁϫⲓ	He did not speak.
		ⲙ̀ⲡⲉⲥⲁϫⲓ	You (sing. fem.) did not speak.	ⲙ̀ⲡⲉⲥⲥⲁϫⲓ	She did not speak.
ⲙ̀ⲡⲉⲛⲥⲁϫⲓ	We did not speak.	ⲙ̀ⲡⲉⲧⲉⲛⲥⲁϫⲓ	You (pl.) did not speak.	ⲙ̀ⲡⲟⲩⲥⲁϫⲓ	They did not speak.

Examples:

ā	ⲡⲓⲁⲗⲟⲩ ⲙ̀ⲡⲉϥⲥⲱ ⲙ̀ⲡⲓⲉⲣⲱϯ.	The child did not drink the milk.
ⲃ̄	ⲙ̀ⲡⲉⲕⲉⲙⲓ ⲉ̀ϯⲙⲉⲑⲙⲏⲓ.	You did not know the truth.
ⲅ̄	ⲙ̀ⲡⲓⲱϣ ⲙ̀ⲡⲓⲱϣ.	I did not read the lesson.
ⲇ̄	ⲙ̀ⲡⲉⲛⲥϧⲁⲓ ⲙ̀ⲡⲉⲛⲱϣ.	We did not write our lesson.
ē	ⲙ̀ⲡⲟⲩⲟⲩⲱⲙ ⲙ̀ⲡⲓⲟⲩⲱⲙ.	They did not eat the food.
ⲋ̄	ⲙ̀ⲡⲉⲛⲉⲣⲃⲱⲕ ⲛ̀ϩⲗⲓ ⲉ̀ⲛⲉϩ.	We were never subjugated to anyone.
ⲍ̄	ⲙ̀ⲡⲉⲧⲉⲛⲉⲣ ⲫⲁⲓ ⲓⲉ ⲫⲏ.	You did not do this or that.

Note: In the same way we can write the negative form of the sentence in five ways without changing the meaning:

ā	ⲡⲓⲥⲟⲛ ⲙ̀ⲡⲉϥϭⲓ ⲙ̀ⲡⲉϥϫⲱⲙ.	The brother did not take his book.
ⲃ̄	ⲙ̀ⲡⲉ ⲡⲓⲥⲟⲛ ϭⲓ ⲙ̀ⲡⲉϥϫⲱⲙ.	The brother did not take his book.
ⲅ̄	ⲙ̀ⲡⲉϥϭⲓ ⲛ̀ϫⲉ ⲡⲓⲥⲟⲛ ⲙ̀ⲡⲉϥϫⲱⲙ.	The brother did not take his book.
ⲇ̄	ⲙ̀ⲡⲉϥϭⲓ ⲙ̀ⲡⲉϥϫⲱⲙ ⲛ̀ϫⲉ ⲡⲓⲥⲟⲛ.	He did not take his book, I mean, the bother.
ē	ⲙ̀ⲡⲉϥϭⲓ ⲙ̀ⲡⲉϥϫⲱⲙ.	He did not take his book.

Exercises

1. Put the following sentences in the negative form:

ā	ⲁ ⲡⲓⲟⲩⲏⲃ ⲓ̀ ⲛ̀ⲥⲁϥ.
ⲃ̄	ⲁⲓⲛⲁⲩ ⲉ̀ⲡⲉϥⲱⲟⲩ.
ⲅ̄	ⲁⲕⲟⲩⲱⲙ ⲙ̀ⲡⲓⲁϥ.
ⲇ̄	ⲁⲣⲉϣⲉⲙϣⲓ ⲙ̀Ⲡⲓϭⲟⲓⲥ.
ē	ⲁϥⲥⲱⲧⲉⲙ ⲉ̀ⲧⲉⲕⲥⲙⲏ.
ⲋ̄	ⲁⲥϭⲓ ⲛ̀ⲟⲩϩⲙⲟⲧ.
ⲍ̄	ⲁⲛⲥⲱ ⲙ̀ⲡⲓⲉⲣⲱϯ.
ⲏ̄	ⲁⲧⲉⲧⲉⲛⲕⲁϯ ⲛ̀ⲛⲉⲧⲉⲛⲱϣ.
ⲑ̄	ⲁⲩⲛⲁϩϯ ⲛⲉⲙⲱⲧⲉⲛ.

Lesson 14 ✣ The Past Tense ✣

2. Answer once in the affirmative form and then in the negative form:

ⲁ̄	ⲙⲏ ⲁⲕϩⲱⲥ ⲛⲉⲙ ⲛⲉⲕⲥ̄ⲛⲏⲟⲩ ⲙ̀ⲫⲟⲟⲩ?	ⲥⲉ,
		ⲙ̀ⲙⲟⲛ,
β̄	ⲙⲏ ⲁⲓⲙⲟϣⲓ ⲉ̀ϯⲉⲕⲕⲗⲏⲥⲓⲁ ⲛ̀ⲭⲱⲗⲉⲙ?	ⲥⲉ,
		ⲙ̀ⲙⲟⲛ,
ⲅ̄	ⲙⲏ ⲁϥⲛⲟϩⲉⲙ ⲛ̀ϫⲉ ⲡⲟⲩⲣⲟ ⲙ̀ⲡⲉϥⲗⲁⲟⲥ?	ⲥⲉ,
		ⲙ̀ⲙⲟⲛ,
ⲇ̄	ⲙⲏ ⲁⲧⲉⲧⲉⲛⲱϣ ⲛ̀ⲛⲉⲧⲉⲛϫⲱⲙ?	ⲥⲉ,
		ⲙ̀ⲙⲟⲛ,
ⲉ̄	ⲙⲏ ⲁⲛⲥ̀ϩⲁⲓ ⲙ̀ⲡⲁⲓϣϣ?	ⲥⲉ,
		ⲙ̀ⲙⲟⲛ,
ⲋ̄	ⲙⲏ ⲁⲩϭⲓⲛⲓ ⲛ̀ⲧⲁⲓⲃⲁⲕⲓ?	ⲥⲉ,
		ⲙ̀ⲙⲟⲛ,

3. Form a meaningful sentence from each group of the following words:

ⲁ̄ ⲛⲟⲩϯ, ⲑⲁⲙⲓⲟ, ⲣⲱⲙⲓ.
β̄ ⲙⲟⲛⲁⲭⲟⲥ, ϩⲱⲥ, ϭⲟⲓⲥ.
ⲅ̄ ⲥⲱⲛⲓ, ⲁ̀ⲣⲉϩ, ⲯⲁⲗⲙⲟⲥ.
ⲇ̄ ϩⲁⲗⲏⲧ, ⲥⲱ, ⲙⲱⲟⲩ.
ⲉ̄ ⲉ̀ⲃⲓⲁⲓⲕ, ⲛⲁⲩ, ⲟⲩⲣⲟ.
ⲋ̄ ϩⲏⲕⲓ, ⲟⲩⲱⲙ, ⲱⲓⲕ.
ⲍ̄ ⲥ̀ϩⲓⲙⲓ, ⲙⲓⲥⲓ, ⲁ̀ⲗⲟⲩ.

4. Write the meaning of the following phrases:

ⲁ̄	ⲁⲓⲥⲱⲧⲉⲙ ⲉ̀ⲣⲟϥ ⲛⲉⲙⲱⲧⲉⲛ.	ⲋ̄	ϩⲁⲛⲓⲟϯ ⲛ̀ⲧⲁϥ.
β̄	ⲁⲣⲉⲛⲁⲩ ⲉ̀ⲣⲟⲥ ⲛⲉⲙⲱⲟⲩ.	ⲍ̄	ⲟⲩϣⲉⲣⲓ ⲛ̀ⲧⲁⲥ.
ⲅ̄	ⲁⲕϣⲗⲏⲗ ⲛⲉⲙⲁⲛ ⲛ̀ⲥⲁϥ.	ⲏ̄	ϩⲁⲛϧⲉⲗⲗⲟⲓ ⲛ̀ⲧⲱⲟⲩ.
ⲇ̄	ⲁⲛϩⲱⲥ ⲛⲉⲙⲁϥ ⲙ̀ⲫⲟⲟⲩ.	ⲑ̄	ⲟⲩⲥⲟⲛ ⲛ̀ⲧⲁⲛ.
ⲉ̄	ⲁⲥⲱϣ ⲙ̀ⲙⲟϥ ⲛⲉⲙⲉ.	ⲓ̄	ϩⲁⲛⲡⲣⲓ ⲛ̀ⲧⲱⲧⲉⲛ.

5. Read and translate (ⲱϣ ⲟⲩⲟϩ ⲃⲱⲗ ⲉ̇ⲃⲟⲗ):

Ⲁϥⲑⲁⲙⲓⲟ ⲛ̇ϫⲉ Ⲫϯ ⲙ̇ⲡⲓⲣⲱⲙⲓ ⲕⲁⲧⲁ ⲡⲉϥⲓ̇ⲛⲓ ⲛⲉⲙ ⲧⲉϥϩⲓⲕⲱⲛ. ⲁ ⲡⲓⲣⲱⲙⲓ ⲉⲣⲛⲟⲃⲓ ⲟⲩⲃⲉ Ⲡⲓϭⲟⲓⲥ. Ⲡ̇ϣⲏⲣⲓ ⲙ̇Ⲫϯ ⲁϥϭⲓⲥⲁⲣⲝ ⲟⲩⲟϩ ⲁϥⲉⲣⲣⲱⲙⲓ. ⲁⲥⲙⲓⲥⲓ ⲙ̇ⲙⲟϥ ⲛ̇ϫⲉ ϯⲡⲁⲣⲑⲉⲛⲟⲥ Ⲙⲁⲣⲓⲁ ⲟⲩⲟϩ ⲁϥⲥⲱϯ ⲙ̇ⲙⲟⲛ. ⲛ̇ⲑⲟϥ ⲁϥⲓ̇ ⲟⲩⲟϩ ⲁϥⲙⲟϣⲓ ⲛⲉⲙ ⲛⲓⲣⲱⲙⲓ. ⲁϥⲧⲟⲩⲃⲟ ⲛ̇ⲛⲉⲛϩⲏⲧ ⲟⲩⲟϩ ⲁϥⲧⲁⲗϭⲟ ⲛ̇ⲛⲓϣⲱⲛⲓ ⲛ̇ⲧⲉ ⲛⲉⲛⲯⲩⲭⲏ ⲛⲉⲙ ⲛⲉⲛⲥⲱⲙⲁ. ⲁⲩⲓ̇ϣⲓ ⲙ̇ⲙⲟϥ ⲛ̇ϫⲉ ⲛⲓⲓⲟⲩⲇⲁⲓ. ⲁϥⲙⲟⲩ ⲟⲩⲟϩ ⲁϥϯ ⲛⲁⲛ ⲙ̇ⲡⲓⲱⲛϧ. ⲁϥⲟⲩⲱⲛ ⲙ̇ⲫ̇ⲣⲟ ⲙ̇ⲡⲓⲡⲁⲣⲁⲇⲓⲥⲟⲥ ⲟⲩⲟϩ ⲁϥⲧⲁⲥⲑⲟ ⲛ̇Ⲁ̇ⲇⲁⲙ ⲉ̇ⲧⲉϥⲁⲣⲭⲏ ⲛ̇ⲕⲉⲥⲟⲡ. ⲧⲉⲛϣⲉⲡϩ̇ⲙⲟⲧ ⲛ̇ⲧⲟⲧϥ ⲉ̇ⲙⲁϣⲱ.

Lesson 15
ⲡⲓⲱϣ ⲙ̄ⲙⲁϩ ⲓ̅ⲉ̅

✝

ϩⲁⲛϫⲓⲛϩⲱⲧⲡ

APPLICATIONS

ⲁϥⲟⲩⲱⲙ ⲛ̄ϫⲉ Ⲁⲇⲁⲙ ⲉ̀ⲃⲟⲗϧⲉⲛ ⲡ̀ⲟⲩⲧⲁϩ ⲙ̀ⲡⲓ̀ϣϣⲏⲛ. ⲁϥⲓ̀ ϩⲓϫⲉⲛ ⲡⲉⲛⲅⲉⲛⲟⲥ ⲛ̄ϫⲉ ⲡⲓⲉⲣϣⲓϣⲓ ⲛ̄ⲧⲉ ⲫ̀ⲙⲟⲩ ⲛⲉⲙ ⲡ̀ⲧⲁⲕⲟ.

Adam ate from the fruit of the tree. The authority of death and perdition came on our race.

Ⲫϯ ϥ̀ⲟⲩⲱϣ ⲙ̀ⲫ̀ⲙⲟⲩ ⲁⲛ ⲙ̀ⲡⲓⲣⲉϥⲉⲣⲛⲟⲃⲓ.

God does not wish the death of the sinner.

ⲁ Ⲡ̅ⲥ̅ ⲥⲱⲧⲡ ⲛ̀ⲟⲩⲡⲁⲣⲑⲉⲛⲟⲥ.

The Lord chose a virgin.

ⲡⲓⲁⲅⲅⲉⲗⲟⲥ ⲁϥⲧⲁⲙⲟ ⲉ̀ⲣⲟⲥ: ⲁⲣⲉϫⲓⲙⲓ ⲛ̀ⲟⲩϩ̀ⲙⲟⲧ ϧⲁⲧⲉⲛ Ⲫϯ. ⲧⲉⲣⲁⲙⲓⲥⲓ ⲙ̀ⲡ̀ϣⲏⲣⲓ ⲙ̀Ⲫϯ. ⲛ̀ⲑⲟϥ ϥ̀ⲛⲁⲛⲟϩⲉⲙ ⲙ̀ⲡⲉϥⲗⲁⲟⲥ ⲉ̀ⲃⲟⲗϧⲉⲛ ⲛⲟⲩⲁ̀ⲛⲟⲙⲓⲁ ⲟⲩⲟϩ ⲥⲉⲛⲁⲱⲛϧ ⲛ̀ϫⲉ ⲛⲟⲩⲯⲩⲭⲏ.

The angel told her: You found grace with God; you will give birth to the Son of God. He will save His people from their sins, and their souls will live.

ϯⲡⲁⲣⲑⲉⲛⲟⲥ ⲁⲥϫⲱ: ϯⲥⲱⲟⲩⲛ ⲛ̀ϩ̀ⲗⲓ ⲁⲛ ⲉ̀ⲃⲏⲗ ⲉ̀ϯⲥⲙⲏ ⲛ̀ⲧⲉ ⲡⲓⲁⲅⲅⲉⲗⲟⲥ.

The Virgin said: I know nothing except the voice of the angel.

ⲁⲣⲉⲙⲟⲣⲧ ⲛ̀ⲟⲩϫⲟⲙ ⲱ̄ ⲧ̀ϣⲉⲣⲓ ⲛ̀Ⲥⲓⲱⲛ.

You girded yourself with power, O daughter of Zion.

Ⲫϯ ⲁϥⲓ̀ ⲉ̀ⲑ̀ⲙⲏⲧⲣⲁ ⲛ̀ϯⲡⲁⲣⲑⲉⲛⲟⲥ. ⲁϥϭⲓⲥⲁⲣⲝ ⲉ̀ⲃⲟⲗϧⲉⲛ ⲡⲓⲡ̀ⲛⲉⲩⲙⲁ ⲉⲑⲟⲩⲁⲃ ⲛⲉⲙ ⲉ̀ⲃⲟⲗϧⲉⲛ Ⲙⲁⲣⲓⲁ ϯϣⲉⲗⲉⲧ ⲉⲑⲟⲩⲁⲃ.

God came to the womb of the Virgin. He was incarnate (took flesh) from the Holy Spirit and from Mary the pure bride.

ⲁϥⲉⲣⲣⲱⲙⲓ ⲙ̀ⲡⲉⲛⲣⲏϯ.
He became Man like us.

ⲙ̀ⲡⲉ ⲟⲩⲅⲁⲙⲟⲥ ⲉⲣϣⲟⲣⲡ ⲉ̀ⲡⲓϫⲓⲛⲙⲓⲥⲓ.
Marriage did not precede the birth.

ⲙ̀ⲡⲉϥⲃⲱⲗ ⲉ̀ⲃⲟⲗ ⲛ̀ⲧⲉⲥⲡⲁⲣⲑⲉⲛⲓⲁ.
It [The birth] did not loosen her virginity.

ⲙ̀ⲡⲉ ϩⲗⲓ ϣ̀ⲫⲟϩ ⲉ̀ⲡⲧⲁⲓⲟ ⲛ̀ϯⲡⲁⲣⲑⲉⲛⲟⲥ.
No one was able to attain the honor of the Virgin.

ⲁ ⲡⲓⲟⲩⲱⲓⲛⲓ ϣⲁⲓ ⲉ̀ⲃⲟⲗϧⲉⲛ Ⲙⲁⲣⲓⲁ.
The light shone from Mary.

ⲁ Ⲉ̇ⲗⲓⲥⲁⲃⲉⲧ ⲙⲓⲥⲓ ⲙ̀ⲡⲓⲡⲣⲟⲇⲣⲟⲙⲟⲥ.
Elizabeth gave birth to the forerunner.

ⲱ̀ ϯⲡⲁⲣⲑⲉⲛⲟⲥ, ⲥ̀ⲣⲁϣⲓ ⲛⲉⲙⲉ ⲛ̀ϫⲉ ϯⲕⲧⲏⲥⲓⲥ ⲧⲏⲣⲥ.
O Virgin, the whole creation rejoices with you. [Literally, "O Virgin, it rejoices with you, I mean, the whole creation."]

ⲉⲑⲃⲉ ⲫⲁⲓ ⲧⲉⲛϭⲓⲥⲓ ⲙ̀ⲙⲟ ⲁ̀ⲝⲓⲱⲥ.
For the sake of this we exalt you worthily.

ⲫⲏⲉⲧⲁϥϣⲱⲡⲓ ⲛ̀ⲣⲱⲙⲓ ⲉⲑⲃⲉ ⲡⲉⲛⲟⲩϫⲁⲓ.
He who became Man for the sake of our salvation.

ⲑⲏⲉⲧⲁⲥⲙⲓⲥⲓ ⲛⲁⲛ ⲙ̀Ⲫϯ ⲡⲓⲗⲟⲅⲟⲥ.
She who gave birth to us God the Word.

ⲧⲉⲛⲛⲁⲩ ⲉ̀ϯⲁⲛⲁⲥⲧⲁⲥⲓⲥ ⲙ̀Ⲡⲓⲭⲣⲓⲥⲧⲟⲥ.
We look to the resurrection of Christ.

ⲧⲉⲛⲟⲩⲱϣⲧ ⲙ̀ⲡⲉⲕⲥ̀ⲧⲁⲩⲣⲟⲥ, ⲱ̀ Ⲡ̅ⲭ̅ⲥ̅.
We worship Your cross, O Christ.

ⲁⲕϧⲟⲙϧⲉⲙ ⲛ̀ϯϫⲟⲙ ⲛ̀ⲧⲉ ⲫ̀ⲙⲟⲩ.
You destroyed (crushed) the power of death.

ⲁϥϩⲱⲙⲓ ⲙ̀ⲫ̀ⲙⲟⲩ ϩⲓⲧⲉⲛ ⲡⲉϥⲙⲟⲩ.
He trampled death by His death.

ⲁϥϯ ⲛⲁⲛ ⲙ̀ⲡⲓⲱⲛϧ ⲉ̀ⲃⲟⲗϩⲓⲧⲉⲛ ⲧⲉϥⲁⲛⲁⲥⲧⲁⲥⲓⲥ.
He granted us life through His resurrection.

ⲁⲩⲓ̀ ⲛ̀ϫⲉ ⲛⲓϩⲓⲟⲙⲓ ⲉ̀ⲡⲓⲙ̀ϩⲁⲩ ⲟⲩⲟϩ ⲁⲩⲛⲁⲩ ⲉ̀ⲡⲓⲁⲅⲅⲉⲗⲟⲥ.
They came, I mean, the women, to the tomb and they saw the angel.

ⲁⲥⲓ ⲛ̀ϫⲉ Ⲙⲁⲣⲓⲁ ϣⲁ ⲛⲓⲙⲁⲑⲏⲧⲏⲥ ⲟⲩⲟϩ ⲁⲥⲧⲁⲙⲟ ⲉ̀ⲣⲱⲟⲩ: ⲁⲓⲛⲁⲩ ⲉ̀Ⲡ̅ⲟ̅ⲥ̅.

She came, I mean, Mary, to the disciples and told them: I saw the Lord.

ⲧⲉⲛⲛⲁⲩ ⲉ̀ⲣⲟⲕ ⲙ̀ⲙⲏⲛⲓ ϩⲓϫⲉⲛ ⲡⲓⲙⲁ̀ⲛⲉⲣϣⲱⲟⲩϣⲓ: ⲧⲉⲛϭⲓ ⲉ̀ⲃⲟⲗϧⲉⲛ ⲡⲉⲕⲥⲱⲙⲁ ⲛⲉⲙ ⲡⲉⲕⲥⲛⲟϥ ⲉⲧⲧⲁⲓⲏⲟⲩⲧ.

We see you everyday upon the altar, and we partake of Your honored Body and Blood.

ⲧⲉⲛⲛⲁϩϯ ϫⲉ ⲫⲁⲓ ⲡⲉ ϧⲉⲛ ⲟⲩⲙⲉⲑⲙⲏⲓ. ⲁⲙⲏⲛ.

We believe that this is in truth. Amen.

Ⲉⲙⲙⲁⲛⲟⲩⲏⲗ ⲡⲉⲛⲛⲟⲩϯ ϧⲉⲛ ⲧⲉⲛⲙⲏϯ ϯⲛⲟⲩ ϧⲉⲛ ⲡ̀ⲱⲟⲩ ⲛ̀ⲧⲉ ⲡⲉϥⲓⲱⲧ ⲛⲉⲙ ⲡⲓⲡ̀ⲛⲉⲩⲙⲁ ⲉⲑⲟⲩⲁⲃ.

Emmanuel our God [is] now in our midst, with the glory of His Father and the Holy Spirit.

ⲧⲉⲛⲟⲩⲱϣⲧ ⲙ̀ⲙⲟⲕ ⲱ̀ Ⲡ̅ⲭ̅ⲥ̅ ⲛⲉⲙ ⲡⲉⲕⲓⲱⲧ ⲛ̀ⲁ̀ⲅⲁⲑⲟⲥ ⲛⲉⲙ ⲡⲓⲡ̀ⲛⲉⲩⲙⲁ ⲉⲑⲟⲩⲁⲃ ϫⲉ ⲁⲕⲓ̀ ⲟⲩⲟϩ ⲁⲕⲥⲱϯ ⲙ̀ⲙⲟⲛ.

We worship You, O Christ, with Your good Father and the Holy Spirit, for You came and saved us.

ⲧⲉⲛϩⲱⲥ ⲉ̀ⲡⲉⲛⲛⲟⲩϯ ⲙ̀ⲙⲏⲛⲓ ⲛ̀ϣⲟⲣⲡ ϧⲉⲛ ϯⲉⲕ̀ⲕⲗⲏⲥⲓⲁ.

We praise our God every day early in the church.

Exercises

1. Complete what is missing in the following table, according to the given example in the first row:

Person	Present	Future	Past Perfect
ⲁⲛⲟⲕ	ϯϩⲱⲥ	ϯⲛⲁϩⲱⲥ	ⲁⲓϩⲱⲥ
ⲛ̀ⲑⲟⲕ	ⲕⲱϣ ⲁⲛ	………	………
ⲛ̀ⲑⲟ	ⲧⲉⲥϧⲁⲓ	………	………
ⲛ̀ⲑⲟϥ	………	ϥⲛⲁϣⲗⲏⲗ	………
ⲛ̀ⲑⲟⲥ	………	………	ⲙ̀ⲡⲉⲥⲟⲩⲱⲙ
ⲁⲛⲟⲛ	ⲧⲉⲛⲥⲱⲧⲉⲙ	………	………
ⲛ̀ⲑⲱⲧⲉⲛ	………	ⲧⲉⲧⲉⲛⲛⲁϭⲓ ⲁⲛ	………
ⲛ̀ⲑⲱⲟⲩ	………	………	ⲁⲩϩⲉⲙⲥⲓ

2. Write the meaning of the following:

1. ⲫⲏⲉⲧϩⲉⲙⲥⲓ
2. ⲑⲏⲉⲧⲥⲱⲧⲉⲙ
3. ⲛⲏⲉⲧⲱϣ
4. ⲫⲏⲉⲑⲛⲁⲥⲱⲧⲡ
5. ⲑⲏⲉⲑⲛⲁϣⲉⲙϣⲓ
6. ⲛⲏⲉⲑⲛⲁⲛⲁϩϯ
7. ⲫⲏⲉⲧⲁϥⲓ
8. ⲑⲏⲉⲧⲁⲥⲙⲓⲥⲓ
9. ⲛⲏⲉⲧⲁⲩⲉⲛⲕⲟⲧ
10. ⲫⲏⲉⲧⲁϥϯ
11. ⲑⲏⲉⲧⲁⲥϭⲓ
12. ⲛⲏⲉⲧⲁⲩϣⲗⲏⲗ

3. Make the object a pronoun:

1. ⲥⲙⲓⲥⲓ ⲛ̀ⲟⲩⲁⲗⲟⲩ.
2. ϥϩⲱⲥ ⲉ̀Ⲫϯ.
3. ⲧⲉⲛⲱϣ ⲛ̀ⲛⲓϫⲱⲙ.
4. ⲥⲉⲛⲁⲩ ⲉ̀ϯⲉⲕⲕⲗⲏⲥⲓⲁ.
5. ⲕ̀ⲥϧⲁⲓ ⲙ̀ⲡⲓⲱϣ.
6. ⲁϥⲥⲙⲟⲩ ⲉ̀ⲡⲉϥⲗⲁⲟⲥ.
7. ⲁⲣⲉⲛⲁⲩ ⲉ̀ⲛⲉⲥⲛⲏⲟⲩ.
8. ⲁⲛⲙⲉⲓ ⲙ̀ⲡⲉⲛⲛⲟⲩϯ.
9. ⲁⲧⲉⲧⲉⲛⲕⲁϯ ⲛ̀ⲛⲉⲧⲉⲛⲱϣ.
10. Ⲫϯ ⲁϥⲥⲱⲧⲡ ⲛ̀ϯⲡⲁⲣⲑⲉⲛⲟⲥ.

4. Write the meaning of the following phrases:

1. ϯⲥϧⲁⲓ ⲛⲱⲧⲉⲛ.
2. ϥⲥⲁϫⲓ ⲛⲉⲙⲁⲕ.
3. ⲕⲱϣ ⲛⲱⲟⲩ.
4. ⲧⲉⲛϯ ⲛⲁⲕ ⲛⲉⲙⲁϥ.
5. ⲥ̀ⲛⲁⲟⲩⲱⲙ ⲛⲉⲙⲉ.
6. ⲧⲉⲣⲁⲓ ⲛⲉⲙⲁⲛ.
7. ⲥⲉϭⲓ ⲛⲉⲙⲱⲧⲉⲛ.
8. ⲧⲉⲛⲛⲁϩⲉⲙⲥⲓ ⲛⲉⲙⲱⲟⲩ.
9. ⲁⲕϯ ⲛⲁⲛ ⲙ̀ⲙⲟϥ.
10. ⲁϥⲥⲱⲧⲡ ⲛⲱⲟⲩ ⲙ̀ⲙⲟⲕ.
11. ϩⲁⲛⲥⲁϫⲓ ⲛ̀ⲧⲁϥ.
12. ⲟⲩϣⲉⲣⲓ ⲛ̀ⲧⲁⲥ.
13. ϩⲁⲛϫⲱⲙ ⲛ̀ⲧⲱⲟⲩ.
14. ϩⲁⲛⲥ̀ⲛⲏⲟⲩ ⲛ̀ⲧⲁⲛ.

5. The following sentences are in the negative form; write them in the affirmative form:

ⲁ̄ ⲙ̀ⲡⲉ ⲡⲓⲣⲱⲙⲓ ⲟⲩⲱⲙ.
ⲃ̄ ⲥⲉⲛⲁⲩ ⲉ̀ⲣⲟϥ ⲁⲛ.
ⲅ̄ ⲙ̀ⲡⲉⲛⲁⲣⲉϩ ⲉ̀ⲡⲉⲛⲱϣ.
ⲇ̄ ⲙ̀ⲡⲟⲩⲥⲁϫⲓ ⲛⲉⲙⲏⲓ.

Lesson 15 ✣ Applications ✣

ⲉ̄   ⲥ̀ϩⲉⲙⲥⲓ ⲁⲛ ⲛⲉⲙⲉ.
ⲋ̄   ⲙ̀ⲡⲉϥⲧⲁⲙⲟ ⲉ̀ⲣⲱⲧⲉⲛ.
ⲍ̄   ⲙ̀ⲡⲉⲕϣⲓⲛⲓ ⲉ̀ⲣⲟⲓ.
ⲏ̄   ⲙ̀ⲡⲓⲥⲱⲧⲡ ⲙ̀ⲙⲱⲧⲉⲛ.
ⲑ̄   ⲧⲉⲧⲉⲛⲛⲁⲥⲱ ⲛ̀ⲟⲩⲏⲣⲡ ⲁⲛ.
ⲓ̄   ⲙ̀ⲡⲉⲛⲁϩϯ ⲉ̀ⲣⲟϥ.
ⲓ̄ⲁ ⲭ̀ⲛⲁⲟⲩⲱⲣⲡ ⲛⲁⲛ ⲁⲛ.
ⲓ̄ⲃ ⲙ̀ⲡⲉⲥⲕⲁϯ ⲙ̀ⲡⲉⲥⲱϣ.
ⲓ̄ⲅ ϥⲛⲁⲛⲟϩⲉⲙ ⲁⲛ ⲙ̀ⲙⲟϥ.
ⲓ̄ⲇ ⲙ̀ⲡⲉⲛⲥⲱⲧⲉⲙ ⲉ̀ϯⲥⲙⲏ.
ⲓ̄ⲉ ⲙ̀ⲡⲟⲩⲛⲉϩⲥⲓ ⲛ̀ϣⲟⲣⲡ.
ⲓ̄ⲋ ⲙ̀ⲡⲉⲧⲉⲛϣⲗⲏⲗ ⲙ̀ⲫⲟⲟⲩ.

Review Exercises 3
On Lessons 11 to 15

1. Write the meaning:

1.	ⲁϥⲕⲓⲙ	9.	ⲥⲱϣ	17.	ϯⲛⲁⲥⲙⲟⲩ	25.	ⲭⲛⲁⲙⲟϣⲓ
2.	ϯⲥⲱⲧⲉⲙ	10.	ⲧⲉⲧⲉⲛⲕⲁϯ	18.	ⲙ̀ⲡⲉⲧⲉⲛⲓ̀	26.	ⲁⲣⲉⲙⲟⲥϯ
3.	ⲙ̀ⲡⲉⲥⲙⲓⲥⲓ	11.	ⲥⲉⲙⲉⲓ	19.	ⲧⲉⲛⲛⲁⲉⲙⲓ	27.	ⲙ̀ⲡⲓⲥⲱⲧⲡ
4.	ⲁⲕⲛⲁⲩ	12.	ϥ̀ϣⲉⲙϣⲓ	20.	ⲙ̀ⲡⲉⲟⲩⲱⲙ	28.	ⲥⲉⲛⲁⲙⲉⲩⲓ̀
5.	ⲧⲉⲛϩⲉⲙⲥⲓ	13.	ⲁⲛⲛⲁϩϯ	21.	ⲥ̀ⲛⲁⲥⲱ	29.	ⲁⲓⲭⲱⲗⲉⲙ
6.	ⲁⲩϣⲗⲏⲗ	14.	ⲙ̀ⲡⲉⲕⲁⲣⲉϩ	22.	ⲭⲟⲩⲱϣⲧ	30.	ⲧⲉⲧⲉⲛⲛⲁϯ
7.	ⲧⲉⲣⲁⲃⲓ	15.	ⲁⲥⲛⲉϩⲥⲓ	23.	ⲙ̀ⲡⲉϥⲕⲱⲧ	31.	ⲙ̀ⲡⲉⲛⲕⲁϯ
8.	ⲙ̀ⲡⲟⲩⲥ̀ⲇⲁⲓ	16.	ⲧⲉϩⲱⲥ	24.	ⲁⲧⲉⲧⲉⲛⲥⲓⲛⲓ	32.	ϥⲛⲁⲥⲁϫⲓ

33.	ⲁϥⲭⲱ ⲛⲁⲛ ⲛⲉⲙⲱⲧⲉⲛ.	38.	ⲁⲓⲛⲁⲩ ⲉ̀ⲣⲱⲧⲉⲛ ⲛⲉⲙⲁϥ.
34.	ⲕ̀ϯ ⲛⲱⲟⲩ ⲛ̀ⲧⲉⲕϩⲓⲣⲏⲛⲏ.	39.	ⲁⲛϩⲱⲥ ⲉ̀ⲣⲟϥ ⲛⲉⲙⲱⲟⲩ.
35.	ⲧⲉⲛⲥⲁϫⲓ ⲛⲉⲙⲁⲕ ϯⲛⲟⲩ.	40.	ⲭⲛⲁϣ ⲙ̀ⲙⲟϥ ⲛⲉⲙⲁⲛ.
36.	ϯⲛⲁⲃⲓ ⲛⲁⲕ ⲛⲉⲙⲏⲓ.	41.	ⲁⲣⲉⲥⲁϫⲓ ⲛⲉⲙⲁⲥ ⲛ̀ⲥⲁϥ.
37.	ϩⲁⲛⲓⲟϯ ⲛ̀ⲧⲱⲟⲩ.	42.	ⲟⲩⲉⲕⲕ̀ⲗⲏⲥⲓⲁ ⲛ̀ⲧⲁⲥ.

2. Put the suitable object mark:

1.	ϯⲙⲉⲓ … ⲛⲁⲥ̀ⲛⲏⲟⲩ.	8.	ⲥⲉⲃⲓ … ⲛⲟⲩϫⲱⲙ.
2.	ⲁⲕⲁⲣⲉϩ … ⲛⲓⲯⲁⲗⲙⲟⲥ.	9.	ⲧⲉⲛⲛⲁϩⲱⲥ … ⲡⲉⲛⲛⲟⲩϯ.

Review Exercises 3 ✠ On Lessons 11 to 15 ✠

3. ϥ̀ⲥϧⲁⲓ ... ⲡⲉϥⲱϣ.
4. ⲧⲉⲣⲁⲙⲓⲥⲓ ... ⲟⲩⲁⲗⲟⲩ.
5. ⲧⲉⲧⲉⲛⲥⲱ ... ⲡⲓⲉⲣⲱϯ.
6. ⲁⲛⲛⲁⲩ ... ⲡⲉϥⲱⲟⲩ.
7. ⲁϥϣⲱⲗⲉⲙ ... ⲡⲓⲥⲑⲟⲓⲛⲟⲩϥⲓ.
10. ⲙ̀ⲡⲉⲥⲟⲩⲱⲙ ... ⲡⲓⲱⲓⲕ.
11. ⲁⲩⲛⲁϩϯ ... ⲡⲟⲩϬⲟⲓⲥ.
12. ⲁⲓⲥⲱⲧⲉⲙ ... ⲧⲉϥⲥⲙⲏ.
13. ⲭ̀ⲛⲁⲱϣ ... ⲡⲁⲓϫⲱⲙ.
14. ⲁⲥⲧⲁⲙⲟ ... ⲛⲓⲙⲁⲑⲏⲧⲏⲥ.

3. Form meaningful sentences from every group of the following words:

ⲁ̄ ⲓⲱⲧ, ϩⲱⲥ, ⲛⲟⲩϯ.
ⲃ̄ ⲉ̀ⲃⲓⲁⲓⲕ, ϣⲉⲙϣⲓ, ⲟⲩⲣⲟ.
ⲅ̄ ⲟⲩⲏⲃ, ϣ̀ⲗⲏⲗ, ⲉⲣⲫⲉⲓ.
ⲇ̄ ϩⲁⲗⲁϯ, ⲥⲱ, ⲙⲱⲟⲩ.
ⲉ̄ ⲙⲁⲣⲧⲩⲣⲟⲥ, ⲛⲁⲩ, Ϭⲟⲓⲥ.
ⲋ̄ ⲥⲛⲏⲟⲩ, ⲕⲁϯ, ⲱϣ.
ⲍ̄ ⲡⲁⲣⲑⲉⲛⲟⲥ, Ϭⲓ, ϩ̀ⲙⲟⲧ.
ⲏ̄ ⲥⲱⲛⲓ, ⲟⲩⲱⲙ, ⲱⲓⲕ.

4. Answer once in the affirmative form and then in the negative form:

ⲁ̄ ⲙⲏ ⲁ ⲡⲓⲥⲟⲛ ⲓ̀ ⲛ̀ⲥⲁϥ?   ⲥⲉ,
                              ⲙ̀ⲙⲟⲛ,

ⲃ̄ ⲙⲏ ⲁⲧⲉⲧⲉⲛⲥ̀ϧⲁⲓ ⲙ̀ⲡⲉⲧⲉⲛⲱϣ? ⲥⲉ,
                                  ⲙ̀ⲙⲟⲛ,

ⲅ̄ ⲙⲏ ⲭ̀ⲛⲁⲁⲣⲉϩ ⲉ̀ⲛⲁⲓⲯⲁⲗⲙⲟⲥ? ⲥⲉ,
                                ⲙ̀ⲙⲟⲛ,

ⲇ̄ ⲙⲏ ⲁⲩϯ ⲛⲱⲧⲉⲛ ⲛ̀ⲛⲉⲧⲉⲛϫⲱⲙ? ⲥⲉ,
                                ⲙ̀ⲙⲟⲛ,

ⲉ̄ ⲙⲏ ⲁⲣⲉⲛⲁⲩ ⲉ̀ⲣⲟⲥ ⲙ̀ⲫⲟⲟⲩ?   ⲥⲉ,
                              ⲙ̀ⲙⲟⲛ,

ⲋ̄ ⲙⲏ ⲁϥⲟⲩⲱⲣⲡ ⲛⲁⲕ ⲙ̀ⲡⲉϥϣⲏⲣⲓ? ⲥⲉ,
                                ⲙ̀ⲙⲟⲛ,

ⲍ̄ ⲙⲏ ⲧⲉⲧⲉⲛⲛⲁⲩ ⲉ̀ⲧⲁⲓϩⲓⲕⲱⲛ?   ⲥⲉ,
                              ⲙ̀ⲙⲟⲛ,

Exam 3
On Lessons 11 to 15

1. Put the following in the negative form:

1. ⲧⲉⲛⲛⲁⲩ	7. ⲁϥⲥⲙⲟⲩ	13. ⲁⲕϣⲗⲏⲗ
2. ⲁⲥⲟⲩⲱϣⲧ	8. ⲁⲧⲉⲧⲉⲛⲥⲱ	14. ⲁⲩⲥⲁϫⲓ
3. ⲁⲓⲥϭⲁⲓ	9. ⲁⲛϭⲓ	15. ⲧⲉⲛⲕⲱϯ
4. ⲁⲣⲉϩⲱⲥ	10. ⲥⲉⲛⲁⲓ	16. ⲁⲛⲕⲁϯ
5. ϯⲛⲁⲙⲟϣⲓ	11. ⲧⲉⲣⲁⲛⲉϩⲥⲓ	17. ⲁⲕⲓⲣⲓ
6. ⲧⲉϣⲉⲙϣⲓ	12. ϥⲛⲁϩϯ	18. ⲁⲥⲙⲟⲩ

2. Write the meaning of the following:

1. ⲁϥⲥⲁϫⲓ ⲛⲉⲙⲁⲛ.	7. ϯⲭⲱ ⲛⲱⲧⲉⲛ.
2. ϫⲟⲩⲱⲙ ⲛⲉⲙⲁϥ.	8. ⲁϥϣⲁⲓ ⲛⲁⲛ.
3. ⲧⲉⲣⲁϩⲉⲙⲥⲓ ⲛⲉⲙⲱⲟⲩ.	9. ⲧⲉⲛϯ ⲛⲁⲕ.
4. ⲁⲣⲉϣⲗⲏⲗ ⲛⲉⲙⲁⲥ.	10. ⲁⲕⲱϣ ⲛⲏⲓ.
5. ϯϩⲱⲥ ⲛⲉⲙⲱⲧⲉⲛ.	11. ⲥⲛⲁⲥϭⲁⲓ ⲛⲱⲟⲩ.
6. ⲧⲉⲧⲉⲛⲙⲟϣⲓ ⲛⲉⲙⲏⲓ.	12. ⲁⲩϭⲓ ⲛⲁϥ.

3. Make the object a pronoun:

1. ⲧⲉⲛⲛⲁⲩ ⲉⲡⲉϥⲱⲟⲩ.	6. ϥⲥⲙⲟⲩ ⲉⲛⲉϥϣⲏⲣⲓ.

Exam 3 ✠ On Lessons 11 to 15 ✠

2. ⲁⲓⲱϣ ⲙ̀ⲡⲁⲓϫⲱⲙ.
3. ⲥⲉϩⲱⲥ ⲉ̀ⲡⲟⲩⲛⲟⲩϯ.
4. ϯⲥⲱⲧⲉⲙ ⲉ̀ⲧⲉϥⲥⲙⲏ.
5. ⲁⲕϭⲓ ⲛ̀ⲛⲉⲕϫⲱⲙ.
7. ⲥⲟⲩⲱⲙ ⲙ̀ⲡⲓⲱⲓⲕ.
8. ⲁϥⲭⲱ ⲛ̀ⲧⲉϥⲕⲩⲑⲁⲣⲁ.
9. ⲥⲉⲁⲣⲉϩ ⲉ̀ⲛⲓⲉⲛⲧⲟⲗⲏ.
10. ⲧⲉⲥⲱⲧⲡ ⲛ̀ⲧⲁⲓⲃⲁⲕⲓ.

4. Write the meaning of the following phrases:

ⲁ̅ ϥϩⲱⲥ ⲉ̀ⲫⲏⲉⲧⲉ ⲫⲱϥ ⲛ̀ⲛⲟⲩϯ.
ⲃ̅ ⲧⲉⲛⲕⲁϯ ⲛ̀ⲛⲏⲉ̀ⲧⲉ ⲛⲟⲩⲛ ⲛ̀ⲱϣ.
ⲅ̅ ⲕ̀ⲱⲛϧ ϧⲉⲛ ⲑⲏⲉ̀ⲧⲉ ⲑⲱⲕ ⲛ̀ⲣⲓ.
ⲇ̅ ϯϥⲁⲓ ⲙ̀ⲫⲏⲉ̀ⲧⲉ ⲫⲱⲓ ⲛ̀ⲥⲧⲁⲩⲣⲟⲥ.
ⲉ̅ ⲧⲉⲥⲱⲧⲉⲙ ⲉ̀ⲑⲏⲉ̀ⲧⲉ ⲑⲱϥ ⲛ̀ⲥⲙⲏ.
ⲋ̅ ⲥⲉⲙⲉⲓ ⲛ̀ⲛⲏⲉ̀ⲧⲉ ⲛⲟⲩⲟⲩ ⲛ̀ϣⲏⲣⲓ.

5. Choose from every left column the suitable number for every word from the opposing right column:

1.	ⲛ̀ⲑⲱⲟⲩ	ⲧⲉⲣⲁⲙⲓⲥⲓ	9.	ⲡⲉⲕⲣⲁⲛ	ⲛ̀ⲧⲁϥ
2.	ⲁⲛⲟⲛ	ϥ̀ϣⲗⲏⲗ	10.	ⲛⲉⲧⲉⲛϫⲱⲙ	ⲛ̀ⲧⲁⲛ
3.	ⲛ̀ⲑⲟⲥ	ⲙ̀ⲡⲟⲩⲅϩⲁⲓ	11.	ⲡⲁⲓⲱⲧ	ⲛ̀ⲧⲱⲟⲩ
4.	ⲛ̀ⲑⲱⲧⲉⲛ	ⲁⲕⲥⲁϫⲓ	12.	ⲧⲟⲩⲙⲁⲩ	ⲛ̀ⲧⲉ
5.	ⲛ̀ⲑⲟⲕ	ⲧⲉⲛⲁⲣⲉϩ	13.	ⲡⲉⲥϣⲏⲣⲓ	ⲛ̀ⲧⲱⲧⲉⲛ
6.	ⲁⲛⲟⲕ	ⲧⲉⲧⲉⲛⲛⲁⲓ	14.	ⲛⲉϥϫⲓϫ	ⲛ̀ⲧⲏⲓ
7.	ⲛ̀ⲑⲟϥ	ⲁⲓⲙⲟϣⲓ	15.	ⲧⲉⲥⲱⲛⲓ	ⲛ̀ⲧⲁⲥ
8.	ⲛ̀ⲑⲟ	ⲥⲛⲁⲱϣ	16.	ⲛⲉⲛⲃⲁⲗⲁⲩϫ	ⲛ̀ⲧⲁⲕ

6. Translate the following:

ⲁ̅ ϯϩⲱⲥ ⲛⲉⲙ ⲛⲁⲥⲛⲏⲟⲩ ϧⲉⲛ ⲧⲁⲓⲉⲕⲕⲗⲏⲥⲓⲁ.
ⲃ̅ ϯⲡⲁⲣⲑⲉⲛⲟⲥ ⲁⲥⲙⲓⲥⲓ ⲙ̀ⲡⲉⲛⲥⲱⲧⲏⲣ Ⲓⲏⲥⲟⲩⲥ.
ⲅ̅ ⲡⲉⲛϭⲟⲓⲥ ⲁϥⲓ̀ ⲟⲩⲟϩ ⲁϥⲙⲟϣⲓ ⲛⲉⲙ ⲛⲓⲣⲱⲙⲓ.
ⲇ̅ ⲧⲉⲛϣⲱ ⲛ̀ⲛⲓⲥⲁϫⲓ ⲙ̀Ⲫⲛⲟⲩϯ ϧⲉⲛ ⲡⲓϫⲱⲙ ⲉⲑⲟⲩⲁⲃ.
ⲉ̅ ⲁⲩⲛⲁϩϯ ⲉ̀ⲡⲟⲩϭⲟⲓⲥ ⲟⲩⲟϩ ⲁⲩⲥⲙⲟⲩ ⲉ̀ⲡⲉϥⲣⲁⲛ.
ⲋ̅ ⲁⲕⲛⲁⲩ ⲉ̀ⲡⲉⲕⲥⲟⲛ ⲟⲩⲟϩ ⲁⲕⲥⲁϫⲓ ⲛⲉⲙⲁϥ.
ⲍ̅ ⲧⲉⲙⲉⲓ ⲙ̀ⲡⲉⲓⲱⲧ ⲛⲉⲙ ⲧⲉⲙⲁⲩ ⲟⲩⲟϩ ⲧⲉϣⲗⲏⲗ ⲛⲉⲙⲱⲟⲩ.

Lesson 16
ⲡⲓⲱϣ ⲙ̀ⲙⲁϩ ⲓ̅ⲋ̅

✝

Classification of Verbs

1. Simple Verbs

These consist of the base of the verb only, for example:

ⲭⲱ	To leave behind, to place	ϣⲓ	To measure, to weigh	ⲥⲱⲛⲧ	To create	ϫⲓⲙⲓ	To find
ϫⲱ	to say, to sing	ⲙⲉⲓ	to love	ⲥⲱⲧⲡ	to choose	ⲙⲓⲥⲓ	to beget
ⲥⲱ	to drink	ϥⲁⲓ	to carry	ⲫⲱⲣϣ	to spread	ⲫⲉⲣⲓ	to shine
ϯ	to give	ⲱ̀ⲗⲓ	to lift	ϩ̀ⲙⲟⲙ	to heat up	ⲃⲟⲣⲃⲉⲣ	to throw, to cast
ϭⲓ	to take, to be granted	ⲃⲱⲗ	to untie, to unfasten	ⲭ̀ⲃⲟⲃ	to cool down	ⲥⲟⲗⲥⲉⲗ	to adorn, to console
ⲥⲓ	to be satiated	ⲣⲱⲧ	to grow	ⲥⲱⲧⲉⲙ	to hear	ⲥⲟⲃϯ	to prepare, to be ready
ⲓ̀ⲣⲓ	to make, to do	ⲕⲱⲧ	to build	ⲑⲱϩⲉⲙ	to call	ⲙⲟⲥϯ	to hate
ⲓ̀ⲛⲓ	to bring, to offer	ϣⲱⲧ	to cut	ⲛⲟϩⲉⲙ	to redeem	ϫⲱⲓⲗⲓ	to sojourn
ⲓ̀ϣⲓ	to hang, to crucify	ⲙⲟϩ	to fill	ⲥⲟϭⲛⲓ	to take cousel	ⲟⲩⲛⲟϥ	to rejoice

2. Causative Verbs

These consist of the base of the verb with an additive attached to their beginning, to make them transitive (a verb that has an object):

1. By adding the letter ⲥ to their beginning:

ϩⲱⲛ	→	ⲥⲁϩⲛⲓ	To command, to provide	ⲧⲱⲟⲩⲛ → ⲥⲱⲟⲩⲧⲉⲛ		to manage, to correct
ⲙⲟⲩⲛ	→	ⲥⲉⲙⲛⲓ	to establish, to confirm	ⲭⲱ → ⲥⲁϫⲓ		to say
ⲟⲩⲁⲃ	→	ⲥⲉⲃⲓ	to circumcise	ⲉ̀ⲙⲓ → ⲥⲉⲙⲓ		to plead, to accuse
ò ϩⲓ	→	ⲥⲟϩⲓ	to reprove, to rebuke	ⲱⲛϧ → ϣⲁⲛϣ		to nourish, to rear, to support

2. By adding the letter ⲧ to their beginning:

ⲁⲕⲱ	→	ⲧⲁⲕⲟ	to destroy, to deprive of	ⲟⲩϫⲁⲓ → ⲧⲟⲩϫⲟ		to heal
ⲱⲛϧ	→	ⲧⲁⲛϧⲟ	to revive	ⲱ̀ⲗⲓ → ⲧⲁⲗⲟ		to carry, to lift up
ⲟⲩⲱⲙ	→	ⲧⲉⲙⲙⲟ	to feed	ⲥⲁⲃⲉ → ⲧ̀ⲥⲁⲃⲟ		to teach
ⲥⲓ	→	ⲧ̀ⲥⲓⲟ	to satiate	ⲙⲟϩ → ⲧⲉⲙϩⲟ		to burn
ⲥⲱ	→	ⲧ̀ⲥⲟ	to water, to quench	ⲟⲩⲁⲃ → ⲧⲟⲩⲃⲟ		to sanctify, to purify
ò ϩⲓ	→	ⲧⲁϩⲟ	to build, to establish	ϩⲉⲙⲥⲓ → ⲧ̀ϩⲉⲙⲥⲟ		to seat

3. Compound Verbs

1. By adding the verb ϯ, meaning "to give":

ϯⲱⲟⲩ	to glorify	ϯⲧⲁⲓⲟ	to honor	ϯϣⲉⲃⲏⲟⲩ	to compensate
ϯ̀ⲥⲃⲱ	to teach, to rear	ϯϫⲟⲙ	to strengthen	ϯⲏⲡⲓ	to count

ϯϩⲁⲡ	to judge	ϯⲙⲁϯ	to console, to gladden	ϯⲉ̇ⲃⲟⲗ	to sell
ϯϭⲓ	to suckle	ϯⲉ̇ⲑⲏ	to pay attention	ϯⲭ̇ⲣⲱⲙ	to kindle
ϯϩⲟ	to ask, to beseech	ϯⲟⲩⲃⲉ	to resist, to confront
ϯⲕⲁϯ	to give insight	ϯⲱⲙⲥ	to baptize, to immerse

2. By adding the verb ϭⲓ, meaning "to take":

ϭⲓⲱⲟⲩ	to be glorified	ϭⲓⲥⲙⲟⲩ	to be blessed	ϭⲓⲥⲃⲱ	to learn
ϭⲓⲟⲩⲱⲓⲛⲓ	to be enlightened	ϭⲓⲫⲁϩⲣⲓ	to be healed	ϭⲓⲭⲣⲱⲙ	to burn
ϭⲓⲱⲙⲥ	to be baptized	ϭⲓⲏ̇ⲡⲓ	to take account	ϭⲓϣⲫⲏⲣⲓ	to be amazed
ϭⲓⲥⲁⲣⲝ	to be incarnate	ϭⲓⲥϩⲓⲙⲓ	to be married	ϭⲓⲥⲁⲛⲓⲥ	to doubt
ϭⲓϫⲟⲙ	to be strengthened	ϭⲓⲕⲁϩⲥ	to be accustomed to
ϭⲓϩⲁⲡ	to judge, to condemn	ϭⲓϣⲓⲡⲓ	to disgrace, to embarrass

3. By adding the syllable ⲉⲣ- from the verb ⲓ̇ⲣⲓ, meaning "to make," "to do," or "to become":

ⲉⲣⲉ̇ⲙⲟⲧ	to grant	ⲉⲣⲣⲱⲙⲓ	to become man	ⲉⲣϩⲏⲧⲥ	to begin
ⲉⲣⲟⲩⲱⲓⲛⲓ	to enlighten	ⲉⲣⲟⲩⲣⲟ	to become king	ⲉⲣϩⲟϯ	to fear
ⲉⲣⲛⲟⲃⲓ	to sin	ⲉⲣϩⲟⲩⲟ	to increase	ⲉⲣⲡ̇ⲉⲙⲡ̇ϣⲁ	to be worthy
ⲉⲣⲟⲩⲱ	to answer	ⲉⲣϩⲱⲃ	to work, to labor	ⲉⲣⲛⲓϣϯ	to become great
ⲉⲣⲃⲱⲕ	to enslave, to serve as a slave	ⲉⲣⲃⲟⲓⲥ	to exercise authority
ⲉⲣϣⲟⲣⲡ	to precede, to come earlier	ⲉⲣⲫⲙⲉⲩⲓ̇	to mention, to remember

Lesson 16 ✠ *Classification of Verbs* ✠

The syllable **ⲉⲣ-** is introduced to the Greek verbs in the infinitive form, for example:

ⲉⲣⲯⲁⲗⲓⲛ	to sing	ⲉⲣⲡ̅ⲣⲉⲥⲃⲉⲩⲓⲛ	to intercede
ⲉⲣⲁⲅⲓⲁⲍⲓⲛ	to sanctify	ⲉⲣⲡ̅ⲣⲟⲥⲉⲩⲭⲉⲥⲑⲉ	to pray
ⲉⲣⲡⲓⲣⲁⲍⲓⲛ	to tempt	ⲉⲣⲛⲏⲥⲧⲉⲩⲓⲛ	to fast

4. By adding **ϣⲉⲡ-** from the verb **ϣⲱⲡ**, meaning "to accept" or "to receive":

ϣⲉⲡϩ̇ⲙⲟⲧ	to thank	ϣⲉⲡⲙ̅ⲕⲁϩ	to suffer, to accept pain	ϣⲉⲡϧⲓⲥⲓ	to labor, to accept toil

5. By adding **ϫⲉⲙ-** from the verb **ϫⲓⲙⲓ**, meaning "to find":

ϫⲉⲙϯⲡⲓ	to taste	ϫⲉⲙⲛⲟⲙϯ	to find consolation	ϫⲉⲙⲡ̅ϣⲓⲛⲓ	to visit, to take care of

6. By adding **ϣ̇**, meaning "to be able to":

ϣ̇ⲥⲁϫⲓ	to be able to speak	ϣ̇ⲓⲣⲓ	to be able to make	ϣ̇ⲛⲁⲩ	to be able to see

Exercises

1. Conjugate the following, according to the given example:

Present	Future	Past perfect (affirmative)	Past perfect (negative)
ϭⲓ	ϥⲛⲁϭⲓ	ⲁϥϭⲓ	ⲙ̅ⲡⲉϥϭⲓ
ⲕ̇ⲱ	....	....	....
ϯⲥⲱⲧⲉⲙ	....	....	....
ⲥ̇ⲙⲓⲥⲓ	....	....	....
ⲧⲉⲛⲱϣ	....	....	....
ⲧⲉϫⲓⲙⲓ	....	....	....
ⲧⲉⲧⲉⲛⲓ̇	....	....	....
ⲥⲉϫⲱ	....	....	....

2. If you know that:

ⲱⲛϧ	to live	ⲟⲩⲱⲛ	to open	ⲟⲩⲱⲣⲡ	to send
ϥⲁⲓ	to carry, to lift up	ⲥⲓⲛⲓ	to pass, to cross	ⲙⲟϣⲓ	to walk

Then write the meaning of the following:

1. We crossed.
2. You (sing. mas.) sent.
3. We will live.
4. She did not carry.
5. I raised (carried).
6. You (sing. fem.) will cross.
7. You (pl.) live.
8. They opened.
9. He will carry.
10. You (sing. fem.) open.
11. He sent.
12. We walked.
13. We send.
14. She lives.
15. You (pl.) carry.
16. You (sing. mas.) cross.

3. Translate to the English language:

ⲁ̅ Ⲫϯ ϥⲧⲟⲩⲃⲟ ⲛ̀ⲛⲉⲛϩⲏⲧ.

ⲃ̅ ϥⲛⲁⲱϣ ⲛ̀ϫⲉ ⲡⲓⲇⲓⲁⲕⲟⲛ ⲙ̀ⲡⲓⲉⲩⲁⲅⲅⲉⲗⲓⲟⲛ.

ⲅ̅ ⲫ̀ⲛⲟⲃⲓ ⲁϥⲧⲁⲕⲟ ⲙ̀ⲡⲉⲛⲅⲉⲛⲟⲥ.

ⲇ̅ ⲛⲓⲣⲱⲙⲓ ⲁⲩⲉⲣⲛⲟⲃⲓ ⲟⲩⲃⲉ Ⲡ̅ⲟ̅ⲥ̅.

ⲉ̅ ⲁ Ⲫϯ ϣⲁⲛϣ ⲙ̀Ⲡⲓⲥⲣⲁⲏⲗ ϧⲉⲛ ⲡ̀ϣⲁϥⲉ ⲛ̀Ⲥⲓⲛⲁ.

ⲋ̅ ⲁϥⲉⲣⲟⲩⲣⲟ ⲛ̀ϫⲉ Ⲇⲁⲩⲓⲇ ⲉ̀ϫⲉⲛ Ⲡⲓⲥⲣⲁⲏⲗ.

ⲍ̅ Ⲫϯ ⲁϥⲉⲣⲁⲅⲓⲁⲍⲓⲛ ⲛ̀ϯⲡⲁⲣⲑⲉⲛⲟⲥ.

ⲏ̅ ⲁ ⲡⲉⲛⲥⲱⲧⲏⲣ ϣⲉⲡⲙ̀ⲕⲁϩ ⲉⲑⲃⲉ ⲡⲉⲛⲟⲩϫⲁⲓ.

ⲑ̅ ⲛⲓⲓⲟⲩⲇⲁⲓ ⲁⲩⲓ̀ⲱⲓ ⲙ̀ⲙⲟϥ.

ⲓ̅ ⲁϥϫⲉⲙϯⲡⲓ ⲙ̀ⲫ̀ⲟⲩⲟⲩ ϧⲉⲛ ⲧ̀ⲥⲁⲣⲝ.

ⲓⲁ̅ ⲡⲉⲛϭⲟⲓⲥ ⲁϥⲛⲟϩⲉⲙ ⲙ̀ⲡⲉϥⲗⲁⲟⲥ.

ⲓⲃ̅ ⲥ̀ⲉⲣⲡ̀ⲣⲉⲥⲃⲉⲩⲓⲛ ⲛ̀ϫⲉ ϯⲡⲁⲣⲑⲉⲛⲟⲥ ⲉⲑⲃⲉ ⲛⲉⲥϣⲏⲣⲓ.

ⲓⲅ̅ ⲧⲉⲛϭⲓⲥⲃⲱ ⲛ̀ⲧ̀ⲁⲥⲡⲓ ⲛ̀ⲣⲉⲙⲛ̀ⲭⲏⲙⲓ.

ⲓⲇ̅ ⲛⲓⲙⲁⲣⲧⲩⲣⲟⲥ ⲁⲩϣⲉⲡϧⲓⲥⲓ ⲉⲑⲃⲉ ⲡⲓⲛⲁϩϯ.

ⲓⲉ̅ ⲛⲓⲉ̀ⲃⲓⲁⲓⲕ ⲥⲉⲉⲣⲃⲱⲕ ⲙ̀ⲡⲟⲩϭⲟⲓⲥ.

ⲓⲋ̅ ϥⲉⲣⲟⲩⲱⲓⲛⲓ ⲙ̀ⲡⲉⲛⲛⲟⲩⲥ ⲛ̀ϫⲉ ⲡⲓⲡ̀ⲛⲉⲩⲙⲁ ⲉⲑⲟⲩⲁⲃ.

ⲓⲍ̅ ⲡⲉⲕⲣⲁⲛ ⲉⲑⲟⲩⲁⲃ ⲁϥϭⲓⲱⲟⲩ ϧⲉⲛ ⲣⲱⲟⲩ ⲛ̀ⲛⲏⲉⲑⲟⲩⲁⲃ ⲛ̀ⲧⲁⲕ.

ιη	ⲛⲓⲁⲅⲓⲟⲥ ⲁⲩⲉⲣⲛⲓϣϯ ϧⲉⲛ ϯⲭⲱⲣⲁ ⲛ̀ⲧⲉ Ⲭⲏⲙⲓ.
ιθ	ⲧⲉⲛϯⲱⲟⲩ ⲛ̀ϯⲡⲁⲣⲑⲉⲛⲟⲥ ⲟⲩⲟϩ ⲧⲉⲛϯⲧⲁⲓⲟ ⲛⲁⲥ.
ⲕ̄	ⲡⲁⲛⲟⲩϯ ϥ̀ϣⲉⲃⲛⲟⲩ ⲙ̀ⲙⲱⲧⲉⲛ.

4. Complete the following conjugation, with what suits the given personal pronoun:

ⲁⲛⲟⲕ	I	ⲡⲁⲥⲟⲛ	My brother	ⲫⲱⲓ	Mine	ⲛⲏⲓ	Mine	ⲉ̀ⲣⲟⲓ	To me
ⲛ̀ⲑⲟⲕ									
ⲛ̀ⲑⲟ									
ⲛ̀ⲑⲟϥ									
ⲛ̀ⲑⲟⲥ									
ⲁⲛⲟⲛ									
ⲛ̀ⲑⲱⲧⲉⲛ									
ⲛ̀ⲑⲱⲟⲩ									

Lesson 17
ⲡⲓⲱϣ ⲙ̀ⲙⲁϩ ⲓⲍ̄

✜

ⲛⲓⲑⲟ ⲛ̀ⲛⲓⲣⲁ

KINDS OF VERBS

Intransitive Verb

It is the verb that does not accept an object, for example:

ⲓ̀	To come, to arrive	ϣⲉ	To go	ⲙⲟϣⲓ	To walk	ϩⲉⲙⲥⲓ	To sit
ⲱⲛϧ	To live	ⲙⲟⲩ	To die	ϧⲱⲛⲧ	To draw near, to approach	ⲛⲉϩⲡⲓ	To mourn

Transitive Verb

It is the verb that accepts an object, for example:

ϯⲛⲁϩⲱⲥ ⲉ̀ⲡⲁⲛⲟⲩϯ.	ⲁϥⲑⲁⲙⲓⲟ ⲙ̀ⲡⲓⲣⲱⲙⲓ.
I will praise my God.	He created man.
ⲧⲉⲛⲥ̀ⲙⲟⲩ ⲉ̀ⲡⲉϥⲣⲁⲛ.	ⲁⲩϭⲓ ⲙ̀ⲡⲓⲭ̀ⲗⲟⲙ.
We bless His name.	They received the crown.

The Verbs that Combine Between the Intransitive and Transitive Verbs

For example: ⲟⲩⲱⲛ (to open, to be opened).

| ⲡⲓⲣⲟ ⲁϥⲟⲩⲱⲛ. | The door was opened. (Intransitive). |

| ⲁϥⲟⲩⲱⲛ ⲛ̀ϫⲉ ⲡⲓⲣⲟ. | The door was opened. |
| ϯⲟⲩⲱⲛ ⲙ̀ⲡⲓⲣⲟ. | I open the door. (Transitive). |

Two-pronoun Verbs

These are verbs that take two pronouns: the first refers to the subject, and the second confirms the character of the subject.

ϣⲉ To go (in the past tense)	ⲕⲟⲧ To return (in the present tense)	ⲧⲱⲛ To arise (in the future tense)
ⲁⲓϣⲉⲛⲏⲓ — I went	ϯⲕⲟⲧ — I return	ϯⲛⲁⲧⲱⲛⲧ — I will arise
ⲁⲕϣⲉⲛⲁⲕ — You (sing. mas.) went	ⲕ̀ⲕⲟⲧⲕ — You (sing. mas.) return	ⲭ̀ⲛⲁⲧⲱⲛⲕ — You (sing. mas.) will arise
ⲁⲣⲉϣⲉⲛⲉ — You (sing. fem.) went	ⲧⲉⲕⲟϯ — You (sing. fem.) return	ⲧⲉⲣⲁⲧⲱⲟⲩⲛⲓ — You (sing. fem.) will arise
ⲁϥϣⲉⲛⲁϥ — He went	ϥ̀ⲕⲟⲧϥ — He returns	ϥ̀ⲛⲁⲧⲱⲛϥ — He will arise
ⲁⲥϣⲉⲛⲁⲥ — She went	ⲥ̀ⲕⲟⲧⲥ — She returns	ⲥ̀ⲛⲁⲧⲱⲛⲥ — She will arise
ⲁⲛϣⲉⲛⲁⲛ — We went	ⲧⲉⲛⲕⲟⲧ(ⲧ)ⲉⲛ — We return	ⲧⲉⲛⲛⲁⲧⲱⲛⲧⲉⲛ — We will arise
ⲁⲧⲉⲧⲉⲛϣⲉⲛⲱⲧⲉⲛ — You (pl.) went	ⲧⲉⲧⲉⲛⲕⲉⲧ ⲑⲏⲛⲟⲩ — You (pl.) return	ⲧⲉⲧⲉⲛⲛⲁⲧⲉⲛ ⲑⲏⲛⲟⲩ — You (pl.) will arise
ⲁⲩϣⲉⲛⲱⲟⲩ — They went	ⲥⲉⲕⲟⲧⲟⲩ — They return	ⲥⲉⲛⲁⲧⲱⲟⲩⲛⲟⲩ — They will arise

Verbs that are Joined to Words to Lead to Special Meanings

1. The word ⲉ̀ⲃⲟⲗ:

ⲭⲱ ⲉ̀ⲃⲟⲗ	To forgive	ⲟⲩⲱⲛϩ ⲉ̀ⲃⲟⲗ	To confess, to reveal
ⲭⲟⲩϣⲧ ⲉ̀ⲃⲟⲗ	To wait	ⲱϣ ⲉ̀ⲃⲟⲗ	To cry out
ⲥⲟⲩⲧⲱⲛ ⲉ̀ⲃⲟⲗ	To spread, to stretch out	ϫⲱⲕ ⲉ̀ⲃⲟⲗ	To complete
ⲱ̀ⲗⲓ ⲉ̀ⲃⲟⲗ	To take away	ⲫⲱⲣϣ ⲉ̀ⲃⲟⲗ	To spread, to unfold
ϩⲉⲓ ⲉ̀ⲃⲟⲗ	To fall	ϫⲱⲣ ⲉ̀ⲃⲟⲗ	To scatter, to disperse

ⲥⲟⲗⲥⲉⲗ ⲉ̀ⲃⲟⲗ	To adorn	ⲥⲓⲛⲓ ⲉ̀ⲃⲟⲗ	To separate, to pass by
ⲃⲱⲗ ⲉ̀ⲃⲟⲗ	To loosen, to destroy	ⲙⲟⲩⲛ ⲉ̀ⲃⲟⲗ	To continue
ⲥⲱⲣⲉⲙ ⲉ̀ⲃⲟⲗ	To go astray, to lose way	ⲫⲓⲣⲓ ⲉ̀ⲃⲟⲗ	To blossom
ⲫⲱⲧ ⲉ̀ⲃⲟⲗ	To run away	ϫⲱⲗ ⲉ̀ⲃⲟⲗ	To deny, to turn back

2. The word ⲛ̀ⲥⲁ:

ⲕⲱϯ ⲛ̀ⲥⲁ	To seek	ⲥⲱⲧⲉⲙ ⲛ̀ⲥⲁ	To obey
ⲥⲁϫⲓ ⲛ̀ⲥⲁ	To slander, to gossip	ⲙⲟϣⲓ ⲛ̀ⲥⲁ	To follow
ⲟⲩⲉϩ ⲛ̀ⲥⲁ	To follow	ϭⲟϫⲓ ⲛ̀ⲥⲁ	To chase away

Verbs that Accept the Pronoun with ⲙ̀ⲙⲟ″

The most famous verbs:

ⲟⲩⲛⲟϥ ⲙ̀ⲙⲟ″ To rejoice	ⲙ̀ⲧⲟⲛ ⲙ̀ⲙⲟ″ To rest, to repose	ϣⲟⲩϣⲟⲩ ⲙ̀ⲙⲟ″ To boast	ϩⲉⲣⲓ ⲙ̀ⲙⲟ″ To calm down, to be still
ϯⲟⲩⲛⲟϥ ⲙ̀ⲙⲟⲓ	ϯⲙ̀ⲧⲟⲛ ⲙ̀ⲙⲟⲓ	ϯϣⲟⲩϣⲟⲩ ⲙ̀ⲙⲟⲓ	ϯϩⲉⲣⲓ ⲙ̀ⲙⲟⲓ
ⲭ̀ⲟⲩⲛⲟϥ ⲙ̀ⲙⲟⲕ	ⲭ̀ⲙ̀ⲧⲟⲛ ⲙ̀ⲙⲟⲕ	ⲕϣⲟⲩϣⲟⲩ ⲙ̀ⲙⲟⲕ	ⲕϩⲉⲣⲓ ⲙ̀ⲙⲟⲕ
ⲧⲉⲟⲩⲛⲟϥ ⲙ̀ⲙⲟ	ⲧⲉⲙ̀ⲧⲟⲛ ⲙ̀ⲙⲟ	ⲧⲉϣⲟⲩϣⲟⲩ ⲙ̀ⲙⲟ	ⲧⲉϩⲉⲣⲓ ⲙ̀ⲙⲟ
ϥⲟⲩⲛⲟϥ ⲙ̀ⲙⲟϥ	ϥⲙ̀ⲧⲟⲛ ⲙ̀ⲙⲟϥ	ϥϣⲟⲩϣⲟⲩ ⲙ̀ⲙⲟϥ	ϥϩⲉⲣⲓ ⲙ̀ⲙⲟϥ
ⲥⲟⲩⲛⲟϥ ⲙ̀ⲙⲟⲥ	ⲥⲙ̀ⲧⲟⲛ ⲙ̀ⲙⲟⲥ	ⲥϣⲟⲩϣⲟⲩ ⲙ̀ⲙⲟⲥ	ⲥϩⲉⲣⲓ ⲙ̀ⲙⲟⲥ
ⲧⲉⲛⲟⲩⲛⲟϥ ⲙ̀ⲙⲟⲛ	ⲧⲉⲛⲙ̀ⲧⲟⲛ ⲙ̀ⲙⲟⲛ	ⲧⲉⲛϣⲟⲩϣⲟⲩ ⲙ̀ⲙⲟⲛ	ⲧⲉⲛϩⲉⲣⲓ ⲙ̀ⲙⲟⲛ
ⲧⲉⲧⲉⲛⲟⲩⲛⲟϥ ⲙ̀ⲙⲱⲧⲉⲛ	ⲧⲉⲧⲉⲛⲙ̀ⲧⲟⲛ ⲙ̀ⲙⲱⲧⲉⲛ	ⲧⲉⲧⲉⲛϣⲟⲩϣⲟⲩ ⲙ̀ⲙⲱⲧⲉⲛ	ⲧⲉⲧⲉⲛϩⲉⲣⲓ ⲙ̀ⲙⲱⲧⲉⲛ
ⲥⲉⲟⲩⲛⲟϥ ⲙ̀ⲙⲱⲟⲩ	ⲥⲉⲙ̀ⲧⲟⲛ ⲙ̀ⲙⲱⲟⲩ	ⲥⲉϣⲟⲩϣⲟⲩ ⲙ̀ⲙⲱⲟⲩ	ⲥⲉϩⲉⲣⲓ ⲙ̀ⲙⲱⲟⲩ

Lesson 17 ✠ Kinds of Verbs ✠

Exercises

1. Write the meaning of the following:

1. ϥⲧⲁⲓⲟ	8. ϥⲉⲣⲟⲩⲣⲟ	15. ⲧⲉⲧⲉⲛⲭⲟⲩϣⲧ ⲉ̀ⲃⲟⲗ
2. ⲕⲉⲣϩⲟⲧ	9. ϥⲛⲁϯϩⲁⲡ	16. ⲧⲉⲛⲟⲩⲛⲟⲩ ⲙ̀ⲙⲟⲛ
3. ⲧⲉⲛϯⲱⲟⲩ	10. ⲥⲉⲛⲁⲱⲛϧ	17. ⲁϥⲃⲱⲗ ⲉ̀ⲃⲟⲗ
4. ⲁⲥⲙⲟⲩ	11. ⲁⲣⲉⲧⲱⲟⲩⲛⲓ	18. ⲁⲧⲉⲣⲛⲏⲥⲧⲉⲩⲓⲛ
5. ⲁⲩⲛⲉϩⲡⲓ	12. ⲕⲱϣ ⲉ̀ⲃⲟⲗ	19. ⲧⲉⲧⲉⲛϣⲉⲛⲱⲧⲉⲛ
6. ⲁϥⲧⲱⲛϥ	13. ⲁⲥϥⲓⲣⲓ ⲉ̀ⲃⲟⲗ	20. ⲁϥⲉⲣϩ̀ⲙⲟⲧ ⲛⲁⲛ
7. ϯⲕⲟⲧ	14. ⲥⲉⲟⲩⲱⲛϩ ⲉ̀ⲃⲟⲗ	21. ⲥ̀ⲉⲣⲡ̀ⲣⲉⲥⲃⲉⲩⲓⲛ

2. The following verbs are in the negative form; write them in the affirmative form:

1. ⲙ̀ⲡⲟⲩϩⲉⲙⲥⲓ	5. ⲙ̀ⲡⲉϥϭⲓⲱⲙⲥ
2. ⲙ̀ⲡⲉⲛϣⲉⲛⲁⲛ	6. ⲙ̀ⲡⲉⲧⲉⲛⲙⲟϣⲓ
3. ⲙ̀ⲡⲓⲧⲱⲛⲧ	7. ⲙ̀ⲡⲉⲥⲁϫⲓ
4. ⲙ̀ⲡⲉⲥⲕⲟⲧⲥ	8. ⲙ̀ⲡⲉⲕⲉⲣϩⲱⲃ

3. Complete the following, according to the given example, by changing what is necessary to suit the subject:

1. ϯϣⲉⲛⲏⲓ ⲉ̀ⲧⲁⲣⲓ ⲟⲩⲟϩ ϯⲟⲩⲛⲟⲩ ⲙ̀ⲙⲟⲓ ϫⲉ Ⲫϯ ⲛⲉⲙⲏⲓ.
2. ⲕ̀ . . . .
3. ⲧⲉ . . . .
4. ϥ̀ . . . .
5. ⲥ̀ . . . .
6. ⲧⲉⲛ . . . .
7. ⲧⲉⲧⲉⲛ . . . .
8. ⲥⲉ . . . .

4. Translate the following to the English language:

ā. ⲁϥⲟⲩⲱⲛ ⲛ̀ϫⲉ Ⲫϯ ⲙ̀ⲫⲣⲟ ⲙ̀ⲡⲓⲡⲁⲣⲁⲇⲓⲥⲟⲥ ⲛ̀ⲧⲉ ⲡ̀ⲟⲩⲛⲟϥ.

ⲃ̄. ⲁϥⲧⲁⲥⲑⲟ ⲙ̀ⲡⲓⲣⲱⲙⲓ ⲉⲧⲉϥⲁⲣⲭⲏ ⲛ̀ⲕⲉⲥⲟⲡ.

ⲅ̄. ⲁⲕⲧⲱⲛⲕ ⲟⲩⲟϩ ⲁⲕⲥⲱϯ ⲙ̀ⲙⲟⲛ.

ⲇ̄. ⲧⲉⲛϣⲉⲛⲁⲛ ⲉ̀ϯⲉⲕⲕⲗⲏⲥⲓⲁ ⲛ̀ϣⲟⲣⲡ.

ⲉ̄. ⲥⲉⲕⲟⲧⲟⲩ ⲉ̀ⲡⲟⲩϭⲟⲓⲥ ϯⲛⲟⲩ.

ⲋ̄. ⲧⲉⲧⲉⲛⲛⲁϭⲓ ⲙ̀ⲡⲓⲭ̀ⲗⲟⲙ ϧⲉⲛ ⲧ̀ⲫⲉ.

ⲍ̄. ⲧⲉⲛϣⲉⲡϩ̀ⲓⲥⲓ ⲙ̀ⲙⲁⲓ ϧⲉⲛ ⲡⲁⲓⲕⲟⲥⲙⲟⲥ.

ⲏ̄. ⲥ̀ⲛⲁϩⲉⲙⲥⲓ ⲛⲉⲙ ⲛⲓⲙⲁⲣⲧⲩⲣⲟⲥ.

ⲑ̄. ⲛⲏⲉⲧⲁⲩϭⲓⲱⲙⲥ ⲁⲩⲭⲱⲗ ⲙ̀ⲡⲓⲇⲓⲁⲃⲟⲗⲟⲥ ⲉ̀ⲃⲟⲗ.

ⲓ̄. ⲡⲁϭⲟⲓⲥ Ⲓⲏⲥⲟⲩⲥ ⲛⲁⲭⲱ ⲛ̀ⲛⲁⲛⲟⲃⲓ ⲛⲏⲓ ⲉ̀ⲃⲟⲗ.

ⲓ̄ⲁ̄. ⲛⲓⲙⲁⲑⲏⲧⲏⲥ ⲁⲩⲙⲟϣⲓ ⲛ̀ⲥⲁ ⲡⲉⲛⲥⲱⲧⲏⲣ.

ⲓ̄ⲃ̄. ⲡ̀ϣⲏⲣⲓ ϥ̀ⲥⲱⲧⲉⲙ ⲛ̀ⲥⲁ ⲡⲉϥⲓⲱⲧ.

ⲓ̄ⲅ̄. ⲧⲉⲛⲕⲱϯ ⲛ̀ⲥⲁ ⲡⲉϥϩⲟ ⲙ̀ⲙⲏⲛⲓ.

ⲓ̄ⲇ̄. ⲛⲓⲁⲅⲓⲟⲥ ⲥⲉⲙ̀ⲧⲟⲛ ⲙ̀ⲙⲱⲟⲩ ϧⲉⲛ ⲡⲓⲡⲁⲣⲁⲇⲓⲥⲟⲥ ⲛ̀ⲧⲉ ⲡ̀ⲟⲩⲛⲟϥ.

ⲓ̄ⲉ̄. ⲧⲉⲛϣⲟⲩϣⲟⲩ ⲙ̀ⲙⲟⲛ ϧⲉⲛ ⲡⲓⲥ̀ⲧⲁⲩⲣⲟⲥ ⲛ̀ⲧⲉ ⲡⲉⲛϭⲟⲓⲥ Ⲓⲏ̄ⲥ̄.

ⲓ̄ⲋ̄. Ⲫϯ ϥ̀ϫⲱⲣ ⲉ̀ⲃⲟⲗ ⲛ̀ⲛⲓϫⲁϫⲓ ⲛ̀ⲧⲉ ϯⲉⲕⲕⲗⲏⲥⲓⲁ.

ⲓ̄ⲍ̄. ⲥⲉⲛⲁⲱⲛϧ ⲛ̀ϫⲉ ⲛⲏⲉⲧⲁⲩⲉⲛⲕⲟⲧ.

5. Translate to the Coptic language:

1. I will rise early and praise my God.

2. The Son was incarnate and became man.

3. The monk is still (calm) in his cell.

4. We went to church today.

5. The Lord did not destroy the Law, but fulfilled it.

6. The saints seek the face of the Lord always.

Lesson 18

ⲡⲓⲱϣ ⲙⲙⲁϩ ⲓⲏ

SPECIAL VERBS

Verbs that are Joined to Adverbs to Lead to Particular Meanings

ϣⲉ	To go	ⲓ̀	To come, to arrive
ϣⲉ ⲉ̀ϧⲟⲩⲛ	To go in (go inside)	ⲓ̀ ⲉ̀ϧⲟⲩⲛ	To come in (come inside)
ϣⲉ ⲉ̀ⲃⲟⲗ	To go out (go outside)	ⲓ̀ ⲉ̀ⲃⲟⲗ	To come out (come outside)
ϣⲉ ⲉ̀ⲡϣⲱⲓ	To ascend (go up)	ⲓ̀ ⲉ̀ⲡϣⲱⲓ	To ascend (come up)
ϣⲉ ⲉ̀ⲡⲉⲥⲏⲧ	To descend (go down)	ⲓ̀ ⲉ̀ⲡⲉⲥⲏⲧ	To descend (come down)
	ⲓ̀ⲛⲓ To offer, to bring		
ⲓ̀ⲛⲓ ⲉ̀ϧⲟⲩⲛ	To bring in	ⲓ̀ⲛⲓ ⲉ̀ⲃⲟⲗ	To bring out
ⲓ̀ⲛⲓ ⲉ̀ⲡϣⲱⲓ	To send up	ⲓ̀ⲛⲓ ⲉ̀ⲡⲉⲥⲏⲧ	To bring down

There are other verbs that accept the same four previous adverbs, for example:

ⲱ̀ⲗⲓ	To lift up, to raise	ϥⲁⲓ	To carry, to lift	ⲙⲟϣⲓ	To walk

We find in the Second Canticle the verb ⲓ̀ⲛⲓ ⲉ̀ⲙⲏⲣ (made pass through). Also we find in the litany of the travelers the verb ϣⲉ ⲉ̀ⲡϣⲉⲙⲙⲟ (to travel abroad).

Examples:

ⲁ̄ ⲁϥϣⲉ ⲉϧⲟⲩⲛ ⲟⲩⲟϩ ⲁϥⲓ ⲉⲃⲟⲗ.   He went in and he came out.

ⲃ̄ ⲁϥϣⲉⲛⲁϥ ⲉⲡϣⲱⲓ ⲉⲛⲓⲫⲏⲟⲩⲓ.   He ascended into the heavens.

ⲅ̄ ⲁϥⲓ ⲉⲡⲉⲥⲏⲧ ⲉⲁⲙⲉⲛϯ.   He descended to hades.

Verbs whose Object Comes in Their Middle

ⲉⲣⲫⲙⲉⲩⲓ	To mention, to remember	ϫⲉⲙⲡϣⲓⲛⲓ	To visit, to take care of
ⲉⲣⲡⲱⲃϣ	To forget, to neglect	ⲑⲱⲧⲡϩⲏⲧ	To console, to reassure

ⲁ̄ Ⲫϯ ϥⲥⲙⲟⲩ ⲉⲣⲟⲛ ⲟⲩⲟϩ ϥϫⲉⲙⲡⲉⲛϣⲓⲛⲓ ϧⲉⲛ ⲡⲉϥⲟⲩϫⲁⲓ.

ⲃ̄ ⲁⲛⲁⲣⲉϩ ⲉⲛⲉⲛⲱϣ ⲟⲩⲟϩ ⲙⲡⲉⲛⲉⲣⲡⲟⲩⲱⲃϣ.
We memorized our lessons and did not forget them.

ⲅ̄ ⲛⲁⲥⲛⲏⲟⲩ ⲥⲉⲉⲣⲡⲁⲙⲉⲩⲓ ϧⲉⲛ ⲛⲟⲩϣⲗⲏⲗ.
My brothers mention me in their prayers.

ⲇ̄ ϯⲡⲁⲣⲑⲉⲛⲟⲥ ⲥⲛⲁⲑⲱⲧⲡⲉⲕϩⲏⲧ ϧⲉⲛ ⲡⲥⲁϫⲓ ⲙⲠ̄ϭⲟⲓⲥ.

Derived Verbs

These verbs consist of two parts: one part is a noun of one of the members of the body which accept the possessor pronoun in its end, and the other part is a suitable verb for the mentioned member noun, for example:

1. The verb derived from **ⲣⲁⲧ** (foot) and **ⲟϩⲓ** (to stand) = to stand on his feet (to stand).

2. The verb derived from **ⲧⲟⲧ** (hand) and **ⲁⲙⲟⲛⲓ** (to hold) = to hold his hand (to be patient, to endure).

3. The verb derived from **ϫⲱ** (head) and **ϭⲛⲉ** (to subdue) = to bow his head (to submit, to obey).

4. The verb derived from **ⲣⲱ** (mouth) and **ⲭⲁ** (to put): to be silent (literally "to put the mouth").

Lesson 18 ✠ Special Verbs ✠

ὃϩι	To stand	ἀμονι	To hold	ϭνε	To bow, to incline	χα	To put
ρατ	Foot	τοτ	Hand	ϫω	Head	ρω	Mouth
αιὁϩι ἐρατ I stood [on my feet]		αιἀμονι ν̀τοτ I was patient		αιϭνεϫωι I submitted		αιχαρωι I was silent	
ακὁϩι ἐρατκ		ακἀμονι ν̀τοτκ		ακϭνεϫωκ		ακχαρωκ	
αρεὁϩι ἐρατϯ		αρεἀμονι ν̀τοτϯ		αρεϭνεϫω		αρεχαρω	
αϥὁϩι ἐρατϥ		αϥἀμονι ν̀τοτϥ		αϥϭνεϫωϥ		αϥχαρωϥ	
ασὁϩι ἐρατσ		ασἀμονι ν̀τοτσ		ασϭνεϫωσ		ασχαρωσ	
ανὁϩι ἐρατεν		ανἀμονι ν̀τοτεν		ανϭνεϫων		ανχαρων	
ατετενὁϩι ἐρατεν θηνοτ		ατετενἀμονι ν̀τεν θηνοτ		ατετενϭνεϫωτεν		ατετενχαρωτεν	
ατὁϩι ἐρατοτ		ατἀμονι ν̀τοτοτ		ατϭνεϫωοτ		ατχαρωοτ	

Examples

ᾱ ϯεκκλησια σϭνεϫωσ μ̀Πιχριστοσ.
The Church submits to Christ.

β̄ τενὁϩι ἐρατεν οτοϩ πιδιακον ϥὡϣ μ̀πιετατγελιον.
We stand and the deacon reads the Gospel.

γ̄ νιμαρτυροσ ατϣεπϧισι οτοϩ ατἀμονι ν̀τοτοτ.
The martyrs accepted the suffering and endured.

δ̄ ϯναϥαι μ̀πασταυροσ οτοϩ ϯναχαρωι.
I will carry my cross and be silent.

✠ Foundations of the Coptic Language ✠

Exercises

1. Write the meaning of the following:

1. ⲥⲉⲓⲛⲓ ⲉ̀ⲡϣⲱⲓ	6. ⲁⲧⲉⲣⲡⲉⲕⲙⲉⲩⲓ̀	11. ⲁⲛⲟ̀ϩⲓ ⲉ̀ⲣⲁⲧⲉⲛ
2. ⲧⲉⲧⲉⲛⲓ̀ ⲉ̀ⲡⲉⲥⲏⲧ	7. ⲁⲣⲉⲉⲣⲡⲉⲥⲱⲃϣ	12. ⲁϥⲁ̀ⲙⲟⲛⲓ ⲛ̀ⲧⲟⲧϥ
3. ⲁϥⲓⲛⲓ ⲉ̀ϧⲟⲩⲛ	8. ⲕ̀ⲭⲉⲙⲡⲟⲩϣⲓⲛⲓ	13. ⲧⲉⲧⲉⲛϭ̀ⲛⲉϫⲱⲧⲉⲛ
4. ⲧⲉⲣⲁϣⲉ ⲉ̀ⲃⲟⲗ	9. ϥ̀ϩⲱⲧⲡⲉⲛϩⲏⲧ	14. ⲥ̇ⲭⲁⲣⲱⲥ
5. ϯⲱⲗⲓ ⲉ̀ⲡϣⲱⲓ	10. ⲁⲓⲉⲣⲡⲉϥⲙⲉⲩⲓ̀	15. ⲁⲩⲟ̀ϩⲓ ⲉ̀ⲣⲁⲧⲟⲩ

2. Form a sentence from each group of the following words:

ⲁ̄ Ⲓⲏⲥⲟⲩⲥ, ⲥⲱⲧⲡ, ⲙⲁⲑⲏⲧⲏⲥ.
ⲃ̄ ⲁⲡⲟⲥⲧⲟⲗⲟⲥ, ϣⲉ ⲉ̀ⲃⲟⲗ, ⲗⲁⲟⲥ, ⲕⲁϩⲓ.
ⲅ̄ ⲓⲱⲧ, ϣⲁⲛϣ, ϣⲏⲣⲓ.
ⲇ̄ ⲡⲁⲣⲑⲉⲛⲟⲥ, ϫⲓⲙⲓ, ϩ̀ⲙⲟⲧ.
ⲉ̄ Ⲇⲓⲁⲃⲟⲗⲓⲥ, ⲉⲣⲡⲓⲣⲁⲍⲓⲛ, ϭⲟⲓⲥ.
ⲋ̄ ⲁⲅⲓⲟⲥ, ⲕⲱϯ ⲛ̀ⲥⲁ, ϩⲟ, Ⲫϯ.

3. Put the suitable number before every word in very vertical column:

1.	ⲡⲁϩⲏⲧ	ϫⲱϥ	ⲙ̀ⲙⲟⲕ	ϣⲉⲛⲁⲥ	ⲣⲁⲧϯ
2.	ⲡⲉⲕϩⲏⲧ	ϫⲱⲛ	ⲙ̀ⲙⲱⲟⲩ	ϣⲉⲛⲏⲓ	ⲣⲁⲧⲉⲛ ⲑⲏⲛⲟⲩ
3.	ⲡⲉϩⲏⲧ	ϫⲱⲧⲉⲛ	ⲙ̀ⲙⲟ	ϣⲉⲛⲁⲛ	ⲣⲁⲧϥ
4.	ⲡⲉϥϩⲏⲧ	ϫⲱ	ⲙ̀ⲙⲟⲥ	ϣⲉⲛⲱⲟⲩ	ⲣⲁⲧⲉⲛ
5.	ⲡⲉⲥϩⲏⲧ	ϫⲱⲓ	ⲙ̀ⲙⲱⲧⲉⲛ	ϣⲉⲛⲁⲕ	ⲣⲁⲧ
6.	ⲡⲉⲛϩⲏⲧ	ϫⲱⲟⲩ	ⲙ̀ⲙⲟⲓ	ϣⲉⲛⲁϥ	ⲣⲁⲧⲥ
7.	ⲡⲉⲧⲉⲛϩⲏⲧ	ϫⲱⲕ	ⲙ̀ⲙⲟⲛ	ϣⲉⲛⲱⲧⲉⲛ	ⲣⲁⲧⲟⲩ
8.	ⲡⲟⲩϩⲏⲧ	ϫⲱⲥ	ⲙ̀ⲙⲟϥ	ϣⲉⲛⲉ	ⲣⲁⲧⲕ

4. Translate to the English language:

ⲁ̄ Ⲫⲛⲟⲩϯ ϥ̀ⲱⲗⲓ ⲛ̀ⲛⲓⲛⲟⲃⲓ ⲛ̀ⲧⲉ ⲡⲓⲗⲁⲟⲥ.
ⲃ̄ ⲧⲉⲧⲉⲛϯ ⲛ̀ⲱⲟⲩ ⲙ̀ⲡⲓⲱⲓⲕ ⲛⲉⲙ ⲡⲓⲙⲱⲟⲩ.
ⲅ̄ ⲛⲓϫⲱⲙ ⲛⲏⲉ̀ⲧⲉⲙⲙⲁⲩ ⲛⲉ ⲛⲟⲩⲥ.

Lesson 18 ✠ Special Verbs ✠

ⲇ̄ ⲡⲓⲣⲱⲙⲓ ⲉⲧⲧⲏ ⲡⲉ ⲡ̇ⲟⲩⲣⲟ ⲛ̇ⲧⲉ ⲡⲁⲓⲗⲁⲟⲥ.

ⲉ̄ ⲁϥϯ ⲛⲁⲛ ⲙ̇ⲫⲏⲉⲧⲉ ⲫⲱⲛ ⲛ̇ⲟⲩϫⲁⲓ.

ⲋ̄ ϯⲛⲏⲥⲧⲓⲁ ⲛⲉⲙ ⲡⲓϣ̇ⲗⲏⲗ ⲥⲉⲓ̇ⲛⲓ ⲉⲃⲟⲗ ⲙ̇ⲡⲓⲇⲓⲁⲃⲟⲗⲟⲥ.

ⲍ̄ Ⲡⲓϭⲟⲓⲥ ϥ̇ⲥⲙⲟⲩ ⲉ̇ⲛⲁⲓϧⲉⲗⲗⲟⲓ ⲉⲧⲧⲁⲓⲏⲟⲩⲧ.

ⲏ̄ ⲛⲟⲩⲉⲩⲭⲏ ⲥⲉϣⲉⲛⲱⲟⲩ ⲉ̇ⲡϣⲱⲓ ϩⲱⲥ ϩⲁⲛⲑⲏⲥⲓⲁ ⲉⲩϣⲏⲡ.

ⲑ̄ ⲡⲓⲙⲟⲛⲁⲭⲟⲥ ϥ̇ϭⲓⲟⲩⲱⲓⲛⲓ ⲉⲃⲟⲗϩⲓⲧⲉⲛ ⲡⲓϣ̇ⲗⲏⲗ ⲛⲉⲙ ⲛⲓϩⲱⲥ.

ⲓ̄ Ⲫϯ ⲁϥⲉⲣϩⲙⲟⲧ ⲛⲁⲛ ⲙ̇ⲡⲓⲭⲱ ⲉⲃⲟⲗ ⲛ̇ⲧⲉ ⲛⲉⲛⲛⲟⲃⲓ.

ⲓⲁ̄ ⲧⲉⲛϣⲉⲡϩ̇ⲙⲟⲧ ⲛ̇ⲧⲟⲧϥ ⲟⲩⲟϩ ⲧⲉⲛⲟⲩⲱϣⲧ ⲙ̇ⲙⲟϥ.

ⲓⲃ̄ ⲛⲉⲛⲓⲟϯ ⲉⲑⲟⲩⲁⲃ ⲥⲉⲉⲣⲡⲉⲛⲙⲉⲩⲓ̇ ⲙ̇ⲡⲉⲙ̇ⲑⲟ ⲙ̇ⲡⲉⲛϭⲟⲓⲥ.

ⲓⲅ̄ ⲁⲣⲉⲓ̇ⲛⲓ ⲉ̇ϧⲟⲩⲛ ⲛ̇ⲟⲩⲗⲁⲟⲥ ⲉϥⲟϣ.

5. Sections from the Psalmody for analysis and translation:

✠ ⲁⲕϣⲉⲛⲁⲕ ⲉ̇ⲁ̇ⲙⲉⲛϯ: ⲁⲕⲓ̇ⲛⲓ ⲉ̇ⲡϣⲱⲓ:

ⲛ̇ⲧⲉⲭⲙⲁⲗⲱⲥⲓⲁ: ϧⲉⲛ ⲡⲓⲙⲁ ⲉ̇ⲧⲉⲙ̇ⲙⲁⲩ.

✠ ⲁⲕⲉⲣϩ̇ⲙⲟⲧ ⲛⲁⲛ ⲛ̇ⲕⲉⲥⲟⲡ: ⲛ̇ϯⲉⲗⲉⲩⲑⲉⲣⲓⲁ:

ϩⲱⲥ ⲛⲟⲩϯ ⲛ̇ⲁⲅⲁⲑⲟⲥ: ϫⲉ ⲁⲕⲧⲱⲛⲕ ⲁⲕⲥⲱϯ ⲙ̇ⲙⲟⲛ.

✠ ⲕⲁⲧⲁ ⲕⲟⲩϫⲓ ⲕⲟⲩϫⲓ: ⲧⲉⲛⲓ̇ⲣⲓ ⲙ̇ⲡⲉⲕⲙⲉⲩⲓ̇:

ⲧⲉⲛϯⲱⲟⲩ ⲙ̇ⲡⲉⲕⲣⲁⲛ: ⲱ̇ Ⲡⲁϭⲟⲓⲥ Ⲓⲏⲥⲟⲩⲥ.

✠ Ⲫⲁⲣⲁⲱ̇ ⲛⲉⲙ ⲛⲉϥϩⲁⲣⲙⲁ: ⲁⲩⲱⲙⲥ ⲉ̇ⲡⲉⲥⲏⲧ:

ⲛⲉⲛϣⲏⲣⲓ ⲙ̇Ⲡⲓⲥⲗ: ⲁⲩⲉⲣⲭⲓⲛⲓⲟⲣ ⲙ̇ⲫⲓⲟⲙ.

✠ ⲫⲁⲓ ⲡⲉ ⲡⲁⲛⲟⲩϯ: ϯⲛⲁϯⲱⲟⲩ ⲛⲁϥ.

Lesson 19
ⲡⲓⲱϣ ⲙ̅ⲙⲁϩ ⲓ̅ⲑ̅

Agent Nouns

An agent noun is formulated in the Coptic language by adding some articles with meanings to the beginning of a verb or word; therefore, the meaning of the agent noun is derived from the meaning of the verb or word.

1. An agent noun from ⲣⲉϥ- with a verb, meaning "maker"

ⲡⲓⲣⲉϥⲑⲁⲙⲓⲟ	The creator	ⲡⲓⲣⲉϥϯⲱⲙⲥ	The baptizer
ⲡⲓⲣⲉϥⲉⲣⲡⲉⲑⲛⲁⲛⲉϥ	The beneficent	ⲡⲓⲣⲉϥⲥⲱⲛⲧ	The creator
ⲡⲓⲣⲉϥⲉⲣⲛⲟⲃⲓ	The sinner	ⲡⲓⲣⲉϥⲥⲱϯ	The savior
ⲡⲓⲣⲉϥϯϩⲁⲡ	The judge	ⲡⲓⲣⲉϥⲉⲣϩⲉⲙⲓ	The guide, the leader
ⲡⲓⲣⲉϥⲛⲟϩⲉⲙ	The redeemer	ⲡⲓⲣⲉϥϯⲫⲁϩⲣⲓ	The healer
ⲡⲓⲣⲉϥϣⲉⲙϣⲓ	The servant	ⲡⲓⲣⲉϥⲧⲁⲛϧⲟ	The life-giver
ⲡⲓⲣⲉϥϣⲁⲛϣ	The provider	ⲡⲓⲣⲉϥⲙⲱⲟⲩⲧ	The dead
ⲡⲓⲣⲉϥϣⲉⲛϩⲏⲧ	The compassionate	ⲡⲓⲣⲉϥϯⲥⲃⲱ	The teacher
ⲡⲓⲣⲉϥⲥϧⲁⲓ	The writer	ⲡⲓⲣⲉϥⲭⲱ ⲉ̇ⲃⲟⲗ	The forgiver
ⲡⲓⲣⲉϥϩⲓⲱⲓϣ	The preacher	ϯⲣⲉϥϫⲫⲉ	The mother

2. An agent noun from ⲥⲁⲛ- with a noun, meaning "the worker in" or "the worker with"

ⲥⲁⲛⲱⲓⲕ	Baker	ⲥⲁⲛϣⲁⲣ	Book-binder
ⲥⲁⲛⲑⲱⲟⲩⲓ	Cobbler	ⲥⲁⲛⲁϥ	Butcher
ⲥⲁⲛⲁϫⲡ	Watchmaker	ⲥⲁⲛⲡⲉⲧϩⲱⲟⲩ	Evil doer

3. An agent noun composed of a relative pronoun (ⲛⲏⲉⲧ, ⲑⲏⲉⲧ, or ⲫⲏⲉⲧ) and a verb

ⲫⲏⲉⲧϩⲉⲙⲥⲓ	The one sitting	ⲑⲏⲉⲧϫⲟⲗϩ	The one clothed
ⲛⲏⲉⲑⲛⲁϩϯ	The believers	ⲫⲏⲉⲧϯ	The giver
ⲫⲏⲉⲧϣⲟⲡ	The one who exists	ⲛⲏⲉⲧⲉⲣϩⲟϯ	The ones who are afraid
ⲫⲏⲉⲧⲱⲗⲓ	The bearer	ⲫⲏⲉⲧϫⲟⲣ	The strong
ⲛⲏⲉⲧⲕⲱϯ	The seekers	ⲑⲏⲉⲧϫⲏⲕ ⲉ̀ⲃⲟⲗ	The perfect
ⲫⲏⲉⲑⲙⲟⲧⲉⲛ ⲙ̀ⲙⲟϥ	The one resting	ⲛⲏⲉⲑⲙⲏⲛ ⲉ̀ⲃⲟⲗ	The ones who perseveres on

Note that the agent noun of the verb ⲛⲁⲓ (to have mercy) is ⲛⲁⲏⲧ (merciful).

4. An agent noun composed of a verb and the relative pronoun ⲡⲉⲧ

ⲡⲉⲧⲥⲁϫⲓ	The speaker	ⲡⲉⲧⲱϣ	The reader
ⲡⲉⲧⲉ̀ⲙⲓ	The knower	ⲡⲉⲧⲁⲣⲉϩ	The guard

5. An agent noun with ⲉⲧ

ⲉⲧⲓⲣⲓ	The maker	ⲉⲧⲭⲏ	The one who is, who exists
ⲉⲧϭⲟⲥⲓ	The exalted	ⲉⲧⲱⲗⲓ	The bearer
ⲉⲑⲙⲏⲛ ⲉ̀ⲃⲟⲗ	The everlasting	ⲉⲧϣⲟⲡ	The one who exists, who dwells
ⲉⲧⲑⲱϩⲉⲙ	The one who calls (invites)	ⲉⲧⲥⲓⲛⲓ	The transient
ⲉⲧⲉⲣⲫⲁϧⲣⲓ	The healer	ⲉⲧϩⲏⲗ	The flying
ⲉⲑⲛⲏⲟⲩ	The coming	ⲉⲑⲙⲟϣⲓ	The walker

6. The agent noun is formulated from the following three verbs by using the letter `ⲉ̀`

ⲟⲩⲟⲛ	To own	→	ⲉ̀ⲟⲩⲟⲛ	Owner
ϣⲱⲧ	To trade	→	ⲉ̀ϣⲱⲧ	Trader
ⲕⲱⲧ	To build	→	ⲉ̀ⲕⲱⲧ	Builder

7. The agent noun from ϥⲁⲓ, meaning "bearer"

ⲡⲓϥⲁⲓⲟⲩⲧⲁϩ	The fruitful (the bearer of fruit)	ⲡⲓϥⲁⲓϣⲉⲛⲛⲟⲩϥⲓ	The preacher (the bearer of good news)

8. Various other kinds of agent nouns

1. ⲙⲁⲛ is an agent noun from the verb ⲙⲟⲛⲓ (to shepherd): ⲡⲓⲙⲁⲛⲉ̀ⲥⲱⲟⲩ (the shepherd).

2. ⲙⲁⲓ is an agent noun from the verb ⲙⲉⲓ (to love):

ⲡⲓⲙⲁⲓⲣⲱⲙⲓ	The lover of mankind	ⲡⲓⲙⲁⲓϩⲁⲧ	The lover of silver
ⲡⲓⲙⲁⲓϣⲉⲙⲙⲟ			The lover of strangers

3. ϣⲁⲙ is an agent noun from the verb ϣⲉⲙϣⲓ (to serve): ⲡⲓϣⲁⲙϭⲱⲙ (the gardener; the servant of the garden).

4. The leader or the guide, ⲡⲓϭⲁⲩⲙⲱⲓⲧ, originates from ϭⲓⲟⲩⲙⲱⲓⲧ, that is, "to take a way."

5. The two following agent nouns have the following composition:

ϩⲁⲙ (as a particle)	+	ϣⲉ (wood)	→	ϩⲁⲙϣⲉ (carpenter)
ϩⲁ (as a particle)	+	ⲛⲟⲩⲃ (gold)	→	ϩⲁⲛⲟⲩⲃ (goldsmith)

Exercises

1. Translate the following sentences:

ⲁ̄ Ⲫϯ ⲡⲉ ⲡⲓⲣⲉϥⲥⲱⲛⲧ ⲛ̀ⲧⲉ ⲡⲓⲕⲟⲥⲙⲟⲥ (ⲧ̀ⲫⲉ ⲛⲉⲙ ⲡ̀ⲕⲁϩⲓ).

ⲃ̄ Ⲓⲏⲥⲟⲩⲥ ⲡⲉ ⲡⲓⲣⲉϥⲛⲟϩⲉⲙ ⲛ̀ⲧⲉ ⲛⲓⲣⲱⲙⲓ.

ⲅ̄ ⲡⲉⲛϭⲟⲓⲥ ⲡⲉ ⲡⲓⲛⲁⲏⲧ ⲛⲉⲙ ⲡⲓⲣⲉϥϣⲉⲛϩⲏⲧ.

ⲇ̄ ⲡ̀ϣⲏⲣⲓ ⲙ̀Ⲫϯ ⲡⲉ ⲡⲓⲣⲉϥⲧⲁϩⲛⲟ ⲛ̀ⲧⲉ ⲛⲓⲣⲉϥⲉⲣⲛⲟⲃⲓ.

ⲉ̅ Ⲅⲁⲃⲣⲓⲏⲗ ⲡⲉ ⲡⲓϥⲁⲓϣⲉⲛⲛⲟⲩϥⲓ ⲛ̀ⲧⲉ ϯⲡⲁⲣⲑⲉⲛⲟⲥ.
ⲋ̅ Ⲓⲱⲁⲛⲛⲏⲥ ⲡⲉ ⲡⲓⲣⲉϥϯⲱⲙⲥ ⲛ̀ⲧⲉ Ⲓⲏⲥⲟⲩⲥ.
ⲍ̅ ⲡⲉⲛⲥⲱⲧⲏⲣ ⲡⲉ ⲡⲓⲣⲉϥⲭⲱ ⲉ̀ⲃⲟⲗ ⲛ̀ⲧⲉ ⲛⲉⲛⲁ̀ⲛⲟⲙⲓⲁ.
ⲏ̅ ⲛⲓⲁⲡⲟⲥⲧⲟⲗⲟⲥ ⲛⲉ ⲛⲓⲣⲉϥϯⲥⲃⲱ ⲛ̀ⲧⲉ ϯⲉⲕⲕⲗⲏⲥⲓⲁ.
ⲑ̅ Ⲙⲁⲣⲕⲟⲥ ⲡⲉ ⲡⲓⲣⲉϥϩⲓⲱⲓϣ ⲛ̀ⲧⲉ Ⲭⲏⲙⲓ.
ⲓ̅ ⲡⲓⲥⲓⲛⲓ ⲙ̀ⲙⲏⲓ ⲡⲉ ⲡⲓⲣⲉϥⲫⲁϧⲣⲓ ⲛ̀ⲧⲉ ⲛⲏⲉⲧϣⲱⲛⲓ.
ⲓⲁ̅ ⲡⲓⲉ̀ⲡⲓⲥⲕⲟⲡⲟⲥ ⲡⲉ ⲡⲓⲣⲉϥⲉⲣⲅⲉⲙⲓ ⲛ̀ⲧⲉ ⲛⲏⲉⲑⲛⲁϩϯ.
ⲓⲃ̅ ⲡⲓⲟⲩⲏⲃ ⲡⲉ ⲡⲓⲣⲉϥϣⲉⲙϣⲓ ⲛ̀ⲧⲉ ⲡⲓⲉⲣⲫⲉⲓ.
ⲓⲅ̅ ⲡⲟⲩⲣⲟ ⲡⲉ ⲡⲓⲣⲉϥϣⲁⲛϣ ⲛ̀ⲧⲉ ⲡⲓⲗⲁⲟⲥ.
ⲓⲇ̅ Ⲫⲛⲟⲩϯ ⲡⲉ ⲡⲓⲣⲉϥϯϩⲁⲡ ⲛ̀ⲧⲉ ϯⲟⲓⲕⲟⲩⲙⲉⲛⲏ.
ⲓⲉ̅ ⲁⲛⲟⲛ ⲛⲉ ⲛⲏⲉⲧⲕⲱϯ ⲛ̀ⲥⲁ ⲡ̀ϩⲟ ⲙ̀Ⲡⲓϭⲟⲓⲥ.
ⲓⲋ̅ ⲛ̀ⲑⲟϥ ⲡⲉ ⲫⲏⲉⲧϯ ϧⲣⲉ ⲛ̀ⲥⲁⲣⲝ ⲛⲓⲃⲉⲛ ⲉⲧⲟⲛϧ.
ⲓⲍ̅ Ⲓⲏⲥⲟⲩⲥ ⲡⲉ ⲫⲏⲉⲧⲱ̀ⲗⲓ ⲙ̀ⲫ̀ⲛⲟⲃⲓ ⲙ̀ⲡⲓⲕⲟⲥⲙⲟⲥ.
ⲓⲏ̅ ⲛ̀ⲑⲟϥ ⲡⲉ ⲡⲉⲛⲣⲉϥⲥⲱϯ ⲉ̀ⲃⲟⲗϧⲉⲛ ⲡ̀ⲧⲁⲕⲟ.
ⲓⲑ̅ ⲡⲉⲛⲟⲩⲣⲟ ⲡⲉ ⲫⲏⲉⲧϩⲉⲙⲥⲓ ϩⲓϫⲉⲛ ⲛⲓⲭⲉⲣⲟⲩⲃⲓⲙ.
ⲕ̅ Ⲓⲏⲥⲟⲩⲥ ⲡⲉ ⲡⲓⲙⲁⲓⲣⲱⲙⲓ ⲛ̀ⲁ̀ⲅⲁⲑⲟⲥ.
ⲕⲁ̅ Ⲙⲱⲩ̀ⲥⲏⲥ ⲡⲉ ⲡⲓⲃⲁⲧⲙⲱⲓⲧ ⲛ̀ⲧⲉ ⲛⲉⲛϣⲏⲣⲓ ⲙ̀Ⲡⲓⲥⲣⲁⲏⲗ.
ⲕⲃ̅ ⲛ̀ⲑⲟⲕ ⲟⲩⲙⲁⲓϣⲉⲙⲙⲟ ⲡⲉ.
ⲕⲅ̅ ⲡⲓⲥⲁⲛⲱⲓⲕ ⲡⲉ ⲡⲓⲣⲱⲙⲓ ⲉⲧⲓⲣⲓ ⲙ̀ⲡⲓⲱⲓⲕ.
ⲕⲇ̅ ⲡⲓⲥⲁⲛⲁϥ ⲡⲉ ⲡⲓⲣⲱⲙⲓ ⲉⲧϯ ⲉ̀ⲃⲟⲗ ⲙ̀ⲡⲓⲁϥ.
ⲕⲉ̅ ⲡⲓⲥⲁⲛⲁϫⲡ ⲡⲉ ⲡⲓⲣⲱⲙⲓ ⲉⲧⲉⲣϩⲱⲃ ϧⲉⲛ ⲛⲓⲁϫⲡ.
ⲕⲋ̅ ⲡⲓⲥⲁⲛⲑⲱⲟⲩⲓ̀ ⲡⲉ ⲡⲓⲣⲱⲙⲓ ⲉⲧⲓⲣⲓ ⲛ̀ⲛⲓⲑⲱⲟⲩⲓ̀.
ⲕⲍ̅ ⲡⲓϩⲁⲙϣⲉ ⲡⲉ ⲡⲓⲣⲱⲙⲓ ⲉⲧⲉⲣϩⲱⲃ ϧⲉⲛ ⲛⲓϣⲉ.
ⲕⲏ̅ ⲡⲓϩⲁⲛⲟⲩⲃ ⲡⲉ ⲡⲓⲣⲱⲙⲓ ⲉⲧⲉⲣϩⲱⲃ ϧⲉⲛ ⲡⲓⲛⲟⲩⲃ.
ⲕⲑ̅ ⲡⲓϣⲁⲙϭⲱⲙ ⲡⲉ ⲡⲓⲣⲉϥϣⲉⲙϣⲓ ⲛ̀ⲧⲉ ⲡⲓϭⲱⲙ.
ⲗ̅ ⲧⲉⲛϣϣ ϧⲉⲛ ⲡⲓϭⲱⲙ ⲛ̀ⲧⲉ ⲛⲓⲙⲟⲛⲁⲭⲟⲥ.

2. Analyze and translate:

✠ ⲡⲓⲱⲓⲕ ⲛ̀ⲧⲉ ⲡ̀ⲱⲛϧ: ⲉⲧⲁϥⲓ̀ ⲉ̀ⲡⲉⲥⲏⲧ:
ⲛⲁⲛ ⲉ̀ⲃⲟⲗϧⲉⲛ ⲧ̀ⲫⲉ: ⲁϥϯ ⲙ̀ⲡ̀ⲱⲛϧ ⲙ̀ⲡⲓⲕⲟⲥⲙⲟⲥ.

✠ ⲛ̀ⲑⲟ ϩⲱⲓ Ⲙⲁⲣⲓⲁ: ⲁⲣⲉϥⲁⲓ ϧⲉⲛ ⲧⲉⲛⲉϩⲓ:
ⲙ̀ⲡⲓⲙⲁⲛⲛⲁ ⲛ̀ⲛⲟⲏⲧⲟⲛ: ⲉⲧⲁϥⲓ̀ ⲉ̀ⲃⲟⲗϧⲉⲛ Ⲫⲓⲱⲧ.

✠ ⲁⲣⲉⲙⲁⲥϥ ⲁ̀ⲃⲛⲉ ⲑⲱⲗⲉⲃ: ⲁϥϯ ⲛⲁⲛ ⲙ̀ⲡⲉϥⲥⲱⲙⲁ:
ⲛⲉⲙ ⲡⲉϥⲥⲛⲟϥ ⲉⲧⲧⲁⲓⲏⲟⲩⲧ: ⲁⲛⲱⲛϧ ϣⲁ ⲉ̀ⲛⲉϩ.

3. Translate to the Coptic language:
1. The Creator of the heavens and the earth.
2. The Giver of life to the dead [people].
3. The judge of the city.
4. The Forgiver of our sins.
5. The Redeemer of our life.
6. This tree is fruitful.
7. The one who calls the sinners.
8. The giver (the one granting) of gifts.

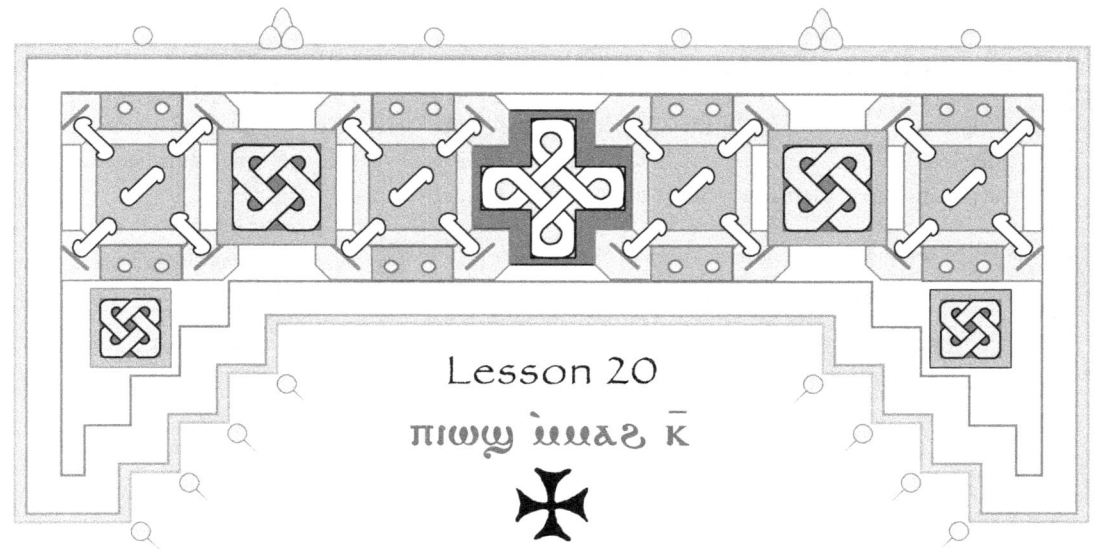

Lesson 20
ⲡⲓⲱϣ ⲙ̄ⲙⲁϩ ⲕ̄

VERBAL AND ABSTRACT NOUNS

1. The Gerund (the Verbal Noun)

It is formulated in two ways:

1. From the substance of the verb itself with the definite article, for example:

| ϯⲟⲩⲱⲙ | The eating (that is, the act of eating) | ⲡⲓⲛⲟϩⲉⲙ | The salvation (that is, the act of salvation) |

2. By using ϫⲓⲛ with the substance of the verb:

ⲡⲓϫⲓⲛⲙⲓⲥⲓ The birth	ⲡⲓϫⲓⲛⲓ̀ The coming	ⲡⲓϫⲓⲛⲥⲱⲧⲉⲙ The hearing
ⲡⲓϫⲓⲛϯⲱⲙⲥ The baptism	ⲡⲓϫⲓⲛϯ The giving	ⲡⲓϫⲓⲛⲥⲁϫⲓ The speaking
ⲡⲓϫⲓⲛⲙⲟϣⲓ The walking, the pursuit	ⲡⲓϫⲓⲛⲓⲣⲓ The work	ⲡⲓϫⲓⲛⲉⲣⲫⲙⲉⲩⲓ̀ The remembrance
ⲡⲓϫⲓⲛⲉⲣⲃⲟⲕⲓ The conception	ⲡⲓϫⲓⲛϭⲓⲥⲃⲱ The learning	ⲡⲓϫⲓⲛⲉⲣⲡⲱⲃϣ The forgetting
ⲡⲓϫⲓⲛⲟⲩⲱϣⲧ The worship	ⲡⲓϫⲓⲛⲙⲟⲩ The death	ⲡⲓϫⲓⲛⲉⲣϩⲩⲙⲛⲟⲥ The praising

When the definite article for singular masculine is used, the gerund here means the event itself, but if the definite article for singular feminine is used, the gerund indicates the way or manner in which the work is achieved, or how the event is completed.

ϯϫⲓⲛⲥⲁϫⲓ	ϯϫⲓⲛⲱϣ	ϯϫⲓⲛⲟⲩⲱϣⲧ
The manner of speaking	The way of reading	The manner of worshipping
ϯϫⲓⲛⲉⲣϩⲱⲃ	ϯϫⲓⲛⲉⲣⲟⲩⲱ	ϯϫⲓⲛⲉⲣⲃⲟⲕⲓ
The manner of work	The way of answering	The means of conception

The two marks ⲡϫⲓⲛⲧⲉ and ⲡϫⲓⲛⲑⲣⲉ are used also to obtain a gerund when there is a particular subject in the sentence, for example:

ⲧⲟⲧⲉ Ⲓⲏⲥⲟⲩⲥ ⲁ ⲡⲓⲡⲛⲉⲩⲙⲁ ⲟⲗϥ ⲉⲡϣⲁϥⲉ ⲉⲡϫⲓⲛⲧⲉ ⲡⲓⲇⲓⲁⲃⲟⲗⲟⲥ ⲉⲣⲡⲓⲣⲁⲍⲓⲛ ⲙ̄ⲙⲟϥ.

"Then Jesus was led up by the Spirit into the wilderness to be tempted by the devil" (Matthew 4:1).

The connected pronouns are attached to the previous marks, and they are conjugated as follows:

ⲡϫⲓⲛⲧⲁ-	ⲡϫⲓⲛⲧⲉⲥ-	ⲡϫⲓⲛⲑⲣⲓ-	ⲡϫⲓⲛⲑⲣⲉⲥ-
ⲡϫⲓⲛⲧⲉⲕ-	ⲡϫⲓⲛⲧⲉⲛ-	ⲡϫⲓⲛⲑⲣⲉⲕ-	ⲡϫⲓⲛⲑⲣⲉⲛ-
ⲡϫⲓⲛⲧⲉ-	ⲡϫⲓⲛⲧⲉⲧⲉⲛ-	ⲡϫⲓⲛⲑⲣⲉ-	ⲡϫⲓⲛⲑⲣⲉⲧⲉⲛ-
ⲡϫⲓⲛⲧⲉϥ-	ⲡϫⲓⲛⲧⲟⲩ-	ⲡϫⲓⲛⲑⲣⲉϥ-	ⲡϫⲓⲛⲑⲣⲟⲩ-

The two marks ⲡϫⲓⲛⲧⲉ and ⲡϫⲓⲛⲑⲣⲉ accept two prepositions ⲉ̀ and ϧⲉⲛ before them:

ⲁ̄ ⲉ̀ⲡϫⲓⲛⲧⲉⲧⲉⲛϣⲱⲡⲓ ⲛⲏⲓ.
That you (pl.) be mine.

ⲃ̄ ⲥⲱⲧⲉⲙ Ⲫϯ ⲉ̀ⲧⲁⲡⲣⲟⲥⲉⲩⲭⲏ ϧⲉⲛ ⲡϫⲓⲛⲧⲁⲧⲱⲃϩ.
O God, listen to my prayer at my praying; (or, when I pray).

ⲅ̄ ⲁϥⲣⲁϣⲓ ⲛ̀ϫⲉ ⲡⲓⲁⲗⲟⲩ ϧⲉⲛ ⲡϫⲓⲛⲑⲣⲉϥⲥⲱⲧⲉⲙ ⲉ̀ⲡⲁⲓⲥⲁϫⲓ.
The boy rejoiced at his hearing this word; (or, when he heard this word).

ⲇ̄ ϧⲉⲛ ⲡϫⲓⲛⲑⲣⲉⲛⲟϩⲓ ⲉ̀ⲣⲁⲧⲉⲛ ⲙ̀ⲡⲉⲕⲙ̀ⲑⲟ ⲥⲱⲙⲁⲧⲓⲕⲱⲥ.
When we stand before You bodily. (At our standing before You bodily).

Lesson 20 ✠ Verbal and Abstract Nouns ✠

ⲉ̄ ϧⲉⲛ ⲡ̀ϫⲓⲛⲑⲣⲟⲩⲛⲁⲩ ⲉ̀ⲣⲟⲕ.
When they saw you. (At their seeing you).

ⲋ̄ ϧⲉⲛ ⲡ̀ϫⲓⲛⲑⲣⲉϥⲓ̀ ⲛⲁⲛ ⲉ̀ϧⲟⲩⲛ ⲛ̀ϫⲉ ⲫ̀ⲛⲁⲩ ⲛ̀ϣⲱⲣⲡ.
When the morning hour comes to us. (At the coming of the morning hour to us).

2. Abstract Nouns

This is always in the feminine form, and it is formulated using the mark **ⲙⲉⲧ-** (**ⲙⲉⲑ-**):

ϯⲙⲉⲧⲓⲱⲧ	The fatherhood	ϯⲙⲉⲑⲛⲟⲩϯ	The divinity
ϯⲙⲉⲧⲁⲡⲟⲥⲧⲟⲗⲟⲥ	The apostolicity	ϯⲙⲉⲧϣⲏⲣⲓ	The sonship
ϯⲙⲉⲧⲣⲱⲙⲓ	The humanity	ϯⲙⲉⲧⲙⲁⲣⲧⲩⲣⲟⲥ	The martyrdom
ϯⲙⲉⲧⲟⲩⲣⲟ	The kingdom	ϯⲙⲉⲧϧⲉⲗⲗⲟ	The old age
ϯⲙⲉⲧⲙⲉⲑⲣⲉ	The testimony	ϯⲙⲉⲧⲟⲩⲏⲃ	The priesthood
ϯⲙⲉⲧⲁ̀ⲗⲟⲩ	The youth	ϯⲙⲉⲧⲙⲟⲛⲁⲭⲟⲥ	The monasticism
ϯⲙⲉⲧϭⲟⲓⲥ	The lordship	ϯⲙⲉⲧϫⲱⲣⲓ	The strength
ϯⲙⲉⲧⲙⲁⲓⲣⲱⲙⲓ	The love of mankind	ϯⲙⲉⲧⲟⲩⲁⲓ	The unity
ϯⲙⲉⲑⲛⲁⲏⲧ	The mercy	ϯⲙⲉⲧⲉ̀ⲡⲓⲕⲏⲥ	The humility
ϯⲙⲉⲧⲥⲁⲃⲉ	The wisdom	ϯⲙⲉⲧⲥⲟⲛ	The brotherhood
ϯⲙⲉⲧⲣⲉⲙⲣⲁⲩϣ	The meekness	ϯⲙⲉⲧⲛⲓϣϯ	The greatness
ϯⲙⲉⲧⲃⲱⲕ	The servitude	ϯⲙⲉⲧϣⲉⲛϩⲏⲧ	The compassion
ϯⲙⲉⲧϥⲁⲓⲣⲱⲟⲩϣ	The care	ϯⲙⲉⲑⲙⲏⲓ	The truth
ϯⲙⲉⲧϫⲁϫⲓ	The enmity	ϯⲙⲉⲧⲥⲁⲓⲉ̀	The beauty, splendor
ϯⲙⲉⲧⲣⲁⲙⲁⲟ̀	The richness	ϯⲙⲉⲧⲁ̀ⲅⲁⲑⲟⲥ	The goodness
ϯⲙⲉⲑⲛⲟⲩϫ	The lying	ϯⲙⲉⲧϩⲏⲕⲓ	The poverty
ϯⲙⲉⲧⲱⲟⲩⲛ̀ϩⲏⲧ	The patience	ϯⲙⲉⲧϭⲉⲛⲛⲉ	The laziness
ϯⲙⲉⲧⲣⲉϥⲉⲣⲛⲏⲫⲓⲛ	The watchfulness	ϯⲙⲉⲧⲕⲟⲩϫⲓ	The smallness

✠ Foundations of the Coptic Language ✠

Exercises

1. Write the meaning of the following:

1. ⲡⲉϥϫⲓⲛⲙⲓⲥⲓ	9. ⲡⲟⲩϫⲓⲛϯ	17. ⲡⲉϫⲓⲛⲉⲣⲃⲟⲕⲓ
2. ⲡⲉⲕϫⲓⲛⲓ̀	10. ⲡⲉϥϫⲓⲛⲙⲟⲩ	18. ⲡⲉⲛϫⲓⲛⲉⲣϩⲩⲙⲛⲟⲥ
3. ⲡⲟⲩϫⲓⲛⲓ̀ⲣⲓ	11. ⲡⲉϫⲓⲛⲙⲟϣⲓ	19. ⲡⲉⲧⲉⲛϫⲓⲛⲟⲩⲱϣⲧ
4. ⲧⲉⲕϫⲓⲛⲥⲁϫⲓ	12. ⲧⲉⲥϫⲓⲛⲉⲣⲃⲟⲕⲓ	20. ⲧⲁϫⲓⲛⲉⲣⲟⲩⲱ
5. ⲧⲉϥⲙⲉⲑⲛⲟⲩϯ	13. ⲧⲉⲛⲙⲉⲧⲃⲱⲕ	21. ⲧⲟⲩⲙⲉⲧⲁⲡⲟⲥⲧⲟⲗⲟⲥ
6. ⲧⲉⲛⲙⲉⲧⲥⲟⲛ	14. ⲧⲉⲧⲉⲛⲙⲉⲧϫⲱⲣⲓ	22. ⲧⲉⲥⲙⲉⲧⲣⲁⲙⲁⲟ̀
7. ⲧⲁⲙⲉⲧϩⲏⲕⲓ	15. ⲧⲉⲕⲙⲉⲧⲓⲱⲧ	23. ⲧⲟⲩⲙⲉⲧⲙⲁⲣⲧⲩⲣⲟⲥ
8. ⲧⲉⲙⲉⲧⲛⲓϣϯ	16. ⲧⲉϥⲙⲉⲧⲟⲩⲏⲃ	24. ⲧⲉⲕⲙⲉⲧⲱⲟⲩⲛ̀ϩⲏⲧ

2. Translate to the English language:

ā. ⲡⲓϫⲓⲛⲓ̀ ⲛ̀ⲧⲉ ⲡⲓⲙⲁⲓⲣⲱⲙⲓ.
b̄. ⲡⲓϫⲓⲛⲙⲓⲥⲓ ⲛ̀ⲧⲉ Ⲉⲙⲙⲁⲛⲟⲩⲏⲗ.
c̄. ϯⲙⲉⲑⲛⲟⲩϯ ⲛ̀ⲧⲉ ⲡⲓϣⲏⲣⲓ ⲙ̀ⲙⲟⲛⲟⲅⲉⲛⲏⲥ.
d̄. ⲧⲉⲛⲙⲉⲧⲟⲩⲁⲓ ϧⲉⲛ Ⲡⲓϭⲟⲓⲥ.
ē. ⲡⲓϫⲓⲛⲥⲱⲧⲉⲙ ⲛ̀ⲥⲁ ⲛⲓⲥⲁϫⲓ ⲛ̀ⲧⲉ Ⲫⲛⲟⲩϯ.
f̄. ⲧⲉϥⲙⲉⲧⲟⲩⲏⲃ ⲛⲉⲙ ⲧⲉϥⲙⲉⲧϭⲟⲓⲥ.
z̄. ⲧⲟⲩⲙⲉⲧⲥⲁⲃⲉ ⲛⲉⲙ ⲧⲟⲩⲙⲉⲧⲣⲉⲙⲣⲁⲩϣ.
h̄. ⲧⲉⲕⲙⲉⲑⲛⲁⲏⲧ ⲛⲉⲙ ⲛⲉⲕⲙⲉⲧϣⲉⲛϩⲏⲧ.
θ̄. ⲁⲕⲉⲣⲫⲙⲉⲩⲓ̀ ⲙ̀ⲡⲓⲥⲟⲛⲓ ϧⲉⲛ ⲧⲉⲕⲙⲉⲧⲟⲩⲣⲟ.
ī. ⲡⲓϧⲏⲃⲥ ⲛ̀ⲧⲉ ϯⲙⲉⲧⲙⲟⲛⲁⲭⲟⲥ.
īā. ⲡⲓⲭ̀ⲗⲟⲙ ⲛ̀ⲧⲉ ϯⲙⲉⲧⲙⲁⲣⲧⲩⲣⲟⲥ.
īb̄. ⲧⲉϥⲙⲉⲧⲣⲁⲙⲁⲟ̀ ⲛⲉⲙ ⲧⲉⲛⲙⲉⲧϩⲏⲕⲓ.
īc̄. ⲧⲉⲕⲙⲉⲧⲛⲓϣϯ ϧⲉⲛ ⲧⲉⲕⲙⲉⲧⲙⲁⲓⲣⲱⲙⲓ.

3. Write the meaning of the following sentences:

1. ϧⲉⲛ ⲡ̀ϫⲓⲛⲧⲁⲓ̀ ⲉ̀ϧⲟⲩⲛ.	6. ϧⲉⲛ ⲡ̀ϫⲓⲛⲧⲉⲕⲟⲩⲱϣⲧ.
2. ⲉ̀ⲡ̀ϫⲓⲛⲧⲟⲩⲁⲣⲉϩ ⲉ̀ⲛⲟⲩⲱϣ.	7. ⲉ̀ⲡ̀ϫⲓⲛⲧⲁϭⲓⲥⲃⲱ.
3. ϧⲉⲛ ⲡ̀ϫⲓⲛⲑⲣⲉϥⲟ̀ϩⲓ ⲉ̀ⲣⲁⲧϥ.	8. ϧⲉⲛ ⲡ̀ϫⲓⲛⲑⲣⲟⲩϣⲉⲡⲓⲕⲁϩ.

Lesson 20 ✠ Verbal and Abstract Nouns ✠

4. ⲉ̀ⲡϫⲓⲛⲑⲣⲉⲛⲉⲣϩⲩⲙⲛⲟⲥ.
5. ϧⲉⲛ ⲡ̀ϫⲓⲛⲑⲣⲉⲥⲙⲓⲥⲓ.
9. ⲉ̀ⲡϫⲓⲛⲑⲣⲉⲧⲉⲛⲉⲣⲫⲙⲉⲩⲓ̀.
10. ϧⲉⲛ ⲡ̀ϫⲓⲛⲑⲣⲉⲕϣⲉⲛⲁⲕ ⲉ̀ⲡϣⲱⲓ.

4. From the Psalmody, for analysis and translation:

ⲁ̅ ⲟⲩⲁⲓ ⲡⲉ ⲉ̀ⲃⲟⲗϧⲉⲛ ⲥ̀ⲛⲁⲩ: ⲟⲩⲙⲉⲑⲛⲟⲩϯ ⲉⲥⲧⲟⲩⲃⲏⲟⲩⲧ: ⲛⲉⲙ ⲟⲩⲙⲉⲧⲣⲱⲙⲓ ⲉⲥⲟⲩⲁⲃ. (From Sunday Theotokia)

ⲃ̅ ⲁⲩⲉⲣϣⲁⲓ ⲛⲉⲙⲁϥ ϧⲉⲛ ⲧⲉϥⲙⲉⲧⲟⲩⲣⲟ. (From Morning Doxology)

ⲅ̅ ϧⲉⲛ ⲟⲩⲙⲉⲧϥⲁⲓⲣⲱⲟⲩϣ ⲛ̀ⲧⲉ ⲧⲉⲕⲙⲉⲧⲁⲅⲁⲑⲟⲥ: ⲁⲕⲣⲓⲕⲓ ⲛ̀ⲛⲓⲫⲏⲟⲩⲓ̀: ⲁⲕⲓ̀ ⲉ̀ⲡⲉⲥⲏⲧ ϣⲁⲣⲟⲛ. (From Monday Psali)

ⲇ̅ ⲁϥϧⲱⲧⲉⲃ ϧⲉⲛ ⲟⲩϫⲱⲕ ⲛ̀ⲧⲙⲉⲧϫⲁϫⲓ. (From Monday Theotokia)

ⲉ̅ ⲱ̀ ϯⲧⲓⲙⲏ ⲛ̀ⲧⲉ ϯϫⲓⲛⲉⲣⲃⲱⲕⲓ ⲛ̀ⲧⲉ ϯⲛⲉϣⲓ ⲙ̀ⲡⲁⲣⲑⲉⲛⲓⲕⲏ ⲟⲩⲟϩ ⲛ̀ⲑⲉⲟⲧⲟⲕⲟⲥ. (From Thursday Theotokia)

ⲋ̅ ⲙ̀ⲡⲉⲟⲩⲁⲅⲙⲟⲥ ⲉⲣϣⲟⲣⲡ ⲉ̀ⲡⲓϫⲓⲛⲙⲓⲥⲓ. ⲙ̀ⲡⲉ ⲡⲓϫⲓⲛⲙⲓⲥⲓ ⲃⲱⲗ ⲉ̀ⲃⲟⲗ ⲛ̀ⲧⲉⲥⲡⲁⲣⲑⲉⲛⲓⲁ. (From Thursday Theotokia)

5. Translate to the Coptic language:

1. The fatherhood and the sonship and the brotherhood.
2. The youth and the manhood and the old age.
3. The learning and the remembrance and the forgetfulness.
4. The divinity of the Holy Spirit.
5. The monasticism of the fathers and their unity.
6. The manner of your speech and the way of your answer.

Review Exercises 4

On Lessons 16 to 20

1. Write the meaning of the following:

1. ϥⲉⲣϩⲙⲟⲧ ⲛⲁⲛ	12. ⲥⲉⲟⲩⲛⲟϥ ⲙ̀ⲙⲱⲟⲩ	23. ⲛⲏⲉⲑⲛⲁϩϯ
2. ⲧⲉⲛϯⲱⲟⲩ ⲛⲁϥ	13. ⲁⲛⲓ ⲉ̀ϧⲟⲩⲛ	24. ⲡⲉϥϫⲓⲛⲓ
3. ⲥⲉϭⲓⲱⲙⲥ	14. ⲧⲉϣⲟⲩϣⲟⲩ ⲙ̀ⲙⲟ	25. ⲡⲟⲩϫⲓⲛϯ
4. ⲧⲉⲧⲉⲛϭⲓⲥⲃⲱ	15. ⲁⲩⲧⲟⲛ ⲙ̀ⲙⲱⲟⲩ	26. ⲧⲁⲙⲉⲧϣⲏⲣⲓ
5. ⲁϥⲓⲛⲓ ⲉ̀ⲡ̀ϣⲱⲓ	16. ⲡⲁⲣⲉϥϩⲛⲟϩⲉⲙ	27. ⲡⲉⲕϫⲓⲛⲓⲣⲓ
6. ϯϣⲉⲡϩ̀ⲙⲟⲧ	17. ⲡⲉⲛⲣⲉϥⲧⲁⲛϧⲟ	28. ⲧⲉϥⲙⲉⲧⲛⲓϣϯ
7. ϥⲛⲁⲧⲱⲛϥ	18. ⲧⲉϥⲣⲉϥϫ̀ⲫⲉ	29. ⲧⲟⲩⲙⲉⲧⲣⲁⲙⲁⲟ
8. ⲁⲕϣⲉⲛⲁⲕ	19. ⲡⲟⲩⲣⲉϥϩⲓⲱⲓϣ	30. ⲧⲉⲛⲙⲉⲧⲟⲩⲁⲓ
9. ⲁⲥⲉⲣϩⲟϯ	20. ⲡⲉⲕⲣⲉϥϣⲉⲙϣⲓ	31. ⲧⲉⲕⲙⲉⲧⲓⲱⲧ
10. ϥ̀ⲭⲱ ⲉ̀ⲃⲟⲗ	21. ⲡⲉⲥϥⲁⲓϣⲉⲛⲛⲟⲩϥⲓ	32. ⲧⲉⲧⲉⲛⲙⲉⲧⲥⲟⲛ
11. ⲧⲉⲛϫⲟⲩϣⲧ ⲉ̀ⲃⲟⲗ	22. ⲫⲏⲉⲧϣⲟⲡ	33. ⲡⲉⲛϫⲓⲛⲉⲣϩⲩⲙⲛⲟⲥ

2. Translate to the English language:

ⲁ̄ ⲁϥⲓ ⲉ̀ⲡⲉⲥⲏⲧ ⲉ̀ⲡⲉⲛⲕⲟⲥⲙⲟⲥ ⲟⲩⲟϩ ⲁϥϣⲉⲛⲁϥ ⲉ̀ⲡ̀ϣⲱⲓ ⲉ̀ⲛⲓⲫⲏⲟⲩⲓ ⲟⲩⲟϩ ⲁϥϩⲉⲙⲥⲓ ϧⲉⲛ ⲛⲏⲉⲧϭⲟⲥⲓ.

ⲃ̄ ⲛⲓⲁⲅⲅⲉⲗⲟⲥ ⲥⲉⲟ̀ϩⲓ ⲉ̀ⲣⲁⲧⲟⲩ ⲙ̀ⲡⲉϥⲙ̀ⲑⲟ ⲛ̀ⲥⲏⲟⲩ ⲛⲓⲃⲉⲛ.

ⲅ̄ ⲁⲩϩⲓⲱⲓϣ ⲛ̀ϫⲉ ⲛⲓⲁⲡⲟⲥⲧⲟⲗⲟⲥ ϧⲉⲛ ⲡⲓⲉⲩⲁⲅⲅⲉⲗⲓⲟⲛ.

ⲇ̄ Ⲫϯ ϥⲉⲣⲡ̀ⲱⲃϣ ⲁⲛ ⲛ̀ⲧⲉϥⲇⲓⲁⲑⲏⲕⲏ.

Review Exercises 4 ✠ On Lessons 16 to 20 ✠

ⲉ̄   ϧⲉⲛ ⲡ̇ϫⲓⲛⲧⲉ ⲡⲓⲇⲓⲁⲕⲟⲛ ⲱϣ ⲛ̇ⲛⲓϫⲓⲛⲱϣ ⲉⲑⲟⲩⲁⲃ ϧⲉⲛ ϯⲉⲕⲕⲗⲏⲥⲓⲁ, ⲧⲉⲛⲭⲁⲣⲱⲛ ⲟⲩⲟϩ ⲧⲉⲛⲥⲱⲧⲉⲙ ϧⲉⲛ ⲟⲩϩⲟϯ ⲟⲩⲟϩ ϧⲉⲛ ⲟⲩⲙⲉⲧϥⲁⲓⲣⲱⲟⲩϣ.

3. There is a single mistake in each sentence. Correct it:

ⲁ̄   ⲁⲥⲙⲓⲥⲓ ϯⲡⲁⲣⲑⲉⲛⲟⲥ ⲛ̇Ⲓⲏⲥⲟⲩⲥ.
ⲃ̄   ⲧⲉⲛⲁϣⲗⲏⲗ ϧⲉⲛ ⲧⲉⲣⲓ.
ⲅ̄   ⲁϥⲉⲣⲟⲩⲣⲟ ⲁⲛ.
ⲇ̄   ⲁⲕⲁⲣⲉϩ ⲛ̇ⲛⲓⲯⲁⲗⲙⲟⲥ.
ⲉ̄   ⲕ̇ⲛⲁϩⲱⲥ ⲛⲉⲙ ⲛⲉⲕⲥ̅ⲛⲏⲟⲩ.

4. The following verses are from the gospel of St. John. Find out their meaning:

ⲁ̄   Ⲫ̇ⲓⲱⲧ ⲙⲉⲓ ⲙ̇ⲡⲓϣⲏⲣⲓ.
ⲃ̄   ⲁⲛⲟⲕ ⲡⲉ ⲡⲓⲱⲓⲕ ⲛ̇ⲧⲉ ⲡ̇ⲱⲛϧ.
ⲅ̄   ⲁⲛⲟⲕ ⲡⲉ ⲫ̇ⲟⲩⲱⲓⲛⲓ ⲙ̇ⲡⲓⲕⲟⲥⲙⲟⲥ.
ⲇ̄   ⲫⲁⲓ ⲡⲉ ⲡⲓⲡ̇ⲣⲟⲫⲏⲧⲏⲥ ⲉⲑⲛⲏⲟⲩ ⲉ̇ⲡⲓⲕⲟⲥⲙⲟⲥ.
ⲉ̄   ⲛⲉⲛⲓⲟϯ ⲁⲩⲟⲩⲱϣⲧ ϩⲓϫⲉⲛ ⲡⲁⲓⲧⲱⲟⲩ.
ⲋ̄   ⲁⲛⲟⲕ ⲡⲉ ⲫⲏⲉⲧⲥⲁϫⲓ ⲛⲉⲙⲉ.
ⲍ̄   ⲁⲛⲟⲕ ⲁⲓ̇ⲓ ϧⲉⲛ ⲫ̇ⲣⲁⲛ ⲙ̇ⲡⲁⲓⲱⲧ.
ⲏ̄   ⲁⲛⲟⲕ ⲡⲉ ⲡⲓⲱⲓⲕ ⲉⲧⲟⲛϧ ⲉⲧⲁϥⲓ̇ ⲉ̇ⲡⲉⲥⲏⲧ ⲉ̇ⲃⲟⲗϧⲉⲛ ⲧ̇ⲫⲉ.
ⲑ̄   ⲡⲓⲡ̅ⲛⲉⲩⲙⲁ ⲡⲉ ⲉⲧⲧⲁⲛϧⲟ.
ⲓ̄   ⲡⲓⲙⲓⲥⲓ ⲉ̇ⲃⲟⲗϧⲉⲛ ϯⲥⲁⲣⲝ ⲟⲩⲥⲁⲣⲝ ⲡⲉ ⲟⲩⲟϩ ⲡⲓⲙⲓⲥⲓ ⲉ̇ⲃⲟⲗϧⲉⲛ ⲡⲓⲡ̅ⲛⲉⲩⲙⲁ ⲟⲩⲡ̅ⲛⲉⲩⲙⲁ ⲡⲉ.
ⲓ̄ⲁ   ⲙ̇ⲙⲟⲛ ⲟⲩⲡ̇ⲣⲟⲫⲏⲧⲏⲥ ⲉϥⲧⲁⲓⲏⲟⲩⲧ ϧⲉⲛ ⲑⲏⲉ̇ⲧⲉ ⲑⲱϥ ⲙ̇ⲃⲁⲕⲓ.
ⲓ̄ⲃ   ⲁϥⲛⲁϩϯ ⲛⲉⲙ ⲡⲉϥⲏⲓ ⲧⲏⲣϥ.
ⲓ̄ⲅ   ⲁⲛⲟⲛ ⲁⲛⲉ̇ⲙⲓ ⲟⲩⲟϩ ⲁⲛⲛⲁϩϯ ϫⲉ ⲛ̇ⲑⲟⲕ ⲡⲉ Ⲡⲓⲭⲣⲓⲥⲧⲟⲥ ⲡ̇ϣⲏⲣⲓ ⲙ̇Ⲫ̇ⲛⲟⲩϯ ⲉⲧⲟⲛϧ.
ⲓ̄ⲇ   ⲟⲩⲟⲛ ⲛⲓⲃⲉⲛ ⲉⲧⲓ̇ⲣⲓ ⲙ̇ⲡⲓⲛⲟⲃⲓ ⲟⲩⲃⲱⲕ ⲛ̇ⲧⲉ ⲫ̇ⲛⲟⲃⲓ ⲡⲉ.
ⲓ̄ⲉ   ⲡⲁⲓⲱⲧ ⲉⲑⲛⲁϯⲱⲟⲩ ⲛⲏⲓ.

Exam 4
On Lessons 16 to 20

1. Write the meaning of the following words:

1. ⲧⲁⲙⲉⲧⲟⲩⲣⲟ	7. ⲧⲉⲕⲙⲉⲧⲉⲡⲓⲕⲏⲥ	13. ⲧⲁⲓⲙⲉⲧⲙⲟⲛⲁⲭⲟⲥ
2. ⲡⲁⲓϫⲓⲛⲙⲓⲥⲓ	8. ⲡⲁⲓⲣⲉϥⲉⲣⲛⲟⲃⲓ	14. ⲡⲁⲓϫⲓⲛⲉⲣϩⲩⲙⲛⲟⲥ
3. ⲧⲁⲓⲙⲉⲧϭⲟⲓⲥ	9. ⲧⲉⲧⲉⲛⲙⲉⲧⲓⲱⲧ	15. ⲧⲉⲕⲙⲉⲧⲙⲁⲓⲣⲱⲙⲓ
4. ⲡⲉⲛϫⲓⲛⲓ̀	10. ⲡⲟⲩϫⲓⲛⲟⲩⲱϣⲧ	16. ⲛⲁⲓⲙⲉⲧⲑⲉⲣⲉⲧ
5. ⲧⲁⲓⲙⲉⲧⲟⲩⲁⲓ	11. ⲧⲉⲛⲙⲉⲧϣⲏⲣⲓ	17. ⲧⲟⲩⲙⲉⲧⲱⲟⲩⲛϩⲏⲧ
6. ⲡⲁⲓⲣⲉϥϩⲓⲱⲓϣ	12. ⲛⲁⲓⲣⲉϥϣⲉⲙϣⲓ	18. ⲡⲉⲧⲉⲛϫⲓⲛⲓⲣⲓ

2. Write the meaning of the following verbs:

1. ϯⲛⲁϩⲱⲥ	7. ⲕⲃⲓⲟⲩⲱⲓⲛⲓ	13. ⲁⲥⲟϩⲓ ⲉⲣⲁⲧⲥ
2. ⲁϥⲭⲁⲣⲱϥ	8. ⲧⲉⲛⲉⲣⲯⲁⲗⲓⲛ	14. ϯϣⲟⲩϣⲟⲩ ⲙ̀ⲙⲟⲓ
3. ⲥⲉϯⲧⲁⲓⲟ	9. ⲁⲓⲱϣ ⲉ̀ⲃⲟⲗ	15. ⲁⲛϫⲉⲙⲡⲟⲩⲱⲓⲛⲓ
4. ⲁϥⲉⲣⲟⲩⲣⲟ	10. ⲧⲉⲟⲩⲛⲟϥ ⲙ̀ⲙⲟ	16. ⲥⲉⲙ̀ⲧⲟⲛ ⲙ̀ⲙⲱⲟⲩ
5. ⲥⲉⲓ̀ ⲉ̀ⲡϣⲱⲓ	11. ⲁϥⲑⲱⲧⲡⲉⲕϩⲏⲧ	17. ⲁⲕϣⲉⲛⲁⲕ ⲉ̀ⲡⲉⲥⲏⲧ
6. ⲕ̀ⲉⲣⲡⲁⲙⲉⲩⲓ̀	12. ⲧⲉⲛϣⲉ ⲉ̀ϧⲟⲩⲛ	18. ⲁϥⲓⲛⲓ ⲉ̀ⲃⲟⲗ

3. Translate to the English language:

ⲁ̄ Ⲫϯ ⲁϥⲉⲣϩⲙⲟⲧ ⲛⲁⲛ ⲙ̀ⲡⲓⲭⲱ ⲉ̀ⲃⲟⲗ ⲛ̀ⲧⲉ ⲛⲉⲛⲛⲟⲃⲓ.

ⲃ̄ ⲧⲉⲛⲕⲱϯ ⲛ̀ⲥⲁ ⲡ̀ϩⲟ ⲙ̀Ⲡⲓϭⲟⲓⲥ ⲛ̀ⲥⲏⲟⲩ ⲛⲓⲃⲉⲛ.

Exam 4 ✠ On Lessons 16 to 20 ✠

ⲅ̄ ⲁϥⲓ̀ ⲉⲡⲉⲥⲏⲧ ⲉⲡⲉⲛⲕⲟⲥⲙⲟⲥ ⲉ̀ⲡϫⲓⲛⲑⲣⲉϥⲥⲱϯ ⲙ̀ⲙⲟⲛ.

ⲇ̄ ⲡⲉⲛⲥⲱⲧⲏⲣ Ⲓⲏⲥⲟⲩⲥ ⲡⲉ ⲡⲓⲣⲉϥⲧⲁⲛϧⲟ ⲛ̀ⲧⲉ ⲛⲉⲛⲯⲩⲭⲏ.

ⲉ̄ ⲧⲉⲛϣⲉⲡ̀ϩⲙⲟⲧ ⲛ̀ⲧⲟⲧϥ ⲙ̀Ⲫⲛⲟⲩϯ ϧⲉⲛ ⲡ̀ϫⲓⲛⲧⲉⲛⲓ̀ ⲉ̀ϧⲟⲩⲛ ⲉ̀ϯⲉⲕⲕⲗⲏⲥⲓⲁ.

4. Consider the sentence: ⲁϥϣⲉⲛⲁϥ ⲉ̀ⲧⲉϥⲣⲓ.

1. Put the sentence in the negative form.
2. Make the sentence in the present tense, and the subject in the first person, changing what needs to be changed.
3. Make the sentence in the future tense, and the subject in the second person, changing what needs to be changed.
4. Replace ⲧⲉϥⲣⲓ with a suitable pronoun and write the sentence, changing what needs to be changed.
5. Begin the sentence with ⲁⲩ- instead of ⲁϥ-, changing what needs to be changed.

5. Find out the meaning of the following verses:

ⲁ̄ ⲁⲛⲟⲕ ⲡⲉ ⲡⲓⲙⲱⲓⲧ ⲛⲉⲙ ϯⲙⲉⲑⲙⲏⲓ ⲛⲉⲙ ⲡⲓⲱⲛϧ.

ⲃ̄ ⲁⲛⲟⲕ ⲡⲉ ⲡⲓⲙⲁⲛⲉ̀ⲥⲱⲟⲩ ⲉⲑⲛⲁⲛⲉϥ: ϯⲥⲱⲟⲩⲛ ⲛ̀ⲛⲏⲉ̀ⲧⲉ ⲛⲟⲩⲓ ⲟⲩⲟϩ ⲛⲏⲉ̀ⲧⲉ ⲛⲟⲩⲓ ⲥⲱⲟⲩⲛ ⲙ̀ⲙⲟⲓ.

ⲅ̄ ⲉⲑⲃⲉ ⲫⲁⲓ ϥ̀ⲙⲉⲓ ⲙ̀ⲙⲟⲓ ⲛ̀ϫⲉ ⲡⲁⲓⲱⲧ.

ⲇ̄ ϥ̀ⲛⲁⲧⲱⲛϥ ⲛ̀ϫⲉ ⲡⲉⲥⲟⲛ.

ⲉ̄ ⲁⲛⲟⲕ ⲡⲉ ϯⲁⲛⲁⲥⲧⲁⲥⲓⲥ ⲛⲉⲙ ⲡⲓⲱⲛϧ.

ⲋ̄ ⲛ̀ⲑⲟⲕ ⲡⲉ Ⲡⲓⲭⲣⲓⲥⲧⲟⲥ ⲡ̀ϣⲏⲣⲓ ⲙ̀Ⲫϯ ⲫⲏⲉⲑⲛⲏⲟⲩ ⲉ̀ⲡⲓⲕⲟⲥⲙⲟⲥ.

ⲍ̄ ⲁⲓⲧⲱⲟⲩⲛ ⲟⲩⲟϩ ϯⲛⲁⲧⲱⲟⲩⲛ.

ⲏ̄ ϯⲛⲟⲩ ⲁϥϭⲓⲱⲟⲩ ⲛ̀ϫⲉ ⲡ̀ϣⲏⲣⲓ ⲙ̀ⲫ̀ⲣⲱⲙⲓ.

6. Translate to the Coptic language:

1. The Son of God was incarnate and became man.
2. The martyrs suffered for the sake of Christ.
3. The sinners return to the Lord.
4. The saints will rise with the apostles.
5. I carry my cross with thanksgiving, and I endure [or am patient].
6. We were granted [took] the grace of monasticism.
7. I saw him when he came [at his coming].

Lesson 21
ⲡⲓⲱϣ ⲙ̀ⲙⲁϩ ⲕⲁ

✠

ⲛⲓ̀ⲥⲙⲟⲧ ⲛ̀ⲧⲉ ⲡⲓⲣⲁ

The Morphological Forms of the Verb

The Coptic language is characterized by the presence of four forms of verbs, each having its way of use.

1. The perfect form or the absolute tense of the verb (ⲡⲓⲥⲙⲟⲧ ⲉⲧϫⲏⲕ)

It is the form of the verb before any changes are done to it, and this form of the verb accepts the mark of the object. And the object in this case is either a noun or a separate pronoun, for example:

Ⲫϯ ⲁϥϣⲱⲡ ⲛ̀ϯⲑⲩⲥⲓⲁ.	God accepted the sacrifice.
Ⲫϯ ⲁϥϣⲱⲡ ⲙ̀ⲙⲟⲥ.	God accepted it.

2. The imperfect form or the phrasal (construct) tense of the verb (ⲡⲓⲥⲙⲟⲧ ⲉⲧϫⲟⲣϩ (ⲉⲧⲥⲟⲃⲕ))

It is also called the "softened" form of the verb. The object here is a noun without being preceded by a mark, for example:

Ⲫϯ ⲁϥϣⲉⲡ ϯⲑⲩⲥⲓⲁ.	God accepted the sacrifice.

This form of the verb is indicated by putting a dash after the verb (ϣⲉⲡ-).

3. The connected form or the pronominal tense of the verb (ⲡⲓⲥⲙⲟⲧ ⲛ̀ⲣⲉⲙⲡⲣⲟⲛⲟⲙⲉⲛ)

The pronoun of the object attaches to the end of this form, for example:

Ⲫϯ ⲁϥϣⲟⲡⲥ.   God accepted it.

This form of the verb is indicated by putting (″) after the verb (ϣⲟⲡ″).

4. The qualitative tense of the verb (ⲡⲓⲥⲙⲟⲧ ⲛ̀ⲣⲉⲙⲙⲓⲛⲓ)

It is a special form of the verb, showing:

1. The state which the object is described to be in, in case of the completion of the action [verb] on it. (Transitive verb).
2. The characteristic which the verb reaches and ends in. (Intransitive verb). Or briefly it is the form in which the verb changes into qualitative adjective.

ϯⲑⲩⲥⲓⲁ ⲉⲧϣⲏⲡ.   The acceptable sacrifice.

ⲟⲩⲑⲩⲥⲓⲁ ⲉⲥϣⲏⲡ.   An acceptable sacrifice.

The qualitative tense of the verb is one of the ways of description in the Coptic language.

Notes:

✠ Some verbs have no qualitative form, such as ⲙⲉⲩⲓ (to think) and ⲛⲁⲩ (to see).

✠ There are verbs that have only the absolute form, and are called the invariable verbs, that is, indeclinable or defective. The other verbs, however, are called the variable verbs, that is, the ones that are conjugated.

Absolute form		Phrasal F.	Pronominal F.	Qualitative form	
ϣⲱⲡ	To accept, buy	ϣⲉⲡ-	ϣⲟⲡ″	ϣⲏⲡ	Acceptable
ⲃⲱⲗ	To loosen, untie, dissolve	ⲃⲉⲗ-	ⲃⲟⲗ″	ⲃⲏⲗ	Loosened, untied
ⲕⲱⲧ	To build	ⲕⲉⲧ-	ⲕⲟⲧ″	ⲕⲏⲧ	Built, edified
ϫⲱⲕ	To complete, perfect	ϫⲉⲕ-	ϫⲟⲕ″	ϫⲏⲕ	Complete, perfect
ϣⲱⲕ	To dig, deepen	ϣⲉⲕ-	ϣⲟⲕ″	ϣⲏⲕ	Deep
ⲕⲱⲥ	To shroud, embalm	ⲕⲉⲥ-	ⲕⲟⲥ″	ⲕⲏⲥ	Shrouded, embalmed

ⲥⲱϯ	To save, rescue, redeem	ⲥⲉⲧ-	ⲥⲟⲧ″	-------	
ⲱⲡ	To count, number	ⲉⲡ-	ⲟⲡ″	ⲏⲡ	Counted, numbered
ⲱⲗ, ⲱⲗⲓ	To carry, lift up	ⲉⲗ-	ⲟⲗ″	ⲟⲗ, ⲏⲗ	Lifted
ⲥⲱ	To drink	ⲥⲉ-	ⲥⲟ″	-------	
ⲥⲱⲧⲡ	To choose	ⲥⲉⲧⲡ-	ⲥⲟⲧⲡ″	ⲥⲟⲧⲡ	Chosen
ⲧⲁⲓⲟ	To honor	ⲧⲁⲓⲉ-	ⲧⲁⲓⲟ″	ⲧⲁⲓⲏⲟⲩⲧ	Honored
ⲥ̀ϧⲁⲓ	To write	ⲥ̀ϧⲉ-	ⲥ̀ϧⲏⲧ″	ⲥ̀ϧⲏⲟⲩⲧ	Written
ⲟⲩⲱⲣⲡ	To send	ⲟⲩⲉⲣⲡ-	ⲟⲩⲟⲣⲡ″	-------	
ⲭⲱ	To leave behind, place	ⲭⲁ-	ⲭⲁ″	ⲭⲏ	Placed, left behind
ⲓ̀ⲛⲓ	To bring, offer	ⲉⲛ-	ⲉⲛ″	-------	
ⲓ̀ⲣⲓ	To work, make, become	ⲉⲣ-	ⲁⲓ″, ⲁⲓⲧ″	ⲟⲓ	Become
ⲙⲓⲥⲓ	To beget	ⲙⲉⲥ-, ⲙⲁⲥ-	ⲙⲁⲥ″	ⲙⲟⲥⲓ	Begotten, born
ⲃⲟⲣⲃⲉⲣ	To cast, throw	ⲃⲉⲣⲃⲉⲣ-	ⲃⲉⲣⲃⲱⲣ″	ⲃⲉⲣⲃⲱⲣ	Cast, thrown
ⲥⲟⲗⲥⲉⲗ	To adorn, console	ⲥⲉⲗⲥⲉⲗ-	ⲥⲉⲗⲥⲱⲗ″	ⲥⲉⲗⲥⲱⲗ	Adorned, consoled

In the previous table, we saw some verbs in their different forms. Now the person who is adept at the language can form a single sentence in various ways, without violating the one meaning.

Concerning the arrangement of the words of a sentence:

ⲁⲩⲥ̀ϧⲁⲓ ⲛ̀ϫⲉ ⲛⲓ̀ⲥⲛⲏⲟⲩ ⲙ̀ⲡⲓⲱϣ.   ⲁϥⲥⲱⲧⲡ ⲛ̀ϫⲉ Ⲓⲏⲥⲟⲩⲥ ⲛ̀ⲛⲉϥⲙⲁⲑⲏⲧⲏⲥ.

ⲛⲓ̀ⲥⲛⲏⲟⲩ ⲁⲩⲥ̀ϧⲁⲓ ⲙ̀ⲡⲓⲱϣ.   Ⲓⲏⲥⲟⲩⲥ ⲁϥⲥⲱⲧⲡ ⲛ̀ⲛⲉϥⲙⲁⲑⲏⲧⲏⲥ.

ⲁ ⲛⲓ̀ⲥⲛⲏⲟⲩ ⲥ̀ϧⲁⲓ ⲙ̀ⲡⲓⲱϣ.   ⲁ Ⲓⲏⲥⲟⲩⲥ ⲥⲱⲧⲡ ⲛ̀ⲛⲉϥⲙⲁⲑⲏⲧⲏⲥ.

Changing the object from a noun to pronoun:

ⲁⲩⲥ̀ϧⲁⲓ ⲛ̀ϫⲉ ⲛⲓ̀ⲥⲛⲏⲟⲩ ⲙ̀ⲙⲟϥ.   ⲁϥⲥⲱⲧⲡ ⲛ̀ϫⲉ Ⲓⲏⲥⲟⲩⲥ ⲙ̀ⲙⲱⲟⲩ.

ⲛⲓ̀ⲥⲛⲏⲟⲩ ⲁⲩⲥ̀ϧⲁⲓ ⲙ̀ⲙⲟϥ.   Ⲓⲏⲥⲟⲩⲥ ⲁϥⲥⲱⲧⲡ ⲙ̀ⲙⲱⲟⲩ.

ⲁ ⲛⲓ̀ⲥⲛⲏⲟⲩ ⲥ̀ϧⲁⲓ ⲙ̀ⲙⲟϥ.   ⲁ Ⲓⲏⲥⲟⲩⲥ ⲥⲱⲧⲡ ⲙ̀ⲙⲱⲟⲩ.

Lesson 21 ✣ The Morphological Forms of the Verb ✣

Using the defective form (the phrasal form) of the verb:

ⲁⲩⲥⲱⲧⲡ ⲛ̀ϫⲉ ⲛⲓⲥⲛⲏⲟⲩ ⲡⲓⲱϣ.	ⲁϥⲥⲉⲧⲡ ⲛ̀ϫⲉ Ⲓⲏⲥⲟⲩⲥ ⲛⲉϥⲙⲁⲑⲏⲧⲏⲥ.
ⲛⲓⲥⲛⲏⲟⲩ ⲁⲩⲥⲱⲧⲡ ⲡⲓⲱϣ.	Ⲓⲏⲥⲟⲩⲥ ⲁϥⲥⲉⲧⲡ ⲛⲉϥⲙⲁⲑⲏⲧⲏⲥ.
ⲁ ⲛⲓⲥⲛⲏⲟⲩ ⲥⲱⲧⲡ ⲡⲓⲱϣ.	ⲁ Ⲓⲏⲥⲟⲩⲥ ⲥⲉⲧⲡ ⲛⲉϥⲙⲁⲑⲏⲧⲏⲥ.

Using the connected form (the pronominal form) of the verb:

ⲁⲩⲥⲟⲧⲡϥ ⲛ̀ϫⲉ ⲛⲓⲥⲛⲏⲟⲩ.	ⲁϥⲥⲟⲧⲡⲟⲩ ⲛ̀ϫⲉ Ⲓⲏⲥⲟⲩⲥ.
ⲛⲓⲥⲛⲏⲟⲩ ⲁⲩⲥⲟⲧⲡϥ.	Ⲓⲏⲥⲟⲩⲥ ⲁϥⲥⲟⲧⲡⲟⲩ.
ⲁ ⲛⲓⲥⲛⲏⲟⲩ ⲥⲟⲧⲡϥ.	ⲁ Ⲓⲏⲥⲟⲩⲥ ⲥⲟⲧⲡⲟⲩ.

Expressing the subject with only pronoun:

ⲁⲩⲥⲟⲧⲡⲓ ⲙ̀ⲙⲟϥ.	ⲁϥⲥⲱⲧⲡ ⲙ̀ⲙⲱⲟⲩ.
ⲁⲩⲥⲟⲧⲡϥ.	ⲁϥⲥⲟⲧⲡⲟⲩ.

Note that in the last row the sentence became one word, which includes the verb, subject, object, and also the tense mark. And this is a distinguishing characteristic of the Coptic language.

Using the qualitative tense of the verb:

ⲡⲓⲱϣ ⲉⲧⲥϧⲏⲟⲩⲧ. The written lesson.	ⲛⲓⲙⲁⲑⲏⲧⲏⲥ ⲉⲧⲥⲟⲧⲡ. The chosen disciples.
ⲟⲩⲱϣ ⲉϥⲥϧⲏⲟⲩⲧ. A written lesson.	ϩⲁⲛⲙⲁⲑⲏⲧⲏⲥ ⲉⲧⲥⲟⲧⲡ. Chosen disciples.

✠ Foundations of the Coptic Language ✠

Exercises

1. Write the meaning of the following:

1. ⲁϥⲟⲩⲉⲣⲡ ⲡⲉϥϣⲏⲣⲓ.
2. ⲁⲕⲥⲉⲧ ⲛⲓⲗⲁⲟⲥ.
3. ⲁⲥⲉⲛ ⲡⲓϫⲱⲙ.
4. ⲁⲩⲥⲉ ⲡⲓⲙⲱⲟⲩ.
5. ⲁⲛⲭⲁ ⲡⲓⲕⲟⲥⲙⲟⲥ.
6. ⲛⲓⲛⲟⲃⲓ ⲉⲧⲏⲗ.
7. ⲟⲩⲙⲱⲟⲩ ⲉϥⲃⲏⲗ ⲉ̀ⲃⲟⲗ.
8. ⲡⲓⲛⲟⲙⲟⲥ ⲉⲧϫⲏⲕ ⲉ̀ⲃⲟⲗ.
9. ⲁϥⲥⲟⲧⲡⲉⲛ.
10. ⲁⲩⲕⲟⲥϥ.
11. ⲧⲉⲛⲧⲁⲓⲟⲥ.
12. ⲁϥⲟⲩⲟⲣⲡⲟⲩ.
13. ⲁϥⲉⲛϥ ⲉ̀ⲡϣⲱⲓ.
14. ⲡⲓϣⲗⲏⲗ ⲉⲧϣⲏⲡ.
15. ϩⲁⲛϭⲉⲗⲗⲟⲓ ⲉⲩⲧⲁⲓⲏⲟⲩⲧ.
16. ⲟⲩϩⲁⲡ ⲉϥⲥϧⲏⲟⲩⲧ.

2. Complete according to the given example:

1. ⲁⲥⲙⲓⲥⲓ ⲙ̀ⲡⲓⲗⲟⲅⲟⲥ.	ⲁⲥⲙⲉⲥ ⲡⲓⲗⲟⲅⲟⲥ.	ⲁⲥⲙⲁⲥϥ.
2. ⲁϥⲭⲱ ⲛ̀ϯⲃⲁⲕⲓ.		
3. ⲁϥⲱⲗⲓ ⲛ̀ⲛⲓⲛⲟⲃⲓ.		
4. ⲁⲩⲧⲁⲓⲟ ⲙ̀ⲡⲟⲩⲓⲱⲧ.		
5. ⲥⲉⲕⲱⲧ ⲛ̀ϯⲉⲕⲕⲗⲏⲥⲓⲁ.		

3. Translate to the English language:

ⲁ̄ ⲁϥⲓ ⲟⲩⲟϩ ⲁϥⲥⲟⲧⲡⲉⲛ ϧⲉⲛ ⲛⲉⲛⲛⲟⲃⲓ.

ⲃ̄ ⲁⲕⲭⲁ ⲛⲟⲩⲛⲟⲃⲓ ⲛⲱⲟⲩ ⲉ̀ⲃⲟⲗ.

ⲅ̄ Ⲫⲛⲟⲩϯ ⲉⲧϣⲏⲕ ⲁϥϣⲱⲡⲓ ⲛ̀ⲟⲩⲙⲁⲓⲙⲟϣⲓ.

ⲇ̄ ⲛⲓⲥⲁϫⲓ ⲉⲧⲁϥⲥϧⲏⲧⲟⲩ ⲛ̀ϫⲉ ⲡⲓⲑⲏⲃ ⲛ̀ⲧⲉ Ⲫϯ.

ⲉ̄ ⲁ Ⲡϭⲟⲓⲥ ⲉⲛ ⲡⲓⲙⲱⲟⲩ ⲛ̀ⲧⲉ ⲫⲓⲟⲙ ⲉ̀ϩⲣⲏⲓ ⲉ̀ϫⲱⲟⲩ.

ⲋ̄ ⲡⲉⲛⲛⲟⲩϯ ϭⲉⲡ ⲁⲛ ⲛⲉⲛⲁⲛⲟⲙⲓⲁ.

ⲍ̄ Ⲓⲏⲥⲟⲩⲥ ⲁϥⲥⲉⲧⲡ ⲛⲉϥⲙⲁⲑⲏⲧⲏⲥ ⲟⲩⲟϩ ⲁϥⲟⲩⲟⲣⲡⲟⲩ ⲉ̀ⲡⲓⲕⲟⲥⲙⲟⲥ.

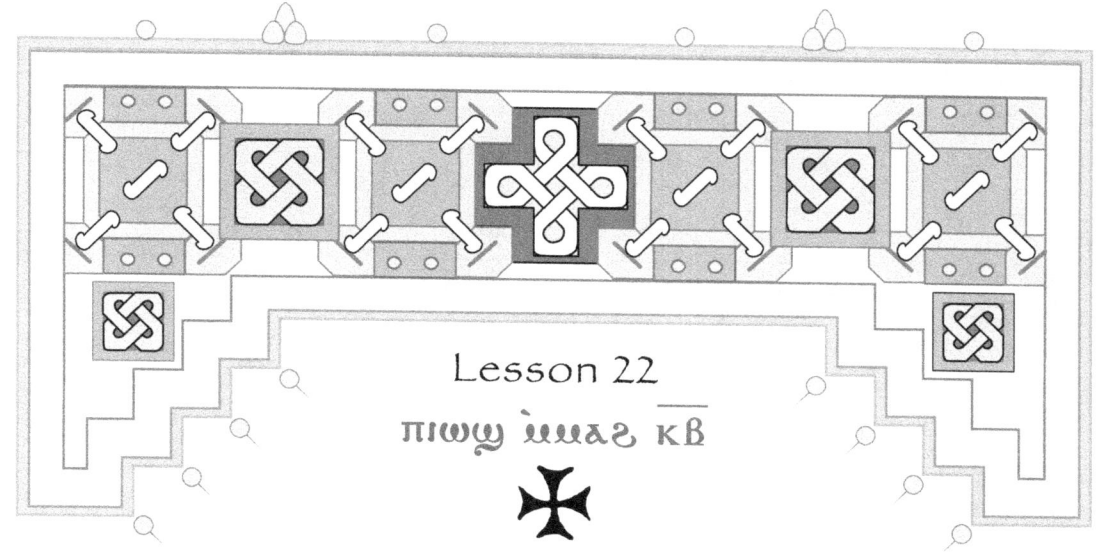

Lesson 22
ⲡⲓⲱϣ ⲙ̇ⲙⲁϩ ⲕ̅ⲃ̅

✠

The Forms (Tenses) of the Simple Verbs [Part I]

1. Verbs consisting of two radical letters

Absolute form		Phrasal F.	Pronominal F.	Qualitative form	
Rule:	ⲱ	ⲉ	ⲟ	ⲏ	
Examples:					
ⲃⲱⲗ	To loosen, untie, dissolve	ⲃⲉⲗ-	ⲃⲟⲗ"	ⲃⲏⲗ	Loose, untied
ⲕⲱⲥ	To shroud, embalm	ⲕⲉⲥ-	ⲕⲟⲥ"	ⲕⲏⲥ	Shrouded, embalmed
ⲕⲱⲧ	To build	ⲕⲉⲧ-	ⲕⲟⲧ"	ⲕⲏⲧ	Built, edified
ⲣⲱⲧ	To grow, sprout	ⲣⲉⲧ-	ⲣⲟⲧ"	ⲣⲏⲧ	grown, sprouted
ⲑⲱⲧ	To mix	ⲑⲉⲧ-	ⲑⲟⲧ"	ⲑⲏⲧ	Mixed
ϣⲱⲡ	To accept, buy	ϣⲉⲡ-	ϣⲟⲡ"	ϣⲏⲡ	Acceptable, bought
ϣⲱⲕ	To dig, deepen	ϣⲉⲕ-	ϣⲟⲕ"	ϣⲏⲕ	Dug, deep
ϩⲱⲡ	To hide, conceal	ϩⲉⲡ-	ϩⲟⲡ"	ϩⲏⲡ	Hidden, concealed

ⲭⲱⲕ	To complete, perfect	ⲭⲉⲕ-	ⲭⲟⲕ″	ⲭⲏⲕ	Complete, perfect
ⲱⲡ	To count, number	ⲉⲡ-	ⲟⲡ″	ⲏⲡ	Counted, numbered
ϩⲱⲗ	To go, fly	-------	-------	ϩⲏⲗ	Flying
ⲟⲩⲱⲙ	To eat	ⲟⲩⲉⲙ-	ⲟⲩⲟⲙ″	-------	
ⲟⲩⲱⲛ	To open	ⲟⲩⲉⲛ-	ⲟⲩⲟⲛ″	ⲟⲩⲏⲛ	Opened
ⲥⲱϯ	To save, rescue	ⲥⲉⲧ-	ⲥⲟⲧ″	-------	
ⲱⲗ, ⲱ̀ⲗⲓ	To carry, lift up	ⲉⲗ-	ⲟⲗ″	ⲟⲗ, ⲏⲗ	Lifted, carried
ⲥⲱ	To drink	ⲥⲉ-	ⲥⲟ″	-------	
ϫⲱ	To say	ϫⲉ-	ϫⲟ″	-------	
ⲭⲱ	To leave behind, place	ⲭⲁ-	ⲭⲁ″	ⲭⲏ	Placed, left behind

The following verbs beginning with ⲙ or ⲛ also follow the verbs above, and have the vowel ⲟⲩ, for example:

ⲙⲟⲩⲛ	To continue, to last	-------	-------	ⲙⲏⲛ	continuous, lasting
ⲙⲟⲩⲣ	To tie	ⲙⲉⲣ-	ⲙⲟⲣ″	ⲙⲏⲣ	Tied
ⲛⲟⲩϫ	To cast, throw	ⲛⲉϫ-	ⲛⲟϫ″	ⲛⲏϫ	Cast, thrown

Sample sentences:

ⲁ̅ ⲟⲩⲙⲱⲟⲩ ⲉϥⲃⲏⲗ ⲉ̀ⲃⲟⲗ ⲁϥⲟ̀ϩⲓ ⲉ̀ⲣⲁⲧϥ.
A flowing water stood upright. (Adam Psali for the First Canticle).

ⲃ̅ ⲁⲣⲓⲯⲁⲗⲓⲛ ⲉ̀ⲫⲏⲉⲧⲁⲩⲁ̲ϣ̲ϥ ⲉ̀ϩⲣⲏⲓ ⲉ̀ϫⲱⲛ ⲟⲩⲟϩ ⲁⲩⲕⲟⲥϥ.
O sing unto Him who was crucified for us, and buried.

ⲅ̅ ⲁⲩⲕⲟⲥϥ ⲁⲩⲭⲁϥ ϧⲉⲛ ⲟⲩⲙ̀ϩⲁⲩ.
They shrouded him and placed him in a tomb.

ⲇ̅ Ⲫϯ ⲡⲓⲛⲓϣϯ ⲡⲓϣⲁ ⲉ̀ⲛⲉϩ ⲫⲏⲉⲧⲁϥⲕⲱⲧ ⲙ̀ⲡⲓⲣⲱⲙⲓ ⲉ̀ϩⲣⲏⲓ ⲉ̀ϫⲉⲛ ϯⲙⲉⲧⲁⲧⲧⲁⲕⲟ.
O God, the Great, the Eternal, who formed [or built] man in incorruption.

ⲉ̅ ⲡⲁⲓⲣⲏϯ ⲟⲛ ⲡⲓⲕⲉⲁ̀ⲫⲟⲧ ⲙⲉⲛⲉⲛⲥⲁ ⲡⲓⲇⲓⲡⲛⲟⲛ: ⲁϥⲑⲟⲧϥ ⲉ̀ⲃⲟⲗϧⲉⲛ ⲟⲩⲏⲣⲡ

Lesson 22 ✠ The Forms (Tenses) of the Simple Verbs [Part 1] ✠

ⲛⲉⲙ ⲟⲩⲙⲱⲟⲩ.
Likewise also, the cup, after supper, He mixed it of wine and water.

ⲋ̄ ⲁϥⲟⲗϥ ⲉⲡϣⲱⲓ ⲛ̀ⲟⲩⲥⲑⲟⲓⲛⲟⲩϥⲓ ϣⲁ Ⲫϯ ⲡⲉϥⲓⲱⲧ.
He lifted up Himself [as] incense to God His Father.

ⲍ̄ ⲁϥⲓ ⲁϥⲥⲟⲧⲧⲉⲛ ⲉ̀ⲃⲟⲗϧⲉⲛ ⲛⲉⲛⲛⲟⲃⲓ.
He came [and] saved us from our sins.

ⲏ̄ ϯ̀ⲧⲣⲓⲁⲥ ⲉⲧϫⲏⲕ ⲉ̀ⲃⲟⲗ.
The perfect Trinity.

ⲑ̄ ⲉⲑⲙⲏⲛ ⲉ̀ⲃⲟⲗ ϣⲁ ⲉ̀ⲛⲉϩ.
Everlasting. [Lasting forever].

ⲓ̄ ⲉⲧϩⲏⲗ ⲉ̀ⲡϭⲓⲥⲓ ⲛⲉⲙ ⲡⲁⲓϩⲩⲙⲛⲟⲥ.
Flying on high with this hymn.

ⲓ̄ⲁ ⲟⲡⲧⲉⲛ ϩⲱⲛ ⲛⲉⲙ ⲛⲉⲕⲉ̀ⲥⲱⲟⲩ.
Number us with Your sheep.

ⲓ̄ⲃ ϯϯϩⲟ ⲉ̀ⲣⲟ ⲱ̄ ϯⲑⲉⲟⲧⲟⲕⲟⲥ: ϫⲁ ⲫⲣⲟ ⲛ̀ⲛⲓⲉⲕⲕⲗⲏⲥⲓⲁ ⲉⲩⲟⲩⲏⲛ ⲛ̀ⲛⲓⲡⲓⲥⲧⲟⲥ.
I ask you, O Mother of God: keep the doors of the churches open to the believers.

ⲓ̄ⲅ ⲉⲩϩⲱⲥ ⲉ̀ⲡⲟⲩⲣⲉϥⲥⲱⲛⲧ ⲉϥⲭⲏ ϧⲉⲛ ⲧⲉⲛⲉϫⲓ.
Praising their Creator who is in your womb.

ⲓ̄ⲇ ⲁϥⲃⲉⲗ ϯⲙⲉⲧϫⲁϫⲓ ⲉ̀ⲃⲟⲗϩⲁⲣⲟⲛ.
He loosened the enmity from us.

ⲓ̄ⲉ ⲁϥⲟⲩⲟⲙⲟⲩ ⲙ̀ⲫⲣⲏϯ ⲛ̀ϩⲁⲛⲣⲱⲟⲩⲓ̀.
He ate them like hay.

ⲓ̄ⲋ ⲡⲓⲙⲁⲛⲛⲁ ⲉⲧϩⲏⲡ ⲛ̀ϧⲏⲧϥ.
The manna that is hidden in it.

Exceptions: Verbs ending with one of the letters ϣ, ϧ, ϩ:

1. Before ϣ, ⲉ is sometimes changed to ⲁ, and ⲟ is always changed to ⲁ, for example:

ⲑⲱϣ	To determine, appoint, decide	ⲑⲉϣ-	ⲑⲁϣ″	ⲑⲏϣ	Determined, appointed, decided
ⲫⲱϣ	To divide	ⲫⲉϣ-	ⲫⲁϣ″	ⲫⲏϣ	Divided
ⲟⲩⲱϣ	To wish, desire, want	ⲟⲩⲁϣ-	ⲟⲩⲁϣ″	-------	

2. Before ϧ, ⲟ is always changed to ⲁ, but rarely to ⲉ, for example:

| ⲑⲱϧ | To mix | ⲑⲉϧ- | ⲑⲁϧ" | ⲑⲏϧ | Mixed |
| ⲫⲱϧ | To tear apart, rip | ⲫⲉϧ- | ⲫⲁϧ" | ⲫⲏϧ | Torn apart, ripped |

3. Before ϩ, (1) ⲱ is changed to ⲟ; (2) ⲉ is changed to ⲁ, in most cases; (3) ⲟ is changed to ⲁ; (4) ⲏ is changed to ⲉ; for example:

ⲙⲟϩ	To fill, be filled	ⲙⲁϩ-	ⲙⲁϩ"	ⲙⲉϩ	Filled
ⲫⲟϩ	To attain, mature	ⲫⲉϩ-	-------	ⲫⲉϩ	Attained, matured
ⲟⲩⲟϩ	To add, follow	ⲟⲩⲁϩ-	ⲟⲩⲁϩ"	ⲟⲩⲉϩ	Added, followed

Sample Sentences:

ⲁ̄ Ⲫϯ ⲛⲁⲓ ⲛⲁⲛ: ⲑⲉⲱ ⲟⲩⲛⲁⲓ ⲉⲣⲟⲛ.
O God, have mercy upon us, settle mercy to us.

ⲃ̄ ⲙ̀ⲡⲉϥⲭⲱϣ ⲙ̀ⲡⲉϥⲑⲱϧ ⲟⲩⲇⲉ ⲙ̀ⲡⲉϥⲫⲱⲣϫ.
He did not overflow, was not mixed and was not separated.

ⲅ̄ ⲁϥⲁⲓⲥ ⲛ̀ⲟⲩⲁⲓ ⲛⲉⲙ ⲧⲉϥⲙⲉⲑⲛⲟⲩϯ ϧⲉⲛ ⲟⲩⲙⲉⲧⲁⲧⲙⲟⲩϫⲧ ⲛⲉⲙ ⲟⲩⲙⲉⲧⲁⲧⲑⲱϧ ⲛⲉⲙ ⲟⲩⲙⲉⲧⲁⲧϣⲓⲃϯ.
He made It one with His divinity without mingling, without confusion, and without alteration.

ⲇ̄ ⲁϥⲫⲁϣϥ ⲁϥⲧⲏⲓϥ ⲛ̀ⲛⲏⲉⲧⲉ ⲛⲟⲩϥ.
He broke it, and gave it to His own.

ⲉ̄ ⲁⲪϯ ⲟⲩⲁϣⲥ.
God desired her. [Tuesday Theolotkia, Part 5].

ⲋ̄ ⲁϥⲫⲱϧ ⲙ̀ⲡⲓⲥϧⲓ ⲛ̀ϫⲓϫ ⲛ̀ⲧⲉ ϯⲙⲉⲧⲃⲱⲕ.
He tore the handwriting of slavery.

ⲍ̄ ⲁ ⲡⲓⲡ̅ⲛ̅ⲁ̅ ⲉⲑⲩ ⲙⲟϩ ⲙ̀ⲙⲁⲓ ⲛⲓⲃⲉⲛ ⲛ̀ⲧⲉ.
The Holy Spirit filled every part of you.

ⲏ̄ ⲙⲟϩ ⲛ̀ⲛⲉⲛϩⲏⲧ ϧⲉⲛ ⲧⲉⲕϩⲓⲣⲏⲛⲏ.
Fill our hearts with Your peace.

ⲑ̄ Ⲧⲫⲉ ⲛⲉⲙ ⲡⲕⲁϩⲓ ⲙⲉϩ ⲉ̀ⲃⲟⲗϧⲉⲛ ⲡⲉⲕⲱⲟⲩ.
The heaven and the earth are full of Your glory.

Lesson 22 ✠ The Forms (Tenses) of the Simple Verbs [Part 1] ✠

ⲓ̄ ϯⲥⲙⲏ ⲉⲑⲙⲉϩ ⲛ̀ⲣⲁϣⲓ.
The voice [which is] full of joy.

ⲓ̄ⲁ̄ ⲭⲉⲣⲉ ⲑⲏⲉⲑⲙⲉϩ ⲛ̀ϩ̀ⲙⲟⲧ.
Hail to you, O full of grace.

Exercises

1. Write the meaning of the following:

1.	ⲧⲉⲧⲉⲛϫⲉⲕ ⲡⲁⲓϩⲱⲃ.	9.	ⲁϥϫⲟⲕϥ ⲉ̀ⲃⲟⲗ.
2.	ⲁϥϣⲉⲡ ⲧⲁⲓⲑⲩⲥⲓⲁ.	10.	ⲁⲕⲥⲟⲧⲥ.
3.	ⲁⲓⲉϣ ⲡⲁⲓϫⲱⲙ.	11.	ⲁⲛⲟⲩⲟⲛⲟⲩ.
4.	ⲥⲉⲟⲩⲉⲙ ⲡⲁⲓⲱⲓⲕ.	12.	ⲁⲥⲭⲁ ⲑⲏⲛⲟⲩ.
5.	ⲁⲣⲉⲥⲉⲧ ⲡⲁⲓⲁ̀ⲗⲟⲩ.	13.	ϫⲛⲁⲟⲩⲟⲙϥ.
6.	ϩⲁⲛⲣⲱⲟⲩ ⲉⲩⲟⲩⲏⲛ.	14.	ⲫⲛⲟⲩⲛ ⲉⲧϣⲏⲕ.
7.	ⲡⲓⲁⲅⲅⲉⲗⲟⲥ ⲉⲧϩⲏⲗ.	15.	ⲟⲩϣ̀ϣⲏⲛ ⲉϥⲣⲏⲧ.
8.	ⲟⲩⲙⲉⲧϫⲁϫⲓ ⲉⲥⲫⲏⲇ.	16.	ⲛⲁⲓⲥⲁⲣⲝ ⲉⲧⲕⲏⲥ.

2. Complete according to the given example:

1.	ⲁϥⲕⲱⲧ ⲙ̀ⲡⲓⲣⲱⲙⲓ.	ⲁϥⲕⲉⲧ ⲡⲓⲣⲱⲙⲓ.	ⲁϥⲕⲟⲧϥ.
2.	ⲁⲥⲟⲩⲱⲛ ⲛ̀ⲛⲁⲓⲣⲱⲟⲩ.		
3.	ⲁⲕⲥⲱϯ ⲛ̀ϯⲡⲟⲣⲛⲏ.		
4.	ⲁϥⲫⲱϣ ⲙ̀ⲡⲉϥⲥⲱⲙⲁ.		
5.	ϫ̀ⲙⲟϩ ⲛ̀ⲛⲉⲛϩⲏⲧ.		

3. Translate to the English language:

ⲁ̄ ⲟⲩⲥⲁⲣⲝ ⲉⲥϫⲏⲕ ⲉ̀ⲃⲟⲗ.
ⲃ̄ ⲟⲩϣ̀ϣⲏⲛ ⲉϥⲙⲉϩ ϧⲉⲛ ⲡⲓⲭⲣⲱⲙ.
ⲅ̄ ⲁϥⲟⲗⲟⲩ ⲉ̀ⲡⲃⲓⲥⲓ ⲛⲉⲙⲁϥ.
ⲇ̄ Ⲫϯ ϥϣⲉⲡ ⲛⲓⲑⲩⲥⲓⲁ ⲛ̀ⲧⲉ ⲛⲉⲛϩⲏⲧ.
ⲉ̄ ⲁⲓϭⲓ ⲛ̀ⲟⲩϫⲱⲙ ⲟⲩⲟϩ ⲁⲓⲁϣϥ.
ⲋ̄ ϥⲟⲡⲟⲩ ⲛⲉⲙ ⲛⲉϥϩⲓⲛⲃ.
ⲍ̄ ⲁⲕⲑⲉⲧ ⲟⲩⲏⲣⲡ ⲛⲉⲙ ⲟⲩⲙⲱⲟⲩ.

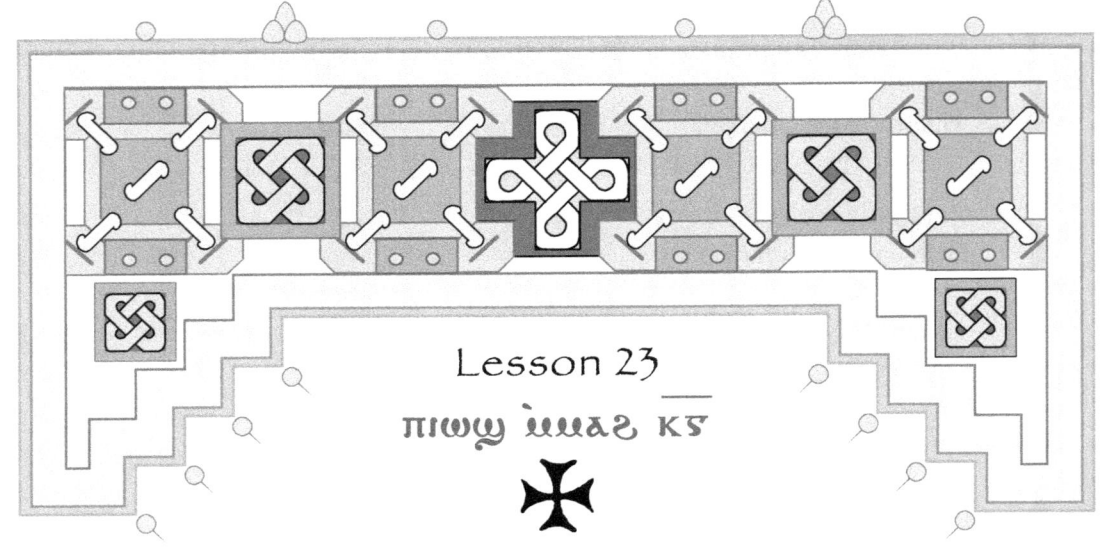

Lesson 23
ⲡⲓⲱϣ ⲙⲙⲁϩ ⲕⲅ

The Forms (Tenses) of the Simple Verbs [Part 2]

2. The Bi-radical Verbs

Absolute form		Phrasal F.	Pronominal F.	Qualitative form	
Rule: ⲟ		---	---	ⲏ	
Examples:					
ϩⲙⲟⲙ	To heat up, become hot	-------	-------	ϩⲏⲙ	Hot, heated
ϫⲃⲟⲃ	To cool off, become wet	-------	-------	ⲕⲏⲃ	Cold, wet
ϫⲙⲟⲙ	To become black	-------	-------	ϫⲏⲙ	Black

3. The Tri-radical Verbs

These contain three radical letters.

Absolute form		Phrasal F.	Pronominal F.	Qualitative form	
Rule: ⲱ		ⲉ	ⲟ	ⲟ	
Examples:					
ⲥⲱⲧⲡ	To choose, select	ⲥⲉⲧⲡ-	ⲥⲟⲧⲡ⸗	ⲥⲟⲧⲡ	Chosen

Lesson 23 ✠ The Forms (Tenses) of the Simple Verbs [Part 2] ✠

ⲥⲱϫⲡ	To remain, leave behind	ⲥⲉϫⲡ-	ⲥⲟϫⲡ⸗	ⲥⲟϫⲡ	Remaining, left behind
ⲑⲱⲙⲥ	To bury	ⲑⲉⲙⲥ-	ⲑⲟⲙⲥ⸗	ⲑⲟⲙⲥ	Buried
ⲫⲱⲛϩ	To turn, replace	ⲫⲉⲛϩ-	ⲫⲟⲛϩ⸗	ⲫⲟⲛϩ	Turned
ⲫⲱⲣϣ	To spread, unfold	ⲫⲉⲣϣ-	ⲫⲟⲣϣ⸗	ⲫⲟⲣϣ	Spread, unfolded
ϩⲱⲃⲥ	To clothe, cover	ϩⲉⲃⲥ-	ϩⲟⲃⲥ⸗	ϩⲟⲃⲥ	Covered
ϩⲱⲧⲡ	To unite, reconcile	ϩⲉⲧⲡ-	ϩⲟⲧⲡ⸗	ϩⲟⲧⲡ	United, reconciled
ϫⲱⲗⲕ	To drown, immerse	-------	ϫⲟⲗⲕ⸗	ϫⲟⲗⲕ	Drowned, immersed
ϫⲱⲗϩ	To wear, put on	-------	ϫⲟⲗϩ⸗	ϫⲟⲗϩ	Worn, clothed
ⲙⲟⲩⲛⲕ	To form, make	ⲙⲉⲛⲕ-	ⲙⲟⲛⲕ⸗	ⲙⲟⲛⲕ	Formed, made
ⲙⲟⲩϫⲧ	To mix	ⲙⲉϫⲧ-	ⲙⲟϫⲧ⸗	ⲙⲟϫⲧ	Mixed
ⲛⲟⲩϫϧ	To wet, sprinkle	-------	ⲛⲟϫϧ⸗	ⲛⲟϫϧ	Wet, sprinkled
ⲱⲃϣ	To forget	ⲉⲃϣ-	ⲟⲃϣ⸗	ⲟⲃϣ	Forgotten
ⲱⲙⲕ	To swallow	ⲉⲙⲕ-	ⲟⲙⲕ⸗	-------	
ⲱⲙⲥ	To immerse	ⲉⲙⲥ-	ⲟⲙⲥ⸗	ⲟⲙⲥ	Immersed
ⲱⲛϧ	To live	-------	-------	ⲟⲛϧ	Alive
ⲱϣϫ	To anoint, paint	-------	ⲟϣϫ⸗	ⲟϣϫ	Anointed, painted
ⲱϥⲧ	To nail	ⲉϥⲧ-	ⲟϥⲧ⸗	ⲟϥⲧ	Nailed
ⲟⲩⲱⲛϩ	To reveal, appear	ⲟⲩⲉⲛϩ-	ⲟⲩⲟⲛϩ⸗	ⲟⲩⲟⲛϩ	Revealed
ⲑⲱⲕⲉⲙ	To draw out, pull	ⲑⲉⲕⲉⲙ-	ⲑⲟⲕⲙ⸗	ⲑⲟⲕⲉⲙ	Drawn
ⲑⲱⲗⲉⲃ	To defile	ⲑⲉⲗⲉⲃ-	ⲑⲟⲗⲃ⸗	ⲑⲟⲗⲉⲃ	Defiled
ⲥⲱⲧⲉⲙ	To hear, listen	ⲥⲉⲧⲉⲙ-	ⲥⲟⲑⲙ⸗	ⲥⲟⲧⲉⲙ	Heard
ⲛⲟϩⲉⲙ	To save, rescue, redeem	ⲛⲁϩⲉⲙ-	ⲛⲁϩⲙ⸗	ⲛⲟϩⲉⲙ	Saved, rescued

Sample Sentences

ⲁ̄ ⲫⲁⲓ ⲉⲧⲁⲕⲥⲟⲧⲡϥ.
This [is he] whom you chose.

ⲃ̄ ⲑⲏⲉⲧϫⲟⲗϩ ⲙ̀ⲡⲓⲱⲟⲩ ⲛ̀ⲧⲉ Ⲡ̄ⲥ̄ Ⲥⲁⲃⲁⲱⲑ.
The [one] clothed with the glory of the Lord of hosts.

ⲅ̄ ⲁϥϫⲟⲗⲕⲟⲩ ϧⲉⲛ ⲫⲓⲟⲙ ⲛ̀ϣⲁⲣⲓ.
He drowned (immersed) them in the Red Sea.

ⲇ̄ ⲁϥⲟⲙⲕⲟⲩ ⲛ̀ϫⲉ ⲡⲕⲁϩⲓ.
The earth swallowed them.

ⲉ̄ ⲁⲕⲟⲩⲱⲣⲡ ⲙ̀ⲡⲉⲕⲡ̀ⲛⲉⲩⲙⲁ ⲁϥϩⲟⲃⲥⲟⲩ ⲛ̀ϫⲉ ⲫⲓⲟⲙ.
You sent Your wind, [so] the sea covered them.

ⲋ̄ ⲡ̀ϣⲏⲣⲓ ⲙ̀Ⲫⲛⲟⲩϯ ⲉⲧⲟⲛϧ.
The living Son of God.

ⲍ̄ ⲛⲁϩⲙⲉⲛ ϧⲉⲛ ⲡⲉⲕⲣⲁⲛ.
Save us in Your name.

ⲏ̄ ⲁⲛⲥⲟⲑⲙⲉⲥ ϧⲉⲛ Ⲉⲫⲣⲁⲑⲁ.
We heard it in Ephratha.

ⲑ̄ ϧⲉⲛ ⲫⲁⲓ ⲁϥⲟⲩⲟⲛϩⲥ ⲉⲃⲟⲗ : ϫⲉ ⲟⲩⲑⲉⲟⲧⲟⲕⲟⲥ ⲧⲉ.
By this He revealed her, that she is the Mother of God.

ⲓ̄ ⲁϥϩⲟⲧⲡⲉⲛ ⲉ̀ⲣⲟϥ.
He united us in Him.

ⲓ̄ⲁ ⲁϥⲛⲁϩⲙⲟⲩ.
He saved them (rescued them).

ⲓ̄ⲃ ⲛⲁⲓ ⲉⲧⲁϥϩⲟⲧⲡⲟⲩ ⲉⲩⲥⲟⲡ ⲛ̀ϫⲉ ⲡⲓⲡ̀ⲛⲉⲩⲙⲁ ⲉⲑⲟⲩⲁⲃ.
These whom the Holy Spirit united (them) together.

The intransitive verbs, however, which belong to this group of verbs, have only the absolute and qualitative tenses. Also there is no one rule to deduce the qualitative tense from the absolute, for example:

Absolute form		Qualitative form	
ϩⲗⲟϫ	To be sweet	ϩⲟⲗϫ	Sweet
ⲙ̀ⲕⲁϩ	To suffer	ⲙⲟⲕϩ	Suffering
ⲟⲩⲃⲁϣ	To become white	ⲟⲩⲟⲃϣ	White

Lesson 23 ✠ The Forms (Tenses) of the Simple Verbs [Part 2] ✠

ⲁϣⲁⲓ	To increase	ⲟϣ	Abundance
ϩⲕⲟ	To hunger	ϩⲟⲕⲉⲣ	Hungry
ⲟⲩϫⲁⲓ	To be safe, be saved	ⲟⲩⲟϫ	Safe, healthy
ⲛ̀ϣⲟⲧ	To be cruel	ⲛⲁϣⲧ	Cruel
ϭⲑⲁⲓ	To become fat, become thick	ϭⲟⲧ	Fat, thick
ϣⲱⲡⲓ	To be, become	ϣⲟⲡ	Existing, become
ϫⲱⲣⲓ	Strong (noun)	ϫⲟⲣ	Strong

As for the verbs ⲥⲱⲟⲩⲛ (to know) and ⲧⲱⲟⲩⲛ (to arise), they are conjugated as follows:

Absolute form		Phrasal F.	Pronominal F.	Qualitative form	
ⲥⲱⲟⲩⲛ	To know	ⲥⲟⲩⲉⲛ-	ⲥⲟⲩⲱⲛ″	ⲥⲟⲩⲏⲛ, ⲥⲟⲩⲉⲛ	Known (famous)
ⲧⲱⲟⲩⲛ	To arise	ⲧⲉⲛ-	ⲧⲱⲛ″	-------	

We also find ⲥⲱⲟⲩⲛⲟⲩ and ⲧⲱⲟⲩⲛⲟⲩ as perfect forms of the absolute tense:

ⲥⲉⲧⲱⲟⲩⲛⲟⲩ ϩⲁⲣⲟⲕ ⲛ̀ϫⲉ ⲛⲓⲭⲉⲣⲟⲩⲃⲓⲙ ⲛⲉⲙ ⲛⲓⲥⲉⲣⲁⲫⲓⲙ: ⲥⲉϣⲛⲁⲩ ⲉⲣⲟⲕ ⲁⲛ.
The cherubim and seraphim arise around You, [and] they cannot see You.

Sample sentences:

ⲁ̄	ϥϩⲟⲗϫ ⲛ̀ϫⲉ ⲡⲉⲕⲛⲁϩⲃⲉϥ.	Your yoke is sweet.
ⲃ̄	ⲡⲉⲕⲣⲁⲛ ϩⲟⲗϫ ⲟⲩⲟϩ ϥ̀ⲥⲙⲁⲣⲱⲟⲩⲧ.	Your name is sweet and blessed.
ⲅ̄	Ⲡ̅ⲟ̅ⲥ̅ ϣⲟⲡ ⲛⲉⲙⲉ.	The Lord is with you (sing. fem.).
ⲇ̄	ⲫⲏⲉⲧϣⲟⲡ ϧⲉⲛ ⲡⲓⲟⲩⲱⲓⲛⲓ.	He who is [dwells] in light.
ⲉ̄	ⲡⲓⲣⲉϥⲉⲣϩⲉⲙⲓ ⲉⲧϫⲟⲣ.	The strong manager.
ⲋ̄	ϩⲟⲥ ⲉⲛⲟⲛϧ ⲧⲉⲛⲥ̀ⲙⲟⲩ ⲉⲣⲟⲕ: ϩⲟⲥ ⲉⲛϣⲟⲡ ⲧⲉⲛϯⲱⲟⲩ ⲛⲁⲕ. As long as we live, we praise You; as long as we exist, we glorify You.	
ⲍ̄	ⲁⲛⲥⲟⲩⲉⲛ ⲡⲓϣⲟⲩϣⲱⲟⲩϣⲓ ⲙ̀ⲙⲏⲓ: ⲛ̀ϫⲁ ⲛⲟⲃⲓ ⲉ̀ⲃⲟⲗ. We knew the true sacrifice for the forgiveness of sins.	

✠ Foundations of the Coptic Language ✠

Exercises

1. Write the absolute tense of each of the following verbs:

1. ⲟϣ	7. ϫⲏⲙ	13. ⲙⲟⲕϩ
2. ⲥⲟⲟⲩⲙ″	8. ⲛⲟϫϭ″	14. ⲭⲁ″
3. ϩⲉⲃⲥ-	9. ⲉⲙⲥ-	15. ⲟⲩⲉⲙ-
4. ϣⲟⲡ	10. ⲟⲛϭ	16. ⲟϣϫ
5. ⲥⲟⲧⲡ″	11. ⲟⲙⲕ″	17. ⲃⲟⲗ″
6. ϩⲉⲧⲡ-	12. ⲉϥⲧ-	18. ϣⲉⲡ-

2. Complete according to the given example:

1. ⲁⲓⲥⲱⲧⲡ ⲙ̀ⲡⲁⲓⲙⲱⲓⲧ.	ⲁⲓⲥⲉⲧⲡ ⲡⲁⲓⲙⲱⲓⲧ.	ⲁⲓⲥⲟⲧⲡϥ.
2. ⲁϥⲟⲩⲱⲛϩ ⲛ̀ⲧⲉϥϫⲟⲙ.		
3. ⲁⲩⲱϣⲧ ⲛ̀Ⲓⲏⲥⲟⲩⲥ.		
4. ⲁϥⲫⲱⲣϣ ⲛ̀ⲛⲉϥϫⲓϫ.		
5. ⲁⲛⲥⲱⲟⲩⲛ ⲛ̀ϯⲙⲉⲑⲙⲏⲓ.		
6. ⲁϥⲛⲟϩⲉⲙ ⲛ̀ⲛⲓⲗⲁⲟⲥ.		

3. Translate to the English language:

ⲁ̄ Ⲡϭⲟⲓⲥ ϣⲟⲡ ⲛⲉⲙⲁⲛ.

ⲃ̄ ⲟⲩϩⲓⲙⲓ ⲉⲥϫⲟⲗϩ ⲙ̀ⲫⲣⲏ.

ⲅ̄ ϯⲕⲓⲃⲱⲧⲟⲥ ⲉⲧⲟϣϫ ⲛ̀ⲛⲟⲩⲃ.

ⲇ̄ ⲁϥⲥⲱⲧⲡ ⲙ̀ⲙⲱⲟⲩ ⲟⲩⲟϩ ⲁϥⲟⲩⲟⲣⲡⲟⲩ ⲉ̀ⲡⲓⲕⲟⲥⲙⲟⲥ.

ⲉ̄ ⲁⲓⲱϣ ⲙ̀ⲡⲉⲕϫⲱⲙ ⲟⲩⲟϩ ⲁⲓⲭⲁϥ ϩⲓϫⲉⲛ ϯⲧⲣⲁⲡⲉⲍⲁ.

ⲋ̄ ⲁⲛⲛⲁⲩ ⲉ̀ⲡⲉⲧⲉⲛϣⲏⲣⲓ ⲟⲩⲟϩ ⲁⲛⲥⲟⲩⲱⲛϥ ⲛ̀ⲭⲱⲗⲉⲙ.

ⲍ̄ ⲁⲩϭⲓ ⲛ̀ⲛⲓⲱⲓⲕ ⲟⲩⲟϩ ⲁⲩⲟⲩⲟⲙⲟⲩ.

Lesson 24
ⲡⲓⲱϣ ⲙⲙⲁϩ ⲕⲇ

The Forms (Tenses) of the Simple Verbs [Part 3]

4. The Imperfect Tri-radical Verbs

That is, in these the third radical letter is weak. They are divided into three kinds.

1. In these verbs the main vowel letter is ⲓ after the first radical letter. Some of these verbs are transitive and some intransitive.

	Absolute form	Phrasal F.	Pronominal F.		Qualitative form
Rule:	ⲓ . ⲓ	ⲉ	ⲁ		ⲟ . ⲓ
Examples:					
ⲙⲓⲥⲓ	To beget, give birth	ⲙⲉⲥ-, ⲙⲁⲥ-	ⲙⲁⲥ″	ⲙⲟⲥⲓ	Born
ϭⲓⲥⲓ	To elevate, exalt	ϭⲉⲥ-	ϭⲁⲥ″	ϭⲟⲥⲓ	Elevated, exalted
ⲫⲓⲥⲓ	To cook	ⲫⲉⲥ-	ⲫⲁⲥ″	ⲫⲟⲥⲓ	Cooked
ⲫⲓⲣⲓ	To blossom	ⲫⲉⲣ-	-------	ⲫⲟⲣⲓ	Blossoming, radiating
ϩⲓⲥⲓ	To toil, weary	-------	ϩⲁⲥ″	ϩⲟⲥⲓ	Wearied, tired

ⲁ *changes to* ⲉ *in the pronominal form before the letter* ⲃ, ⲙ, ⲛ:

ϫⲓⲙⲓ	To find	ϫⲉⲙ-	ϫⲉⲙ″	-------	
ϣⲓⲛⲓ	To ask	ϣⲉⲛ-	ϣⲉⲛ″	-------	
ⲓⲛⲓ	To bring, offer	ⲉⲛ-	ⲉⲛ″	-------	
ⲓⲛⲓ	To resemble	ⲉⲛ-	-------	ⲟⲛⲓ	Similar

ⲟ *changes to* ⲁ *in the qualitative form before the letter* ⲕ, ϣ, ϭ:

ⲣⲓⲕⲓ	To bend, tilt	ⲣⲉⲕ-	ⲣⲁⲕ″	ⲣⲁⲕⲓ	Bent, tilted
ⲙⲓϣⲓ	To strike, fight	ⲙⲉϣ-, ⲙⲁϣ-	ⲙⲁϣ″	ⲙⲁϣⲓ	Stricken
ⲓϣⲓ	To hang, crucify	ⲉϣ-	ⲁϣ″	ⲁϣⲓ	Hung, crucified
ⲑⲓϭⲓ	To get drunk	-------	-------	ⲑⲁϭⲓ	Drunk

The following verbs are an exception to this rule:

ⲓⲣⲓ	To work, make, become	ⲉⲣ-	ⲁⲓ″, ⲁⲓⲧ″	ⲟⲓ	Made, become
ϯ	To give	ϯ-	ⲧⲏⲓ″, ⲧⲏⲓⲧ″	ⲧⲟⲓ	Given
ϩⲓⲟⲩⲓ	To throw, cast	ϩⲓ-	ϩⲓⲧ″	ϩⲱⲟⲩⲓ	Cast, thrown

2. Verbs whose main vowel letter is different in the absolute form, and their qualitative form is formed by the letters ⲱⲟⲩ, and they are all intransitive verbs.

Absolute form		Qualitative form	
ⲫⲉⲣⲓ	To shine, sparkle	ⲫⲉⲣⲓⲱⲟⲩ	Shining, sparkling
ϣⲁⲓ	To shine, rise (sun)	ϣⲁⲓⲱⲟⲩ	Sunny
ϩⲉⲣⲓ	To be still, be quiet	ϩⲟⲣⲡⲱⲟⲩ	Still
ⲁⲥⲓⲁⲓ	To be healed, to be active	ⲁⲥⲓⲱⲟⲩ	Light (weight), active
ϣⲁϥⲓ	To swell	ϣⲁϥⲓⲱⲟⲩ	Swollen
ϣⲱⲟⲩⲓ	To dry up	ϣⲟⲩⲱⲟⲩ	Dry

Lesson 24 ✠ The Forms (Tenses) of the Simple Verbs [Part 3] ✠

3. Four verbs whose qualitative form is formed by the letters ϩⲟⲩ.

Absolute form		Phrasal F.	Pronominal F.	Qualitative form	
ϣⲓ	To measure, weigh (trans.)	ϣⲓ-	ϣⲓⲧ"	ϣⲏⲟⲩ	Measured, weighed
ϭⲓ	To take, be granted (trans.)	ϭⲓ-	ϭⲓⲧ"	ϭⲏⲟⲩ	Taken
ⲥⲓ	To be sated (intrans.)	-------	-------	ⲥⲏⲟⲩ	Sated
ⲟⲩⲉⲓ	To be far (intrans.)	-------	-------	ⲟⲩⲏⲟⲩ	Far

The following two verbs are included in this group:

| ⲙⲉⲓ | To love | ⲙⲉⲛⲣⲉ- | ⲙⲉⲛⲣⲓⲧ" | ⲙⲉⲛⲣⲓⲧ | Beloved |
| ϥⲁⲓ | To lift, carry | ϥⲓ- | ϥⲓⲧ" | ------- | |

Application:

The phrasal tenses (ϯ-, ϭⲓ-, ⲉⲣ-, ϫⲉⲙ-, ϣⲉⲛ-, ϣⲉⲡ-, ϩⲓ-) of the verbs (ϯ, ϭⲓ, ⲓⲣⲓ, ϫⲓⲙⲓ, ϣⲓⲛⲓ, ϣⲱⲡ, ϩⲓⲟⲩⲓ) are used to form phrasal verbs, for example:

ϯⲱⲟⲩ	To glorify	ϯⲧⲁⲓⲟ	To honor	ϯⲥⲃⲱ	To teach
ϯⲱⲙⲥ	To baptize	ϭⲓⲱⲟⲩ	To be glorified	ϭⲓⲥⲁⲣⲝ	To be incarnate
ϭⲓⲥⲃⲱ	To learn	ϭⲓϩⲓⲙⲓ	To marry	ⲉⲣⲣⲱⲙⲓ	To become man
ⲉⲣⲟⲩⲱⲓⲛⲓ	To illuminate	ⲉⲣϩⲙⲟⲧ	To grant	ⲉⲣⲙⲉⲑⲣⲉ	To testify
ϫⲉⲙⲛⲟⲙϯ	To be consoled	ϫⲉⲙϯⲡⲓ	To taste	ϫⲉⲙϫⲟⲙ	To be strong
ϫⲉⲙⲡϣⲓⲛⲓ	To visit	ϣⲉⲛϩⲏⲧ	To be compassionate	ϣⲉⲛⲟⲩⲱⲙ	To fast
ϣⲉⲛⲛⲟⲩϥⲓ	Good news (noun)	ϣⲉⲡϩⲙⲟⲧ	To give thanks	ϣⲉⲡⲙ̀ⲕⲁϩ	To suffer, accept pain
ϣⲉⲡϭⲓⲥⲓ	To suffer, accept suffering	ϩⲓⲥⲉⲛϯ	To found, lay the foundation of	ϩⲓϣⲉⲛⲛⲟⲩϥⲓ	To preach, to announce good news

Sample Sentences:

ⲁ̄ ⲭⲉⲣⲉ ⲑⲏⲉⲑⲙⲉϩ ⲛ̀ϩⲙⲟⲧ: ⲭⲉⲣⲉ ⲑⲏⲉⲧⲁⲥϫⲉⲙ ϩ̀ⲙⲟⲧ: ⲭⲉⲣⲉ ⲑⲏⲉⲧⲁⲥⲙⲉⲥ Ⲡⲭⲥ̅: ⲟⲩⲟϩ Ⲡ̅ⲟ̅ⲥ̅ ϣⲟⲡ ⲛⲉⲙⲉ.
Hail to you O full of grace; hail to you who found grace; hail to you who gave birth to Christ; the Lord is with you.

ⲃ̄ Ⲓⲏⲥ ⲫⲏⲉⲧⲁⲥⲙⲁⲥϥ ⲛ̀ϫⲉ ϯⲡⲁⲣⲑⲉⲛⲟⲥ.
Jesus whom the Virgin bore.

ⲅ̄ ϯⲥⲁⲣⲝ, ⲑⲁⲓ ⲉⲧⲁϥϭⲓⲧⲥ ⲛ̀ϩⲏⲧ̀.
The body, this which He took from you.

ⲇ̄ ⲡⲁⲓⲣⲏϯ ⲁ Ⲫϯ ⲙⲉⲛⲣⲉ ⲡⲓⲕⲟⲥⲙⲟⲥ.
God so loved the world.

ⲉ̄ ⲁⲩⲉⲛ ⲡⲓϣⲃⲱⲧ ⲛ̀ⲧⲉ Ⲁⲁⲣⲱⲛ ϩⲓϫⲉⲛ ⲡϣⲉ ⲛ̀ⲧⲉ ⲡⲓⲥ̅ⲧⲁⲩⲣⲟⲥ ⲉⲧⲁⲩⲉϣ ⲡⲁⲟ̅ⲥ̅ ⲉ̀ⲣⲟϥ.
They likened the rod of Aaron to the wood of the cross, on which my Lord was crucified.

[ⲁⲩⲓⲛⲓ . . . ϩⲓϫⲉⲛ = they bring ... upon = they liken ... to]

ⲋ̄ ⲫⲏⲉⲧⲁⲩⲁϣϥ ⲉ̀ⲡⲓⲥ̅ⲧⲁⲩⲣⲟⲥ ⲛ̀ϫⲉ ⲛⲓⲓⲟⲩⲇⲁⲓ.
That whom the Jews hung (crucified) on the cross.

ⲍ̄ ⲁϥⲉⲣ ⲡⲉⲛⲅⲉⲛⲟⲥ ⲛ̀ⲣⲉⲙϩⲉ.
He made our race free. [He freed our race.]

ⲏ̄ ϥⲛⲁⲁⲓⲧⲉⲛ ⲛ̀ⲣⲁⲙⲁⲟ̀.
He will make us rich.

ⲑ̄ ⲛⲓⲙ ⲅⲁⲣ ϧⲉⲛ ⲛⲓⲛⲟⲩϯ ⲉⲧⲟⲛⲓ ⲙ̀ⲙⲟⲕ Ⲡ̅ⲟ̅ⲥ̅?
Who is likened unto You, O Lord, among the gods?

ⲓ̄ ⲙ̀ⲡⲉϥϫⲉⲙ ⲫⲏⲉⲧⲟⲛⲓ ⲙ̀ⲙⲟ.
He did not find that who is like you.

ⲓ̄ⲁ̄ ⲁϥⲣⲉⲕ ⲛⲓⲫⲏⲟⲩⲓ̀ ⲛ̀ⲧⲉ ⲛⲓⲫⲏⲟⲩⲓ̀.
He bent the heavens of the heavens.

ⲓ̄ⲃ̄ ⲁⲕϭⲓⲙⲱⲓⲧ ϧⲁϫⲱϥ ⲙ̀ⲡⲉⲕⲗⲁⲟⲥ.
You guided Your people. [You took a way before Your people.]

ⲓ̄ⲅ̄ ⲫⲁⲓ ⲉⲧⲁϥⲉⲛϥ ⲉ̀ⲡ̀ϣⲱⲓ ⲛ̀ⲟⲩⲑⲩⲥⲓⲁ ⲉⲥϣⲏⲡ.
This is [He] who offered Himself as an acceptable sacrifice.

Lesson 24 ✤ The Forms (Tenses) of the Simple Verbs [Part 3] ✤

ⲓⲃ̄ ⲁ Ⲡⳓⲥ̄ ⲉⲛ ⲡⲓⲙⲱⲟⲩ ⲛ̀ⲧⲉ ⲫⲓⲟⲙ ⲉ̀ϩⲣⲏⲓ ⲉ̀ϫⲱⲟⲩ.
The Lord brought the water of the sea upon them.

ⲓⲉ̄ ⲟⲩⲥⲑⲉⲣⲧⲉⲣ ⲉⲧⲁϥϭⲓⲧⲟⲩ.
A trembling which took them.

ⲓⲋ̄ ⲁⲩϭⲓⲥⲓ ⲛ̀ϫⲉ ⲛⲓⲙⲱⲟⲩ ⲙ̀ⲫⲣⲏϯ ⲛ̀ⲟⲩⲥⲟⲃⲧ.
The waters rose up like a wall.

ⲓⲍ̄ ⲥⲱⲥ ⲉ̀ⲣⲟϥ ⲁⲣⲓϩⲟⲩⲟ́ ϭⲁⲥϥ.
Praise Him and exalt Him. [Praise Him and make increase of His exaltedness].

ⲓⲏ̄ ⲉⲧⲁ Ⲙⲱⲩ̈ⲥⲓⲥ ⲙⲉϣ ϯⲡⲉⲧⲣⲁ ⲛ̀ϧⲏⲧϥ.
With which Moses struck the rock.

ⲓⲑ̄ ⲕⲁⲧⲁ ϣⲉⲛⲛⲓϥⲓ ⲛⲓⲃⲉⲛ ⲉ̀ϯⲛⲁⲑⲏⲓⲧⲟⲩ: ϯⲛⲁⲥⲙⲟⲩ ⲉ̀ⲡⲉⲕⲣⲁⲛ ⲉⲑⲟⲩⲁⲃ.
Every breath that I will give [draw], I will bless Your holy name.

ⲕ̄

ⲟⲩϣⲱⲃϣ ⲉϥϭⲟⲥⲓ.
A high arm.

ⲧⲉⲕⲉⲧⲫⲱ ⲁⲥⲓⲱⲟⲩ.
Your light burden.

ⲛⲓⲛⲟⲃⲓ ⲉⲧⲁⲓⲁⲓⲧⲟⲩ.
The sins that I committed.

ⲁϥⲉⲣ ⲟⲩⲛⲁⲓ ⲛⲉⲙⲁⲛ.
He made mercy with us.

ⲛⲓⲧⲱⲟⲩ ⲉⲧϭⲟⲥⲓ.
The high mountains.

ϩⲁⲛⲁⲥⲕⲏⲥⲓⲥ ⲉⲧϭⲟⲥⲓ.
Laborious asceticism [ascetical practices].

Exercises

1. Complete the conjugation of the following verbs:

Absolute form	Phrasal form	Pronominal form	Qualitative form
-----	ϣⲉⲡ-	-----	ϣⲏⲡ
ⲙⲟϩ	-----	ⲙⲁϩ"	-----
-----	ⲭⲁ-	-----	-----
ⲱⲡ	-----	ⲟⲡ"	-----
-----	ⲥⲉⲧⲡ-	-----	ⲥⲟⲧⲡ
ⲱϥⲧ	-----	ⲟϥⲧ"	-----
ⲙⲓⲥⲓ	-----	-----	-----
-----	ⲉⲣ	-----	ⲟⲓ

†	-----	-----	ⲧⲟⲓ
-----	-----	ϭⲁⲥ″	-----
-----	ϭⲓ	-----	-----
ⲓⲱⲓ	-----	-----	ⲁϣⲓ

2. Complete according to the given example:

   1. ⲁⲣⲉⲭⲓⲙⲓ ⲛ̀ⲟⲩϩⲙⲟⲧ.   ⲁⲣⲉⲭⲉⲙ ⲟⲩϩⲙⲟⲧ.   ⲁⲣⲉⲭⲉⲙϥ.
   2. ⲁⲓ̈ⲣⲓ ⲛ̀ⲛⲁⲓⲛⲟⲃⲓ.
   3. ⲧⲉⲣⲁⲙⲓⲥⲓ ⲙ̀ⲫⲏⲉⲑⲟⲩⲁⲃ.
   4. ⲁϥⲓⲛⲓ ⲛ̀ⲧⲉϥⲕⲩⲑⲁⲣⲁ.
   5. ϥⲙⲉⲓ ⲙ̀ⲡⲉϥϣⲏⲣ.
   6. ⲁⲩⲙⲓϣⲓ ⲛ̀ⲛⲟⲩⲭⲁϫⲓ.

3. Translate to the English language:

   1. ϯⲧⲣⲓⲁⲥ ⲉⲧϫⲏⲕ ⲉ̀ⲃⲟⲗ.
   2. ⲟⲩⲁⲗⲟⲩ ⲉϥⲙⲟⲥⲓ.
   3. ϩⲁⲛϫⲱⲙ ⲉⲩϭⲛⲟⲩ.
   4. ⲛⲓⲙⲁ ⲉⲧϭⲟⲥⲓ.
   5. ⲟⲩⲗⲁⲟⲥ ⲉϥⲟϣ.
   6. ⲛⲓⲥⲛⲏⲟⲩ ⲉⲑⲙⲉⲛⲣⲓⲧ.
   7. ⲉⲑⲙⲉϩ ⲛ̀ⲱⲟⲩ.
   8. ⲟⲩⲡⲉⲧⲣⲁ ⲉϥⲙⲁϣⲓ.
   9. ⲡⲉⲕⲣⲁⲛ ⲉⲧϩⲟⲗϫ.
   10. ⲟⲩⲟⲩⲥⲓⲁ ⲉⲥϣⲏⲡ.
   11. ⲉⲑⲙⲏⲛ ⲉ̀ⲃⲟⲗ ϣⲁ ⲉ̀ⲛⲉϩ.
   12. ϩⲁⲛϩ̀ⲃⲏⲟⲩⲓ̈ ⲉⲩϭⲟⲥⲓ.

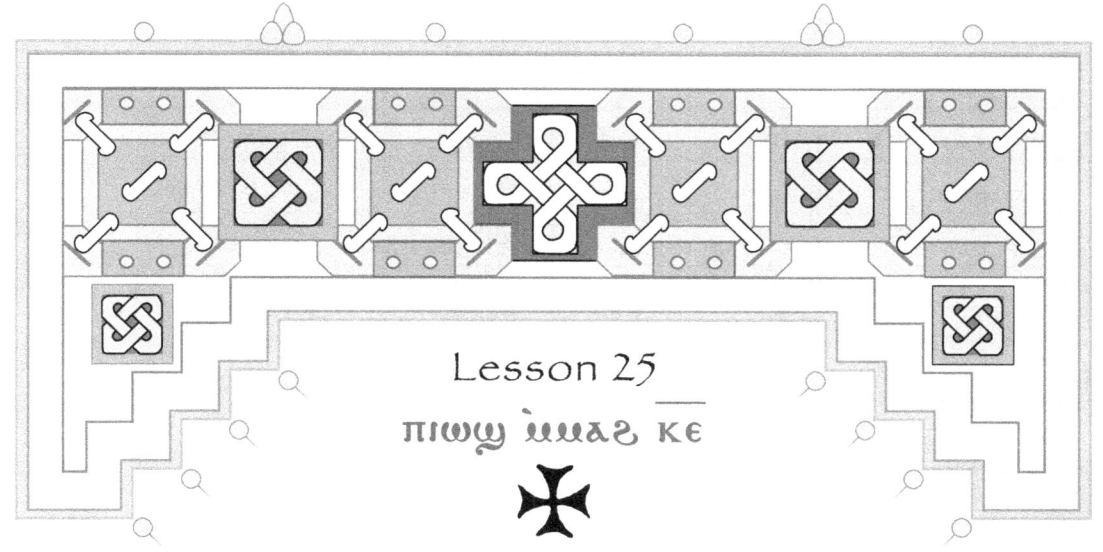

Lesson 25

ⲡⲓⲱϣ ⲙ̄ⲙⲁϩ ⲕ̅ⲉ̅

✠

The Forms (Tenses) of the Simple Verbs [Part 4]

5 and 6. The Quadri-radical and Penta-radical Verbs

Absolute form	Phrasal F.	Pronominal F.	Qualitative form
Rule: ⲟ . ⲉ	ⲉ . ⲉ	ⲉ . ⲱ	ⲉ . ⲱ

Quadri-radical verbs:

ⲃⲟⲣⲃⲉⲣ	To cast, throw	ⲃⲉⲣⲃⲉⲣ-	ⲃⲉⲣⲃⲱⲣ″	ⲃⲉⲣⲃⲱⲣ	Thrown, cast
ⲥⲟⲗⲥⲉⲗ	To adorn, console	ⲥⲉⲗⲥⲉⲗ-	ⲥⲉⲗⲥⲱⲗ″	ⲥⲉⲗⲥⲱⲗ	Adorned
ϧⲟⲗϧⲉⲗ	To slaughter	ϧⲉⲗϧⲉⲗ-	ϧⲉⲗϧⲱⲗ″	ϧⲉⲗϧⲱⲗ	Slaughtered
ϧⲟⲙϧⲉⲙ	To crush, mash	ϧⲉⲙϧⲉⲙ-	ϧⲉⲙϧⲱⲙ″	ϧⲉⲙϧⲱⲙ	Crushed
ϧⲟⲧϧⲉⲧ	To examine, test	ϧⲉⲧϧⲉⲧ-	ϧⲉⲧϧⲱⲧ″	ϧⲉⲧϧⲱⲧ	Examined
ϩⲟⲛϩⲉⲛ	To order, command	ϩⲉⲛϩⲉⲛ-	ϩⲉⲛϩⲱⲛ″	-------	
ϩⲟⲭϩⲉⲭ	To annoy, be annoyed	ϩⲉⲭϩⲉⲭ-	ϩⲉⲭϩⲱⲭ″	ϩⲉⲭϩⲱⲭ	Annoyed, troubled
ⲫⲟⲧⲫⲉⲧ	To crumble, cut	-------	ⲫⲉⲧⲫⲱⲧ″	ⲫⲉⲧⲫⲱⲧ	Crumbled

ϣⲟⲣϣⲉⲣ	To demolish	-------	ϣⲉⲣϣⲱⲣ″	ϣⲉⲣϣⲱⲣ	Demolished
ϫⲟⲩϫⲉⲛ	To touch	-------	ϫⲉⲛϫⲱⲛ″	-------	
ⲙⲟⲕⲙⲉⲕ	To think	ⲙⲉⲕⲙⲉⲕ-	ⲙⲉⲕⲙⲟⲩⲕ″	-------	
ⲑⲟⲛⲧⲉⲛ	To be like, be similar	-------	ⲧⲉⲛⲑⲱⲛ-	ⲧⲉⲛⲑⲱⲛ″	ⲧⲉⲛⲑⲱⲛⲧ	Similar, like

Penta-radical verbs:

ⲥ̀ⲕⲟⲣⲕⲉⲣ	To roll	ⲥ̀ⲕⲉⲣⲕⲉⲣ-	ⲥ̀ⲕⲉⲣⲕⲱⲣ″	ⲥ̀ⲕⲉⲣⲕⲱⲣ	Rolled
ϣ̀ⲑⲟⲣⲧⲉⲣ	To be disturbed	ϣ̀ⲑⲉⲣⲧⲉⲣ-	ϣ̀ⲧⲉⲣⲑⲱⲣ″	ϣ̀ⲧⲉⲣⲑⲱⲣ	Disturbed
ⲉ̀ⲣⲟϣⲣⲉϣ	To be red	-------	-------	ⲉ̀ⲣⲉϣⲣⲱϣ	Red

Note: The absolute form of some of these verbs is sometimes formed by the letter ⲉ instead of ⲟ:

ⲃⲉⲣⲃⲉⲣ	To boil		ⲧⲉⲗⲧⲉⲗ	To drip, trickle
ⲥ̀ⲕⲉⲣⲕⲉⲣ	To roll, be rolled		ⲭⲣⲉⲙⲣⲉⲙ	To complain

7. Tri-radical verbs with repeated third consonant

None has remained of these verbs in the Coptic language except the verb ⲥⲟⲃϯ:

ⲥⲟⲃϯ	To prepare, be ready	ⲥⲉⲃⲧⲉ-	ⲥⲉⲃⲧⲱⲧ″	ⲥⲉⲃⲧⲱⲧ	Prepared, ready

Noteworthy is that the repetition of the third letter (ⲧ) appears in the pronominal and qualitative forms.

8. Quadri-radical verbs ending with a vowel

That is, the fourth letter, following the third consonant letter, is a vowel. Some verbs have remained of this kind, such as:

ⲙⲟⲥϯ	To hate	ⲙⲉⲥⲧⲉ-	ⲙⲉⲥⲧⲱ″	-------	
ⲙⲟⲛⲓ	To shepherd	-------	ⲙⲁⲛⲟⲩ″	-------	
ϫⲱⲓⲗⲓ	To reside, sojourn	ϫⲁⲗⲉ-	ϫⲁⲗⲱ″	ϫⲁⲗⲏⲟⲩⲧ	Sojourner
ⲥⲟϭⲛⲓ	To plot, deliberate	-------	-------	-------	

Lesson 25 ✣ The Forms (Tenses) of the Simple Verbs [Part 4] ✣

Sample Sentences:

ⲁ̄ ⲁϥⲃⲟⲣⲃⲉⲣ ⲙ̀Ⲫⲁⲣⲁⲱ ⲛⲉⲙ ⲧⲉϥϫⲟⲙ ⲧⲏⲣⲥ ⲉ̀ϥⲓⲟⲙ ⲛ̀ϣⲁⲣⲓ.
He cast Pharaoh and all his power in the Red Sea.

ⲃ̄ ⲛⲓⲃⲉⲣⲉϭⲱⲟⲩⲧⲥ ⲛ̀ⲧⲉ Ⲫⲁⲣⲁⲱ ⲛⲉⲙ ⲧⲉϥϫⲟⲙ ⲧⲏⲣⲥ ⲁϥⲃⲉⲣⲃⲱⲣⲟⲩ ⲉ̀ϥⲓⲟⲙ.
The chariots of Pharaoh and all his power He cast in the sea.

ⲅ̄ ⲡ̀ⲧⲁⲓⲟ ⲛ̀ϯⲥⲕⲏⲛⲏ ⲉⲧⲁϥⲥⲉⲗⲥⲱⲗⲥ ⲉ̀ⲃⲟⲗ ⲛ̀ϫⲉ ⲡⲓⲡ̀ⲣⲟⲫⲏⲧⲏⲥ.
The honor of the tabernacle which the prophet [Moses] adorned.

ⲇ̄ ⲭⲉⲣⲉ ⲡⲓⲙⲁⲛ̀ϣⲉⲗⲉⲧ ⲉⲧⲥⲉⲗⲥⲱⲗ ϧⲉⲛ ⲟⲩⲑⲟ ⲛ̀ⲣⲏϯ ⲛ̀ⲧⲉⲡⲓⲛⲩⲙⲫⲓⲟⲥ ⲙ̀ⲙⲏⲓ.
Hail to the bridal chamber, adorned with various kinds [of adornments] of the true Bridegroom.

ⲉ̄ ⲑⲏⲉⲧⲥⲉⲗⲥⲱⲗ ϧⲉⲛ ⲧⲁⲓⲟ ⲛⲓⲃⲉⲛ.
Who is adorned with all honor.

ⲋ̄ ⲁⲕⲥⲟⲗⲥⲉⲗ ⲛ̀ⲛⲉⲛⲯⲩⲭⲏ: ⲱ̀ Ⲙⲱⲩ̀ⲥⲏⲥ ⲡⲓⲡ̀ⲣⲟⲫⲏⲧⲏⲥ: ϧⲉⲛ ⲡ̀ⲧⲁⲓⲟ ⲛ̀ϯⲥⲕⲏⲛⲏ: ⲉⲧⲁⲕⲥⲉⲗⲥⲱⲗⲥ ⲉ̀ⲃⲟⲗ.
You adorned (consoled) our souls, O Moses the prophet, with the honor of the tabernacle, which you adorned.

ⲍ̄ ⲕϧⲟⲧϧⲉⲧ ⲛ̀ⲛⲁϭ̀ⲗⲱⲧ.
You examine my kidneys [i.e. my inwards parts].

ⲏ̄ ⲁⲕϧⲟⲙϧⲉⲙ ⲛ̀ϯⲥⲟⲩⲣⲓ ⲛ̀ⲧⲉ ⲫ̀ⲙⲟⲩ.
You crushed the sting of death.

ⲑ̄ ⲁϥϧⲟⲙϧⲉⲙ ⲙ̀ⲫ̀ⲙⲟⲩ ϩⲓⲧⲉⲛ ⲡⲉϥⲙⲟⲩ.
He crushed death by His death.

ⲓ̄ ⲉⲕⲉ̀ϧⲟⲙϧⲉⲙ ⲙ̀ⲡ̀ⲥⲁⲧⲁⲛⲁⲥ ⲥⲁⲡⲉⲥⲏⲧ ⲛ̀ⲛⲉⲛϭⲁⲗⲁⲩϫ.
Crush [always] the devil under our feet.

ⲓⲁ̄ ⲫ̀ⲙⲟⲩ ⲉⲧⲁϥⲓ̀ ⲉ̀ϧⲟⲩⲛ ⲉ̀ⲡⲓⲕⲟⲥⲙⲟⲥ ϩⲓⲧⲉⲛ ⲡⲓⲫ̀ⲑⲟⲛⲟⲥ ⲛ̀ⲧⲉ ⲡⲓⲇⲓⲁⲃⲟⲗⲟⲥ ⲁⲕϣⲉⲣϣⲱⲣϥ ϩⲓⲧⲉⲛ ⲡⲓⲟⲩⲱⲛϩ ⲉ̀ⲃⲟⲗ ⲛ̀ⲣⲉϥⲧⲁⲛϧⲟ.
The death, which entered into the world through the envy of the devil, You destroyed by the life-giving manifestation.

ⲓⲃ̄ ⲡⲓⲁⲧϣ̀ⲧⲁϩⲟϥ ⲁⲩϫⲉⲙϫⲱⲙϥ.
The incomprehensible they touched.

ⲓⲅ̄ ⲉⲧⲉⲣϧⲁⲉ̀ ⲉⲩϩⲉϫϩⲱϫ ⲟⲩⲟϩ ⲉⲩϯⲙⲕⲁϩ.
They were needy, distressed, and suffering.

ⲓⲇ̄ ⲁⲣⲉⲧⲉⲛⲟⲩⲱⲛϯ ⲉ̀ⲙⲟⲩⲕⲓ ⲑⲏⲉⲧⲁ Ⲓⲁⲕⲱⲃ ⲛⲁⲩ ⲉ̀ⲣⲟⲥ.
You resembled the ladder which Jacob saw.

ι̅ε̅	ⲥⲉⲧⲉⲛⲑⲱⲛϯ ⲉⲡⲓϣⲃⲱⲧ ⲛ̀ⲧⲉ Ⲁⲁⲣⲱⲛ.	

ι̅ε̅ ⲥⲉⲧⲉⲛⲑⲱⲛϯ ⲉⲡⲓϣⲃⲱⲧ ⲛ̀ⲧⲉ Ⲁⲁⲣⲱⲛ.
They liken you to the rod of Aaron.

ι̅ⲋ̅ ⲁϥⲥⲕⲉⲣⲕⲉⲣ ⲡⲓⲱⲛⲓ ⲉ̀ⲃⲟⲗϩⲁ ⲣⲱϥ ⲙ̀ⲡⲓⲙϩⲁⲩ.
He rolled the rock from the mouth of the tomb.

ι̅ⲍ̅ ⲁϥⲥⲕⲉⲣⲕⲱⲣϥ.
He rolled it.

ι̅ⲏ̅ ⲁⲩϫⲓⲙⲓ ⲙ̀ⲡⲓⲱⲛⲓ ⲉ̀ⲁⲩⲥⲕⲉⲣⲕⲱⲣϥ ⲥⲁⲃⲟⲗ ⲙ̀ⲡⲓⲙϩⲁⲩ.
They found the rock rolled far from the tomb.

ι̅ⲑ̅ ⲉⲑⲃⲉⲟⲩ ⲧⲉⲧⲉⲛϣⲧⲉⲣⲑⲱⲣ?
"Why are you troubled?" (Luke 24:38).

ⲕ̅ ⲡⲉⲕⲙⲁⲛ̀ϣⲱⲡⲓ ⲉⲧⲥⲉⲃⲧⲱⲧ.
Your prepared dwelling.

ⲕ̅ⲁ̅ ⲁⲩⲥⲉⲃⲧⲉ ⲡⲓⲡⲁⲥⲭⲁ.
They prepared the Passover.

ⲕ̅ⲃ̅ ⲡⲉⲕⲙⲁ ⲉⲑⲟⲩⲁⲃ Ⲡ⳪ ⲫⲏⲉⲧⲁⲩⲥⲉⲃⲧⲱⲧϥ ⲛ̀ϫⲉ ⲛⲉⲕϫⲓϫ.
Your holy place, O Lord, which Your hands prepared.

ⲕ̅ⲅ̅ ϫⲉ ⲁⲩⲛⲁⲩ ⲛ̀ϫⲉ ⲛⲁⲃⲁⲗ ⲉ̀ⲡⲉⲕⲛⲟϩⲉⲙ: ⲫⲏⲉⲧⲁⲕⲥⲉⲃⲧⲱⲧϥ ⲙ̀ⲡⲉⲙⲑⲟ
ⲛ̀ⲛⲓⲗⲁⲟⲥ ⲧⲏⲣⲟⲩ.
For my eyes have seen Your salvation which You have prepared before [the face of] all peoples.

ⲕ̅ⲇ̅ ⲫⲁⲓ ⲡⲉ ⲡⲁⲛⲟⲩϯ ϯⲛⲁϯⲱⲟⲩ ⲛⲁϥ: Ⲫϯ ⲙ̀ⲡⲁⲓⲱⲧ ϯⲛⲁϭⲁⲥϥ.
This is my God, I will glorify Him; God of my father, I will exalt Him.

Exercises

1. Put the verb in the suitable tense in the following sentences:

ⲁ̅	(ϣⲟⲣϣⲉⲣ)	ⲡⲉⲛⲥⲱⲧⲏⲣ ⲁϥ---------ϥ.
ⲃ̅	(ϩⲟⲙϩⲉⲙ)	ⲫⲓⲟⲩ ⲉⲧ---------.
ⲅ̅	(ⲥⲟⲗⲥⲉⲗ)	ⲛⲏⲉⲑⲟⲩⲁⲃ ⲥⲉ--------- ⲛⲉⲛⲯⲩⲭⲏ.
ⲇ̅	(ϩⲟⲧϩⲉⲧ)	Ⲫⲛⲟⲩϯ ⲁϥ---------ⲟⲩ.
ⲉ̅	(ⲥⲕⲟⲣⲕⲉⲣ)	ⲡⲓⲱⲛⲓ ⲉⲧ---------.
ⲋ̅	(ⲥⲟⲃϯ)	ⲛⲓⲙⲁⲑⲏⲧⲏⲥ ⲁⲩ--------- ⲡⲓⲡⲁⲥⲭⲁ.
ⲍ̅	(ⲙⲓⲥⲓ)	ϯⲡⲁⲣⲑⲉⲛⲟⲥ ⲁⲥ--------- Ⲡⲓⲭⲣⲓⲥⲧⲟⲥ.

Lesson 25 ✠ *The Forms (Tenses) of the Simple Verbs [Part 4]* ✠

2. Complete according to the given example:

1. ⲁϥϩⲟⲧϩⲉⲧ ⲛ̀Ⲁⲃⲣⲁⲁⲙ.	ⲁϥϩⲉⲧϩⲉⲧ Ⲁⲃⲣⲁⲁⲙ.	ⲁϥϩⲉⲧϩⲱⲧϥ.
2. ⲁⲕⲃⲟⲣⲃⲉⲣ ⲛ̀ⲛⲓϫⲁϫⲓ.		
3. ⲁⲩ̀ⲥⲕⲟⲣⲕⲉⲣ ⲙ̀ⲡⲓⲱⲛⲓ.		
4. ⲥⲉϩⲟⲗϩⲉⲗ ⲛ̀ϯϣⲟϣ.		
5. ⲁϥⲥⲟⲛϩⲉⲛ ⲛ̀ⲛⲉϥϣⲏⲣⲓ.		
6. ⲧⲉⲛϭⲓ ⲛ̀ⲧⲉϥϩⲓⲣⲏⲛⲏ.		

3. Write the absolute tense for the following verbs:

1. ⲉⲡ-	7. ϩⲟⲃⲥ"	13. ⲙⲉϩ
2. ⲫⲉⲣϣ-	8. ⲛⲁϩⲙ"	14. ⲭⲏ
3. ϫⲉⲙ-	9. ⲁϣ"	15. ϭⲟⲥⲓ
4. ⲉⲣ-	10. ⲟⲙⲥ"	16. ϫⲏⲕ
5. ⲙⲉⲛⲣⲉ-	11. ⲁⲓ"	17. ⲧⲉⲛⲑⲱⲛⲧ
6. ϣ̀ⲑⲉⲣⲧⲉⲣ-	12. ⲥⲉⲗⲥⲱⲗ"	18. ⲑ̀ⲣⲉϣⲣⲱϣ

Review Exercises 5
On Lessons 21 to 25

1. Write the meaning of the following:

1. Ⲫⲛⲟⲩϯ ⲉⲧⲟⲛϧ.
2. ⲛⲓⲥⲛⲏⲟⲩ ⲉⲑⲙⲉⲛⲣⲓⲧ.
3. ⲁⲕϭⲓⲥⲁⲣⲝ ⲟⲩⲟϩ ⲁⲕⲉⲣⲣⲱⲙⲓ.
4. ⲁϥⲃⲉⲗ ϯⲙⲉⲧϫⲁϫⲓ.
5. ⲁⲩⲁϣϥ ⲉ̀ⲡⲓⲥ̅ⲧⲁⲩⲣⲟⲥ.
6. ⲁϥⲁⲓⲧⲉⲛ ⲛ̀ⲣⲉⲙϩⲉ.
7. ⲡⲓⲣⲉϥⲉⲣϩⲉⲙⲓ ⲉⲧⲭⲟⲣ.
8. ϩⲁⲛⲁⲥⲕⲏⲥⲓⲥ ⲉⲩϭⲟⲥⲓ.
9. ⲕϭⲉⲧϭⲉⲧ ⲛⲁⲃ̀ⲗⲱⲧ.
10. ⲁⲥⲟⲩⲉⲙ ⲟⲩⲱⲓⲕ.
11. ⲁⲩⲭⲁϥ ϧⲉⲛ ⲟⲩⲙϩⲁⲩ.
12. ⲁϥⲥ̀ⲕⲉⲣⲕⲱⲣϥ.

2. Put the verb in the qualitative form according to the given example:

1. ⲁϥϣⲱⲡ ⲛ̀ⲟⲩⲑⲩⲥⲓⲁ.   ⲟⲩⲑⲩⲥⲓⲁ ⲉⲥϣⲏⲡ.
2. ⲁⲓⲟⲩⲱⲛ ⲛ̀ϩⲁⲛⲣⲱⲟⲩ.   ϩⲁⲛⲣⲱⲟⲩ ----------.
3. ⲁⲕⲫⲱⲣϣ ⲛ̀ⲛⲉⲕϫⲓϫ.   ⲛⲉⲕϫⲓϫ ----------.
4. ⲁϥⲃⲱⲗ ⲛ̀ⲟⲩⲙⲱⲟⲩ ⲉ̀ⲃⲟⲗ. ⲟⲩⲙⲱⲟⲩ ---------- ⲉ̀ⲃⲟⲗ.
5. ⲁⲩⲁ̀ϣⲁⲓ ⲛ̀ϫⲉ ⲛⲁⲛⲟⲃⲓ.   ⲛⲁⲛⲟⲃⲓ ----------.

3. Complete according to the given example:

1. ⲁⲛϫⲓⲙⲓ ⲙ̀Ⲙⲁⲥⲓⲁⲥ. | ⲁⲛϫⲉⲙ Ⲙⲁⲥⲓⲁⲥ. | ⲁⲛϫⲉⲙϥ.
2. ⲁϥⲥⲱϯ ⲛ̀ϯⲡⲟⲣⲛⲏ. |

3. ⲁⲩⲓⲛⲓ ⲛ̀ϩⲁⲛⲇⲱⲣⲟⲛ.
4. ⲁⲕϭⲟⲙϭⲉⲙ ⲙ̀ⲡⲥⲁⲧⲁⲛⲁⲥ.
5. ⲧⲉⲛⲥⲟⲃϯ ⲛ̀ϯⲧⲣⲁⲡⲉⲍⲁ.
6. ⲁⲓϭⲓ ⲛ̀ⲛⲁⲓϫⲱⲙ.
7. ⲁⲥⲙⲓⲥⲓ ⲛ̀Ⲉⲙⲙⲁⲛⲟⲩⲏⲗ.

4. Put the verb in the suitable form in every sentence:

ⲁ̄	(ⲃⲟⲣⲃⲉⲣ)	ⲁϥ--------ⲟⲩ ⲉ̀ϥⲓⲟⲙ.
ⲃ̄	(ⲙⲓⲥⲓ)	ⲁⲥ--------ϥ ⲛ̀ϫⲉ ϯⲡⲁⲣⲑⲉⲛⲟⲥ.
ⲅ̄	(ⲟⲩⲱⲣⲡ)	Ⲓⲏⲥ ⲁϥ-------- ⲛⲉϥⲙⲁⲑⲏⲧⲏⲥ ⲉ̀ⲡⲓⲕⲟⲥⲙⲟⲥ.
ⲇ̄	(ϫⲱⲕ)	ⲛⲓⲁⲡⲟⲥⲧⲟⲗⲟⲥ ⲁⲩ-------- ⲡⲓϩⲱⲃ ⲉ̀ⲃⲟⲗ.
ⲉ̄	(ϭⲓⲥⲓ)	Ⲫϯ ⲙ̀ⲡⲁⲓⲱⲧ ϯⲛⲁ--------ϥ.
ⲋ̄	(ⲑⲟⲛⲧⲉⲛ)	ⲁⲣⲉ--------ϯ ⲉ̀ⲧⲙⲟⲩⲕⲓ ⲑⲏⲉⲧⲁ Ⲓⲁⲕⲱⲃ ⲛⲁⲩ ⲉ̀ⲣⲟⲥ.
ⲍ̄	(ⲥⲱⲟⲩⲛ)	ⲁⲛ-------- ⲡⲓϣⲟⲩϣⲱⲟⲩϣⲓ ⲙ̀ⲙⲏⲓ.

5. Translate to the English language:

ⲁ̄ ⲧⲉⲛⲙⲟⲥϯ ⲙ̀ⲡⲓⲛⲟⲃⲓ, ⲁⲗⲗⲁ ⲧⲉⲛⲙⲉⲛⲣⲉ ⲛⲓⲣⲉϥⲉⲣⲛⲟⲃⲓ.

ⲃ̄ ⲁⲓⲭⲁ ⲛⲁⲓϫⲱⲙ ϩⲓϫⲉⲛ ϯⲧⲣⲁⲡⲉⲍⲁ ⲉⲧⲉⲙⲙⲁⲩ ⲟⲩⲟϩ ⲡⲁⲥⲟⲛ ⲁϥⲉⲛⲟⲩ ⲉ̀ⲙ̀ⲛⲁⲓ.

ⲅ̄ ⲡⲓⲁⲅⲅⲉⲗⲟⲥ ⲁϥϣⲉⲛⲛⲟⲩϥⲓ ⲛ̀Ⲍⲁⲭⲁⲣⲓⲁⲥ ⲡⲓⲟⲩⲏⲃ ⲉ̀ⲡ̀ϫⲓⲛⲙⲓⲥⲓ ⲛ̀Ⲓⲱⲁⲛⲛⲏⲥ ⲡⲓⲣⲉϥϯⲱⲙⲥ, ⲟⲩⲟϩ ⲁϥϣⲉⲛⲛⲟⲩϥⲓ ⲙ̀Ⲙⲁⲣⲓⲁ ϯⲡⲁⲣⲑⲉⲛⲟⲥ ⲉ̀ⲡ̀ϫⲓⲛⲙⲓⲥⲓ ⲙ̀ⲡⲉⲛⲥⲱⲧⲏⲣ Ⲓⲏⲥⲟⲩⲥ.

ⲇ̄ Ⲫϯ ⲁϥϭⲓ ⲛ̀ⲧⲉⲛⲥⲁⲣⲝ, ⲁϥϯ ⲛⲁⲛ ⲙ̀ⲡⲉϥⲡ̀ⲛⲉⲩⲙⲁ ⲉⲑⲟⲩⲁⲃ ⲟⲩⲟϩ ⲁϥϩⲟⲧⲡⲉⲛ ⲉ̀ⲣⲟϥ.

ⲉ̄ ⲁϥⲁⲓⲧⲉⲛ ⲛ̀ⲟⲩⲁⲓ ⲛⲉⲙⲁϥ.

ⲋ̄ ⲁⲛⲟⲕ ⲡⲉ ⲡⲓⲱⲓⲕ ⲉⲧⲟⲛϧ ⲫⲏⲉⲧⲁϥⲓ̀ ⲉ̀ⲡⲉⲥⲏⲧ ⲉ̀ⲃⲟⲗϧⲉⲛ ⲧ̀ⲫⲉ.

ⲍ̄ ⲡⲓⲱⲓⲕ ⲁⲛⲟⲕ ⲉ̀ϯⲛⲁⲧⲏⲓϥ ⲧⲁⲥⲁⲣⲝ ⲧⲉ, ⲑⲏ ⲉ̀ϯⲛⲁⲧⲏⲓⲥ ⲉⲑⲃⲉ ⲡ̀ⲱⲛϧ ⲙ̀ⲡⲓⲕⲟⲥⲙⲟⲥ.

ⲏ̄ ⲛⲓⲥⲁϫⲓ ⲁⲛⲟⲕ ⲉⲧⲁⲓϫⲟⲧⲟⲩ ⲛⲱⲧⲉⲛ ⲟⲩⲡ̀ⲛⲉⲩⲙⲁ ⲡⲉ ⲟⲩⲟϩ ⲟⲩⲱⲛϧ ⲡⲉ.

ⲑ̄ ⲕⲁⲧⲁⲫ̀ⲣⲏϯ ⲉⲧⲁⲕⲟⲩⲟⲣⲡⲧ ⲉ̀ⲡⲓⲕⲟⲥⲙⲟⲥ ⲁⲛⲟⲕ ϩⲱ ⲁⲓⲟⲩⲟⲣⲡⲟⲩ ⲉ̀ⲡⲓⲕⲟⲥⲙⲟⲥ.

Exam 5

On Lessons 21 to 25

1. Write the meaning of the following:

1. ⲁϥⲉⲣ ⲟⲩⲛⲁⲓ ⲛⲉⲙⲁⲛ.
2. ⲁⲕϣⲉⲡ ⲧⲁⲓⲑⲩⲥⲓⲁ.
3. ⲁⲩϥϯ Ⲓⲏⲥⲟⲩⲥ.
4. ⲁⲛⲭⲁ ⲡⲓⲕⲟⲥⲙⲟⲥ.
5. ⲁⲥⲟⲩⲉⲛ ⲡⲁⲓⲣⲟ.
6. ⲡⲓⲛⲟⲙⲟⲥ ⲉⲧϫⲏⲕ ⲉⲃⲟⲗ.
7. ⲡⲓⲁⲅⲅⲉⲗⲟⲥ ⲉⲧϩⲏⲗ ⲉⲡϭⲓⲥⲓ.
8. ⲁϥⲥⲟⲧⲧⲉⲛ.
9. ⲁⲕϣⲟⲡⲧⲉⲛ ⲉⲣⲟⲕ.
10. ⲁϥⲁⲓⲧⲟⲩ ⲛ̀ⲣⲁⲙⲁⲟ.
11. ⲁⲓⲥⲟⲧⲡϥ.
12. ⲁⲕⲃⲉⲣⲃⲱⲣⲟⲩ ⲉ̀ⲫⲓⲟⲙ.
13. ϩⲁⲛⲥ̀ⲛⲏⲟⲩ ⲉⲩⲙⲉⲛⲣⲓⲧ.
14. ϯⲡⲁⲣⲑⲉⲛⲟⲥ ⲉⲑⲙⲉϩ ⲛ̀ⲧⲁⲓⲟ.

2. Write the absolute form for each of the following:

1. ⲉⲗ-
2. ⲉϣ-
3. ⲉⲡ-
4. ⲉⲛ-
5. ⲭⲁ"
6. ⲟⲙⲥ"
7. ⲙⲉⲛⲣⲓⲧ"
8. ⲙⲉⲥⲧⲱ"
9. ϭⲟⲥⲓ
10. ⲟⲛϧ
11. ⲃⲏⲗ
12. ⲙⲉϩ

3. Complete according to the given example:

1. ⲥ̀ⲛⲁⲙⲓⲥⲓ ⲛ̀ⲟⲩⲁⲗⲟⲩ. | ⲥ̀ⲛⲁⲙⲉⲥ ⲟⲩⲁⲗⲟⲩ. | ⲥ̀ⲛⲁⲙⲁⲥϥ.
2. | ⲁϥⲥⲉⲧⲡ ⲛⲉϥⲙⲁⲑⲏⲧⲏⲥ. |

3.	ⲁⲩⲥⲉⲃⲧⲉ ⲡⲓⲡⲁⲥⲭⲁ.	
4.	ⲁⲣⲉⲭⲉⲙ ⲟⲩϩⲙⲟⲧ.	
5.	ⲁⲛⲥⲟⲩⲉⲛ ϯⲙⲉⲑⲙⲏⲓ.	
6.	ⲁϥⲥⲉⲗⲥⲉⲗ ⲛⲉⲛⲯⲩⲭⲏ.	
7.	ⲁⲛⲉϣ ⲡⲁⲓⲭⲱⲙ.	

4. Read this passage and translate it:

Ⲫϯ ⲁϥⲙⲉⲓ ⲙ̀ⲡⲓⲣⲱⲙⲓ ⲉ̀ⲙⲁϣⲱ. ⲁϥⲟⲩⲉⲣⲡ ⲡⲉϥϣⲏⲣⲓ ⲉⲑⲙⲉⲛⲣⲓⲧ ⲉ̀ⲡⲁⲓⲕⲟⲥⲙⲟⲥ. ⲛ̀ⲑⲟϥ ⲁϥϭⲓⲥⲁⲣⲝ ⲟⲩⲟϩ ⲁϥⲉⲣⲣⲱⲙⲓ. ⲁⲥⲙⲁⲥϥ ⲛ̀ϫⲉ ϯⲡⲁⲣⲑⲉⲛⲟⲥ. ⲁϥϣⲱⲡ ⲉ̀ⲣⲟϥ ⲙ̀ⲡⲓⲥⲉⲃⲓ. ⲁⲩⲟⲩⲱϣⲧ ⲙ̀ⲙⲟϥ ⲛ̀ϫⲉ ⲛⲓⲙⲁⲅⲟⲥ. ⲁϥϭⲓⲱⲙⲥ ϧⲉⲛ ⲡⲓⲓⲟⲣⲇⲁⲛⲏⲥ ⲉ̀ⲃⲟⲗϩⲓⲧⲉⲛ Ⲓⲱⲁⲛⲛⲏⲥ ⲡⲓⲣⲉϥϯⲱⲙⲥ. ϧⲉⲛ Ⲕⲁⲛⲁ ⲛ̀ⲧⲉ ϯⲄⲁⲗⲓⲗⲉⲁ, ⲁϥⲥⲙⲟⲩ ⲉ̀ⲛⲓⲙⲱⲟⲩ ⲁϥⲁⲓⲧⲟⲩ ⲛ̀ⲏⲣⲡ. Ⲓⲏⲥⲟⲩⲥ ⲁϥⲉⲣ ϩⲁⲛϣⲫⲏⲣⲓ ⲛⲉⲙ ϩⲁⲛⲙⲏⲓⲛⲓ ϧⲉⲛ ⲑⲙⲏϯ ⲙ̀ⲡⲓⲗⲁⲟⲥ. ⲁⲩⲁϣϥ ⲛ̀ϫⲉ ⲛⲓⲓⲟⲩⲇⲁⲓ ⲉ̀ⲡⲓⲥ̀ⲧⲁⲩⲣⲟⲥ. ⲁϥⲙⲟⲩ ⲟⲩⲟϩ ⲁϥϯ ⲛⲁⲛ ⲙ̀ⲡⲓⲱⲛϧ. ⲁϥⲧⲱⲛϥ ⲟⲩⲟϩ ⲁϥⲟⲗⲧⲉⲛ ⲉ̀ⲡϭⲓⲥⲓ ⲛⲉⲙⲁϥ. ⲁϥⲓⲛⲓ ⲛⲁⲛ ⲛ̀ⲟⲩⲥⲱⲧⲏⲣⲓⲁ ⲉⲥⲭⲏⲕ ⲉ̀ⲃⲟⲗ. ⲧⲉⲛϣⲉⲡϩ̀ⲙⲟⲧ ⲛ̀ⲧⲟⲧϥ ⲉ̀ⲙⲁϣⲱ.

Rewrite the underlined verbs, clarify their form, and then write their absolute form:

The given verb	Its form	Its absolute form	The given verb	Its form	Its absolute form
ⲙⲉⲓ	absolute	ⲙⲉⲓ			
ⲟⲩⲉⲣⲡ	phrasal	ⲟⲩⲱⲣⲡ			

Lesson 26
ⲡⲓⲱϣ ⲙⲙⲁϩ ⲕⲋ

The Forms (Tenses) of the Derived Verbs

1. The verbs that are derived by adding the letter ⲥ to their beginning:

Absolute form		Phrasal F.	Pronominal F.	Qualitative form	
The first group: its qualitative form is formed by adding ⲏⲟⲩⲧ to its end, for example:					
ⲥⲁϩⲛⲓ	To command, place, provide	ⲥⲉϩⲛⲉ-	ⲥⲁϩⲛⲏⲧ″	ⲥⲉϩⲛⲏⲟⲩⲧ	Placed, provided
ⲥⲉⲙⲛⲓ	To confirm, establish	ⲥⲉⲙⲛⲉ-	ⲥⲉⲙⲛⲏⲧ″	ⲥⲉⲙⲛⲏⲟⲩⲧ	Decided, confirmed
ⲥⲉⲃⲓ	To circumcise, purify	ⲥⲟⲩⲃⲉ-	ⲥⲟⲩⲃⲏⲧ″	ⲥⲉⲃⲏⲟⲩⲧ	Circumcised, pure
The second group: These are derived from the tri-radical verbs, and are conjugated as follows:					
ⲥⲱⲟⲩⲧⲉⲛ	To manage, straighten, extend	ⲥⲟⲩⲧⲉⲛ-	ⲥⲟⲩⲧⲱⲛ″	ⲥⲟⲩⲧⲱⲛ	Upright, straight
ⲥⲁϩⲟⲩⲓ	To curse, insult	ⲥ̀ϩⲟⲩⲉⲣ-	ⲥ̀ϩⲟⲩⲱⲣ″	ⲥ̀ϩⲟⲩⲱⲣⲧ	Cursed
ϣⲁⲛϣ	To support, nourish, rear	ϣⲁⲛⲉϣ-	ϣⲁⲛⲟⲩϣ″	ϣⲁⲛⲉⲩϣ	Nourished, reared

Lesson 26 ✤ The Forms (Tenses) of the Derived Verbs ✤

2. The verbs that are derived by adding the letter ⲧ to their beginning:

Absolute form		Phrasal F.	Pronominal F.	Qualitative form	
Rule	ⲟ	ⲉ	ⲟ	ⲏⲟⲩⲧ	
Examples:					
ⲧⲁⲓⲟ	To honor, respect	ⲧⲁⲓⲉ-	ⲧⲁⲓⲟ″	ⲧⲁⲓⲏⲟⲩⲧ	Honored
ⲧⲁⲕⲟ	To lose, perish	ⲧⲁⲕⲉ-	ⲧⲁⲕⲟ″	ⲧⲁⲕⲏⲟⲩⲧ	Lost, perished
ⲧⲁⲗⲟ	To burden, cause to lift	ⲧⲁⲗⲉ-	ⲧⲁⲗⲟ″	ⲧⲁⲗⲏⲟⲩⲧ	Lifted up, burdened
ⲧⲁⲟⲩⲟ	To send	ⲧⲁⲟⲩⲉ-	ⲧⲁⲟⲩⲟ″	ⲧⲁⲟⲩⲏⲟⲩⲧ	Sent
ⲧⲁⲥⲑⲟ	To return, bring back	ⲧⲁⲥⲑⲉ-	ⲧⲁⲥⲑⲟ″	ⲧⲁⲥⲑⲏⲟⲩⲧ	Returned, brought back
ⲧⲁϩⲟ	To establish, comprehend	ⲧⲁϩⲉ-	ⲧⲁϩⲟ″	ⲧⲁϩⲏⲟⲩⲧ	Comprehended, established
ⲧⲁϫⲣⲟ	To confirm	ⲧⲁϫⲣⲉ-	ⲧⲁϫⲣⲟ″	ⲧⲁϫⲣⲏⲟⲩⲧ	Confirmed
ⲧⲟⲩⲃⲟ	To purify, clean	ⲧⲟⲩⲃⲉ-	ⲧⲟⲩⲃⲟ″	ⲧⲟⲩⲃⲏⲟⲩⲧ	Purified, chaste
ⲧⲟⲩϫⲟ	To be healed, heal	ⲧⲟⲩϫⲉ-	ⲧⲟⲩϫⲟ″	ⲧⲟⲩϫⲏⲟⲩⲧ	Healing, healthy
ϯⲥⲁⲃⲟ	To teach	ϯⲥⲁⲃⲉ-	ϯⲥⲁⲃⲟ″	ϯⲥⲁⲃⲏⲟⲩⲧ	Educated
ϯⲥⲓⲟ	To satiate, sate	ϯⲥⲓⲉ-	ϯⲥⲓⲟ″	ϯⲥⲏⲟⲩⲧ	Sated
ϯϩⲉⲙⲕⲟ	To torment	ϯϩⲉⲙⲕⲉ-	ϯϩⲉⲙⲕⲟ″	ϯϩⲉⲙⲕⲏⲟⲩⲧ	Tormented
ϯϩⲉⲙⲥⲟ	To seat	ϯϩⲉⲙⲥⲉ-	ϯϩⲉⲙⲥⲟ″	ϯϩⲉⲙⲥⲏⲟⲩⲧ	Seated

Verbs that begin with the letter ⲑ instead of the letter ⲧ, and have the same conjugation, for example:

ⲑⲁⲙⲓⲟ	To create, make	ⲑⲁⲙⲓⲉ-	ⲑⲁⲙⲓⲟ″	ⲑⲁⲙⲓⲏⲟⲩⲧ	Created
ⲑⲉⲃⲓⲟ	To subject, to be humble	ⲑⲉⲃⲓⲉ-	ⲑⲉⲃⲓⲟ″	ⲑⲉⲃⲓⲏⲟⲩⲧ	Subjected, humble
ⲑⲙⲁⲓⲟ	To justify	ⲑⲙⲁⲓⲉ-	ⲑⲙⲁⲓⲟ″	ⲑⲙⲁⲓⲏⲟⲩⲧ	Justified

Verbs that have no qualitative form:

ⲧⲁⲗϭⲟ	To heal	ⲧⲁⲗϭⲉ-	ⲧⲁⲗϭⲟ″	-------
ⲧⲁⲙⲟ	To tell, inform	ⲧⲁⲙⲉ-	ⲧⲁⲙⲟ″	-------
ⲧⲁⲛϩⲟ	To give life	ⲧⲁⲛϩⲉ-	ⲧⲁⲛϩⲟ″	-------
ⲧ̇ⲥⲟ	To water, give to drink	ⲧ̇ⲥⲉ-	ⲧ̇ⲥⲟ″	-------
ⲧ̇ⲫⲟ	To reach, accompany, return	ⲧ̇ⲫⲉ-	ⲧ̇ⲫⲟ″	-------
ⲧⲟⲩϩⲟ	To add, increase	ⲧⲟⲩϩⲉ-	ⲧⲟⲩϩⲟ″	-------

Notes:

1. There are some transitive verbs that follow the rule of these verbs although they are not formed by adding ⲥ or ⲧ:

ϭⲟ	To plant	ϭⲉ-	ϭⲟ″	ϭⲏⲟⲩⲧ	Planted
ϭⲉⲣⲟ	To burn, kindle	ϭⲉⲣⲉ-	ϭⲉⲣⲟ″	ϭⲉⲣⲏⲟⲩⲧ	Lit, burning

2. The pronominal form of some verbs is formed with the letter ⲱ instead of the letter ⲟ, for example:

ⲗⲁⲗⲟ	To paint	ⲗⲁⲗⲉ-	ⲗⲁⲗⲱ″	ⲗⲁⲗⲏⲟⲩⲧ	Painted, coated
ϫⲁⲗⲟ	To deposit, feed, graze	ϫⲁⲗⲉ-	ϫⲁⲗⲱ″	ϫⲁⲗⲏⲟⲩⲧ	Deposited, fed

Sample Sentences

ⲁ̄ ⲧⲉⲕϫⲓϫ ⲛ̇ⲟⲩⲓ̇ⲛⲁⲙ ⲡⲁⲛⲟⲩϯ ⲁⲥⲧⲁⲕⲉ ⲛⲉⲕϫⲁϫⲓ.
Your right hand, O my God, destroyed Your enemies.

ⲃ̄ ⲁⲕⲥⲟⲩⲧⲉⲛ ⲧⲉⲕⲟⲩⲓ̇ⲛⲁⲙ ⲉ̇ⲃⲟⲗ ⲁϥⲟⲙⲕⲟⲩ ⲛ̇ϫⲉ ⲡ̇ⲕⲁϩⲓ.
You stretched out Your right [hand], the earth swallowed them.

ⲅ̄ ⲫⲏⲉⲧⲁϥⲧⲁϫⲣⲟ ⲙ̇ⲡⲓⲕⲁϩⲓ ϩⲓϫⲉⲛ ⲛⲓⲙⲱⲟⲩ.
Who established the earth upon the waters.

ⲇ̄ ⲁϥϯⲥⲟ ⲙ̇ⲡⲉϥⲗⲁⲟⲥ ⲛ̇ϩ̇ⲣⲏⲓ ϩⲓ ⲡ̇ϣⲁϥⲉ.
He gave His people to drink in the wilderness. [He watered His people in the wilderness].

Lesson 26 ✠ The Forms (Tenses) of the Derived Verbs ✠

$\overline{ⲉ}$ ⲛⲏⲉⲧⲑⲉⲃⲓⲏⲟⲩⲧ ϧⲉⲛ ⲡⲟⲩϩⲏⲧ.
Those who are humble in their hearts.

$\overline{ⲋ}$ ϯⲇⲓⲁⲑⲏⲕⲏ ⲑⲏⲉⲧⲁⲕⲥⲉⲙⲛⲏⲧⲥ ⲛⲉⲙ ⲛⲉⲛⲓⲟϯ.
The covenant which You established with our fathers.

$\overline{ⲍ}$ ⲫⲏⲉⲧⲁⲕⲑⲁⲙⲓⲟϥ.
That whom You created.

$\overline{ⲏ}$ ⲛⲏⲉⲧⲧⲁⲓⲏⲟⲩⲧ.
Those who are honored.

$\overline{ⲑ}$ ⲡⲓⲥⲧⲁⲙⲛⲟⲥ ⲉⲧⲧⲁⲓⲏⲟⲩⲧ.
The precious [or honored] jar.

$\overline{ⲓ}$ ϯϣⲟⲩⲣⲏ ⲉⲧⲧⲟⲩⲃⲏⲟⲩⲧ.
The pure censer.

$\overline{ⲓⲁ}$ ⲥⲉⲙⲛⲉ ⲛⲟⲙⲟⲥ ⲛⲏⲓ.
Appoint a law to me.

$\overline{ⲓⲃ}$ ⲁϥⲥⲟⲩⲧⲉⲛ ⲛⲉⲛϭⲁⲗⲁⲩϫ ⲉⲫⲙⲱⲓⲧ ⲛ̀ⲧⲉ ϯϩⲓⲣⲏⲛⲏ.
He straightened our feet to the path of peace.

$\overline{ⲓⲅ}$ ⲫⲁⲓ ⲡⲉ ⲡⲓⲉϩⲟⲟⲩ ⲉⲧⲁ Ⲡ⳪ ⲑⲁⲙⲓⲟϥ.
This is the day which the Lord made.

$\overline{ⲓⲇ}$ ϣⲁⲛⲟⲩϣⲟⲩ ϧⲉⲛ ⲟⲩⲙⲁ ⲛ̀ⲭⲗⲟⲏ: ϩⲓϫⲉⲛ ⲫⲙⲟⲩ ⲛ̀ⲧⲉ ⲡⲉⲙⲧⲟⲛ: ϧⲉⲛ ⲡⲓⲡⲁⲣⲁⲇⲓⲥⲟⲥ ⲛ̀ⲧⲉ ⲡⲟⲩⲛⲟϥ.
Sustain them in a green pasture beside the water of rest in the Paradise of joy. [Litany of the Departed].

$\overline{ⲓⲉ}$ ⲟⲩⲟⲛ ⲟⲩⲕⲓⲃⲱⲧⲟⲥ ⲭⲏ ϧⲉⲛ ϯⲥⲕⲏⲛⲏ: ⲉⲥⲗⲁⲗⲏⲟⲩⲧ ⲛ̀ⲛⲟⲩⲃ: ⲥⲁϧⲟⲩⲛ ⲛⲉⲙ ⲥⲁⲃⲟⲗ.
There is an ark in the tabernacle, coated with gold within and without.

$\overline{ⲓⲋ}$ ⲁϥⲑⲁⲙⲓⲟⲥ ϧⲉⲛ ⲟⲩⲱⲟⲩ ⲕⲁⲧⲁ ⲡⲥⲁϫⲓ ⲙ̀Ⲡ⳪.
He made it with glory according to the word of the Lord.

$\overline{ⲓⲍ}$ ⲫⲁⲓ ⲉⲧⲁⲕⲧⲁⲥⲑⲟϥ ⲉⲧⲉϥⲁⲣⲭⲏ ⲛ̀ⲕⲉⲥⲟⲡ.
This [is he] whom You brought back to his authority again.

Exercises

1. Complete according to the given example:

1. ϥⲥⲉⲙⲛⲓ ⲛ̀ⲧⲉϥϩⲓⲣⲏⲛⲏ. | ϥⲥⲉⲙⲛⲉ ⲧⲉϥϩⲓⲣⲏⲛⲏ. | ϥⲥⲉⲙⲛⲏⲧⲥ.
2. ⲁϥⲧⲁϫⲣⲟ ⲙ̀ⲡⲉϥⲥⲁϫⲓ.
3. ⲁⲥⲧⲁⲙⲟ ⲛ̀ⲛⲓⲙⲁⲑⲏⲧⲏⲥ.
4. ⲥⲉⲧⲥⲁⲃⲟ ⲙ̀ⲡⲓⲗⲁⲟⲥ.
5. ⲁϥⲧⲁⲗϭⲟ ⲛ̀ⲛⲓϣⲱⲛⲓ.
6. ⲧⲉⲧⲥⲟ ⲛ̀ⲧⲉⲁⲗⲟⲩ.

2. Write the verb in the qualitative form:

1. ⲧⲉⲛⲧⲁⲓⲟ ⲛ̀ⲧⲉⲥⲡⲁⲣⲑⲉⲛⲓⲁ. | ⲧⲉⲥⲡⲁⲣⲑⲉⲛⲓⲁ ⲉⲧⲧⲁⲓⲏⲟⲩⲧ.
2. ⲁϥⲧⲁⲥⲑⲟ ⲙ̀ⲡⲓⲣⲱⲙⲓ. | ⲡⲓⲣⲱⲙⲓ ⲉⲧ----------.
3. ϥⲧⲟⲩⲃⲟ ⲛ̀ⲛⲉⲛϩⲏⲧ. | ⲛⲉⲛϩⲏⲧ ⲉⲧ----------.
4. ⲁϥⲗⲁⲗⲟ ⲛ̀ϯⲕⲓⲃⲱⲧⲟⲥ. | ϯⲕⲓⲃⲱⲧⲟⲥ ⲉⲧ----------.
5. ⲕⲃⲉⲣⲟ ⲙ̀ⲡⲓⲗⲁⲙⲡⲁⲥ. | ⲡⲓⲗⲁⲙⲡⲁⲥ ⲉⲧ----------.
6. ⲁϥϣⲁⲛϣ ⲙ̀ⲡⲉϥⲗⲁⲟⲥ. | ⲡⲉϥⲗⲁⲟⲥ ⲉⲧ----------.

3. Translate to the English language:

ⲁ̄ ⲱ̀ ⲡⲉⲛϭⲟⲓⲥ, ⲕ̀ⲥⲟⲩⲧⲉⲛ ⲛⲉⲛⲙⲱⲓⲧ ⲛ̀ⲥⲏⲟⲩ ⲛⲓⲃⲉⲛ.
ⲃ̄ ⲁϥⲧⲁⲕⲟ ⲙ̀ⲡⲉⲛⲅⲉⲛⲟⲥ ⲛ̀ϫⲉ ⲡⲓⲛⲟⲃⲓ.
ⲅ̄ ⲡⲉⲛⲥⲱⲧⲏⲣ ⲁϥⲧⲁⲥⲑⲉ ⲡⲓⲣⲱⲙⲓ ⲛ̀ⲕⲉⲥⲟⲡ ⲉ̀ⲧⲉϥⲁⲣⲭⲏ.
ⲇ̄ ⲟⲩⲓⲱⲧ ⲉϥⲧⲁⲓⲏⲟⲩⲧ ⲛⲉⲙ ϩⲁⲛϣⲏⲣⲓ ⲉⲩⲑⲉⲃⲓⲏⲟⲩⲧ.
ⲉ̄ Ⲫϯ ⲁϥⲑⲁⲙⲓⲟⲛ ⲕⲁⲧⲁ ⲡⲉϥⲓⲛⲓ ⲛⲉⲙ ⲧⲉϥϩⲓⲕⲱⲛ.
ⲋ̄ ⲁϥⲧϩⲉⲙⲥⲟⲛ ⲛⲉⲙⲁϥ ϧⲉⲛ ⲛⲁ ⲛⲓⲫⲏⲟⲩⲓ ϧⲉⲛ Ⲡⲭⲥ Ⲓⲏⲥ.
ⲍ̄ ⲛⲓⲁⲡⲟⲥⲧⲟⲗⲟⲥ ⲁⲩⲧⲥⲁⲃⲉ ⲛⲓⲗⲁⲟⲥ ⲛ̀ⲧⲉ ⲡⲓⲕⲁϩⲓ.

The Imperative Mood

If the verb is said by an elder or higher ranking [person] to a young or lower ranking, it indicates a command. If it is said by a younger or lower ranking [person] to an elder or higher ranking, it indicates a question, entreaty, and request.

The imperative verb can be translated to mean the second person, feminine or masculine, singular or plural, for example:

The phrase ⲁⲣⲉϩ ⲉⲡⲓⲱϣ can be translated to "Memorize the lesson," for singular or plural, feminine or masculine. However, the different forms can be distinguished if there is a pronoun, for example:

ⲁⲣⲉϩ ⲉⲡⲉⲱϣ.	Memorize your [sing. fem.] lesson.
ⲁⲣⲉϩ ⲉⲡⲉⲕⲱϣ.	Memorize your [sing. mas.] lesson.
ⲁⲣⲉϩ ⲉⲡⲉⲧⲉⲛⲱϣ.	Memorize your [pl. both genders] lesson.

1. In most verbs, the base (infinitive) form of the verb is used, without addition or change, as an imperative mood, for example:

ϣⲗⲏⲗ.	Pray.	ⲣⲁϣⲓ.	Rejoice.	ⲙⲟϣⲓ ⲛⲥⲱⲓ.	Follow me.
ϩⲱⲥ.	Praise.	ⲥϧⲁⲓ.	Write.	ⲙⲉⲛⲣⲉ Ⲡϭⲟⲓⲥ.	Love the Lord.
ⲥⲙⲟⲩ.	Bless.	ⲛⲉϩⲥⲓ.	Wake up.	ⲥⲱⲧⲉⲙ ⲉⲧⲁⲥⲙⲏ.	Listen to my voice.

2. **The imperative mood of some verbs is formed by adding the prefix ⲁ- to the verb, for example:**

ⲁⲛⲁⲩ.	Look.	ⲁⲟⲩⲱⲛ.	Open.
ⲁⲟⲩⲱⲙ.	Eat.	ⲁϫⲱ, ⲁϫⲉ-, ⲁϫⲟ″	Say.

Sample Examples:

ⲁ̄ ⲁϫⲟⲥ ⲛ̇ⲧⲙⲉⲑⲙⲏⲓ ⲙ̇ⲙⲏⲛⲓ.
Say the truth always.

ⲃ̄ ⲁⲛⲁⲩ ⲉ̇ⲡⲓϩⲏⲕⲓ.
Look to the poor.

ⲅ̄ ⲁⲟⲩⲱⲛ ⲛ̇ⲛⲉⲕⲃⲁⲗ.
Open your eyes.

ⲇ̄ ⲁⲟⲩⲱⲙ ⲙ̇ⲡⲓⲱⲓⲕ.
Eat the bread.

3. **The three verbs ⲓ̇ⲣⲓ, ⲓ̇ⲛⲓ, and ⲱ̇ⲗⲓ, their imperative mood is formed as follows:**

The absolute form	ⲁⲣⲓⲟⲩⲓ̇	ⲁⲛⲓⲟⲩⲓ̇	ⲁⲗⲓⲟⲩⲓ̇
The phrasal form	ⲁⲣⲓ-	ⲁⲛⲓ-	ⲁⲗⲓ-
The pronominal form	ⲁⲣⲓⲧ″	ⲁⲛⲓⲧ″	ⲁⲗⲓⲧ″

1. Examples of the absolute form:

ⲁ̄ ⲁⲣⲓⲟⲩⲓ̇ ⲛⲉⲙⲁⲛ ⲕⲁⲧⲁ ⲧⲉⲕⲙⲉⲧⲉ̇ⲡⲓⲕⲏⲥ.
Deal [do] with us according to Your meekness.

ⲃ̄ ⲁⲛⲓⲟⲩⲓ̇ ⲛ̇ⲛⲁⲓϫⲱⲙ ⲛⲉⲙⲁⲕ.   Bring these books with you.

ⲅ̄ ⲁⲗⲓⲟⲩⲓ̇ ⲉ̇ⲃⲟⲗϩⲁⲣⲱⲟⲩ ⲛ̇ⲛⲓϣⲱⲛⲓ.   Take away sicknesses from them.

2. Examples of the phrasal form:

ⲁ̄ ⲁⲣⲓ ⲟⲩⲛⲁⲓ ⲛⲉⲙⲁⲛ.   Do mercy with us.

ⲃ̄ ⲁⲣⲓⲡⲁⲙⲉⲩⲓ̇ ϧⲉⲛ ⲧⲉⲕⲙⲉⲧⲟⲩⲣⲟ.   Remember me in Your kingdom.

Lesson 27 ✠ The Imperative Mood ✠

e̅	ⲁⲣⲓϩⲙⲟⲧ ⲛⲁⲛ ⲛ̀ⲧⲉⲕϩⲓⲣⲏⲛⲏ ϣⲁ ⲉ̀ⲃⲟⲗ. Grant us Your mercy to the end.	
ⲍ̅	ⲁⲣⲓⲟⲩⲱⲓⲛⲓ ⲛ̀ⲛⲁⲃⲁⲗ.	Enlighten my eyes.
ⲉ̅	ⲁⲛⲓⲟⲩⲧⲁϩ.	Bear fruit. [Mas., sing. and pl.]
ⲋ̅	ⲁⲛⲓ ⲛⲉⲧⲉⲛϩⲏⲧ ⲛ̀ⲟⲩⲑⲩⲥⲓⲁ.	Offer your hearts a sacrifice.

All the verbs that begin with the syllable ⲉⲣ-, their imperative mood is formulated by using ⲁⲣⲓ-, but there are verbs that do not begin with the syllable ⲉⲣ- and their imperative mood is formulated by using ⲁⲣⲓ-, for example the verb ⲉ̀ⲙⲓ (to know). The imperative mood of this is ⲁⲣⲓⲉ̀ⲙⲓ (know).

3. Examples of the pronominal form:

ⲁ̅	ⲁⲣⲓⲧⲧ ⲙ̀ⲫⲣⲏϯ ⲙ̀ⲡⲓⲧⲉⲗⲱⲛⲏⲥ.	Make me like the publican.
ⲃ̅	ⲁⲛⲓⲧⲟⲩ ⲉ̀ⲡϣⲱⲓ.	Raise them.
ⲅ̅	ⲁⲗⲓⲧⲟⲩ ⲉ̀ⲃⲟⲗϩⲁⲣⲟⲛ ⲛⲉⲙ ⲉ̀ⲃⲟⲗϩⲁ ⲡⲉⲕⲗⲁⲟⲥ ⲧⲏⲣϥ. Take them away from us and from all Your people.	
ⲇ̅	ⲁⲣⲓⲧⲉⲛ ⲛ̀ⲉⲙⲡϣⲁ.	Make us worthy.

4. The imperative from the verb ϯ (to give):

The absolute form	ⲙⲟⲓ
The phrasal form	ⲙⲁ-
The pronominal form	ⲙⲏⲓ″

ⲁ̅	ⲙⲟⲓ ⲛⲁⲛ ⲛ̀ⲧⲉⲕϩⲓⲣⲏⲛⲏ.	Give to us [give us] Your peace.
ⲃ̅	ⲙⲁ ⲛⲏⲓ ⲡⲉⲕϫⲱⲙ.	Give to me [give me] your book.
ⲅ̅	ⲡⲉⲛⲱⲓⲕ ⲛ̀ⲧⲉ ⲣⲁⲥϯ ⲙⲏⲓϥ ⲛⲁⲛ ⲙ̀ⲫⲟⲟⲩ. Our bread of tomorrow give to us today.	

✠ Foundations of the Coptic Language ✠

The phrasal form (ⲙⲁ-) is used to formulate the following verbs:

1. Phrasal verbs beginning with the verb ϯ (to give), for example:

ϯⲱⲟⲩ	To glorify	→	ⲙⲁⲱⲟⲩ	Glorify
ϯⲥⲃⲱ	To teach	→	ⲙⲁⲥ̀ⲃⲱ	Teach
ϯϩⲁⲡ	To judge	→	ⲙⲁϩⲁⲡ	Judge
ϯⲱⲙⲥ	To baptize	→	ⲙⲁⲱⲙⲥ	Baptize
ϯⲁⲥⲟ	To have compassion	→	ⲙⲁ̀ⲁⲥⲟ	Have compassion
ϯϭⲓ	To nurse (a baby)	→	ⲙⲁϭⲓ ⲛⲁϥ	Nurse him

And sometimes the ϯ is not removed, for example:

ϯϩⲟ	To ask, to beseech	→	ⲙⲁϯϩⲟ	Ask, beseech
ϯⲟⲩⲱ	To end	→	ⲙⲁϯⲟⲩⲱ	End

2. The derived verbs beginning with the letter ⲧ, the imperative is formulated from them by adding ⲙⲁ- to their beginning, for example:

ⲧⲟⲩⲃⲟ	To purify	→	ⲙⲁⲧⲟⲩⲃⲟ	Purify
ⲧⲁⲥⲑⲟ	To return, to bring back	→	ⲙⲁⲧⲁⲥⲑⲟ	Bring back
ⲧⲁⲛϧⲟ	To give life	→	ⲙⲁⲧⲁⲛϧⲟ	Give life
ⲧⲁⲗϭⲟ	To heal	→	ⲙⲁⲧⲁⲗϭⲟ	Heal
ⲧⲁϫⲣⲟ	To confirm	→	ⲙⲁⲧⲁϫⲣⲟ	Confirm
ⲑⲉⲃⲓⲟ	To be humble, to be subject	→	ⲙⲁⲑⲉⲃⲓⲟ	Be humble

3. Other verbs from which the imperative mood is formulated by adding ⲙⲁ- to their beginning, for example:

ⲕⲁϯ	To understand	→	ⲙⲁⲕⲁϯ	Understand
ϣⲉ	To go	→	ⲙⲁϣⲉⲛⲁⲕ	Go
ϣ̀ⲑⲁⲙ	To close	→	ⲙⲁϣⲑⲁⲙ	Close
ϭⲛⲉϫⲱ	To subdue	→	ⲙⲁϭⲛⲉϫⲱ	Subdue

Lesson 27 ✠ The Imperative Mood ✠

5. Verbs that exist only in the imperative mood and are not derived from other verbs:

ⲁⲙⲟⲩ	Come (sing. mas.)	ⲁⲙⲏ	Come (sing. fem.)	ⲁⲙⲱⲓⲛⲓ	Come (pl.)
ⲙⲟ	Take (sing. mas.)	ⲙⲉ	Take (sing. fem.)	ⲙⲱⲓⲛⲓ	Take (pl.)
ⲁⲩⲓⲥ	Bring, give (sing. mas., sing. fem., and pl.)				

Examples:

ⲁ̄	ⲁⲙⲟⲩ ϣⲁⲣⲟⲛ ⲙ̇ⲫⲟⲟⲩ: ⲱ ⲡⲉⲛⲛⲏⲃ Ⲡ̅ⲭ̅ⲥ̅. Come to us today, O our master Christ.
ⲃ̄	ⲁⲙⲱⲓⲛⲓ ⲛⲓⲗⲁⲟⲥ ⲧⲏⲣⲟⲩ. Come, O all peoples.

The Negative Imperative Mood (ⲡⲓⲣⲏϯ ⲙ̇ⲡⲓϩⲱⲛ ⲛ̇ⲭⲱⲗ)

There are three kinds of this negative tense.

1. The Simple Negative

Its mark is ⲙ̇ⲡⲉⲣ-, and it is used for the singular and plural, masculine and feminine:

ⲙ̇ⲡⲉⲣⲉⲣϩⲟϯ	Do not fear	ⲙ̇ⲡⲉⲣⲣⲓⲙⲓ	Do not cry
ⲙ̇ⲡⲉⲣⲥⲁϫⲓ	Do not speak	ⲙ̇ⲡⲉⲣϯϩⲁⲡ	Do not judge, do not condemn
ⲙ̇ⲡⲉⲣϩⲉⲙⲥⲓ	Do not sit	ⲙ̇ⲡⲉⲣϯϣⲓⲡⲓ ⲛⲁⲛ	Do not put us to shame

ⲁ̄	ⲙ̇ⲡⲉⲣⲉⲣⲡⲱⲃϣ ⲛ̇ϯⲇⲓⲁⲑⲏⲕⲏ.	Do not forget the covenant.
ⲃ̄	ⲡⲉⲕⲡⲛ̅ⲁ̅ ⲉⲑⲩ ⲙ̇ⲡⲉⲣⲟⲗϥ ⲉⲃⲟⲗϩⲁⲣⲟⲓ. Your Holy Spirit do not take away from me.	
ⲅ̄	ⲙ̇ⲡⲉⲣⲥⲟϩⲓ ⲙ̇ⲙⲟⲓ ϧⲉⲛ ⲡⲉⲕϫⲱⲛⲧ.	Do not rebuke me in Your anger.
ⲇ̄	ⲙ̇ⲡⲉⲣⲥⲟⲙⲥ ⲉⲣⲟⲓ ϧⲉⲛ ⲟⲩⲃⲟⲛ.	Do not look to me in wrath.

2. The Emphasized Negative

Its mark is ⲛ̀ⲛⲉ-, and it is attached to the singular and plural pronouns, masculine and feminine:

ⲁ̅	ⲛ̀ⲛⲉⲕϧⲱⲧⲉⲃ.	Do not kill (sing. mas.).
	ⲛ̀ⲛⲉⲕϭⲓⲟⲩⲓ̀.	Do not steal (sing. mas.).
ⲃ̅	ⲛ̀ⲛⲉⲥⲁϫⲓ ⲛ̀ⲥⲁ ⲟⲩϩⲗⲓ.	Do not slander [speak against] (sing. fem.) anyone.
ⲅ̅	ⲛ̀ⲛⲉⲧⲉⲛⲙⲟⲥϯ ⲛ̀ⲛⲓⲣⲉϥⲉⲣⲛⲟⲃⲓ.	Do not hate (pl.) the sinners.

3. The Exaggerated Negative

Its mark is ⲙ̀ⲡⲉⲛⲑⲣⲉ-, and it is used to mean the necessity and importance of the negative:

ⲁ̅ ⲙ̀ⲡⲉⲛⲑⲣⲉ ⲡⲓⲡⲉⲧϩⲱⲟⲩ ϭⲣⲟ ⲉ̀ⲣⲟⲕ, ⲁⲗⲗⲁ ϧⲉⲛ ⲟⲩⲡⲉⲑⲛⲁⲛⲉϥ ϭⲣⲟ ⲉ̀ⲡⲓⲡⲉⲧϩⲱⲟⲩ.
Do not let evil overcome you, but by good overcome evil.

ⲃ̅ ⲙ̀ⲡⲉⲛⲑⲣⲉⲛⲥⲱⲧⲉⲙ ϧⲉⲛ ⲟⲩⲥⲑⲉⲣⲧⲉⲣ: ϫⲉ ϯⲥⲱⲟⲩⲛ ⲙ̀ⲙⲱⲧⲉⲛ ⲁⲛ.
Do not make us hear with trembling: "I do not know you."

Exercises

1. Write the imperative mood of the following verbs:

1. ϩⲱⲥ	5. ⲉⲣⲟⲩⲱⲓⲛⲓ	9. ⲟⲩⲱⲛ
2. ⲛⲁⲩ	6. ϯϩⲟ	10. ⲱ̀ⲗⲓ
3. ϯⲱⲟⲩ	7. ⲉ̀ⲙⲓ	11. ⲧⲟⲩⲃⲟ
4. ⲓⲣⲓ	8. ⲥ̀ⲙⲟⲩ	12. ⲕⲁϯ

2 Translate the following phrases and sentences:

ⲁ̅	ⲙⲁⲧⲁⲛϧⲟⲓ.	ⲃ̅	ⲁⲣⲓ̀ⲡⲣⲉⲥⲃⲉⲩⲓⲛ.
	ⲁⲣⲓⲃⲟⲏⲑⲓⲛ ⲉ̀ⲣⲟⲛ.		ⲙⲁⲱⲟⲩ ⲙ̀Ⲡϭⲟⲓⲥ.
	ⲙⲁⲧⲁⲙⲉ ⲛⲁⲥⲛⲏⲟⲩ.		ⲁⲣⲓⲯⲁⲗⲓⲛ ⲉ̀ⲫⲏⲉⲧⲁⲩϣϥ.

ⲅ̅ ϩⲱⲥ ⲉ̀ⲣⲟϥ ⲁⲣⲓϩⲟⲩⲟ̀ ϭⲁⲥϥ.

ⲇ̅ ⲙ̀ⲡⲉⲣⲉⲣⲡⲱⲃϣ ⲛ̀ⲧⲉⲕⲇⲓⲁⲑⲏⲕⲏ.

Lesson 27 ✠ The Imperative Mood ✠

ⲉ̄ ⲙⲁⲧⲁⲥⲑⲟ ⲙ̀ⲡⲉⲕϩⲟ ⲥⲁⲃⲟⲗ ⲛ̀ⲛⲁⲛⲟⲃⲓ.

ⲋ̄ ⲭⲱ ⲛⲏⲓ ⲉ̀ⲃⲟⲗ ⲙ̀ⲡⲁ̀ϣⲁⲓ ⲛ̀ⲧⲉ ⲛⲁⲁ̀ⲛⲟⲙⲓⲁ.

ⲍ̄ ⲱⲟⲩⲛ̀ϩⲏⲧ ⲛⲉⲙⲏⲓ: ⲙ̀ⲡⲉⲣⲧⲁⲕⲟⲓ ⲛ̀ⲭⲱⲗⲉⲙ.

ⲏ̄ ⲙⲁⲧⲁⲥⲑⲟⲛ Ⲫϯ ⲉ̀ϧⲟⲩⲛ ⲉ̀ⲡⲉⲕⲟⲩϫⲁⲓ.

ⲑ̄ ⲁⲣⲓⲟⲩⲓ̀ ⲛⲉⲙⲁⲛ ⲕⲁⲧⲁ ⲧⲉⲕⲙⲉⲧⲁ̀ⲅⲁⲑⲟⲥ.

ⲓ̄ ⲣⲁϣⲓ ⲟⲩⲟϩ ⲑⲉⲗⲏⲗ: ⲱ̀ ⲡ̀ⲅⲉⲛⲟⲥ ⲛ̀ⲛⲓⲣⲱⲙⲓ.

ⲓ̄ⲁ ⲁⲣⲓⲟⲩⲱⲓⲛⲓ ⲉ̀ⲣⲟⲛ ϧⲉⲛ ⲧⲉⲕⲙⲉⲑⲛⲟⲩϯ ⲉⲧϭⲟⲥⲓ.

ⲓ̄ⲃ ⲥⲱϯ ⲙ̀ⲙⲟⲛ ⲟⲩⲟϩ ⲛⲁⲓ ⲛⲁⲛ.

ⲓ̄ⲅ ⲙⲁⲧϩⲟ ⲙ̀ⲫⲏⲉⲧⲁⲣⲉⲙⲁⲥϥ.

ⲓ̄ⲇ ⲁⲙⲱⲓⲛⲓ ϩⲁⲣⲟⲓ ⲛⲏⲉⲧⲥ̀ⲙⲁⲣⲱⲟⲩⲧ ⲛ̀ⲧⲉ ⲡⲁⲓⲱⲧ: ⲁⲣⲓⲕ̀ⲗⲏⲣⲟⲛⲟⲙⲓⲛ ⲙ̀ⲡⲓⲱⲛϧ ⲉⲑⲙⲏⲛ ⲉ̀ⲃⲟⲗ ϣⲁ ⲉ̀ⲛⲉϩ.

ⲓ̄ⲉ ⲛⲏⲉⲧϣⲱⲛⲓ ⲙⲁⲧⲁⲗϭⲱⲟⲩ: ⲛⲏⲉⲧⲁⲩⲉⲛⲕⲟⲧ Ⲡ̄ϭ̄ⲟ̄ⲓ̄ⲥ̄ ⲙⲁⲙ̀ⲧⲟⲛ ⲛⲱⲟⲩ: ⲛⲉⲛⲥ̀ⲛⲏⲟⲩ ⲉⲧⲭⲏ ϧⲉⲛ ϩⲟϫϩⲉϫ ⲛⲓⲃⲉⲛ: Ⲡ̄ⲁ̄ⲥ̄ ⲁⲣⲓⲃⲟⲏ̀ⲑⲓⲛ ⲉ̀ⲣⲟⲛ ⲛⲉⲙⲱⲟⲩ.

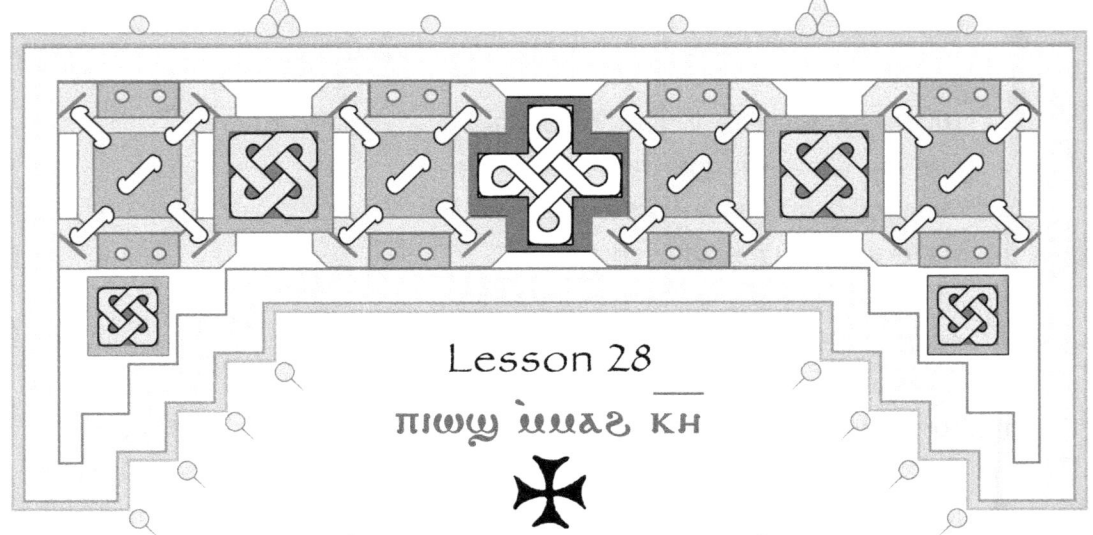

Lesson 28

ⲠⲒⲰϢ ⲘⲘⲀϨ ⲔⲎ

✠

ⲚⲒⲤⲎⲞⲨ ⲚⲦⲈ ⲠⲒⲢⲀ ϦⲈⲚ ⲠⲒⲢⲎϮ ⲚⲦⲀⲘⲞ

VERB TENSES IN THE INDICATIVE MOOD

Verb tenses in the Coptic language are divided into three categories: present, past, and future. And for each of the following tenses, there are various kinds: The present has four kinds, the past five kinds, and the future five kinds. And for every one of these fourteen kinds, there is a mark indicating its tense. Also each of them is conjugated with different pronouns indicating the person of the subject. These pronouns are divided into two groups:

	The first group			The second group		
	1st person	2nd person	3rd person	1st person	2nd person	3rd person
Sing. mas.	Ϯ-	Ⲕ̀-, Ⲭ̀-	ϥ̀-	-Ⲓ-	-Ⲕ-, -Ⲭ-	-ϥ-
Sing. fem.	Ϯ-	ⲦⲈ-	Ⲥ̀-	-Ⲓ-	-ⲠⲈ-	-Ⲥ-
Pl. both	ⲦⲈⲚ-	ⲦⲈⲦⲈⲚ-	ⲤⲈ-	-Ⲛ-	-ⲠⲈⲦⲈⲚ-	-Ⲩ-

The first group is used to conjugate two tenses only: The first present and first future.

The second group is used to conjugate the remaining twelve tenses:

1. The remaining present tenses, and they are three: The second present; the unlimited present; the habitual present.
2. The past tenses, and they are five: The past perfect; antecedent past tense (preceding another); the past imperfect; the past pluperfect; the habitual past imperfect.
3. The remaining future tenses, and they are four: The second future; the future imperfect; the unlimited future; the emphatic future.

Lesson 28 ✠ Verb Tenses in the Indicative Mood ✠

Verbs in the Present Tense (ⲡⲓⲣⲁ ϧⲉⲛ ⲡⲓⲥⲏⲟⲩ ⲉⲧϣⲟⲡ)

It consists of four kinds, different in form and meaning, and these are conjugated as follows:

Tense / Subject	First Present	Second Present	Unlimited Present	Habitual Present	
				Affirmative	Negative
ⲁⲛⲟⲕ	ϯⲥⲙⲟⲩ	ⲁⲓⲛⲁϩϯ	ⲉⲓϩⲱⲥ	ϣⲁⲓϣⲗⲏⲗ	ⲙ̀ⲡⲁⲓⲥⲁϫⲓ
ⲛ̀ⲑⲟⲕ	ⲕ̀-, ⲭ̀-	ⲁⲕ-	ⲉⲕ-	ϣⲁⲕ-	ⲙ̀ⲡⲁⲕ-
ⲛ̀ⲑⲟ	ⲧⲉ-	ⲁⲣⲉ-	ⲉⲣⲉ-	ϣⲁⲣⲉ-	ⲙ̀ⲡⲁⲣⲉ-
ⲛ̀ⲑⲟϥ	ϥ̀-	ⲁϥ-	ⲉϥ-	ϣⲁϥ-	ⲙ̀ⲡⲁϥ-
ⲛ̀ⲑⲟⲥ	ⲥ̀-	ⲁⲥ-	ⲉⲥ-	ϣⲁⲥ-	ⲙ̀ⲡⲁⲥ-
ⲁⲛⲟⲛ	ⲧⲉⲛ-	ⲁⲛ-	ⲉⲛ-	ϣⲁⲛ-	ⲙ̀ⲡⲁⲛ-
ⲛ̀ⲑⲱⲧⲉⲛ	ⲧⲉⲧⲉⲛ-	ⲁⲣⲉⲧⲉⲛ-	ⲉⲣⲉⲧⲉⲛ-	ϣⲁⲣⲉⲧⲉⲛ-	ⲙ̀ⲡⲁⲣⲉⲧⲉⲛ-
ⲛ̀ⲑⲱⲟⲩ	ⲥⲉ-	ⲁⲩ-	ⲉⲩ-	ϣⲁⲩ-	ⲙ̀ⲡⲁⲩ-
Before a subject when it is a noun	N/A	ⲁⲣⲉ	ⲉⲣⲉ	ϣⲁⲣⲉ	ⲙ̀ⲡⲁⲣⲉ
Negative	...ⲁⲛ / ⲛ̀ ... ⲁⲛ	ⲛ̀ ... ⲁⲛ	...ⲁⲛ		

1. The First Present Tense (Simple) [ⲡⲓⲥⲏⲟⲩ ⲉⲧϣⲟⲡ ⲛ̀ϩⲟⲩⲓⲧ]

It indicates an event that is taking place at the moment when the statement is spoken. Examples:

ⲁ̅	ϯϫⲱ ⲙ̀ⲙⲟⲥ ⲛⲁⲕ: ⲧⲱⲛⲕ.	I say to you, "Arise."
ⲃ̅	ϥ̀ⲥϧⲁⲓ ⲙ̀ⲡⲉϥϣ.	He writes his lesson.
ⲅ̅	ⲧⲉⲛⲥⲱⲧⲉⲙ ⲉ̀ⲟⲩⲥⲙⲏ.	We hear a voice.
ⲇ̅	ⲥⲉϩⲱⲥ ⲉ̀ⲡⲟⲩⲣⲉϥⲥⲱⲛⲧ.	They praise their Creator.

But if the subject is a noun instead of a pronoun, it precedes the verb. And the verb may take the pronoun of the subject, or it may not take it, for example:

ⲡⲁⲓⲣⲱⲙⲓ ϩⲉⲙⲥⲓ. ⲓⲉ   ⲡⲁⲓⲣⲱⲙⲓ ϥ̀ϩⲉⲙⲥⲓ.

But if the verb comes before the noun, then there must be attached to the beginning of the verb a pronoun that indicates the subject, and the subject noun must be preceded by the mark **ⲛ̀ϫⲉ**, for example:

ϥϩⲉⲙⲥⲓ ⲛ̀ϫⲉ ⲡⲁⲓⲣⲱⲙⲓ.

The negative form of this tense is formulated by the negative article **ⲁⲛ**, and it comes after the verb:

ⲧⲉⲛⲥϧⲁⲓ ⲁⲛ.   We do not write.

And in case of the emphasis of the negative form, the letter **ⲛ̀** is placed before the subject pronoun, and **ⲁⲛ** after the verb, for example:

ⲛ̀ⲥⲉⲙⲟⲥϯ ⲁⲛ ⲛ̀ϩⲗⲓ.   They do not hate anyone at all.

Note:

The singular, masculine pronoun for the first person **ϫ**- is used before the verbs beginning with the letters **ⲙ**, **ⲛ**, or **ⲟⲩ**, for example:

ϫⲙⲉⲓ.   You love. | ϫⲛⲁϩϯ.   You believe. | ϫⲟⲩⲱⲙ   You eat.

As for **ⲕ̀**, it is used with the remaining verbs, for example: **ⲕⲱϣ** (You read).

2. The Second Present Tense (ⲡⲓⲙⲁϩⲥ̀ⲛⲁⲩ ⲛ̀ⲥⲏⲟⲩ ⲉⲧϣⲟⲡ)

It is used in two cases:
1. To ask a question (interrogative sentences).
2. To state a known truth or one that must be known.

ā ⲁⲕⲑⲱⲛ Ⲁⲇⲁⲙ?
   Where are you, Adam?

β̄ ⲁⲩϭⲱⲣⲉⲙ ⲉ̀ⲡⲉϥⲓⲱⲧ ϫⲉ: ⲁⲕⲟⲩⲱϣ ⲉ̀ⲙⲟⲩϯ ⲉ̀ⲣⲟϥ ϫⲉ ⲛⲓⲙ?
   They pointed (made signs) to his father: "What do you want to name him?"

γ̄ ⲡⲉⲛⲛⲟⲩϯ ⲁϥϣⲱⲡⲓ ϧⲉⲛ ⲧ̀ⲫⲉ ⲟⲩⲟϩ ϧⲉⲛ ⲙⲁⲓ ⲛⲓⲃⲉⲛ.
   Our God is in heaven and in every place.

When the subject is a noun, it is preceded by the mark of the tense **ⲁⲣⲉ**, for example:

ⲁⲣⲉ ⲡⲉϥⲥⲙⲟⲩ ϧⲉⲛ ϯⲉⲕⲕⲗⲏⲥⲓⲁ ⲛ̀ⲧⲉ ⲛⲏⲉⲑⲟⲩⲁⲃ.
His praise in the church of the saints. (The fourth canticle).

3. The Unlimited Present [ⲡⲓⲥⲏⲟⲩ ⲉⲧϣⲟⲡ ⲛ̀ⲁⲧⲑⲁϣϥ (ⲉⲑⲙⲏⲛ)]

ⲛ̀ⲁⲧⲑⲁϣϥ = unlimited

ⲉⲑⲙⲏⲛ = continuous

It is used to express the state of being, for example:

- ⲁ̄ ⲁⲓ̇ⲓ̇ ⲉⲓⲙⲟϣⲓ.
  I came walking.

- ⲃ̄ ⲁⲓⲛⲁⲩ ⲉⲣⲟϥ ⲉϥϩⲉⲙⲥⲓ.
  I saw him sitting.

- ⲅ̄ ⲁϥϫⲉⲙⲟⲩ ⲉⲩⲉⲛⲕⲟⲧ.
  I found them sleeping [or dead].

- ⲇ̄ ⲁⲥⲉⲣⲟⲩⲱ ⲉⲥϫⲱ ⲙ̀ⲙⲟⲥ.
  She answered, saying.

- ⲉ̄ ⲛⲓⲁⲅⲅⲉⲗⲟⲥ ⲥⲉϩⲱⲥ ⲉⲣⲟϥ ⲉⲩⲱϣ ⲉ̇ⲃⲟⲗ ⲉⲩϫⲱ ⲙ̀ⲙⲟⲥ.
  The angels praise Him, crying out and saying.

- ⲋ̄ ⲉⲕϩⲱⲥ ⲛⲉⲙ ⲛⲓⲁⲅⲅⲉⲗⲟⲥ: ⲉⲕϯⲱⲟⲩ ⲛ̀ϯⲧⲣⲓⲁⲥ.
  You are praising with the angels, glorifying the Trinity.

- ⲍ̄ ⲉⲣⲉ ⲡⲥⲟⲗⲥⲉⲗ ⲙ̀Ⲙⲁⲣⲓⲁⲙ ϧⲉⲛ ⲛⲓⲫⲏⲟⲩⲓ̇ ⲉⲧⲥⲁ ⲡ̀ϣⲱⲓ.
  The adornment [or consolation] of Mary in the high heavens [always].

4. The Habitual Present Tense (ⲡⲓⲥⲏⲟⲩ ⲛ̀ⲣⲉⲙⲕⲁϩⲥ ⲉⲧϣⲟⲡ)

ⲛ̀ⲣⲉⲙⲕⲁϩⲥ = habitual

It indicates a repeated event or a habit that occurs frequently.

- ⲁ̄ ϣⲁⲓⲧⲱⲛⲧ ⲙ̀ⲫⲛⲁⲩ ⲛ̀ϣⲱⲣⲡ: ⲛ̀ⲧⲁⲥⲙⲟⲩ ⲉ̇ⲡⲉⲕⲣⲁⲛ.
  I [habitually] arise at the time of dawn to bless Your name.

- ⲃ̄ ϣⲁⲩϩⲱⲥ ϣⲁⲩϯⲱⲟⲩ ⲙ̀Ⲡⲁϭⲟⲓⲥ Ⲓⲏⲥⲟⲩⲥ.
  [The cherubim are accustomed to] praising and glorifying my Lord Jesus.

- ⲅ̄ ϩⲱⲃ ⲛⲓⲃⲉⲛ ⲉ̇ϣⲁϥⲁⲓⲧⲟⲩ ϣⲁϥⲧⲙⲁϯ ⲛ̀ϧⲏⲧⲟⲩ.
  Every matter [or thing] he is accustomed to doing, he is accustomed to succeeding in it.

- ⲇ̄ ϣⲁⲣⲉ Ⲫϯ ⲟⲩⲱⲣⲡ ⲛⲁⲛ ⲛ̀ⲛⲉϥⲛⲁⲓ ⲛⲉⲙ ⲛⲉϥϣⲉⲛϩⲏⲧ.
  God sends to us His mercy and His compassion [repeatedly].

- ⲉ̄ ⲙ̀ⲡⲁⲣⲉ ⲡⲉⲥϩⲏⲃⲥ ϭⲉⲛⲟ ⲙ̀ⲡⲓⲉ̇ϫⲱⲣϩ ⲧⲏⲣϥ.
  Her lamp is not quenched all night.

- ⲋ̄ ⲙ̀ⲡⲁⲩⲛⲁⲩ ⲟⲩⲇⲉ ⲙ̀ⲡⲁⲩⲥⲱⲧⲉⲙ.
  [Gods which] do not see nor hear.

Exercises

1. Write the following verbs in the negative form:

1. ⲕϩⲉⲙⲥⲓ.
2. ϣⲁⲥⲟⲩⲱⲙ.
3. ⲉⲛⲙⲟϣⲓ.
4. ⲧⲉⲧⲉⲛⲛⲁⲩ.
5. ϣⲁⲓⲥⲱⲧⲉⲙ.
6. ⲉϥⲥⲁϫⲓ.
7. ⲁⲧⲱⲛϩ.
8. ϫⲛⲁϩϯ.
9. ϣⲁⲕϣⲗⲏⲗ.
10. ⲉⲩⲥⲙⲟⲩ.

2. Translate to the English language:

ⲁ̅ ⲧⲉⲛⲛⲁⲩ ⲉ̀ⲣⲱⲧⲉⲛ ⲉⲣⲉⲧⲉⲛϩⲉⲙⲥⲓ.

ⲃ̅ ⲧⲉⲧⲉⲛⲥⲱⲧⲉⲙ ⲉ̀ⲣⲟⲥ ⲉⲥⲱϣ ⲉ̀ⲃⲟⲗ.

ⲅ̅ ϫ̀ⲟⲩⲱϣ ⲙ̀ⲫⲙⲟⲩ ⲁⲛ ⲙ̀ⲡⲓⲣⲉϥⲉⲣⲛⲟⲃⲓ.

ⲇ̅ ϣⲁϥⲧⲟⲩⲃⲟ ⲛ̀ⲛⲓⲛⲟⲃⲓ ⲙ̀ⲡⲉϥⲗⲁⲟⲥ.

ⲉ̅ ⲧⲉⲛϯϩⲟ ⲟⲩⲟϩ ⲧⲉⲛⲧⲱⲃϩ.

ⲋ̅ ⲉⲩϩⲱⲥ ⲉ̀ⲡⲟⲩⲣⲉϥⲥⲱⲛⲧ: ⲉϥⲭⲏ ϧⲉⲛ ⲧⲉⲛⲉϫⲓ.

ⲍ̅ ⲁϥϯ ⲛⲁⲛ ⲙ̀ⲡⲉϥⲥⲱⲙⲁ ⲛⲉⲙ ⲡⲉϥⲥⲛⲟϥ ⲉⲧⲧⲁⲓⲏⲟⲩⲧ: ⲁⲛⲱⲛϩ ϣⲁ ⲉ̀ⲛⲉϩ.

ⲏ̅ ⲉⲣⲉ ⲡⲓⲙⲁⲛⲛⲁ ϩⲏⲡ ⲛ̀ϧⲏⲧϥ.

ⲑ̅ ϣⲁⲩⲭⲁϥ ϧⲉⲛ ϯⲥⲕⲏⲛⲏ.

ⲓ̅ ⲉⲣⲉ Ⲫϯ ⲭⲏ ⲙ̀ⲡⲟⲩⲑⲟ ⲉ̀ⲃⲟⲗ: ⲉⲣⲉ ⲡⲉϥⲣⲁⲛ ⲉⲑⲟⲩⲁⲃ ϧⲉⲛ ⲣⲱⲟⲩ ⲛ̀ⲥⲏⲟⲩ ⲛⲓⲃⲉⲛ.

ⲓ̅ⲁ̅ ϣⲁⲩϫⲱⲕ ⲉ̀ⲃⲟⲗ ⲛ̀ϫⲉ ⲛⲓⲕⲁⲣⲡⲟⲥ: ϩⲓⲧⲉⲛ ⲛⲉⲛⲧⲱⲃϩ ⲙ̀Ⲙⲓⲭⲁⲏⲗ.

ⲓ̅ⲃ̅ ⲉⲩⲉⲣϩⲁⲉ ⲉⲩϩⲉϫϩⲱϫ ⲟⲩⲟϩ ⲉⲩϭⲓⲙⲕⲁϩ.

ⲓ̅ⲅ̅ ⲍ̅ ⲛ̀ⲁⲣⲭⲏ ⲁⲅⲅⲉⲗⲟⲥ: ⲥⲉⲟ̀ϩⲓ ⲉ̀ⲣⲁⲧⲟⲩ ⲉⲩⲉⲣϩⲩⲙⲛⲟⲥ: ⲙ̀ⲡⲉ̀ⲙⲑⲟ ⲙ̀ⲡⲓⲡⲁⲛⲧⲟⲕⲣⲁⲧⲱⲣ: ⲉⲩϣⲉⲙϣⲓ ⲙ̀ⲙⲩⲥⲧⲏⲣⲓⲟⲛ ⲉⲧϩⲏⲡ.

Lesson 29
ⲡⲓⲱϣ ⲙ̀ⲙⲁϩ ⲕⲑ

✠

ⲡⲓⲣⲁ ϧⲉⲛ ⲡⲓⲥⲏⲟⲩ ⲉⲧⲥⲓⲛⲓ

Verbs in the Past Tense

The past tense has five kinds differing in form and meaning:

1. The past perfect tense; 2. The past pluperfect tense; 3. The past imperfect tense; 4. The antecedent past tense (preceding another); 5. The habitual past imperfect tense.

These kinds are conjugated as follows:

Tense / Subject	1. Past Perfect Affir.	1. Past Perfect Negative	2. Past Pluperfect Affir.	2. Past Pluperfect Negative	3. Past Imperfect Affir.	3. Past Imperfect Negative
ⲁⲛⲟⲕ	ⲁⲓⲥⲙⲟⲩ	ⲙ̀ⲡⲓⲱϣ	ⲛⲉⲁⲓϭⲓ	ⲛⲉⲙ̀ⲡⲓⲓ	ⲛⲁⲓϯ ⲡⲉ	ⲛⲁⲓⲥⲁϫⲓ ⲁⲛ ⲡⲉ ←
ⲛ̀ⲑⲟⲕ	ⲁⲕ-	ⲙ̀ⲡⲉⲕ-	ⲛⲉⲁⲕ-	ⲛⲉⲙ̀ⲡⲉⲕ-	ⲛⲁⲕ- ⲡⲉ	
ⲛ̀ⲑⲟ	ⲁⲣⲉ-	ⲙ̀ⲡⲉ-	ⲛⲉⲁⲣⲉ-	ⲛⲉⲙ̀ⲡⲉ-	ⲛⲁⲣⲉ- ⲡⲉ	
ⲛ̀ⲑⲟϥ	ⲁϥ-	ⲙ̀ⲡⲉϥ-	ⲛⲉⲁϥ-	ⲛⲉⲙ̀ⲡⲉϥ-	ⲛⲁϥ- ⲡⲉ	
ⲛ̀ⲑⲟⲥ	ⲁⲥ-	ⲙ̀ⲡⲉⲥ-	ⲛⲉⲁⲥ-	ⲛⲉⲙ̀ⲡⲉⲥ-	ⲛⲁⲥ- ⲡⲉ	
ⲁⲛⲟⲛ	ⲁⲛ-	ⲙ̀ⲡⲉⲛ-	ⲛⲉⲁⲛ-	ⲛⲉⲙ̀ⲡⲉⲛ-	ⲛⲁⲛ- ⲡⲉ	
ⲛ̀ⲑⲱⲧⲉⲛ	ⲁⲣⲉⲧⲉⲛ-	ⲙ̀ⲡⲉⲧⲉⲛ-	ⲛⲉⲁⲣⲉⲧⲉⲛ	ⲛⲉⲙ̀ⲡⲉⲧⲉⲛ	ⲛⲁⲣⲉⲧⲉⲛ	
ⲛ̀ⲑⲱⲟⲩ	ⲁⲩ-	ⲙ̀ⲡⲟⲩ-	ⲛⲉⲁⲩ-	ⲛⲉⲙ̀ⲡⲟⲩ-	ⲛⲁⲩ- ⲡⲉ	
Before a noun	ⲁ	ⲙ̀ⲡⲉ	ⲛⲉⲁ (ⲓⲉ) ⲛⲉⲁⲣⲉ	ⲛⲉⲙ̀ⲡⲉ	ⲛⲁⲣⲉ... ⲡⲉ	ⲛⲁⲣⲉ... ⲁⲛ ⲡⲉ

Tense Subject	4. The Antecedent Past (preceding another)		5. Habitual Past Imperfect	
	Affir.	Negative	Affir.	Negative
ⲁⲛⲟⲕ	ⲉⲧⲁⲓϫⲱ	Three ways for negative: ----ⲁⲛ, ⲛ----ⲁⲛ, ⲉⲧⲉⲙⲡⲉ	ⲛⲉϣⲁⲓⲥⲱ ⲡⲉ	ⲛⲉⲙⲡⲁⲓⲱⲥⲕ
ⲛ̀ⲑⲟⲕ	ⲉⲧⲁⲕ-		ⲛⲉϣⲁⲕ- ⲡⲉ	ⲛⲉⲙⲡⲁⲕ-
ⲛ̀ⲑⲟ	ⲉⲧⲁⲣⲉ-		ⲛⲉϣⲁⲣⲉ- ⲡⲉ	ⲛⲉⲙⲡⲁⲣⲉ-
ⲛ̀ⲑⲟϥ	ⲉⲧⲁϥ-		ⲛⲉϣⲁϥ- ⲡⲉ	ⲛⲉⲙⲡⲁϥ-
ⲛ̀ⲑⲟⲥ	ⲉⲧⲁⲥ-		ⲛⲉϣⲁⲥ- ⲡⲉ	ⲛⲉⲙⲡⲁⲥ-
ⲁⲛⲟⲛ	ⲉⲧⲁⲛ-		ⲛⲉϣⲁⲛ- ⲡⲉ	ⲛⲉⲙⲡⲁⲛ-
ⲛ̀ⲑⲱⲧⲉⲛ	ⲉⲧⲁⲣⲉⲧⲉⲛ-		ⲛⲉϣⲁⲣⲉⲧⲉⲛ- ⲡⲉ	ⲛⲉⲙⲡⲁⲣⲉⲧⲉⲛ-
ⲛ̀ⲑⲱⲟⲩ	ⲉⲧⲁⲩ-		ⲛⲉϣⲁⲩ- ⲡⲉ	ⲛⲉⲙⲡⲁⲩ-
Before a noun	ⲉⲧⲁ or ⲉⲧⲁⲣⲉ		ⲛⲉϣⲁⲣⲉ	ⲛⲉⲙⲡⲁⲣⲉ

1. **The Past Perfect Tense** (ⲡⲓⲥⲏⲟⲩ ⲉⲧⲥⲓⲛⲓ ⲉⲧϫⲏⲕ ⲉ̀ⲃⲟⲗ)

It indicates that the event took place in the past, and it ended, for example:

ⲁ̄	ⲁϥⲱⲣⲕ ⲛ̀ϫⲉ Ⲡ̀ⲟ̅ⲥ̅.	The Lord swore. [Thursday Theotokia]
ⲃ̄	ⲁⲓⲛⲁⲩ ⲟⲩⲟϩ ⲁⲓϣⲫⲏⲣⲓ.	I looked and marveled.
ⲅ̄	ⲁⲥⲉⲣⲃⲟⲕⲓ ⲛ̀ϫⲉ Ⲙⲁⲣⲓⲁⲙ ⲟⲩⲟϩ ⲁⲥⲙⲓⲥⲓ ⲛ̀Ⲓⲏⲥⲟⲩⲥ. Mary conceived and gave birth to Jesus.	
ⲇ̄	ⲁⲩϣⲗⲏⲗ ⲛ̀ϫⲉ ⲛⲏⲉⲑⲛⲁϩϯ ⲟⲩⲟϩ ⲁ Ⲡ̀ⲟ̅ⲥ̅ ⲥⲱⲧⲉⲙ ⲉ̀ⲧⲟⲩⲥⲙⲏ. The believers prayed and the Lord heard their voice.	
ⲉ̄	ⲁ ⲡⲓⲗⲟⲅⲟⲥ ϭⲓⲥⲁⲣⲝ ⲟⲩⲟϩ ⲁϥⲉⲣⲣⲱⲙⲓ. The Word took flesh and became man.	
ⲋ̄	Ⲫϯ ⲙ̀ⲡⲉ ϩⲗⲓ ⲛⲁⲩ ⲉⲣⲟϥ ⲛ̀ⲉⲛⲉϩ.	No one ever saw God.
ⲍ̄	ⲙ̀ⲡⲓⲱϣ ⲙ̀ⲡⲁⲓϫⲱⲙ.	I did not read this book.
ⲏ̄	ⲙ̀ⲡⲉⲧⲉⲛⲓ̀ ⲛ̀ⲥⲁϥ.	You did not come yesterday.
ⲑ̄	ⲁ Ⲫ̀ⲓⲱⲧ ϫⲟⲩϣⲧ ⲉ̀ⲃⲟⲗϧⲉⲛ ⲧ̀ⲫⲉ ⲙ̀ⲡⲉϥϫⲉⲙ ⲫⲏⲉⲧⲟ̀ⲛⲓ ⲙ̀ⲙⲟ. The Father looked from heaven [and] He did not find that who resembles you.	
ⲓ̄	ⲙ̀ⲡⲟⲩϣϥⲟϩ ⲉ̀ⲡⲓϭⲓⲥⲓ ⲛ̀ⲛⲉⲕⲙⲁⲕⲁⲣⲓⲥⲙⲟⲥ. They could not reach the height of your blessedness.	

Lesson 29 ✣ Verbs in the Past Tense ✣

This tense is used in the narration of history, where it expresses the occurrence of the action once in the past.

2. The Past Pluperfect Tense (ⲡⲓⲥⲏⲟⲩ ⲉⲧϭⲓⲛⲓ ⲛ̀ⲑⲟⲩⲟϫⲏⲕ)

This is one of the compound tenses, composed of two parts, concerning the mark: one from the past perfect and the other from the past imperfect. Its counterpart in the English language is "had."

Examples:

ⲁ̄	ⲛⲉⲁⲓ ⲛⲁⲩ ⲉ̀ⲣⲟϥ.	I had seen him.
ⲃ̄	ⲛⲉⲁϥⲛⲁϩϯ ⲉ̀ⲫⲛⲟⲩϯ.	He had believed in God.
ⲅ̄	ⲛⲉ ⲁ Ⲡϭⲟⲓⲥ ⲣⲉϧⲧ ⲛⲓⲃⲁⲕⲓ ⲡⲉ.	The Lord had struck the cities.
ⲇ̄	Ⲏⲣⲱⲇⲏⲥ ⲅⲁⲣ ⲛⲉⲁϥⲁⲙⲟⲛⲓ ⲛ̀ⲓⲱⲁⲛⲛⲏⲥ.	Because Herod had seized John.
ⲉ̄	ⲛⲉⲁⲩϩⲣⲟϣ ⲡⲉ ⲛ̀ϫⲉ ⲛⲉⲛⲃⲁⲗ ⲛ̀ⲓⲁⲕⲱⲃ. Jacob's eyes had become heavy. [Genesis 48]	

This tense is made in the negative form in the same way as that of the past perfect tense, while keeping ⲛⲉ which indicates the past pluperfect tense:

ⲁ̄	ⲛⲉ ⲙ̀ⲡⲓⲟⲩⲱⲙ ⲙ̀ⲡⲓⲧⲉⲃⲧ ϧⲉⲛ ϯⲛⲏⲥⲧⲓⲁ. I had not eaten fish in the fast.
ⲃ̄	ⲛⲉ ⲙ̀ⲡⲉ ⲛⲓⲥⲛⲏⲟⲩ ϣⲉ ⲉ̀ϧⲟⲩⲛ ⲉ̀ϯⲉⲕⲕⲗⲏⲥⲓⲁ. The brothers had not gone into the church.
ⲅ̄	ⲛⲉ ⲙ̀ⲡⲟⲩⲛⲁϩϯ ⲉ̀ⲡⲓⲉⲩⲁⲅⲅⲉⲗⲓⲟⲛ. They had not believed in the gospel.

Note: This tense is rarely used, considering that there are past perfect and past imperfect tenses.

3. The Past Imperfect Tense (ⲡⲓⲥⲏⲟⲩ ⲉⲧϭⲓⲛⲓ ⲛ̀ⲁⲧϫⲏⲕ ⲉ̀ⲃⲟⲗ)

It expresses the continuation of an event or state in the past, but it is considered finished. In other words, we can say that it is the present [tense] that has been completed or has ended.

So if the present is ϥⲥⲁϫⲓ (He speaks), then the past imperfect is ⲛⲁϥⲥⲁϫⲓ (He was speaking).

The negative form of this tense is formulated by the article ⲁⲛ.

Every incomplete sentence in the past imperfect tense is followed by the syllable ⲡⲉ, and this is not a "to be" verb, but it is rather complementary to the incomplete sentence. Also it does not change with changing the subject, whether masculine or feminine, singular or plural, for example:

ⲛⲁⲓϣⲗⲏⲗ ⲡⲉ.	I was praying.
ⲛⲁⲥϣⲗⲏⲗ ⲡⲉ.	She was praying.
ⲛⲁⲛϣⲗⲏⲗ ⲡⲉ.	We were praying.

ⲡⲉ here gives the complete meaning to the imperfect sentence.

ⲛⲁϥⲱϣ ⲁⲛ ϧⲉⲛ ⲡⲉϥϫⲱⲙ ⲡⲉ.

He was not reading his book. (This is an incomplete sentence whose meaning was completed by putting ⲡⲉ in its end).

ⲛⲁϥⲱϣ ⲁⲛ ϧⲉⲛ ⲡⲉϥϫⲱⲙ ⲁⲗⲗⲁ ϧⲉⲛ ⲫⲁ ⲡⲉϥⲥⲟⲛ.

He was not reading in his book, but in his brother's book. (This is a complete sentence, and there is no need to put ⲡⲉ in its end).

Examples:

ⲁ̄ **ⲛⲁϥⲛⲁⲩ ϧⲉⲛ ⲛⲓⲃⲁⲗ ⲙ̄ⲡⲣⲟⲫⲏⲧⲓⲕⲟⲛ.**
He was looking with the prophetic eyes.

ⲃ̄ **ⲁⲛⲟⲕ ⲛⲁⲓⲥⲱⲟⲩⲛ ⲙ̄ⲙⲟϥ ⲁⲛ ⲡⲉ.**
I did not know him [I was not knowing him.]

ⲅ̄ **ⲟⲩⲇⲉ ⲅⲁⲣ ⲛⲉϥⲕⲉⲥⲛⲏⲟⲩ ⲛⲁⲩⲛⲁϩϯ ⲉⲣⲟϥ ⲁⲛ ⲡⲉ.**
For nor his brothers were believing in Him.

ⲇ̄ **ⲛⲁⲛⲟⲓ ⲛ̄ⲙ̄ⲕⲁϩⲛ̄ϩⲏⲧ ⲡⲉ ⲉⲛⲕⲱϯ ⲛ̄ⲥⲱⲕ.**
We were seeking you, tormented.

ⲉ̄ **ⲛⲁⲣⲉⲧⲉⲛⲉ̀ⲙⲓ ⲁⲛ ⲡⲉ ϫⲉ ϩⲱϯ ⲉ̀ⲣⲟⲓ ⲛ̄ⲧⲁϣⲱⲡⲓ ϧⲉⲛ ⲛⲁ ⲡⲁⲓⲱⲧ?**
Did you not know that I must be about my Father's business? [Luke 2:49 NKJV]

Note: Before the noun, **ⲛⲁⲣⲉ** is used in the verbal sentence, and **ⲛⲉ** is used in the nominal sentence.

ⲛⲁⲣⲉ Ⲫϯ ⲭⲏ ⲛⲉⲙⲁϥ ⲡⲉ.
God was with him.

ⲛⲉ Ⲍⲁⲭⲁⲣⲓⲁⲥ ⲟⲩⲟⲩⲏⲃ ⲡⲉ.
Zacharias was a priest.

Lesson 29 ✣ *Verbs in the Past Tense* ✣

4. The Antecedent Past Tense (ⲡⲓⲥⲏⲟⲩ ⲉⲧⲥⲓⲛⲓ ⲉⲧⲉⲣϣⲟⲣⲡ ⲛ̀ⲕⲉ)

1. It refers to an event preceding another in the same sentence:

   ⲉⲧⲁϥⲓ̀ⲃⲓ ⲁϥⲥⲱ ⲛ̀ⲟⲩⲙⲱⲟⲩ.
   He thirsted, [so] he drank water. [Both verbs are for one subject].

   ⲛⲉⲧⲁⲓⲉ̀ⲙⲓ ⲁⲛ ⲙ̀ⲡⲓⲓ̀.
   I did not know, [so] I did not come. [Both verbs are for one subject].

   ⲉⲧⲁⲛϣⲗⲏⲗ ⲙ̀Ⲫϯ ⲁϥⲥⲱⲧⲉⲙ ⲉ̀ⲣⲟⲛ.
   As we prayed to God, He answered us. [Two different subjects].

   ⲛⲉⲧⲁⲕⲙⲟⲩϯ ⲉ̀ⲣⲟϥ ⲁⲛ ⲙ̀ⲡⲉϥⲓ̀ ⲉ̀ϧⲟⲩⲛ.
   As you did not invite him, he did not come in. [Two different subjects].

2. ⲉⲧⲁ is adverbial: ⲉⲧⲁ ⲡⲓⲛⲁⲩ ϣⲱⲡⲓ. When the time came.

3. ⲉⲧⲁ is infinitive if preceded by ⲙⲉⲛⲉⲛⲥⲁ or ⲕⲁⲧⲁ:

   ⲙⲉⲛⲉⲛⲥⲁ ⲉⲧⲁⲓϫⲱⲕ ⲉ̀ⲃⲟⲗ ⲙ̀ⲡⲁϩⲱⲃ ⲁⲓⲓ̀.
   After I finished my work, I came.

   ⲧⲉⲛⲛⲁⲓ̀ⲣⲓ ⲕⲁⲧⲁ ⲉⲧⲁⲛⲥⲉⲙⲛⲓ.
   We will do as we established.

Examples of the negative form: three ways to form the negative:

ā ⲉⲧⲁⲥϣⲱⲡⲓ ⲁⲛ ⲉⲑⲃⲏⲧ ⲛ̀ϫⲉ ⲧⲁⲓⲥⲙⲏ.
   This voice did not happen for my sake.

b̄ ⲛⲉⲧⲁⲓⲓ̀ ⲉ̀ⲃⲱⲗ ⲉ̀ⲃⲟⲗ ⲁⲛ ⲁⲗⲗⲁ ⲉ̀ϫⲱⲕ ⲉ̀ⲃⲟⲗ.
   I did not come to destroy but to fulfill.

ḡ ⲉ̀ⲧⲉⲙⲡⲉ ϯϭⲣⲟⲙⲡⲓ ϫⲉⲙ-ⲙⲁⲛⲉⲙⲧⲟⲛ ⲛ̀ⲛⲉⲥϭⲁⲗⲁⲩϫ ⲁⲥⲧⲁⲥⲑⲟ.
   When the dove did not find a place for its feet, it returned.

5. The Habitual Past Imperfect Tense (ⲡⲓⲥⲏⲟⲩ ⲉⲑⲃⲏⲕ ⲛ̀ⲣⲉⲙⲕⲁϩⲥ)

This is one of the compound tenses, for it derives its mark from two tenses: The habitual present tense and the past imperfect tense. It indicates an event that used to happen in the past in a repeated manner, but it stopped or was cancelled.

ā ⲛⲉϣⲁⲩϩⲱⲥ ⲛ̀ϣⲱⲣⲡ ⲙ̀ⲙⲏⲛⲓ. Their habit was to praise early daily.

b̄ ⲛⲉϣⲁϥⲓ̀ ⲉ̀ⲃⲟⲗ ⲙ̀ⲫⲛⲁⲩ ⲙ̀ⲡⲓⲕⲁⲩⲙⲁ.
   His habit was to go out in the hot time.

ⲅ̄	ⲟⲩⲟϩ ⲛⲉϣⲁⲩϣⲉⲛⲱⲟⲩ ⲡⲉ ⲛ̀ϫⲉ ⲛⲉϥⲓⲟϯ ⲛ̀ⲧⲉⲙ ⲣⲟⲙⲡⲓ ⲉ̀ⲓⲉⲣⲟⲩⲥⲁⲗⲏⲙ ⲉ̀ⲡⲓϣⲁⲓ ⲛ̀ⲧⲉ ⲡⲓⲡⲁⲥⲭⲁ. "His parents went to Jerusalem every year at the Feast of the Passover." [Luke 2:41 NKJV]	
ⲇ̄	ⲛⲉⲙ̀ⲡⲁⲛⲱⲥⲕ ⲛ̀ⲉⲛⲉϩ.	We were not in the habit of being late.
ⲉ̄	ⲛⲉⲙ̀ⲡⲁⲓⲛⲉϩⲥⲓ ⲛ̀ⲱⲥⲕ.	It was not my habit to wake up late.

Exercises

1. Write the meaning of the following:

   1. ⲛⲁϥϣⲗⲏⲗ ⲡⲉ.
   2. ⲛⲉⲙ̀ⲡⲟⲩⲓ̀.
   3. ⲁⲓϣⲉ ⲉ̀ϧⲟⲩⲛ.
   4. ⲛⲉⲁⲥⲙⲓⲥⲓ.
   5. ⲙ̀ⲡⲉⲧⲉⲛⲥⲁϫⲓ.
   6. ⲛⲁⲕⲟⲩⲱⲙ ⲁⲛ ⲡⲉ.
   7. ⲉⲧⲁⲛϭⲓⲥⲓ ⲁⲛϩⲉⲙⲥⲓ.
   8. ⲛⲉⲧⲁⲕⲙⲟⲩϯ ⲉⲣⲟϥ ⲙ̀ⲡⲉϥⲓ̀.
   9. ⲛⲉϣⲁⲧϩⲱⲥ ⲉ̀ⲡⲟⲩⲛⲟⲩϯ.
   10. ⲛⲉⲙ̀ⲡⲁⲓⲱⲥⲕ ϧⲉⲛ ⲡⲓϩⲱⲃ.

2. Put the following sentences in the negative form:

   ⲁ̄ ⲁⲩⲓ̀ ⲛ̀ⲥⲁϥ.
   ⲃ̄ ⲛⲁϥϣⲗⲏⲗ ⲡⲉ.
   ⲅ̄ ⲉⲧⲁϥⲧⲱⲛϥ ⲁϥⲙⲟϣⲓ.
   ⲇ̄ ⲛⲉϣⲁⲓϣⲉ ⲉ̀ⲃⲟⲗ ⲉ̀ⲡϣⲁϥⲉ.
   ⲉ̄ ⲛⲉⲁⲕϫⲉⲕ ⲡⲓϩⲱⲃ ⲉ̀ⲃⲟⲗ.

3. Translate to the English language:

   ⲁ̄ ⲉⲧⲁϥϭⲓⲥⲁⲣⲝ ⲁϥϣⲱⲡⲓ ⲛ̀ϧⲏⲧⲉⲛ ⲁⲛⲛⲁⲩ ⲉ̀ⲡⲉϥⲱⲟⲩ.
   ⲃ̄ ⲛⲁⲣⲉ Ⲫⲛⲟⲩϯ ⲭⲏ ⲛⲉⲙⲱⲟⲩ ⲡⲉ.
   ⲅ̄ ϧⲉⲛ ⲧ̀ⲁⲣⲭⲏ ⲛⲉ ⲡⲓⲥⲁϫⲓ ⲡⲉ ⲟⲩⲟϩ ⲡⲓⲥⲁϫⲓ ⲛⲁϥⲭⲏ ϧⲁⲧⲉⲛ Ⲫϯ.
   ⲇ̄ ⲛ̀ⲑⲟⲕ ⲡⲉ ⲉⲧⲁⲕⲓⲣⲓ ⲙ̀ⲡⲁⲓϩⲱⲃ.
   ⲉ̄ ⲉⲧⲁⲣⲉⲧⲉⲛϣⲗⲏⲗ ⲙ̀Ⲫⲛⲟⲩϯ ⲁϥⲥⲱⲧⲉⲙ ⲉ̀ⲣⲱⲧⲉⲛ.
   ⲋ̄ ⲁ ⲡⲟⲩϩⲣⲱⲟⲩ ϣⲉⲛⲁϥ ⲉ̀ⲃⲟⲗ ⲉ̀ⲡⲓⲕⲟⲥⲙⲟⲥ ⲧⲏⲣϥ.
   ⲍ̄ ⲛⲉⲛϣⲏⲣⲓ ⲙ̀Ⲡⲓⲥⲗ ⲛⲁⲩⲙⲟϣⲓ ϧⲉⲛ ⲡⲉⲧϣⲟⲩⲱⲟⲩ ϧⲉⲛ ⲑⲙⲏϯ ⲙ̀ⲫⲓⲟⲙ.
   ⲏ̄ ⲙⲉⲛⲉⲛⲥⲁ ⲉⲧⲁⲛⲥⲙⲟⲩ ⲉ̀Ⲫⲛⲟⲩϯ ⲁⲛⲓ ⲉ̀ⲃⲟⲗ ⲉⲛⲙⲉϩ ⲛ̀ϩⲙⲟⲧ.
   ⲑ̄ ⲛⲉϣⲁⲓⲓ̀ ⲉ̀ⲃⲟⲗ ⲛ̀ϣⲱⲣⲡ ⲉ̀ⲃⲟⲗϧⲉⲛ ⲧⲁⲣⲓ ⲛ̀ⲧⲁϩⲱⲗ ⲉ̀ⲡⲁϩⲱⲃ ϧⲉⲛ ⲡⲓⲥⲛⲟⲩ ⲉⲧⲉⲙⲙⲱ.

Lesson 30
ⲡⲓⲱϣ ⲙ̄ⲙⲁϩ ⲗ̄
✠
ⲡⲓⲣⲁ ϧⲉⲛ ⲡⲓⲥⲏⲟⲩ ⲉⲑⲛⲏⲟⲩ

VERBS IN THE FUTURE TENSE

Tense / Subject	The First Future	The Second Future	The Unlimited Future	The Future Imperfect	The Emphatic Future	
					Affir.	Negative
ⲁⲛⲟⲕ	ϯⲛⲁⲥⲱ	ⲁⲓⲛⲁϭⲓ	ⲉⲓⲛⲁⲭⲱ	ⲛⲁⲓⲛⲁⲓ ⲡⲉ	ⲉⲓⲉⲙⲉⲓ	ⲛ̀ⲛⲁⲙⲟⲥϯ
ⲛ̀ⲑⲟⲕ	ⲭⲛⲁ-	ⲁⲭⲛⲁ-	ⲉⲭⲛⲁ-	ⲛⲁⲭⲛⲁ- ⲡⲉ	ⲉⲕⲉ̀-	ⲛ̀ⲛⲉⲕ-
ⲛ̀ⲑⲟ	ⲧⲉⲣⲁ-	ⲁⲣⲉⲛⲁ-	ⲉⲣⲉⲛⲁ-	ⲛⲁⲣⲉⲛⲁ- ⲡⲉ	ⲉⲣⲉⲉ̀-	ⲛ̀ⲛⲉ-
ⲛ̀ⲑⲟϥ	ϥⲛⲁ-	ⲁϥⲛⲁ-	ⲉϥⲛⲁ-	ⲛⲁϥⲛⲁ- ⲡⲉ	ⲉϥⲉ̀-	ⲛ̀ⲛⲉϥ-
ⲛ̀ⲑⲟⲥ	ⲥⲛⲁ-	ⲁⲥⲛⲁ-	ⲉⲥⲛⲁ-	ⲛⲁⲥⲛⲁ- ⲡⲉ	ⲉⲥⲉ̀-	ⲛ̀ⲛⲉⲥ-
ⲁⲛⲟⲛ	ⲧⲉⲛⲛⲁ-	ⲁⲛⲛⲁ-	ⲉⲛⲛⲁ-	ⲛⲁⲛⲛⲁ- ⲡⲉ	ⲉⲛⲉ̀-	ⲛ̀ⲛⲉⲛ-
ⲛ̀ⲑⲱⲧⲉⲛ	ⲧⲉⲧⲉⲛⲛⲁ	ⲁⲣⲉⲧⲉⲛⲛⲁ	ⲉⲣⲉⲧⲉⲛⲛⲁ	ⲛⲁⲣⲉⲧⲉⲛⲛⲁ	ⲉⲣⲉⲧⲉⲛⲉ̀	ⲛ̀ⲛⲉⲧⲉⲛ-
ⲛ̀ⲑⲱⲟⲩ	ⲥⲉⲛⲁ-	ⲁⲩⲛⲁ-	ⲉⲩⲛⲁ-	ⲛⲁⲩⲛⲁ- ⲡⲉ	ⲉⲩⲉ̀-	ⲛ̀ⲛⲟⲩ-
Before a noun	N/A	ⲁⲣⲉ…ⲛⲁ	ⲉⲣⲉ…ⲛⲁ	ⲛⲁⲣⲉ…ⲛⲁ	ⲉⲣⲉⲉ̀	ⲛ̀ⲛⲉ
Negative	…ⲁⲛ ⲛ̀…ⲁⲛ	ⲛ̀…ⲁⲛ	…ⲁⲛ	…ⲁⲛ		

✠ Foundations of the Coptic Language ✠

Formulating the Future Tense

The first, second, and unlimited future tenses are formulated from the first, second, and unlimited present tenses, respectively, by adding the mark **ⲛⲁ** (indicative of the future tense) directly before the verb.

The future imperfect tense is formulated by adding **ⲛⲁ** to the past imperfect.

The emphatic future tense is formulated by adding **ⲉ̀** to the unlimited present tense.

1. The First Future Tense (ⲡⲓϩⲟⲩⲓⲧ ⲛ̀ⲥⲏⲟⲩ ⲉⲑⲛⲏⲟⲩ)

[This was previously spoken of in lesson 13]

It is used to state truths and questions, and it expresses an event that will happen in the future. We note that if the subject is a noun, then it begins the sentence without any supportive letters, exactly like the first present tense. It is also noted that the feminine second person [pronoun] takes **ⲧⲉⲣⲁ** instead of **ⲧⲉⲛⲁ**.

1. The meaning of affirmation:

   Ⲡ̅ⲟ̅ⲥ̅ ⲛⲁϣⲓⲛⲓ ⲉ̀ⲣⲱⲧⲉⲛ.   The Lord will visit you.

   Ⲫⲁⲣⲁⲱ̀ ⲛⲁⲥⲱⲧⲉⲙ ⲛ̀ⲥⲁ ⲑⲏⲛⲟⲩ ⲁⲛ.   Pharoah will not listen to you.

2. Interrogative form:

   Ⲡ̅ⲟ̅ⲥ̅ ⲟⲩ ⲡⲉⲧⲁϥϣⲱⲡⲓ ϫⲉ ⲭ̀ⲛⲁⲟⲩⲟⲛϩⲕ ⲉ̀ⲣⲟⲛ ⲁⲛⲟⲛ ⲟⲩⲟϩ ⲡⲓⲕⲟⲥⲙⲟⲥ ⲛ̀ⲑⲟϥ ⲁⲛ?
   "Lord, how is it that You will manifest Yourself to us, and not to the world?" [John 14:22 NKJV]

3. Negative form:

   ⲛ̀ϯⲛⲁϫⲉ ⲟⲩⲙⲏϣ ⲛ̀ⲥⲁϫⲓ ⲛⲉⲙⲱⲧⲉⲛ ⲁⲛ.   I will not talk much with you.

2. The Second Future Tense (ⲡⲓⲙⲁϩⲥ̀ⲛⲁⲩ ⲛ̀ⲥⲏⲟⲩ ⲉⲑⲛⲏⲟⲩ)

This tense specializes in examples, proverbs, common sayings, description, and interrogative sentences.

ⲁ̅	ⲁⲩⲛⲁⲉⲣ ⲙ̀ⲫⲣⲏϯ ⲛ̀ⲛⲓⲁⲅⲅⲉⲗⲟⲥ.	They will be as the angels.
ⲃ̅	ϫⲉ ⲁϥⲛⲁϭⲓ ⲉ̀ⲃⲟⲗϧⲉⲛ ⲡⲉⲧⲉⲫⲱⲓ.	He will take of what is mine.
ⲅ̅	ⲁⲣⲉ ⲛⲁⲓ ⲛⲁϣⲱⲡⲓ ⲛ̀ⲑⲛⲁⲩ?	When will these be?

ⲁ̄	ϦⲈⲚ ϮⲀⲚⲀⲤⲦⲀⲤⲒⲤ ⲀⲤⲚⲀⲈⲢ ⲤϨⲒⲘⲒ ⲚⲚⲒⲘ?
	In the resurrection, whose wife will she be? [In the resurrection, of whom will she be a wife?]
ⲉ̄	ⲀⲢⲈⲦⲈⲚⲚⲀⲔⲰϮ ⲚⲤⲀ ⲞⲨ? What will you look for?

3. The Unlimited Future Tense [ⲠⲒⲤⲎⲞⲨ ⲈⲐⲚⲎⲞⲨ ⲚⲀⲦⲞⲨⲰϢϤ (ⲈⲐⲘⲎⲚ)]

It indicates a state coming in the future.

ⲁ̄	ⲈϤⲚⲀⲞⲨⲚⲞϤ ⲈϤⲚⲀⲢⲰⲦ.
	He will rejoice and will grow. [It has the meaning of continuation].
ⲃ̄	ⲈⲨⲚⲀϮϨⲀⲠ ⲈⲢⲰⲦⲈⲚ.
	They will judge you (pl.). [You (pl.) will be judged.]
ⲅ̄	ⲈⲨⲚⲀϪⲞⲤ ⲚⲎⲒ ⲘⲎ ϦⲈⲚ ⲠⲈⲔⲢⲀⲚ ⲀⲚ ⲀⲚⲈⲢⲠⲢⲞⲪⲎⲦⲈⲨⲒⲚ?
	They will say to Me, "Did we not prophesy in Your name?" [Matthew 7:22 NKJV]
ⲇ̄	ⲤⲚⲎⲞⲨ ⲚϪⲈ ⲞⲨⲞⲨⲚⲞⲨ ϨⲞⲦⲈ ⲈⲒⲚⲀⲤⲀϪⲒ ⲚⲈⲘⲰⲦⲈⲚ ⲀⲚ ϦⲈⲚ ϨⲀⲚⲠⲀⲢⲀⲂⲞⲖⲎ.
	An hour comes when I will not talk with you in parables.
ⲉ̄	ⲈⲢⲈ ⲠⲈϤⲤⲘⲞⲨ ⲚⲀϢⲰⲠⲒ ⲈϤⲘⲎⲚ ⲈⲂⲞⲖ ϦⲈⲚ ⲢⲰⲚ.
	His praise will be always in our mouths.

4. The Future Imperfect Tense (ⲠⲒⲤⲎⲞⲨ ⲈⲐⲚⲎⲞⲨ ⲚⲀⲦϪⲎⲔ)

It is used to indicate what was about to happen. (An event that would have happened in the future, which is viewed from the past). It is considered to have ended from the speaker's point of view.

ⲁ̄	ⲚⲀⲢⲈ ⲠⲀⲤⲞⲚ ⲚⲀⲘⲞⲨ ⲀⲚ ⲠⲈ.	My brother would not have died.
ⲃ̄	ⲚⲀⲒⲚⲀⲞⲨⲞⲢⲠⲔ ⲠⲈ ϦⲈⲚ ⲞⲨⲞⲨⲚⲞϤ.	I would have sent you joyfully.
ⲅ̄	ⲚⲀⲢⲈⲦⲈⲚⲚⲀⲢⲀϢⲒ ⲠⲈ.	You would have rejoiced.
ⲇ̄	ⲚⲀⲨⲚⲀⲚⲞϨⲈⲘ ⲀⲚ ⲠⲈ ⲚϪⲈ ⲤⲀⲢⲜ ⲚⲒⲂⲈⲚ.	All flesh would not have been saved.
ⲉ̄	ⲚⲀⲢⲈ ⲠⲒⲢⲰⲘⲒ ⲚⲀⲰⲚϦ ⲈⲰⲒⲔ ⲘⲘⲀⲨⲀⲦϤ ⲀⲚ.	Man would not have lived by bread alone.

5. The Emphatic Future Tense (ⲡⲓⲥⲏⲟⲩ ⲉⲑⲛⲏⲟⲩ ⲉⲧⲧⲁϫⲣⲏⲟⲩⲧ)

It is used to indicate the future that will certainly happen, or the future that bears certainty, will (volition), and execution in its meaning. With the second person form (feminine and masculine, singular and plural), it signifies a command, a request, and an appeal.

ⲁ̅ ⲉⲥⲉ̀ⲉⲣⲃⲟⲕⲓ ⲟⲩⲟϩ ⲉⲥⲉ̀ⲙⲓⲥⲓ.
She will conceive and give birth [with all certainty].

ⲃ̅ ⲉⲓⲉⲭⲱ ⲙ̀ⲡⲁⲡⲛⲉⲩⲙⲁ ϩⲓϫⲱϥ ⲉϥⲉ̀ⲧⲁⲙⲉ ⲛⲓⲉⲑⲛⲟⲥ ⲉⲩϩⲁⲡ.
"I will [certainly] put My Spirit upon Him, and He will declare [with certainty] justice to the Gentiles" (Matthew 12:18).

ⲅ̅ ⲁⲛⲟⲕ ϯⲱⲛϧ ⲟⲩⲟϩ ⲛ̀ⲑⲱⲧⲉⲛ ⲉⲣⲉⲧⲉⲛⲉ̀ⲱⲛϧ.
I live and you will live [with all certainty].

ⲇ̅ ⲉⲩⲉ̀ϣⲟⲩϣⲟⲩ ⲙ̀ⲙⲱⲟⲩ ⲛ̀ϫⲉ ⲛⲏⲉⲑⲟⲩⲁⲃ ϧⲉⲛ ⲟⲩⲱⲟⲩ: ⲉⲩⲉ̀ⲑⲉⲗⲏⲗ ⲙ̀ⲙⲱⲟⲩ ϩⲓϫⲉⲛ ⲛⲟⲩⲙⲁⲛ̀ⲉⲛⲕⲟⲧ.
The saints will [certainly] boast in glory, and will rejoice [with all certainty] upon their beds.

ⲉ̅ ⲉⲕⲉ̀ⲙⲉⲛⲣⲉ ⲡⲉⲕϣⲫⲏⲣ ⲙ̀ⲡⲉⲕⲣⲏϯ.
You will love your fellow as yourself. [Love your fellow as yourself.]

ⲋ̅ ⲉⲕⲉ̀ⲧⲟⲩⲛⲟⲥ ⲛ̀ⲧⲟⲩⲥⲁⲣⲝ ϧⲉⲛ ⲡⲓⲉ̀ϩⲟⲟⲩ ⲉⲧⲁⲕⲑⲁϣϥ.
Raise [You will raise] their bodies in the day which You have appointed.

ⲍ̅ ⲛ̀ⲛⲉϥϭⲛⲏⲛ ⲟⲩⲇⲉ ⲛ̀ⲛⲉϥⲱϣ ⲉ̀ⲃⲟⲗ ⲟⲩⲇⲉ ⲛ̀ⲛⲉ ⲟⲩⲁⲓ ⲥⲱⲧⲉⲙ ⲉ̀ⲧⲉϥⲥⲙⲏ ϧⲉⲛ ⲛⲓⲡⲗⲁⲧⲓⲁ.
"He will not quarrel nor cry out, nor will anyone hear His voice in the streets." [Matthew 12:19 NKJV]

ⲏ̅

ⲛ̀ⲛⲉⲕϧⲱⲧⲉⲃ	ⲛ̀ⲛⲉⲕϭⲓⲟⲩⲓ̀	ⲛ̀ⲛⲉⲕⲱⲣⲕ
You shall not murder.	You shall not steal.	You shall not swear.

Note that the negative form, with respect to the second person speaker, changes to the prohibition (negative imperative) form.

Lesson 30 ✠ *Verbs in the Future Tense* ✠

Exercises

1. Write the meaning of the following:

1. ⲧⲉⲣⲁⲉⲣϩⲱⲃⲓ.
2. ⲛⲁⲅⲛⲁⲓ ⲡⲉ.
3. ⲛ̀ⲛⲉⲕⲱⲣⲕ.
4. ⲉϥⲉⲟⲩⲛⲟϥ.
5. ⲛ̀ⲛⲉⲧⲉⲛⲙⲟⲥϯ.
6. ⲭⲛⲁⲥⲱⲧⲉⲙ ⲁⲛ.
7. ⲁϥⲛⲁϯ ⲉⲣⲱⲧⲉⲛ.
8. ⲛⲁⲛⲛⲁⲥϭⲁⲓ ⲁⲛ ⲡⲉ.
9. ⲉⲣⲉⲧⲉⲛⲛⲁϩⲉⲙⲥⲓ.
10. ⲉⲓⲉⲙⲟϣⲓ ⲛ̀ⲥⲱϥ.

2. Put the following sentences in the negative form:

ⲁ̄ ⲉⲓⲉⲥⲁϫⲓ ⲛⲉⲙⲁϥ.
ⲃ̄ ⲛⲁϥⲛⲁϣⲉ ⲉϧⲟⲩⲛ ⲡⲉ.
ⲅ̄ ⲉⲣⲉⲧⲉⲛⲉ̀ⲙⲟϣⲓ ⲛ̀ⲥⲁ Ⲡ⳪.
ⲇ̄ ⲥⲉⲛⲁⲁⲣⲉϩ ⲉ̀ⲛⲟⲩⲱϣ.

3. Translate to the English language:

ⲁ̄ ⲉⲥⲉ̀ⲙⲓⲥⲓ ⲛ̀ⲟⲩϣⲏⲣⲓ: ⲉⲩⲉ̀ⲙⲟⲩϯ ⲉⲡⲉϥⲣⲁⲛ ϫⲉ Ⲉⲙⲙⲁⲛⲟⲩⲏⲗ.
ⲃ̄ ⲁⲓⲛⲁⲙⲟⲩϯ ⲉⲣⲟ ϫⲉ ⲛⲓⲙ ⲱ̀ ϯⲡⲁⲛⲁⲅⲓⲁ ⲙ̀ⲡⲁⲣⲑⲉⲛⲟⲥ.
ⲅ̄ ⲉⲩⲉ̀ⲥⲙⲟⲩ ⲉⲡⲉⲕⲣⲁⲛ ⲉⲑⲟⲩⲁⲃ ⲛ̀ϫⲉ ⲛⲓⲫⲩⲗⲏ ⲧⲏⲣⲟⲩ ⲛ̀ⲧⲉ ⲡⲕⲁϩⲓ.
ⲇ̄ ⲧⲉⲛⲛⲁϭⲓⲥⲓ ⲁⲛ ⲉ̀ⲛⲉϩ: ⲧⲉⲛⲛⲁⲕⲏⲛ ⲁⲛ ⲉⲛ̀ⲥⲙⲟⲩ ⲉⲣⲟⲕ.
ⲉ̄ ϫⲉ Ⲡ⳪ ⲛⲁϯⲙⲁϯ ⲉϫⲉⲛ ⲡⲉϥⲗⲁⲟⲥ: ϥⲛⲁϭⲓⲥⲓ ⲛ̀ⲛⲓⲣⲉⲙⲣⲁⲩϣ ϧⲉⲛ ⲟⲩⲟⲩϫⲁⲓ.
ⲋ̄ ⲟⲩϩⲏⲧ ⲉϥⲟⲩⲁⲃ ⲉⲕⲉ̀ⲥⲟⲛⲧϥ ⲛ̀ϩⲏⲧ.
ⲍ̄ ⲉϥⲉ̀ⲥⲙⲟⲩ ⲉⲣⲟⲛ ⲛ̀ϫⲉ Ⲫϯ: ⲧⲉⲛⲛⲁⲥⲙⲟⲩ ⲉⲡⲉϥⲣⲁⲛ ⲉⲑⲟⲩⲁⲃ.
ⲏ̄ ⲉⲕⲉ̀ⲙⲉⲛⲣⲉ Ⲡⲓϭⲟⲓⲥ ⲡⲉⲕⲛⲟⲩϯ ⲉ̀ⲃⲟⲗϧⲉⲛ ⲡⲉⲕϩⲏⲧ ⲧⲏⲣϥ ⲛⲉⲙ ⲉ̀ⲃⲟⲗϧⲉⲛ ⲧⲉⲕⲯⲩⲭⲏ ⲧⲏⲣⲥ ⲛⲉⲙ ⲉ̀ⲃⲟⲗϧⲉⲛ ⲧⲉⲕϫⲟⲙ ⲧⲏⲣⲥ ⲛⲉⲙ ⲉ̀ⲃⲟⲗϧⲉⲛ ⲛⲉⲕⲙⲉⲩⲓ ⲧⲏⲣⲟⲩ.

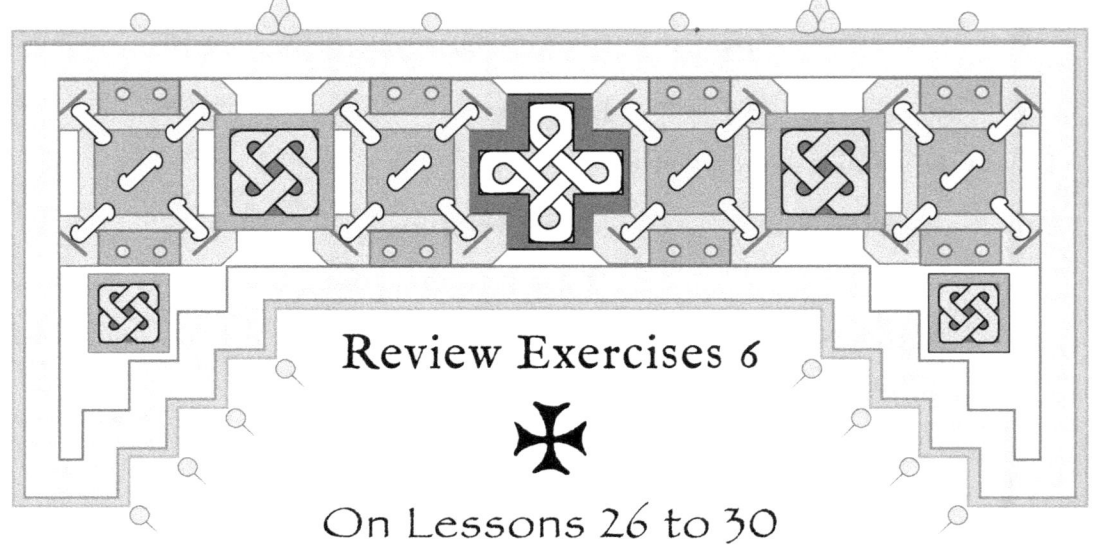

Review Exercises 6

On Lessons 26 to 30

1. Write the meaning of the following phrases:

1. ⲉⲕⲉϣⲱⲡⲓ ϧⲉⲛ ⲧⲉⲛⲙⲏϯ.
2. ϯⲇⲓⲁⲑⲏⲕⲏ ⲉⲧⲥⲉⲙⲛⲏⲟⲩⲧ.
3. ⲁⲣⲓⲡⲉⲛⲙⲉⲩⲓ.
4. ⲁⲟⲩⲱⲛ ⲛ̀ⲣⲱⲕ.
5. ⲉⲩⲛⲁϩⲱⲥ ⲉ̀ⲡⲟⲩⲛⲟⲩϯ.
6. ϣⲁϥϣⲉ ⲉ̀ϧⲟⲩⲛ ⲉ̀ϯⲉⲕⲕⲗⲏⲥⲓⲁ.
7. ⲛⲁⲕⲱϣ ⲙ̀ⲡⲁⲓⲭⲱⲙ ⲡⲉ.
8. ϯⲓⲣⲓ ⲕⲁⲧⲁ ⲉⲧⲁϥϫⲱ ⲛⲏⲓ.
9. ⲧⲉⲧⲉⲛϭⲓⲙⲕⲁϩ ⲉⲣⲉⲧⲉⲛⲣⲁϣⲓ.
10. ⲉϥⲉⲁⲓⲧⲉⲛ ⲛ̀ⲥⲁ ⲧⲉϥϭⲟⲩⲓ̀ⲛⲁⲙ.

2. Put the verb in the pronominal form, making the necessary changes:

ⲁ̄ ⲁⲕⲥⲉⲙⲛⲓ ⲛⲁⲛ ⲛ̀ⲧⲉⲕϩⲓⲣⲏⲛⲏ.
ⲃ̄ ⲫ̀ⲛⲟⲃⲓ ⲁϥⲧⲁⲕⲟ ⲙ̀ⲡⲓⲣⲱⲙⲓ.
ⲅ̄ ⲁϥϣⲁⲛϣ ⲛ̀ⲛⲉⲛϣⲏⲣⲓ ⲙ̀Ⲡⲓⲥⲣⲁⲏⲗ.
ⲇ̄ Ⲫϯ ⲁϥⲑⲁⲙⲓⲟ ⲛ̀Ⲇⲁⲙ.
ⲉ̄ ⲡⲉϥϫⲓⲛⲙⲟⲩ ⲁϥⲧⲁⲛϧⲟ ⲙ̀ⲙⲟⲓ.
ⲋ̄ ⲁⲕⲧⲁⲗϭⲟ ⲛ̀ⲛⲉⲛϣⲱⲛⲓ.
ⲍ̄ ⲁϥⲥⲱϯ ⲙ̀ⲙⲟⲛ.

3. Write the following verbs in the imperative mood:

1. ⲛⲟϩⲉⲙ
2. ⲟⲩⲱⲙ
3. ⲉⲣϩⲙⲟⲧ
7. ⲧⲁⲥⲑⲟ
8. ⲉⲣⲟⲩⲱⲓⲛⲓ
9. ⲱ̀ϣⲁⲙ
13. ⲓ̀ⲣⲓ
14. ϩⲱⲥ
15. ϯⲥⲃⲱ

4. ⲧⲁϫⲣⲟ	10. ⲙⲟϣⲓ	16. ⲓⲛⲓ
5. ϣⲗⲏⲗ	11. ϯⲱⲟⲩ	17. ⲕⲁϯ
6. ⲛⲁⲩ	12. ⲧⲟⲩⲃⲟ	18. ⲱⲗⲓ

4. The following sentences are in the negative form, put them in the affirmative:

ⲁ̄ ⲙ̀ⲡⲉⲣϩⲉⲙⲥⲓ ⲙ̀ⲛⲁⲓ.
ⲃ̄ ⲧⲉⲛⲥⲱⲟⲩⲛ ⲁⲛ ⲙ̀ⲡⲁⲓⲣⲱⲙⲓ.
ⲅ̄ ⲙ̀ⲡⲁⲧⲱϣ ⲛ̀ⲛⲁⲓϫⲱⲙ.
ⲇ̄ ⲙ̀ⲡⲉϥⲥⲁϫⲓ ⲛⲉⲙⲏⲓ.
ⲉ̄ ⲛⲁⲕϣⲗⲏⲗ ⲁⲛ ⲡⲉ.
ⲋ̄ ⲛ̀ⲛⲉϥⲱⲛϧ ⲟⲩⲟϩ ⲛ̀ⲛⲟⲩⲱⲛϧ.

5. Translate to the English language:

ⲁ̄ ⲙⲟⲓ ⲛⲁⲛ Ⲡ̅ⲟ̅ⲥ̅ ⲛ̀ⲟⲩⲙⲉⲧⲣⲉϥⲉⲣⲛⲩⲫⲓⲛ.
ⲃ̄ Ⲡ̅ⲟ̅ⲥ̅ ⲉϥⲉ̀ⲥⲙⲟⲩ ⲉ̀ⲣⲟⲕ ⲉ̀ⲃⲟⲗϧⲉⲛ Ⲥⲓⲱⲛ.
ⲅ̄ ⲉ̀ⲣⲉ ⲛⲁⲥⲫⲟⲧⲟⲩ ⲃⲉⲃⲓ ⲛ̀ⲟⲩⲥⲙⲟⲩ.
ⲇ̄ ⲕⲱϯ ⲛ̀ⲥⲁ ⲡⲉⲕⲃⲱⲕ ϫⲉ ⲛⲉⲕⲉⲛⲧⲟⲗⲏ ⲙ̀ⲡⲓⲉⲣⲡⲟⲩⲱⲃϣ.
ⲉ̄ ⲛ̀ⲑⲟⲕ ⲡⲉ ⲡⲉⲛⲛⲟⲩϯ ⲟⲩⲟϩ ⲛ̀ⲧⲉⲛⲥⲱⲟⲩⲛ ⲛ̀ⲕⲉⲟⲩⲁⲓ ⲁⲛ ⲉ̀ⲃⲏⲗ ⲉ̀ⲣⲟⲕ.
ⲋ̄ ⲉ̀ⲃⲟⲗϩⲓⲧⲉⲛ ⲡⲉϥⲥⲧⲁⲩⲣⲟⲥ ⲁϥⲓ̀ ⲛ̀ϫⲉ ⲫⲣⲁϣⲓ ⲉ̀ϧⲟⲩⲛ ⲉ̀ⲡⲓⲕⲟⲥⲙⲟⲥ ⲧⲏⲣϥ.
ⲍ̄ ⲁⲕϧⲟⲙϧⲉⲙ ⲛ̀ϯϫⲟⲙ ⲛ̀ⲧⲉ ⲫⲙⲟⲩ ⲱ̅ Ⲡⲓⲥⲱⲧⲏⲣ: ⲟⲩⲟϩ ⲁⲕⲧⲟⲩⲛⲟⲥ Ⲁⲇⲁⲙ ⲛⲉⲙⲁⲕ ⲟⲩⲟϩ ⲁⲕⲁⲓϥ ⲛ̀ⲣⲉⲙϩⲉ ⲉ̀ⲃⲟⲗϧⲉⲛ ⲁⲙⲉⲛϯ.
ⲏ̄ ⲡ̀ⲥⲛⲟϥ ⲙ̀ⲡⲓⲣⲱⲙⲓ ⲁϥϣⲉⲣⲓ: ⲙ̀ⲡⲉⲣⲣⲓⲙⲓ: ⲁⲗⲗⲁ ⲁⲣⲓϩⲓϣⲱ ⲛ̀ϯⲁⲛⲁⲥⲧⲁⲥⲓⲥ ⲛ̀ⲛⲓⲁⲡⲟⲥⲧⲟⲗⲟⲥ.
ⲑ̄ ⲁⲩⲏⲥ ⲙ̀ⲙⲱⲟⲩ ⲉ̀ⲡⲉⲕⲙ̀ϩⲁⲩ ⲛ̀ϫⲉ ⲛⲓϩⲓⲟⲙⲓ ⲙ̀ϥⲁⲓⲥⲟϫⲉⲛ ⲉⲩⲛⲉϩⲡⲓ.
ⲓ̄ ⲁⲥⲛⲁⲩ ⲉ̀ⲡⲓⲁⲅⲅⲉⲗⲟⲥ ⲉϥϩⲉⲙⲥⲓ ϩⲓϫⲉⲛ ⲡⲓⲱ̀ⲛⲓ.
ⲓⲁ̄ ⲫⲁⲓ ⲉⲧⲁϥⲉⲛϥ ⲉ̀ⲡ̀ϣⲱⲓ ⲛ̀ⲟⲩⲑⲩⲥⲓⲁ ⲉⲥϣⲏⲡ.
ⲓⲃ̄ ⲁⲟⲩⲱⲛ ⲛⲁⲛ Ⲡ̅ⲟ̅ⲥ̅ ⲙ̀ⲫ̀ⲣⲟ ⲛ̀ⲧⲉ ϯⲉⲕⲕⲗⲏⲥⲓⲁ.
ⲓⲅ̄ ⲛⲓⲛⲟⲃⲓ ⲉⲧⲁⲓⲁⲓⲧⲟⲩ: Ⲡⲁ̅ⲟ̅ⲥ̅ ⲛ̀ⲛⲉⲕⲣ̀ⲡⲟⲩⲙⲉⲩⲓ.

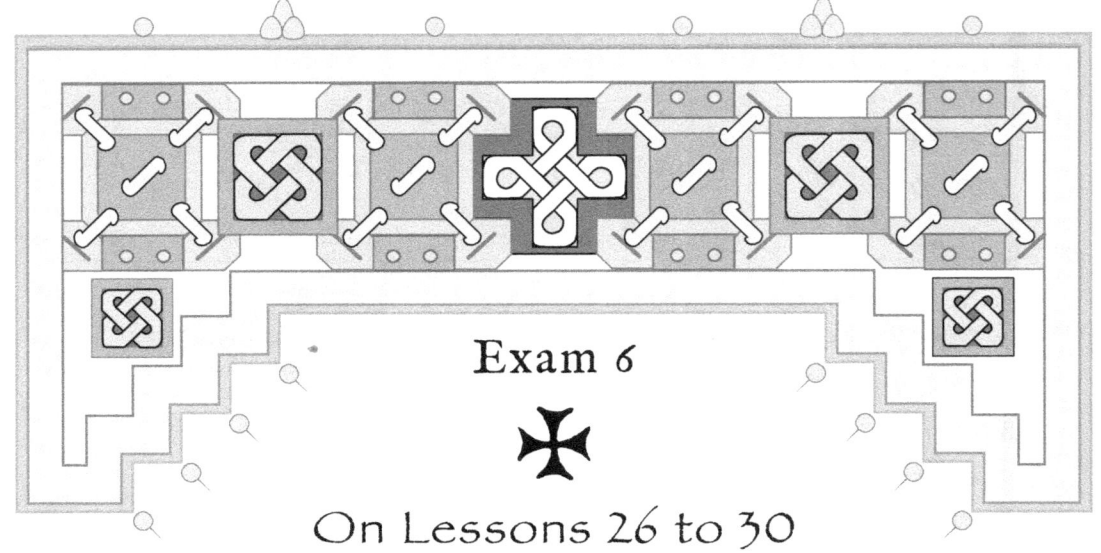

Exam 6

On Lessons 26 to 30

1. Write the meaning of the following phrases:

1. ⲁϥⲧⲁⲕⲉ ⲡⲉⲛⲅⲉⲛⲟⲥ.
2. ϩⲁⲛϣⲏⲣⲓ ⲉⲩϣⲁⲛⲉⲩϣ.
3. ⲙⲟⲓ ⲛⲁⲛ ⲛ̀ⲧⲉⲕϩⲓⲣⲏⲛⲏ.
4. ⲙⲁ̀ⲧⲥⲁⲃⲟⲓ ⲛ̀ⲛⲉⲕⲙⲉⲑⲙⲏⲓ.
5. ⲛⲁⲣⲉⲧⲉⲛⲛⲁⲣⲁϣⲓ ⲡⲉ.
6. ϣⲁⲛⲥ̀ⲙⲟⲩ ⲉ̀ⲡⲓⲣⲁⲛ ⲙ̀ⲡⲉⲛⲛⲟⲩϯ.
7. ⲙⲉⲛⲉⲛⲥⲁ ⲉⲧⲁⲓⲟⲩⲱⲙ ⲁⲓ̈.
8. ⲛⲉϣⲁⲥϣⲗⲏⲗ ⲡⲉ ⲛⲉⲙ ⲛⲉⲥϣⲏⲣⲓ.
9. ⲧⲉⲣⲁϩⲉⲙⲥⲓ ⲛⲉⲙ ⲛⲓⲁⲡⲟⲥⲧⲟⲗⲟⲥ.
10. ⲧⲉⲛⲥⲱⲧⲉⲙ ⲉ̀ⲣⲱⲟⲩ ⲉⲩϩⲱⲥ.

2. Put the verb in the qualitative form:

1. ⲧⲉⲛⲧⲁⲓⲟ ⲛ̀ϯⲡⲁⲣⲑⲉⲛⲟⲥ.   ϯⲡⲁⲣⲑⲉⲛⲟⲥ ⲉⲧ . . . .
2. ⲁϥⲧⲁⲥⲑⲟ ⲛ̀ⲟⲩⲣⲉϥⲉⲣⲛⲟⲃⲓ.   ⲟⲩⲣⲉϥⲉⲣⲛⲟⲃⲓ ⲉϥ . . . .
3. ⲁⲕⲧⲁϫⲣⲟ ⲙ̀ⲡⲉϥⲑⲣⲟⲛⲟⲥ.   ⲡⲉϥⲑⲣⲟⲛⲟⲥ ⲉⲧ . . . .
4. ϥ̀ⲧⲟⲩⲃⲟ ⲛ̀ⲛⲉⲛϩⲏⲧ.   ⲛⲉⲛϩⲏⲧ ⲉⲧ . . . .
5. ⲁⲩⲗⲁⲗⲟ ⲛ̀ⲟⲩⲕⲓⲃⲱⲧⲟⲥ.   ⲟⲩⲕⲓⲃⲱⲧⲟⲥ ⲉⲥ . . . .
6. ⲁⲛⲧⲁⲗⲟ ⲛ̀ϩⲁⲛⲱ̀ⲛⲓ.   ϩⲁⲛⲱ̀ⲛⲓ ⲉⲩ . . . .
7. ⲁⲩ̀ⲧⲥⲁⲃⲟ ⲛ̀ⲛⲓⲗⲁⲟⲥ.   ⲛⲓⲗⲁⲟⲥ ⲉⲧ . . . .

3. The following verbs are in the imperative mood, give the base form from them:

1. ⲙⲁϩⲁⲡ
7. ⲙⲁⲕⲁϯ
13. ⲁⲗⲓⲟⲩⲓ̀

2. ⲁⲣⲓϩⲙⲟⲧ	8. ⲁⲛⲓⲟⲩⲧⲁϩ	14. ⲁⲛⲁⲩ
3. ⲥ̇ⲙⲟⲩ	9. ⲙⲁⲧⲁⲛϧⲟ	15. ⲙⲁⲱⲛⲥ
4. ⲙⲁⲧⲁⲗϭⲟ	10. ⲁⲭⲱ	16. ⲁⲣⲓⲫⲙⲉⲩⲓ̇
5. ⲁⲟⲩⲱⲛ	11. ⲙⲁϣⲉⲛⲁⲕ	17. ⲙⲁⲧⲟⲩⲃⲟ
6. ⲙⲁϣⲟⲩ	12. ⲥⲱⲧⲉⲙ	18. ⲁⲛⲓⲟⲩⲓ̇

4. Put the following sentences in the negative form:

ⲁ̄   ⲁⲛⲱϣ ⲛ̇ⲛⲉⲛϣⲱ.

ⲃ̄   ϣⲁⲕⲥ̇ϭⲁⲓ ⲉⲣⲟϥ.

ⲅ̄   ⲛⲁⲣⲉϩⲉⲙⲥⲓ ⲡⲉ ⲛⲉⲙ ⲛⲉⲁ̇ⲗⲱⲟⲩⲓ̇.

ⲇ̄   ⲁϥⲭⲱ ⲛⲏⲓ ⲙ̇ⲡⲁⲓⲥⲁϫⲓ.

ⲉ̄   ⲧⲉⲛⲛⲁⲛⲉϩⲥⲓ ⲛ̇ϣⲱⲣⲡ.

ⲋ̄   ⲉⲣⲉⲧⲉⲛⲉ̇ⲓ̇ ⲛⲉⲙⲁⲕ.

5. Translate to the English language:

ⲁ̄   ⲁⲓⲛⲁⲩ ⲉ̇Ⲡ̅ⲥ̅.

ⲃ̄   ⲙⲁⲧⲁⲙⲉ ⲛⲁⲥⲛⲏⲟⲩ.

ⲅ̄   ⲁⲣⲉⲙⲁⲥϥ ⲁϥⲧⲁⲗϭⲟⲛ.

ⲇ̄   ϣⲁϥⲧⲟⲩⲃⲟ ⲛ̇ⲛⲓⲛⲟⲃⲓ.

ⲉ̄   ⲁⲙⲱⲓⲛⲓ ⲧⲏⲣⲟⲩ ⲛⲓⲡⲓⲥⲧⲟⲥ.

ⲋ̄   ⲉⲧⲁ Ⲙⲱⲩⲥⲏⲥ ⲑⲁⲙⲓⲟⲥ.

ⲍ̄   ϣⲁϥⲭⲁϥ ϧⲉⲛ ϯⲥⲕⲏⲛⲏ.

ⲏ̄   ⲉⲣⲉ Ⲫϯ ⲥⲁϧⲟⲩⲛ ⲙ̇ⲙⲟⲥ.

ⲑ̄   ⲙ̇ⲡⲉⲣⲉⲣⲡⲱϣ ⲛ̇ϯⲇⲓⲁⲑⲏⲕⲏ: ⲑⲏⲉⲧⲁⲕⲥⲉⲙⲛⲏⲧⲥ ⲛⲉⲙ ⲛⲉⲛⲓⲟϯ.

ⲓ̄   ⲉⲣⲉ ⲡⲟⲩⲥ̇ⲙⲟⲩ ⲉⲑⲟⲩⲁⲃ ϣⲱⲡⲓ ⲛⲉⲙⲁⲛ.

ⲓ̄ⲁ   ⲟⲩϩⲏⲧ ⲉϥⲟⲩⲁⲃ ⲉⲕⲉ̇ⲥⲟⲛⲧϥ ⲛ̇ϧⲏⲧ.

ⲓ̄ⲃ   ⲙⲁⲧⲁⲥⲑⲟⲛ Ⲫ̇ⲛⲟⲩϯ ⲉ̇ϧⲟⲩⲛ ⲉ̇ⲡⲉⲕⲟⲩϫⲁⲓ.

ⲓ̄ⲅ   ⲉⲩϩⲱⲥ ⲉ̇ⲡⲟⲩⲣⲉϥⲥⲱⲛⲧ ⲉϥⲭⲏ ϧⲉⲛ ⲧⲉⲛⲉϫⲓ: ⲫⲁⲓ ⲉⲧⲁϥϭⲓ ⲙ̇ⲡⲉⲛⲓⲛⲓ.

ⲓ̄ⲇ   ⲁⲕⲧⲱⲛⲕ ⲁⲕⲥⲱϯ ⲙ̇ⲙⲟⲛ.

ⲓ̄ⲉ   ϧⲉⲛ ⲟⲩⲥⲏⲟⲩ ⲉϥϣⲏⲡ ⲉⲕⲉ̇ⲥⲱⲧⲉⲙ ⲉ̇ⲣⲟⲓ.

ⲓ̄ⲋ   ⲁⲛⲁⲩ ⲛ̇ⲑⲱⲧⲉⲛ ⲟⲩⲟϩ ⲁⲣⲓⲉⲙⲓ ϫⲉ ⲁϥⲟ̇ϩⲓ ⲉ̇ⲣⲁⲧϥ ⲛ̇ϫⲉ ⲡⲓⲥⲱⲧⲏⲣ ⲟⲩⲟϩ ⲁϥⲧⲱⲛϥ ⲉ̇ⲃⲟⲗϧⲉⲛ ⲛⲏⲉⲑⲙⲱⲟⲩⲧ.

ⲓ̄ⲍ   ⲉⲥⲉ̇ⲱⲛϧ ⲛ̇ϫⲉ ⲧⲁⲯⲩⲭⲏ ⲟⲩⲟϩ ⲉⲥⲉ̇ⲥⲙⲟⲩ ⲉ̇ⲣⲟⲕ ⲟⲩⲟϩ ⲛⲉⲕϩⲁⲡ ⲉⲩⲉ̇ⲉⲣⲃⲟⲏⲑⲓⲛ ⲉ̇ⲣⲟⲓ.

ⲓ̄ⲏ   Ⲡ̅ⲥ̅ ⲉⲕⲉ̇ⲁⲟⲩⲱⲛ ⲛ̇ⲛⲁⲥⲫⲟⲧⲟⲩ: ⲟⲩⲟϩ ⲉⲣⲉ ⲣⲱⲓ ϫⲱ ⲙ̇ⲡⲉⲕⲥ̇ⲙⲟⲩ.

Lesson 31

ⲡⲓⲱϣ ⲙ̀ⲙⲁϩ ⲗ̅ⲁ̅

✠

ⲡⲓⲥ̀ⲙⲟⲧ

ADJECTIVES

Definition: an adjective is a word added to a noun to describe its state.

Kinds of Adjectives (ⲛⲓⲑⲟ ⲛ̀ⲛⲓⲥ̀ⲙⲟⲧ)

1. Original Adjectives

These are adjectives that are not taken from other words, and are a small group in the Coptic language:

ⲃⲉⲣⲓ	New, modern	ⲁⲡⲁⲥ	Old, ancient	ⲛⲓϣϯ	Great, big
ⲕⲟⲩϫⲓ	Small, little	ⲙⲏⲓ	True, just	ⲁ̀ϣⲓⲣⲓ	Diligent
ⲥⲁⲓⲉ̀	Beautiful, splendid	ϩⲏⲕⲓ	Poor, needy	ⲙⲏϣ	Multitude, many

These original adjectives are sometimes treated as nouns and accept definite and indefinite articles:

ⲡⲓⲕⲟⲩϫⲓ	The baby, the little one	ⲛⲓⲕⲟⲩϫⲓ	The babies, the little ones
ⲡⲓⲛⲓϣϯ	The great one, the big one	ⲛⲓϩⲏⲕⲓ	The poor ones, the needy ones

Lesson 31 ✠ Adjectives ✠

There are adjectives whose end changes in the feminine and plural forms, for example:

Singular, masculine	Singular, feminine	Meaning	Plural	
ⲥⲁⲃⲉ	ⲥⲁⲃⲏ	Wise, rational	ⲥⲁⲃⲉⲩ	Wise, rational
ⲑⲉϣⲉ	ⲑⲉϣⲏ	Neighbor	ⲑⲉϣⲉⲩ	Neighbors
ⲃⲉⲗⲗⲉ	ⲃⲉⲗⲗⲏ	Blind	ⲃⲉⲗⲗⲉⲩ	Blind [people]
ϫⲁϭⲉ	ϫⲁϭⲏ	Left-handed	ϫⲁϭⲉⲩ	Left-handed
ϣⲁϥⲉ	ϣⲁϥⲏ	Desolate, desert	ϣⲁϥⲉⲩ	Desolate, desert [places]
ϭⲁⲗⲉ	ϭⲁⲗⲏ	Crippled	ϭⲁⲗⲉⲩ	Crippled
ϧⲁⲉ̀	ϧⲁⲏ̀	Last	ϧⲁⲉⲩ	Last
ϩⲟⲩⲓⲧ	ϩⲟⲩⲓϯ	First	ϩⲟⲩⲁϯ	First
ⲛⲁⲛⲉϥ	ⲛⲁⲛⲉⲥ	Good	ⲛⲁⲛⲉⲩ	Good
ϣⲉⲙⲙⲟ	ϣⲉⲙⲙⲱ	Stranger, foreigner	ϣⲉⲙⲙⲱⲟⲩ	Strangers, foreigners
ϧⲉⲗⲗⲟ	ϧⲉⲗⲗⲱ	Elder, old man (mas.) Eldress, old woman (fem.)	ϧⲉⲗⲗⲟⲓ	Elders, eldresses
			ϧⲉⲗⲗⲱⲟⲩ	Elders, eldresses
ⲣⲁⲙⲁⲟ̀	ⲣⲁⲙⲁⲱ̀	Rich	ⲣⲁⲙⲁⲟⲓ	Rich
			ⲣⲁⲙⲁⲱⲟⲩ	Rich

2. Derived Adjectives:

These are derived from verbs, and are expressed by the qualitative form of the verb, for example:

ⲧⲁⲕⲟ	To perish	→	ⲧⲁⲕⲏⲟⲩⲧ	Perished
ⲧⲁⲓⲟ	To honor	→	ⲧⲁⲓⲏⲟⲩⲧ	Honored
ⲧⲟⲩⲃⲟ	To sanctify	→	ⲟⲩⲁⲃ	Holy, sanctified
ⲧⲟⲩⲃⲟ	To purify	→	ⲧⲟⲩⲃⲏⲟⲩⲧ	Pure
ⲑⲉⲃⲓⲟ	To be humble	→	ⲑⲉⲃⲓⲏⲟⲩⲧ	Humble

ⲥⲙⲟⲩ	To bless	→	ⲥⲙⲁⲣⲱⲟⲩⲧ	Blessed
ⲕⲉⲛⲓ	To fatten up	→	ⲕⲉⲛⲓⲱⲟⲩⲧ	Fattened
ϣⲱⲕ	To deepen	→	ϣⲏⲕ	Deep

It should be noted whether the described noun starts with definite or indefinite article.

1. If the described noun starts with a definite article, the adjective (the qualitative form of the verb) is preceded by the relative pronoun ⲉⲧ (or ⲉⲑ):

ⲡⲓⲡⲛⲉⲩⲙⲁ ⲉⲑⲟⲩⲁⲃ The Holy Spirit	ⲛⲓⲣⲱⲙⲓ ⲉⲑⲟⲩⲁⲃ The holy men
ⲡⲓⲟⲩⲏⲃ ⲉⲧⲧⲁⲓⲏⲟⲩⲧ The honored priest	ⲛⲓϧⲉⲗⲗⲟⲓ ⲉⲧⲧⲁⲓⲏⲟⲩⲧ The honored elders
ⲫⲛⲟⲩⲛ ⲉⲧϣⲏⲕ The deep depth	ⲛⲓϣⲏⲣⲓ ⲉⲧⲥⲙⲁⲣⲱⲟⲩⲧ The blessed sons

2. If the described noun starts with an indefinite article, the adjective (the qualitative form of the verb) is preceded by the letter ⲉ and by the personal pronoun referring to the described [noun]: ϥ for the singular masculine, ⲥ for the singular feminine, and ⲩ for both kinds of plural:

ⲟⲩⲣⲱⲙⲓ ⲉϥⲧⲁⲓⲏⲟⲩⲧ	ⲟⲩⲡⲛⲉⲩⲙⲁ ⲉϥⲟⲩⲁⲃ
ⲟⲩⲥϩⲓⲙⲓ ⲉⲥⲧⲁⲓⲏⲟⲩⲧ	ϩⲁⲛⲁⲅⲅⲉⲗⲟⲥ ⲉⲩⲟⲩⲁⲃ
ϩⲁⲛⲣⲱⲙⲓ ⲉⲩⲥⲙⲁⲣⲱⲟⲩⲧ	ⲟⲩⲙⲉⲑⲛⲟⲩϯ ⲉⲥⲧⲟⲩⲃⲏⲟⲩⲧ
ϩⲁⲛⲥⲱⲛⲓ ⲉⲩⲑⲉⲃⲓⲏⲟⲩⲧ	ⲟⲩⲙⲉⲧⲣⲱⲙⲓ ⲉⲥⲟⲩⲁⲃ
ϩⲁⲛⲉⲃⲏⲟⲩⲓ ⲉⲩⲧⲁⲓⲏⲟⲩⲧ	ϩⲁⲛⲙⲁⲥⲓ ⲉⲩⲕⲉⲛⲓⲱⲟⲩⲧ Fatted calves
ϧⲉⲛ ⲟⲩϫⲓϫ ⲉⲥⲁⲙⲁϩⲓ ⲛⲉⲙ ⲟⲩϣⲱⲃϣ ⲉϥϭⲟⲥⲓ	

3. Compound Adjective

They are composed of an article added to the beginning of the noun.

1. ⲗⲁ which signifies abundance:

ⲥⲁϫⲓ	Word	→	ⲗⲁⲥⲁϫⲓ	Talkative
ⲥⲱⲃⲓ	Laughter	→	ⲗⲁⲥⲱⲃⲓ	Prone to much laughter
ϥⲱⲓ	Hair	→	ⲗⲁϥⲱⲓ	Hairy
ϫⲁⲗ	Branch	→	ⲗⲁϫⲁⲗ	Having many branches
ⲙⲁϧⲧ	Intestines	→	ⲗⲁⲙⲁϧⲧ	Gluttonous
ϫⲱⲃⲓ	Leaf	→	ⲗⲁϫⲱⲃⲓ	Leafy

2. ⲁⲧ (ⲁⲑ) which signifies negation or reversing of the adjective:

ϩⲏⲧ	Heart	→	ⲁⲧϩⲏⲧ	Heartless
ⲛⲁϩϯ	Belief	→	ⲁⲑⲛⲁϩϯ	Unbelieving
ⲛⲟⲃⲓ	Sin	→	ⲁⲑⲛⲟⲃⲓ	Sinless
ⲙⲟⲩ	Death	→	ⲁⲑⲙⲟⲩ	Immortal
ⲥⲙⲏ	Voice	→	ⲁⲧⲥⲙⲏ	Voiceless, mute
ⲥⲁⲣⲝ	Body	→	ⲁⲧⲥⲁⲣⲝ	Bodiless
ⲑⲱⲗⲉⲃ	Defilement	→	ⲁⲧⲑⲱⲗⲉⲃ	Undefiled
ⲟⲩⲱⲛϩ	Manifest	→	ⲁⲑⲟⲩⲱⲛϩ	Hidden
ⲥⲱⲧⲉⲙ	To hear	→	ⲁⲧⲥⲱⲧⲉⲙ	Disobedient
ⲥⲓⲛⲓ	To traverse	→	ⲁⲧⲥⲓⲛⲓ	Impassable
ⲉⲙⲓ	To know	→	ⲁⲧⲉⲙⲓ	Ignorant, unaware
ⲕⲁϯ	To understand	→	ⲁⲧⲕⲁϯ	Foolish, not understanding
ⲁⲣⲭⲏ	Beginning	→	ⲁⲧⲁⲣⲭⲏ	Without a beginning
ⲛⲁⲩ	To see	→	ⲁⲑⲛⲁⲩ	Invisible
ⲭⲟⲩ	Time	→	ⲁⲧⲭⲟⲩ	Timeless
ⲑⲱⲟⲩⲓ	Shoe	→	ⲁⲧⲑⲱⲟⲩⲓ	Barefoot

ⲁⲧ is especially used with the infinitive denoting power (ability), which is the infinitive that is formed by adding the letter ϣ̀- (can or to be able) to the beginning of the word, for example:

ⲧⲁϩⲟ	To comprehend	→	ⲁⲧϣ̀ⲧⲁϩⲟϥ	Incomprehensible
ϧⲟⲧϧⲉⲧ	To examine	→	ⲁⲧϣ̀ϧⲟⲧϧⲉⲧ	Unsearchable
ⲥⲁϫⲓ	To speak, to utter	→	ⲁⲧϣ̀ⲥⲁϫⲓ ⲙ̀ⲙⲟϥ	Unutterable

3. **ⲥⲁ** *which signifies profession, occupation, or specialization in:*

ⲱⲓⲕ	Bread	→	ⲥⲁⲛ̀ⲱⲓⲕ	Baker
ϣⲁⲣ	Skin	→	ⲥⲁⲛ̀ϣⲁⲣ	Bookbinder
ⲁϥ	Meat	→	ⲥⲁⲛ̀ⲁϥ	Butcher
ⲑⲱⲟⲩⲓ	Shoe	→	ⲥⲁⲛⲑⲱⲟⲩⲓ	Cobbler

ⲥⲁ is also attached to moral adjectives, for example:

ⲡⲉⲧϩⲱⲟⲩ	Evil	→	ⲥⲁⲙ̀ⲡⲉⲧϩⲱⲟⲩ	Evil doer
ⲙⲉⲑⲛⲟⲩϫ	Lie	→	ⲥⲁⲙ̀ⲙⲉⲑⲛⲟⲩϫ	Liar (accustomed to lying)

4. **ϣⲟⲩ** *which signifies qualification and worthiness; worthy of.*

ϣ̀ⲧⲉⲙ which signifies negation, being unqualified, and unworthiness.

The condition for using it is that it must be prefixed by the article ⲛ̀, and suffixed by a pronoun that refers to the described noun and that follows it regarding whether it is feminine or masculine, singular or plural.

ⲡⲁⲓⲱⲧ ⲛ̀ϣⲟⲩⲙⲉⲛⲣⲓⲧϥ.	My father, the worthy to be loved.
ϯⲡⲁⲣⲑⲉⲛⲟⲥ ⲛ̀ϣⲟⲩⲧⲁⲓⲟⲥ.	The virgin, the worthy to be honored.
ⲛⲁⲓⲟϯ ⲛ̀ϣⲟⲩⲙⲉⲛⲣⲓⲧⲟⲩ.	My fathers, the worthy of love.
Ⲫϯ ⲛ̀ϣⲟⲩϯⲱⲟⲩ ⲛⲁϥ.	God, the worthy to be glorified.
ⲡⲓⲣⲱⲙⲓ ⲛ̀ϣ̀ⲧⲉⲙⲧⲁⲓⲟϥ.	The man, the unworthy of respect.
ϯⲥⲱⲛⲓ ⲛ̀ϣ̀ⲧⲉⲙⲉⲣϣⲫⲏⲣⲓ ⲙ̀ⲙⲟⲥ.	The sister, the unworthy of admiration.

Lesson 31 ✠ Adjectives ✠

ⲛⲓϫⲁϫⲓ ⲛ̀ϣⲧⲉⲙⲙⲉⲛⲣⲓⲧⲟⲩ.	The hated enemies. (The enemies, the unworthy of love).
ⲛⲓⲁ̀ⲗⲱⲟⲩ̀ⲓ ⲛ̀ϣⲧⲉⲙⲉⲣϣ̀ⲫⲏⲣⲓ ⲙ̀ⲙⲱⲟⲩ.	The children, the unworthy of admiration.

Using the method of genitive construction to express an adjective

Considering that original adjectives are few in the Coptic language, this method, the method of genitive construction, is used to compensate for the deficiency in original adjectives. To convert the first and second nouns using genitive construction into an adjective and a described noun, the second noun is stripped of the definite articles, so that it may change to an adjective, and the first noun in the genitive construction to the described noun. And if ⲛ̀ⲧⲉ is present as a genitive article, it is substituted with ⲛ̀ or ⲙ̀.

First and second nouns in genitive construction		Adjective and the described noun	
ⲡⲓⲣⲁⲛ ⲛ̀ⲧⲉ ⲡⲓⲟⲩϫⲁⲓ	The name of salvation	ⲡⲓⲣⲁⲛ ⲛ̀ⲟⲩϫⲁⲓ	The salvific name
ϯⲥⲙⲏ ⲛ̀ⲧⲉ Ⲫ̀ⲛⲟⲩϯ	The voice of God	ϯⲥⲙⲏ ⲛ̀ⲛⲟⲩϯ	The divine voice
ⲛⲓϫⲟⲙ ⲛ̀ⲧⲉ ⲧ̀ⲫⲉ	The powers of the heaven	ⲛⲓϫⲟⲙ ⲙ̀ⲫⲉ	The heavenly powers
ⲡⲓⲭ̀ⲗⲟⲙ ⲛ̀ⲧⲉ ⲡⲓⲛⲟⲩⲃ	The crown of gold	ⲡⲓⲭ̀ⲗⲟⲙ ⲛ̀ⲛⲟⲩⲃ	The golden crown

When the described noun is in the indefinite form:

ϩⲁⲛⲁⲅⲅⲉⲗⲟⲥ ⲛ̀ⲟⲩⲱⲓⲛⲓ	Luminous angels
ⲟⲩϩⲓⲣⲏⲛⲏ ⲛ̀ⲛⲟⲩϯ	Divine peace

Exercises

1. Write the meaning of the following:

1. ϯⲇⲓⲁⲑⲏⲕⲏ ⲙ̀ⲃⲉⲣⲓ
2. ⲡⲓⲁⲗⲟⲩ ⲛ̀ⲁ̀ϣⲓⲣⲓ
3. ⲛⲓⲥⲛⲏⲟⲩ ⲉⲑⲛⲁⲛⲉⲩ
7. ⲡⲓϫⲱⲙ ⲛ̀ⲁⲡⲁⲥ
8. ϯⲭⲏⲣⲁ ⲛ̀ⲥⲁⲃⲏ
9. ⲛⲓϧⲉⲗⲗⲟⲓ ⲉⲧⲧⲁⲓⲏⲟⲩⲧ

4. ⲡⲓⲣⲱⲙⲓ ⲛ̀ⲣⲁⲙⲁ̀ⲟ	10. ϯⲥϩⲓⲙⲓ ⲛ̀ϣⲉⲙⲙⲱ
5. ⲟⲩϣϣⲏⲛ ⲛ̀ⲗⲁϫⲱⲃⲓ	11. ⲟⲩⲙⲟⲛⲁⲭⲟⲥ ⲙ̀ⲫⲁⲓⲟⲩⲧⲁϩ
6. ϩⲁⲛϫ̀ⲗⲟⲙ ⲛ̀ⲁⲑⲗⲱⲙ	12. ⲡⲁⲓⲱⲧ ⲛ̀ϣⲟⲩⲙⲉⲛⲣⲓⲧϥ

2. Write the feminine and plural adjectives from the following original adjectives:

	Masculine	Feminine	Plural		Masculine	Feminine	Plural
1.	ϩⲟⲩⲓⲧ			6.	ⲛⲁⲛⲉϥ		
2.	ⲃⲉⲗⲗⲉ			7.	ⲣⲁⲙⲁ̀ⲟ		
3.	ⲥⲁⲃⲉ			8.	ⲑⲉϣⲉ		
4.	ϣⲁϥⲉ			9.	ϫⲁⲉ̀		
5.	ⲉϥϭⲟⲥⲓ			10.	ⲉϥϫⲏⲕ		

3. Translate the following:

ⲁ̅   ⲧⲉⲛⲱϣ ϧⲉⲛ ⲛⲓϫⲱⲙ ⲛ̀ⲧⲉ ⲛⲓⲇⲓⲁⲑⲏⲕⲏ ⲛ̀ⲁⲡⲁⲥ ⲛⲉⲙ ⲙ̀ⲃⲉⲣⲓ.

ⲃ̅   ϯⲥⲕⲏⲛⲏ ⲛ̀ϩⲟⲩⲓϯ ⲉ̀ⲧⲁ Ⲙⲱⲩⲥⲏⲥ ⲑⲁⲙⲓⲟⲥ.

ⲅ̅   ⲡⲁⲗⲁⲥ ⲉⲧϫⲱϧⲉⲃ ⲟⲩⲟϩ ⲛ̀ⲣⲉϥⲉⲣⲛⲟⲃⲓ.

ⲇ̅   ⲁⲥⲛⲁⲩ ⲉ̀ⲟⲩⲁⲅⲅⲉⲗⲟⲥ ⲛ̀ⲟⲩⲱⲓⲛⲓ.

ⲉ̅   ⲱⲟⲩⲛⲓⲁϯ ⲛ̀ⲑⲟ Ⲙⲁⲣⲓⲁ: ϯⲥⲁⲃⲏ ⲟⲩⲟϩ ⲛ̀ⲥⲉⲙⲛⲉ: ϯⲙⲁϩⲥ̀ⲛⲟⲩϯ ⲛ̀ⲥⲕⲏⲛⲏ: ⲡⲓⲁϩⲟ ⲙ̀ⲡⲛⲉⲩⲙⲁⲧⲓⲕⲟⲛ.

ⲋ̅   ⲫⲏⲉⲧⲁϥϣⲱⲡⲓ ⲛ̀ⲟⲩⲗⲩⲭⲛⲓⲁ ⲛ̀ⲛⲟⲩⲃ.

ⲍ̅   ⲁⲕⲁ̀ⲣⲉϩ ⲉ̀ⲛⲓⲉⲛⲧⲟⲗⲏ ⲉⲧⲥ̀ϧⲏⲟⲩⲧ ϧⲉⲛ ⲡⲓⲉⲩⲁⲅⲅⲉⲗⲓⲟⲛ.

ⲏ̅   ⲛⲉⲛⲓⲟϯ ⲉⲑⲟⲩⲁⲃ ⲁⲩϣⲱⲡⲓ ⲛ̀ϩⲁⲛⲗⲓⲙⲏⲛ ⲛ̀ⲟⲩϫⲁⲓ.

Lesson 32

ⲡⲓⲱϣ ⲙⲙⲁϩ ⳰ⲗⲃ

Place of Adjectives with Respect to Described Nouns

The general rule is that the described noun comes first, followed by the adjective.

1. Original Adjectives

Original adjectives are allowed to come before or after the described noun, on the condition that the preceding one of them be prefixed by definite or indefinite articles, while the one following be prefixed by the linker letter ⲛ̀ which changes to ⲙ̀ in the words beginning with one of the letters articulated at the lips (ⲃ, ⲙ, ⲡ, ⲫ, and ⲯ).

Examples:

1. The described noun precedes, and the adjective follows:

| ⲡⲓⲣⲱⲙⲓ ⲛ̀ⲥⲁⲃⲉ | The wise man | ⲡⲓϩⲱⲥ ⲙ̀ⲃⲉⲣⲓ | The new hymn |
| ⲟⲩⲣⲱⲙⲓ ⲛ̀ⲥⲁⲃⲉ | A wise man | ⲟⲩϩⲱⲥ ⲙ̀ⲃⲉⲣⲓ | A new hymn |

2. The adjective precedes, and the described noun follows:

| ⲡⲓⲥⲁⲃⲉ ⲛ̀ⲣⲱⲙⲓ | The wise man | ⲡⲓⲃⲉⲣⲓ ⲛ̀ϩⲱⲥ | The new hymn |
| ⲟⲩⲥⲁⲃⲉ ⲛ̀ⲣⲱⲙⲓ | A wise man | ⲟⲩⲃⲉⲣⲓ ⲛ̀ϩⲱⲥ | A new hymn |

The following adjectives are an exception to the general rule, for they always precede the described noun:

ⲕⲟⲩϫⲓ	Small	ϣⲟⲣⲡ	First (beginning)	ϣⲏⲙ	Little
ⲛⲓϣϯ	Great	ϩⲟⲩⲓⲧ	First	ⲙⲏϣ	Much, many
ϩⲏⲕⲓ	Poor	ϧⲁⲉ	Last	ⲑⲟ	Abundant, various

Examples:

ⲡⲓⲕⲟⲩϫⲓ ⲛ̀ⲁⲗⲟⲩ	The small child	ⲟⲩϩⲏⲕⲓ ⲛ̀ⲣⲱⲙⲓ	A poor man
ⲡⲓⲛⲓϣϯ ⲛ̀ⲟⲩⲣⲟ	The great king	ⲟⲩϣⲏⲙ ⲛ̀ⲛⲉϩ	A little oil
ⲡⲓϣⲟⲣⲡ ⲙ̀ⲙⲓⲥⲓ	The first offspring	ⲡⲓϧⲁⲉ ⲛ̀ⲉϩⲟⲟⲩ	The last day
ⲡⲓϩⲟⲩⲓⲧ ⲛ̀ⲁⲃⲟⲧ	The first month	ϩⲁⲛⲙⲏϣ ⲛ̀ⲣⲟⲙⲡⲓ	Many years
ϧⲉⲛ ⲟⲩⲑⲟ ⲛ̀ⲣⲏϯ ⲛⲉⲙ ⲟⲩⲙⲏϣ ⲛ̀ⲥⲙⲟⲧ In various ways and many analogies			

Some of these adjectives might sometimes come after the described noun, and are considered a substitute, for example:

Ⲫϯ ⲡⲓⲛⲓϣϯ ⲡⲓϣⲁ ⲉ̀ⲛⲉϩ	God, the great, the eternal

If there are two adjectives for one described noun, only one of them is permitted to come before the described noun, for example:

ⲡⲓⲡⲓⲥⲧⲟⲥ ⲛ̀ⲥⲟⲛ ⲟⲩⲟϩ ⲛ̀ⲥⲁⲃⲉ	The faithful and wise brother
ⲟⲩⲕⲟⲩϫⲓ ⲛ̀ⲁⲗⲟⲩ ⲛ̀ⲥⲁⲓⲉ̀	A small, beautiful child.

2. Derived Adjectives

They always come after the described noun and are not prefixed by the letter ⲛ̀ or ⲙ̀:

ⲛⲓϣⲏⲣⲓ ⲉⲧⲥⲙⲁⲣⲱⲟⲩⲧ The blessed sons	ⲡⲓⲡⲛⲉⲩⲙⲁ ⲉⲑⲟⲩⲁⲃ The Holy Spirit
ϩⲁⲛϧⲉⲗⲗⲟⲓ ⲉⲧⲧⲁⲓⲏⲟⲩⲧ Honored elders	ⲟⲩⲙⲱⲓⲧ ⲉϥⲥⲟⲩⲧⲱⲛ An upright way (a straight road)

3. Compound Adjectives

They come after the described noun and are prefixed by the letter ⲛ̀ or ⲙ̀:

ⲡⲓⲟⲩⲏⲃ ⲛ̀ϣⲟⲩⲙⲉⲛⲣⲓⲧϥ	The priest, the worthy to be loved.
ϯⲁⲗⲟⲩ ⲛ̀ⲗⲁⲙⲁϣⲧ	The gluttonous girl.
ⲟⲩⲃⲱⲕ ⲛ̀ⲁⲑⲛⲁϩϯ	An unbelieving servant.

4. Adjectives of Greek Origin

Most of them come after the described noun, for example:

ⲡⲉⲕⲓⲱⲧ ⲛ̀ⲁⲅⲁⲑⲟⲥ	ⲡⲉϥⲥⲛⲟϥ ⲛ̀ⲁⲗⲏⲑⲓⲛⲟⲛ
Your good father	His true blood
ϯⲛⲉϫⲓ ⲙ̀ⲡⲁⲣⲑⲉⲛⲓⲕⲏ	ⲟⲩⲥⲁⲣⲝ ⲛ̀ⲗⲟⲅⲓⲕⲏ
The virginal womb	A rational body

And there are Greek adjectives that come before the described noun, for example:

ⲡⲓⲁⲅⲓⲟⲥ ⲙ̀ⲙⲁⲣⲧⲩⲣⲟⲥ	ⲡⲓⲙⲟⲛⲟⲅⲉⲛⲏⲥ ⲛ̀ⲛⲟⲩϯ
The holy martyr	The only God
ⲛⲉⲕⲁⲅⲓⲟⲥ ⲙ̀ⲙⲁⲑⲏⲧⲏⲥ	ⲛⲓⲁⲑⲗⲓⲧⲏⲥ ⲙ̀ⲙⲁⲣⲧⲩⲣⲟⲥ
Your holy disciples	The struggling martyrs

5. The word ⲛⲓⲃⲉⲛ, meaning "every"

This is considered an adjective and always comes after the described noun, without the linking letter ⲛ̀. And the described noun remains in the singular form and without an article, neither definite nor indefinite articles.

| ⲛⲓϥⲓ ⲛⲓⲃⲉⲛ | Every breath | ⲃⲁⲗ ⲛⲓⲃⲉⲛ | Every eye |
| ϩⲱⲃ ⲛⲓⲃⲉⲛ | Every work, everything | ⲗⲁⲥ ⲛⲓⲃⲉⲛ | Every tongue |

The word ⲙⲁ (place) is an exception to this rule, for its plural, ⲙⲁⲓ (places) is the one [more often] used with the word ⲛⲓⲃⲉⲛ than the singular.

| ⲙⲁⲓ ⲛⲓⲃⲉⲛ | Every place, everywhere |

If an adjective comes after that, this adjective must be prefixed by the letter ⲛ̀ or ⲙ̀ as a general rule:

ϩⲱⲃ ⲛⲓⲃⲉⲛ ⲛ̀ⲁⲅⲁⲑⲟⲥ	Every good work.
ⲥⲟⲛ ⲛⲓⲃⲉⲛ ⲙ̀ⲙⲉⲛⲣⲓⲧ	Every beloved brother.

As for the verb or pronoun referring to the described noun, it is in the plural form, for example:

ⲛⲓϥⲓ ⲛⲓⲃⲉⲛ ⲥⲉⲥⲙⲟⲩ ⲉⲣⲟⲕ.	Every breath blesses You.
ϩⲱⲃ ⲛⲓⲃⲉⲛ ⲁⲩϣⲱⲡⲓ ⲉⲃⲟⲗϩⲓⲧⲟⲧϥ.	Everything became through him.
ⲣⲱⲙⲓ ⲛⲓⲃⲉⲛ ⲉⲩⲉ̀ⲧⲱⲟⲩⲛⲟⲩ ϧⲉⲛ ⲡⲓϩⲁⲉ̀ ⲛ̀ⲉϩⲟⲟⲩ. All people will rise on the last day.	

The verb might be sometimes mentioned in the singular form, and in this case, by the word **ⲛⲓⲃⲉⲛ** is meant the determination of persons individually, for example:

ⲟⲩⲟⲛ ⲛⲓⲃⲉⲛ ⲉⲑⲛⲁϭⲁⲥϥ ⲥⲉⲛⲁⲑⲉⲃⲓⲟϥ.
"For whoever exalts himself will be humbled," (Luke 14:11).

The agreement between the adjective and the described noun

The adjectives that have masculine and feminine forms, and singular and plural forms, follow the described noun in gender and number (singular and plural), for example:

ⲟⲩⲥⲁⲃⲉ ⲛ̀ⲣⲱⲙⲓ	A wise man	ϩⲁⲛⲥⲁⲃⲉⲩ ⲛ̀ⲣⲱⲙⲓ	Wise men
ⲟⲩⲥⲁⲃⲏ ⲛ̀ⲥϩⲓⲙⲓ	A wise woman	ϩⲁⲛⲥⲁⲃⲉⲩ ⲛ̀ⲥⲱⲛⲓ	Wise sisters

But if the adjective is an object or predicate, then it remains without change, for example:

ϥⲛⲁⲁⲓⲧⲉⲛ ⲛ̀ⲣⲁⲙⲁⲟ̀.	ⲉⲥⲟⲓ ⲛ̀ⲣⲉⲙϩⲉ.
He will make us rich.	She is free.

Also the word that comes in the second position remains usually without change, despite the fact that sometimes it follows the described noun, for example:

ϩⲁⲛⲣⲱⲙⲓ ⲛ̀ⲥⲁⲃⲉ	Wise men	ϩⲁⲛⲥⲁⲃⲏ ⲛ̀ⲥϩⲓⲙⲓ	Wise women

Lesson 32 ✠ Place of Adjectives with Respect to Described Nouns ✠

Exercises

Translate the following:

ⲁ̄ ⲡⲉⲕⲛⲓϣϯ ⲛ̀ⲛⲁⲓ.   ϯϣⲟⲩⲣⲏ ⲛ̀ⲛⲟⲩⲃ.

   ⲧⲉⲕⲙⲁⲩ ⲛ̀ϣⲉⲗⲉⲧ.   ⲫⲓⲟⲙ ⲛ̀ϣⲁⲣⲓ.

   ϯⲥⲕⲏⲛⲏ ⲙ̀ⲙⲏⲓ.   ⲡⲓⲟⲩϫⲁⲓ ⲛ̀ⲉⲱⲛⲓⲟⲛ.

ⲃ̄ ⲡⲓⲱⲟⲩ ⲛⲁⲕ ⲡⲓⲙⲁⲓⲣⲱⲙⲓ ⲛ̀ⲁⲅⲁⲑⲟⲥ.

ⲅ̄ ⲉ̀ⲛⲁⲩⲱⲥ ⲉ̀Ⲫϯ ϧⲉⲛ ⲧⲁⲓϣⲱⲗⲏ ⲙ̀ⲃⲉⲣⲓ.

ⲇ̄ ⲧⲉⲕⲙⲉⲧⲟⲩⲣⲟ ⲡⲁⲛⲟⲩϯ ⲟⲩⲙⲉⲧⲟⲩⲣⲟ ⲛ̀ⲉⲛⲉϩ.

ⲉ̄ ⲗⲁⲥ ⲛⲓⲃⲉⲛ ⲉⲩⲥⲟⲡ ⲥⲉⲥⲙⲟⲩ ⲉ̀ⲡⲉⲕⲣⲁⲛ.

ⲋ̄ ϫⲉ ⲁⲩⲥⲁϫⲓ ⲉⲑⲃⲏϯ: ⲛ̀ϩⲁⲛϩⲃⲏⲟⲩⲓ̀ ⲉⲩⲧⲁⲓⲏⲟⲩⲧ: ϯⲃⲁⲕⲓ ⲉⲑⲟⲩⲁⲃ: ⲛ̀ⲧⲉ ⲡⲓⲛⲓϣϯ ⲛ̀ⲟⲩⲣⲟ.

ⲍ̄ ϩⲁⲛⲩⲙⲛⲟⲗⲟⲅⲓⲁ ⲙ̀ⲡⲣⲟⲫⲏⲧⲓⲕⲟⲛ.

   ⲛⲓⲥⲧⲣⲁⲧⲓⲁ ⲛ̀ⲁⲅⲅⲉⲗⲓⲕⲟⲛ.

   ⲛⲓⲧⲁⲅⲙⲁ ⲛ̀ⲉ̀ⲡⲟⲩⲣⲁⲛⲓⲟⲛ.

   ϩⲁⲛϣⲱⲏⲗ ⲙ̀ⲡⲛⲉⲩⲙⲁⲧⲓⲕⲟⲛ.

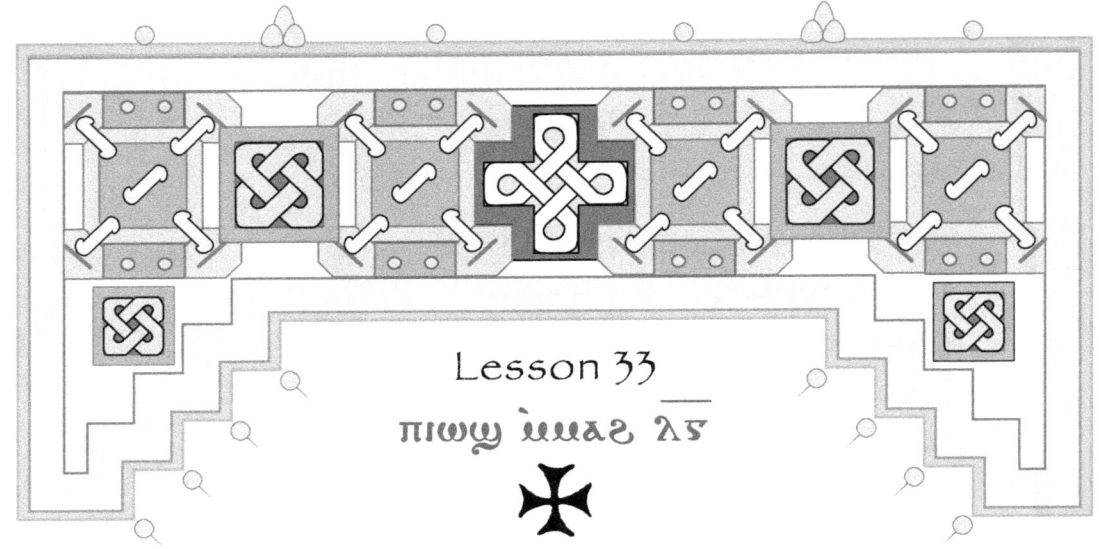

Lesson 33
ⲡⲓⲱϣ ⲙ̄ⲙⲁϩ ⲗ̄ⲅ̄

✠

DEGREES OF DESCRIPTION

There are three degrees of description:

1. Simple Description

It consists of an adjective and the described noun, for example:

ⲡⲓⲙⲁⲓⲣⲱⲙⲓ ⲛ̀ⲁⲅⲁⲑⲟⲥ	ϯⲡⲁⲣⲑⲉⲛⲟⲥ ⲛ̀ⲁⲧⲑⲱⲗⲉⲃ
ϯϥⲉ ⲙ̀ⲃⲉⲣⲓ	ϯⲛⲉϫⲓ ⲙ̀ⲡⲁⲣⲑⲉⲛⲓⲕⲏ
ⲡⲓⲛⲓϣϯ ⲛ̀ⲟⲩⲣⲟ	ⲛⲓϩⲉⲗⲗⲟⲓ ⲉⲧⲧⲁⲓⲏⲟⲩⲧ
ϯⲟⲩⲣⲱ ⲙ̀ⲙⲏⲓ	ⲛⲓⲥⲛⲏⲟⲩ ⲛ̀ϣⲟⲩⲙⲉⲛⲣⲓⲧⲟⲩ

2. Comparing Between Two Sides (Similar or Match)

1. That the described nouns are equal in the degree of description, and it is called the **equal match**. Its articles are the following:

ⲉ̀ - ⲙ̀ⲫⲣⲏϯ ⲛ̀ (ⲙ̀) - ϩⲱⲥ

Examples:

ⲁ̄ ϣⲁⲥϣⲱⲡⲓ ⲉ̀ⲟⲩϣϣⲏⲛ.
She becomes like a tree.

ⲃ̄ ⲡⲁⲥⲟⲛ ⲟⲩⲙⲁⲑⲏⲧⲏⲥ ⲡⲉ ⲙ̀ⲫⲣⲏϯ ⲙ̀ⲡⲉⲕⲥⲟⲛ.
My brother is a disciple like your brother.

Lesson 33 ✠ Degrees of Description ✠

- ⲉ̄ ⲁⲩϭⲓⲥⲓ ⲛ̀ϫⲉ ⲛⲓⲙⲱⲟⲩ ⲙ̀ⲫⲣⲏϯ ⲛ̀ⲟⲩⲥⲟⲃⲧ.
  The waters rose up like a wall. [First Canticle]

- ⲇ̄ ⲁⲓⲥⲱⲣⲉⲙ ⲙ̀ⲫⲣⲏϯ ⲛ̀ⲟⲩⲉⲥⲱⲟⲩ ⲉⲁϥⲧⲁⲕⲟ.
  I went astray like a sheep that perished.

- ⲉ̄ ⲙⲟϣⲓ ϩⲱⲥ ϩⲁⲛϣⲏⲣⲓ ⲛ̀ⲧⲉ ⲡⲓⲟⲩⲱⲓⲛⲓ.
  Walk like sons of the light.

- ⲋ̄ ϩⲱⲥ ϣⲏⲣⲓ ⲛ̀ⲧⲉ ⲛⲉⲕⲉⲩⲭⲏ.
  Like sons of your prayers.

- ⲍ̄ ⲙ̀ⲫⲣⲏϯ ϧⲉⲛ ⲧ̀ⲫⲉ: ⲛⲉⲙ ϩⲓϫⲉⲛ ⲡⲓⲕⲁϩⲓ.
  As [or like] in the heaven, so on the earth. [On earth as it is in heaven].

- ⲏ̄ ⲁⲛⲛⲁⲩ ⲉⲡⲉϥⲱⲟⲩ ⲙ̀ⲫⲣⲏϯ ⲙ̀ⲡ̀ⲱⲟⲩ ⲛ̀ⲟⲩϣⲏⲣⲓ ⲙ̀ⲙⲁⲩⲁⲧϥ ⲛ̀ⲧⲟⲧϥ ⲙ̀ⲡⲉϥⲓⲱⲧ.
  We saw His glory, like the glory of an only Son of His Father.

2. That one of the sides is greater in description than the other, and it is called the **greater match**. Its articles are the following:

ⲉϩⲟⲧⲉ, ⲉ̀, ⲡⲁⲣⲁ	Before the noun to which a comparison is made
ⲉϩⲟⲧⲉ ⲛ̀ⲧⲉ-, ⲉϩⲟⲧⲉ ⲉ̀-	Before the verb
ⲉϩⲟⲧⲉⲣⲟ″, ⲉϩⲟⲧⲉ ⲉⲣⲟ″	With the attached personal pronouns
ⲛ̀ϩⲟⲩⲟ̀, ⲟⲩϩⲟⲩⲟ̀	After the noun to which a comparison is made

Examples:

- ⲁ̄ ⲉⲕⲉ̀ⲣⲁϧⲧ ⲉⲓⲉ̀ⲟⲩⲃⲁϣ ⲉϩⲟⲧⲉ ⲟⲩⲭⲓⲱⲛ.
  You wash me, so I become whiter than snow.

- ⲃ̄ ⲡⲉⲱⲟⲩ Ⲙⲁⲣⲓⲁ ϭⲟⲥⲓ ⲉϩⲟⲧⲉ ⲧ̀ⲫⲉ, ⲧⲉⲧⲁⲓⲏⲟⲩⲧ ⲉ̀ⲡⲕⲁϩⲓ ⲛⲉⲙ ⲛⲏⲉⲧϣⲟⲡ ⲛ̀ϧⲏⲧϥ.
  Your glory, O Mary, is higher than the heaven, you are more honorable than the earth and those dwelling in it. [Sunday Theotokia]

- ⲅ̄ ⲟⲩⲛⲓϣϯ ⲡⲉ ⲡ̀ⲧⲁⲓⲟ ⲙ̀Ⲙⲁⲣⲓⲁ ⲡⲁⲣⲁ ⲛⲏⲉⲑⲟⲩⲁⲃ ⲧⲏⲣⲟⲩ.
  Great is the honor of Mary, more than all the saints. [Wednesday Theotokia]

- ⲇ̄ ⲛⲁⲛⲉⲥ ⲉ̀ⲧⲏⲓⲥ ⲛⲁⲕ ⲉϩⲟⲧⲉ ⲉ̀ⲧⲏⲓⲥ ⲛ̀ⲕⲉⲣⲱⲙⲓ.
  That she be given to you is better than she be given to another man. [Gen. 29:19]

- ⲉ̄ ⲛⲁⲛⲉⲥ ⲛ̀ⲧⲉⲛⲉⲣⲃⲱⲕ ⲛ̀ⲛⲓⲣⲉⲙⲛ̀ⲭⲏⲙⲓ ⲉϩⲟⲧⲉ ⲛ̀ⲧⲉⲛⲙⲟⲩ ⲛ̀ϩⲣⲏⲓ ϩⲓ ⲡ̀ϣⲁϥⲉ.
  It is better for us to serve the Egyptians than to die in the desert. [Exodus 14:12]

⳥ ⲁ ⲟⲩⲙⲏϣ ⲛ̀ⲥϩⲓⲙⲓ ϭⲓⲧⲁⲓⲟ: ⲁⲣⲉϭⲓⲥⲓ ⲛ̀ⲑⲟ ⲉ̀ϩⲟⲧⲉⲣⲱⲟⲩ ⲧⲏⲣⲟⲩ.

Many women received honor; you are more exalted than all of them. [Friday Theotokia]

ⲍ̅ ⲛ̀ⲑⲟⲕ ⲟⲩϩⲟⲩⲟ̀ ⲙ̀ⲡ̀ⲡⲣⲟⲫⲏⲧⲏⲥ.

You are better than a prophet. [Doxology of John the Baptist]

If the comparison is general, that is, without mentioning the second term which comes after "than," then we use the article **ⲛ̀ϩⲟⲩⲟ̀** which means "much more," and it comes after the word it describes, for example:

| ⲟⲩⲥⲁⲃⲉ ⲛ̀ϩⲟⲩⲟ̀. | Wiser. | ⲟⲩϩⲁⲡ ⲛ̀ϩⲟⲩⲟ̀. | A greater condemnation. |

ϯⲙⲉⲧⲙⲉⲑⲣⲉ ⲛ̀ⲧⲉ Ⲫ̀ϯ ⲟⲩⲛⲓϣϯ ⲧⲉ ⲛ̀ϩⲟⲩⲟ̀.
The testimony of God is much greater. [1 John 5:9]

3. That one of them is less in description than the other, and it is called the **lesser match**. In the Coptic language, it is expressed using the greater match with reversing the adjective, for example: poorer, instead of less rich; more ignorant, instead of less educated; more unjust, instead of less just; and so on. Therefore, the articles of the lesser match are the same as the articles of the greater match.

Examples:

| ⲁ̅ | ⲁⲛⲟⲕ ⲟⲩⲁⲧϩⲏⲧ ⲡⲉ ⲉ̀ϩⲟⲧⲉⲣⲟⲕ.
I am more ignorant [less educated] than you. |
| ⲃ̅ | ⲡⲁⲓⲣⲱⲙⲓ ⲟⲩϩⲏⲕⲓ ⲡⲉ ⲉ̀ϩⲟⲧⲉ ⲫⲏ.
This man is poorer [less rich] than that. |

3. A Noun Preferred Over Others

1. **Relative preference**: If a person or thing excels in its description over many of its counterparts, it is called the relative preferred [noun]. Its articles are:

| ϧⲉⲛ | In, in between | ⲟⲩⲧⲉ | Between, among |

Examples:

ⲁ̅	ⲧⲉⲥⲙⲁⲣⲱⲟⲩⲧ ⲛ̀ⲑⲟ ϧⲉⲛ ⲛⲓϩⲓⲟⲙⲓ.	Blessed are you among women.
ⲃ̅	ⲡⲓⲛⲓϣϯ ϧⲉⲛ ⲛⲓⲁ̀ⲅⲓⲟⲥ.	The great among the saints.
ⲅ̅	ⲡⲓⲕⲟⲩϫⲓ ⲉ̀ⲃⲟⲗ ⲟⲩⲧⲉ ⲛⲓⲁ̀ⲡⲟⲥⲧⲟⲗⲟⲥ.	The smallest among the apostles.

Lesson 33 ✠ Degrees of Description ✠

ⲇ̅ ⲫⲏ ⲉⲧⲟⲓ ⲛ̀ⲕⲟⲩϫⲓ ϧⲉⲛ ⲑⲏⲛⲟⲩ.
That who is the youngest among you.

2. **Absolute preference**: if a person or thing excels in description irrespective of their counterparts, it is called the absolute preferred [noun]. And its article is ⲉⲙⲁϣⲱ (very).

ⲁ̅ ⲟⲩⲛⲓϣϯ ⲛ̀ⲣⲁϣⲓ ⲉⲙⲁϣⲱ. A very great joy.

ⲃ̅ ⲁϥⲉⲣⲣⲁⲙⲁⲟ ⲛ̀ϫⲉ ⲡⲓⲣⲱⲙⲓ ⲉⲙⲁϣⲱ ⲉⲙⲁϣⲱ.
The man became very rich. [Genesis 30:43]

Exercises

Translate the following, mentioning the kind of adjective, the degree of description, and its article in each sentence:

ⲁ̅ ⲥⲉ ⲅⲁⲣ ⲁⲗⲏⲑⲱⲥ: ⲁⲥϭⲓⲥⲓ ⲉⲙⲁϣⲱ: ⲛ̀ϫⲉ ⲧⲁⲓⲡⲁⲣⲑⲉⲛⲟⲥ ⲉⲑⲙⲉϩ ⲛ̀ⲧⲁⲓⲟ. [Sunday Psali]

ⲃ̅ ⲧⲉⲃⲟⲥⲓ ⲉⲙⲁϣⲱ ⲉϩⲟⲧⲉ ⲛⲓⲭⲉⲣⲟⲩⲃⲓⲙ: ⲧⲉⲧⲁⲓⲏⲟⲩⲧ ⲛ̀ϩⲟⲩ'ⲟ ⲉⲛⲓⲥⲉⲣⲁⲫⲓⲙ. [Sunday Psali]

ⲅ̅ ⲧⲉϩⲓⲁⲕⲧⲓⲛ ⲉ̀ⲃⲟⲗ ⲉϩⲟⲧⲉ ⲫⲣⲏ: ⲧⲉⲟⲓ ⲛ̀ⲗⲁⲙⲡⲣⲟⲥ ⲉϩⲟⲧⲉ ⲛⲓⲭⲉⲣⲟⲩⲃⲓⲙ. [Sunday Theotokia]

ⲇ̅ ⲁⲣⲉϭⲓⲥⲓ ⲉ̀ⲛⲓⲫⲩⲥⲓⲥ ⲛ̀ⲛⲟⲏⲣⲟⲛ ⲉⲧⲥⲁ̀ⲡϣⲱⲓ. [Tuesday Lobsh]

ⲉ̅ ⲁⲣⲉ ⲉⲙⲡϣⲁ ⲛ̀ⲧⲁⲓⲟ ⲛⲓⲃⲉⲛ: ⲡⲁⲣⲁ ⲟⲩⲟⲛ ⲛⲓⲃⲉⲛ ⲉⲧ ϩⲓϫⲉⲛ ⲡⲓⲕⲁϩⲓ. [Wednesday Lobsh]

ⲋ̅ ⲧⲉⲥⲙⲁⲣⲱⲟⲩⲧ ⲉϩⲟⲧⲉ ⲧ̀ⲫⲉ: ⲧⲉⲧⲁⲓⲏⲟⲩⲧ ⲉϩⲟⲧⲉ ⲡ̀ⲕⲁϩⲓ. [Friday Theotokia]

ⲍ̅ ⲥϭⲟⲥⲓ ⲉ̀ⲛⲓⲭⲉⲣⲟⲩⲃⲓⲙ: ⲥⲧⲁⲓⲏⲟⲩⲧ ⲉ̀ⲛⲓⲥⲉⲣⲁⲫⲓⲙ. [Wednesday Theotokia]

ⲏ̅ ⲙⲓⲭⲁⲏⲗ ⲡⲁⲣⲭⲱⲛ ⲛ̀ⲛⲁ ⲛⲓⲫⲏⲟⲩⲓ̀: ⲛ̀ⲑⲟϥ ⲉⲧⲟⲓ ⲛ̀ϣⲟⲣⲡ: ϧⲉⲛ ⲛⲓⲧⲁⲝⲓⲥ ⲛ̀ⲁⲅⲅⲉⲗⲓⲕⲟⲛ: ⲉϥϣⲉⲙϣⲓ ⲙ̀ⲡⲉⲙⲑⲟ ⲙ̀Ⲡ̅ⲥ̅.

ⲑ̅ ⲛⲁⲛⲉ ⲫ̀ⲣⲁϣⲓ ⲛ̀Ⲥⲟⲩⲣⲓⲏⲗ: ⲉⲛⲓⲣⲓ ⲙ̀ⲙⲟϥ ϧⲉⲛ ⲛⲓⲉⲕⲕⲗⲏⲥⲓⲁ: ⲉϩⲟⲧⲉ ⲫ̀ⲣⲁϣⲓ ⲛ̀ⲟⲩⲡⲁⲧϣⲉⲗⲉⲧ: ⲛ̀ⲧⲉ ⲡⲁⲓⲕⲟⲥⲙⲟⲥ ⲉⲑⲛⲁⲥⲓⲛⲓ. [Doxology of Archangel Suriel]

ⲓ̅ ⲛ̀ⲑⲟⲕ ⲟⲩⲛⲓϣϯ ϧⲉⲛ ⲛⲏⲉⲑⲟⲩⲁⲃ ⲧⲏⲣⲟⲩ. [Doxology of John the Baptist]

ⲓⲁ̅ ⲁ ⲡⲓⲥⲑⲟⲓⲛⲟⲩϥⲓ ⲛ̀ⲧⲉ ⲛⲉϥⲁⲣⲉⲧⲏ: ϯ ⲙ̀ⲡⲟⲩⲛⲟϥ ⲛ̀ⲛⲉⲛⲯⲩⲭⲏ: ⲙ̀ⲫⲣⲏϯ ⲙ̀ⲡⲓⲁⲣⲱⲙⲁⲧⲁ: ⲉⲧⲣⲏⲧ ϧⲉⲛ ⲡⲓⲡⲁⲣⲁⲇⲓⲥⲟⲥ. [Doxology of Abba Anthony]

ⲓⲃ̅ ⲁⲗⲏⲑⲱⲥ ⲁⲕϭⲓⲥⲓ ⲉⲙⲁϣⲱ: ϧⲉⲛ ⲑⲙⲏϯ ⲛ̀ⲧⲥⲩⲛⲟⲇⲟⲥ: ⲛ̀ⲧⲉ ⲛⲉⲛⲓⲟϯ ⲛ̀ⲟⲣⲑⲟⲇⲟⲝⲟⲥ: ϧⲉⲛ ϯⲡⲟⲗⲓⲥ Ⲉⲫⲉⲥⲟⲥ. [Abba Shenouda]

ⲓⲅ̅ ⲁⲛⲟⲕ ⲡⲉ ⲡⲓⲕⲟⲩϫⲓ ⲛ̀ϩⲣⲏⲓ ϧⲉⲛ ⲛⲁⲥⲛⲏⲟⲩ. [Psalm 151]

Lesson 34

ⲡⲓⲱϣ ⲙ̅ⲙⲁϩ ⲗ̅ⲇ̅

† ϯⲏⲡⲓ

NUMBERS [PART 1]

Numbers are written in the Coptic language using the alphabet with placing a horizontal dash above the numbers—this horizontal dash is called the perfector **ⲡⲓⲣⲉϥϫⲱⲕ ⲉ̀ⲃⲟⲗ**—to denote numbers from 1 to 999.

1. Simple Numbers

	Ones			Tens			Hundreds	
#	Pronun.	Meaning	#	Pronun.	Meaning	#	Pronun.	Meaning
ⲁ̅	ⲟⲩⲁⲓ	1	ⲓ̅	ⲙⲏⲧ	10	ⲣ̅	ϣⲉ	100
ⲃ̅	ⲥⲛⲁⲩ	2	ⲕ̅	ϫⲟⲩⲧ	20	ⲥ̅	ⲥⲛⲁⲩϣⲉ	200
ⲅ̅	ϣⲟⲙⲧ	3	ⲗ̅	ⲙⲁⲡ	30	ⲧ̅	ϣⲟⲙⲧϣⲉ	300
ⲇ̅	ϥⲧⲟⲩ	4	ⲙ̅	ϩⲙⲉ	40	ⲩ̅	ϥⲧⲟⲩϣⲉ	400
ⲉ̅	ϯⲟⲩ	5	ⲛ̅	ⲧⲉⲃⲓ	50	ⲫ̅	ϯⲟⲩϣⲉ	500
ⲋ̅	ⲥⲟⲟⲩ	6	ⲝ̅	ⲥⲉ	60	ⲭ̅	ⲥⲟⲟⲩϣⲉ	600
ⲍ̅	ϣⲁϣϥ	7	ⲟ̅	ϣ̀ⲃⲉ	70	ⲯ̅	ϣⲁϣϥϣⲉ	700
ⲏ̅	ϣⲙⲏⲛ	8	ⲡ̅	ϩⲁⲙⲛⲉ	80	ⲱ̅	ϣⲙⲏⲛϣⲉ	800
ⲑ̅	ⲯⲓⲧ	9	ϥ̅	ⲡⲓⲥⲧⲁⲩ	90	ϣ̅	ⲯⲓⲧϣⲉ	900

Lesson 34 ✠ Numbers [Part 1] ✠

To denote numbers from a thousand (that is, thousands), either two horizontal dashes are placed above the alphabetical letter, or a diagonal dash is placed under the alphabetical letter, which is called "the maker of thousands" ⲡⲓⲣⲉϥⲉⲣϣⲟ.

Ones of thousands			Tens of thousands			Hundreds of thousands		
#	Pronun.	Meaning	#	Pronun.	Meaning	#	Pronun.	Meaning
ⲁ̿, ⲁ̗	ϣⲟ	1000	ⲓ̿, ⲓ̗	ⲙⲏⲧⲛ̀ϣⲟ	10000	ⲣ̿, ⲣ̗	ϣⲉⲛ̀ϣⲟ	100000
ⲃ̿, ⲃ̗	ϣⲟⲥ̀ⲛⲁⲩ	2000	ⲕ̿, ⲕ̗	ϫⲟⲩⲧⲛ̀ϣⲟ	20000	ⲥ̿, ⲥ̗	ⲃ̇ϣⲉⲛ̀ϣⲟ	200000
ⲅ̿, ⲅ̗	ϣⲟⲙⲧⲛ̀ϣⲟ	3000	ⲗ̿, ⲗ̗	ⲙⲁⲡⲛ̀ϣⲟ	30000	ⲧ̿, ⲧ̗	ⲅ̇ϣⲉⲛ̀ϣⲟ	300000
:	:	:	:	:	:	:	:	:
ⲑ̿, ⲑ̗	ⲯⲓⲧⲛ̀ϣⲟ	9000	ϥ̿, ϥ̗	ⲡⲓⲥⲧⲁⲩⲛ̀ϣⲟ	90000	ϣ̿, ϣ̗	ⲑ̇ϣⲉⲛ̀ϣⲟ	900000

To obtain the number of millions, either a third horizontal dash is placed above the previous numbers, or two diagonal dashes are placed under the alphabetical letter:

Original numbers ⁻			Thousands ⸴ or ⁼			Millions ⸴⸴ or ⁼		
#	Pronun.	Meaning	#	Pronun.	Meaning	#	Pronun.	Meaning
ⲁ̄	ⲟⲩⲁⲓ	1	ⲁ̿, ⲁ̗	ϣⲟ	1000	ⲁ̿, ⲁ̗̗	ϣⲟⲛ̀ϣⲟ	1×10^6
ⲓ̄	ⲙⲏⲧ	10	ⲓ̿, ⲓ̗	ⲙⲏⲧⲛ̀ϣⲟ	10000	ⲓ̿, ⲓ̗̗	ⲓ̄ϣⲟⲛ̀ϣⲟ	10×10^6
ⲣ̄	ϣⲉ	100	ⲣ̿, ⲣ̗	ϣⲉⲛ̀ϣⲟ	100000	ⲣ̿, ⲣ̗̗	ⲣ̄ϣⲟⲛ̀ϣⲟ	100×10^6
ⲧ̄	ϣⲟⲙⲧϣⲉ	300	ⲧ̿, ⲧ̗	ⲅ̇ϣⲉⲛ̀ϣⲟ	300000	ⲧ̿, ⲧ̗̗	ⲧ̄ϣⲟⲛ̀ϣⲟ	300×10^6
ϣ̄	ⲯⲓⲧϣⲉ	900	ϣ̿, ϣ̗	ⲑ̇ϣⲉⲛ̀ϣⲟ	900000	ϣ̿, ϣ̗̗	ϣ̄ϣⲟⲛ̀ϣⲟ	900×10^6

2. Compound Numbers:

1. Ones and tens:

ⲓ̄ⲁ	ⲙⲉⲧ-ⲟⲩⲁⲓ	11	ⲕ̄ⲏ	ϫⲟⲩⲧ-ϣ̇ⲙⲏⲛ	28
ⲓ̄ⲃ	ⲙⲉⲧ-ⲥ̀ⲛⲁⲩ	12	ⲗ̄ⲉ	ⲙⲁⲡ-ⲧ̇ⲓⲟⲩ	35
ⲓ̄ⲅ	ⲙⲉⲧ-ϣⲟⲙⲧ	13	ⲙ̄ⲑ	ϩ̇ⲙⲉ-ⲯⲓⲧ	49
ⲓ̄ⲍ	ⲙⲉⲧ-ϣⲁϣϥ	17	ⲛ̄ⲍ	ⲧⲉⲃⲓ-ϣⲁϣϥ	57
ⲓ̄ⲑ	ⲙⲉⲧ-ⲯⲓⲧ	19	ⲟ̄ⲃ	ϣ̇ⲃⲉ-ⲥ̀ⲛⲁⲩ	72
ⲕ̄ⲇ	ϫⲟⲩⲧ-ϥ̇ⲧⲟⲩ	24	ϥ̄ⲑ	ⲡⲓⲥⲧⲁⲩ-ⲯⲓⲧ	99

2. Ones with tens with hundreds:

p̄ḡ	ϣⲉ-ϣⲟⲙⲧ	103	т̄ιн	ϣⲟⲙⲧϣⲉ-ⲙⲉⲧ-ϣⲙⲏⲛ	318
p̄ⲓⲁ	ϣⲉ-ⲙⲉⲧ-ⲟⲩⲁⲓ	111	ⲫ̄ⲟⲅ	ⲧⲓⲟⲩϣⲉ-ϣ̄ⲃⲉ-ⲥⲟⲟⲩ	576
p̄ⲙⲇ	ϣⲉ-ϩⲙⲉ-ϥⲧⲟⲩ	144	x̄π̄ⲅ	ⲥⲟⲟⲩϣⲉ-ϣ̄ⲙⲛⲉ-ϣⲟⲙⲧ	683
ⲥ̄ⲁ	ⲥⲛⲁⲩϣⲉ ⲛⲉⲙ ⲟⲩⲁⲓ	201	ψ̄ⲛⲃ	ϣⲁϣϥϣⲉ-ⲧⲉⲃⲓ-ⲥⲛⲁⲩ	752
ⲥ̄ⲕⲉ	ⲥⲛⲁⲩϣⲉ ⲛⲉⲙ ϫⲟⲩⲧ-ⲧⲓⲟⲩ	225	ψ̄ϥⲑ	ψⲓⲧϣⲉ-ⲡⲓⲥⲧⲁⲩ-ψⲓⲧ	999

3. Ones with tens with hundreds with thousands:

ⲁ̿ⲁ	ϣⲟ ⲛⲉⲙ ⲟⲩⲁⲓ	1001
ⲁ̿ⲧⲙⲇ	ϣⲟ ⲛⲉⲙ ϣⲟⲙⲧϣⲉ-ϩⲙⲉ-ϥⲧⲟⲩ	1344
ⲁ̿ⲗⲉ	ϣⲟ ⲛⲉⲙ ⲙⲁⲡ-ϣⲙⲏⲛ	1038
ⲁ̿ϣⲟⲍ	ϣⲟ ⲛⲉⲙ ψⲓⲧϣⲉ-ϣ̄ⲃⲉ-ϣⲁϣϥ	1977

Notes:

1. We can express the thousands by using the hundreds after the tens and linking them by the letter ⲛ̀:

ⲃ̿	=	ϣⲟ ⲥⲛⲁⲩ	=	ϫⲟⲩⲧ ⲛ̀ϣⲉ	=	2000 (twenty hundred)
ⲁ̿ⲣ	=	ϣⲟ ⲛⲉⲙ ϣⲉ	=	ⲙⲉⲧ-ⲟⲩⲁⲓ ⲛ̀ϣⲉ	=	1100 (eleven hundred)

2. To express the tens of thousands, we can use the term ⲑⲃⲁ (ten thousand, myriad), as follows, noting that the number ⲥⲛⲁⲩ comes always subsequently:

ⲕ̿	=	ϫⲟⲩⲧ ⲛ̀ϣⲟ	=	ⲑⲃⲁ-ⲥⲛⲁⲩ	=	20000 (twenty thousand)
ⲣ̿	=	ϣⲉ ⲛ̀ϣⲟ	=	ⲙⲏⲧ ⲛ̀ⲑⲃⲁ	=	100000 (a hundred thousand)

3. There is no difference between writing the discontinuous dash or the continuous dash above the compound letters:

ⲁ̿ⲩⲛⲍ	=	ⲁ̿ⲩ̿ⲛ̿ⲍ̿	=	ⲁ ⲩ̿ⲛ̿ⲍ̿	=	1457

Lesson 34 ✠ Numbers [Part 1] ✠

Numbers that have a feminine form: from 1 to 29, according to grammar books:

Masculine		Feminine		Masculine		Feminine	
ⲁ̄	ⲟⲩⲁⲓ		ⲟⲩⲓ̀	ⲓ̄	ⲙⲏⲧ	ⲓ̄†	ⲙⲏϯ
ⲃ̄	ⲥⲛⲁⲩ	ⲃ̄†	ⲥⲛⲟⲩϯ	ⲓ̄ⲁ	ⲙⲉⲧ-ⲟⲩⲁⲓ	ⲓ̄ⲁ†	ⲙⲏϯ-ⲟⲩⲓ̀
ⲅ̄	ϣⲟⲙⲧ	ⲅ̄†	ϣⲟⲙϯ	ⲓ̄ⲃ	ⲙⲉⲧ-ⲥⲛⲁⲩ	ⲓ̄ⲃ†	ⲙⲏϯ-ⲥⲛⲟⲩϯ
ⲇ̄	ϥ̀ⲧⲟⲩ	ⲇ̄†	ϥ̀ⲧⲟⲩⲉ̀	ⲓ̄ⲍ	ⲙⲉⲧ-ϣⲁϣϥ	ⲓ̄ⲍ†	ⲙⲏϯ-ϣⲁϣϥⲓ
ⲉ̄	ϯⲟⲩ	ⲉ̄†	ϯⲉ, ϯⲉ̀	ⲓ̄ⲑ	ⲙⲉⲧ-ⲯⲓⲧ	ⲓ̄ⲑ†	ⲙⲏϯ-ⲯⲓϯ
ⲋ̄	ⲥⲟⲟⲩ	ⲋ̄†	ⲥⲟ	ⲕ̄	ϫⲟⲩⲧ	ⲕ̄†	ϫⲱϯ
ⲍ̄	ϣⲁϣϥ	ⲍ̄†	ϣⲁϣϥⲓ	ⲕ̄ⲁ	ϫⲟⲩⲧ-ⲟⲩⲁⲓ	ⲕ̄ⲁ†	ϫⲱϯ-ⲟⲩⲓ̀
ⲏ̄	ϣⲙⲏⲛ	ⲏ̄†	ϣⲙⲏⲛⲓ	ⲕ̄ⲉ	ϫⲟⲩⲧ-ϯⲟⲩ	ⲕ̄ⲉ†	ϫⲱϯ-ϯⲉ
ⲑ̄	ⲯⲓⲧ	ⲑ̄†	ⲯⲓϯ	ⲕ̄ⲑ	ϫⲟⲩⲧ-ⲯⲓⲧ	ⲕ̄ⲑ†	ϫⲱϯ-ⲯⲓϯ

Ordinal Numbers

It is formulated by using the article **ⲙⲁϩ**, except the first and last which have a special form:

ⲡⲓϩⲟⲩⲓⲧ	The first (mas.)	ϯϩⲟⲩⲓϯ	The first (fem.)	ⲛⲓϩⲟⲩⲁϯ	The first (pl.)
ⲡⲓϧⲁⲉ̀	The last (mas.)	ϯϫⲁⲏ̀	The last (fem.)	ⲛⲓϧⲁⲉⲩ	The last (pl.)

As for the rest of the ordinal numbers, they are formulated as follows:

ⲡⲓⲙⲁϩⲥⲛⲁⲩ	The second (mas.)	ϯⲙⲁϩⲥⲛⲟⲩϯ	The second (fem.)
ⲡⲓⲙⲁϩϣⲟⲙⲧ	The third (mas.)	ϯⲙⲁϩϣⲟⲙϯ	The third (fem.)
ⲡⲓⲙⲁϩϣⲁϣϥ	The seventh (mas.)	ϯⲙⲁϩϣⲁϣϥⲓ	The seventh (fem.)
ⲡⲓⲙⲁϩⲙⲏⲧ	The tenth (mas.)	ϯⲙⲁϩⲙⲏϯ	The tenth (fem.)
ⲡⲓⲙⲁϩⲙⲉⲧⲥⲛⲁⲩ	The twelfth	ⲡⲓⲙⲁϩϣⲉϩⲙⲉ	The hundred and fortieth
ⲡⲓⲙⲁϩϫⲟⲩⲧ	The twentieth	ⲡⲓⲙⲁϩϣⲟⲙⲧϣⲉ	The three hundredth
ⲡⲓⲙⲁϩⲙⲁⲡϥ̀ⲧⲟⲩ	The thirty fourth	ⲡⲓⲙⲁϩϣⲟ	The thousandth

The article ⲥⲟⲩ is used in the ordering of numbers in the days of months only:

ϧⲉⲛ ⲥⲟⲩⲁⲓ ⲙ̇ⲡⲓⲁⲃⲟⲧ	In the first day of the month.
ϧⲉⲛ ⲥⲟⲩⲙⲏⲧ ⲙ̇ⲡⲓⲁⲃⲟⲧ	In the tenth day.
ⲥⲟⲩ ⲙⲉⲧϣⲟⲙⲧ ⲙ̇ⲡⲓⲁⲃⲟⲧ ⲧⲱⲃⲓ	The thirteenth day of the month of Tobe.

Linking the Number with the Counted Word

The counted noun is linked with the number by the letter ⲛ̇. The letter ⲛ̇ is changed to ⲙ̇ before the letters ⲃ, ⲙ, ⲡ, ⲫ, and ⲯ.

ⲡⲓϣⲟⲙⲧ ⲛ̇ⲁⲗⲟⲩ	The three youths	ⲡⲓⲙⲉⲧ̇ⲥⲛⲁⲩ ⲙ̇ⲙⲁⲑⲏⲧⲏⲥ	The twelve disciples
ⲡⲓϥⲧⲟⲩ ⲛ̇ⲍⲱⲟⲛ	The four living creatures	ⲡⲓⲭⲟⲩⲧϥ̇ⲧⲟⲩ ⲙ̇ⲡⲣⲉⲥⲃⲩⲧⲉⲣⲟⲥ	The 24 priests
ⲡⲓϣⲁϣϥ ⲛ̇ⲭⲱⲙ	The seven books	ⲡⲓⲙ̇ⲯⲓⲧ ⲙ̇ⲙⲁⲣⲧⲩⲣⲟⲥ	The 49 martyrs
ϯⲙⲏϯ ⲙ̇ⲃⲁⲕⲓ	The ten cities	ⲡⲓϣⲉⲧⲉⲃⲓ ⲛ̇ⲉⲡⲓⲥⲕⲟⲡⲟⲥ	The 150 bishops

It is clear that the number is prefixed by the definite article, while the counted noun comes after the number and is prefixed by the letter ⲛ̇ or ⲙ̇.

As for number 2, it has a special position, for the counted noun comes first and then the number 2, for example:

ⲡⲓⲧⲉⲃⲧ ⲃ̄	The two fish	ⲡⲓⲙⲟⲛⲁⲭⲟⲥ ⲥ̇ⲛⲁⲩ	The two monks
ϯⲉⲛⲧⲟⲗⲏ ⲃ̄ϯ	The two commandments	ϯⲥⲱⲛⲓ ⲥ̇ⲛⲟⲩϯ	The two sisters

As for linking the counted noun with the ordinal numbers, it is as follows:

ⲡⲓⲉ̇ϩⲟⲟⲩ ⲙ̇ⲙⲁϩϣⲟⲙⲧ	=	ⲡⲓⲙⲁϩϣⲟⲙⲧ ⲛ̇ⲉ̇ϩⲟⲟⲩ	=	The third day
ϯⲫⲉ ⲙ̇ⲙⲁϩⲥⲛⲟⲩϯ	=	ϯⲙⲁϩⲥⲛⲟⲩϯ ⲙ̇ⲫⲉ	=	The second heaven

If numbers come as a subject in a sentence, the verb comes in the plural form, for example:

ⲁⲩⲓ̇ ⲛ̇ϫⲉ ⲡⲓⲙⲉⲧ̇ⲥⲛⲁⲩ ⲛ̇ⲁⲡⲟⲥⲧⲟⲗⲟⲥ.
ⲥⲉϩⲱⲥ ⲛ̇ϫⲉ ⲡⲓϣⲁϣϥ ⲛ̇ⲧⲁⲅⲙⲁ ⲛ̇ⲁⲅⲅⲉⲗⲓⲕⲟⲛ.

Lesson 34 ✠ Numbers [Part 1] ✠

Exercises

1. Write the pronunciation of the following numbers:

b̄	=	ō	=	c̄	=
ē	=	m̄	=	t̄	=
h̄	=	z̄	=	x̄	=
ῑz	=	p̄oh	=	ȳpa	=
k̄ⲩ	=	n̄ⲗ	=	ϣ̄ϥⲑ	=
b̄ⲧⲗⲉ	=				

2. Write the feminine form of the following numbers:

1. ⲟⲩⲁⲓ
2. ⲥⲛⲁⲩ
3. ⲥⲟⲟⲩ
4. ϣⲁϣϥ
5. ⲯⲓⲧ
6. ⲙⲏⲧ
7. ⲙⲉⲧ-ϣⲟⲙⲧ
8. ⲙⲉⲧ-ϯⲟⲩ
9. ϫⲟⲩⲧ-ⲥⲛⲁⲩ
10. ϫⲟⲩⲧ-ϣⲙⲏⲛ

3. Write the meaning of the following:

1. ⲡⲓϩⲟⲩⲓⲧ ⲛ̀ϫⲱⲙ
2. ϯϫⲁϩ ⲛ̀ⲧⲣⲁⲡⲉⲍⲁ
3. ⲛⲓϩⲟⲩⲁϯ ⲙ̀ⲙⲁⲑⲏⲧⲏⲥ
4. ϯⲙⲁϩⲥⲛⲟⲩϯ ⲛ̀ⲥⲕⲏⲛⲏ
5. ⲡⲓⲙⲁϩϣⲁϣϥ ⲛ̀ⲉϩⲟⲟⲩ
6. ⲛⲓϫⲁⲉⲩ ⲛ̀ⲁⲗⲱⲟⲩⲓ̀
7. ϯⲙⲁϩϫⲟⲩϯ ⲛ̀ⲣⲓ
8. ⲡⲓϥⲧⲟⲩ ⲛ̀ⲍⲱⲟⲛ ⲛ̀ⲁⲥⲱⲙⲁⲧⲟⲥ
9. ϯⲙⲁϩϣⲟⲙϯ ⲛ̀ⲥⲱⲛⲓ
10. ⲡⲓⲙⲟⲛⲁⲭⲟⲥ ⲥ̀ⲛⲁⲩ
11. ϯⲙⲏϯ ⲛ̀ⲉⲛⲧⲟⲗⲏ
12. ⲡⲓⲥⲛⲁⲩ ϣⲉ ⲛ̀ⲉⲡⲓⲥⲕⲟⲡⲟⲥ
13. ⲥⲉϩⲱⲥ ⲛ̀ϫⲉⲡⲓϫⲟⲩⲧ-ϥⲧⲟⲩ
14. ⲁⲩⲑⲉⲗⲏⲗ ⲛ̀ϫⲉ ⲡⲓϩⲙⲉⲯⲓⲧ

Lesson 35
ⲡⲓⲱϣ ⲙ̄ⲙⲁϩ ⳉⲉ

✠

Numbers [Part 2]

Fractions

"Half" in the Coptic language is called either ⲧ̇ⲫⲁϣⲓ, which is derived from ⲫⲱϣ (to divide), or ⲟⲩϫⲟⲥ, which is always prefixed by the indefinite article ⲟⲩ-, for example:

ⲟⲩⲙⲁϩⲓ ⲟⲩϫⲟⲥ	An arm and a half.
ϣⲟⲙⲧ ⲟⲩϫⲟⲥ ⲛ̄ⲣⲟⲙⲡⲓ	Three years and a half.

Note that ⲟⲩϫⲟⲥ comes between the number and the counted noun, but in the case of the number ⲥⲛⲁⲩ, ⲥⲛⲁⲩ always comes after the counted noun, so we say:

ⲙⲁϩⲓ ⲥⲛⲁⲩ ⲟⲩϫⲟⲥ ⲛ̇ϣⲓⲏ	Two arms and a half in length.

The fractions which are smaller than a half are formulated by adding ⲣⲉ-, meaning "part," to the beginning of the number:

ⲣⲉ ⲅ̄	=	ⲣⲉϣⲟⲙⲧ	=	1/3 (one third)	ⲣⲉ ⲍ̄	=	ⲣⲉϣⲁϣϥ	=	1/7 (one seventh)
ⲣⲉ ⲇ̄	=	ⲣⲉϥⲧⲟⲩ	=	1/4 (one fourth)	ⲣⲉ ⲏ̄	=	ⲣⲉϣⲙⲏⲛ	=	1/8 (one eighth)
ⲣⲉ ⲉ̄	=	ⲣⲉ̇ⲧⲓⲟⲩ	=	1/5 (one fifth)	ⲣⲉ ⲑ̄	=	ⲣⲉⲯⲓⲧ	=	1/9 (one ninth)
ⲣⲉ ⲋ̄	=	ⲣⲉⲥⲟⲟⲩ	=	1/6 (one sixth)	ⲣⲉ ⲓ̄	=	ⲣⲉⲙⲏⲧ	=	1/10 (one tenth)

Lesson 35 ✠ Numbers [Part 2] ✠

As for the fractions whose numerator is greater than one, we can formulate them as follows:

B̄ pe ḡ	=	c̀naⲩ pe ϣoⲙⲧ	=	2/3
ḡ pe ⲇ̄	=	ϣoⲙⲧ pe ϥ̀ⲧoⲩ	=	3/4
ē pe ⲏ̄	=	ϯoⲩ pe ϣⲙⲏⲛ	=	5/8

Notes:

✠ **naⲩ** means approximately, about, or time:

ⲫ̀naⲩ ⲙ̀ⲙⲉⲣⲓ	ⲙ̀ⲫnaⲩ ⲛ̀ⲣoⲩϩⲓ
Noontime or shortly before noon.	Approximately evening.
naⲩ ϣⲉ ⲛ̀ⲣoⲙⲡⲓ	naⲩoⲓ ⲇⲉ naⲩ ⲉ̄ ⲛ̀ϣo ⲛ̀ⲣⲱⲙⲓ.
About a hundred years.	They were about five thousand men.

✠ **ⲕⲉ** is added between the noun and the article, meaning "another" or "second," for example:

oⲩⲕⲉⲣⲱⲙⲓ	Another (a second) man	ⲛ̀ⲕⲉcoⲡ	Another (a second) time
ⲡⲓⲕⲉcoⲛ	The other brother	ϯⲕⲉϣoⲩⲣⲏ	The other censer

✠ The word **aⲛ**, which means several or bulk, is used in:

aⲛϣaϣϥ	Week (a bulk of seven)	aⲛϣo	Several thousands
aⲛⲑ̀Ba	Several myriads		

✠ The word **aⲛaⲛ**, the repetition of **aⲛ**, multiplies the addition, for example:

aⲛaⲛϣaϣϥ	Several weeks	aⲛaⲛϣo	Thousands of thousands

The first **aⲛ** might go back to its origin **ϩaⲛ**, for example:

ϩaⲛaⲛϣaϣϥ	Several weeks

✠ Repeating the number denotes division, for example:

ā ā	=	oⲩaⲓ oⲩaⲓ	One one	=	each one

✠ Foundations of the Coptic Language ✠

B̄ B̄	=	ⲥⲛⲁⲩ ⲥⲛⲁⲩ	Two two =	each two
N̄ N̄	=	ⲧⲉⲃⲓ ⲧⲉⲃⲓ	Fifty fifty =	each fifty
P̄ P̄	=	ϣⲉ ϣⲉ	Hundred hundred =	each hundred

✠ As for dividing time intervals, it is done by repeating the original number, then linking it to the noun by the letter ⲛ̀:

ⲥⲛⲁⲩ ⲥⲛⲁⲩ ⲛ̀ⲉϩⲟⲟⲩ	Every two days

✠ To multiply the number—forming multiples or folds—the article ⲕⲱⲃ is used:

Ḡ ⲛ̀ⲕⲱⲃ	Threefold (times)	Ī ⲛ̀ⲕⲱⲃ	Tenfold
Z̄ ⲛ̀ⲕⲱⲃ	Sevenfold	K̄ ⲛ̀ⲕⲱⲃ	Twentyfold

Days of the Week (ⲛⲓⲉϩⲟⲟⲩ ⲛ̀ⲧⲉ ⲡⲓⲁⲛϣⲁϣϥ)

ⲡⲓⲁ̄	=	ⲡⲓⲟⲩⲁⲓ	=	ϯⲕⲩⲣⲓⲁⲕⲏ	Sunday (the Day of the Lord)
ⲡⲓⲃ̄	=	ⲡⲓⲥⲛⲁⲩ	=		Monday
ⲡⲓḠ	=	ⲡⲓϣⲟⲙⲧ	=		Tuesday
ⲡⲓⲇ̄	=	ⲡⲓϥⲧⲟⲩ	=		Wednesday
ⲡⲓⲉ̄	=	ⲡⲓ̀ⲧⲓⲟⲩ	=		Thursday
ⲡⲓⲋ̄	=	ⲡⲓⲥⲟⲟⲩ	=	ϯⲡⲁⲣⲁⲥⲕⲉⲩⲏ	Friday
ⲡⲓⲍ̄	=	ⲡⲓϣⲁϣϥ	=	ⲡⲓⲥⲁⲃⲃⲁⲧⲟⲛ	Saturday

Arithmetical Operations in the Coptic Language

1. Addition:

The first method:

ⲛⲉⲙ + (plus, and, with)

ⲉⲩϣⲏϣ = (equal)

Lesson 35 ✟ Numbers [Part 2] ✟

Example:

$\overline{\theta}$	ⲛⲉⲙ	$\overline{\Delta}$	ⲛⲉⲙ	$\overline{\text{B}}$	ⲉⲧϣⲏϣ	$\overline{\text{ⲓⲉ}}$
9	+	4	+	2	=	15

The second method:

ⲧⲁⲗⲉ . . . . ϩⲓϫⲉⲛ . . . .   Lift up… over…

ⲧⲁⲗⲉ ⲟ̄ ϩⲓϫⲉⲛ ⲣ̄   Lift up 70 over 100

2. Subtraction:

| ⲉⲩⲃⲟⲣⲃⲉⲣ ⲛ̀ | (ⲓⲉ) | ⲉⲩⲃⲟⲣⲃⲉⲣ ⲙ̀ | Excluded from (-) |
| ⲉ̀ⲃⲟⲗ ⲛ̀ | (ⲓⲉ) | ⲉ̀ⲃⲟⲗ ⲙ̀ | Out of (-) |

Example:

ⲥ̄ⲛⲁⲩ	ⲉ̀ⲃⲟⲗ	ⲛ̀ϣⲁϣϥ	ⲉⲧϣⲏϣ	ⲧ̄ⲓⲟⲩ	[Two taken out of seven leaves five]
2	-	7	=	5	

3. Multiplication:

ⲥⲟⲡ ⲛ̀ Time   (ⲓⲉ)   ⲕⲱⲃ ⲛ̀ Fold

Examples:

| ϣⲁϣϥ | ⲛ̀ϣⲙⲏⲛ | ⲛ̀ⲥⲟⲡ | ⲉⲧϣⲏϣ | ⲧⲉⲃⲓ-ⲥⲟⲟⲩ | 7 × 8 = 56 |
| ⲯⲓⲧ | ⲛ̀ⲧⲓⲟⲩ | ⲛ̀ⲕⲱⲃ | ⲉⲧϣⲏϣ | ϩⲙⲉ-ⲧⲓⲟⲩ | 9 × 5 = 45 |

4. Division:

ⲉⲩⲫⲏϣ ϧⲁ ÷ Divided by

Examples:

| $\overline{\text{ⲛ}}$ | ⲉⲩⲫⲏϣ | ϧⲁ | $\overline{\text{ⲕⲉ}}$ | ⲉⲩϣⲏϣ | $\overline{\text{B}}$ | 50 ÷ 25 = 2 |
| $\overline{\text{ⲓⲃ}}$ | ⲉⲩⲫⲏϣ | ϧⲁ | $\overline{\text{ⲅ}}$ | ⲉⲩϣⲏϣ | $\overline{\Delta}$ | 12 ÷ 3 = 4 |

The Principal Directions [the Four Winds of the Earth (ⲡⲓϥⲧⲉⲑⲟⲩ ⲙ̀ⲡⲕⲁϩⲓ)]

ⲡⲉⲙϩⲓⲧ	The north	ⲫⲣⲏⲥ	The south
ⲡⲉⲓⲉⲃⲧ	The east	ⲡⲉⲙⲉⲛⲧ	The west
ⲙⲁⲛϣⲁⲓ	East (sunrise)	ⲙⲁⲛϩⲱⲧⲡ	West (sunset)

The Four Seasons of the Year (ⲡⲓϥⲧⲉⲥⲛⲟⲩ ⲛ̀ⲧⲣⲟⲙⲡⲓ)

ⲡⲓϩⲏⲛϣⲱⲙ	The spring	ⲡⲓϣⲱⲙ	The summer
ⲡⲓϩⲏⲛⲉⲫⲣⲱ	The fall	ϯⲫⲣⲱ	The winter

Coptic Months (ⲛⲓⲁⲃⲟⲧ ⲛ̀ⲣⲉⲙⲛ̀ⲭⲏⲙⲓ)

Bohairic Coptic	Sahidic Coptic	English	Bohairic Coptic	Sahidic Coptic	English
ⲑⲱⲟⲩⲧ	ⲑⲟⲟⲩⲧ	Thoout	ⲫⲁⲙⲉⲛⲱⲑ	ⲡⲁⲣⲉⲙϩⲁⲧ	Paremhotep
ⲡⲁⲟ̀ⲡⲓ	ⲡⲁⲁⲡⲉ	Paope	ⲫⲁⲣⲙⲟⲩⲑⲓ	ⲡⲁⲣⲙⲟⲩⲧⲉ	Parmoute
ⲁⲑⲱⲣ	ϩⲁⲑⲱⲣ	Hathor	ⲡⲁϣⲟⲛⲥ	ⲡⲁϣⲟⲛⲥ	Pashons
ⲭⲟⲓⲁⲕ	ⲕⲓⲁϩⲕ	Koiahk	ⲡⲁⲱ̀ⲛⲓ	ⲡⲁⲱⲛⲉ	Paone
ⲧⲱⲃⲓ	ⲧⲱⲃⲉ	Tobe	ⲉⲡⲏⲡ	ⲉⲡⲉⲡ	Epep
ⲙⲉϣⲓⲣ	ⲙⲉϣⲏⲣ	Meshir	ⲙⲉⲥⲱⲣⲏ	ⲙⲉⲥⲱⲣⲏ	Mesore

Then the Little Month (Nesi) ⲡⲓⲕⲟⲩϫⲓ ⲛ̀ⲁⲃⲟⲧ

ⲡⲓⲥⲟⲩⲁⲓ ⲙ̀ⲡⲓⲁⲃⲟⲧ	ⲡⲓⲁⲗⲕⲉ ⲙ̀ⲡⲓⲁⲃⲟⲧ
The beginning of the month	The end of the month

Hour

ϯⲁϫⲡ	The hour (and a number comes after it)	ⲫⲁϣⲓ	Half
ϯⲟⲩⲛⲟⲩ	The hour (60 minutes)	ⲣⲉ ϣⲟⲙⲧ	A third
ⲡⲓⲥⲟⲩⲥⲟⲩ	The minute	ⲣⲉ ϥⲧⲟⲩ	A quarter
ⲡⲓⲁⲧ	The second	ⲉ̀ⲃⲏⲗ (ⲓⲉ) ϣⲁⲧⲉⲛ	Except
ⲡⲓⲣⲓⲕⲓ ⲙ̀ⲃⲁⲗ	The blink of an eye	ⲛⲉⲙ	And

Review Exercises 7
On Lessons 31 to 35

1. Write the meaning of the following adjectives:

1. ⲛⲓϣϯ	11. ⲧⲁⲓⲏⲟⲩⲧ	21. ⲁⲑⲛⲟⲃⲓ
2. ⲃⲉⲣⲓ	12. ⲟⲩⲁⲃ	22. ⲁⲧⲑⲱⲗⲉⲃ
3. ⲕⲟⲩϫⲓ	13. ⲥⲙⲁⲣⲱⲟⲩⲧ	23. ⲁⲑⲛⲁⲩ
4. ϩⲏⲕⲓ	14. ϭⲟⲥⲓ	24. ⲁⲧⲥⲁⲣⲝ
5. ⲙⲏⲓ	15. ⲧⲟⲩⲃⲏⲟⲩⲧ	25. ⲁⲧⲥⲱⲧⲉⲙ
6. ⲥⲁⲃⲉ	16. ⲁⲑⲙⲟⲩ	26. ⲁⲧϣⲧⲁϩⲟϥ
7. ϩⲟⲩⲓⲧ	17. ⲁⲧⲥⲛⲟⲩ	27. ⲁⲧϣⲃⲉⲧϥⲱⲧϥ
8. ϣⲁϥⲉ	18. ⲗⲁⲥⲁϫⲓ	28. ⲥⲁⲛⲱⲓⲕ
9. ⲛⲁⲛⲉϥ	19. ⲗⲁϫⲱⲃⲓ	29. ϣⲟⲩⲙⲉⲛⲣⲓⲧϥ
10. ⲣⲁⲙⲁⲟ	20. ⲗⲁⲙⲁϩⲧ	30. ϣⲟⲩⲧⲁⲓⲟⲥ

2. Write the pronunciation of the following numbers:

ā	=	ī	=	p̄	=
s̄	=	λ̄	=	т̄	=
z̄	=	ō	=	ω̄	=
īⲉ	=		pⲙλ	=	
κλ̄	=		т̄ⲓⲏ	=	
ⲙⲑ̄	=		ⲫ̄ⲝⲍ	=	

ⲁ̄ϣϥⲥ̄ = _____

3. Put the following in the plural form:

ⲁ̄	ⲟⲩⲥⲁⲃⲉ ⲛ̀ⲣⲱⲙⲓ	ⲃ̄	ⲟⲩⲇⲁⲉ̀ ⲙ̀ⲙⲁⲑⲏⲧⲏⲥ
ⲅ̄	ⲡⲓϧⲉⲗⲗⲟ ⲛ̀ⲟⲩⲏⲃ	ⲇ̄	ⲡⲓϩⲟⲩⲓⲧ ⲛ̀ⲭⲱⲙ

4. Write the meaning of the following phrases:

1. Ⲫ̇ϯ ⲙ̀ⲙⲏⲓ.
2. ⲟⲩⲥⲙⲏ ⲛ̀ⲑⲉⲗⲏⲗ.
3. ⲛⲓⲧⲱⲟⲩ ⲉⲧϭⲟⲥⲓ.
4. ⲟⲩⲛⲓϣϯ ⲛ̀ϣⲣⲱⲓⲥ.
5. ⲡⲓⲭⲱⲣⲓ ⲉⲑⲟⲩⲁⲃ.
6. ϩⲁⲛⲙⲱⲟⲩ ⲉⲧⲟϣ.
7. ⲡⲓⲍ̄ ⲛ̀ⲥⲁϫⲓ.
8. ϯⲉⲗⲉⲩⲑⲉⲣⲓⲁ ⲛ̀ⲉⲱⲛⲓⲟⲛ.
9. ⲡⲓⲁⲧⲩϣϭⲛⲧ ⲉ̀ⲣⲟϥ.
10. ϯⲙⲁϩⲥⲛⲟⲩϯ ⲛ̀ⲥⲕⲏⲛⲏ.
11. ⲧⲉⲕⲙⲁⲩ ⲛ̀ϣⲉⲗⲉⲧ.
12. ⲟⲩϩⲁⲡ ⲉϥⲥϧⲏⲟⲩⲧ.

5. Translate to the English language:

ⲁ̄ ⲟⲩⲕⲁϩⲓ ⲛ̀ⲁⲑⲟⲩⲱⲛϩ: ⲁ̀ ⲫ̇ⲣⲏ ϣⲁⲓ ϩⲓϫⲱϥ:
   ⲟⲩⲙⲱⲓⲧ ⲛ̀ⲁⲧⲥⲓⲛⲓ: ⲁⲩⲙⲟϣⲓ ϩⲓⲱⲧϥ.

ⲃ̄ ϧⲉⲛ ⲟⲩⲥⲛⲟⲩ ⲉϥϣⲏⲡ: ⲉⲕⲉ̀ⲥⲱⲧⲉⲙ ⲉ̀ⲣⲟⲓ.

ⲅ̄ ⲍ̄ ⲛ̀ⲥⲟⲡ ⲙ̀ⲙⲏⲛⲓ: ϯⲛⲁⲥⲙⲟⲩ ⲉ̀ⲡⲉⲕⲣⲁⲛ.

ⲇ̄ ⲕⲉⲗⲓ ⲛⲓⲃⲉⲛ ⲥⲉⲕⲱⲗϫ: ⲙ̀ⲡⲉⲕⲙ̀ⲑⲟ ⲉ̀ⲃⲟⲗ.

ⲉ̄ ⲡⲓⲇ̄ ⲛ̀ⲍⲱⲟⲛ ⲛ̀ⲁⲥⲱⲙⲁⲧⲟⲥ ⲛ̀ⲗⲓⲧⲟⲩⲣⲅⲟⲥ ⲛ̀ϣⲁϩ ⲛ̀ⲭⲣⲱⲙ.

ⲋ̄ ⲃⲱϣ ⲙ̀ⲡⲓⲣⲱⲙⲓ ⲙ̀ⲡⲁⲗⲉⲟⲥ: ⲟⲩⲟϩ ⲭⲱⲗϩ ⲙ̀ⲡⲓⲃⲉⲣⲓ ⲉⲩⲕⲗⲉⲟⲥ.

ⲍ̄ ⲭⲉⲣⲉ ⲛⲉ Ⲙⲁⲣⲓⲁ: ϯϭⲣⲟⲙⲡⲓ ⲉⲑⲛⲉⲥⲱⲥ: ⲉⲑⲙⲉϩ ⲛ̀ⲥⲟⲫⲓⲁ: ⲑ̀ⲙⲁⲩ ⲛ̀Ⲓⲏ̄ⲥ Ⲡⲭ̄ⲥ.

ⲏ̄ ⲧⲉϭⲟⲥⲓ ⲉ̀ⲙⲁϣⲱ: ⲉ̀ϩⲟⲧⲉ ⲛⲓⲡⲁⲧⲣⲓⲁⲣⲭⲏⲥ:
   ⲟⲩⲟϩ ⲧⲉⲧⲁⲓⲏⲟⲩⲧ: ⲉ̀ϩⲟⲧⲉ ⲛⲓⲡⲣⲟⲫⲏⲧⲏⲥ.

ⲑ̄ ⲉⲑⲃⲉ ⲫⲁⲓ ⲟⲩⲟⲛ ⲛⲓⲃⲉⲛ: ⲥⲉⲃⲓⲥⲓ ⲙ̀ⲙⲟ:
   ⲧⲁϭⲟⲓⲥ ϯⲑⲉⲟⲧⲟⲕⲟⲥ: ⲉⲑⲟⲩⲁⲃ ⲛ̀ⲥⲏⲟⲩ ⲛⲓⲃⲉⲛ.

ⲓ̄ ⲁⲩⲉⲛ ϯⲗⲩⲭⲛⲓⲁ ⲛ̀ⲛⲟⲩⲃ: ϩⲓϫⲉⲛ ϯⲉⲕⲕⲗⲏⲥⲓⲁ:
   ⲡⲉⲥⲕⲉϩ̄ ⲛ̀ϩⲏⲃⲥ: ϩⲓϫⲉⲛ ⲡⲓⲍ̄ ⲛ̀ⲧⲁⲅⲙⲁ.

ⲓⲁ̄ ⲡⲓⲧⲓⲏ ⲉⲧⲁⲩⲑⲱⲟⲩϯ ϧⲉⲛ Ⲛⲓⲕⲉⲁ ⲉⲑⲃⲉ ⲡⲓⲛⲁϩϯ.

ⲓⲃ̄ ⲡⲓⲣⲛ ⲛ̀ⲧⲉ Ⲕⲱⲥⲧⲁⲛⲧⲓⲛⲟⲩ ⲡⲟⲗⲓⲥ.

ⲓⲅ̄ ⲡⲓⲥⲛⲁⲩ ϣⲉ ⲛ̀ⲧⲉ Ⲉ̀ⲫⲉⲥⲟⲥ.

Exam 7

On Lessons 31 to 35

1. Complete the following table:

Phrase	Meaning of phrase	Write the adjective and mention its kind: original, derived, or compound.
ⲡⲉⲕⲓⲱⲧ ⲛ̀ⲁⲅⲁⲑⲟⲥ.		
ⲡⲓⲡⲛⲉⲩⲙⲁ ⲉⲑⲟⲩⲁⲃ.		
ⲟⲩϩⲱⲥ ⲙ̀ⲃⲉⲣⲓ.		
Ⲫ̇ⲛⲟⲩϯ ⲛ̀ⲁⲑⲛⲁⲩ.		
ⲛⲉⲛⲓⲟϯ ⲛ̀ⲁⲥⲕⲏⲧⲏⲥ.		
ⲡⲓϣϩⲛ ⲛ̀ⲗⲁⲭⲁⲗ.		
ⲟⲩⲟⲩⲥⲓⲁ ⲉⲥϣⲏⲡ.		
ⲟⲩⲥⲟⲛ ⲛ̀ϣⲟⲩⲙⲉⲛⲣⲓⲧϥ.		

2. Write the abbreviation of the following numbers:

ⲥ̇ⲛⲁⲩ	=	ⲧⲉⲃⲓ	=	ⲥ̇ⲛⲁⲩ ϣⲉ	=
ⲥⲟⲟⲩ	=	ⲥⲉ	=	ⲃ̇ⲧⲟⲩ ϣⲉ	=
ϣ̇ⲙⲏⲛ	=	ⲡⲓⲥⲧⲁⲩ	=	ϣⲁϣϥ ϣⲉ	=
ⲭⲟⲩⲧ-ⲧⲓⲟⲩ	=			ϣⲉ-ⲙⲉⲧ-ϥ̇ⲧⲟⲩ	=
ⲙⲁⲡ-ϣⲟⲙⲧ	=			ϣⲟⲙⲧ ϣⲉ-ϩ̇ⲙⲉ-ⲥⲟⲟⲩ	=
ϫⲁⲙⲛⲉ-ⲯⲓⲧ	=			ⲧ̇ⲓⲟⲩ ϣⲉ-ϣ̇ⲃⲉ-ⲟⲩⲁⲓ	=

3. Write the meaning of the following:

ⲁ̅	ⲡⲓⲉ̄ ⲛ̄ⲱⲓⲕ.	ⲋ̅	ⲡⲓⲙⲁϩⲥⲛⲁⲩ ⲛ̄Ⲁⲇⲁⲙ.
ⲃ̅	ⲡⲓ ⲍ̄ ⲛ̄ⲥⲁϫⲓ.	ⲍ̅	ϯⲙⲁϩⲥⲛⲟⲩϯ ⲛ̄ϥⲉ.
ⲅ̅	ⲡⲓⲕⲇ̅ ⲙ̄ⲡⲣⲉⲥⲃⲩⲧⲉⲣⲟⲥ.	ⲏ̅	ⲡⲓϣⲟⲣⲡ ⲙ̄ⲙⲁⲣⲧⲩⲣⲟⲥ.
ⲇ̅	ⲡⲓⲙⲑ̄ ⲙ̄ⲙⲁⲣⲧⲩⲣⲟⲥ.	ⲑ̅	ⲡⲓϫⲁⲉ ⲛ̄ⲉϩⲟⲟⲩ.
ⲉ̅	ⲡⲓⲣⲙⲇ̄ ⲛ̄ϣⲟ.	ⲓ̅	ϯⲥⲕⲏⲛⲏ ⲛ̄ϩⲟⲩϯ.

4. Write the following phrases in the singular form:

ⲁ̅	ϩⲁⲛⲥⲁⲃⲉⲩ ⲛ̄ⲥⲱⲛⲓ	→
ⲃ̅	ⲛⲓϣⲉⲙⲙⲱⲟⲩ ⲛ̄ⲣⲱⲙⲓ	→
ⲅ̅	ϩⲁⲛϣⲁϥⲉⲩ ⲛ̄ⲧⲟⲡⲟⲥ	→
ⲇ̅	ⲛⲓϩⲉⲗⲗⲱⲟⲩ ⲛ̄ⲥϩⲓⲙⲓ	→
ⲉ̅	ϩⲁⲛⲑⲉϣⲉⲩ ⲛ̄ϩⲏⲕⲓ	→

5. Translate to the English language:

ⲁ̅ ⲛⲓⲥⲉⲣⲁⲫⲓⲙ ⲛⲁ ⲡⲓⲉ̄ ⲛ̄ⲧⲉⲛϩ.

ⲃ̅ ⲙⲟϣⲓ ϩⲱⲥ ϩⲁⲛϣⲏⲣⲓ ⲛ̄ⲧⲉ ⲡⲓⲟⲩⲱⲓⲛⲓ.

ⲅ̅ ⲁⲛⲛⲁⲩ ⲉⲡⲉϥⲱⲟⲩ ⲙ̄ⲫⲣⲏϯ ⲙ̄ⲡⲱⲟⲩ ⲛ̄ⲟⲩϣⲏⲣⲓ ⲙ̄ⲙⲁⲩⲁⲧϥ.

ⲇ̅ ⲭⲉⲣⲉ ⲑⲏⲉⲑⲙⲉϩ ⲛ̄ϩⲙⲟⲧ: ϯⲡⲁⲣⲑⲉⲛⲟⲥ ⲛⲁⲧⲑⲱⲗⲉⲃ: ⲡⲓⲕⲩⲙⲓⲗⲗⲓⲟⲛ ⲉⲧⲥⲱⲧⲡ: ⲛ̄ⲧⲉ ϯⲟⲓⲕⲟⲩⲙⲉⲛⲏ ⲧⲏⲣⲥ.

ⲉ̅ ⲗⲁⲟⲥ ⲛⲓⲃⲉⲛ ⲥⲉϩⲱⲥ: ⲛⲉⲙ ⲛⲓⲁⲥⲡⲓ ⲛ̄ⲗⲁⲥ: ⲉ̇ϯⲑⲉⲟⲧⲟⲕⲟⲥ: ⲑⲙⲁⲩ ⲙ̄Ⲙⲁⲥⲓⲁⲥ.

ⲋ̅ ⲧⲉⲃⲟⲥⲓ ⲁⲗⲏⲑⲱⲥ ⲉϩⲟⲧⲉ ⲡⲓϣⲃⲱⲧ ⲛ̄ⲧⲉ Ⲁⲁⲣⲱⲛ.

ⲍ̅ ⲭⲉⲣⲉ ϯⲫⲉ ⲙ̄ⲃⲉⲣⲓ: ⲑⲏⲉⲧⲁ Ⲫⲓⲱⲧ ⲑⲁⲙⲓⲟⲥ.

ⲏ̅ ϩⲁⲛⲁⲛϣⲟ ⲛ̄ϣⲟ: ⲛⲉⲙ ϩⲁⲛⲑⲃⲁ ⲛ̄ⲑⲃⲁ: ⲛ̄ⲁⲣⲭⲏⲁⲅⲅⲉⲗⲟⲥ: ⲛⲉⲙ ⲁⲅⲅⲉⲗⲟⲥ ⲉⲧⲟⲩⲁⲃ: ⲉⲩⲟϩⲓ ⲉⲣⲁⲧⲟⲩ: ⲙ̄ⲡⲉⲙⲑⲟ ⲙ̄ⲡⲓⲑⲣⲟⲛⲟⲥ: ⲛ̄ⲧⲉ ⲡⲓⲡⲁⲛⲧⲟⲕⲣⲁⲧⲱⲣ.

ⲑ̅ Ⲙⲓⲭⲁⲏⲗ ⲡⲉ ⲡⲓϩⲟⲩⲓⲧ: Ⲅⲁⲃⲣⲓⲏⲗ ⲡⲉ ⲡⲓⲙⲁϩⲃ̄: Ⲣⲁⲫⲁⲏⲗ ⲡⲉ ⲡⲓⲙⲁϩ ⲅ̄: ⲕⲁⲧⲁ ⲡⲧⲩⲡⲟⲥ ⲛ̄ⲥⲧⲣⲁⲧⲓⲁⲥ.

ⲓ̅ ⲧⲱⲃϩ ⲙ̄Ⲡ̄ⲟ̄ⲥ̄ ⲉ̇ϩⲣⲏⲓ ⲉ̇ϫⲱⲛ: ⲱ̄ ⲛⲁϭⲟⲓⲥ ⲛ̄ⲓⲟϯ ⲛ̄ⲁⲡⲟⲥⲧⲟⲗⲟⲥ: ⲛⲉⲙ ⲡⲓⲟ̄ⲃ̄ ⲙ̄ⲙⲁⲑⲏⲧⲏⲥ: ⲛ̄ⲧⲉϥⲭⲁ ⲛⲉⲛⲛⲟⲃⲓ ⲛⲁⲛ ⲉ̇ⲃⲟⲗ.

6. Translate to the Coptic language:

1. The great mercy, the true peace.
2. Christ arose on the third day.
3. The holy city, the golden censer.
4. The twelve apostles preached to the peoples of the world.

Appendix A

Answers of the Lessons' Exercises

Answers of the Exercises of the First Lesson

1. The meaning of the words:

1. A prayer; 2. Hands; 3. An honor; 4. Heavens; 5. A city; 6. Servants; 7. A servant; 8. Cells (rooms); 9. A sky; 10. Sons; 11. A censer; 12. Sisters; 13. A fast; 14. Praises; 15. A brother; 16. Daughter; 17. A head; 18. Names; 19. A harp; 20. Men (human beings; people); 21. A woman; 22. Trees; 23. A question; 24. Brothers; 25. A star; 26. Fathers; 27. A book; 28. Pens; 29. A sun; 30. Virgins; 31. A dove; 32. Women; 33. An elder; 34. Mountains; 35. A cell (a room); 36. Deserts; 37. A maidservant; 38. Mothers; 39. A blessing.

2. The plural form of the nouns:

1. ϩⲁⲛⲓⲟϯ. 2. ϩⲁⲛⲓⲁⲣⲱⲟⲩ. 3. ϩⲁⲛⲉⲃⲓⲁⲓⲕ. 4. ϩⲁⲛⲁⲗⲱⲟⲩⲓ. 5. ϩⲁⲛⲥⲛⲏⲟⲩ. 6. ϩⲁⲛⲁⲙⲁⲓⲟⲩ. 7. ϩⲁⲛϣⲁϥⲉⲩ. 8. ϩⲁⲛϩⲓⲟⲙⲓ. 9. ϩⲁⲛⲫⲏⲟⲩⲓ. 10. ϩⲁⲛⲁⲫⲏⲟⲩⲓ. 11. ϩⲁⲛϫⲉⲗⲗⲟⲓ. 12. ϩⲁⲛⲛⲏⲥⲧⲓⲁ. 13. ϩⲁⲛⲓⲟϩ. 14. ϩⲁⲛⲥⲓⲟⲩ.

Answers of the Exercises of the Second Lesson

1. Translation to the English language:

1. The God and the man; 2. The sin and the death; 3. The faith and the light; 4. The sun and the moon; 5. The brother and the sister; 6. The son and the daughter; 7. The maidservant and the mother; 8. The heaven and the earth; 9. The death and the life; 10. A man and sons; 11. A king and servants.

Appendix A ✠ Answers of the Lessons' Exercises ✠

2. Translation to the Coptic language:

ⲁ̅. ⲡⲓⲱⲓⲕ ⲛⲉⲙ ⲡⲓⲙⲱⲟⲩ. ⲃ̅. ϩⲁⲛϣⲗⲏⲗ ⲛⲉⲙ ϩⲁⲛⲛⲏⲥⲧⲓⲁ. ⲅ̅. ⲡ̅ϭⲟⲓⲥ (ⲡⲓϭⲟⲓⲥ) ⲛⲉⲙ ⲫ̅ⲃⲱⲕ (ⲡⲓⲃⲱⲕ). ⲇ̅. ⲡⲟⲩⲧⲁϩ (ⲡⲓⲟⲩⲧⲁϩ) ⲛⲉⲙ ⲡ̅ⲱⲛϧ (ⲡⲓⲱⲛϧ). ⲉ̅. ϯⲁⲫⲉ (ϯⲁⲫⲉ) ⲛⲉⲙ ϯⲃⲁⲗⲟϫ. ⲋ̅. ϩⲁⲛϩⲉⲗⲗⲟⲓ ⲛⲉⲙ ϩⲁⲛⲡⲁⲣⲑⲉⲛⲟⲥ. ⲍ̅. ϯϣⲟⲩⲣⲏ ⲛⲉⲙ ϯⲫⲟⲣϣⲓ. ⲏ̅. ⲡⲟⲩϫⲁⲓ ⲛⲉⲙ ⲡⲟⲩⲛⲟϥ. ⲑ̅. ⲟⲩⲥⲟⲛ ⲛⲉⲙ ⲟⲩⲥⲱⲛⲓ. ⲓ̅. ⲑⲛⲉϫⲓ (ϯⲛⲉϫⲓ) ⲛⲉⲙ ⲫ̅ⲗⲁⲥ (ⲡⲓⲗⲁⲥ). ⲓⲁ̅. ⲑⲣⲓ (ϯⲣⲓ) ⲛⲉⲙ ⲧ̅ⲫⲉ (ϯⲫⲉ).

Answers of the Exercises of the Third Lesson

1. Translation to the English language:

1. The fathers and the brothers; 2. The kings and the servants; 3. Elders and children; 4. The seas and the rivers; 5. A bird and birds; 6. The heavens and the deserts; 7. Men and women; 8. Hands and feet; 9. The earth and the works; 10. The soul and the faith; 11. The servants of the Lord; 12. The city of God; 13. The sons of Zion; 14. The kings of the earth; 15. The prayers of the fathers; 16. The birds of the sky; 17. The works of the human being; 18. The bread of life; 19. The fathers of the deserts; 20. The years of the life.

2. Putting the suitable definite article for the plural noun [ⲛⲓ or ⲛⲉⲛ]:

1. ⲛⲓ-. 2. ⲛⲉⲛ-. 3. ⲛⲉⲛ-. 4. ⲛⲓ-. 5. ⲛⲉⲛ-. 6. ⲛⲉⲛ-.

3. Translation to the Coptic language:

ⲁ̅. ⲛⲓϩⲁⲗⲁϯ ⲛⲉⲙ ⲛⲓⲫⲏⲟⲩⲓ. ⲃ̅. ⲛⲓⲥⲛⲏⲟⲩ ⲛⲉⲙ ⲛⲓⲥⲱⲛⲓ. ⲅ̅. ϩⲁⲛⲓⲁⲣⲱⲟⲩ ⲛⲉⲙ ϩⲁⲛⲁⲙⲁⲓⲟⲩ. ⲇ̅. ϩⲁⲛⲓⲟϯ ⲛⲉⲙ ϩⲁⲛⲙⲁⲩ. ⲉ̅. ϯⲁⲫⲉ ⲛⲉⲙ ⲛⲓⲃⲁⲗⲁⲩϫ. ⲋ̅. ⲛⲓⲭⲱⲙ ⲛⲉⲙ ⲛⲓⲉ̅ⲃⲏⲟⲩⲓ. ⲍ̅. ϩⲁⲛⲙⲉⲛⲣⲁϯ ⲛⲉⲙ ϩⲁⲛⲥⲛⲏⲟⲩ. ⲏ̅. ⲛⲓϣⲏⲣⲓ ⲛ̅ⲧⲉ ⲡⲓⲟⲩⲱⲓⲛⲓ (ⲛⲉⲛϣⲏⲣⲓ ⲙ̅ⲡⲓⲟⲩⲱⲓⲛⲓ). ⲑ̅. ⲫ̅ⲛⲁϩϯ ⲛ̅ⲛⲓⲣⲱⲙⲓ (ⲡⲓⲛⲁϩϯ ⲛ̅ⲧⲉ ⲛⲓⲣⲱⲙⲓ). ⲓ̅. ⲛⲓⲙⲟⲛⲁⲭⲟⲥ ⲛ̅ⲧⲉ ⲡⲓϣⲁϥⲉ. ⲓⲁ̅. ⲛⲉⲛⲉ̅ⲃⲏⲟⲩⲓ ⲙ̅ⲡ̅ϭⲟⲓⲥ (ⲛⲓⲉ̅ⲃⲏⲟⲩⲓ ⲛ̅ⲧⲉ ⲡ̅ϭⲟⲓⲥ). ⲓⲃ̅. ⲡⲟⲩⲧⲁϩ ⲛ̅ⲧⲉ ⲡⲓⲱⲛϧ (ⲡⲟⲩⲧⲁϩ ⲙ̅ⲡⲱⲛϧ). ⲓⲅ̅. ⲧ̅ϫⲓϫ ⲙ̅ⲫ̅ⲛⲟⲩϯ (ϯϫⲓϫ ⲛ̅ⲧⲉ ⲫ̅ⲛⲟⲩϯ). ⲓⲇ̅. ⲡⲟⲩⲛⲟϥ ⲛ̅ⲛⲓⲙⲉⲛⲣⲁϯ (ⲡⲓⲟⲩⲛⲟϥ ⲛ̅ⲧⲉ ⲛⲓⲙⲉⲛⲣⲁϯ).

Answers of the Exercises of the Fourth Lesson

1. Translation to the English language:

1. This is the Son of Man; 2. This is the mother of Jesus; 3. These are the fathers of the

Church; 4. This day is the feast of the Apostles; 5. This fast is the fast of the Virgin; 6. These books are the books of this monk; 7. This is Saint Mark the Apostle; 8. This is the icon of Saint Mary the Virgin; 9. These are the monks Maximus and Dometius; 10. This man is the father of this desert; 11. This is a brother; 12. This is a cell; 13. These are birds; 14. These are brothers.

2. Translation to the Coptic language:

ⲁ̅. ⲫⲁⲓ ⲡⲉ ⲡⲓⲗⲟⲅⲟⲥ ⲛ̀ⲧⲉ Ⲫⲓⲱⲧ. ⲃ̅. ⲑⲁⲓ ⲧⲉ ϯϣⲉⲗⲉⲧ ⲛ̀ⲧⲉ Ⲡⲓⲭⲣⲓⲥⲧⲟⲥ. ⲅ̅. ⲛⲁⲓ ⲛⲉ ⲛⲓϩⲉⲗⲗⲟⲓ ⲛ̀ⲧⲉ ⲡⲓϣⲁϥⲉ (ⲛⲉⲛϩⲉⲗⲗⲟⲓ ⲙ̀ⲡϣⲁϥⲉ). ⲇ̅. ⲡⲁⲓⲣⲱⲙⲓ ⲡⲉ ⲫⲓⲱⲧ ⲛ̀ⲧⲉ ⲛⲓⲙⲟⲛⲁⲭⲟⲥ. ⲉ̅. ⲧⲁⲓⲉⲕⲕⲗⲏⲥⲓⲁ ⲧⲉ ϯⲉⲕⲕⲗⲏⲥⲓⲁ ⲛ̀ⲧⲉ ⲡⲓⲁⲅⲅⲉⲗⲟⲥ. ⲋ̅. ⲛⲁⲓⲥⲁϫⲓ ⲛⲉ ⲛⲓⲥⲁϫⲓ ⲛ̀ⲧⲉ ⲡⲓⲱⲛϧ (ⲛⲉⲛⲥⲁϫⲓ ⲙ̀ⲡⲱⲛϧ). ⲍ̅. ⲫⲁⲓ ⲡⲉ ⲡⲓⲕⲁϣ ⲛ̀ⲧⲉ ⲡⲓⲥⲟⲛ Ⲗⲟⲩⲕⲁⲥ. ⲏ̅. ⲫⲁⲓ ⲟⲩⲏⲓ ⲡⲉ. ⲑ̅. ⲛⲁⲓ ϩⲁⲛϣⲏⲣⲓ ⲛⲉ. ⲓ̅. ⲑⲁⲓ ⲟⲩϥⲉ ⲧⲉ. ⲓⲁ̅. ⲛⲁⲓ ϩⲁⲛϣ̀ϣⲏⲛ ⲛⲉ.

Answers of the Exercises of the Fifth Lesson

1. The meaning of the following:

1. This day; 2. This virgin; 3. These elders; 4. This fast; 5. These birds; 6. This book; 7. These children; 8. This life; 9. This power.

2. Translation to the English language:

1. I am the bread of life; 2. You are the King of kings [lit. the kings]; 3. You are the daughter of Zion; 4. He is the head of the Church; 5. She is the bride of Christ; 6. We are the sons of the martyrs; 7. You are the servants of the Lord; 8. They are the beloved of Christ.

3. Translation to the Coptic language:

ⲁ̅. ⲛ̀ⲑⲟⲥ ⲧⲉ ⲑⲙⲁⲩ ⲙ̀ⲡⲓⲟⲩⲱⲓⲛⲓ. ⲃ̅. ⲛ̀ⲑⲟⲕ ⲡⲉ ⲡⲓⲥⲱⲧⲏⲣ ⲛ̀ⲧⲉ ⲡⲓⲕⲟⲥⲙⲟⲥ. ⲅ̅. ⲛ̀ⲑⲟϥ ⲡⲉ ⲡⲓⲛⲟⲩϯ ⲛ̀ⲧⲉ ⲛⲓⲣⲱⲙⲓ. ⲇ̅. ⲛ̀ⲑⲟ ⲧⲉ ϯⲡⲁⲣⲑⲉⲛⲟⲥ ⲛⲉⲙ ϯⲙⲁⲩ. ⲉ̅. ⲛ̀ⲑⲱⲧⲉⲛ ⲛⲉ ⲛⲓⲥⲛⲏⲟⲩ ⲛ̀ⲧⲉ Ⲡⲓϭⲟⲓⲥ (ⲛⲉⲛⲥⲛⲏⲟⲩ ⲙ̀Ⲡ̅ⲥ̅). ⲋ̅. ⲛ̀ⲑⲱⲟⲩ ⲛⲉ ⲛⲓϩⲁⲗⲁϯ ⲛ̀ⲧⲉ ϯⲫⲉ (ⲛⲉⲛϩⲁⲗⲁϯ ⲛ̀ⲧⲫⲉ). ⲍ̅. ⲁⲛⲟⲕ ⲟⲩϣⲏⲣⲓ ⲡⲉ. ⲏ̅. ⲁⲛⲟⲛ ϩⲁⲛⲥⲛⲏⲟⲩ ⲛⲉ.

Answers of the Review Exercises 1: On Lessons 1 to 5

1. Putting the appropriate definite article for the words:

Appendix A ✠ Answers of the Lessons' Exercises ✠

ⲛⲓⲓⲟⲧ	ⲧ̀ϫⲓϫ	ⲡⲓⲥⲟⲛ	ⲧ̀ⲥϩⲓⲙⲓ	ⲛⲓⲫⲏⲟⲩⲓ̀
ⲧ̀ⲃⲁⲗⲟϫ	ⲡⲓⲃⲱⲕ	ⲧ̀ⲫⲉ	ⲛⲓⲥⲛⲏⲟⲩ	ⲡ̀ⲟⲩⲣⲟ
ⲛⲓⲉ̀ⲃⲓⲁⲓⲕ	ⲑ̀ⲃⲁⲕⲓ	ⲛⲓϩ̀ⲃⲏⲟⲩⲓ̀	ⲛⲓϩⲉⲗⲗⲟⲓ	ⲡ̀ϣⲁϥⲉ
ⲡⲓϩⲁⲗⲏⲧ	ⲛⲓⲙⲉⲛⲣⲁϯ	ⲫ̀ⲓⲁⲣⲟ	ⲛⲓϩⲓⲟⲙⲓ	ⲛⲓⲟⲩⲣⲱⲟⲩ
ⲡⲓϩⲱⲃ	ϯⲟⲩⲣⲱ	ⲛⲓⲁⲙⲁⲓⲟⲩ	ⲑ̀ⲃⲱⲕⲓ	ⲛⲓⲁⲗⲱⲟⲩⲓ̀

2. The meaning of the words:

1. This monk; 2. These birds; 3. This faith; 4. This virgin; 5. This mercy; 6. This cell (room); 7. These sins; 8. This soul; 9. These men; 10. This peace; 11. This bread; 12. This daughter.

3. How do you ask about:

ⲡⲓϣⲏⲣⲓ	ⲛⲓⲙ ⲡⲉ ⲫⲁⲓ?	ⲫⲁⲓ ⲡⲉ ⲡⲓϣⲏⲣⲓ.
ϩⲁⲛϣ̀ϣⲏⲛ	ⲁϣ ⲛⲉ ⲛⲁⲓ?	ⲛⲁⲓ ϩⲁⲛϣ̀ϣⲏⲛ ⲛⲉ.
ϯϣⲟⲩⲣⲏ	ⲁϣ ⲧⲉ ⲑⲁⲓ?	ⲑⲁⲓ ⲧⲉ ϯϣⲟⲩⲣⲏ.
ⲛⲓⲙⲟⲛⲁⲭⲟⲥ	ⲛⲓⲙ ⲛⲉ ⲛⲁⲓ?	ⲛⲁⲓ ⲛⲉ ⲛⲓⲙⲟⲛⲁⲭⲟⲥ.
ⲟⲩⲥⲱⲛⲓ	ⲛⲓⲙ ⲧⲉ ⲑⲁⲓ?	ⲑⲁⲓ ⲟⲩⲥⲱⲛⲓ ⲧⲉ.
ⲡⲓⲣⲏ	ⲁϣ ⲡⲉ ⲫⲁⲓ?	ⲫⲁⲓ ⲡⲉ ⲡⲓⲣⲏ.
ϩⲁⲛⲓⲟϯ	ⲛⲓⲙ ⲛⲉ ⲛⲁⲓ?	ⲛⲁⲓ ϩⲁⲛⲓⲟϯ ⲛⲉ.

4. Translation to the English language:

1. The light and the darkness; 2. The sin and the salvation; 3. Prayers and fasts; 4. The heavens and the earth; 5. Seas and rivers; 6. A son and a daughter; 7. The praises of the monks; 8. The joy of the brothers; 9. The servants of the Lord; 10. The hand of God; 11. The house of the angels; 12. The birds of the sky; 13. This is the light; 14. This is the censer; 15. These are the fruits; 16. This is a river; 17. This is a church; 18. These are books; 19. I am a son; 20. You are fathers; 21. She is a sister; 22. We are beloved; 23. He is the beloved; 24. You are the virgin.

5. Translation to the Coptic language:

ⲁ̄. ⲫⲁⲓ ⲡⲉ ⲡⲓⲟⲩⲏⲃ ⲛ̀ⲧⲉ ⲡⲓϣⲁϥⲉ. ⲃ̄. ⲛⲁⲓ ϩⲁⲛⲓⲟϯ ⲛⲉⲙ ϩⲁⲛⲥⲛⲏⲟⲩ ⲛⲉ. ⲅ̄. ⲑⲁⲓ ⲧⲉ ⲑ̀ⲙⲁⲩ ⲙ̀ⲡⲓⲟⲩⲱⲓⲛⲓ. ⲇ̄. ⲛⲑⲱⲟⲩ ⲛⲉ ⲛⲓⲁⲅⲅⲉⲗⲟⲥ ⲛ̀ⲧⲉ ⲧ̀ⲫⲉ. ⲉ̄. ⲁⲛⲟⲛ ⲛⲉ ⲛⲉⲛϣⲏⲣⲓ ⲛ̀ϯⲉⲕⲕⲗⲏⲥⲓⲁ. ⲉ̅. ⲛ̀ⲑⲟⲕ ⲡⲉ ⲡ̀ϣⲏⲣⲓ ⲙ̀Ⲫⲛⲟⲩϯ. Ⲍ̅. ⲛ̀ⲑⲟϥ ⲡⲉ ⲡⲓⲥⲱⲧⲏⲣ ⲛ̀ⲧⲉ ⲡⲓⲕⲟⲥⲙⲟⲥ. Ⲏ̅. ⲛ̀ⲑⲟⲥ ⲧⲉ ϯⲃⲁⲕⲓ ⲛ̀ⲧⲉ Ⲫⲛⲟⲩϯ. ⲑ̅. ⲛⲑⲟ ⲧⲉ Ⲧ̀ϣⲉⲣⲓ ⲛ̀Ⲥⲓⲱⲛ. Ⲓ̅. ⲛ̀ⲑⲱⲧⲉⲛ ⲛⲉ ⲛⲓⲥⲛⲏⲟⲩ ⲛ̀ⲧⲉ Ⲡⲓϭⲟⲓⲥ.

Answers of the Exam 1: On Lessons 1 to 5

1. The meaning of the words:

1. A book; 2. Cells (rooms); 3. A man (human being); 4. Names; 5. A servant; 6. Years; 7. A tree; 8. Fasts; 9. A city; 10. Sons; 11. A moon; 12. Sins.

2. For the following singular, masculine nouns, putting the appropriate definite article:

ⲡ̀ϭⲟⲓⲥ, ⲫ̀ⲙⲟⲩ, ⲡ̀ϣⲏⲣⲓ, ⲫ̀ⲣⲁⲛ, ⲫ̀ⲛⲁϩϯ, ⲫ̀ⲗⲁⲥ, ⲡ̀ⲱⲛϧ, ⲡ̀ⲥⲟⲛ, ⲫ̀ⲛⲟⲩϯ, ⲡ̀ⲱⲓⲕ, ⲡ̀ⲟⲩⲣⲟ, ⲡ̀ⲟⲩϫⲁⲓ, ⲡ̀ⲕⲁϩⲓ, ⲫ̀ⲛⲟⲃⲓ, ⲫ̀ⲃⲱⲕ, ⲡ̀ⲏⲓ.

3. For the following singular, feminine nouns, putting the appropriate definite article:

ⲧ̀ⲥⲱⲛⲓ, ⲧ̀ⲫⲉ, ⲑ̀ⲃⲁⲕⲓ, ⲧ̀ⲁⲫⲉ, ⲑ̀ⲛⲉϫⲓ, ⲑ̀ⲙⲁⲩ, ⲧ̀ϫⲓϫ, ⲑ̀ⲃⲱⲕⲓ, ⲑ̀ⲣⲓ, ⲧ̀ϣⲉⲣⲓ, ⲧ̀ⲃⲁⲗⲟϫ, ⲧ̀ϣⲟⲩⲣⲏ.

4. The singular of the plural nouns:

1. ⲓⲱⲧ. 2. ⲫⲉ. 3. ⲙⲉⲛⲣⲓⲧ. 4. ⲟⲩⲣⲟ. 5. ϩⲁⲗⲏⲧ. 6. ⲃⲱⲕ. 7. ϧⲉⲗⲗⲟ. 8. ϣⲁϥⲉ. 9. ⲁⲗⲟⲩ. 10. ⲥ̀ϩⲓⲙⲓ. 11. ⲓⲁⲣⲟ. 12. ⲥⲟⲛ.

5. The appropriate demonstrative pronoun:

1. ⲫⲁⲓ. 2. ⲛⲁⲓ. 3. ⲑⲁⲓ. 4. ⲫⲁⲓ. 5. ⲛⲁⲓ. 6. ⲑⲁⲓ.

6. The meaning of the words:

1. This heaven; 2. These books; 3. This son; 4. These hands; 5. This sister; 6. These sins; 7. This sun; 8. This bread; 9. This mother.

7. Translation to the English language:

1. They are the fathers of the Church; 2. We are the sons of the light; 3. He is the angel of the Lord; 4. You are the mother of Jesus; 5. You are the Lord of hosts; 6. I am the light of the world; 7. She is the daughter of Zion; 8. You are the servants of God.

Appendix A ✷ Answers of the Lessons' Exercises ✷

8. Translation to the Coptic language:

ⲁ̅. ⲡⲓⲱⲓⲕ ⲛ̀ⲧⲉ ⲡⲓⲱⲛϩ. ⲃ̅. ⲡⲓⲟⲩⲱⲓⲛⲓ ⲛ̀ⲧⲉ Ⲡϭⲟⲓⲥ. ⲅ̅. ⲡⲓⲏⲓ ⲛ̀ⲧⲉ ⲛⲓⲁⲅⲅⲉⲗⲟⲥ.
ⲇ̅. ⲡⲟⲩⲛⲟϥ ⲛ̀ⲧⲉ ⲛⲓ̀ⲥⲛⲏⲟⲩ.

Answers of the Exercises of the Sixth Lesson

1. The meaning of the following:

1. This book; 2. This censer; 3. These monks; 4. The brother who is there (that brother); 5. The sister who is there (that sister); 6. The fathers who are there (those fathers); 7. That book which is there (that book); 8. That censer which is there (that censer); 9. Those monks who are there (those monks); 10. The moon which is there (that moon); 11. The icon (image) which is there (that icon); 12. The cells (rooms) which are there (those cells or rooms).

2. Translation to the English language:

1. This is a father, and those are sons; 2. This is an icon, and that is a book; 3. These are brothers, and that is a sister; 4. That is the priest, and these are the deacons (servants); 5. That is the censer, and this is the sanctuary (temple); 6. Those are the fathers, and this is the mother; 7. The man who is there is the king of this city; 8. The woman who is there is the mother of these children; 9. The brothers who are there are the sons of this priest; 10. Who is that? He is the father of these monks; 11. Who is that? She is the daughter of this sister; 12. Who are those? They are the fathers of this desert.

Answers of the Exercises of the Seventh Lesson

1. The meaning of the following:

1. My God; 2. Our Lord; 3. Your head; 4. Her hands; 5. His eyes; 6. Your face; 7. His nose; 8. Your ear; 9. Our tongue; 10. His mercy; 11. Your peace; 12. Your teeth; 13. Their throat; 14. Their heart; 15. Our flesh; 16. Your womb; 17. My kidneys; 18. Your arm; 19. My elbow; 20. His finger; 21. Her feet; 22. My knees; 23. His soul; 24. Our thought; 25. Their mind; 26. My senses; 27. His shoulder; 28. Your throat; 29. His sons; 30. Their king; 31. Her mother; 32. My lips; 33. Your name; 34. Your sister; 35. Their mother; 36. Your names.

2. Translation to the Coptic language:

1. ⲛⲟⲩⲛⲁϩⲃⲓ.   2. ⲡⲉⲛⲛⲟⲩⲥ.   3. ⲡⲉϥⲣⲁⲛ.   4. ⲛⲉⲛⲃⲁⲗⲁⲩϫ.   5. ⲛⲟⲩϣⲏⲣⲓ.

6. ⲡⲉⲕⲥⲟⲛ. 7. ⲧⲉⲁⲫⲉ. 8. ⲛⲉⲥⲙⲁϣϫ. 9. ⲡⲁϩⲏⲧ. 10. ⲧⲉϥϩⲓⲣⲏⲛⲏ. 11. ⲡⲉⲛⲛⲟⲩϯ. 12. ⲡⲟⲩⲱⲛϩ. 13. ⲧⲉⲯⲩⲭⲏ. 14. ⲛⲉⲛⲧⲏⲃ. 15. ⲛⲁⲓⲟϯ. 16. ⲡⲉⲕⲛⲁⲓ. 17. ⲡⲁϭⲟⲓⲥ. 18. ⲛⲉⲕⲃⲁⲗ. 19. ⲡⲉϥⲗⲁⲥ. 20. ⲧⲉⲧⲉⲛⲥⲱⲛⲓ.

3. Translation to the English language:

1. The salvation of our souls; 2. Your mercy and your peace; 3. My sister and my friend; 4. The sons of your prayers; 5. My sins and my iniquities; 6. Our God and our king; 7. Your glory and your honor; 8. Pharaoh and his chariots; 9. The fruit of your womb; 10. Elizabeth your relative; 11. Your books and your pens; 12. Your sister and her daughters; 13. Cosman and his brothers and their mother.

Answers of the Exercises of the Eighth Lesson

1. Putting the appropriate possessive adjective or pronoun in the blank:

ā. ⲑⲱϥ. B̄. ⲛⲟⲩⲥ. ḡ. ⲫⲱⲕ. Δ̄. ⲑⲱⲛ. Ē. ⲛⲟⲩⲟⲩ. S̄. ⲛⲉⲧⲉⲛ-. Z̄. ⲧⲟⲩ-. H̄. ⲡⲉⲕ-. Θ̄. ⲧⲉⲥ-. Ī. ⲛⲉⲛ-.

2. Translation to the English language:

1. This fast is the fast of the Virgin (this fast is the Virgin's); 2. This feast is the feast of the martyrs; 3. The owner of the harp is David; 4. Yours be the power and the glory; 5. The heavens and the earth are Yours, O God; 6. These children belong to you, beloved; 7. This day is the day of St. Maximus; 8. This church is the church of St. Mary the Virgin; 9. The books which are there are his.

Answers of the Exercises of the Seventh and Eighth Lessons

1. The meaning of the words:

1. My name; 2. Their heart; 3. His icon (his image); 4. Our God; 5. My recitation; 6. Our sins; 7. My peace; 8. Her son; 9. Your relative; 10. Your salvation; 11. Your king; 12. His midst; 13. Their land; 14. His father; 15. Your prayers; 16. My lord (my master); 17. My masters; 18. Your face; 19. His glory; 20. Your honor; 21. Their enemies; 22. Her God; 23. Your names; 24. Their throat; 25. Your son; 26. His mother; 27. Your womb; 28. Our souls.

Appendix A ✠ Answers of the Lessons' Exercises ✠

2. Translation to the Coptic language:

1. ⲡⲁⲥⲟⲛ. 2. ⲡⲉⲕⲛⲁⲓ. 3. ⲡⲉⲛⲟⲩⲣⲟ. 4. ⲧⲉⲛⲉⲭⲓ. 5. ⲛⲉⲥⲥⲱⲛⲓ. 6. ⲡⲉⲥⲓⲱⲧ. 7. ⲧⲉⲛⲙⲁⲩ. 8. ⲧⲉϥⲥⲱⲛⲓ. 9. ⲡⲁⲛⲟⲩϯ. 10. ⲧⲉⲧⲉⲛⲟⲩⲣⲱ. 11. ⲛⲁⲛⲟⲃⲓ. 12. ⲡⲉⲕⲱⲟⲩ. 13. ⲡⲉϥϩⲟ. 14. ⲛⲉⲧⲉⲛϣⲏⲣⲓ. 15. ⲛⲉϥϫⲱⲙ. 16. ⲡⲉⲕⲡ̅ⲛ̅ⲁ̅. 17. ⲛⲁⲓⲟϯ. 18. ⲡⲉⲥϭⲟⲓⲥ. 19. ⲛⲟⲩⲥⲁϫⲓ. 20. ⲧⲉⲕϩⲓⲣⲏⲛⲏ.

3. Completing the table:

ⲁⲛⲟⲕ	ⲡⲁϩⲏⲧ	ⲧⲁⲯⲩⲭⲏ	ⲛⲁϫⲓϫ	ⲫⲱⲓ	ⲛⲟⲩⲓ
ⲛ̅ⲑⲟⲕ	ⲡⲉⲕϩⲏⲧ	ⲧⲉⲕⲯⲩⲭⲏ	ⲛⲉⲕϫⲓϫ	ⲫⲱⲕ	ⲛⲟⲩⲕ
ⲛ̅ⲑⲟ	ⲡⲉϩⲏⲧ	ⲧⲉⲯⲩⲭⲏ	ⲛⲉϫⲓϫ	ⲫⲱ	ⲛⲟⲩ
ⲛ̅ⲑⲟϥ	ⲡⲉϥϩⲏⲧ	ⲧⲉϥⲯⲩⲭⲏ	ⲛⲉϥϫⲓϫ	ⲫⲱϥ	ⲛⲟⲩϥ
ⲛ̅ⲑⲟⲥ	ⲡⲉⲥϩⲏⲧ	ⲧⲉⲥⲯⲩⲭⲏ	ⲛⲉⲥϫⲓϫ	ⲫⲱⲥ	ⲛⲟⲩⲥ
ⲁⲛⲟⲛ	ⲡⲉⲛⲥⲟⲛ	ⲧⲉⲛⲥⲱⲛⲓ	ⲛⲉⲛⲥⲛⲏⲟⲩ	ⲫⲱⲛ	ⲛⲟⲩⲛ
ⲛ̅ⲑⲱⲧⲉⲛ	ⲡⲉⲧⲉⲛⲥⲟⲛ	ⲧⲉⲧⲉⲛⲥⲱⲛⲓ	ⲛⲉⲧⲉⲛⲥⲛⲏⲟⲩ	ⲫⲱⲧⲉⲛ	ⲛⲟⲩⲧⲉⲛ
ⲛ̅ⲑⲱⲟⲩ	ⲡⲟⲩⲥⲟⲛ	ⲧⲟⲩⲥⲱⲛⲓ	ⲛⲟⲩⲥⲛⲏⲟⲩ	ⲫⲱⲟⲩ	ⲛⲟⲩⲟⲩ

4. Complete; put the suitable possessive pronoun or adjective in the blanks:

3. ⲫⲱ, 4. ⲡⲉϥ-, 5. ⲫⲱⲥ, 6. ⲡⲉⲛ-, 7. ⲫⲱⲧⲉⲛ, 8. ⲡⲟⲩ-, 10. ⲑⲱⲕ, 11. ⲧⲉ-, 12. ⲑⲱϥ, 13. ⲧⲉⲥ-, 14. ⲑⲱⲛ, 15. ⲧⲉⲧⲉⲛ-, 16. ⲑⲱⲟⲩ, 17. ⲛⲟⲩⲓ, 18. ⲛⲉⲕ-, 19. ⲛⲟⲩ, 20. ⲛⲉϥ-, 21. ⲛⲟⲩⲥ, 22. ⲛⲉⲛ-, 23. ⲛⲟⲩⲧⲉⲛ, 24. ⲛⲟⲩ-.

5. Complete, putting the suitable possessive pronoun or adjective in the blanks:

2. ⲫⲱⲕ, 3. ⲡⲉ-, 4. ⲫⲱϥ, 5. ⲡⲉⲥ-, 6. ⲫⲱⲛ, 7. ⲡⲉⲧⲉⲛ-, 8. ⲫⲱⲟⲩ, 9. ⲑⲱⲓ, 10. ⲧⲉⲕ-, 11. ⲑⲱ, 12. ⲧⲉϥ-, 13. ⲑⲱⲥ, 14. ⲧⲉⲛ-, 15. ⲑⲱⲧⲉⲛ, 16. ⲧⲟⲩ-, 17. ⲛⲁ-, 18. ⲛⲟⲩⲕ, 19. ⲛⲉ-, 20. ⲛⲟⲩϥ, 21. ⲛⲉⲥ-, 22. ⲛⲟⲩⲛ, 23. ⲛⲉⲧⲉⲛ-, 24. ⲛⲟⲩ-.

6. Choose from the column on right what suits every word in the column on the left:

ⲡⲉⲕⲣⲁⲛ	ⲫⲱⲕ	ⲧⲟⲩⲃⲁⲕⲓ	ⲑⲱⲟⲩ	ⲡⲁⲥⲙⲟⲩ	ⲫⲱⲓ
ⲛⲟⲩⲥⲁϫⲓ	ⲛⲟⲩⲟⲩ	ⲛⲉⲓⲟϯ	ⲛⲟⲩ	ⲛⲉⲥϫⲱⲙ	ⲛⲟⲩⲥ
ⲧⲉⲙⲁⲩ	ⲑⲱ	ⲡⲉϥϩⲏⲧ	ⲫⲱϥ	ⲧⲉⲕϩⲓⲣⲏⲛⲏ	ⲑⲱⲕ

✠ Foundations of the Coptic Language ✠

ⲡⲉⲧⲉⲛⲓⲱⲧ	ⲫⲱⲧⲉⲛ	ⲛⲉⲕⲃⲁⲗ	ⲛⲟⲩⲕ	ⲡⲟⲩⲛⲟⲩϯ	ⲫⲱⲟⲩ
ⲧⲉϥⲣⲓ	ⲑⲱϥ	ⲧⲁⲛⲉⲭⲓ	ⲑⲱⲓ	ⲛⲉϥϣⲏⲣⲓ	ⲛⲟⲩϥ
ⲛⲉⲛϫⲁϫⲓ	ⲛⲟⲩⲛ	ⲡⲉⲥⲗⲁⲥ	ⲫⲱⲥ	ⲧⲉⲛⲥⲱⲛⲓ	ⲑⲱⲛ
ⲧⲉⲥϣⲉⲣⲓ	ⲑⲱⲥ	ⲧⲉⲧⲉⲛⲁⲥⲡⲓ	ⲑⲱⲧⲉⲛ	ⲛⲉⲧⲉⲛϫⲓϫ	ⲛⲟⲩⲧⲉⲛ
ⲛⲁⲥⲛⲏⲟⲩ	ⲛⲟⲩⲓ	ⲡⲉⲛⲥⲱⲧⲏⲣ	ⲫⲱⲛ	ⲡⲉⲣⲁⲛ	ⲫⲱ

7. Translation to the English language:

O Jesus, You are our God and our Savior and our King. You are the way and the truth and the life. You are the bread of our life and the light of our world. Your Father is our Father. His throne is in heaven. The earth is the place of His feet.

We are Your people. We are Your sons and Your beloved. Your mother is the saint Mary the Virgin. She is our mother and the pride of our race.

O Mary, you are our queen, the queen of the heavenly and the earthly. You are the golden censer. Your Son is our Lord. We are your sons.

I am Your servant, O Jesus. My brothers are Your servants. The saints are our fathers. We are their sons and their beloved. Our life is in Your hand, O our Lord.

Answers of the Exercises of the Ninth Lesson

1. The meaning of the following:

1. The heavenly (pl.); 2. The door-keeper; 3. The owner of this house; 4. The earthly (pl.); 5. The Egyptians; 6. Belonging to (the daughter of) this church; 7. Your name; 8. His peace; 9. Our fathers; 10. Your brothers; 11. Their king; 12. Our city; 13. Your foot; 14. His bosom; 15. My hands; 16. Our mouth; 17. Its end; 18. Their head; 19. Books I have or some of my books; 20. A brother he has or one of his brothers; 21. Works we have or some of our works; 22. A daughter she has or one of her daughters; 23. Fathers they have or some of their fathers; 24. A father of yours or one of your fathers; 25. Those disciples who are yours; 26. That sister who is yours; 27. That creation which is His; 28. Those sons who are hers; 29. That mother who is ours; 30. That teacher who is mine.

2. Translation to the English language:

1. The body of the Lord and His blood; 2. The prayers of the monks and their praises; 3. Our Lord and our God and our King; 4. The man who is there is your priest; 5. Those are their sons and their daughters; 6. This icon is the Virgin's (or is the icon of the Virgin); 7.

Appendix A ✣ *Answers of the Lessons' Exercises* ✣

Mine is all the earth; 8. These are the ritualists [who are] of that church; 9. Your sons are my brothers and my beloved.

Answers of the Exercises of the Tenth Lesson

1. The meaning of the phrases:

1. An honorable man; 2. An upright path; 3. An acceptable time; 4. Many books; 5. Open doors; 6. A pure hand; 7. Our coming Lord (who will come); 8. The perfect man; 9. The strong God; 10. The Virgin [who is] full of honor; 11. The blessed brothers; 12. Your tomb [which is] full of grace.

2. The translation:

1. The man who is from Egypt; 2. The sister who is from this city; 3. The fathers who are from this desert; 4. The book which is on this table is yours [your book]; 5. The icon which is on that wall is the icon of the Virgin; 6. The children who are in the house that is there are your children; 7. This is the brother who is coming through our king; 8. This is the blessed daughter who is from the church that is there [from that church]; 9. There are the honored elders who are from those holy mountains.

Answers of the Review Exercises 2: On Lessons 6 to 10

1. The meaning of the phrases:

1. That light which is there [that light]; 2. The church which is there [that church]; 3. The monks who are there [those monks]; 4. His mercy and His peace; 5. Your words and your works; 6. Our king and our queen; 7. Their sins and their iniquities; 8. The heavenly [those of the heavens]; 9. Of the glory [the owner of the glory]; 10. The owner of this place; 11. Fathers of mine [some of my fathers]; 12. A brother of his [one of his brothers]; 13. Books of theirs [some of their books]; 14. A city of theirs [one of their cities].

2. Put the suitable possessive pronoun or adjective:

ⲡⲉⲛⲟⲩϫⲁⲓ, ⲛⲉϥϣⲏⲣⲓ, ⲧⲟⲩⲙⲁⲩ, ⲡⲁⲓⲱⲧ, ⲛⲉⲧⲉⲛⲃⲁⲗ, ⲧⲉⲕϫⲓϫ. ⲫⲱⲧⲉⲛ, ⲛⲟⲩⲥ, ⲑⲱⲟⲩ, ⲫⲱⲕ, ⲛⲟⲩⲓ, ⲑⲱ.

3. The meaning of the words:

1. Our mouth; 2. My bosom; 3. Your foot; 4. His head; 5. Their hands; 6. Our belly; 7. Your heart; 8. His face; 9. Her womb; 10. Your hand; 11. Your head; 12. Its price; 13. Its end; 14. Your feet; 15. Our face; 16. His bosom; 17. Your hand; 18. His eye.

4. The meaning of the phrases:

1. Who are from the heaven; 2. Who is through God; 3. Who is from Egypt; 4. Who is to everlasting [eternal]; 5. Who are on the earth; 6. Who is from this city; 7. An upright heart; 8. The honored man; 9. Holy [pure] angels; 10. The holy [pure] Virgin; 11. An acceptable sacrifice; 12. The blessed brothers.

5. The translation to the English language:

1. That man is their father; 2. The church which is there is [the church] of the Virgin; 3. Those brothers are our brothers; 4. Our Lord and our God and our Savior is Jesus; 5. My books and your books are in this cell (room); 6. He and his sons are there; 7. The coming feast is the feast of the martyrs; 8. Yours is the glory and honor; 8. The icons that are on the wall which is there are icons of the saints; 10. Those are the blessed sons who are through the honored elders.

6. The translation to the Coptic language:

1. ⲫⲁⲓ ⲟⲩⲓⲱⲧ ⲡⲉ ⲟⲩⲟϩ ⲛⲏ ϩⲁⲛⲥⲛⲏⲟⲩ ⲛⲉ. 2. ⲡⲁⲡⲛⲉⲩⲙⲁ ⲛⲉⲙ ⲧⲁⲯⲩⲭⲏ ⲛⲉⲙ ⲡⲁⲥⲱⲙⲁ. 3. ⲛⲁⲓϫⲱⲙ ⲛⲉ ⲛⲟⲩⲛ. 4. ϯⲡⲁⲣⲑⲉⲛⲟⲥ ⲑⲏⲉⲑⲙⲉϩ ⲛ̀ϩⲙⲟⲧ.

Answers of the Exam 2: On Lessons 6 to 10

1. The meaning of the phrases:

1. The bird which is there [that bird]; 2. The censer which is there [that censer]; 3. The trees which are there [those trees]; 4. The man who is there [that man]; 5. The sister who is there [that sister]; 6. The sons who are there [those sons]; 7. His mercy; 8. My sins; 9. Your faces; 10. His soul; 11. Their blessing; 12. Our God; 13. Her prayers; 14. Your honor; 15. My Savior.

2. Completed with the suitable possessive pronouns or adjectives:

1. ⲫⲱⲓ. 2. ⲧⲉϥ-. 3. ⲛⲟⲩⲥ. 4. ⲡⲉⲛ-. 5. ⲑⲱⲧⲉⲛ. 6. ⲛⲉⲕ-. 7. ⲫⲱⲟⲩ. 8. ⲧⲉ-. 9. ⲛⲟⲩⲓ. 10. ⲧⲁ-. 11. ⲧⲉⲕ-. 12. ⲧⲉϥ-. 13. ⲡⲉⲕ-. 14. ⲧⲉⲕ-. 15. ⲧⲉϥ-. 16.

ⲛⲉⲥ-. 17. ⲧⲉ-. 18. ⲧⲉ-. 19. ⲡⲉϥ-. 20. ⲡⲉⲛ-. 21. ⲛⲉⲛ-.

3. Putting the suitable definite article:

1. ⲡⲓ, ⲡⲓ. 2. ⲛⲓ, ⲛⲓ. 3. ϯ, ϯ.

4. The meaning of phrases:

1. Our coming God [who will come]; 2. The honored elder; 3. Our blessed fathers; 4. The holy mountains; 5. A pure hand; 6. Holy angels; 7. An open book; 8. Many sons.

5. Translation to the English language:

1. He is God of our fathers; 2. His name is Emanuel; 3. His mother is the holy Virgin; 4. O Mary, the mother of our God: Yours is the honor, yours is the glorification; 5. That is a book and that is an icon; 6. Those elders are the fathers of these deserts; 7. This is the brother who is from the church which is there [that church].

6. Translation to the Coptic language:

1. ⲡⲁϩⲏⲧ ⲛⲉⲙ ⲡⲁⲗⲁⲥ ⲛⲉⲙ ⲛⲁⲗⲟⲅⲓⲥⲙⲟⲥ. 2. ⲛⲁ ⲛⲓⲫⲏⲟⲩⲓ ⲛⲉⲙ ⲛⲁ ⲡ̄ⲕⲁϩⲓ. 3. ⲟⲩⲥⲟⲛ ⲉϥⲥⲙⲁⲣⲱⲟⲩⲧ ⲛⲉⲙ ⲟⲩⲁⲅⲅⲉⲗⲟⲥ ⲉϥⲟⲩⲁⲃ.

Answers of the General Exam on Lessons 1 to 10

1. The meaning of the phrases:

1. A book; 2. The book; 3. This book; 4. That book [the book which is there]; 5. His book; 6. My book [one of my books]; 7. Books; 8. The books; 9. These books; 10. Those books [the books which are there]; 11. Your books; 12. Her books [some of her books].

2. Choosing the suitable words from the opposite column:

1.	ⲛⲁⲓⲟϯ	ⲛⲟⲩⲓ	9.	ⲧⲁⲣⲓ	ⲑⲱⲓ
2.	ⲧⲟⲩⲙⲁⲩ	ⲑⲱⲟⲩ	10.	ⲡⲉⲛⲗⲁⲥ	ⲫⲱⲛ
3.	ⲡⲉⲥⲣⲁⲛ	ⲫⲱⲥ	11.	ⲛⲉⲕⲁⲗⲱⲟⲩⲓ	ⲛⲟⲩⲕ
4.	ⲧⲉⲥⲱⲛⲓ	ⲑⲱ	12.	ⲧⲉϥϫⲟⲙ	ⲑⲱϥ
5.	ⲛⲉϥϣⲏⲣⲓ	ⲛⲟⲩϥ	13.	ⲡⲟⲩⲕⲁϩⲓ	ⲫⲱⲟⲩ

6.	ⲡⲉⲧⲉⲛⲟⲩⲣⲟ	ⲫⲱⲧⲉⲛ	14.	ⲛⲉⲧⲉⲛϣⲗⲏⲗ	ⲛⲟⲩⲧⲉⲛ
7.	ⲧⲉⲕϩⲓⲣⲏⲛⲏ	ⲑⲱⲕ	15.	ⲛⲉⲥⲁϫⲓ	ⲛⲟⲩ
8.	ⲛⲉⲛϫⲓϫ	ⲛⲟⲩⲛ	16.	ⲧⲉⲥϣⲉⲣⲓ	ⲑⲱⲥ

3. Putting the suitable definite article:

1. ⲛⲓ, ⲛⲓ, ⲛⲓ   2. ⲡⲓ, ⲡⲓ   3. ϯ, ϯ

4. Writing the meaning of the phrases:

1. The believing man; 2. A pure heart; 3. Your perfect peace; 4. An honored virgin; 5. The open doors; 6. Many sons; 7. Our mighty Lord; 8. The blessed brothers.

5. Completing with the suitable possessive adjectives:

1. ⲧⲉϥ-.   2. ⲡⲉⲕ-.   3. ⲧⲁ-.   4. ⲧⲉⲥ-.   5. ⲛⲉⲧⲉⲛ-.   6. ⲛⲉⲛ-.   7. ⲛⲉ-.   8. ⲛⲟⲩ-.   9. ⲡⲁ-.

6. Translation to the English language:

1. We are His people, and they are our fathers; 2. This is a man, and those are sons of his [some of his sons]; 3. Who is this? She is our holy mother; 4. The heavens and the earth are yours, O our God; 5. That is a child, and that is a virgin; 6. Yours is the glory and the honor and the thankgiving; 7. The monk who is there [that monk] is the elder of this desert; 8. These are the priests who are of that church [the church which is there].

7. Translation to the Coptic language:

1. ⲧⲉⲕⲁ̀ⲫⲉ ⲛⲉⲙ ⲛⲉⲕⲃⲁⲗ ⲛⲉⲙ ⲡⲉⲕⲙⲉⲧⲓ̀.

2. ⲛⲁ Ⲭⲏⲙⲓ ⲛⲉⲙ ⲛⲟⲩϣⲏⲣⲓ.

3. ϩⲁⲛⲁⲅⲅⲉⲗⲟⲥ ⲉⲧⲟⲩⲁⲃ ⲛⲉⲙ ⲟⲩⲥⲱⲛⲓ ⲉⲥⲥⲙⲁⲣⲱⲟⲩⲧ.

Answers of the Exercises of the Eleventh Lesson

1. Writing the meaning of the verbs:

1. We write; 2. He moves; 3. You worship; 4. You see; 5. You come; 6. She hates; 7. We seek; 8. They eat; 9. You read; 10. They praise; 11. I ask; 12. He saves [rescues]; 13. You walk; 14. We bless; 15. I wake up; 16. You give; 17. He prays; 18. You keeps [guards or memorizes];

19. You drink; 20. They take; 21. We understand; 22. He serves; 23. She gives birth; 24. You hurry; 25. We pass [cross]; 26. You sit; 27. I believe.

2. Translation:

1. I do not read, but I write; 2. You do not eat, but you drink; 3. You do not talk, but you listen; 4. He does not memorize, but he understands; 5. She does not see, but she smells; 6. We do not send, but we come; 7. You do not take, but you give; 8. They do not sit, but they pray; 9. We never hate, but we love.

3. Example sentences for translation:

I speak with my tongue, hear with my ears, see with my eyes, smell with my nose, eat with my teeth, drink with my mouth, point with my finger, work with my hands, walk with my feet, write with my pen, understand with my mind, read in my Holy Book, pray from my heart, praise with my fathers and my brothers.

4. Answering the questions according to the example:

ce, ⲧⲁⲓⲣⲓ ⲧⲉ ⲧⲁⲣⲓ.	ⲙ̀ⲙⲟⲛ, ⲧⲁⲓⲣⲓ ⲧⲉ ⲁⲛ ⲧⲁⲣⲓ.
ce, ⲛⲁⲓⲥⲛⲏⲟⲩ ⲛⲉ ⲛⲁⲥⲛⲏⲟⲩ.	ⲙ̀ⲙⲟⲛ, ⲛⲁⲓⲥⲛⲏⲟⲩ ⲛⲉ ⲁⲛ ⲛⲁⲥⲛⲏⲟⲩ.
ce, ϯⲥϧⲁⲓ ϧⲉⲛ ⲡⲉⲭⲱⲣϩ.	ⲙ̀ⲙⲟⲛ, ϯⲥϧⲁⲓ ⲁⲛ ϧⲉⲛ ⲡⲉⲭⲱⲣϩ.
ce, ϯϩⲉⲙⲥⲓ ϯⲛⲟⲩ.	ⲙ̀ⲙⲟⲛ, ϯϩⲉⲙⲥⲓ ⲁⲛ ϯⲛⲟⲩ.

5. Translation to the English language:

1. A father and elders and brothers; 2. The censer is in the hand of the priest; 3. You are the light of the world; 4. The Virgin Mary is the mother of Jesus; 5. She is the daughter of Zion; 6. We are the servants of Christ; 7. He is the tree of life; 8. This is a child, but that is a virgin; 9. This is your watch, and that is mine [or my watch]; 10. These books are his, but those [books] are hers; 11. This man who is from this city is your father; 12. These icons which are on the wall are those of our holy fathers.

Answers of the Exercises of the Twelfth Lesson

1. Beginning the sentences with the verb:

ⲁ̄ ϥⲱϣ ⲛ̀ϫⲉ ⲡⲓⲁⲗⲟⲩ. ⲃ̄ ⲥⲉϣⲉⲙϣⲓ ⲛ̀ϫⲉ ⲛⲓⲉ̀ⲃⲓⲁⲓⲕ. ⲅ̄ ⲥ̀ϩⲉⲙⲥⲓ ⲛ̀ϫⲉ ϯⲥⲱⲛⲓ.

✠ Foundations of the Coptic Language ✠

2. Putting the suitable object mark:

ⲁ̅ ⲙ̄, ⲃ̅ ⲉ̀, ⲅ̅ ⲙ̄, ⲇ̅ ⲉ̀, ⲉ̅ ⲛ̀, ⲋ̅ ⲙ̄, ⲍ̅ ⲛ̀, ⲏ̅ ⲛ̀.

3. Choosing the verb for each sentence:

ⲁ̅ ϣⲁⲣⲓ, ⲃ̅ ⲟⲩⲱⲙ, ⲅ̅ ϣⲉⲙϣⲓ, ⲇ̅ ϩⲱⲥ, ⲉ̅ ⲱϣ, ⲋ̅ ⲥⲱⲧⲉⲙ, ⲍ̅ ϣⲓⲛⲓ, ⲏ̅ ⲛⲁⲩ.

4. Making the object a pronoun:

ⲁ̅ ϯϩⲱⲥ ⲉⲣⲟϥ. ⲃ̅ ϫⲛⲁⲩ ⲉⲣⲱⲟⲩ. ⲅ̅ ⲧⲉⲥⲱⲉⲙ ⲉⲣⲟⲥ. ⲇ̅ ϥⲥϧⲁⲓ ⲙ̀ⲙⲱⲟⲩ. ⲉ̅ ⲥⲱϣ ⲙ̀ⲙⲟϥ. ⲋ̅ ⲧⲉⲛⲙⲉⲓ ⲙ̀ⲙⲟϥ. ⲍ̅ ⲥⲉⲭⲱ ⲙ̀ⲙⲟⲥ. ⲏ̅ ⲧⲉⲧⲉⲛⲥⲙⲟⲩ ⲉⲣⲟϥ.

5. Translating to the English language:

1. You keep the commandments of the Lord; 2. They [that is the commandments] are the path of the life; 3. We love the light, and we hate the works of the dankness; 4. He praises his Lord with his brothers; 5. The priest and the deacons pray in the sanctuary; 6. I believe [in] You, O my God, I have hope [in] You, and I serve You; 7. You read in your Holy Book, and you write the words of the Lord; 8. They beseech their God from their hearts; 9. We receive [partake of] His honored Body and Blood; 10. We call Him at all times; 11. God hears His servants, and He saves them from their enemies.

Answers of the Exercises of the Thirteenth Lesson

1. Writing the sentences in the future tense:

ⲁ̅	ϫⲛⲁⲓ ⲉ̀ϯⲉⲕⲕⲗⲏⲥⲓⲁ.	ⲃ̅	ⲧⲉⲛⲛⲁϩⲱⲥ ⲛⲉⲙⲱⲟⲩ.
ⲅ̅	ⲧⲉⲣⲁⲥϧⲁⲓ ⲙ̀ⲡⲉϣϣ.	ⲇ̅	ϫⲛⲁⲥⲁϫⲓ ⲛⲉⲙⲱⲟⲩ.
ⲉ̅	ⲧⲉⲣⲁⲁⲣⲉϩ ⲉ̀ⲛⲓⲉⲛⲧⲟⲗⲏ.	ⲋ̅	ⲧⲉⲧⲉⲛⲛⲁⲛⲁⲩ ⲉ̀ⲧⲫⲉ.

2. Answering in the affirmative form and then in the negative form:

ⲁ̅	ⲥⲉ, ϥⲛⲁⲓ ⲛ̀ϫⲉ ⲡⲓⲟⲩⲏⲃ.	ⲙ̀ⲙⲟⲛ, ϥⲛⲁⲓ ⲁⲛ ⲛ̀ϫⲉ ⲡⲓⲟⲩⲏⲃ.
ⲃ̅	ⲥⲉ, ϯⲛⲁⲩ ⲉ̀ⲡⲓⲁⲅⲅⲉⲗⲟⲥ.	ⲙ̀ⲙⲟⲛ, ϯⲛⲁⲩ ⲁⲛ ⲉ̀ⲡⲓⲁⲅⲅⲉⲗⲟⲥ.
ⲅ̅	ⲥⲉ, ⲧⲉⲛⲥⲱ ⲙ̀ⲡⲓⲉ̀ⲣⲱϯ.	ⲙ̀ⲙⲟⲛ, ⲧⲉⲛⲥⲱ ⲁⲛ ⲙ̀ⲡⲓⲉ̀ⲣⲱϯ.
ⲇ̅	ⲥⲉ, ⲕⲱϣ ⲙ̀ⲡⲁⲓϫⲱⲙ.	ⲙ̀ⲙⲟⲛ, ⲕⲱϣ ⲁⲛ ⲙ̀ⲡⲁⲓϫⲱⲙ.
ⲉ̅	ⲥⲉ, ⲥⲉⲛⲁⲁⲣⲉϩ ⲉ̀ⲛⲟⲩⲱϣ.	ⲙ̀ⲙⲟⲛ, ⲥⲉⲛⲁⲁⲣⲉϩ ⲁⲛ ⲉ̀ⲛⲟⲩⲱϣ.

Appendix A ☥ Answers of the Lessons' Exercises ☥

3. Writing the meaning of the words:

1. That (mas.) who makes [works]; 2. That (fem.) who hears; 3. Those who praise; 4. That (mas.) who asks; 5. That (fem.) who gives; 6. Those who walk.

4. Writing the meaning of the phrases:

1. I say to you; 2. You pray to Him; 3. You hear with her the word of God; 4. He gives to us with them; 5. Sons of hers [some of her sons]; 6. We keep them; 7. You will serve Him; 8. They give to You with us; 9. A father of theirs; 10. His saints [the saints who are His]; 11. Sisters of yours.

5. Translation to the English language:

1. The Lord saves His people; 2. I choose you, my beloved; 3. We have hope in You, O our God; 4. She will beget a child [she will give birth to a child]; 5. You will sit with the Apostles; 6. You will receive grace with your brothers; 7. You hear his voice quickly; 8. They will seek the face of the Lord; 9. God sends to us His Son; 10. We choose the way of life; 11. They love their fathers and their brothers; 12. O our Savior, do with us according to Your mercy.

Answers of the Exercises of the Fourteenth Lesson

1. Putting the sentence in the negative form:

ⲁ̄   ⲙ̀ⲡⲉ ⲡⲓⲟⲩⲏⲃ ⲓ̀ ⲛ̀ⲥⲁϥ.   ⲃ̄   ⲙ̀ⲡⲓⲛⲁⲩ ⲉ̀ⲡⲉϥϣⲟⲩ.

ⲅ̄   ⲙ̀ⲡⲉⲕⲟⲩⲱⲙ ⲙ̀ⲡⲓⲁϥ.   ⲇ̄   ⲙ̀ⲡⲉϣⲉⲙϣⲓ ⲙ̀Ⲡⲓϭⲟⲓⲥ.

ⲉ̄   ⲙ̀ⲡⲉϥⲥⲱⲧⲉⲙ ⲉ̀ⲧⲉⲕⲥⲙⲏ.   ⲋ̄   ⲙ̀ⲡⲉⲥϭⲓ ⲛ̀ⲟⲩϩ̀ⲙⲟⲧ.

ⲍ̄   ⲙ̀ⲡⲉⲛⲥⲱ ⲙ̀ⲡⲓⲉ̀ⲣⲱϯ.   ⲏ̄   ⲙ̀ⲡⲉⲧⲉⲛⲕⲁϯ ⲛ̀ⲛⲉⲧⲉⲛϣ.

ⲑ̄   ⲙ̀ⲡⲟⲩⲛⲁϩϯ ⲛⲉⲙⲱⲧⲉⲛ.

2. Answering in the affirmative form and then in the negative form:

ⲁ̄   ⲥⲉ, ⲁⲓϩⲱⲥ ⲛⲉⲙ ⲛⲁⲥ̀ⲛⲏⲟⲩ ⲙ̀ⲫⲟⲟⲩ.

ⲙ̀ⲙⲟⲛ, ⲙ̀ⲡⲓϩⲱⲥ ⲛⲉⲙ ⲛⲁⲥ̀ⲛⲏⲟⲩ ⲙ̀ⲫⲟⲟⲩ.

ⲃ̄   ⲥⲉ, ⲁⲕⲙⲟϣⲓ ⲉ̀ϯⲉⲕⲕⲗⲏⲥⲓⲁ ⲛ̀ⲭⲱⲗⲉⲙ.

ⲙ̀ⲙⲟⲛ, ⲙ̀ⲡⲉⲕⲙⲟϣⲓ ⲉ̀ϯⲉⲕⲕⲗⲏⲥⲓⲁ ⲛ̀ⲭⲱⲗⲉⲙ.

ⲅ̄   ⲥⲉ, ⲁϥⲛⲟϩⲉⲙ ⲛ̀ϫⲉ ⲡⲟⲩⲣⲟ ⲙ̀ⲡⲉϥⲗⲁⲟⲥ.

ⲙ̀ⲙⲟⲛ, ⲙ̀ⲡⲉϥⲛⲟϩⲉⲙ ⲛ̀ϫⲉ ⲡⲟⲩⲣⲟ ⲙ̀ⲡⲉϥⲗⲁⲟⲥ.

ⲁ̄	ⲥⲉ, ⲁⲛⲱϣ ⲛ̀ⲛⲉⲛϫⲱⲙ.	ⲙ̀ⲙⲟⲛ, ⲙ̀ⲡⲉⲛⲱϣ ⲛ̀ⲛⲉⲛϫⲱⲙ.
ⲉ̄	ⲥⲉ, ⲁⲧⲉⲧⲉⲛⲥϧⲁⲓ ⲙ̀ⲡⲁⲓⲱϣ.	ⲙ̀ⲙⲟⲛ, ⲙ̀ⲡⲉⲧⲉⲛⲥϧⲁⲓ ⲙ̀ⲡⲁⲓⲱϣ.
ⲋ̄	ⲥⲉ, ⲁⲩⲥⲓⲛⲓ ⲛ̀ⲧⲁⲓⲃⲁⲕⲓ.	ⲙ̀ⲙⲟⲛ, ⲙ̀ⲡⲟⲩⲥⲓⲛⲓ ⲛ̀ⲧⲁⲓⲃⲁⲕⲓ.

3. Forming meaningful sentences:

ⲁ̄	Ⲫⲛⲟⲩϯ ⲁϥⲑⲁⲙⲓⲟ ⲙ̀ⲡⲓⲣⲱⲙⲓ.	ⲃ̄	ⲛⲓⲙⲟⲛⲁⲭⲟⲥ ⲥⲉϩⲱⲥ ⲉ̀ⲡⲓϭⲟⲓⲥ.
ⲅ̄	ϯⲥⲱⲛⲓ ⲥ̀ⲛⲁⲁⲣⲉϩ ⲉ̀ⲛⲓⲯⲁⲗⲙⲟⲥ.	ⲇ̄	ⲡⲓϩⲁⲗⲏⲧ ϥ̀ⲥⲱ ⲙ̀ⲡⲓⲙⲱⲟⲩ.
ⲉ̄	ⲛⲓⲉ̀ⲃⲓⲁⲓⲕ ⲁⲩⲛⲁⲩ ⲉ̀ⲡⲟⲩⲣⲟ.	ⲋ̄	ⲥⲉⲟⲩⲱⲙ ⲛ̀ϫⲉ ⲛⲓϩⲏⲕⲓ ⲙ̀ⲡⲓⲱⲓⲕ.
ⲍ̄	ϯⲥϩⲓⲙⲓ ⲁⲥⲙⲓⲥⲓ ⲛ̀ⲟⲩⲁⲗⲟⲩ.		

4. Meaning of phrases:

1. I heard him with you; 2. You saw her with them; 3. You prayed with us yesterday; 4. We praised with him today; 5. She read it with you; 6. Fathers of his [some of his fathers]; 7. A daughter of hers [one of her daughters]; 8. Elders of theirs [some of their elders]; 9. A brother of ours [one of our brothers]; 10. Cells (rooms) of yours [some of your cells (rooms)].

5. Translation:

God created man according to His likeness and His image. Man sinned against the Lord. The Son of God was incarnate [took flesh] and became man. The Virgin Mary gave birth to Him and He saved us. He came and walked with men. He purified our hearts and healed the sicknesses of our souls and our bodies. The Jews crucified Him. He died and gave to us life. He opened the gate of Paradise and returned Adam to his authority once more. We give thanks to Him exceedingly.

Answers of the Exercises of the Fifteenth Lesson

1. Completing what is missing in the table:

Person	Present	Future	Past Perfect
ⲁⲛⲟⲕ	ϯϩⲱⲥ	ϯⲛⲁϩⲱⲥ	ⲁⲓϩⲱⲥ
ⲛ̀ⲑⲟⲕ	ⲕⲱϣ ⲁⲛ	ⲭⲛⲁⲱϣ ⲁⲛ	ⲙ̀ⲡⲉⲕⲱϣ
ⲛ̀ⲑⲟ	ⲧⲉⲥϧⲁⲓ	ⲧⲉⲣⲁⲥϧⲁⲓ	ⲁⲣⲉⲥϧⲁⲓ
ⲛ̀ⲑⲟϥ	ϥϣⲗⲏⲗ	ϥⲛⲁϣⲗⲏⲗ	ⲁϥϣⲗⲏⲗ

Appendix A ⊹ Answers of the Lessons' Exercises ⊹

ⲛ̀ⲑⲟⲥ	ⲥⲟⲧⲱⲙ ⲁⲛ	ⲥ̀ⲛⲁⲟⲩⲱⲙ ⲁⲛ	ⲙ̀ⲡⲉⲥⲟⲩⲱⲙ
ⲁⲛⲟⲛ	ⲧⲉⲛⲥⲱⲧⲉⲙ	ⲧⲉⲛⲛⲁⲥⲱⲧⲉⲙ	ⲁⲛⲥⲱⲧⲉⲙ
ⲛ̀ⲑⲱⲧⲉⲛ	ⲧⲉⲧⲉⲛϭⲓ ⲁⲛ	ⲧⲉⲧⲉⲛⲛⲁϭⲓ ⲁⲛ	ⲙ̀ⲡⲉⲧⲉⲛϭⲓ
ⲛ̀ⲑⲱⲟⲩ	ⲥⲉϩⲉⲙⲥⲓ	ⲥⲉⲛⲁϩⲉⲙⲥⲓ	ⲁⲩϩⲉⲙⲥⲓ

2. Writing the meaning of the phrases:

1. The one seated [that who sits]; 2. The hearer [that who hears]; 3. The readers [those who read]; 4. That who will choose; 5. That who will serve; 6. Those who will believe; 7. That who came; 8. That who gave birth; 9. Those who passed away; 10. That who gave; 11. That who took; 12. Those who prayed.

3. Making the object a pronoun:

1. ⲥ̀ⲙⲥⲓ ⲙ̀ⲙⲟϥ. 2. ϥϩⲱⲥ ⲉ̀ⲣⲟϥ. 3. ⲧⲉⲛⲱϣ ⲙ̀ⲙⲱⲟⲩ. 4. ⲥⲉⲛⲁⲩ ⲉ̀ⲣⲟⲥ. 5. ⲕ̀ⲥϧⲁⲓ ⲙ̀ⲙⲟϥ. 6. ⲁϥⲥⲙⲟⲩ ⲉ̀ⲣⲟϥ. 7. ⲁⲣⲉⲛⲁⲩ ⲉ̀ⲣⲱⲟⲩ. 8. ⲁⲛⲙⲉⲓ ⲙ̀ⲙⲟϥ. 9. ⲁⲧⲉⲧⲉⲛⲕⲁϯ ⲙ̀ⲙⲱⲟⲩ. 10. Ⲫϯ ⲁϥⲥⲱⲧⲡ ⲙ̀ⲙⲟⲥ.

4. Writing the meaning of the phrases:

1. I write to you; 2. He speaks with you; 3. You read to them; 4. We give to you with him; 5. She will eat with you; 6. You will come with us; 7. They take with you; 8. We will sit with them; 9. You gave him/it to us; 10. He chose you to them; 11. Words of his [some of his words]; 12. A daughter of hers [one of her daughters]; 13. Books of theirs [some of their books]; 14. Brothers of ours [some of our brothers].

5. Putting the senctences in the affirmative form:

ⲁ̄ ⲁ ⲡⲓⲣⲱⲙⲓ ⲟⲩⲱⲙ. ⲃ̄ ⲥⲉⲛⲁⲩ ⲉ̀ⲣⲟϥ. ⲅ̄ ⲁⲛⲁⲣⲉϩ ⲉ̀ⲡⲉⲛⲱϣ. ⲇ̄ ⲁⲩⲥⲁϫⲓ ⲛⲉⲙⲏⲓ. ⲉ̄ ϭϩⲉⲙⲥⲓ ⲛⲉⲙⲉ. ⲋ̄ ⲁϥⲧⲁⲙⲟ ⲉ̀ⲣⲱⲧⲉⲛ. ⲍ̄ ⲁⲕϣⲓⲛⲓ ⲉ̀ⲣⲟⲓ. ⲏ̄ ⲁⲓⲥⲱⲧⲡ ⲙ̀ⲙⲱⲧⲉⲛ. ⲑ̄ ⲧⲉⲧⲉⲛⲛⲁⲥⲱ ⲛ̀ⲟⲩⲏⲣⲡ. ⲓ̄ ⲁⲛⲛⲁϩϯ ⲉ̀ⲣⲟϥ. ⲓ̄ⲁ ⲭ̀ⲛⲁⲟⲩⲱⲣⲡ ⲛⲁⲛ. ⲓ̄ⲃ ⲁⲥⲕⲁϯ ⲙ̀ⲡⲉⲥⲱϣ. ⲓ̄ⲅ ϥⲛⲁⲛⲟϩⲉⲙ ⲙ̀ⲙⲟϥ. ⲓ̄ⲇ ⲁⲛⲥⲱⲧⲉⲙ ⲉ̀ϯⲥⲙⲏ. ⲓ̄ⲉ ⲁⲩⲛⲉϩⲥⲓ ⲛ̀ϣⲟⲣⲡ. ⲓ̄ⲋ ⲁⲧⲉⲧⲉⲛϣⲗⲏⲗ ⲙ̀ⲫⲟⲟⲩ.

Answers of the Review Exercises 3: On Lessons 11 to 15

1. The meaning of phrases:

1. He moved; 2. I hear; 3. She did not give birth; 4. You saw; 5. We sit; 6. They prayed; 7. You will take; 8. They did not write; 9. She reads; 10. You understand; 11. They love; 12. He serves; 13. We believed; 14. You did not keep [memorize]; 15. She woke up; 16. You praise; 17. I will bless; 18. You did not come; 19. We will tell; 20. You did not eat; 21. She will drink; 22. You worship; 23. He did not ask; 24. You passed; 25. You will walk; 26. You hate; 27. I did not choose; 28. They will think; 29. I hurried; 30. You will give; 31. We did not understand; 32. He will speak;

33. He said to us with you; 34. You give to them Your peace; 35. We speak to you now; 36. I will take for you with me; 37. Fathers of theirs or some of their fathers; 38. I saw you with him; 39. We praised Him with them; 40. You will read it with us; 41. You spoke with her yesterday; 42. A church of hers [one of her churches].

2, Putting the suitable object mark:

1. ⲛ̀ 2. ⲉ̀ 3. ⲙ̀ 4. ⲛ̀ 5. ⲙ̀ 6. ⲉ̀ 7. ⲉ̀
8. ⲛ̀ 9. ⲉ̀ 10. ⲙ̀ 11. ⲉ̀ 12. ⲉ̀ 13. ⲙ̀ 14. ⲉ̀

3. Forming meaningful sentences:

ⲁ̄ ⲥⲉϩⲱⲥ ⲛ̀ϫⲉ ⲛⲉⲛⲓⲟϯ ⲉ̀ⲡⲟⲩⲛⲟⲩϯ.
ⲃ̄ ⲛⲓⲉ̀ⲃⲓⲁⲓⲕ ⲁⲩϣⲉⲙϣⲓ ⲙ̀ⲡⲟⲩⲟⲩⲣⲟ.
ⲅ̄ ϥ̀ϣⲗⲏⲗ ⲛ̀ϫⲉ ⲡⲓⲟⲩⲏⲃ ϧⲉⲛ ⲡⲓⲉⲣⲫⲉⲓ.
ⲇ̄ ⲥⲉⲥⲱ ⲛ̀ϫⲉ ⲛⲓϩⲁⲗⲁϯ ⲛ̀ⲛⲓⲙⲱⲟⲩ.
ⲉ̄ ⲛⲓⲙⲁⲣⲧⲩⲣⲟⲥ ⲥⲉⲛⲁⲛⲁⲩ ⲉ̀ⲡⲓϭⲟⲓⲥ.
ⲋ̄ ⲁⲩⲕⲁϯ ⲛ̀ϫⲉ ⲛⲁⲥⲛⲏⲟⲩ ⲛ̀ⲛⲟⲩⲱϣ.
ⲍ̄ ϯⲡⲁⲣⲑⲉⲛⲟⲥ ⲁⲥϭⲓ ⲛ̀ⲟⲩϩⲙⲟⲧ.
ⲏ̄ ⲥ̀ⲛⲁⲟⲩⲱⲙ ⲛ̀ϫⲉ ϯⲥⲱⲛⲓ ⲙ̀ⲡⲓⲱⲓⲕ.

4. Answering in the affirmative form and then in the negative form:

ⲁ̄. ⲥⲉ, ⲁ ⲡⲓⲥⲟⲛ ⲓ̀ ⲛ̀ⲥⲁϥ.   ⲙ̀ⲙⲟⲛ, ⲙ̀ⲡⲉ ⲡⲓⲥⲟⲛ ⲓ̀ ⲛ̀ⲥⲁϥ.
ⲃ̄. ⲥⲉ, ⲁⲛⲥϧⲁⲓ ⲙ̀ⲡⲉⲛⲱϣ.   ⲙ̀ⲙⲟⲛ, ⲙ̀ⲡⲉⲛⲥϧⲁⲓ ⲙ̀ⲡⲉⲛⲱϣ.
ⲅ̄. ⲥⲉ, ϯⲛⲁⲁ̀ⲣⲉϩ ⲉ̀ⲛⲁⲓⲯⲁⲗⲙⲟⲥ.   ⲙ̀ⲙⲟⲛ, ϯⲛⲁⲁ̀ⲣⲉϩ ⲁⲛ ⲉ̀ⲛⲁⲓⲯⲁⲗⲙⲟⲥ.
ⲇ̄. ⲥⲉ, ⲁⲩϯ ⲛⲁⲛ ⲛ̀ⲛⲉⲛϫⲱⲙ.   ⲙ̀ⲙⲟⲛ, ⲙ̀ⲡⲟⲩϯ ⲛⲁⲛ ⲛ̀ⲛⲉⲛϫⲱⲙ.
ⲉ̄. ⲥⲉ, ⲁⲓⲛⲁⲩ ⲉ̀ⲣⲟⲥ ⲙ̀ⲫⲟⲟⲩ.   ⲙ̀ⲙⲟⲛ, ⲙ̀ⲡⲓⲛⲁⲩ ⲉ̀ⲣⲟⲥ ⲙ̀ⲫⲟⲟⲩ.
ⲋ̄. ⲥⲉ, ⲁϥⲟⲩⲱⲣⲡ ⲛⲏⲓ ⲙ̀ⲡⲉϥϣⲏⲣⲓ. ⲙ̀ⲙⲟⲛ, ⲙ̀ⲡⲉϥⲟⲩⲱⲣⲡ ⲛⲏⲓ ⲙ̀ⲡⲉϥϣⲏⲣⲓ.
ⲍ̄. ⲥⲉ, ⲧⲉⲛⲛⲁⲩ ⲉ̀ⲧⲁⲓϩⲓⲕⲱⲛ.   ⲙ̀ⲙⲟⲛ, ⲧⲉⲛⲛⲁⲩ ⲁⲛ ⲉ̀ⲧⲁⲓϩⲓⲕⲱⲛ.

Answers of the Exam 3: On Lessons 11 to 15

1. Putting the phrases in the negative form:

Appendix A ✣ Answers of the Lessons' Exercises ✣

1. ⲧⲉⲛⲛⲁⲩ ⲁⲛ
2. ⲙ̄ⲡⲉⲥⲟⲩⲱϣⲧ
3. ⲙ̄ⲡⲓⲥϭⲁⲓ
4. ⲙ̄ⲡⲉϩⲱⲥ
5. ϯⲛⲁⲙⲟϣⲓ ⲁⲛ
6. ⲧⲉϣⲉⲙϣⲓ ⲁⲛ
7. ⲙ̄ⲡⲉϥⲥⲙⲟⲩ
8. ⲙ̄ⲡⲉⲧⲉⲛⲥⲱ
9. ⲙ̄ⲡⲉⲛϭⲓ
10. ⲥⲉⲛⲁⲓ ⲁⲛ
11. ⲧⲉⲣⲁⲛⲉϩⲥⲓ ⲁⲛ
12. ϥⲛⲁϩϯ ⲁⲛ
13. ⲙ̄ⲡⲉⲕϣⲗⲏⲗ
14. ⲙ̄ⲡⲟⲩⲥⲁϫⲓ
15. ⲧⲉⲛⲕⲱϯ ⲁⲛ
16. ⲙ̄ⲡⲉⲛⲕⲁϯ
17. ⲙ̄ⲡⲉⲕⲓⲣⲓ
18. ⲙ̄ⲡⲉⲥⲙⲟⲩ

2. Writing the meaning:

1. He spoke with us; 2. You eat with him; 3. You will sit with them; 4. You prayed with her; 5. I praise with you; 6. You walk with me; 7. I say to you; 8. He shone to us; 9. We give to you; 10. You read to me; 11. She will write to them; 12. They took to him.

3. Changing the object to a pronoun:

1. ⲧⲉⲛⲛⲁⲩ ⲉⲣⲟϥ.
2. ⲁⲓⲱϣ ⲙ̄ⲙⲟϥ.
3. ⲥⲉϩⲱⲥ ⲉⲣⲟϥ.
4. ϯⲥⲱⲧⲉⲙ ⲉⲣⲟⲥ.
5. ⲁⲕϭⲓ ⲙ̄ⲙⲱⲟⲩ.
6. ϥ̄ⲥⲙⲟⲩ ⲉⲣⲱⲟⲩ.
7. ⲥⲟⲩⲱⲙ ⲙ̄ⲙⲟϥ.
8. ⲁϥϫⲱ ⲙ̄ⲙⲟⲥ.
9. ⲥⲉⲁⲣⲉϩ ⲉⲣⲱⲟⲩ.
10. ⲧⲉⲥⲱⲧⲡ ⲙ̄ⲙⲟⲥ.

4. Writing the meaning of the phrases:

1. He praises that God who is his; 2. We understand those lessons which are ours; 3. You live in that cell (room) which is yours; 4. I carry that cross which is mine; 5. You hear that voice which is his; 6. They love those sons who are theirs.

5. Choosing what is suitable:

1.	ⲛ̄ⲑⲱⲟⲩ	ⲙ̄ⲡⲟⲩⲥϭⲁⲓ	9.	ⲡⲉⲕⲣⲁⲛ	ⲛ̄ⲧⲁⲕ
2.	ⲁⲛⲟⲛ	ⲧⲉⲛⲁⲣⲉϩ	10.	ⲛⲉⲧⲉⲛϫⲱⲙ	ⲛ̄ⲧⲱⲧⲉⲛ
3.	ⲛ̄ⲑⲟⲥ	ⲥ̄ⲛⲁϣ	11.	ⲡⲁⲓⲱⲧ	ⲛ̄ⲧⲏⲓ
4.	ⲛ̄ⲑⲱⲧⲉⲛ	ⲧⲉⲧⲉⲛⲛⲁⲓ	12.	ⲧⲟⲩⲙⲁⲩ	ⲛ̄ⲧⲱⲟⲩ
5.	ⲛ̄ⲑⲟⲕ	ⲁⲕⲥⲁϫⲓ	13.	ⲡⲉⲥϣⲏⲣⲓ	ⲛ̄ⲧⲁⲥ
6.	ⲁⲛⲟⲕ	ⲁⲓⲙⲟϣⲓ	14.	ⲛⲉϥϫⲓϫ	ⲛ̄ⲧⲁϥ
7.	ⲛ̄ⲑⲟϥ	ϥ̄ϣⲗⲏⲗ	15.	ⲧⲉⲥⲱⲛⲓ	ⲛ̄ⲧⲉ
8.	ⲛ̄ⲑⲟ	ⲧⲉⲣⲁⲙⲓⲥⲓ	16.	ⲛⲉⲛⲃⲁⲗⲁⲩϫ	ⲛ̄ⲧⲁⲛ

6. Translating the sentences:

1. I praise with my brothers in this church; 2. The Virgin gave birth to our Savior Jesus; 3. Our Lord came and walked with men; 4. We read the words of God in the Holy Book; 5. They believed their Lord and blessed His name; 6. You saw your brother and spoke with him; 7. You love your father and your mother, and you pray with them.

Answers of the Exercises of the Sixteenth Lesson

1. Completing the table:

Present	Future	Past perfect (affirmative)	Past perfect (negative)
ϥϭⲓ	ϥⲛⲁϭⲓ	ⲁϥϭⲓ	ⲙ̄ⲡⲉϥϭⲓ
ⲕ̄ⲥⲱ	ⲭⲛⲁⲥⲱ	ⲁⲕⲥⲱ	ⲙ̄ⲡⲉⲕⲥⲱ
ϯⲥⲱⲧⲉⲙ	ϯⲛⲁⲥⲱⲧⲉⲙ	ⲁⲓⲥⲱⲧⲉⲙ	ⲙ̄ⲡⲓⲥⲱⲧⲉⲙ
ⲥ̄ⲙⲓⲥⲓ	ⲥ̄ⲛⲁⲙⲓⲥⲓ	ⲁⲥⲙⲓⲥⲓ	ⲙ̄ⲡⲉⲥⲙⲓⲥⲓ
ⲧⲉⲛⲱϣ	ⲧⲉⲛⲛⲁⲱϣ	ⲁⲛⲱϣ	ⲙ̄ⲡⲉⲛⲱϣ
ⲧⲉⲧⲣⲁϫⲓⲙⲓ	ⲧⲉⲧⲣⲁϫⲓⲙⲓ	ⲁⲣⲉϫⲓⲙⲓ	ⲙ̄ⲡⲉϫⲓⲙⲓ
ⲧⲉⲧⲉⲛⲓ	ⲧⲉⲧⲉⲛⲛⲁⲓ	ⲁⲧⲉⲧⲉⲛⲓ	ⲙ̄ⲡⲉⲧⲉⲛⲓ
ⲥⲉⲭⲱ	ⲥⲉⲛⲁϫⲱ	ⲁⲩϫⲱ	ⲙ̄ⲡⲟⲩϫⲱ

2. Writing the meaning of the verbs:

1. ⲁⲛϭⲓⲛⲓ   2. ⲁⲕⲟⲩⲱⲣⲡ   3. ⲧⲉⲛⲛⲁⲱⲛϧ   4. ⲙ̄ⲡⲉⲥϥⲁⲓ
5. ⲁⲓϥⲁⲓ   6. ⲧⲉⲣⲁⲥⲓⲛⲓ   7. ⲧⲉⲧⲉⲛⲱⲛϧ   8. ⲁⲩⲟⲩⲱⲛ
9. ϥ̄ⲛⲁϥⲁⲓ   10. ⲧⲉⲟⲩⲱⲛ   11. ⲁϥⲟⲩⲱⲣⲡ   12. ⲁⲛⲙⲟϣⲓ
13. ⲧⲉⲛⲟⲩⲱⲣⲡ   14. ⲥ̄ⲱⲛϧ   15. ⲧⲉⲧⲉⲛϥⲁⲓ   16. ⲕ̄ⲥⲓⲛⲓ

3. Translation to the English language:

1. God purifies our hearts; 2. The deacon will read the gospel; 3. The sin destroyed our race; 4. Men sinned against the Lord; 5. God sustained Israel in the wilderness of Sinai; 6. David became king over Israel; 7. God sanctified the Virgin; 8. Our Savior accepted the suffering for the sake of our salvation; 9. The Jews crucified Him; 10. He tasted death in the flesh; 11. Our Lord saved His people; 12. The Virgin intercedes for the sake of her sons; 13. We

learn the Coptic language; 14. The martyrs accepted suffering for the sake of the faith; 15. The servants serve their master; 16. The Holy Spirit enlightens our mind; 17. Your holy name was glorified in the mouths of Your saints; 18. The saints became great in the land of Egypt; 19. We glorify the Virgin and honor her; 20. My God reward you.

4. Complete the conjugation:

ⲁⲛⲟⲕ I	ⲡⲁⲥⲟⲛ My brother	ⲫⲱⲓ Mine	ⲛⲏⲓ Mine	ⲉⲣⲟⲓ To me
ⲛ̀ⲑⲟⲕ	ⲡⲉⲕⲥⲟⲛ	ⲫⲱⲕ	ⲛⲁⲕ	ⲉⲣⲟⲕ
ⲛ̀ⲑⲟ	ⲡⲉⲥⲟⲛ	ⲫⲱ	ⲛⲉ	ⲉⲣⲟ
ⲛ̀ⲑⲟϥ	ⲡⲉϥⲥⲟⲛ	ⲫⲱϥ	ⲛⲁϥ	ⲉⲣⲟϥ
ⲛ̀ⲑⲟⲥ	ⲡⲉⲥⲥⲟⲛ	ⲫⲱⲥ	ⲛⲁⲥ	ⲉⲣⲟⲥ
ⲁⲛⲟⲛ	ⲡⲉⲛⲥⲟⲛ	ⲫⲱⲛ	ⲛⲁⲛ	ⲉⲣⲟⲛ
ⲛ̀ⲑⲱⲧⲉⲛ	ⲡⲉⲧⲉⲛⲥⲟⲛ	ⲫⲱⲧⲉⲛ	ⲛⲱⲧⲉⲛ	ⲉⲣⲱⲧⲉⲛ
ⲛ̀ⲑⲱⲟⲩ	ⲡⲟⲩⲥⲟⲛ	ⲫⲱⲟⲩ	ⲛⲱⲟⲩ	ⲉⲣⲱⲟⲩ

Answers of the Exercises of the Seventeen Lesson

1. Writing the meaning:

1. He honors (he gives honor); 2. You fear; 3. We glorify; 4. She died; 5. They mourned; 6. He rose up; 7. I return; 8. He became king; 9. He will judge; 10. They will live; 11. You (sing. fem.) arose; 12. You (sing. masc.) cry out; 13. She blossomed; 14. They confess (reveal); 15. You wait; 16. We rejoice; 17. He loosened (abolished); 18. They fasted; 19. You go; 20. He granted to us; 21. She intercedes.

2. Writing the verbs in the affirmative form:

1. ⲁⲩϩⲉⲙⲥⲓ   2. ⲁⲛϣⲉⲛⲁⲛ   3. ⲁⲓⲧⲱⲛⲧ   4. ⲁⲥⲕⲟⲧⲥ
5. ⲁϥϭⲓⲱⲙⲥ   6. ⲁⲧⲉⲧⲉⲛⲙⲟϣⲓ   7. ⲁⲣⲉⲥⲁϫⲓ   8. ⲁⲕⲉⲣϩⲱⲃ

3. Completing according to the given example:

1. ϯϣⲉⲛⲏⲓ ⲉ̀ⲧⲁⲣⲓ ⲟⲩⲟϩ ϯⲟⲩⲛⲟϥ ⲙ̀ⲙⲟⲓ ϫⲉ Ⲫϯ ⲛⲉⲙⲏⲓ.
2. ⲕϣⲉⲛⲁⲕ ⲉ̀ⲧⲉⲕⲣⲓ ⲟⲩⲟϩ ⲭⲟⲩⲛⲟϥ ⲙ̀ⲙⲟⲕ ϫⲉ Ⲫϯ ⲛⲉⲙⲁⲕ.
3. ⲧⲉϣⲉⲛⲉ ⲉ̀ⲧⲉⲣⲓ ⲟⲩⲟϩ ⲧⲉⲟⲩⲛⲟϥ ⲙ̀ⲙⲟ ϫⲉ Ⲫϯ ⲛⲉⲙⲉ.
4. ϥϣⲉⲛⲁϥ ⲉ̀ⲧⲉϥⲣⲓ ⲟⲩⲟϩ ϥⲟⲩⲛⲟϥ ⲙ̀ⲙⲟϥ ϫⲉ Ⲫϯ ⲛⲉⲙⲁϥ.
5. ⲥϣⲉⲛⲁⲥ ⲉ̀ⲧⲉⲥⲣⲓ ⲟⲩⲟϩ ⲥⲟⲩⲛⲟϥ ⲙ̀ⲙⲟⲥ ϫⲉ Ⲫϯ ⲛⲉⲙⲁⲥ.

6. ⲧⲉⲛϣⲉⲛⲁⲛ ⲉⲛⲉⲛⲣⲓ ⲟⲩⲟϩ ⲧⲉⲛⲟⲩⲛⲟϥ ⲙ̅ⲙⲟⲛ ϫⲉ Ⲫϯ ⲛⲉⲙⲁⲛ.

7. ⲧⲉⲧⲉⲛϣⲉⲛⲱⲧⲉⲛ ⲉⲛⲉⲧⲉⲛⲣⲓ ⲟⲩⲟϩ ⲧⲉⲧⲉⲛⲟⲩⲛⲟϥ ⲙ̅ⲙⲱⲧⲉⲛ ϫⲉ Ⲫⲛⲟⲩϯ ⲛⲉⲙⲱⲧⲉⲛ.

8. ⲥⲉϣⲉⲛⲱⲟⲩ ⲉⲛⲟⲩⲣⲓ ⲟⲩⲟϩ ⲥⲉⲟⲩⲛⲟϥ ⲙ̅ⲙⲱⲟⲩ ϫⲉ Ⲫϯ ⲛⲉⲙⲱⲟⲩ.

4. Translation to the English language:

1. God opened the door of the paradise of joy; 2. He restored man to his authority once again; 3. You arose and saved us; 4. We go to church early; 5. They return to their Lord now; 6. You will receive the crown in heaven; 7. We accept suffering here in this world; 8. She will sit with the martyrs; 9. Those who were baptized renounced the devil; 10. My Lord Jesus will forgive me my sins; 11. The disciples followed (walked toward) our Savior; 12. The son obeys his father; 13. We seek His face daily (always); 14. The saints rest in the paradise of joy; 15. We boast in the cross of our Lord Jesus; 16. God disperses the enemies of the Church; 17. Those who reposed will live.

5. Translation to the Coptic language:

ⲁ̅. ϯⲛⲁⲧⲱⲛⲧ ⲛ̅ϣⲟⲣⲡ ⲟⲩⲟϩ ϯⲛⲁϩⲱⲥ ⲉⲡⲁⲛⲟⲩϯ. ⲃ̅. ⲁϥϭⲓⲥⲁⲣⲝ ⲛ̅ϫⲉ Ⲡⲓϣⲏⲣⲓ ⲟⲩⲟϩ ⲁϥⲉⲣⲣⲱⲙⲓ. ⲅ̅. ⲡⲓⲙⲟⲛⲁⲭⲟⲥ ϥϣⲉⲣⲓ ⲙ̅ⲙⲟϥ ϧⲉⲛ ⲧⲉϥⲣⲓ. ⲇ̅. ⲁⲛϣⲉⲛⲁⲛ ⲉϯⲉⲕⲕⲗⲏⲥⲓⲁ ⲙ̅ⲫⲟⲟⲩ. ⲉ̅. ⲙ̅ⲡⲉϥⲃⲱⲗ ⲙ̅ⲡⲓⲛⲟⲙⲟⲥ ⲉⲃⲟⲗ ⲛ̅ϫⲉ Ⲡⲓϭⲟⲓⲥ ⲁⲗⲗⲁ ⲁϥϫⲱⲕ ⲙ̅ⲙⲟϥ ⲉⲃⲟⲗ. ⲋ̅. ⲛⲓⲁⲅⲓⲟⲥ ⲥⲉⲕⲱϯ ⲛ̅ⲥⲁ ⲡϩⲟ ⲙ̅Ⲡϭⲟⲓⲥ ⲛ̅ⲥⲏⲟⲩ ⲛⲓⲃⲉⲛ.

Answers of the Exercises of the Eighteenth Lesson

1. Writing the meaning:

1. They send up; 2. You come down; 3. He brought in; 4. You will go out; 5. I lift up; 6. They mentioned you, they remembered you; 7. You forgot her; 8. You visit them; 9. He comforts (calms our hearts) us; 10. I remembered him; 11. We stood up; 12. He endured; 13. You submit; 14. She is silent; 15. They stood up.

2. Forming sentences:

ⲁ̅. ⲡⲉⲛϭⲟⲓⲥ Ⲓⲏⲥⲟⲩⲥ ⲁϥⲥⲱⲧⲡ ⲛ̅ⲛⲉϥⲙⲁⲑⲏⲧⲏⲥ.

ⲃ̅. ⲛⲓⲁⲡⲟⲥⲧⲟⲗⲟⲥ ⲁⲩϣⲉ ⲉⲃⲟⲗ ϣⲁ ⲛⲓⲗⲁⲟⲥ ⲛ̅ⲧⲉ ⲡⲕⲁϩⲓ.

ⲅ̅. Ⲫⲓⲱⲧ ϥϣⲁⲛϣ ⲙ̅ⲡⲉϥϣⲏⲣⲓ.

ⲇ̅. ϯⲡⲁⲣⲑⲉⲛⲟⲥ ⲁⲥϫⲓⲙⲓ ⲛ̅ⲟⲩϩⲙⲟⲧ.

ⲉ̅. ⲡⲓⲇⲓⲁⲃⲟⲗⲟⲥ ⲁϥⲉⲣⲡⲓⲣⲁⲍⲓⲛ ⲙ̅ⲡⲉⲛϭⲟⲓⲥ.

ⲋ̅. ⲛⲓⲁⲅⲓⲟⲥ ⲥⲉⲕⲱϯ ⲛ̅ⲥⲁ ⲡϩⲟ ⲙ̅Ⲫϯ.

Appendix A ✠ Answers of the Lessons' Exercises ✠

3. Putting the suitable number, or arranging the words with what suits them:

1.	ⲡⲁϩⲏⲧ	ϫⲱⲓ	ⲙ̀ⲙⲟⲓ	ϣⲉⲛⲏⲓ	ⲣⲁⲧ
2.	ⲡⲉⲕϩⲏⲧ	ϫⲱⲕ	ⲙ̀ⲙⲟⲕ	ϣⲉⲛⲁⲕ	ⲣⲁⲧⲕ
3.	ⲡⲉϩⲏⲧ	ϫⲱ	ⲙ̀ⲙⲟ	ϣⲉⲛⲉ	ⲣⲁϯ
4.	ⲡⲉϥϩⲏⲧ	ϫⲱϥ	ⲙ̀ⲙⲟϥ	ϣⲉⲛⲁϥ	ⲣⲁⲧϥ
5.	ⲡⲉⲥϩⲏⲧ	ϫⲱⲥ	ⲙ̀ⲙⲟⲥ	ϣⲉⲛⲁⲥ	ⲣⲁⲧⲥ
6.	ⲡⲉⲛϩⲏⲧ	ϫⲱⲛ	ⲙ̀ⲙⲟⲛ	ϣⲉⲛⲁⲛ	ⲣⲁⲧⲉⲛ
7.	ⲡⲉⲧⲉⲛϩⲏⲧ	ϫⲱⲧⲉⲛ	ⲙ̀ⲙⲱⲧⲉⲛ	ϣⲉⲛⲱⲧⲉⲛ	ⲣⲁⲧⲉⲛ ⲑⲏⲛⲟⲩ
8.	ⲡⲟⲩϩⲏⲧ	ϫⲱⲟⲩ	ⲙ̀ⲙⲱⲟⲩ	ϣⲉⲛⲱⲟⲩ	ⲣⲁⲧⲟⲩ

4. Translation to the English language:

1. God lifts the sins of the people; 2. You give to them bread and water; 3. The books which are there are hers; 4. That man is the king of this people; 5. He gave us that salvation which is ours; 6. Fasting and prayer cast out the devil; 7. The Lord blesses these honored elders; 8. Their prayers go up as acceptable sacrifices; 9. The monk is enlightened through prayer and praises; 10. God granted to us the forgiveness of our sins; 11. We give thanks to Him and worship Him; 12. Our holy fathers remember us before our Lord; 13. You brought in many people.

5. Analysis and translation of parts of the Psalmody:

1. You went to Hades, [and] you brought up the captivity, in [from] that place; 2. You granted to us once more the freedom, as a good God, for You rose up [and] saved us; 3. Little by little, we make Your remembrance, [and] we glorify Your name, O my Lord Jesus; 4. Pharaoh and his chariots sank under; the sons of Israel crossed the sea; 5. This is my God; I will glorify Him.

Answers of the Exercises of the Nineteenth Lesson

1. Translation of the sentences:

1. God is the Creator of the world (the heaven and the earth); 2. Jesus is the redeemer of men; 3. Our Lord is the merciful and the compassionate; 4. The Son of God is the giver of live to the sinners; 5. Gabriel is the announcer of the Virgin; 6. John is the baptizer of Jesus; 7. Our Savior is the forgiver of our iniquities; 8. The apostles are the teachers of the Church; 9. Mark is the preacher of Egypt; 10. The true physician is the healer of those who are sick;

11. The bishop is the guide of the believers; 12. The priest is the servant of the sanctuary; 13. The king is the sustainer of the people; 14. God is the judge of the world; 15. We are the seekers of the face of the Lord; 16. He is the giver of food to every living flesh; 17. Jesus is the bearer of the sin of the world; 18. He is our Savior from perdition; 19. Our King is the one sitting upon the cherubim; 20. Jesus is good lover of mankind; 21. Moses is the leader of the sons of Israel; 22. You are a lover of strangers; 23. The baker is the man who makes bread; 24. The butcher is the man who sells meat; 25. The watchmaker is the man who works with watches; 26. The cobbler is the man who makes shoes; 27. The carpenter is the man who works with woods; 28. The goldsmith is the man who works with gold; 29. The gardener is the servant of the garden; 30. We read the paradise (garden) of the monks.

2. Analysis and translation:

1. The bread of life, which came down to us from heaven, gave life to the world; 2. You too, O Mary, carried in your womb the rational Manna who came from the Father; 3. You gave birth to Him without defilement; He gave us His precious body and blood; we lived forever.

3. Translation to the Coptic language:

1. ⲡⲓⲣⲉϥⲑⲁⲙⲓⲟ ⲛ̀ⲧⲉ ⲛⲓⲫⲏⲟⲩⲓ̀ ⲛⲉⲙ ⲡ̀ⲕⲁϩⲓ.   2. ⲡⲓⲣⲉϥⲧⲁⲛϧⲟ ⲛ̀ⲧⲉ ⲛⲓⲣⲉϥⲙⲱⲟⲩⲧ.

3. ⲡⲓⲣⲉϥϯϩⲁⲡ ⲛ̀ⲧⲉ ϯⲃⲁⲕⲓ.   4. ⲡⲓⲣⲉϥⲭⲱ ⲉ̀ⲃⲟⲗ ⲛ̀ⲧⲉ ⲛⲉⲛⲛⲟⲃⲓ.

5. ⲡⲓⲣⲉϥⲛⲟϩⲉⲙ ⲛ̀ⲧⲉ ⲡⲉⲛⲱⲛϧ.   6. ⲡⲁⲓϣϣⲏⲛ ⲟⲩϧⲁⲓⲟⲩⲧⲁϩ ⲡⲉ.

7. ⲫⲏⲉⲧⲟⲩⲱϩⲉⲙ ⲛ̀ⲧⲉ ⲛⲓⲣⲉϥⲉⲣⲛⲟⲃⲓ.   8. ⲡⲓⲣⲉϥϯ ⲛ̀ⲧⲉ ⲛⲓϩ̀ⲙⲟⲧ.

Answers of the Exercises of the Twentieth Lesson

1. Writing the meaning of the phrases:

1. His birth; 2. Your coming; 3. Their work; 4. The manner of your speech; 5. His divinity; 6. Our brotherhood; 7. My poverty; 8. Your greatness; 9. Their giving; 10. His death; 11. Your walking (your way of behaving, conduct); 12. The way of her conception; 13. Our servitude; 14. Your (pl.) power; 15. Your fatherhood; 16. His priesthood; 17. Your conception; 18. Our praising; 19. Your (pl.) worshipping; 20. The way of my answering; 21. Their apostleship; 22. Her richness; 23. Their martyrdom; 24. Your patience.

2. Translation to the English language:

1. The coming of the lover of mankind; 2. The birth of Emmanuel; 3. The divinity of the only begotten Son; 4. Our unity in the Lord; 5. The obedience to the words of God; 6. His priesthood and His lordship; 7. Their wisdom and their meekness; 8. Your mercy and your compassion; 9. You remembered the thief in Your kingdom; 10. The lamp of monasticism;

11. The crown of martyrdom; 12. His richness and our poverty; 13. Your greatness in Your love for mankind.

3. Writing the meaning of the phrases:

1. when I come in (at my coming in); 2. To memorize (for the memorization) their lessons; 3. When he stands (at his standing); 4. For our praising; 5. When she gives birth (at her giving birth); 6. When you worship (at your worshiping); 7. To learn (for my learning); 8. When they suffer (at their suffering); 9. For your remembrance; 10. When You ascended (at Your ascension).

4. From the Psalmody for analysis and translation:

1. One out of two: a pure divinity and a holy humanity; 2. They celebrated with Him in His kingdom; 3. In the care of Your goodness, You bent the heavens [and] came down to us; 4. He killed the enmity completely; 5. O the honor of the way of conception which belongs to the virginal womb and the begetter of God; 6. A marriage did not precede the birth. The birth did not loosen her virginity.

5. Translation to the Coptic language:

1. ϯⲙⲉⲧⲓⲱⲧ ⲛⲉⲙ ϯⲙⲉⲧϣⲏⲣⲓ ⲛⲉⲙ ϯⲙⲉⲧⲥⲟⲛ. 2. ϯⲙⲉⲧⲁⲗⲟⲩ ⲛⲉⲙ ϯⲙⲉⲧⲣⲱⲙⲓ ⲛⲉⲙ ϯⲙⲉⲧϧⲉⲗⲗⲟ. 3. ⲡⲓϫⲓⲛϭⲓⲥⲃⲱ ⲛⲉⲙ ⲡⲓϫⲓⲛⲉⲣⲫⲙⲉⲩⲓ ⲛⲉⲙ ⲡⲓϫⲓⲛⲉⲣⲡⲱⲃϣ. 4. ϯⲙⲉⲑⲛⲟⲩϯ ⲛ̀ⲧⲉ ⲡⲓⲡⲛⲉⲩⲙⲁ ⲉⲑⲟⲩⲁⲃ. 5. ϯⲙⲉⲧⲙⲟⲛⲁⲭⲟⲥ ⲛ̀ⲧⲉ ⲛⲓⲓⲟϯ ⲛⲉⲙ ⲧⲟⲩⲙⲉⲧⲟⲩⲁⲓ. 6. ⲧⲉⲕϫⲓⲛⲥⲁϫⲓ ⲛⲉⲙ ⲧⲉⲕϫⲓⲛⲉⲣⲟⲩⲱ.

Answers of the Review Exercises 4: On Lessons 16 to 20

1. Writing the meaning:

1. He grants to us; 2. We give to Him glory; 3. They receive baptism; 4. You learn; 5. He brought up (he offered up); 6. I give thanks; 7. He will rise; 8. You went; 9. She feared; 10. He forgives; 11. We wait for (we look forward); 12. They rejoice; 13. We came in (entered); 14. You boast; 15. They reposed (rested); 16. My Redeemer (my Savior); 17. Our life-giver; 18. His mother; 19. Their evangelist (their preacher); 20. Your servant; 21. Her announcer; 22. The one who exists; 23. Those believers; 24. His coming; 25. Their giving; 26. My sonship; 27. Your work; 28. His greatness; 29. Their richness; 30. Our unity; 31. Your fatherhood; 32. Your brotherhood; 33. Our praising.

2. Translation to the English language:

1. He came down to our world, and He ascended to the heavens, and He sat on high; 2. The angels stand before Him always; 3. The apostles preached the gospel; 4. God does not forget His covenant; 5. When the deacon reads the holy Scriptures [readings] in the church, we remain silent and listen with fear and with care.

3. Writing the correct sentences:

ⲁ̄ ⲁⲥⲙⲓⲥⲓ ⲛ̀ϫⲉ ϯⲡⲁⲣⲑⲉⲛⲟⲥ ⲙ̀Ⲓⲏⲥⲟⲩⲥ. Ⲃ̄ ⲧⲉⲣⲁϣⲗⲏⲗ ϧⲉⲛ ⲧⲉⲣⲓ.

ⲅ̄ ⲙ̀ⲡⲉϥⲉⲣⲟⲩⲣⲟ (ⲓⲉ) ϥ̀ⲉⲣⲟⲩⲣⲟ ⲁⲛ. Ⲇ̄ ⲁⲕⲁ̀ⲣⲉϩ ⲉ̀ⲛⲓⲯⲁⲗⲙⲟⲥ.

ⲉ̄ ϫ̀ⲛⲁϩⲱⲥ ⲛⲉⲙ ⲛⲉⲕ̀ⲥⲛⲏⲟⲩ.

4. The meaning of the verses:

1. The Father loves the Son; 2. I am the bread of life; 3. I am the light of the world; 4. This is the prophet [who is] coming into the world; 5. Our fathers worshipped on this mountain; 6. I am the one speaking with you; 7. I came in the name of My Father; 8. I am the living bread which came down from heaven; 9. The Spirit is the giver of life; 10. The [one] born from the flesh is flesh, the [one] born from the Spirit is spirit; 11. No prophet is honored in his city; 12. He believed and all his house; 13. We knew and believed that You are the Christ, the Son of the living God; 14. Everyone who sins (does the sin) is a servant of the sin; 15. My Father who will give glory to (will glorify) Me.

Answers of the Exam 4: On Lessons 16 to 20

1. Writing the meaning of the words:

1. My kingdom; 2. This birth; 3. This lordship; 4. Our coming; 5. This unity; 6. This preacher; 7. Your meekness; 8. This sinner; 9. Your (pl.) fatherhood; 10. Their worshipping; 11. Our sonship; 12. These servants; 13. This monasticism; 14. This praising; 15. Your love for mankind; 16. These testimonies; 17. Their long-suffering; 18. Your work (your making).

2. Writing the meaning of the verbs:

1. I will praise; 2. He was silent; 3. They glorify; 4. He became king; 5. They ascend (they come up); 6. You remember me; 7. You are enlightened; 8. We sing; 9. I cried out; 10. You rejoice; 11. He comforted you; 12. We enter (we go in); 13. She stood up; 14. I boast; 15. We visited them; 16. They repose (rest); 17. You descended (went down); 18. He brought out.

Appendix A ✠ Answers of the Lessons' Exercises ✠

3. Translation to the English language:

1. God granted to us the forgiveness of our sins; 2. We seek the face of the Lord always; 3. He came down to our world to save us; 4. Our Savior Jesus is the giver of life to our souls; 5. We give thanks to God at our entrance into the church.

4. Considering the sentence ⲁϥϣⲉⲛⲁϥ ⲉ̀ⲧⲉϥⲣⲓ:

ⲁ̄ ⲙ̀ⲡⲉϥϣⲉⲛⲁϥ ⲉ̀ⲧⲉϥⲣⲓ.   ⲃ̄ ϯϣⲉⲛⲏⲓ ⲉ̀ⲧⲁⲣⲓ.   ⲅ̄ ⲭⲛⲁϣⲉⲛⲁⲕ ⲉ̀ⲧⲉⲕⲣⲓ.
ⲇ̄ ⲁϥϣⲉⲛⲁϥ ⲉ̀ⲣⲟⲥ.   ⲉ̄ ⲁⲩϣⲉⲛⲱⲟⲩ ⲉ̀ⲛⲟⲩⲣⲓ.

5. The meaning of the verses:

1. I am the way and the truth and the life; 2. I am the good Shepherd, I know those who are mine, and those who are mine know Me; 3. For the sake of this the Father loves Me; 4. Your brother will rise; 5. I am the resurrection and the life; 6. You are the Christ, the Son of God, the one who is coming to the world; 7. I glorified and will glorify; 8. Now the Son of Man was glorified (received glory).

6. Translation to the Coptic language:

ⲁ̄. ⲁϥϭⲓⲥⲁⲣⲝ ⲛ̀ϫⲉ Ⲡ̀ϣⲏⲣⲓ ⲙ̀Ⲫⲛⲟⲩϯ ⲟⲩⲟϩ ⲁϥⲉⲣⲣⲱⲙⲓ.
ⲃ̄. ⲛⲓⲙⲁⲣⲧⲩⲣⲟⲥ ⲁⲩϣⲉⲡⲙ̀ⲕⲁϩ ⲉⲑⲃⲉ Ⲡⲓⲭⲣⲓⲥⲧⲟⲥ.
ⲅ̄. ⲛⲓⲣⲉϥⲉⲣⲛⲟⲃⲓ ⲥⲉⲕⲟⲧⲟⲩ ⲉ̀Ⲡⲓϭ̅ⲥ̅.
ⲇ̄. ⲥⲉⲛⲁⲧⲱⲟⲩⲛⲟⲩ ⲛ̀ϫⲉ ⲛⲓⲁⲅⲓⲟⲥ ⲛⲉⲙ ⲛⲓⲁⲡⲟⲥⲧⲟⲗⲟⲥ.
ⲉ̄. ϯϥⲁⲓ ⲙ̀ⲡⲁⲥ̀ⲧⲁⲩⲣⲟⲥ ϧⲉⲛ ⲟⲩϣⲉⲡϩ̀ⲙⲟⲧ ⲟⲩⲟϩ ϯⲁⲙⲟⲛⲓ ⲛ̀ⲧⲟⲧ.
ⲋ̄. ⲁⲛϭⲓ ⲙ̀ⲡⲓϩ̀ⲙⲟⲧ ⲛ̀ⲧⲉ ϯⲙⲉⲧⲙⲟⲛⲁⲭⲟⲥ.
ⲍ̄. ⲁⲓⲛⲁⲩ ⲉ̀ⲣⲟϥ ϧⲉⲛ ⲡ̀ϫⲓⲛⲑⲣⲉϥϣⲓ.

Answers of the Exercises of the Twenty-first Lesson

1. Writing the meaning:

1. He sent His Son; 2. You saved the peoples; 3. She brought the book; 4. They drank the water; 5. We left the world; 6. The lifted sins; 7. A flowing water; 8. The perfect Law; 9. He saved us; 10. They buried Him; 11. We honor her; 12. He sent them; 13. He lifted Himself up; 14. The acceptable prayer; 15. Honorable elders; 16. Written judgment.

2. Completing according to the example:

1.	ⲁⲥⲙⲓⲥⲓ ⲙ̄ⲡⲓⲗⲟⲅⲟⲥ.	ⲁⲥⲙⲉⲥ ⲡⲓⲗⲟⲅⲟⲥ.	ⲁⲥⲙⲁⲥϥ.
2.	ⲁϥⲭⲱ ⲛ̄ϯⲃⲁⲕⲓ.	ⲁϥⲭⲁ ϯⲃⲁⲕⲓ.	ⲁϥⲭⲁⲥ.
3.	ⲁϥⲱⲗⲓ ⲛ̄ⲛⲓⲛⲟⲃⲓ.	ⲁϥⲉⲗ ⲛⲓⲛⲟⲃⲓ.	ⲁϥⲟⲗⲟⲩ.
4.	ⲁⲩⲧⲁⲓⲟ ⲙ̄ⲡⲟⲩⲓⲱⲧ.	ⲁⲩⲧⲁⲓⲉ ⲡⲟⲩⲓⲱⲧ.	ⲁⲩⲧⲁⲓⲟϥ.
5.	ⲥⲉⲕⲱⲧ ⲛ̄ϯⲉⲕⲕⲗⲏⲥⲓⲁ.	ⲥⲉⲕⲉⲧ ϯⲉⲕⲕⲗⲏⲥⲓⲁ.	ⲥⲉⲕⲟⲧⲥ.

3. Translation to the English language:

1. He came and saved us from our sins; 2. You forgave them their sins; 3. The depth of the deep became a path; 4. The words which the finger of God wrote; 5. The Lord brought the water of the sea upon them; 6. Our God does not count our iniquities; 7. Jesus chose His disciples and sent them to the world.

Answers of the Exercises of the Twenty-second Lesson

1. Writing the meaning:

1. You (pl.) complete this work; 2. He accepted this sacrifice; 3. I read this book; 4. They eat this bread; 5. You saved this child; 6. Open doors; 7. The flying angel; 8. A ripped enmity; 9. He completed it; 10. You saved her; 11. We opened them; 12. She left you (pl.); 13. You will eat it; 14. The very deep; 15. A grown tree; 16. These shrouded bodies.

2. Completing according to the example:

2.	ⲁⲥⲟⲩⲱⲛ ⲛ̄ⲛⲁⲓⲣⲱⲟⲩ.	ⲁⲥⲟⲩⲉⲛ ⲛⲁⲓⲣⲱⲟⲩ.	ⲁⲥⲟⲩⲟⲛⲟⲩ.
3.	ⲁⲕⲥⲱϯ ⲛ̄ϯⲡⲟⲣⲛⲏ.	ⲁⲕⲥⲉⲧ ϯⲡⲟⲣⲛⲏ.	ⲁⲕⲥⲟⲧⲥ.
4.	ⲁϥⲫⲱϣ ⲙ̄ⲡⲉϥⲥⲱⲙⲁ.	ⲁϥⲫⲉϣ ⲡⲉϥⲥⲱⲙⲁ.	ⲁϥⲫⲁϣϥ.
5.	ϫⲙⲟϩ ⲛ̄ⲛⲉⲛϩⲏⲧ.	ϫⲙⲁϩ ⲛⲉⲛϩⲏⲧ.	ϫⲙⲁϩⲟⲩ.

3. Translation to the English language:

1. A perfect body; 2. A tree filled with fire; 3. He lifted them with Him to the height; 4. God accepts the sacrifices of our hearts; 5. I took a book, and I read it; 6. He counts them with His lambs; 7. You mixed wine and water.

Appendix A ✠ *Answers of the Lessons' Exercises* ✠

Answers of the Exercises of the Twenty-third Lesson

1. Writing the absolute tense:

1.	ⲟϣ	ⲁϣⲁⲓ	7.	ϧⲏⲙ	ϧⲙⲟⲙ	13.	ⲙⲟⲕϩ	ⲙ̀ⲕⲁϩ
2.	ⲥⲟⲑⲙ"	ⲥⲱⲧⲉⲙ	8.	ⲛⲟⲩϫϭ"	ⲛⲟⲩϫϭ	14.	ⲭⲁ"	ⲭⲱ
3.	ϩⲉⲃⲥ-	ϩⲱⲃⲥ	9.	ⲉⲙⲥ-	ⲱⲙⲥ	15.	ⲟⲩⲉⲙ-	ⲟⲩⲱⲙ
4.	ϣⲟⲡ	ϣⲱⲡⲓ	10.	ⲟⲛϧ	ⲱⲛϧ	16.	ⲟϣϫ	ⲱϣϫ
5.	ⲥⲟⲧⲡ"	ⲥⲱⲧⲡ	11.	ⲟⲙⲕ"	ⲱⲙⲕ	17.	ⲃⲟⲗ"	ⲃⲱⲗ
6.	ϩⲉⲧⲡ-	ϩⲱⲧⲡ	12.	ⲉϥⲧ-	ⲱϥⲧ	18.	ϣⲉⲡ-	ϣⲱⲡ

2. Completing according to the example:

1.	ⲁⲓⲥⲱⲧⲡ ⲙ̀ⲡⲁⲓⲙⲱⲓⲧ.	ⲁⲓⲥⲉⲧⲡ ⲡⲁⲓⲙⲱⲓⲧ.	ⲁⲓⲥⲟⲧⲡϥ.
2.	ⲁϥⲟⲩⲱⲛϩ ⲛ̀ⲧⲉϥϫⲟⲙ.	ⲁϥⲟⲩⲉⲛϩ ⲧⲉϥϫⲟⲙ.	ⲁϥⲟⲩⲟⲛϩⲥ.
3.	ⲁⲧⲱϭⲧ ⲛ̀Ⲓⲏⲥⲟⲩⲥ.	ⲁⲧⲉϭⲧ Ⲓⲏⲥⲟⲩⲥ.	ⲁⲧⲟϭⲧϥ.
4.	ⲁϥⲫⲱⲣϣ ⲛ̀ⲛⲉϥϫⲓϫ.	ⲁϥⲫⲉⲣϣ ⲛⲉϥϫⲓϫ.	ⲁϥⲫⲟⲣϣⲟⲩ.
5.	ⲁⲛⲥⲱⲟⲩⲛ ⲛ̀ϯⲙⲉⲑⲙⲏⲓ.	ⲁⲛⲥⲟⲩⲉⲛ ϯⲙⲉⲑⲙⲏⲓ.	ⲁⲛⲥⲟⲩⲱⲛⲥ.
6.	ⲁϥⲛⲟϩⲉⲙ ⲛ̀ⲛⲓⲗⲁⲟⲥ.	ⲁϥⲛⲁϩⲉⲙ ⲛⲓⲗⲁⲟⲥ.	ⲁϥⲛⲁϩⲙⲟⲩ.

3. Translation to the English language:

1. The Lord is with us; 2. A woman clothed with the sun; 3. The ark overlaid with gold; 4. He chose them and sent them to the world; 5. I read your book, and I put it on the table; 6. We saw your son, and we knew him quickly; 7. They took the loaves of bread, and they ate them.

Answers of the Exercises of the Twenty-fourth Lesson

1. Completing the conjugation of the verbs:

Absolute form	Phrasal form	Pronominal form	Qualitative form
ϣⲱⲡ	ϣⲉⲡ-	ϣⲟⲡ"	ϣⲏⲡ
ⲙⲟϩ	ⲙⲁϩ-	ⲙⲁϩ"	ⲙⲉϩ

✠ Foundations of the Coptic Language ✠

ϫⲱ	ϫⲁ-	ϫⲁ"	ϫⲏ
ⲱⲡ	ⲉⲡ-	ⲟⲡ"	ⲏⲡ
ⲥⲱⲧⲡ	ⲥⲉⲧⲡ-	ⲥⲟⲧⲡ"	ⲥⲟⲧⲡ
ⲱϥⲧ	ⲉϥⲧ-	ⲟϥⲧ"	ⲟϥⲧ
ⲙⲓⲥⲓ	ⲙⲉⲥ-	ⲙⲁⲥ"	ⲙⲟⲥⲓ
ⲓⲣⲓ	ⲉⲣ-	ⲁⲓ"	ⲟⲓ
ϯ	ϯ-	ⲧⲏⲓ"	ⲧⲟⲓ
ϭⲓⲥⲓ	ϭⲉⲥ-	ϭⲁⲥ"	ϭⲟⲥⲓ
ϭⲓ	ϭⲓ-	ϭⲓⲧ"	ϭⲛⲟⲩ
ⲓⲱϣ	ⲉϣ-	ⲁϣ"	ⲁϣⲓ

2. Completing according to the example:

1. ⲁⲣⲉϫⲓⲙⲓ ⲛ̄ⲟⲩⲉ̄ⲙⲟⲧ. | ⲁⲣⲉϫⲉⲙ ⲟⲩⲉ̄ⲙⲟⲧ. | ⲁⲣⲉϫⲉⲙϥ.
2. ⲁⲓ̈ⲓⲣⲓ ⲛ̄ⲛⲁⲓⲛⲟⲃⲓ. | ⲁⲓⲉⲣ ⲛⲁⲓⲛⲟⲃⲓ. | ⲁⲓⲁⲓⲧⲟⲩ.
3. ⲧⲉⲣⲁⲙⲓⲥⲓ ⲙ̄ⲫⲏⲉⲑⲟⲩⲁⲃ. | ⲧⲉⲣⲁⲙⲉⲥ ⲫⲏⲉⲑⲟⲩⲁⲃ. | ⲧⲉⲣⲁⲙⲁⲥϥ.
4. ⲁϥⲓⲛⲓ ⲛ̄ⲧⲉϥⲕⲑⲟⲁⲣⲁ. | ⲁϥⲉⲛ ⲧⲉϥⲕⲑⲟⲁⲣⲁ. | ⲁϥⲉⲛⲥ.
5. ϥⲙⲉⲓ ⲙ̄ⲡⲉϥϣⲏⲣ. | ϥⲙⲉⲛⲣⲉ ⲡⲉϥϣⲏⲣⲓ. | ϥⲙⲉⲛⲣⲓⲧϥ.
6. ⲁⲩⲙⲓϣⲓ ⲛ̄ⲛⲟⲩϫⲁϫⲓ. | ⲁⲩⲙⲉϣ ⲛⲟⲩϫⲁϫⲓ. | ⲁⲩⲙⲁϣⲟⲩ.

3. Translation to the English language:

1. The perfect Trinity; 2. A born child; 3. Taken books; 4. The high places; 5. Many people; 6. The beloved brothers; 7. The full of glory; 8. A stricken rock; 9. Your sweet name; 10. An acceptable sacrifice; 11. The one who endures forever; 12. Laborious works.

Answers of the Exercises of the Twenty-fifth Lesson

1. Putting the verb in the suitable tense:

ⲁ̄ ⲁϥϣⲉⲣϣⲱⲣϥ.	ⲃ̄ ⲉⲧϭⲉⲙϭⲱⲙ.	ⲅ̄ ⲥⲉⲥⲉⲗⲥⲉⲗ.
ⲇ̄ ⲁϥϭⲉⲧϭⲱⲧⲟⲩ.	ⲉ̄ ⲉⲧⲥⲕⲉⲣⲕⲱⲣ.	ⲋ̄ ⲁⲩⲥⲉⲃⲧⲉ.
ⲍ̄ ⲁⲥⲙⲉⲥ.		

Appendix A ✠ Answers of the Lessons' Exercises ✠

2. Completing according to the example:

2. ⲁⲕⲃⲟⲣⲃⲉⲣ ⲛ̄ⲛⲓϫⲁϩⲓ.	ⲁⲕⲃⲉⲣⲃⲉⲣ ⲛⲓϫⲁϩⲓ.	ⲁⲕⲃⲉⲣⲃⲱⲣⲟⲩ.
3. ⲁⲩⲥⲕⲟⲣⲕⲉⲣ ⲙ̄ⲡⲓⲱⲛⲓ.	ⲁⲩⲥⲕⲉⲣⲕⲉⲣ ⲡⲓⲱⲛⲓ.	ⲁⲩⲥⲕⲉⲣⲕⲱⲣϥ.
4. ⲥⲉϩⲟⲗϩⲉⲗ ⲛ̄ⲧϣⲟϣ.	ⲥⲉϩⲉⲗϩⲉⲗ ϯϣⲟϣ.	ⲥⲉϩⲉⲗϩⲱⲗⲥ.
5. ⲁϥϩⲟⲛϩⲉⲛ ⲛ̄ⲛⲉϥϣⲏⲣⲓ.	ⲁϥϩⲉⲛϩⲉⲛ ⲛⲉϥϣⲏⲣⲓ.	ⲁϥϩⲉⲛϩⲱⲛⲟⲩ.
6. ⲧⲉⲛϭⲓ ⲛ̄ⲧⲉϥϩⲓⲣⲏⲛⲏ.	ⲧⲉⲛϭⲓ ⲧⲉϥϩⲓⲣⲏⲛⲏ.	ⲧⲉⲛϭⲓⲧⲥ.

3. Writing the absolute form:

1. ⲱⲡ	7. ϩⲱⲃⲥ	13. ⲙⲟϩ
2. ⲫⲱⲣϣ	8. ⲛⲟϩⲉⲙ	14. ⲭⲱ
3. ϫⲓⲙⲓ	9. ⲓ̇ϣⲓ	15. ϭⲓⲥⲓ
4. ⲓ̇ⲣⲓ	10. ⲱⲙⲥ	16. ϫⲱⲕ
5. ⲙⲉⲓ	11. ⲓ̇ⲣⲓ	17. ⲑⲟⲛⲧⲉⲛ
6. ϣ̇ⲑⲟⲣⲧⲉⲣ	12. ⲥⲟⲗⲥⲉⲗ	18. ⲟ̇ⲣⲟϣⲣⲉϣ

Answers of the Review Exercises 5: On Lessons 21 to 25

1. Writing the meaning:

1. The living God; 2. The beloved brothers; 3. You took flesh, and You became man; 4. He loosened (abolished) the enmity; 5. They crucified (hanged) Him on the cross; 6. He made us free; 7. The strong leader [manager]; 8. Laborious ascetical practices; 9. You search my kidneys; 10. She ate bread; 11. They placed Him in a tomb; 12. He rolled it.

2. Putting the verb in the qualitative form:

2. ϩⲁⲛⲣⲱⲟⲩ ⲉⲧⲟⲩⲏⲛ.	3.	ⲛⲉⲕϫⲓϫ ⲉⲧⲫⲟⲣϣ.
4. ⲟⲩⲙⲱⲟⲩ ⲉϥⲃⲏⲗ ⲉ̇ⲃⲟⲗ.	5.	ⲛⲁⲛⲟⲃⲓ ⲉⲧⲟϣ.

3. Completing according to the example:

1. ⲁⲛϫⲓⲙⲓ ⲙ̇ⲙⲁⲥⲓⲁⲥ.	ⲁⲛϫⲉⲙ ⲙⲁⲥⲓⲁⲥ.	ⲁⲛϫⲉⲙϥ.

2. ⲁϥⲥⲱϯ ⲛ̄ϯⲡⲟⲣⲛⲏ.	ⲁϥⲥⲉⲧ ϯⲡⲟⲣⲛⲏ.	ⲁϥⲥⲟⲧⲥ.
3. ⲁⲧⲓⲛⲓ ⲛ̄ϩⲁⲛⲇⲱⲣⲟⲛ.	ⲁⲧⲉⲛ ϩⲁⲛⲇⲱⲣⲟⲛ.	ⲁⲧⲉⲛⲟⲩ.
4. ⲁⲕϭⲟⲙϭⲉⲙ ⲙ̄ⲡⲥⲁⲧⲁⲛⲁⲥ.	ⲁⲕϭⲉⲙϭⲉⲙ ⲡⲥⲁⲧⲁⲛⲁⲥ.	ⲁⲕϭⲉⲙϭⲱⲙϥ.
5. ⲧⲉⲛⲥⲟⲃϯ ⲛ̄ϯⲧⲣⲁⲡⲉⲍⲁ.	ⲧⲉⲛⲥⲉⲃⲧⲉ ϯⲧⲣⲁⲡⲉⲍⲁ.	ⲧⲉⲛⲥⲉⲃⲧⲱⲧⲥ.
6. ⲁⲓϭⲓ ⲛ̄ⲛⲁⲓϫⲱⲙ.	ⲁⲓϭⲓ ⲛⲁⲓϫⲱⲙ.	ⲁⲓϭⲓⲧⲟⲩ.
7. ⲁⲥⲙⲓⲥⲓ ⲛ̄Ⲉⲙⲙⲁⲛⲟⲩⲏⲗ.	ⲁⲥⲙⲉⲥ Ⲉⲙⲙⲁⲛⲟⲩⲏⲗ.	ⲁⲥⲙⲁⲥϥ.

4. Putting the verb in the suitable form:

ⲁ̄ ⲁϥⲃⲉⲣⲃⲱⲣⲟⲩ.   ⲃ̄ ⲁⲥⲙⲁⲥϥ.   ⲅ̄ ⲁϥⲟⲧⲉⲣⲡ.

ⲇ̄ ⲁⲧϫⲉⲕ.   ⲉ̄ ϯⲛⲁⲃⲁⲥϥ.   ⲋ̄ ⲁⲣⲉⲧⲉⲛⲑⲱⲛϯ.

ⲍ̄ ⲁⲛⲥⲟⲧⲉⲛ.

5. Translation to the English language:

1. We hate the sin, but we love the sinners; 2. I put these books on the table which is there (that table), and my brother brought them here; 3. The angel announced [to] Zacharias the priest the birth of John the Baptist, and he announced to the Virgin Mary the birth of our Savior Jesus; 4. God took our flesh, and He gave us His Holy Spirit, and He united us to Him; 5. He made us one with Him; 6. I am the living bread which came down from heaven; 7. The bread I will give is My body, that which I will give for the life of the world; 8. The words which I said to you are a spirit and a life; 9. As You sent Me to the world, I also sent them to the world.

Answers of the Exam 5: On Lessons 21 to 25

1. Writing the meaning:

1. He did mercy with us; 2. You accepted this sacrifice; 3. They nailed Jesus; 4. We abandoned the world; 5. She opened this door; 6. The perfect Law; 7. The angel flying to the height; 8. He saved us; 9. You accepted us to you; 10. He made them rich; 11. I chose him; 12. You cast them into the sea; 13. Beloved brothers; 14. The Virgin, the full of honor.

2. Writing the absolute form:

1. ⲱⲗⲓ	5. ⲭⲱ	9. ϭⲓⲥⲓ
2. ⲓⲱⲓ (ⲓⲉ) ⲱϣ	6. ⲱⲙⲥ	10. ⲱⲛϩ

Appendix A ✠ Answers of the Lessons' Exercises ✠

3. ⲱⲡ	7. ⲙⲉⲓ	11. ⲃⲱⲗ
4. ⲓⲛⲓ	8. ⲙⲟⲥϯ	12. ⲙⲟⲥ̅

3. Completing according to the example:

2. ⲁϥⲥⲱⲧⲡ ⲛ̅ⲛⲉϥⲙⲁⲑⲏⲧⲏⲥ.	ⲁϥⲥⲉⲧⲡ ⲛⲉϥⲙⲁⲑⲏⲧⲏⲥ.	ⲁϥⲥⲟⲧⲡⲟⲩ.
3. ⲁⲩⲥⲟⲃϯ ⲙ̅ⲡⲓⲡⲁⲥⲭⲁ.	ⲁⲩⲥⲉⲃⲧⲉ ⲡⲓⲡⲁⲥⲭⲁ.	ⲁⲩⲥⲉⲃⲧⲱⲧϥ.
4. ⲁⲣⲉⲭⲓⲙⲓ ⲛ̄ⲟⲩⲥ̅ⲙⲟⲧ.	ⲁⲣⲉⲭⲉⲙ ⲟⲩⲥ̅ⲙⲟⲧ.	ⲁⲣⲉⲭⲉⲙϥ.
5. ⲁⲛⲥⲱⲟⲩⲛ ⲛ̄ϯⲙⲉⲑⲙⲏⲓ.	ⲁⲛⲥⲟⲩⲉⲛ ϯⲙⲉⲑⲙⲏⲓ.	ⲁⲛⲥⲟⲩⲱⲛⲥ.
6. ⲁϥⲥⲟⲗⲥⲉⲗ ⲛ̄ⲛⲉⲛⲯⲩⲭⲏ.	ⲁϥⲥⲉⲗⲥⲉⲗ ⲛⲉⲛⲯⲩⲭⲏ.	ⲁϥⲥⲉⲗⲥⲱⲗⲟⲩ.
7. ⲁⲛⲱϣ ⲙ̄ⲡⲁⲓϫⲱⲙ.	ⲁⲛⲉϣ ⲡⲁⲓϫⲱⲙ.	ⲁⲛⲟϣϥ.

4. Translation of the paragraph:

God loved man greatly. He sent His beloved Son to this world. He took flesh and became man. The Virgin gave birth to Him. He accepted to Himself the circumcision. The Magi worshipped Him. He was baptized in the Jordan through John the Baptizer. In Cana of Galilee, He blessed the water and turned it into wine. Jesus did wonders and signs in the midst of the people. The Jews hanged Him on the cross. He died and gave to us life. He arose and lifted us up to the height with Him. He offered us a perfect salvation. We give thanks to Him greatly.

The given verb	Its form	Its absolute form	The given verb	Its form	Its absolute form
ⲙⲉⲓ	absolute	ⲙⲉⲓ	ⲉⲣ	phrasal	ⲓⲣⲓ
ⲟⲩⲉⲣⲡ	phrasal	ⲟⲩⲱⲣⲡ	ⲁϣ	pronominal	ⲓϣⲓ
ϭⲓ	phrasal	ϭⲓ	ⲙⲟⲩ	absolute	ⲙⲟⲩ
ⲉⲣ	phrasal	ⲓⲣⲓ	ϯ	absolute	ϯ
ⲙⲁⲥ	pronominal	ⲙⲓⲥⲓ	ⲧⲱⲛ	pronominal	ⲧⲱⲟⲩⲛ
ϣⲱⲡ	absolute	ϣⲱⲡ	ⲟⲗ	pronominal	ⲱⲗⲓ
ⲟⲩⲱϣⲧ	absolute	ⲟⲩⲱϣⲧ	ⲓⲛⲓ	absolute	ⲓⲛⲓ
ϭⲓ	phrasal	ϭⲓ	ϫⲏⲕ	qualitative	ϫⲱⲕ
ⲥ̅ⲙⲟⲩ	absolute	ⲥ̅ⲙⲟⲩ	ϣⲉⲡ	phrasal	ϣⲱⲡ

Answers of the Exercises of the Twenty-sixth Lesson

1. Completing according to the example:

2. ⲁϥⲧⲁϫⲣⲟ ⲙ̅ⲡⲉϥⲥⲁϫⲓ.	ⲁϥⲧⲁϫⲣⲉ ⲡⲉϥⲥⲁϫⲓ.	ⲁϥⲧⲁϫⲣⲟϥ.
3. ⲁⲥⲧⲁⲙⲟ ⲛ̅ⲛⲓⲙⲁⲑⲏⲧⲏⲥ.	ⲁⲥⲧⲁⲙⲉ ⲛⲓⲙⲁⲑⲏⲧⲏⲥ.	ⲁⲥⲧⲁⲙⲱⲟⲩ.
4. ⲥⲉⲧⲥⲁⲃⲟ ⲙ̅ⲡⲓⲗⲁⲟⲥ.	ⲥⲉⲧⲥⲁⲃⲉ ⲡⲓⲗⲁⲟⲥ.	ⲥⲉⲧⲥⲁⲃⲟϥ.
5. ⲁϥⲧⲁⲗϭⲟ ⲛ̅ⲛⲓϣⲱⲛⲓ.	ⲁϥⲧⲁⲗϭⲉ ⲛⲓϣⲱⲛⲓ.	ⲁϥⲧⲁⲗϭⲱⲟⲩ.
6. ⲧⲉⲧⲥⲟ ⲛ̅ⲧⲉⲁⲗⲟⲩ.	ⲧⲉⲧⲥⲉ ⲧⲉⲁⲗⲟⲩ.	ⲧⲉⲧⲥⲟⲥ.

2. Putting the verbs in the qualitative form:

2. ⲡⲓⲣⲱⲙⲓ ⲉⲧⲧⲁⲥⲑⲟⲛⲟⲩⲧ.   3. ⲛⲉⲛϩⲏⲧ ⲉⲧⲧⲟⲩⲃⲏⲟⲩⲧ.

4. ϯⲕⲓⲃⲱⲧⲟⲥ ⲉⲧⲗⲁⲗⲏⲟⲩⲧ.   5. ⲡⲓⲗⲁⲙⲡⲁⲥ ⲉⲧϭⲉⲣⲏⲟⲩⲧ.

6. ⲡⲉϥⲗⲁⲟⲥ ⲉⲧϣⲁⲛⲉⲩϣ.

3. Translation to the English language:

1. O our Lord, You straighten our ways always; 2. The sin destroyed our race; 3. Our Savior returned man once again to his authority; 4. An honored father and humble (submissive) sons; 5. God created us according to His likeness and His image; 6. He seated us with Him in the heavenlies in Christ Jesus; 7. The apostles taught the peoples of the earth.

Answers of the Exercises of the Twenty-seventh Lesson

1. Writing the imperative mood:

1. ϩⲱⲥ	5. ⲁⲣⲓⲟⲩⲱⲓⲛⲓ	9. ⲁⲟⲩⲱⲛ
2. ⲁⲛⲁⲩ	6. ⲙⲁϯϩⲟ	10. ⲁⲗⲓⲟⲩⲓ
3. ⲙⲁⲱⲟⲩ	7. ⲁⲣⲓⲉⲙⲓ	11. ⲙⲁⲧⲟⲩⲃⲟ
4. ⲁⲣⲓⲟⲩⲓ	8. ⲥⲙⲟⲩ	12. ⲙⲁⲕⲁϯ

2. Translation to the English language:

1. Revive me. Help us. Tell My brothers.

2. Intercede. Glorify the Lord. Sing to that who was crucified.

3. Praise Him and exalt Him; 4. Do not forget Your covenant; 5. Turn Your face away

from my sins; 6. Forgive me the multitude of my iniquities; 7. Be patient with me, do not destroy me speedily; 8. Return us, O God, to Your salvation; 9. Deal with us according to Your goodness; 10. Be glad and rejoice, O the race of men; 11. Enlighten us with Your exalted divinity; 12. Save us and have mercy on us; 13. Ask of that whom you gave birth to; 14. Come to Me, O blessed of My Father, inherit the life lasting forever; 15. The sick, heal them; the departed, O Lord, repose them; our brethren who are in every hardship, O Lord, help us with them.

Answers of the Exercises of the Twenty-eighth Lesson

1. Writing the verbs in the negative form:

1. ⲕ̀ϩⲉⲙⲥⲓ ⲁⲛ 2. ⲙ̀ⲡⲁⲥⲟⲩⲱⲙ 3. ⲉⲛⲙⲟϣⲓ ⲁⲛ 4. ⲧⲉⲧⲉⲛⲛⲁⲩ ⲁⲛ 5. ⲙ̀ⲡⲁⲓⲥⲱⲧⲉⲙ
6. ⲉϥⲥⲁϫⲓ ⲁⲛ 7. ⲛⲁⲩⲱⲛϧ ⲁⲛ 8. ϫⲛⲁϩϯ ⲁⲛ 9. ⲙ̀ⲡⲁⲕϣⲗⲏⲗ 10. ⲉⲩⲥⲙⲟⲩ ⲁⲛ.

2. Translation to the English language:

1. We see you (pl.) sitting; 2. You hear her crying out; 3. You do not desire the death of the sinner; 4. He is accustomed to cleansing the sins of His people; 5. We ask and entreat; 6. They praise their Creator who is in your womb; 7. He gives to us His honored Body and Blood; we live forever [second present tense]; 8. The manna hidden in it; 9. They are accustomed to placing it in the Tabernacle; 10. God is present before them, and His holy name is always in their mouths; 11. The fruits are [habitually] perfected through the prayers of Michael; 12. Being in need, being troubled, and being afflicted; 13. Seven archangels stand praising before the Almighty, serving the hidden mystery.

Answers of the Exercises of the Twenty-ninth Lesson

1. Write the meaning of the phrases:

1. He was praying; 2. They had not come; 3. I entered; 4. She had given birth; 5. You did not speak; 6. You were not eating; 7. When we became tired, we sat; 8. As I did not call him, he did not come; 9. They were in the habit of praising their God; 10. I was not in the habit of delaying in the work.

2. Putting the sentences in the negative form:

ⲁ̄ ⲙ̀ⲡⲟⲩⲓ̀ ⲛⲥⲁϥ.   ⲃ̄ ⲛⲁϥϣⲗⲏⲗ ⲁⲛ ⲡⲉ.

ⲅ̄ ⲛ̀ⲉⲧⲁϥⲧⲱⲛϥ ⲁⲛ ⲙ̀ⲡⲉϥⲙⲟϣⲓ.   ⲇ̄ ⲛⲉⲙ̀ⲡⲁⲓϣⲉ ⲉ̀ⲃⲟⲗ ⲉ̀ⲡϣⲁϥⲉ.
ⲉ̄ ⲛⲉⲙ̀ⲡⲉⲕϫⲉⲕ ⲡⲓϩⲱⲃ ⲉ̀ⲃⲟⲗ.

3. Translation to the English language:

1. When He took flesh, He dwelt in us [and] we saw His glory; 2. God was present with them; 3. In the beginning was the Word, and the Word was with God; 4. You were the doer of this work; 5. When you prayed to God, He heard you; 6. Their voice went out to all the world; 7. The sons of Israel were walking on (in) dry land in the middle of the sea; 8. After we praised God, we came out full of grace; 9. I was in the habit of coming out of my cell early, that I go to my work at the appointed time.

Answers of the Exercises of the Thirtieth Lesson

1. Writing the meaning of the phrases:

1. You will conceive; 2. They will be coming; 3. Do not swear; 4. He will [certainly] rejoice; 5. Do not hate; 6. You will not hear; 7. He will give to you; 8. We will not be writing; 9. You will be sitting; 10. I will [certainly] follow him.

2. Putting the sentences in the negative form:

ⲁ̄ ⲛ̀ⲛⲁⲥⲁϫⲓ ⲛⲉⲙⲁϥ.   ⲃ̄ ⲛⲁⲥⲛⲁϣⲉ ⲉ̀ϧⲟⲩⲛ ⲁⲛ ⲡⲉ.
ⲅ̄ ⲛ̀ⲛⲉⲧⲉⲛⲙⲟϣⲓ ⲛ̀ⲥⲁ Ⲡ̅ⲟ̅ⲥ̅.   ⲇ̄ ⲥⲉⲛⲁⲁ̀ⲣⲉϩ ⲁⲛ ⲉ̀ⲛⲟⲩⲱϣ.

3. Translation to the English language:

1. She will [certainly] give birth to a son, and His name will [certainly] be called Emmanuel; 2. What will I call you, O all-holy Virgin; 3. All the tribes of the earth will [certainly] bless Your holy name; 4. We will never be weary, we will never cease blessing (praising) You; 5. For the Lord will be pleased in His people, and He will exalt the meek with salvation; 6. Create [certainly] in me a pure heart; 7. God will bless us [with all certainty], and we will bless His holy name; 8. [Certainly] love the Lord your God with all your heart, and with all your soul, and with all your strength, and with all your thoughts.

Answers of the Review Exercises 6: On Lessons 26 to 30

1. Writing the meaning:

1. Be [certainly] in our midst; 2. The determined (appointed) covenant; 3. Remember us;

Appendix A ✠ Answers of the Lessons' Exercises ✠

4. Open your mouth; 5. They will be praising their God; 6. He is in the habit of going into the church; 7. You were reading this book; 8. I do as he said to me; 9. You suffer rejoicing; 10. He will [certainly] make us on His righthand.

2. Putting the verb in the pronominal form:

ā	ⲁⲕⲥⲉⲙⲛⲏⲧⲥ ⲛⲁⲛ.	b̄	ⲫ̇ⲛⲟⲃⲓ ⲁϥⲧⲁⲕⲟϥ.	ḡ	ⲁϥϣⲁⲛⲟⲩⲱⲟⲩ.
d̄	Ⲫϯ ⲁϥⲑⲁⲙⲓⲟϥ.	ē	ⲡⲉϥϫⲓⲛⲙⲟⲩ ⲁϥⲧⲁⲛϩⲟⲓ.		
s̄	ⲁⲕⲧⲁⲗϭⲱⲟⲩ.	z̄	ⲁϥⲥⲟⲧⲧⲉⲛ.		

3. Writing the imperative mood:

1.	ⲛⲟϩⲉⲙ	7.	ⲙⲁⲧⲁⲥⲑⲟ	13.	ⲁⲣⲓⲟⲩⲓ̀
2.	ⲁⲟⲩⲱⲙ	8.	ⲁⲣⲓⲟⲩⲱⲓⲛⲓ	14.	ϩⲱⲥ
3.	ⲁⲣⲓϩⲙⲟⲧ	9.	ⲙⲁϣⲑⲁⲙ	15.	ⲙⲁⲥ̀ⲃⲱ
4.	ⲙⲁⲧⲁϫⲣⲟ	10.	ⲙⲟϣⲓ	16.	ⲁⲛⲓⲟⲩⲓ̀
5.	ⲱ̀ϣⲗⲏⲗ	11.	ⲙⲁⲧⲱⲟⲩ	17.	ⲙⲁⲕⲁϯ
6.	ⲁⲛⲁⲩ	12.	ⲙⲁⲧⲟⲩⲃⲟ	18.	ⲁⲗⲓⲟⲩⲓ̀

4. Putting the sentences in the affirmative form:

ā	ϩⲉⲙⲥⲓ ⲙ̀ⲛⲁⲓ.	b̄	ⲧⲉⲛⲥⲱⲟⲩⲛ ⲙ̀ⲡⲁⲓⲣⲱⲙⲓ.
ḡ	ϣⲁⲧⲱϣ ⲛ̀ⲛⲁⲓϫⲱⲙ.	d̄	ⲁϥⲥⲁϫⲓ ⲛⲉⲙⲏⲓ.
ē	ⲛⲁⲕϣ̀ⲗⲏⲗ ⲡⲉ.	s̄	ⲉϥⲉ̀ⲱⲛϧ ⲟⲩⲟϩ ⲉⲩⲉ̀ⲱⲛϧ.

5. Translation to the English language:

1. Give us, O Lord, watchfulness; 2. The Lord will bless you [with all certainty] from Zion; 3. My lips [certainly] overflow praise (blessing); 4. Seek Your servant, because I did not forget Your commandments; 5. You are our God, and we know no other except You; 6. Through His cross joy entered into all the world; 7. O Savior, You crushed the power of death, and You raised Adam with You and freed him (lit. made him free) from Hades; 8. The time of weeping was passed; do not weep, but preach the resurrection to the apostles; 9. The women carrying the fragrant oil hurried to the tomb, mourning; 10. She saw the angel sitting on the stone; 11. This who offered Himself an acceptable sacrifice; 12. Open to us, O Lord, the door of the church; 13. The sins which I committed, O Lord do not remember.

✠ Foundations of the Coptic Language ✠

Answers of the Exam 6: On Lessons 26 to 30

1. Writing the meaning of the phrases:

1. He destroyed our race; 2. Nourished sons; 3. Give us (to us) Your peace; 4. Teach me Your statutes; 5. You will be rejoicing; 6. We bless the name of our God [We are in the habit of blessing the name of our God]; 7. After I ate, I came; 8. She was in the habit of praying with her sons; 9. You will sit with the apostles; 10. We hear them praising.

2. Putting the verb in the qualitative tense:

ⲁ̄	ϯⲡⲁⲣⲑⲉⲛⲟⲥ ⲉⲧⲧⲁⲓⲏⲟⲩⲧ.	ⲃ̄	ⲟⲩⲣⲉϥⲉⲣⲛⲟⲃⲓ ⲉϥⲧⲁⲥⲟⲏⲟⲩⲧ.
ⲅ̄	ⲡⲉϥⲑⲣⲟⲛⲟⲥ ⲉⲧⲧⲁⲭⲣⲏⲟⲩⲧ.	ⲇ̄	ⲛⲉⲛϩⲏⲧ ⲉⲧⲧⲟⲩⲃⲏⲟⲩⲧ.
ⲉ̄	ⲟⲩⲕⲓⲃⲱⲧⲟⲥ ⲉⲥⲗⲁⲗⲏⲟⲩⲧ.	ⲋ̄	ϩⲁⲛⲱⲛⲓ ⲉⲩⲧⲁⲗⲏⲟⲩⲧ.
ⲍ̄	ⲛⲓⲗⲁⲟⲥ ⲉⲧⲧⲥⲁⲃⲏⲟⲩⲧ.		

3. Writing the base for of the verb from the imperative mood:

1.	ϯϩⲁⲡ	7.	ⲕⲁϯ	13.	ⲱⲗⲓ
2.	ⲉⲣϩⲙⲟⲧ	8.	ⲉⲛⲟⲩⲧⲁϩ	14.	ⲛⲁⲩ
3.	ⲥⲙⲟⲩ	9.	ⲧⲁⲛϧⲟ	15.	ϯⲱⲙⲥ
4.	ⲧⲁⲗϭⲟ	10.	ⲭⲱ	16.	ⲉⲣⲫⲙⲉⲩⲓ
5.	ⲟⲩⲱⲛ	11.	ϣⲉⲛⲁⲕ	17.	ⲧⲟⲩⲃⲟ
6.	ϯⲱⲟⲩ	12.	ⲥⲱⲧⲉⲙ	18.	ⲓⲛⲓ

4. Putting the sentences in the negative:

ⲁ̄	ⲙ̄ⲡⲉⲛⲱϣ ⲛ̄ⲛⲉⲛⲱϣ.	ⲃ̄	ⲙ̄ⲡⲁⲕϭⲁⲓ ⲉⲣⲟϥ.
ⲅ̄	ⲛⲁⲣⲉϩⲉⲙⲥⲓ ⲁⲛ ⲡⲉ ⲛⲉⲙ ⲛⲉⲁⲗⲱⲟⲩⲓ.	ⲇ̄	ⲙ̄ⲡⲉϥⲭⲱ ⲛⲏⲓ ⲙ̄ⲡⲁⲓⲥⲁϫⲓ.
ⲉ̄	ⲧⲉⲛⲛⲁⲛⲉϩⲥⲓ ⲁⲛ ⲛ̄ϣⲱⲣⲡ.	ⲋ̄	ⲛ̄ⲛⲉⲧⲉⲛⲓ ⲛⲉⲙⲁⲕ.

5. Translation to the English language:

1. I saw the Lord; 2. Tell my brothers; 3. You gave birth to Him, [so] He healed us; 4. He purifies the sins [He is in the habit of purifying the sins]; 5. Come, all the believers; 6. Which Moses made; 7. They put it in the tabernacle [they ae in the habit of putting it in the tabernacle]; 8. God is [always] within it [her]; 9. Do not forget the covenant which You established with our fathers; 10. Their holy blessing be with us (always); 11. A pure heart create (certainly) in me; 12. Restore us, O God, into Your salvation; 13. Praising their

Creator who is in your womb, This who took our likeness; 14. You rose up [and] saved us; 15. In an acceptable time, You hear me (with all certainty); 16. You look and know that the Savior stood up and rose up from among the dead; 17. My soul will (certainly) live and bless You, and Your judgments will help me (with all certainty); 18. O Lord, open my lips, and my mouth shall sing Your praise.

Answers of the Exercises of the Thirty-first Lesson

1. Writing the meaning of the phrases:

1. The New Testament; 2. The diligent child; 3. The good brothers; 4. The rich man; 5. A leafy tree; 6. Unperishable crowns; 7. The old book; 8. The wise widow; 9. The honored elders; 10. The foreign woman; 11. A fruitful monk; 12. My father, the worthy of being loved.

2. Adjectives for the feminine and plural:

	Masculine	Feminine	Plural		Masculine	Feminine	Plural
1.	ⲍⲟⲩⲓⲧ	ⲍⲟⲩⲓϯ	ⲍⲟⲩⲁϯ	6.	ⲛⲁⲛⲉϥ	ⲛⲁⲛⲉⲥ	ⲛⲁⲛⲉⲩ
2.	ⲃⲉⲗⲗⲉ	ⲃⲉⲗⲗⲏ	ⲃⲉⲗⲗⲉⲩ	7.	ⲣⲁⲙⲁ̀ⲟ	ⲣⲁⲙⲁⲱ	ⲣⲁⲙⲁⲱⲟⲩ
3.	ⲥⲁⲃⲉ	ⲥⲁⲃⲏ	ⲥⲁⲃⲉⲩ	8.	ⲑⲉⲱⲉ	ⲑⲉⲱⲏ	ⲑⲉⲱⲉⲩ
4.	ϣⲁϥⲉ	ϣⲁϥⲏ	ϣⲁϥⲉⲩ	9.	ϭⲁⲉ̀	ϭⲁⲏ̀	ϭⲁⲉⲩ
5.	ⲉϥϭⲟⲥⲓ	ⲉⲥϭⲟⲥⲓ	ⲉⲩϭⲟⲥⲓ	10.	ⲉϥⲭⲏⲕ	ⲉⲥⲭⲏⲕ	ⲉⲩⲭⲏⲕ

3. Translation to the English language:

1. We read in the books of the Old and New Testaments; 2. The first tabernacle which Moses made; 3. My weak and sinful tongue; 4. She saw a luminous angel; 5. Blessed are you, O Mary, the wise and the chaste, the second tabernacle, the spiritual treasure; 6. He who became a golden lampstand; 7. You kept the written commandments in the Gospel; 8. Our holy fathers became harbors of salvation.

Answers of the Exercises of the Thirty-second Lesson

1. Translation to the English language:

1. Your great mercy; your mother, the bride; the true tabernacle; the golden censer; the Red

Sea; the eternal salvation.

2. Glory [be] to You, the good Lover of mankind; 3. They were praising God with this new hymn; 4. Your kingdom, O my God, is an eternal kingdom; 5. All tongues together bless Your name; 6. For they spoke concerning you honored things, O holy city of the great King.

7. Prophetic glorifications; the angelic hosts; the heavenly orders; spiritual prayers.

Answers of the Exercises of the Thirty-third Lesson

1. Translation to the English language:

1. For truly she was greatly exalted, I mean, this virgin who is full of honor; 2. You are greatly exalted more than the cherubim, more honored than the seraphim; 3. You are brighter than the sun, and more sparkling than the cherubim; 4. You were exalted above the high, rational natures; 5. You are worthy of all honor, more than anyone on earth; 6. You are blessed more than the heaven, [and] honored more than the earth; 7. She is exalted more than the cherubim, and is honored more than the seraphim; 8. Michael, the head of the heavenly, he is the first in the angelic orders, serving before the Lord; 9. Good is the joy of Suriel, which we make to him in the churches, more than the joy of a bridegroom of this world that is passing; 10. You are great among all the saints; 11. The good smell of his virtues gives joy to our souls like the fragrant aroma grown in paradise; 12. Truly you were greatly exalted in the midst of the council of our orthodox fathers in the city of Ephesus; 13. I am the little in my brothers.

2. The adjectives, kinds, the degree of description and its article:

	Adjective	Kind of adjective	Degree of description	Its article
ⲁ̄	ϭⲓⲥⲓ (verb)	Simple original verb	Absolute preference	ⲉⲙⲁϣⲱ
	ⲙⲉϩ	Derived	Simple	ⲛ̀
ⲃ̄	ϭⲟⲥⲓ	Derived	Greater match	ⲉϩⲟⲧⲉ
	ⲧⲁⲓⲏⲟⲩⲧ	Derived	Greater match	ⲛ̀ϩⲟⲩⲟ
ⲅ̄	ϩⲓⲁⲕⲧⲓⲛ (verb)	Compound verb	Greater match	ⲉϩⲟⲧⲉ
	ⲗⲁⲙⲡⲣⲟⲥ	Original	Greater match	ⲉϩⲟⲧⲉ
ⲇ̄	ϭⲓⲥⲓ (verb)	Simple original verb	Greater match	ⲉ̀
ⲉ̄	ⲉⲙⲡϣⲁ	Original	Greater match	ⲡⲁⲣⲁ
ⲋ̄	ⲥⲙⲁⲣⲱⲟⲩⲧ	Derived	Greater match	ⲉϩⲟⲧⲉ

Appendix A ✠ *Answers of the Lessons' Exercises* ✠

	ⲧⲁⲓϩⲟⲩⲧ	Derived	Greater match	ⲉ̀ϩⲟⲧⲉ
z̄	ϭⲟⲥⲓ	Derived	Greater match	ⲉ̀
	ⲧⲁⲓϩⲟⲩⲧ	Derived	Greater match	ⲉ̀
ⲏ̄	ϣⲟⲣⲡ	Original	Relative preference	ϧⲉⲛ
ⲑ̄	ⲛⲁⲛⲉ	Original	Greater match	ⲉ̀ϩⲟⲧⲉ
ⲓ̄	ⲛⲓϣϯ	Original	Relative preference	ϧⲉⲛ
ⲓⲁ̄	ⲥⲑⲟⲓⲛⲟⲩϥⲓ (noun)	Compound noun	Equal match	ⲙ̀ⲫⲣⲏϯ
ⲓⲃ̄	ϭⲓⲥⲓ (verb)	Simple original verb	Absolute preference	ⲉ̀ⲙⲁϣⲱ
ⲓⲅ̄	ⲕⲟⲩϫⲓ	Original	Relative preference	ϧⲉⲛ

Answers of the Exercises of the Thirty-fourth Lesson

1. Writing the pronunciation of the numbers:

ⲃ̄	=	ⲥ̀ⲛⲁⲩ	ⲑ̄	=	ⲯⲓⲧ	ⲥ̄	=	ⲥ̀ⲛⲁⲩ ϣⲉ
ⲉ̄	=	ϯⲟⲩ	ⲙ̄	=	ϩⲙⲉ	ⲩ̄	=	ϥⲧⲟⲩ ϣⲉ
ⲏ̄	=	ϣ̀ⲙⲏⲛ	ⲍ̄	=	ⲥⲉ	ⲭ̄	=	ⲥⲟⲟⲩ ϣⲉ
ⲓⲍ̄	=	ⲙⲉⲧ-ϣⲁϣϥ	ⲣⲟⲏ	=	ϣⲉ ϣ̀ⲃⲉ-ϣ̀ⲙⲏⲛ	ⲩⲡⲁ	=	ϥⲧⲟⲩ ϣⲉ-ϧⲁⲙⲛⲉ-ⲟⲩⲁⲓ
ⲕⲅ̄	=	ϫⲟⲩⲧ-ϣⲟⲙⲧ	ⲛⲇ̄	=	ⲧⲉⲃⲓ-ϥⲧⲟⲩ	ϣϥⲑ	=	ⲯⲓⲧ ϣⲉ-ⲡⲓⲥⲧⲁⲩ-ⲯⲓⲧ
ⲃ̄ⲧⲗⲉ	=	ϣⲟ ⲥ̀ⲛⲁⲩ-ϣⲟⲙⲧ ϣⲉ-ⲙⲁⲡ-ϯⲟⲩ						

2. Writing the feminine form of the numbers:

1. ⲟⲩⲓ̀ 2. ⲥ̀ⲛⲟⲩϯ 3. ⲥⲟ
4. ϣⲁϣϥⲓ 5. ⲯⲓⲧ 6. ⲙⲏϯ
7. ⲙⲏϯ-ϣⲟⲙϯ 8. ⲙⲏϯ-ϯⲉ 9. ϫⲱϯ-ⲥ̀ⲛⲟⲩϯ
10. ϫⲱϯ-ϣ̀ⲙⲏⲛⲓ

3. Writing the meaning:

1. The first book; 2. The last table; 3. The first disciples; 4. The second tabernacle; 5. The seventh day; 6. The last children; 7. The twentieth cell; 8. The four incorporeal creatures; 9. The third sister; 10. The two monks; 11. The ten commandments; 12. The two hundred bishops; 13. The twenty-four [ones] praise; 14. The forty-nine [ones] rejoice.

Answers of the Review Exercises 7: On Lessons 31 to 35

1. The meaning of the adjectives:

1. Great; 2. New; 3. Small; 4. Poor; 5. True; 6. Wise; 7. First; 8. Desolate or deserted; 9. Good; 10. Rich; 11. Honored; 12. Holy; 13. Blessed; 14. Exalted; 15. Purified, clean; 16. Immortal; 17. Timeless; 18. Talkative; 19. Leafy; 20. Glutton; 21. Sinless; 22. Undefiled; 23. Unseen; 24. Bodiless; 25. Disobedient; 26. Incomprehensible; 27. Unsearchable; 28. Baker; 29. Beloved (worthy to be loved); 30. Worthy of honor (worthy to be honored).

2. Writing the pronunciation of the numbers:

ⲁ̄	=	ⲟⲩⲁⲓ	ⲓ̄	=	ⲙⲏⲧ	ⲣ̄	=	ϣⲉ
ⲋ̄	=	ϣⲟⲙⲧ	ⲗ̄	=	ⲙⲁⲡ	ⲧ̄	=	ϣⲟⲙⲧ ϣⲉ
ⲍ̄	=	ϣⲁϣϥ	ⲟ̄	=	ⲯ̄ⲃⲉ	ⲱ̄	=	ϣⲙⲏⲛ ϣⲉ
ⲓⲉ̄	=	ⲙⲉⲧ-ⲧⲓⲟⲩ	ⲣⲙ̄ⲁ	=	ϣⲉ-ϩⲙⲉ-ϥⲧⲟⲩ			
ⲕⲇ̄	=	ϫⲟⲩⲧ-ϥⲧⲟⲩ	ⲧⲓⲏ̄	=	ϣⲟⲙⲧ ϣⲉ-ⲙⲉⲧ-ϣⲙⲏⲛ			
ⲙⲑ̄	=	ϩⲙⲉ-ⲯⲓⲧ	ⲫⲍ̄ⲍ	=	ⲧⲓⲟⲩ ϣⲉ-ⲥⲉ-ϣⲁϣϥ			
ⲁ̄ϣϥ̄ⲉ	=	ϣⲟ ⲛⲉⲙ ⲯⲓⲧ ϣⲉ-ⲡⲓⲥⲧⲁⲩ-ϣⲟⲙⲧ						

3. Writing the phrases in plural:

ⲁ̄ ϩⲁⲛⲥⲁⲃⲉⲩ ⲛ̄ⲣⲱⲙⲓ.   ⲃ̄ ⲛⲓϩⲉⲗⲗⲟⲓ ⲛ̄ⲟⲩⲏⲃ.
ⲋ̄ ϩⲁⲛϭⲁⲉⲩ ⲙ̄ⲙⲁⲑⲏⲧⲏⲥ.   ⲇ̄ ⲛⲓϩⲟⲩⲣⲁϯ ⲛ̄ϫⲱⲙ.

4. Writing the meaning of the phrases:

1. The true God; 2. A voice of rejoicing; 3. The high mountains; 4. A great watchfulness; 5. The strong saint; 6. Abundant waters; 7. The ten words; 8. The eternal freedom; 9. The unapproachable; 10. The second tabernacle; 11. Your mother the bride; 12. A written judgment.

5. Translation to the English language:

1. An unseen earth the sun rose upon, an impassible path they walked upon; 2. In an acceptable time You hear me [with all certainty]; 3. Seven times every day I will bless Your name; 4. All knees bow down before You; 5. The four incorporeal living creatures, the ministers flaming with fire; 6. Take off the old man, and put on the new superior one; 7. Hail to you, O Mary, the beautiful dove, who is full of wisdom, the mother of Jesus Christ; 8. You are greatly exalted more than the patriarchs, and honored more than the prophets; 9. Because of this everyone exalts you, O my lady the Mother of God, the holy at all times; 10. They likened the golden lampstand to the Church, and the seven lamps to the seven orders; 11. The 318 [men] who assembled in Nicea concerning the faith; 12. The 150 of [attributed to] the city of Constantinople; 13. The 200 of [attributed to] Ephesus.

Answers of the Exam 7: On Lessons 31 to 35

1. Completing the table:

Phrase	Meaning of phrase	Write the adjective and mention its kind: original, derived, or compound.	
ⲡⲉⲕⲓⲱⲧ ⲛ̀ⲁⲅⲁⲑⲟⲥ.	Your good Father.	ⲁⲅⲁⲑⲟⲥ	Original
ⲡⲓⲡⲛⲉⲩⲙⲁ ⲉⲑⲟⲩⲁⲃ.	The Holy Spirit.	ⲟⲩⲁⲃ	Derived
ⲟⲩϩⲱⲥ ⲙ̀ⲃⲉⲣⲓ.	A new hymn.	ⲃⲉⲣⲓ	Original
Ⲫⲛⲟⲩϯ ⲛ̀ⲁⲑⲛⲁⲩ.	The unseen God.	ⲁⲑⲛⲁⲩ	Compound
ⲛⲉⲛⲓⲟϯ ⲛ̀ⲁⲥⲕⲏⲧⲏⲥ.	Our ascetic fathers.	ⲁⲥⲕⲏⲧⲏⲥ	Original
ⲡⲓϣϣⲏⲛ ⲛ̀ⲗⲁⲭⲁⲗ.	The leafy tree.	ⲗⲁⲭⲁⲗ	Compound
ⲟⲩⲑⲩⲥⲓⲁ ⲉⲥϣⲏⲡ.	An acceptable sacrifice.	ϣⲏⲡ	Derived
ⲟⲩⲥⲟⲛ ⲛ̀ϣⲟⲩⲙⲉⲛⲣⲓⲧϥ.	A brother worthy of love.	ϣⲟⲩⲙⲉⲛⲣⲓⲧϥ	Compound

2. Writing the abbreviated numbers:

ⲥ̇ⲛⲁⲩ	=	ⲃ̄	ⲧⲉⲃⲓ	=	ⲛ̄	ⲥ̇ⲛⲁⲩ ϣⲉ	=	ⲥ̄
ⲥⲟⲟⲩ	=	ⲉ̄	ⲥⲉ	=	ⲍ̄	ϥ̇ⲧⲟⲩ ϣⲉ	=	ⲩ̄
ϣ̇ⲙⲏⲛ	=	ⲏ̄	ⲡⲓⲥⲧⲁⲩ	=	ϥ̄	ϣⲁϣϥ ϣⲉ	=	ⲯ̄
ⲭⲟⲩⲧ-ⲧⲓⲟⲩ	=		ⲕⲉ̄		ϣⲉ-ⲙⲉⲧ-ϥ̇ⲧⲟⲩ		=	ⲣⲓ̄ⲗ

ⲙⲁⲡ-ϣⲟⲙⲧ	=	ⲗ̄ⲍ̄	ϣⲟⲙⲧ ϣⲉ-ϩⲙⲉ-ⲥⲟⲟⲩ = ⲧⲙ̄ⲍ̄
ϧⲁⲙⲛⲉ-ⲯⲓⲧ	=	ⲡ̄ⲑ̄	ϯⲟⲩ ϣⲉ-ϣⲃⲉ-ⲟⲩⲁⲓ = ⲫ̄ⲟⲇ̄

3. Writing the meaning of the phrases:

1. The five loaves of bread; 2. The ten words; 3. The twenty-four priests; 4. The forty-nine martyrs; 5. The 144000; 6. The second Adam; 7. The second heaven; 8. the first martyr; 9. The last day; 10. The first tabernacle.

4. Writing the phrases in the singular form:

ⲁ̄ ⲟⲩⲥⲁⲃⲏ ⲛ̀ⲥⲱⲛⲓ   ⲃ̄ ⲡⲓϣⲉⲙⲙⲟ ⲛ̀ⲣⲱⲙⲓ

ⲅ̄ ⲟⲩϣⲁϥⲉ ⲛ̀ⲧⲟⲡⲟⲥ   ⲇ̄ ϯϧⲉⲗⲗⲱ ⲛ̀ⲥϩⲓⲙⲓ

ⲉ̄ ⲟⲩⲑⲉⲱϣⲉ ⲛ̀ϩⲏⲕⲓ

5. Translation to the English language:

1. The seraphim with the six wings; 2. Walk as sons of the light; 3. We saw His glory as the glory of an only begotten Son; 4. Hail to that who is the full of glory, the undefiled Virgin, the chosen vessel of all the world; 5. All peoples with all tongues praise the Mother of God, the mother of the Messiah; 6. You are truly exalted more than the rod of Aaron; 7. Hail to the new heaven which the Father made [created]; 8. Thousands of thousands and myriads of myriads of archangels and holy angels, standing before the throne of the Almighty [Pantocrator]; 9. Michael is the first, Gabriel is the second, Raphael is the third, according to the type of soldiers; 10. Ask the Lord on our behalf, O my masters fathers the apostles, and the seventy-two disciples, that He may forgive us our sins.

6. Translation to the Coptic language:

ⲁ̄ ⲡⲓⲛⲓϣϯ ⲛ̀ⲛⲁⲓ. ϯϩⲓⲣⲏⲛⲏ ⲙ̀ⲙⲏⲓ.

ⲃ̄ ⲁϥⲧⲱⲛϥ ⲛ̀ϫⲉ Ⲡⲓⲭ̀ⲣⲓⲥⲧⲟⲥ ϧⲉⲛ ⲡⲓⲉ̀ϩⲟⲟⲩ ⲙ̀ⲙⲁϩ ϣⲟⲙⲧ.

ⲅ̄ ϯⲃⲁⲕⲓ ⲉⲑⲟⲩⲁⲃ. ϯϣⲟⲩⲣⲏ ⲛ̀ⲛⲟⲩⲃ.

ⲇ̄ ⲁⲩϩⲓⲱⲓϣ ⲛ̀ϫⲉ ⲡⲓⲙⲉⲧ-ⲥⲛⲁⲩ ⲛ̀ⲁⲡⲟⲥⲧⲟⲗⲟⲥ ⲉ̀ⲛⲓⲗⲁⲟⲥ ⲛ̀ⲧⲉ ⲡⲓⲕⲟⲥⲙⲟⲥ.

Appendix B

Comprehensive Table of Frequently-Used Verb Forms

Absolute form		Phrasal F.	Pronominal F.	Qualitative form	
ⲁϭⲓⲁⲓ	To be healed, to be active	---	---	ⲁϭⲓⲱⲟⲩ	Light, active
ⲁϣⲁⲓ	To increase	---	---	ⲟϣ	Abundance
ⲃⲟⲣⲃⲉⲣ	To cast, to throw	ⲃⲉⲣⲃⲉⲣ-	ⲃⲉⲣⲃⲱⲣ″	ⲃⲉⲣⲃⲱⲣ	Thrown, cast
ⲃⲟⲩϣⲉϣ	To strike, to smash	ⲃⲉϣⲃⲉϣ-	ⲃⲉϣⲃⲱϣ″	ⲃⲉϣⲃⲱϣ	Struck, smashed
ⲃⲱⲗ	To untie, to unfasten	ⲃⲉⲗ-	ⲃⲟⲗ″	ⲃⲏⲗ	Untied, unfastened
ⲃⲱⲥⲧ	To dry, to roast	ⲃⲁⲥⲧ-	ⲃⲁⲥⲧ″	ⲃⲟⲥⲧ	Dry, roasted
ⲃⲱϣ	To undress, to strip	ⲃⲉϣ-, ⲃⲁϣ-	ⲃⲁϣ″	ⲃⲏϣ	Naked, undressed
ⲑⲁⲙⲓⲟ	To create, to make	ⲑⲁⲙⲓⲉ-	ⲑⲁⲙⲓⲟ″	ⲑⲁⲙⲓⲏⲟⲩⲧ	Created
ⲑⲉⲃⲓⲟ	To subject, to be humble	ⲑⲉⲃⲓⲉ-	ⲑⲉⲃⲓⲟ″	ⲑⲉⲃⲓⲏⲟⲩⲧ	Subjected, humble
ⲑⲙⲁⲓⲟ	To justify, to be justified	ⲑⲙⲁⲓⲉ-	ⲑⲙⲁⲓⲟ″	ⲑⲙⲁⲓⲏⲟⲩⲧ	Justified
ⲑⲟⲕⲧⲉⲕ	To print, to tattoo	ⲑⲉⲕⲧⲉⲕ-	ⲑⲉⲕⲧⲱⲕ″	ⲑⲉⲕⲧⲱⲕ	Printed, tattooed
ⲑⲟⲛⲧⲉⲛ	To be like, to be similar	ⲧⲉⲛⲑⲱⲛ-	ⲧⲉⲛⲑⲱⲛ″	ⲧⲉⲛⲑⲱⲛⲧ	Similar, like

Absolute form		Phrasal F.	Pronominal F.	Qualitative form	
ⲑⲟⲩⲍ	To pierce, to stab	ⲧⲉⲕⲥ-	ⲑⲟⲕⲥ⸗	ⲑⲟⲍ	Pierced, stabbed
ⲑⲟϩ	To muddy, to disturb	ⲑⲁϩ-	ⲑⲁϩ⸗	ⲑⲉϩ	Muddied, disturbed
ⲑⲱⲕⲉⲙ	To draw out (a sword)	ⲑⲉⲕⲙ-	ⲑⲟⲕⲙ⸗	ⲑⲟⲕⲉⲙ	Drawn
ⲑⲱⲗⲉⲃ	To defile, to damage	ⲑⲉⲗⲉⲃ-	ⲑⲟⲗⲃ⸗	ⲑⲟⲗⲉⲃ	Defiled, unclean
ⲑⲱⲙ	To close, to shut	ⲑⲉⲙ-	ⲑⲟⲙ⸗	ⲑⲏⲙ	Closed, shut
ⲑⲱⲙⲥ	To bury, to conceal	ⲑⲉⲙⲥ-	ⲑⲟⲙⲥ⸗	ⲑⲟⲙⲥ	Buried, concealed
ⲑⲱⲟⲩⲧ	To gather, to assemble	ⲑⲟⲩⲉⲧ-	ⲑⲟⲩⲱⲧ⸗	ⲑⲟⲩⲏⲧ	Gathered, healed
ⲑⲱⲧ	To mix	ⲑⲉⲧ-	ⲑⲟⲧ⸗	ⲑⲏⲧ	Mixed
ⲑⲱϣ	To determine, to appoint, to decide	ⲑⲉϣ-	ⲑⲁϣ⸗	ⲑⲏϣ	Determined, appointed, decided
ⲑⲱϧ	To mix	ⲑⲉϧ-	ⲑⲁϧ⸗	ⲑⲏϧ	Mixed
ⲑⲱϩⲙ	To call, to invite	ⲑⲁϩⲙ-	ⲑⲁϩⲙ⸗	ⲑⲁϩⲉⲙ	Called, invited
ⲑⲱϩⲥ	To anoint	ⲑⲉϩⲥ-	ⲑⲁϩⲥ⸗	ⲑⲁϩⲥ	Anointed
ⲓ̀ⲃⲓ	To thirst	---	---	ⲟ̀ⲃⲓ	Thirsty
ⲓ̀ⲛⲓ	To bring, to offer	ⲉⲛ-	ⲉⲛ⸗	---	
ⲓ̀ⲛⲓ	To resemble, to be like	ⲉⲛ-	---	ⲟⲛⲓ	Similar, like
ⲓ̀ⲣⲓ	To do, to make, to become	ⲉⲣ-	ⲁⲓ⸗, ⲁⲓⲧ⸗	ⲟⲓ	Made, become
ⲓⲱ, ⲓⲱⲓ	To wash	ⲓⲁ-	ⲓⲁ⸗	ⲓⲱⲟⲩ	Washed
ⲓⲱⲡⲉⲙ	To stare, to be amazed	---	---	ⲓⲟⲡⲉⲙ	Amazed, astonished
ⲓⲱⲥ	To rush	---	---	ⲓⲏⲥ	Rushed
ⲓ̀ϣⲓ	To hang, to crucify	ⲉϣ-	ⲁϣ⸗	ⲁϣⲓ	Hanged, crucified

Appendix B ✠ Comprehensive Table of Frequently-Used Verb Forms ✠

Absolute form		Phrasal F.	Pronominal F.	Qualitative form	
ⲕⲉⲛⲓ	To become fat	---	---	ⲕⲉⲛⲓⲱⲟⲩⲧ	Fat
ⲕⲓⲙ	To move	ⲕⲉⲙ-	---	---	
ⲕⲟⲧ	To return	ⲕⲉⲧ-	ⲕⲟⲧ″	---	
ⲕⲟⲩⲗⲱⲗ	To wrap, to swaddle	---	ⲕⲟⲩⲗⲟⲗ″	ⲕⲟⲩⲗⲱⲗ	Wrapped, swaddled
ⲕⲟϩ	To carve, to smoothen	ⲕⲉϩ-	ⲕⲁϩ″	ⲕⲉϩ	Carved, smoothed, paved
ⲕⲱⲃ	To multiply, to double	ⲕⲉⲃ-	ⲕⲟⲃ″	ⲕⲏⲃ, ⲕⲏⲡ	Multiplied, doubled
ⲕⲱⲗⲡ	To steal, to rob	ⲕⲉⲗⲡ-	ⲕⲟⲗⲡ″	ⲕⲟⲗⲡ	Stolen, robbed
ⲕⲱⲣϥ	To abolish, to cancel	ⲕⲉⲣϥ-	ⲕⲟⲣϥ″	ⲕⲟⲣϥ	Abolished, cancelled
ⲕⲱⲥ	To shroud, to embalm	ⲕⲉⲥ-	ⲕⲟⲥ″	ⲕⲏⲥ	Shrouded, embalmed
ⲕⲱⲧ	To build, to establish, to edify	ⲕⲉⲧ-	ⲕⲟⲧ″	ⲕⲏⲧ	Built, edified
ⲕⲱⲧϥ	To pick, to glean	ⲕⲉⲧϥ-	ⲕⲟⲧϥ″	ⲕⲟⲧϥ	Picked, gleaned
ⲕⲱϣ	To break	ⲕⲉϣ-	ⲕⲁϣ″	---	
ⲕⲱϯ	To seek, to surround	ⲕⲉⲧ-	ⲕⲟⲧ″	---	
ⲗⲁⲗⲟ	To paint, to coat	ⲗⲁⲗⲉ-	ⲗⲁⲗⲱ″	ⲗⲁⲗⲏⲟⲩⲧ	Painted, coated
ⲗⲱⲙ	To whither, to fade	---	---	ⲗⲟⲙ	Whthered, faded
ⲗⲱϫϩ	To lick	ⲗⲉϫϩ-	ⲗⲟϫϩ″	---	
ⲙⲉⲓ	To love	ⲙⲉⲛⲣⲉ-	ⲙⲉⲛⲣⲓⲧ″	ⲙⲉⲛⲣⲓⲧ	Beloved
ⲙⲓⲥⲓ	To give birth, to beget	ⲙⲉⲥ-, ⲙⲁⲥ-	ⲙⲁⲥ″	ⲙⲟⲥⲓ	Born
ⲙⲓϣⲓ	To strike, to fight	ⲙⲉϣ-, ⲙⲁϣ-	ⲙⲁϣ″	ⲙⲁϣⲓ	Stricken

✠ Foundations of the Coptic Language ✠

Absolute form		Phrasal F.	Pronominal F.	Qualitative form	
ⲙⲕⲁϩ	To suffer	---	---	ⲙⲟⲕϩ	Suffering. in pain
ⲙⲟⲓ	To give, to grant	ⲙⲁ-	ⲙⲏⲓ″, ⲙⲏⲓⲧ″	---	
ⲙⲟⲕⲙⲉⲕ	To think	ⲙⲉⲕⲙⲉⲕ-	ⲙⲉⲕⲙⲟⲩⲕ″	---	
ⲙⲟⲥⲧ	To hate	ⲙⲉⲥⲧⲉ-	ⲙⲉⲥⲧⲱ″	ⲙⲉⲥⲧⲉ	Hated
ⲙⲟⲩ	To die	---	---	ⲙⲱⲟⲩⲧ	Dead
ⲙⲟⲩⲗϩ	To salt	ⲙⲉⲗϩ-	ⲙⲟⲗϩ″	ⲙⲟⲗϩ	Salted, salty
ⲙⲟⲩⲛ	To continue, to remain	---	---	ⲙⲏⲛ	Continuous, incessant
ⲙⲟⲩⲛⲕ	To form, to make	ⲙⲉⲛⲕ-	ⲙⲟⲛⲕ″	ⲙⲟⲛⲕ	Made
ⲙⲟⲩⲣ	To tie, to gird	ⲙⲉⲣ-	ⲙⲟⲣ″	ⲙⲏⲣ	Tied, girded
ⲙⲟⲩϣⲧ	To roam, to inspect	ⲙⲉϣⲧ-	ⲙⲟϣⲧ″	---	
ⲙⲟⲩϫⲧ	To mix, to mingle	ⲙⲉϫⲧ-	ⲙⲟϫⲧ″	ⲙⲟϫⲧ	Mixed, mingled
ⲙⲟⲩϩ	To fill, to complete	ⲙⲁϩ-	ⲙⲁϩ″	ⲙⲉϩ	Filled, fulfilled
ⲙⲧⲟⲛ	To rest, to give rest	---	---	ⲙⲟⲧⲉⲛ	Rested, comforting
ⲛⲁϩϯ	To believe	---	---	ⲉⲛϩⲟⲧ	Believing, faithful
ⲛⲟⲩⲓ	To be about to do	ⲛⲁ-	---	ⲛⲏⲟⲩ	Coming
ⲛⲟⲩϣⲡ	To scare, to frighten	ⲛⲉϣⲡ-	ⲛⲟϣⲡ″	ⲛⲟϣⲡ	Scared, frightened
ⲛⲟⲩϫ	To throw away, to cast off	ⲛⲉϫ-	ⲛⲟϫ″	ⲛⲏϫ, ⲛⲟⲩϫ	Thrown, cast off
ⲛⲟⲩϫϧ	To sprinkle, to wet	ⲛⲉϫϧ-	ⲛⲟϫϧ″	ⲛⲟϫϧ	Sprinkled, wet
ⲛⲟϩⲙ	To save, to redeem	ⲛⲁϩⲙ-	ⲛⲁϩⲙ″	ⲛⲟϩⲙ	Saved, redeemed
ⲛϣⲟⲧ	To be hard	---	---	ⲛⲁϣⲧ	Hard, rough

Appendix B ⚜ Comprehensive Table of Frequently-Used Verb Forms ⚜

Absolute form		Phrasal F.	Pronominal F.	Qualitative form	
ⲟⲩⲃⲁϣ	To become white	---	---	ⲟⲩⲟⲃϣ	White
ⲟⲩⲉⲓ	To be far	---	---	ⲟⲩⲏⲟⲩ	Far
ⲟⲩⲟⲛ	There is	ⲟⲩⲟⲛⲧⲉ-	ⲟⲩⲟⲛⲧⲁ″	---	
ⲟⲩⲟⲥⲑⲉⲛ	To enlarge, to broaden	ⲟⲩⲉⲥⲑⲉⲛ-	ⲟⲩⲉⲥⲑⲱⲛ″	ⲟⲩⲉⲥⲑⲱⲛ	Large, broad
ⲟⲩⲟϩ	To add, to follow	ⲟⲩⲁϩ-	ⲟⲩⲁϩ″	ⲟⲩⲉϩ	Added, followed
ⲟⲩⲱⲙ	To eat	ⲟⲩⲉⲙ-	ⲟⲩⲟⲙ″	---	
ⲟⲩⲱⲛ	To open	ⲟⲩⲉⲛ-	ⲟⲩⲟⲛ″	ⲟⲩⲏⲛ	Opened
ⲟⲩⲱⲛϩ	To reveal, to appear	ⲟⲩⲉⲛϩ-	ⲟⲩⲟⲛϩ″	ⲟⲩⲟⲛϩ	Revealed
ⲟⲩⲱⲣⲡ	To send	ⲟⲩⲉⲣⲡ-	ⲟⲩⲟⲣⲡ″	---	
ⲟⲩⲱⲧⲉⲃ	To move, to excel	ⲟⲩⲉⲧⲉⲃ-	ⲟⲩⲟⲑⲃ″	ⲟⲩⲟⲧⲉⲃ	Moved, Excellent
ⲟⲩⲱϣ	To desire, to want	ⲟⲩⲁϣ-	ⲟⲩⲁϣ″	---	
ⲟⲩⲱϣⲙ	To knead, to mash	ⲟⲩⲉϣⲙ-	ⲟⲩⲟϩⲙ″	ⲟⲩⲟϣⲙ	Kneaded, mixed
ⲟⲩⲱϣⲥ	To widen, to become wide	ⲟⲩⲉϣⲥ-	ⲟⲩⲟϣⲥ″	ⲟⲩⲟϣⲥ	Wide
ⲟⲩⲱϣϥ	To crush, to destroy	ⲟⲩⲉϣϥ-	ⲟⲩⲁϣϥ″	ⲟⲩⲟϣϥ	Crushed, destroyed
ⲟⲩⲱϩ	To add, to follow	ⲟⲩⲁϩ-	ⲟⲩⲁϩ″	ⲟⲩⲉϩ	Added, followed
ⲟⲩⲱϩⲙ	To repeat, to answer	ⲟⲩⲁϩⲙ-	ⲟⲩⲁϩⲙ″	ⲟⲩⲟϩⲙ	Repeated, added
ⲟⲩⲱϫⲡ	To break, to destroy	ⲟⲩⲉϫⲡ-	ⲟⲩⲟϫⲡ″	ⲟⲩⲟϫⲡ	Destroyed, demolished
ⲟⲩϫⲁⲓ	To be healed	---	---	ⲟⲩⲟϫ	Healed, healthy
ⲣⲓⲕⲓ	To bend, to deviate	ⲣⲉⲕ-	ⲣⲁⲕ″	ⲣⲁⲕⲓ	Bent, deviated
ⲣⲱⲓⲥ	To stay awake, to watch	---	---	ⲣⲏⲥ	Awake, watchful

✠ Foundations of the Coptic Language ✠

Absolute form		Phrasal F.	Pronominal F.	Qualitative form	
ⲣⲱⲕϩ	To burn, to be on fire	ⲣⲉⲕϩ-	ⲣⲟⲕϩ″	ⲣⲟⲕϩ	Burned, on fire
ⲣⲱⲧ	To sprout, to spring up	ⲣⲉⲧ-	ⲣⲟⲧ″	ⲣⲏⲧ	Sprouted
ⲣⲱⲧⲉⲃ	To recline	---	ⲣⲟⲑⲃ″	ⲣⲟⲧⲉⲃ	Reclined
ⲣⲱϣⲓ	To suffice, to be enough	ⲣⲉϣ-, ⲣⲁϣ-	ⲣⲁϣ″	ⲣⲁϣⲓ	Sufficient, enough
ⲣⲱϭ, ⲣⲱϭⲓ	To wash	---	ⲣⲁϭ″	ⲣⲁϭⲓ	Clean, washed
ⲣⲱϭⲧ	To convulse, to throw down	ⲣⲉϭⲧ-	ⲣⲁϭⲧ″	ⲣⲁϭⲧ	Convulsing, thrown down
ⲣⲱϫⲡ	To fall, to be thrown down	ⲣⲉϫⲡ-	ⲣⲟϫⲡ″	ⲣⲟϫⲡ	Fallen, thrown down
ⲥⲁⲃⲟ	To learn	ⲥⲁⲃⲉ-	---	ⲥⲁⲃⲏⲟⲩⲧ	Educated
ⲥⲁⲓ	To become beautiful	---	---	ⲥⲁⲓⲱⲟⲩ	Beautiful
ⲥⲁϩⲛⲓ	To command, to place, to provide	ⲥⲉϩⲛⲉ-	ⲥⲁϩⲛⲏⲧ″	ⲥⲉϩⲛⲏⲟⲩⲧ	Placed, provided
ⲥⲁϩⲟ	To eliminate, to remove	ⲥⲁϩⲉ-	ⲥⲁϩⲱ″	ⲥⲁϩⲏⲟⲩⲧ	Eliminated, removed
ⲥⲁϩⲟⲩⲓ	To curse, to insult	ⲥϩⲟⲩⲉⲣ-	ⲥϩⲟⲩⲱⲣ″	ⲥϩⲟⲩⲱⲣⲧ	Cursed
ⲥⲃⲟⲕ	To decrease, to diminish, to become small	---	---	ⲥⲟⲃⲕ	Little, inferior
ⲥⲉⲃⲓ	To circumcise	ⲥⲟⲩⲃⲉ-	ⲥⲟⲩⲃⲏⲧ″	ⲥⲉⲃⲏⲟⲩⲧ	Circumcised
ⲥⲉⲙⲛⲓ	To establish, to confirm	ⲥⲉⲙⲛⲉ-	ⲥⲉⲙⲛⲏⲧ″	ⲥⲉⲙⲛⲏⲟⲩⲧ	Decided, confirmed
ⲥⲓ	To be filled	---	---	ⲥⲏⲟⲩ	Filled, satiated
ⲥⲓⲛⲓ	To pass, to cross	ⲥⲉⲛ-	ⲥⲉⲛ″	ⲥⲓⲛⲓⲱⲟⲩ	Passenger, crossing
ⲥⲓϯ	To sow, to throw	ⲥⲉⲧ-, ⲥⲁⲧ-	ⲥⲁⲧ″	ⲥⲁϯ, ⲥⲏϯ	Planted, thrown

Appendix B ✠ Comprehensive Table of Frequently-Used Verb Forms ✠

Absolute form		Phrasal F.	Pronominal F.	Qualitative form	
ⲥ̀ⲕⲟⲣⲕⲉⲣ	To roll	ⲥ̀ⲕⲉⲣⲕⲉⲣ-	ⲥ̀ⲕⲉⲣⲕⲱⲣ″	ⲥ̀ⲕⲉⲣⲕⲱⲣ	Rolled
ⲥ̀ⲙⲟⲩ	To bless	---	---	ⲥ̀ⲙⲁⲣⲱⲟⲩⲧ	Blessed
				ⲥ̀ⲙⲁⲙⲁⲧ	Blessed
ⲥⲟⲃϯ	To prepare, to be ready	ⲥⲉⲃⲧⲉ-	ⲥⲉⲃⲧⲱⲧ″	ⲥⲉⲃⲧⲱⲧ	Prepared, ready
ⲥⲟⲗⲥⲉⲗ	To adorn, to console	ⲥⲉⲗⲥⲉⲗ-	ⲥⲉⲗⲥⲱⲗ″	ⲥⲉⲗⲥⲱⲗ	Adorned, consoled
ⲥⲟⲡⲥⲉⲡ	To plead, to entreat	ⲥⲉⲡⲥⲉⲡ-	ⲥⲉⲡⲥⲱⲡ″	---	
ⲥⲟϩⲓ	To rebuke, to admonish	ⲥⲁϩⲉ-	ⲥⲁϩⲱ″	---	
ⲥⲱ	To drink	ⲥⲉ-	ⲥⲟ″	---	
ⲥⲱⲕ	To pull, to draw	ⲥⲉⲕ-	ⲥⲟⲕ″	ⲥⲏⲕ	Pulled, drawn
ⲥⲱⲗⲡ	To cut off, to break off	ⲥⲉⲗⲡ-	ⲥⲟⲗⲡ″	ⲥⲟⲗⲡ	Cut off, broken off
ⲥⲱⲗⲝ	To wipe, to obliterate	ⲥⲉⲗⲝ-	ⲥⲟⲗⲝ″	---	
ⲥⲱⲛⲕ	To suck	ⲥⲉⲛⲕ-	ⲥⲟⲛⲕ″	---	
ⲥⲱⲛⲧ	To create	ⲥⲉⲛⲧ-	ⲥⲟⲛⲧ″	---	
ⲥⲱⲛϩ	To bind, to fetter	ⲥⲉⲛϩ-	ⲥⲟⲛϩ″	ⲥⲟⲛϩ	Bound, fettered
ⲥⲱⲟⲩⲛ	To know	ⲥⲟⲩⲉⲛ-	ⲥⲟⲩⲱⲛ″	ⲥⲟⲩⲏⲛ	Known
ⲥⲱⲟⲩⲧⲉⲛ	To manage, to correct	ⲥⲟⲩⲧⲉⲛ-	ⲥⲟⲩⲧⲱⲛ″	ⲥⲟⲩⲧⲱⲛ	Upright, straight
ⲥⲱⲡ	To dip	ⲥⲉⲡ-	ⲥⲟⲡ″	---	
ⲥⲱⲣ	To spread, to lead astray	ⲥⲉⲣ-, ⲥⲁⲣ-	ⲥⲟⲣ″	ⲥⲏⲣ	Widespread, astray
ⲥⲱⲣⲉⲙ	To lead astray, to go astray	ⲥⲉⲣⲉⲙ-	ⲥⲟⲣⲙ″	ⲥⲟⲣⲉⲙ	Lost, astray
ⲥⲱⲧⲉⲙ	To hear	ⲥⲉⲧⲉⲙ-	ⲥⲟⲟⲙ″	---	
ⲥⲱⲧⲟⲩⲛ	To correct, to guide	ⲥⲟⲩⲧⲉⲛ-	ⲥⲟⲩⲧⲱⲛ″	ⲥⲟⲩⲧⲱⲛ	Upright, straight

Absolute form		Phrasal F.	Pronominal F.	Qualitative form	
ⲥⲱⲧⲡ	To choose	ⲥⲉⲧⲡ-	ⲥⲟⲧⲡ″	ⲥⲟⲧⲡ	Chosen
ⲥⲱⲧϥ	To purify, to strain	ⲥⲉⲧϥ-	ⲥⲟⲧϥ″	ⲥⲟⲧϥ	Pure, clean
ⲥⲱϥ	To defile, to pollute	ⲥⲉϥ-	ⲥⲟϥ″	ⲥⲟϥ	Defiled, polluted
ⲥⲱϭⲓ	To weave	---	ⲥⲁϭ″	ⲥⲏϭ, ⲥⲏϭⲓ	Woven
ⲥⲱϩⲓ	To remove	ⲥⲁϩⲉ-	ⲥⲁϩⲱ″	---	
ⲥⲱϫⲡ	To remain, to leave behind	ⲥⲉϫⲡ-	ⲥⲟϫⲡ″	ⲥⲟϫⲡ	Remaining, left behind
ⲥⲱϯ	To save, to redeem	ⲥⲉⲧ-	ⲥⲟⲧ″	---	
ⲥϧⲁⲓ	To write	ⲥϧⲉ-	ⲥϧⲏⲧ″	ⲥϧⲏⲟⲩⲧ	Written
ⲧⲁⲓⲟ	To honor	ⲧⲁⲓⲉ-	ⲧⲁⲓⲟ″	ⲧⲁⲓⲏⲟⲩⲧ	Honored
ⲧⲁⲕⲟ	To destroy, to perish	ⲧⲁⲕⲉ-	ⲧⲁⲕⲟ″	ⲧⲁⲕⲏⲟⲩⲧ	Destroyed, perished
ⲧⲁⲕⲧⲟ	To encircle, to surround	ⲧⲁⲕⲧⲉ-	ⲧⲁⲕⲧⲟ″	ⲧⲁⲕⲧⲏⲟⲩⲧ	Encircled, surrounded
ⲧⲁⲗⲟ	To lift up, to raise up, to mount	ⲧⲁⲗⲉ-	ⲧⲁⲗⲟ″	ⲧⲁⲗⲏⲟⲩⲧ	Raised up, mounted
ⲧⲁⲗϭⲟ	To heal	ⲧⲁⲗϭⲉ-	ⲧⲁⲗϭⲟ″	---	
ⲧⲁⲙⲟ	To inform, to tell	ⲧⲁⲙⲉ-	ⲧⲁⲙⲟ″	---	
ⲧⲁⲛϣⲟ	To increase	ⲧⲁⲛϣⲉ-	ⲧⲁⲛϣⲟ″	---	
ⲧⲁⲛϧⲟ	To give life	ⲧⲁⲛϧⲉ-	ⲧⲁⲛϧⲟ″	---	
ⲧⲁⲟⲩⲟ	To send, to produce	ⲧⲁⲟⲩⲉ-	ⲧⲁⲟⲩⲟ″	ⲧⲁⲟⲩⲏⲟⲩⲧ	Sent
ⲧⲁⲣⲕⲟ	To swear, to make to swear	ⲧⲁⲣⲕⲉ-	ⲧⲁⲣⲕⲟ″	---	
ⲧⲁⲣϣⲟ	To increase, to multiply	ⲧⲁⲣϣⲉ-	ⲧⲁⲣϣⲟ″	ⲧⲁⲣϣⲏⲟⲩⲧ	Increased, multiplied
ⲧⲁⲥⲑⲟ	To return, to bring back	ⲧⲁⲥⲑⲉ-	ⲧⲁⲥⲑⲟ″	ⲧⲁⲥⲑⲏⲟⲩⲧ	Returned, brought back

Appendix B ✣ Comprehensive Table of Frequently-Used Verb Forms ✣

Absolute form		Phrasal F.	Pronominal F.	Qualitative form	
ⲧⲁϩⲛⲟ	To hinder, to prevent	ⲧⲁϩⲛⲉ-	ⲧⲁϩⲛⲟ″	---	
ⲧⲁϩⲟ	To establish, to comprehend	ⲧⲁϩⲉ-	ⲧⲁϩⲟ″	ⲧⲁϩⲏⲟⲩⲧ	Established, comprehended
ⲧⲁϫⲣⲟ	To confirm	ⲧⲁϫⲣⲉ-	ⲧⲁϫⲣⲟ″	ⲧⲁϫⲣⲏⲟⲩⲧ	Firm
ⲧⲉⲙⲙⲟ	To feed	ⲧⲉⲙⲙⲉ-	ⲧⲉⲙⲙⲟ″	---	
ⲧⲉⲛϩⲟⲩⲧ	To believe	ⲧⲉⲛϩⲉⲧ-	ⲧⲉⲛϩⲟⲩⲧ″	ⲧⲉⲛϩⲟⲧ	Faithful, trustworthy
ⲧⲟⲩⲃⲟ	To purify	ⲧⲟⲩⲃⲉ-	ⲧⲟⲩⲃⲟ″	ⲧⲟⲩⲃⲏⲟⲩⲧ	Purified, clean
ⲧⲟⲩⲛⲟⲥ	To raise (revive)	ⲧⲟⲩⲛⲉⲥ-	ⲧⲟⲩⲛⲟⲥ″	---	
ⲧⲟⲩϩⲟ	To add, to increase	ⲧⲟⲩϩⲉ-	ⲧⲟⲩϩⲟ″	---	
ⲧⲟⲩϫⲟ	To heal, to be healed	ⲧⲟⲩϫⲉ-	ⲧⲟⲩϫⲟ″	ⲧⲟⲩϫⲏⲟⲩⲧ	Healthy, sound
ϯⲥⲁⲃⲟ	To teach, to discipline	ϯⲥⲁⲃⲉ-	ϯⲥⲁⲃⲟ″	ϯⲥⲁⲃⲏⲟⲩⲧ	Educated, disciplined
ϯⲥⲓⲟ	To satiate	ϯⲥⲓⲉ-	ϯⲥⲓⲟ″	ϯⲥⲏⲟⲩⲧ	Satiated
ϯⲥⲟ	To give to drink	ϯⲥⲉ-	ϯⲥⲟ″	---	
ⲧⲱⲃ	To seal, to stamp	ⲧⲉⲃ-	ⲧⲟⲃ″	ⲧⲟⲃ, ⲧⲏⲃ	Sealed
ⲧⲱⲃϩ	To entreat, to pray	ⲧⲉⲃϩ-	ⲧⲟⲃϩ″	ⲧⲟⲃϩ	Requested
ⲧⲱⲙ	To join, to connect	ⲧⲉⲙ-	ⲧⲟⲙ″	ⲧⲟⲙ	Joined, connected
ⲧⲱⲙⲧ	To be amazed, to be astonished	ⲧⲉⲙⲧ-	ⲧⲟⲙⲧ″	ⲧⲟⲙⲧ	Amazed, astonished
ⲧⲱⲟⲩⲛ	To arise	ⲧⲉⲛ-	ⲧⲱⲛ″	---	
ⲧⲱⲥ	To dry up, to freeze	ⲧⲉⲥ-	ⲧⲟⲥ″	ⲧⲏⲥ	Dry, frozen
ϯϩⲉⲙⲕⲟ	To torture	ϯϩⲉⲙⲕⲉ-	ϯϩⲉⲙⲕⲟ″	ϯϩⲉⲙⲕⲏⲟⲩⲧ	Tortured

✠ Foundations of the Coptic Language ✠

Absolute form		Phrasal F.	Pronominal F.	Qualitative form	
ⲑⲙⲥⲟ	To seat	ⲑⲙⲥⲉ	ⲑⲙⲥⲟ″	ⲑⲙⲥⲏⲟⲩⲧ	Seated
ϥⲉⲣⲓ	To shine, to sparkle	---	---	ϥⲉⲣⲓⲱⲟⲩ	Shining, sparkling
ϥⲓⲣⲓ	To blossom	ϥⲉⲣ-	---	ϥⲟⲣⲓ	Blossoming, emerging
ϥⲓⲥⲓ	To cook	ϥⲉⲥ-	ϥⲁⲥ″	ϥⲟⲥⲓ	Cooked
ϥⲟⲧϥⲉⲧ	To cut into small pieces	ϥⲉⲧϥⲉⲧ-	ϥⲉⲧϥⲱⲧ″	ϥⲉⲧϥⲱⲧ	Cut into small pieces
ϥⲟϩ	To reach, to attain, to mature	ϥⲉϩ-	ϥⲁϩ″	ϥⲉϩ	Attained, matured
ϥⲱⲗⲝ	To separate, to disconnect	ϥⲉⲗⲝ-	ϥⲟⲗⲝ″	---	
ϥⲱⲛ	To pour out, to shed	ϥⲉⲛ-	ϥⲟⲛ″	ϥⲏⲛ	Poured out, shed
ϥⲱⲛϩ	To turn, to be twisted	ϥⲉⲛϩ-	ϥⲟⲛϩ″	ϥⲟⲛϩ	Turned, twisted
ϥⲱⲣⲕ	To uproot, to pluck out	ϥⲉⲣⲕ-	ϥⲟⲣⲕ″	ϥⲉⲣⲕ	Uprooted, plucked out
ϥⲱⲣϣ	To spread, to unfold	ϥⲉⲣϣ-	ϥⲟⲣϣ″	ϥⲟⲣϣ	Spread, unfolded
ϥⲱⲣⲝ	To divide, to split	ϥⲉⲣⲝ-	ϥⲟⲣⲝ″	ϥⲟⲣⲝ	Divided, split
ϥⲱⲧ	To flee	---	---	ϥⲏⲧ	Fleeing
ϥⲱϣ	To divide, to be divided	ϥⲉϣ-	ϥⲁϣ″	ϥⲏϣ	Divided, halved
ϥⲱϣⲉⲛ	To be a priest, to sanctify	ϥⲉϣⲉⲛ-	ϥⲟϣⲛ″	ϥⲟϣⲉⲛ	Consecrated, ordained
ϥⲱϭ	To tear apart	ϥⲉϭ-, ϥⲁϭ-	ϥⲁϭ″	ϥⲏϭ	Torn apart
ϫⲃⲟⲃ	To cool, to soften	ⲕⲃⲉ-	---	ⲕⲏⲃ, ϫⲏⲃ	Cool
ϫⲙⲟⲩ	To become black	---	---	ϫⲏⲙ	Black, blackened
ϫⲱ	To leave behind, to place	ϫⲁ-	ϫⲁ″	ϫⲏ	Left behind, placed

Appendix B ✠ Comprehensive Table of Frequently-Used Verb Forms ✠

Absolute form		Phrasal F.	Pronominal F.	Qualitative form	
ϩⲱⲡ	To hide, to conceal	ϩⲉⲡ-	ϩⲟⲡ″	ϩⲏⲡ	Hidden, concealed
ⲱⲃϣ	To forget	ⲉⲃϣ-	ⲟⲃϣ″	ⲟⲃϣ	Negligent, inattentive
ⲱⲗ, ⲱ̀ⲗⲓ	To lift up, to carry	ⲉⲗ-	ⲟⲗ″	ⲟⲗ, ⲏⲗ	Lifted up, carried
ⲱⲙⲕ	To swallow	ⲉⲙⲕ-	ⲟⲙⲕ″	---	
ⲱⲙⲥ	To immerse, to drown	ⲉⲙⲥ-	ⲟⲙⲥ″	ⲟⲙⲥ	Immersed, drowned
ⲱⲛϧ	To live	---	---	ⲟⲛϧ	Living, alive
ⲱⲡ	To count, to number	ⲉⲡ-	ⲟⲡ″	ⲏⲡ	Counted, numbered
ⲱⲣϥ	To surround, to live in solitude	ⲉⲣϥ-	ⲟⲣϥ″	ⲟⲣϥ	Isolated, secluded
ⲱⲥⲕ	To delay	---	---	ⲟⲥⲕ	Delayed
ⲱⲥϧ	To reap, to harvest	ⲉⲥϧ-	ⲟⲥϧ″	ⲟⲥϧ	Harvested
ⲱⲧⲡ	To load, to be laden	ⲉⲧⲡ-	ⲟⲧⲡ″	ⲟⲧⲡ	Loaded
ⲱϣ	To read, to study	ⲉϣ-	ⲟϣ″	---	
ⲱϣⲙ	To quench	ⲟϣⲙ-	ⲟϣⲙ″	ⲟϣⲙ	Quenched
ⲱϣⲝ	To anoint, to paint	ⲉϣⲝ-	ⲟϣⲝ″	ⲟϣⲝ	Painted, anointed
ⲱϥⲧ	To nail	ⲉϥⲧ-	ⲟϥⲧ″	ⲟϥⲧ	Nailed, fixed
ⲱϫⲉⲃ	To become cold, to freeze	---	---	ⲟϫⲉⲃ	Cold, frozen
ϣⲁⲓ	To rise	---	---	ϣⲁⲓⲱⲟⲩ	Sunny
ϣⲁⲛϣ	To support, to nourish, to rear	ϣⲁⲛⲉϣ-	ϣⲁⲛⲟⲩϣ″	ϣⲁⲛⲉⲩϣ	Nourished, reared
ϣⲉⲃⲓⲱ	To change, to exchange	ϣⲉⲃⲓⲉ-	ϣⲉⲃⲓⲏⲧ″	ϣⲉⲃⲓⲏⲟⲩⲧ	Variable, different
ϣⲉⲙϣⲓ	To serve	ϣⲉⲙϣⲉ-	ϣⲉⲙϣⲏⲧ″	ϣⲉⲙϣⲏⲧ	Servant
ϣ̀ⲑⲁⲙ	To lock, to close	ϣ̀ⲧⲉⲙ-	---	ϣ̀ⲑⲁⲙⲏⲟⲩⲧ	Locked, closed

Absolute form		Phrasal F.	Pronominal F.	Qualitative form	
ϣⲑⲟⲣⲧⲉⲣ	To be disturbed	ϣⲑⲉⲣⲧⲉⲣ-	ϣⲧⲉⲣⲑⲱⲣ⸗	ϣⲧⲉⲣⲑⲱⲣ	Disturbed
ϣⲓ	To measure, to weigh	ϣⲓ-	ϣⲓⲧ⸗	ϣⲏⲟⲩ	Measured, weighed
ϣⲓⲛⲓ	To ask	ϣⲉⲛ-	ϣⲉⲛ⸗	---	
ϣⲟⲣϣⲉⲣ	To demolish, to ruin	ϣⲉⲣϣⲉⲣ-	ϣⲉⲣϣⲱⲣ⸗	ϣⲉⲣϣⲱⲣ	Ruined, demolished
ϣⲱⲃⲧ	To change	ϣⲉⲃⲧ-	ϣⲟⲃⲧ⸗	---	
ϣⲱⲕ	To dig, to deepen	ϣⲉⲕ-	ϣⲟⲕ⸗	ϣⲏⲕ	Dug, deep
ϣⲱⲗⲉⲙ	To smell	ϣⲉⲗⲉⲙ-	---	---	
ϣⲱⲛⲧ	To plait, to braid	ϣⲉⲛⲧ-	ϣⲟⲛⲧ⸗	ϣⲟⲛⲧ	Plaited
ϣⲱⲡ	To buy, to accept	ϣⲉⲡ-	ϣⲟⲡ⸗	ϣⲏⲡ	Acceptable
ϣⲱⲡⲓ	To be, to become, to dwell	---	---	ϣⲟⲡ	Becoming, existing
ϣⲱⲣⲡ	To be early	ϣⲉⲣⲡ-	ϣⲟⲣⲡ⸗	ϣⲟⲣⲡ	Early, preceding
ϣⲱⲧ	To slaughter, to sever	ϣⲉⲧ-	ϣⲁⲧ⸗	ϣⲁⲧ	Slaughtered, slain
ϣⲱⲧⲉⲙ	To close, to lock	---	---	ϣⲟⲧⲉⲙ	Locked, closed
ϣⲱϣϥ	To despise	ϣⲉϣϥ-	ϣⲟϣϥ⸗	ϣⲟϣϥ	Despised, humiliated
ϣⲱϥ	To lay waste, to desert	ϣⲉϥ-	ϣⲟϥ⸗	ϣⲏϥ	Laid waste, deserted
ϣⲱϥⲧ	To err, to stumble	---	---	ϣⲟϥⲧ	Wrong, mistaken
ϥⲁⲓ	To lift up, to carry	ϥⲓ-	ϥⲓⲧ⸗	ϥⲏⲩ	Lifted up, carried
ϥⲱϯ	To wipe, to wipe out	ϥⲉⲧ-	ϥⲟⲧ⸗	ϥⲏϯ	Wiped, wiped out
ϧⲑⲁⲓ	To become fat, to become thick	---	---	ϧⲟⲧ	Fat, thick
ϧⲓⲥⲓ	To toil, to weary	---	ϧⲁⲥ⸗	ϧⲟⲥⲓ	Wearied, suffering

Appendix B ✠ Comprehensive Table of Frequently-Used Verb Forms ✠

Absolute form		Phrasal F.	Pronominal F.	Qualitative form	
ϧⲙⲟⲙ	To heat up	---	---	ϧⲏⲙ	Hot, heated
ϧⲟⲗϧⲉⲗ	To slaughter	ϧⲉⲗϧⲉⲗ-	ϧⲉⲗϧⲱⲗ″	ϧⲉⲗϧⲱⲗ	Slaughtered
ϧⲟⲙϧⲉⲙ	To crush, to mash	ϧⲉⲙϧⲉⲙ-	ϧⲉⲙϧⲱⲙ″	ϧⲉⲙϧⲱⲙ	Crushed
ϧⲟⲧϧⲉⲧ	To examine, to test	ϧⲉⲧϧⲉⲧ-	ϧⲉⲧϧⲱⲧ″	ϧⲉⲧϧⲱⲧ	Examined
ϧⲱⲛⲧ	To draw near, to approach	ϧⲉⲛⲧ-	ϧⲟⲛⲧ″	ϧⲉⲛⲧ	Near, adjacent
ϧⲱⲧⲉⲃ	To kill, to murder	ϧⲁⲧⲉⲃ-	ϧⲟⲑⲃ″	---	
ϩⲉⲓ	To fall	---	---	ϩⲓⲱⲟⲩⲧ	Fallen
ϩⲉⲣⲓ	To be still, to be quiet	---	---	ϩⲟⲩⲣⲱⲟⲩ	Still, quiet
ϩⲓⲟⲩⲓ	To throw, to cast	ϩⲓ-	ϩⲓⲧ″	ϩⲱⲟⲩⲓ	Thrown, cast
ϩ̀ⲕⲟ	To hunger	---	---	ϩⲟⲕⲉⲣ	Hungry
ϩ̀ⲗⲟϫ	To be sweet	---	---	ϩⲟⲗϫ	Sweet
ϩⲟⲛϩⲉⲛ	To order, to command	ϩⲉⲛϩⲉⲛ-	ϩⲉⲛϩⲱⲛ″	---	
ϩⲟϫϩⲉϫ	To annoy	ϩⲉϫϩⲉϫ-	ϩⲉϫϩⲱϫ″	ϩⲉϫϩⲱϫ	Annoyed
ϩⲱⲃⲥ	To clothe, to cover	ϩⲉⲃⲥ-	ϩⲟⲃⲥ″	ϩⲟⲃⲥ	Covered, clothed
ϩⲱⲗ	To go, to fly	---	---	ϩⲏⲗ	Flying
ϩⲱⲙⲓ	To trample	ϩⲉⲙ-	ϩⲟⲙ″	ϩⲏⲙ, ϩⲟⲙⲓ	Tampled
ϩⲱⲡ	To hide, to conceal	ϩⲉⲡ-	ϩⲟⲡ″	ϩⲏⲡ	Hidden, concealed
ϩⲱⲧⲡ	To reconcile, to unite	ϩⲉⲧⲡ-	ϩⲟⲧⲡ″	ϩⲟⲧⲡ	Reconciled, united
ϫⲓⲙⲓ	To find	ϫⲉⲙ-	ϫⲉⲙ″	---	
ϫⲟⲙϫⲉⲙ	To touch	ϫⲉⲙϫⲉⲙ-	ϫⲉⲙϫⲱⲙ″	---	
ϫ̀ⲫⲟ	To acquire, to beget	ϫ̀ⲫⲉ-	ϫ̀ⲫⲟ″	ϫ̀ⲫⲏⲟⲩⲧ	Acquired, begotten
ϫⲱ	To say	ϫⲉ-	ϫⲟ″, ϫⲟⲧ″	---	

✠ Foundations of the Coptic Language ✠

	Absolute form	**Phrasal F.**	**Pronominal F.**		**Qualitative form**
ϫⲱⲓⲗⲓ	To reside, to sojourn	ϫⲁⲗⲉ-	ϫⲁⲗⲱ″	ϫⲁⲗⲏⲟⲩⲧ	Sojourner, resident
ϫⲱⲕ	To complete, to fulfill	ϫⲉⲕ-	ϫⲟⲕ″	ϫⲏⲕ	Completed, perfect
ϫⲱⲗ	To roll back, to deny	ϫⲉⲗ-	ϫⲟⲗ″	ϫⲏⲗ	Rolled back, denying
ϫⲱⲗϩ	To wear, to put on	---	ϫⲟⲗϩ″	ϫⲟⲗϩ	Clothed
ϫⲱⲣ	To scatter, to disperse	ϫⲉⲣ-	ϫⲟⲣ″	ϫⲏⲣ	Scattered, dispersed
ϫⲱⲣⲓ	To strengthen	---	---	ϫⲟⲣ	Strong
ϫⲱϣ	To pour	ϫⲉϣ-	ϫⲟϣ″	ϫⲏϣ	Poured
ϭⲉⲛⲟ	To quench, to extinguished	ϭⲉⲛⲉ-	ϭⲉⲛⲟ″	ϭⲉⲛⲏⲟⲩⲧ	Quenched
ϭⲉⲣⲟ	To be illuminated	ϭⲉⲣⲉ-	ϭⲉⲣⲱ″	ϭⲉⲣⲏⲟⲩⲧ	Enlightened
ϭⲓ	To take, to receive	ϭⲓ-	ϭⲓⲧ″	ϭⲏⲩ	Taken
ϭⲓⲥⲓ	To elevate, to exalt	ϭⲉⲥ-, ϭⲁⲥ-	ϭⲁⲥ″	ϭⲟⲥⲓ	Elevated, exalted
ϭⲛⲟ	To subject	ϭⲛⲉ-	---	ϭⲛⲏⲟⲩⲧ	Subject
ϭⲟ	To plant	ϭⲉ-	ϭⲟ″	ϭⲏⲟⲩⲧ	Planted
ϭⲟϩ	To arrive, to follow	---	---	ϭⲉϩ	Arrived, reached
ϭⲣⲟ	To triumph, to conquer	---	---	ϭⲣⲏⲟⲩⲧ	Victorious
ϭⲱⲡ	To seize	ϭⲉⲡ-	ϭⲟⲡ″	ϭⲏⲡ	Seized
ϭⲱⲣⲡ	To uncover, to reveal	---	ϭⲟⲣⲡ″	ϭⲟⲣⲡ	Uncovered
ϭⲱⲥ	To freeze, to harden	---	---	ϭⲏⲥ	Frozen
ϭⲱϭⲉⲙ	To defile, to pollute	---	ϭⲁϭⲙ″	ϭⲁϭⲉⲙ	Defiled, unclean
ϭⲱϫ	To stain, to extend	ϭⲉϫ-	ϭⲟϫ″	ϭⲏϫ	Stained, dyed, extended
†	To give	†-	ⲧⲏⲓ″, ⲧⲏⲓⲧ″	ⲧⲟⲓ	Given

Appendix C
Bibliography

Grammar Books:

1. A. S. J. Mallon, *Grammaire Copte*. (Beyrouth, 1926).

2. G. Sobhy, *Qawa'id Al-Lugha Al-Masri'ia Al-Qobtia* [Grammar of the Egyptian Coptic Language]. (1925).

3. A. F. Ibrahim, **Ⲡⲓ Ⲛⲟⲩⲃ** *Li-Ta'leem Al-Lugha Al-Qobtia Al-Joz' Al-Awal* [**Ⲡⲓ Ⲛⲟⲩⲃ** Pinoub : Teaching the Coptic Language Vol. 1]. (1977).

4. A. F. Ibrahim, **Ⲡⲓ Ⲛⲟⲩⲃ** *Li-Ta'leem Al-Lugha Al-Qobtia Al-Joz' Al-Thabi wa Al-Thalith* [**Ⲡⲓ Ⲛⲟⲩⲃ** Pinoub : Teaching the Coptic Language Vol. 2 and 3]. (1965).

5. *Risalat Mar Mina Al-Thamina: Al-Marja' fi Qawa'id Al-Lugha Al-Qobtia* [The Eighth Letter of Mar Mina: Handbook of the Coptic Language Grammar]. (The Association of Mar Mina the Wonderworker in Alexandria, 1969).

6. E. Y. Labib, *Qawa'id Al-Lugha Al-Qobtia* [Grammar of the Coptic Language].

7. A. Awad, *Al-Manhaj Al-Hadeeth Li-Ta'leen Al-Lugha Al-Qobtia* [The Moden Curriculum for Teaching the Coptic Language]. (1937).

8. Fr. Matthew the Poor, *Al-Lugha Al-Qobtia wa Qawa'idaha* [The Coptic Language and its Grammar]. (Unpublished work).

9. Lessons in the Coptic language that were taught in the sixties and seventies in the city of Alexandria.

10. Hegumen Shenouda Mahher, **ⲥⲁϫⲓ ⲛⲉⲙⲁⲛ** *[Saji Neman] Vol. 1 and 2*. (1972).

11. M. A. Salama, **Ⲡⲓϫⲱⲙ ⲛ̀ⲧⲁⲥⲑⲟ ⲛ̀ⲧⲉ ϯⲁⲅⲓⲁ Ⲙⲁⲣⲓⲁ ϧⲉⲛ ⲛⲓⲥⲉⲛϯ ⲛ̀ⲧⲉ ϯⲁⲥⲡⲓ ⲛ̀ⲣⲉⲙⲛ̀ⲭⲏⲙⲓ ⲕⲁⲧⲁ ⲡⲓⲉⲩⲁⲅⲅⲉⲗⲓⲟⲛ ⲉⲑⲟⲩⲁⲃ**. (2003).

12. N. S. Issac, *Dorous fi Ta'leem Al-Lugha Al-Qobtia* **Ⲛⲟϥⲣⲓ ϧⲉⲛ ϯⲁⲥⲡⲓ ⲛ̀ⲣⲉⲙⲛ̀ⲭⲏⲙⲓ** [Lessons in Teaching the Coptic Language]. (2010).

✠ Foundations of the Coptic Language ✠

Holy Books:

13. *The Coptic Version of the New Testament in the Northern Dialect.* (Oxford, at the Clarendon Press, 1898).
14. Ⲡⲓϫⲱⲙ ⲛ̀ⲧⲉ ⲡⲓⲯⲁⲗⲧⲏⲣⲓⲟⲛ ⲛ̀ⲧⲉ Ⲇⲁⲩⲓⲇ *Kitab Zaboor Daoud Al-Nabi wa Al-Malik* [The Book of the Psalms of David the Prophet and the King]. (1744).
15. Ⲡⲓϫⲱⲙ ⲉⲑⲟⲩⲁⲃ, Ϯⲇⲓⲁⲑⲏⲕⲏ ⲛ̀ⲁⲡⲁⲥ (ϯⲅⲉⲛⲉⲥⲓⲥ ⲛⲉⲙ ϯⲉⲝⲟⲇⲟⲥ). (Cairo: Abna' Al-Kaneesa Al-Qobtia, 1939).
16. *Kitab Nobo'at Al-Ahd Al-Qadeem bi Al-Lugha Al-Qobtia* Ⲡⲓϫⲱⲙ ⲛ̀ⲛⲓ̀ⲡⲣⲟⲫⲏⲧⲓⲁ ⲛ̀ⲧⲉ ϯⲇⲓⲁⲑⲏⲕⲏ ⲛ̀ⲁⲡⲁⲥ [The Book of the Prophecies of the Old Testaments in the Coptic Language]. (F. S. Girgis, 2000).
17. *Sifr Ayob Al-Sideek bi Al-Lugha Al-Qobtia* Ⲡⲓϫⲱⲙ ⲛ̀Ⲓⲱⲃ Ⲡⲓⲑⲙⲏⲓ [The Book of Job in the Coptic Language]. (F. S. Girgis, 1999).
18. Ⲡⲓϫⲱⲙ ⲛ̀ⲧⲉ ϯⲇⲓⲁⲑⲏⲕⲏ ⲙ̀ⲃⲉⲣⲓ. (Cairo: Abna' Al-Kaneesa fi Masr, 1934).
19. Ⲡⲓⲉⲩⲁⲅⲅⲉⲗⲓⲟⲛ Ⲉⲑⲟⲩⲁⲃ ⲕⲁⲧⲁ Ⲙⲁⲧⲑⲉⲟⲛ, Ⲙⲁⲣⲕⲟⲛ, Ⲗⲟⲩⲕⲁⲛ ⲛⲉⲙ Ⲓⲱⲁⲛⲛⲏⲛ. (Habib Girgis and others, 1935).

Dictionaries:

20. W. E. Crum, *A Coptic Dictionary.* (Oxford, UK: Oxford Univerity Press, 1939).
21. R. Kasser, *Compléments au Dictionnaire Copte de Crum.* (Institut Français D'Archéologie Orientale, Le Caire, 1964).
22. A. Peyron, *Lexicon Linguae Copticae.* (Taurini, Ex Regio Typographeo, 1835).
23. R. Smith, *A Concise Coptic-English Lexicon.* (Michigan: William B. Eerdmans Publishing Company, 1983).
24. W. Westendorf, *Koptisches Handwörterbuch.* (Heidelberg, 1965).
25. W. Vycichl, *Dictionnaire Étymologique De La Langue Copte.* (Leuven: Peeters, 1983).
26. M. Strasbach, *Dictionnaire Inversé Du Copte.* (Leuven: Peeters, 1976).
27. M. H. Munier, *La Scala Copte 44 De La Bibliothèque Nationale De Paris, Transcription Et Vocabulaire.* (Institut Français D'Archéologie Orientale, Le Caire, 1930).
28. H. G. Liddell and R. Scott, *A Greek-English Lexicon.* (Oxford, at the Clarendon Press, 1968).
29. M. D. Abdel Nour, *Qamous Al-Lugha Al-Qobtia: Qobti-Arabi* Ⲡⲓⲁⲛⲥⲁϫⲓ ⲛ̀ⲧⲁⲥⲡⲓ ⲛ̀ⲣⲉⲙⲛ̀ⲭⲏⲙⲓ [Coptic Language Dictionary: Coptic-Arabic]. (2000).
30. E. Y. Labib, *Qamous Al-Lugha Al-Qobtia Al-Masri'ia* Ⲡⲓⲗⲉⲝⲓⲕⲟⲛ ⲛ̀ⲧⲁⲥⲡⲓ ⲛ̀ⲧⲉ ⲛⲓⲣⲉⲙⲛ̀ⲭⲏⲙⲓ [The Egyptian Coptic Language Dictionary]. (1895).
31. E. H. Abdel Malek, Ⲡⲓⲁⲛⲥⲁϫⲓ ⲛ̀ⲧⲁⲥⲡⲓ ⲛ̀ⲣⲉⲙⲛ̀ⲭⲏⲙⲓ *Qamous Al-Lugha Al-Qobtia Al-Arba' Ahrof* (ⲋ, ϫ, ϭ, ϯ) *Al-Naqisa fi Qamous Ekladios Labib* [Coptic Language

Dictionary: The Four Missing Letters in the Dictionary of Ekladios Labib (ϩ, ϫ, ϭ, ϯ)]. (1997).

32. M. A. Youssef, *Qamous Al-Lugha Al-Qobtia, Arabi-Qobti* [Coptic Language Dictionary, Arabic-Coptic]. (1999).

33. Fr. Andreas of the Monastery of St. Macarius, *Qamous Qobti Arabi Li-Kalimat Al-Lahja Al-Bohairia Lil-Lugha Al-Qobtia wa Al-Kalimat Al-Ma'khotha Min Al-Lugha Al-Youna'nia Al-Mustakhdama fi Salawat Al-Kaneesa wa Al-Nosous Al-Aba'iya* [Coptic-Arabic Dictionary for the Bohairic Dialect of the Coptic Language and the Words that are Taken from the Greek Language Used in the Church Prayers and Patristic Texts]. (2010).

34. Fr. Andreas of the Monastery of St. Macarius, *Qamous Younani-Arabi Li-Kalimat Al-Ahd Al-Jadeed wa Al-Kitabat Al-Mase'hiya Al-Oula* [Greek-Arabic Dictionary for the New Testament Words and the Early Christian Writings]. (2003).

Analysis Books:

35. M. Barsoum, **Ⲃⲱⲗ ⲉⲃⲟⲗ ⲛ̀ⲧⲉ ϯⲁⲛⲁⲫⲟⲣⲁ ⲙ̀Ⲃⲁⲥⲓⲗⲓⲟⲥ** *Tahlil Al-Qodas Al-Baseeli Bi Al-Lugha Al-Qobtia* [Analysis of the Liturgy of St. Basil in the Coptic Language]. (1964).

36. Fr. Andreas of the Monastery of St. Macarius, **Ⲡⲓⲃⲱⲗ ⲉ̀ⲃⲟⲗ ⲛ̀ⲧⲉ ⲡⲓϫⲱⲙ ⲛ̀ⲧⲉ ϯⲯⲁⲗⲙⲟⲇⲓⲁ ⲉⲑⲟⲩⲁⲃ** *Tahlil Kitab Al-Ibsalmoudia Al-Moqadasa* [Analysis of the Holy Psalmody Book]. (2010).

37. Fr. Andreas of the Monastery of St. Macarius, **Ⲡⲓⲃⲱⲗ ⲉ̀ⲃⲟⲗ ⲛ̀ⲧⲉ ⲡⲓϫⲱⲙ ⲛ̀ⲧⲉ ⲡⲓⲉⲩⲭⲟⲗⲟⲅⲓⲟⲛ ⲉⲑⲟⲩⲁⲃ** *Tahlil Kitab Al-Kholaji Al-Moqadas (Raf' Bokhour wa Al-Qodas Al-Baseeli)* [Analysis of the Holy Liturgy Book (Morning Raising of Incense and the Divine Liturgy of St. Basil]. (2010).

www.ingramcontent.com/pod-product-compliance
Lightning Source LLC
Chambersburg PA
CBHW080545230426
43663CB00015B/2706